Motif-Index
of
Folk-Literature
Vol. 6.2

MOTIF-INDEX

OF

FOLK-LITERATURE

A Classification of Narrative Elements in
Folktales, Ballads, Myths, Fables, Mediaeval Romances,
Exempla, Fabliaux, Jest-Books, and
Local Legends

REVISED AND ENLARGED EDITION BY

STITH THOMPSON
Indiana University

VOLUME 6.2
INDEX
(L-Z)

INDIANA UNIVERSITY PRESS
BLOOMINGTON AND INDIANAPOLIS

This book is a publication of

Indiana University Press
601 North Morton Street
Bloomington, IN 47404-3797 USA

http://iupress.indiana.edu

Telephone orders 800-842-6796
Fax orders 812-855-7931
Orders by e-mail iuporder@indiana.edu

Manufactured in the United States of America

Cataloging information is available from the Library of Congress.

Volume 6.1 ISBN: 0-253-34089-6
Volume 6.2 ISBN: 0-253-34091-8

Labor, see also **Childbirth;** contest won by deception K40ff.; — Beginning of division of l. A1472; fairy helps mortal with l. F346; food at first comes without effort: plan changed so that man must l. A1420.4, L482.5; ghosts forced to l. E558; intemperance in undertaking l. J557; king works so subjects cannot complain of enforced l. P15.7; man must l. for a living (at first everything too easy) A1346.2; race of ox and horse: ox must l. A2252.2; results of l. lost in a moment of procrastination J1071; strong man makes l. contract E613ff.; tribal characteristics: l. A1671.

Labors. — Strong man's l. F614ff.

Laboratory. — Substitute specimen for l. test K1858.

Laborer. Animal as farm l. B292.9.

Laborer's. — Stealing l. pajamas H1151.22.

Laborers P410ff. — Fairies as l. F271.

Laboring. — Object l. automatically *D1601ff.; statue l. for owner D1620.1.6; tabu: l. of bearded man C565.1.

Labyrinth F781.1. — Clue to find way out of l. R121.5.

Lac. — Earth made of l. A821.

Lace. — Murder with poisoned l. S111.2.

Lacing bedcovering to shoe J2161.3.

Lack, see also **Without;** of proper education regretted J142. — Absurd l. of logic J2200ff.; animal's l. of hearing A2428.1; why certain animals l. legs A2371.3; why animals l. tail A2378.2; why animals l. tongue *A2344.2ff.; why certain birds l. nests A2235.1, A2431.2; why countries l. certain animals A2434.2; countries with one conspicuous l. F708; why dogs l. restraint A2526.1; why emus l. wings A2377.1; saint's bones for l. of worship remove themselves from church V143; witches l. bread and salt G229.3.

Lacquer. — Seven coats of l. on chopsticks H1199.16.

Ladder to heaven A666; as symbol of upward progress Z139.7; to upper world F52. — Extraordinary l. F848ff.; forbidden l. C611.3; girl's long hair as l. into tower F848.1; lover reaches mistress's room by l. K1348; making l. which whole army cannot set up (task) H1147; stretching fingers to make l. D485; walking on l. of knives H225.1.

Ladders. — Knockers harm miners' l. F456.1.2.1.4; thief says that he is seller of l. J1391.2.

Ladle. — Gigantic l. F881.1.2.

Lady, see also **Woman.** — Chain tale: old l. swallows a fly Z49.14; hero in disguise of foolish knight, then of black knight, rescues l. R169.1; knight's duty to perform as l. bids P52.1; loathly l. D732; magic object received from l. in dream D812.8; magic sword received from L. of Lake D813.1.1; noble l. P60ff.; pardon given if hero produces the l. about whom he has boasted M55; revenant as l. in white E425.1.1.

Lady's. — Crime mitigated if committed at l. request P517.

Ladies in wild hunt E501.2.2. — Devils as l. G303.3.1.17.

Lady-slipper. — Origin of l. A2658.

Laid. — Curse l. on child by fairy F316; treasure l. in lake by serpent B103.5.1; walking ghost l. *E440ff.

Lake becomes bloody D474.2; deeper than the bottomless J2217.2; drunk dry D1641.12.1; entrance to lower world F93.2; magically transported D2136.4; of milk by tree of life A878.2; -monster G308; removes itself D1641.12; -serpent B91.5.2. — Animal dives into l., disappears F989.13; bathing in l. restores blindness F952.7; big l. under the earth A659.2; bringing a l. to king (task) H1023.25; creator emerges from l. A25.1; curse on l. M477; devil builds two islands in a l. G303.9.1.9; disenchantment by following enchanted woman through l. to underwater castle D759.5; diving into l. which makes person old K1072; dragon guards l. B11.7.2; dragon lives in l. B11.3.1.1; drying up l. in one night H1097.1; emptying l. with pail in one day H1143.1; extraordinary l. F713; fairyland at bottom of l. H1286.0.1; fairies' cattle under a l. F241.2.3; forbidden l. C615.1; giant lives under l. F531.6.2.2.2; hero battles under l. F691.0.1; huldra l. F460.2.5; lovers first see each other on shores of l. N715; magic healing l. D1500.1.18.4; magic l. sent against enemy D2091.7; magic light illuminates l. bottom D1478.2; magic spell dries up l. D1542.3.4; magic tree at bottom of l. D950.0.2; magic cauldron received from l. spirit D813.1.2; magic l. D921; magic sword returned to l. whence it was received D878.1; magic sword received from Lady of L. D813.1.1; mankind emerges from l. A1232.2; mermaid lives under l. B81.13.12; monster turning over causes l. to overflow F713.3; rajah sacrifices entire family to purify l. S263.3.3; saint makes l. of milk V229.16; serpent king resides in l. B244.1.2; serpents' palace on l. bottom F127.1.1; sun emerges from l. A719.1; tabu: telling children about l. monster C423.6; tabus concerning fairyland l. F378.2; threat to pull the l. together with a rope K1744; unsuccessful magic production of l. J2411.7; village under l. F725.5.1; water withdrawn from l. C939.1.

Lakes in otherworld F162.6. — Bottomless l. F713.2; extraordinary occurrences concerning l. F934; magic control of l. D2151.7; magic stone makes rivers and l. D1486.1; origin of l. A920.1.

Lake-horse paramour B611.3.2.

Lakshmi A482.2.

Lamb chooses her foster mother, the she-goat J391.1; prefers to be sacrificed in temple rather than to be eaten by a wolf J216.2; without a heart K402; symbolizes Christ Z177. — Daw tries to carry off l. like eagle J2413.3; devastating supernatural l. B16.1.6.1; devil cannot change into a l. G303.3.6.3; dwarf lets l. escape waiting for ram K553.2.1; escaped l. delivers himself to shepherd rather than to slaughter J217.1; golden l. promised to goddess (common l. sacrificed) K231.3.2; king seizes poor man's l. U35.1.1; man disguised as l. K1823.3; man transformed to l. D135.1; only l. punished of all animals U11.1.1.1; revenant as l. E423.1.6; sheep licking her l. is envied by wolf J1909.5; using l. to get lawyer's audience J1653; vegetable l. B95ff.; wolf persuades l. to bring him drink K815.11; wolf unjustly accuses l. and eats him U31.

Lambs. — Fairies cause ewes to have two l. F339.3.2.

Lambskin disguise as hairy man K1821.4.1.

Lame boy (girl) as helper N822; child as hero L112.8; god A128.5; man given hardworking wife T125.1. — Blind girl marries l. man T125.2; blind, l., and deaf as witnesses in court X141; blind man carries l. man N886; blind man carrying l. man treasure guardians N577; curse: horse will be l. M471.3.1; magic power of the l. D1716.2; mother abusing l. son S12.7; thief makes l. excuse J1391; youth made l.: has kicked his mother J225.1; why l. make good soldiers J1494.

Lameness magically cured D2161.3.7. — Animal feigns l. K1818.5; humor of l. X143; trickster pretends l. and is taken on woman's back: violates her K1382.

Lamentations for the dead A1547.3; for heavenly bodies F961.0.3. — Animal's l. for person lost when animal was transformed A2275.1.

Lamia B29.1; eats children G262.0.1.

Laming horse for sale K134.8; as punishment Q451.2. — Fairies l. miller F361.17.1; knockers l. miners F456.1.2.1.5; payment for l. man K251.6; witch l. G263.4.3.

Lamp gives vision of Most High D1323.19; lighted over murderer's body E185.1; lit at least every fortnight A1599.14; unlighted, ghosts take over house E593.3. — Cover face: no need to put out l. W111.2.9; disenchantment by breaking l. D789.2; entrance into woman's room in l. stand K1342.0.2; lighting l. with king's moustache P672.4; lighting empty l. by magic D1933; magic l. *D1162.1, (summons genie) D1421.1.5; miser running back to put out burning l. W153.11.2; oil l. blown out: had thought that it outshone stars L475; suitor brings own l. J1575.1.

Lamps burn with urine F964.3.1; converse overheard N454.2. — Giants with l. under coats F531.4.7.2; saint's breath kindles l. D1566.1.4.

Lampblack. — Magic l. D931.1.3.

Lamplighter, treacherous K2259.2.

Lampoon. — Fear of druidic l. P427.4.1.

Lancaster rose A2656.2.

Lance cast through leaf F661.8.1; foretells owner's defeat D1311.17.3; imbedded in earth cannot be moved D1654.4.3; for witch killing G229.4.1. — Bleeding l. flows into silver cup F991.1; demon occupies l. F408.1; extraordinary l. F832; gae bulga (barbed l. which cannot be withdrawn) F832.1.1; ghost points l. at murderer E231.2; gift to magic l. necessary C835.2.1; magic l. D1086, (flaming) D1645.8.3, (kills) D1402.7.3; skillful marksman casts l. through ring F661.8; stretching l. D482.3.

Lances. — Eyes impervious to l. F541.10.

Lanced. — Cheek l. rather than reveal fig in mouth W111.5.8.

Land, see also **Country, Earth;** of Cimmerians F129.3; of Cokaygne *X1503; of the dead E481; grants M207; made magically fertile D2157.1; measured by amount in view H1584.1; of happiness *F111; of Immortals F116; of Lotus Eaters *F111.3; of Men of Heads Only F129.1; of moon *F16; of Mossynoikoi F129.2; of plenty F701; of Promise F111.2, F979.10; of the Saints V511.4; that has seen the sun only once (riddle) H822; sinks and lake appears as punishment Q552.2.1; -spirits F494; made magically sterile *D2081; of the sun *F17; of Thunders F117; of the Unborn F115; under Water F252.1.0.2; of Women F112; of youth D1338.7. — Building bridge over l. and sea (task) H1131.1; China first l. in world A802; clearing l.: axe broken K1421; curse on l. M474; deceptive l. purchase K185; dwarfs came into the l. by the hundreds F451.3.14.1; eel becomes dry l. D426.1.2; fairies clear l. F271.5; giant immortal so long as he touches l. of his birth D1854; head of divinity as protection of l. D1380.3; leaving l. unoccupied tabu C868; lies about l. features X1510; magic l. features D930ff.; magic l. and water ship D1533.1.1; magic song makes barren l. fruitful D1563.1.2; mortal goes to l. of dwarfs F451.5.4; much l. as reward Q111.8; penniless wooer; patch of l. K1917.1; plowing enormous amount of l. in one day (task) H1103.2; riddle about l. that has seen sun once only H822.1; roots hold l. firm A857.3.1; supplying water in l. where it is lacking (task) H1138; trespasser's defense: standing on his own l. J1161.3.

Landing on gods' island tabu C93.8; on island tabu C755.7; of returning heroes prophesied M369.6. — God's l. place A151.12; voyager l. on sea-beast's back B556.

Landlord. — Woman in disguise outwits tricky l. K1837.5.

Landlord's — Dead supplies l. money E373.4.

Landlords have biggest bellies J1289.17.

Landmarks. — Man who removes l. cannot rest in grave E416; remover of l. punished Q275; removing l. forbidden C846.

Landowner. — Devil punishes l. G303.9.3.1.1.

Landscape of otherworld F162. — Illusions in l. K1886.

Language of heaven A667, A1482.1, B212.0.1; learned by swallowing characters D1735.2; misunderstandings J2496.2. — Angels' l. V249.2; animals, men spoke same l. B210.3; answers in foreign l. C495.2.2; change of l. for breaking tabu *C966; first animals knew human l. B212.0.2; Hebrew as l. of heaven A1482.1; hero invents, teaches Irish l. A541.1; Irish l. A1616.2; king brought to sense of duty by feigned knowledge of bird l. J816.1; learning foreign l. quickly F695.3.1; magic knowledge of animals' l. D1815.2*; origin of l. A1482; poets' difficult l. P427.7.2.1; saints' l. abilities V223.5; sign l. H607; trickster teaches dupe strange l. K1068; use of strange l. to show education W116.7; witness who cannot speak l. of accusation discredited J1152.

Languages. — Animal l. B215ff., (knowledge of) *B216, (learned) *B217;

cold before theft of fire impedes speech: explanation of difficulty of certain l. A1616.1; dupe scalding self to learn l. K1046; magic knowledge of strange l. *D1815; magic object teaches animal l. D1301; murder discovered through knowledge of bird l. N271.4; origin of particular l. A1616; understanding animal l. leads to treasure N547.

Lantern. — Aesop with the l. J1303; cat carrying l. K264.2; ghost carries l. E599.7; Jack o' L. A2817, F491; magic l. heals wounds D1503.5; magic wishing l. D1470.1.17; quest for healing l. H1324.1; quest for magic l. H1341; witch power from swinging red l. G224.6.

Lanterns. — Dwarfs have little l. F451.7.3; "hang out l." J2516.5.

Lap. — Baby placed in bathing queen's l. T589.6.1.1; ball thrown into l. to test sex of girl masking as man H1578.1.4; eagle lays eggs in l. of Zeus L315.7; sleeping with head in wife's l. T299.1.

Lapdog dies when mistress dies B301.7. — Fairy as l. F234.1.9.1; first l. in Ireland H1831.2; hound becomes l. D412.5.2; split l. becomes two rocks A977.5.4.

Lapdogs B182.1.0.1.

Lapis lazuli cart F861.3.1.

Lapland. — Origin of gnats in L. A2033.1.

Lapwing. — Why l. flies in curves A2442.2.3.

Lard made from bark D476.1.4. — Man transformed to l. D271.1; obtaining wild boar's l. H1154.11.

Larder. — Inexhaustible l. D1652.18.

Large, see also **Big, Great;** animal frightened by bluffing smaller K1715.12; loaves need large oven X434.1. — Why animal's mouth is l. A2341.2; beggar with small bag surpasses the one with the l. L251; choices: small inconveniences, l. gain J350ff.; devil as a l. strong man G303.3.1.1; dwarf has small body and l. head F451.2.1.3; exceptionally l. or small men F530ff.; extraordinarily l. fruit F813.0.3; fairies with unusually l. ears F232.3; ghost as l. man E422.3.2; giant with l. (beard) F531.1.6.4, (gleaming eyes) F531.1.1.2; giants l. or small at will F531.6.5.2; lie: remarkably l. person X922; men at first as l. as giants A1301; remarkably l. mouth F544.0.1; remarkably l. nose F543.2; putting a l. squash into a narrow-necked jar H1023.11; small trespasses punished: l. crimes condoned U11.

Larger. — Animal becomes l. A2301ff., D2038; devil becomes l. and l. G303.3.5.1; hero professes to be able to perform much l. task than that assigned K1741; making the earth l. A853; objects become l. D480ff.; person becomes magically l. D55.1; robber promised l. sum at office: cheated K439.7; surprise that king is not l. J1742.4.

Lark causes elephant to fall over precipice L315.5. — Creation of l. A1911; helpful l. B451.1; smallness of offense no excuse when hunter prepares to kill l. U32; wedding of l. B282.3ff.

Larks. — King of l. B242.2.12.

Larvae. — Manking descended from l. A1224.2.

Lash confers invulnerability D1846.4.1.

Lasso. — Priest caught in l. by rival lover K1218.1.6.

Lassoed buzzards rescue man from hole B547.2.1.

Last belongs to devil G303.19.1. — Borrower to get the corn at same place as l. year J1381; devil disappears on l. day G303.17.1.2; devil is to have l. one who leaves "black school" S241.2; evil woman in glass case as l. commodity K216.1; Judas spills salt at L. Supper N131.3.1; knight divides his l. penny Q42.1; payment to be made when l. leaf falls K222; unpromising hero l. to try task H991.

Late bird alone succeeds at bird convocation L147.1. — Animal who arrives l. performs tasks for man B571.2; animal l. at distribution of qualities: hence his characteristics A2235; lover made l. at rendezvous by incessant talker *T35.0.1; too l. for same advice J1363; witch returns home l. G249.4.

Latin. — Boy pretends to speak only L. J1511.11; injuring dupe as he is taught L. K1068.2; prearranged L. answers J1741.3; priests (shoolmasters) ignorant of L. J1741; sham priest repeats few words of L. K1961.1.2; speaking L. so birds won't understand J1894.

Latrine too small for dining room table J2236.

Laugh. — Dwarfs' l. F451.6.6; enigmatical l. reveals secret (knowledge) N456, (prophecy) M304; magic object compels person's l. D1419.1; prophecy from enigmatical l. M304; suitor test: causing princess's l. H341ff.; task: causing person's l. H1194.

Laughing animal B214.3; ass J1169.5; and crying at the same time *F1041.11; fish reveals unjust judgment *D1318.2.1; at ghosts tabu C462; jackal H1194.2; mountain F755.1.1; skull advises hero E366.1; statue reveals crime D1639.4; tabu C460ff.; at thief who gets nothing J1392.4. — Avoiding punishment by getting king l. J823; bean split from l. F662.3, (causes black stripe) A2741.1; bearded man l. tabu C461; deceptive l. contest K87; devil l. when men weep G303.4.8.8; fruits l. or crying D1619.3; magic results from l. *D1773; magic l. object D1617; man l. at blind made blind Q583.1; numskull l. at his child's death J2461.3; patient l. at foolish diagnosis of sham physician breaks his abscess and gets well N641; person never l. F591; philosopher l. at world's sin U15.1; preaching leaves half congregation l., half crying X416; spurned favorite makes rajah l.-stock K1678; thief imagines people are l. at him, confesses N275.4; vow against l. until hero arrives M151.7; women l. (at grave) C181.7, (explained) A1372.2.

Laughter from chagrin F1041.11.1; forbidden A1372.7; produces rain D2143.1.11; thought to be spirits J1784.1. — God of l. A489.4; inordinate l. brings misfortune N399.2; journey to Isle of L. F111.1; magic compels l. D1419.1; man whose l. brings rain H1194.1; origin of l. A1399.1; sick fairy cured by l. D813.2; sister is mourning last year's l. H583.5; wife's l. checks husband J1545.7.

Laundress. — House of l. of clothes for church spared in great fire V137;

stingy dead woman lifts her head to correct exorbitant account of l. W152.3.

Laurel causes forgetfulness D1365.1.3; and olive tree scorn thornbush as umpire in their dispute J411.7. — Magic l. (plant) *D965.9, (tree) D950.17; magic wishing-l. D1470.1.3; man (woman) transformed to l. D215.1; why l. tree is bitter A2771.8.2.

Lava flow as punishment Q552.24. — Ogresses caught in l. flood G514.6.

Laving, see Washing.

Law courts *P510ff.; against rape A1556.1; student forgets speech J2046. — Animals at l. B270ff.; cheating through l. K453; cleverness in l. court J1130—J1199; culture hero establishes l. and order A530ff.; god rewards enacting good l. Q176; magic object helps win in l. court D1406ff.; marriage for a night to evade l. T156; natural l. suspended D2137.

Laws P522; given directly by deity A1580.2; on property division within family A1585. — Absurd disregard of natural l. J1930ff.; dwarfs are subject to l. of nature F451.3.5; king's l. must be kept until his death: sends back bones M14; making of l. P541; natural l. inoperative at end of world A1091; origin of l. A1580ff.; vow to abide by l. M185.

Lawbreaker. — Ungrateful l. seduces magistrate's wife W154.15.

Lawbreakers. — Dogs track down l. B578.

Lawlessness. — Banishment for l. Q431.2.3.

Lawsuit against animals B272.1. — Animal characteristics result of l. A2255ff.; noblemen being ruined by long l. join their families in marriage to save fortunes J552.2; riddle as solution to l. H542.1; wisdom of child decides l. J123.

Lawsuits of animals B270ff.; involving lending horse J1552.3. — Bishop fond of l. J552.2.1.

Lawyer P422; outwitted into settling debt K1623. — Devil follows corpse when a l. is buried G303.25.8; the doubly-feed l. K441.2; woman masks as l. and frees her husband K1825.2.

Lawyer's dog steals meat (double damages as fee) K488; mad client (Pathelin) *K1655. — Thief steals l. hood and robe K362.9; using lamb to get l. attention J1653.

Lawyers. — Jokes on l. X310ff.

Lay. — Division between religious and l. activities A1472.1.

Laying see also **Laid.** — How birds began l. eggs A2486.4; woman l. eggs F569.1.

Layman ignorant of medicine J1734; made to believe he is a monk J2314. — Priest disguises as l. K1824.

Laymen. — Peasant as priest preaches on the troubles of l. K1961.1.1ff.

Laziness *W111ff.; punished *Q321, Q5. — Key in flax reveals bride's l. H382.1; monk falsely accused of l. K2129.1; origin of l. A1377.

Lazy boy asks god to delay plowing season J713.1; boy and industrious girl matched T125; hero L114.1; husband W111.4; pupil reforms by watching home builder J67.1; servant W111.2ff.; wife W111.3, (taken

naked in bundle of straw to a wedding) Q495.1; woman resumes her
work when she sees little bird peck hole in stone J1011. — Ant and l.
cricket J711.1; ass buyer returns ass which has associated with l. companions J451.1; creation of monkey from l. man A1861.3; God throws
sand on l. shepherds (origin of insects) A2005; house dog blames master
for teaching him l. habits J142.1; mother wishes l. daughter may marry
devil C12.4.1; shoving, killing l. child J2465.3.1; tabu: bearded man being
l. C565.2; why shoemakers are l. P453.1; witches punish l. spinning
women G282.

Lead is heaviest (riddle) H645.1. — Bath of molten l. F872.5; dwarf
turns gold into l. F451.3.3.2; murder by hot l. poured into ear S112.3;
punishment: boiling l. Q414.1; reward for the bag of l. K476.2.2; saint
unhurt by melted l. D1841.2.2; sham-dead person tested by hot l.
poured on hand H248.1.

Leader of the Wild Hunt E501.1ff. — Coming of religious l. prophesied
M363; foolish imitation of l. J2417; man transformed to beast becomes
l. of herd B241.3; warriors battle l. as valor test H1561.8; you be l.
and I will follow J1515.

Leader's — Shooting off l. tail X1124.1.

Leaders in single combat for victory H217.1.

Leadership test H1567.

Leading. — Animals l. men B563ff.; drunk men l. one another home
X814.

Leaf falls on altar F962.12.5; sent down stream as a warning to one
below H135; serves as boat D1524.8.1; thrown at animal's rump: hence
tails A2215.1; transformed to another object D451.8; transformed to
person D431.3. — Bringing plantain l. without tearing it H1041; crossing
river on l.: God reposed on one J2495.5; deceptive wage: rice on l.
K256.1; disenchantment from l. by breaking it from tree D711.5; hare
and man contest in watching for l. to fall A2256.1; impregnation by l. of
lettuce T532.1.3; last l. never falls from oak: devil cheated K222; living
on food piled on l. H351.1; magic l. *D955, (bears person aloft) D1532.9;
origin of l.-dress A1453.4; recognition by l. H135.1; resuscitation by l.
E64.18; transformation by eating l. D551.5; why hare skips about like a
l. A2479.2; why rat's tail looks like folded l. A2378.9.5; witch flies on
l. G242.3.

Leaves become gold plates D475.1.19; fall from tree as life token E761.7.3;
of life and death E64.1.1.2; magically enlarged D489.1; of plant
A2760ff.; transformed to animal D441.5; of tree open and close to give
saint passage F979.2. — Beauty contestants covered with l. K98.1;
blister on back from lying in rose l. F647.9; conception from eating l.
T511.2.0.2; counting l. daily falling off tree H1118.2; dead l. changed to
gold D475.1.3; devils put to flight by cross made of l. G303.16.3.3; doing
penance till green l. grow on a dry branch Q521.1; fairies dance on
undisturbed l. F261.2.1; flower with "ave" on l. E631.0.2.1; injury from

rose l. falling F647.3; magic flower pot bears plants with gold letters on l. D1469.1. magic l. turn white bird black D1337.2.1; prophecy on l. blown by winds M301.21; remedy: covering with dry l. K1010.1; resuscitation by l. E105; riddle: how many l. are on the tree? H705; riddle: tree with l. white on one side and black on the other H721.2; riddle: tree with twelve branches, each with thirty l., black and white H721.1; shame for nakedness appears to first women (l. for clothes) A1383.1; sky rests on top of trees: hence flat l. A2741.3; touching l. forbidden C511; tree with extraordinary l. F811.2; tree sheds l. in sympathy F979.15; why all trees have l. A2760.1; why certain l. have holes in them A2763; why certain l. are hollow A2764; why l. hang head downward A2768; why khijur l. are long and narrow: split by arrow A2741.5; waiting in vain for l. to fall J2066.8; wild huntsman repays with l. that turn to gold *E501.15.4.

Leak. — Helpful animal stops l. in Noah's Ark *B527.2; seduction by l. in roof over woman's bed K1339.8; tiger frightened of l. J2633.

Leaky. — Carrying water in l. vessel (task) H1023.2.1; embarkation in l. vessel as punishment Q466; filling l. vessels with water from a bottomless jar as punishment Q512.1; pumping out a l. ship (task) H1023.5.

Lean dogs envy arena-dog his fatness but later see their error L455. — Division of fat and l. fowls J1241.4; fat and l. kine in otherworld F171.1; king grows l. from fear of death U241.

Leander drowned as he swims to Hero T83.

Leap. — Cliff from lovers' l. A968.2; enormous l. F1071.2.1; horse's tremendous l. F989.1.1.

Leaps. — Chasms mark l. of giants A972.5.2.

Leaping a camping place tabu C876; to death with woman in arms Q411.0.1.3; over stone yearly compulsion C684.3. — Cat l. through man like arrow of fire, burns him to ashes B16.1.1.2; corpse l. up in emotion at saint's passing nearby E597; soul l. from body E722.2.5.

Lear, king M21.

Learned man giving away knowledge reincarnated as tree H1292.2.1; person worth two unlearned J252; professions P420ff.; words misunderstood by uneducated J1803. — Animal characteristic l. from another animal A2271; animal language l. B217ff.; ignorant surpasses l. man L143; man gains entrance to l. girl's presence K1321.1.3; means of resuscitation l. E181; remedy l. from overhearing animal meeting *B513; valuable secrets l. *N440—N499.

Learning art of love T4; the Bavarian language X652; fear H1440ff.; to pray V51; quickly to read F695.3; to read by magic D1819.4; as suitor test H327; or wit more important? N141.1. — Choice: doing what you know or l. something J483; god of l. A465.3; saint helps with l. V223.4; test of l. H502; wisdom before l. J1217.2.

Leash. — Dogs on l. in wild hunt E501.4.1.9; life token: dogs pulling on l. E761.7.5.

Leashes. — Forgetting hounds' l. bad omen D1812.5.1.21.

Least loved friend only true H1558.1.1. — Contest: who will eat l.? H81.4.

Leather. — Stirrup l. breaking bad omen D1815.5.1.28.

Leave. — "Have we l. to go?" K475.2.

Leaven tabu for cooking C888.

Leaves, see after **Leaf.**

Leavetaking. — Buffaloes fail to come at god's l. A2231.12; trees fail to come at god's l., punished A2721.7.

Leaving purchase, remembering extra token J2461.5. — Bridegroom l. bride, impelled by magic T177; cat l. house when report is made of death of one of his companions *B342; fairy l. when named F381.1; excuse for returning home after l. wife J1545.3.3; guests l. after shabby hospitality P334; manner of soul's l. body E722.2ff.; punishment for l. holy orders Q226; tabu: women l. hero's land C566.3; Virgin miraculously prevents nun from l. convent V265.

Lecherous, see also **Lustful;** brother T415.1; father T411.1; king glued with feathers K1218.18; prince in disguise to kill grandchildren K1812.14. — Tiger tears l. teacher Q243.6.

Lechery. — Man saved from l. through prayer V52.1.

Led. — Lost king l. from forest by lion *B563.1; man harnessed and l. to dance by witch G269.3; person l. astray by spirit F402.1.1.

Leech. — Girl reborn as l. to avenge murder E693.1; indestructibility of l. B745; origin of l. A2182.2; reincarnation as l. E618.1; why l. is blind A2332.6.8; why l. feeds on human blood A2435.6.3.

Leeches. — Don't pluck off well-fed l. J215.1.3.

Leek in beer poison protection D1383.5. — Magic l. *D983.3; rush becomes l. D451.2.1.

Leeks. — Test of wife's obedience: not to eat l. H473.3; to eat a hundred l. J2095.

Left, see also **Leaving.** — Body l. or entered by soul E720ff.; chaste woman to surrender when rocks have l. the coast M261; earthly bride l. for service of Virgin T376.1; implement l. by mountain-men F460.4.3; man l. by fairy mistress when he breaks tabu F302.6; money l. on hill to repay helpful mountain-men F460.4.2.2; truth deserts city because there is no place l. for her Z121.1; witch's body l. by soul *G229.1.

Left (adjective) eye only vulnerable spot Z311.1; eye renders fairies visible F235.8.2; -handed tribe F515.5; hand's power for evil *D996.0.2.1; -sided giant F525.5. — Amazons cut off l. breast of daughters so that they can handle bow F565.1.1; familiar spirit acquired by carrying egg under l. arm-pit F403.2.1.1; ointment cures l. cheek, not right D1663.2; skillful marksman shoots l. eye (of fly at two miles) F661.5.3, (of serpent) F661.5.1; soul (life) in l. hand E714.7; tabu: turning l. side of chariot toward certain town C643.

Leg, see also **Foot.** — Bringing l. to fit dragon's claw H322.3; broken l. saves man from fatal fight N178.1; child born with one l. T551.12;

clever girl comes with one l. on animal's back, one on ground H1053.3; coyote persuaded to break l.: therefore has thin right l. A2284.5; dwarf carries his knocked-off l. on his shoulder F451.6.13; fairy breaks servant's l. F361.17.4; fairy horse with one l. F241.1.3.1; giant with one l. F531.1.3.3.1; fowl makes another animal believe that he has had his l. cut off J2413.4.1; ghost laid when l. is buried E441.1; giant's l. stops ship at sea F531.3.1.2; god with one l. A128.3.1; goose without a. l. K402.1; horse's l. cut off and replaced *E782.4; -less deity supported on animal A128.3; marvelous runners keeps l. tied up F681.1; mountain stretches l. out to meet beloved A965.1; numskull ties rope to l. as cow grazes on the roof J2132.2; ogre with sharpened l. G341.1; ogress can extend l. or arm any distance G365.2; ox's l. as person F988.1; pumpkin tied to another's l. J2013.3; return from dead to punish theft of l. from grave E235.4.2; sawing l. off J2131.3.3; severed l. regrows E782.4.2; substituted l. E782.4.1; trained deer drinks wine until he breaks his l. but thereafter abstains J133.3; trickster receives power of sharpening l. without harm if he will use it but four times J2424; village of people with one l. F768.3; witch known by hose unbound on one l. G255; wooden l. overawes Indians K547.2.

Leg's length from earth to heaven H682.1.8.

Legs cut off as punishment Q451.2.4. — Animal with two short l. for living on hillside X1381; animal with one head, two bodies, six l. B15.7.11; animal with body of horse, l. of hound B14.2; animal with six l. F451.4.3.9; why animals lift their l. A2473; animals with unusual l. or feet B15.6; armless people have l. growing from their shoulders F516.1.1; breaking l. for prowess in dancing K1013.6; cat devours man's l. B161.1.3; corpse's l. cause murder accusation K2152.2; daddy-long-legs' long l. A2371.2.12; devil will not carry usurers to hell but will drag them by the l. X513; devil's l. G303.4.5ff.; disenchantment by passing between l. D798; earth supported on birds' l. A844.10; ghost with thin l. E422.1.6.2; god with many l. A123.6; Indians and whites from l. of first man A1614.7; loss of eating contest: because of weak l. J2228; magic animal l. D1012.1; magic drink deprives of l. D1410.6; magic sight by looking under one's l. D1821.3.3; man lets l. burn in fire rather than move them W111.1.1; men with two faces, three l., and seven arms F526.5; miser breaks l. trying to retrieve single grain J2146.1; mutilation: cutting off l. *S162; numskulls cannot find their own l. J2021; ogre terrified by woman's l. K1755; origin and nature of animal's l. A2371ff.; person unusual as to his l. F517; putting l. together proves sex H1578.1.4.1; remarkable l. F548; riddle: four l. in the morning, two at midday, and three in the evening H761; riddle: two l., three l., four l. H742; riddle about two l. better than three H761.1; snake with l. B765.23; stag scorns his l. but is proud of his horns L461; witch burns child's l. for wood, heals them D2161.3.3.1.

Leg-wrappers. — Copper l. capture spirit F405.13.

Legal. — Animals in l. relations B270ff.

Legend. — Riddles based on l. H810ff.

Legerdemain. — Deception by l. K1871.

Legible. — Decalogue l. on both sides F883.1.3.

Legitimacy of children tested by dipping them in river H222.1. — Child's missing toe proves l. T318; children not l. T640ff.; wrestling to test son's l. H218.2.

Legitimate. — God reveals self to those of l. birth K445.1; not of l. birth J1803.1.

Leinster. — Broad-headed spears in L. A1459.1.2.

Leisure. — Why women have no l. A1372.8.

Lemon indicates head, foot of couch H506.6; thrown to indicate princess's choice H316.1. — Conception from eating l. T511.1.5.

Lemons, three D211.1.

Lemur looks where forbidden: has big eyes A2234.3; marriage to B601.6.

Lender discredited J21.38.

Lenders. — Practical retorts: borrowers and l. J1550ff.

Lending. — Animal characteristics: l. and refusing to receive back A2243; chain tale: l. and repaying Z41.5; counsel on not l. your horse J21.10; dwarfs l. to mortals F451.5.1.11; ghost l. jewels E363.5.1; promise on l. wife M267; tabu: l. C784; trolls' l. F455.6.2.

Length. — Grave equals five times l. of any person's foot D482.5.1.

Lengthened days in spring A1155. — Day magically l. D2146.1.1; night magically l. D2146.2.2; summer magically l. D2145.2.1.

Lenore (dead lover returns) E215.

Lent V73.6; to be short since winter was J1743.2. — Meat disguised as butter during L. K498.

Lents. — Three l. Z71.1.6.

Lentil in the soup J2469.1. — Monkey and lost l. J344.1.

Lentils. — Chain tale: l. get into sack Z41.9.

Leopard ashamed of lizard bite J411.10; in human form B651.11; leaves victim claiming to hold up sky K547.14; mistaken for calf J1758.4; with nine tails B15.7.7; persuaded to enter bag, see trick K711.2; poses as brother, kills child K2011.1.4; released: grateful B375.7; as suitor B621.5; transformed to person D312.3; traps lion in cave K730.3; tied in bag in water floats to shore, finds mate N228. — Abduction by l. R13.1.9; antelope sends l. for fire, eats game K345.4; why l. cannot capture animal who passes him on right side A2463.1; dog becomes l. D412.5.5; color of l. A2411.1.1.1; enemies of l. A2494.2ff.; friendship of l. and (goat) A2493.8, (cat) A2493.35; (night-jar) A2493.8, (squirrel) A2493.7; helpful l. B431.1; jackal as l. cubs' nurse K2061.11; jackal, l. tie tails together J681.1.1; why l. lives where he does A2433.3.18; why l. cats live in cold, damp, shady places A2433.3.12; lizard defeats l. L315.11; lizard frightens l. away K1715.5; magic l. gall causes death D1402.3.2; man transformed to l. D112.4; marriage to l. B601.4; ox-demon transformed to l. D412.2.4; sham-dead l. betrays self K607.3.3; spots on l. A2412.1.2; strong man kills l. F628.1.1.2;

strong man throws l. F624.1.3; tortoise cheats l. of meat K476.1.2; trickster tells l. he is too dirty to eat K553.6; transformation: handkerchief with three knots to golden l. etc. D454.3.2.2; why l. walks alone A2433.2.3.1; why l. is strong A2528.1; cause of walk of l. A2441.1.9.

Leopard's food A2435.3.17; haunt A2433.3.1.2. — Stone falls, knocks l. teeth out K1015.2.

Leopards as God's messengers A165.2.1.1.5; guide Holy Family to Egypt B563.5. — Children spotted like l. after bestiality T465.4.

Leper P162; controls winds D2142.0.4; as helper N864; hero L112.7.1; intercepts letter and takes paramour's place with princess K1317.2; laid in queen's bed K2112.2; as villain K2276. — Christ disguised as l. V211.2.1.1; curse: man to kiss l. M438.1; disguise as l. K1818.1, (to spy) K2357.11; kissing l. as punishment Q499.1.1; risking life to carry l., Christ in disguise Q25.1; seduction by posing as l. K1315.11; spring flows where l. pulls out rushes A941.5.3; transformation into l. *D27; wisdom from dream: the l. with the cup of water J157.1; woman consorts with l. T232.1; woman disguised as l. seduces, binds enemies K778.2.

Lepers are sacred V293.

Lepidoptera. — Creation of l. A2040ff.

Leprechauns F451.0.1; from Ham's curse A1614.1.1.

Leprosy from breaking tabu C941.1; cured except on thumb Z311.3; as curse M431.7; as punishment Q551.6.0.1; as punishment for desecration church Q222.5.3. — Ashes cause l. D1500.4.6; devil of l. A478.5; escape by shamming l. K523.2; magic object cures l. *D1502.4ff.; mistress accuses wife of l. K2110.1.1; origin of l. A1337.6; saint cures l. V221.3; Satan smites man with l. G303.9.4.0.2; sunlight ray causes l. D1500.4.4.

Leprous. — Wife alone remains with l. husband T215.7.1.

Lesson. — Son learns l. from mother's sufferings P236.7.

Letter believed despite contrary evidence J2528; of Christ V211.10; delivered to wrong man, substitute lover K1317.2.2; falsified for false elopement T92.4.2; from man in hell Q564; of salvation given from grave E373.3; shot into sky F883.2.1; from soul in purgatory E755.3.1; written on human skin F883.2. — Alleged healing l. sold *K115.1; alleged l. from king dupes victim K825.4; angel leaves l. of instructions V246.0.1; bird as l. carrier B291.1.0.1; carrying l. in person: no one else can read it J2242.1; cobra writes l. on prince's tongue B165.1.3; cure by kissing saint's l. V221.7; dead wife's l. to husband E322.7; extraordinary writings (book, l.) F883; forged l. obtains credit L455.8.1; holy man's l. stops devastation D2163.5.2.1; husband discovers love l. to wife K1557.1; husband's l. altered into execution order K2117.1; innocent man compelled to write treasonable l. K2156; intercepted love l. leads to substitute lover K1317.9; king's l. must be explained on pain of death H587.0.1; love l. hidden in apple K1872.3; magic l. protects against attack D1381.24; man desirous of traveling sent six miles to deliver a l. J1076.1; page throws l. in fire, thereby proving his guilt H262; rabbit sold as l.-carrier *K131.1; reading l. written by Christ protects against attack D1381.24.1; sending l. by flooded river J1881.1.7; sham teacher pretends to read document brought him as a l. K1958; substituted l. *K1851; Uriah l.: man carries written order for his own execution K978; Uriah l. changed .*K511.

Letters in book have become small; were big in school J1746.1, J2258; in clouds interpreted as call to ministry ("P. C." in clouds as "preach Christ" or "plow corn") X459.1.1. — Adam's name from initial l. of four stars A1281.6.1; clouds form l. F795.1; flower from grave bears l. E531.0.2; inscription of golden l. on bird B7.3; magic flower pot bears plants with gold l. on leaves D1469.1; magic object from exchanging l. D836; quest for vulture's egg figured with golden l. H1332.2; symbolic meaning of l. H602; taking l. to dead H1252.2..

Lettuce. — Impregnation by leaf of l. T532.1.3; nun eating unblessed l. eats a demon G303.16.2.3.4.

Level. — Student hands back l. bushel and keeps surplus K223.

Leveling. — Magic l. of mountain D2152.1.

Leviathan B61; casts up gorge which spreads disease B16.4.1; keeps sea warm A1119.2; surrounds globe A876.1. — Angels battle l. A1082.7; cataclysm from l. striking earth with tail B16.4.1.1; creation of l. A2135.2; earth rests on l. A844.11; god battles l. A1082.4; god plays with l. A179.9.

Levitation D2135.0.1.

Levites as religious order V453. — Institution of L. as reward Q113.4.1.

Levity about biblical passages J1262.4. — Repartee based on l. toward sacred persons and things J1261ff.

Lewd. — Banishment for l. conduct Q431.5.3.

Lia Fáil H171.5.

Liar brings about fight between dupes K1084; cannot be healed U235.1; discredits own confession J1155.1; escapes from devil H1318; praises apes' beauty and receives reward J815.1. — Attempt to lie out of having called another a l. J1456; give and prove me a l. J1333; greatest l. to get his supper free K455.7; greatest l. made king of Schlaraffenland X905.2.

Liars. — River drowns l. D1318.17.

Libations V12.9.

Liberal girl rewarded with riches Q101.1. — Ruler l., gives more than treasurer writes W11.12.

Liberality as amend for stinginess Q589.4. — Cause l. to be depicted J1576; invitation to continued l. H595.1.

Liberating woman captive in elephant's ear H1151.18.

Liberty. — Wild animal finds his l. better than tame animal's ease L451; wolf prefers l. and hunger to dog's servitude and plenty L451.

Lice, see after **Louse.**

Licked. — First man from maid having l. semen-stained cloth A1211.7; river valley l. out by giant beast A951.1.

Licking brew gives serpent power G224.7; husband's body K1085.1. — Animals l. Christ-child B251.10; boar l. holy man's wounds B256.6.3; conception from l. spittle T512.5; cow l. saint's feet B251.2.6.2; deer l. saint's tomb daily B251.2.6; lion l. sick man J413.1; magic cure by l. D2161.4.17; magic results from l. *D1775; pig heals wounds by l. B511.2.2; water-monsters l. saint's feet B251.2.6.1; wolves l. saint's shoes B251.2.3.

Lid. — Murder by slamming down l. of chest S121; eye with remarkably heavy l. F541.7.

Lie, see also **Liar, Lying;** becomes truth as punishment Q591. — Forcing princess to say, "That is a l." *H342.1; telling skillful l. as test H509.5.

Lies precipitate fight K1084. — Filling a sack full of l. *H1045; flattering l. vs. unflattering truths J267; humor of l. and exaggeration *X900— X1899; hungry apprentice attracts master's attention by telling l. on him J1341.5; shoemaker drinks more than his portion of "drink of l." X242.

Lieutenant. — Lion as king makes ass his l. J421.1.

Life beheads simpleton J27; as ever-decreasing paradox answer H1075; index *E760ff., H1353; kept in special part of body E714; -lights in lower world E765.1.3; -long penance for brother-sister marriage Q520.3; the most beloved (riddle) H647.1; personified as old woman Z113; preferred to death and vengeance J327; prolonged D1855ff.; restored to dead E0—E199; saved by accident N650ff.; spans M341.1.6.1; spared as reward Q151; token *E761ff.; wagered N2.2. — After world-fire, l. recreated from tree A1006.9; animal saves person's l. *B520ff.; how ants can secure longer l. H1292.11; bargains to spare l. M234; belief in future l. V311; bodily member sacrificed to save l. J351; cooked animal comes to l. E168; daily l. of the gods A150ff.; darkness comes in daytime in order to save l. of maiden about to be executed F965.1; dead awaken after three days to new l. and great wisdom E489.1; dead tree comes to l. *E2; deer of gold and jewels possessing l. D1620.2.3; dying man refuses to believe in l. to come V311.2; fairy grateful to mortal for saving his l. F337; forethought in provision for l. J700ff.; fountain miraculously supports l. D1472.1.1; girl demands suitor's l. H333; giving l. for friend P316; guessing with l. as wager H512; hidden l. E712; lake of milk by tree of l. A878.2; law: l. for a life P522.1; long l. by cutting off finger-ends S161.1.1; long l. as reward Q145.1; long l. of first man A1323; man learns the fear of Death by meeting L. J27; married l. *T200—T299; marriage promised as l. saver M268; marvelous things needed to save girl's l. H355.0.1; miraculously long l. as reward Q145; nature of l. U (entire chapter); no time for minor fights when l. is in danger J371; oath taken on person's l. M119.8; ordering of human l. *A1300ff.; patriarchs because of long l. made inventions A1440.3; person comes to l. E1; picture comes to l. D435.2.1; preservation of l. during world calamity A1005; prophecy of long l. M321; quest for apple of l. H1333.3.1.2; quest for water of l. H1321.1; recognition by telling l. history H11.1; resuscitation of wife by husband giving up half his remaining l. *E165; return to l.: see **Resuscitation;** short l. of first man A1325; soldier prefers l. to death with revenge J327; staff of l. and death E64.1.1; tree of l. *E90ff.; unusual manner of l. F560ff.; vampire brought to l. E251.2; wands of l. and death D1663.1; water of l. *E80ff., F162.6.2; water-spirit claims a l. every seven years F420.5.2.1.6; well indicates l. span D1663.5; why animal has long l. A2578; witch offers man his l. if he will marry her G266.

Life's inequalities U0—U99.

Lives. — Giants playing with men's l. F531.3.15.

Lifelike. — Contest in l. painting H504.1.

Lifted. — Sun falls, l. back to sky A721.5; woman can be l. only by lover D1651.13.

Lifter. — Fairy as mighty l. F253.1.1.1; mighty l. F624ff.; remarkable l. X941.

Lifting cat (serpent that embraces the earth) H1149.2; mountain H1149.9; power of widow prepared for suttee H479.1; stone as test of strength H1562.2; strong princess's giant weapon as suitor test H345.1; sword tests strength H1562.2.1. — Cannibal hard l. G92; five men for l. club F835.2.1; magic object l. heavy object D1547.3; miraculous l. into air, dashing to death Q551.10; strong man l. stone F624.2; tree l. person up F979.4; visit to lower world through hole made by l. clumps of grass F92.1.

Light appears at holy man's death F960.2.4; carried into windowless house in baskets J2123; extinguished and woman stolen R31; from hand-of-glory renders person helpless D1410.2; indicates hidden treasure N532; keeps evil from corpse E752.10.2; moving toward cemetery sign of death D1322.2; put out by spear F834.2; seen from tree lodging place at night leads to adventures N776. — Why certain animals avoid l. A2491; angels shed l. on saint's tomb V241.2.1; beams of l. tie sun to earth A733.4; burning l. scares off ghosts E439.7; chariot of l. E754.5; clothes of l. F821.7; cock's elixir makes people l. B739.1; column of l. descends on chosen man V222.1.3; combat between god of l. and dragon of ocean A162.2; crime inevitably comes to l. *N270ff.; dazzling l. marks saint's birth V222.0.1.3; devil gives smith l.: smith known as jack-o'-lantern A2817.1; devil appears in intense l. G303.6.3.4; extinguishing l. to hide paramour K1516.3; extraordinary l. at royal birth F960.1.6; fingers of saint give l. or fire F552.1.2; ghost l. follows ghost E530.1.1; ghost l. reveals murderer E231.3; god of l. A107; hand-of-glory renders l. invisible D1361.7; hero's l.: appears around head of hero aroused to extraordinary feats of valor F969.3.2; holy man emits l. F574.3; illusory l. K1888; ink becomes l. beams D454.14; "letting in the l." J1738.6; life bound up with l. *E765.1; life token: l. goes out E761.7.4; magic l. *D1162; magic object provides l. D1478; man's body emits l. D1645.10;

mankind from peace and quiet fructified by l. A1221.2; marvelous l. F969.3, (accompanying saint) V222.1; moon dragged up to l. earth when sun sinks A735.1; mother shows l. of world to one who has not yet seen it (assists at birth) H583.4.1; mountain-men cannot enter house till l. is quenched F460.2.3; origin of l. A1412; quest for l.-giving child H1396; quest for sword of l. H1337; soul as l. *E742ff.; soul as point of l. E722.1.3; spirit of l. F499.1.1; sun gives l. to stars A769.5; theft of l. *A1411; tree planted on moon to diminish its l. A751.6.1; trying to catch l. in a mouse-trap J1961.1; vast l. at Nativity V211.1.31; white sheep-skin used as source of l. J1961; why some nights are l. A1174.2.

Lights tabu on Sabbath C631.4. — Blue l. follow witches G229.7; exhibition of l. at saint's birth F960.1.3; fairy l. seen in low places F217.1; ghost-like l. E530.1; ghostly l. frighten treasure seekers N576.2; heavenly l. A790ff.; mountain of seven l. F759.8; numskull thinks the extinguishing of l. at the church presages a fight J1823.3; spirit puts out l. F473.2.3; wish: no l. except in own home J2076.1.

Lightbeam renders witch powerless G273.1.1.

Lighted. — Lamp l. every fortnight A1599.14; sacred fire from which all others l. V1.6.3.1.1.

Lighting the cat's tail J2101.1; empty lamp by magic D1933; the road K1412. — Disenchantment by l. fire D784; magic lamp indicates falsehood by l. D1316.2; test of king (pope): candle l. itself H41.3; troll l. fingers G304.2.1.1; Will o' the Wisp l. people to their homes F491.2; woman's face l. up the dark F574.1.

Lightning, see also **Thunder;** effective against serpent B765.17; flashes from hero's armpits A526.9; kills ogre G512.10; made from the old moon J2271.2.1; in magic box kills army D1400.1.23.2; strikes excommunicated person who enters church V84.1; strikes monk who despises humility Q552.1.1; strikes where innocent man is being hanged R341.1; slays devils A162.3.2; as torches of invisible dancer A1141.7.1; weapon of the gods A285.1. — Angel of l. A285.0.1; devil retreats into hell amid thunder and l. G303.17.2.5; disastrous l. as punishment C984.5; eyes flash l. F541.1.2; extraordinary l. F968; giants fear l. F531.6.11.1; giants killed by l. F531.6.12.4; god of l. A285; god clothes self with l. A179.7; god with l. as sword A137.14.4; impregnation by l. T528; man becomes l. D281.2; origin of l. A1141; osprey produces l. B172.8; prophecy: death by l. M341.2.11; resuscitation by striking with l. E29.7; sister's face as l. R321.1; trolls killed by l. F455.8.2; why bija tree often struck by l. A2791.12; why elder tree is never struck by l. A2711.2.1; why l. spares the nut-tree A2791.2; witch produces l. D2149.1.1.

Like. — Quest for woman exactly l. another H1381.3.5.

Likeness of Christ criticized V124. — Devil's l. kills beholder Q338.2; seduction by displaying obscene l. K1385; transformation to l. of another *D40ff., D592.

Likes. — Follow your master's l. U42.

Liking. — Devil's l. for negligence in men G303.25.3.

Lily as chastity index H432.2; from grave E631.1.1; issues from devotee buried in unconsecrated ground V255.1. — Bee rests on water l. which closes over it at night and kills it J2137.3; soul as l. E745.4.1; stretching l. plant D482.2.

Lilies. — Lie: remarkable l. X1481.

Limb. — Animal dupe cuts off l. A2284.1, J2413.4; disenchantment by cutting off animal's l. D712.1.1; murderer torn l. from limb Q469.12; numskull cuts off tree l. on which he sits J2133.4; severed l. prevents detection K407.

Limbs affected by breaking tabu C946; cut off as punishment Q451.2.0.1; of dead fettered to prevent return E431.5; of dead voluntarily reassemble and revive E31; successfully replaced E782. — Animals with unusual l. or members B15ff.; bodies from which l. cut impaled Q461.2; child with extraordinary l. T551ff.; creaking l. (of tree) J1872; escape by catching hold of tree l. K685, R219.1; extraordinary animal l. F988; fairy's l. F231; magic appearance of human l. D61; magic cure of broken l. D2161.3.3; numskull injures his l. J2131.3; ogre revives after l. are severed G635; severed l. as identification H106; severed l. replaced by Virgin Mary D2161.5.2.4; swelling of l. C941.2; why all l. dependent on body A1391.1; witch breaks person's l. G269.12.

Lime sold as gold K121; supply for church miraculously renewed D1652.16, V224.5; used in building church as cure D1500.1.35. — Magic l. *D931.1.4, (healing) D1500.1.2.4; magic l. tree *D950.7; throwing into l. pit as punishment Q465.4; why the l. tree is cursed A2721.6.

Limitations. — Deity's l. A196; peculiar l. of fairies F255.

Limited amount of magic in world D1719.11; number of wives for king P18.2; number of wishes granted *D1761.0.2. — Heaven stay l. F11.3; invulnerability for l. time D1845.

Limitless wishes granted D1761.0.1.

Limping soldier told every step a virtue P711.2.

Linden. — Transformation to l. tree D215.4.

Line. — Birds hatched from broken eggs repaired by skillful tailor have red l. around necks F662.1.1; crossing l. to commit adultery K1588; magic l. D1272.1; hunting wolves with rod and l. X1124.4; stepping outside l. tabu C614.1.0.3.

Lineage. — Son-to-be will destroy l. M342.2.

Linen. — Fairies bleach l. F271.4.1; making sails for a ship from one bundle of l. H1022.3; making shirt from piece of l. three inches square H1022.4; quest for the finest of l. H1306.

Lingering. — Soul l. in body E722.2.8.1.

Lintel. — Death from striking head against door l. N339.13.

Lion approaches too near to horse (kicked in face) *K1121f.; bear, and wolf resuscitate master B515; blows life into cubs three days after birth B751.4; buried in cave with gold letters V61.9; calls insult worse than wound W185.6; carries off child R13.1.2; carries person B557.5; cubs awed by fox's boasting K1715.14; comforted for his fear of the cock J881.2; cub killed by bull gives lioness no right to complain U36; despite his strength is in man's power A1421.1.1; disguised as monk K1822.1; divides the booty J811.1.1; divides slain bullock Q3.2; as domestic servant B292.2.3; follows man who saved him B301.8; freed from net by mouse B363.1; frightened away by stabbing from cage K1715.11; kills wolf at fox's instigation K961.1.1; kills wolf who has killed mistress's sheep B591.1; as king makes ass his lieutenant J421.1; as king of animals *B240.4; leads lost king from forest *B563.1; leaves sleeping hare to follow the shepherd J321.3; licks sick man J413.1; lies down at saint's feet B251.2.11; with magic wisdom B121.6; protects saint's body B773.3; rescued from net by rat eats rat W154.3.1; ridden by drunkard J1758.5; sent to kill a man (frees him from possibility of sinning and sojourn in purgatory) J225.2; spares mouse: mouse later releases lion from net B371.1; and the statue J1454; suitor B621.2, (allows teeth to be pulled and claws to be cut) J642.1; thankful rescued by snake B374.1; thinks man is devil J1786.5; thinks man astride him monster J1786.7; transformed to person D312.1; and wild boar make peace rather than slay each other for benefit of vulture J218.1; worship V1.8.9. — Androcles and the l. B381; animals confess sins to l. U11.1.1.1; arranging for l. to eat adulterous mate K813.1; ass follows after l. and is punished J952.2; ass insults dying l. W121.2.1; ass punished for stealing mouthful of grass: l. and wolf forgiven for eating sheep U11.1; automatic statue of l. D1620.2.4; bringing in fierce l. alive H1154.12; camel killed by l. in game K869.3; deceived l. stuck in cave entrance: eaten by hare K714.9; deity rides l. A136.1.7; devil as l. G303.3.3.2.5; dog follows l. but flees at lion's roar J952.3; dogs tear up l. skin but fear living l. W121.2.4; dragon fight to free l. B11.11.6; dragon flies away with l. B11.6.8.1; enemies of l. (dog) A2494.4.7, (leopard) A2494.2.2, (monkey) A2494.7.1, (wolf) A2494.7.2; enemy horses captured by l. join forces and become friends J891; envious jackal makes l. suspicious of bull K2131.2; fox finally converses with l. whom he had feared at first U131.1; fox deceives l. into entering pit K714.9.1; fox insults caged l. W121.2.2; fox with l. protector goes hunting alone and is killed J684.1; fox as mediator to appease l. B239.1; fox refuses to mediate between l. and lioness J811.2; fox's fables against l. forgotten J811.6; fox's fear of l. wears off J1075.2; friendship between l. and (jackal) A2493.30.1, (monkey) A2493.14.2, (tiger) A2493.30; giant l. B871.2.5, (overcome by hero) B16.2.3; girl saved by l. from ravishment B549.1; glove and the l. L431.1; gnats having overcome l. are in turn killed by spider L478; gold-producing l. B103.0.6; grateful fly warns l. B371.2; hare shows l. his reflection K1715.1; hairs of l., when burnt, get owner out of difficulties D1390.1; helpful l. B431.2; honey-covered l. lures animals K767; killing devastating l. H1161.6; killing l. guarding girl H335.3.2; leopard traps

l. in cave K730.3; lovers transformed into l. and lioness for desecrating temple Q551.3.1; magic l. dismembers perjurer H251.1.1; man in tree so frightened of l. he drops sword, kills it N331.2.1; man-killing l. must not touch certain animals C549.1; man with head of l. B27; man, l., and bear in pit J685.1; man resuscitates a l. which devours him J563; man transformed to l. D112.1; marriage to l. in human form B651.3; oath of truth before magic l. H254; only one, but a l. J281.1; oracular brazen l. D1311.7.2; owner frightened from goods by trickster's l. K335.0.6; precepts of the l. to his sons J22ff.; prophetic l. B142.4; reincarnation as l. E612.1; saint kills l. with slipper D2156.11; sick l. K961; singing l. B214.1.5; shepherd shuts up the l. in the yard with the livestock J2172.2; soul as l. E731.11; speaking l. B211.2.2; stag escapes from hunters to be eaten by l. N255.1; stone l. becomes man D435.1.5; suitor task: saddling, mounting a l. M145.1; why l. stays away from settlement A2433.3.16; strong man kills l. with own hands F628.1.1; the third time fox meets l. she has no fear J1075.2; transformation to l. in order to guard palace D659.4.1; treasure from stone l. D1469.13; war between l. and other animals B263.8; why l. does not attack dog A2464.1; why l. is brave A2524.5; wolf tries to make friends with l. J411.5; yoking together l. and wild boar H1149.1.

Lion's blood venomous B776.5.2; dance B293.4; daughter marries mouse, tramples him to death B363.1; human offspring B631.8; roar causes havoc at 300 miles B741; share J811.1; strong teeth B747.1; tail as broom H1151.11. — Animal lured into l. den K714.6; ass in l. skin unmasked when he raises his voice J951.1; children rescue mother from l. den R154.0.1; creation of cat: sneezed from l. nostrils A1811.2; fox sees all tracks going into l. den but none coming out J644.1; girl removes dog from l. claws B848.2; imprisonment in l. den R45.2; jealous courtiers accuse the jackal of stealing the l. food K2141; magic hair of l. tail D1023.3; quest for l. milk H1361; riddle about bees, honey, l. carcass H804; stone l. eyes become bloody D474.9; thorn removed from l. paw B381; wolves, wild pigs condemned to death in l. court B275.1.3.2.

Lions despise what asses admire U149.1; do not harm falsely accused adulteress B522.3; do not mate with their fellows but prefer leopards *B754.3; fall from furnace instead of golden men (unsuccessful imitation) J2411.1.2; fear cock's crow J2614.3; as God's messengers A165.2.1.1.6; in hell A671.2.12; as king's pets P14.22; placed in city to prevent entrance B847; tamed by Moses' rod B771.2.3; on way to otherworld F144.1. — Being fed to l. Q415.4; captive throws his hat to l. who fight over it while he escapes K671; fight of l. and bulls J1022; hungry l. do not harm saint B771.2.1; king of l. B241.2.1; land of l. B221.3; magic rod tames l. D1442.4.1; man saved from l. as reward Q151.11; presumptious wolf among l. J952.1; quest to land of l. H1289.1.1; seeds cast on l. and tigers render them helpless D1410.1; strong man sent to kill l. F615.2.2.

Lioness bears man child B631.4; helps recover magic D882.1.2; pursuing hare puts head in hole, stuck K771.1. — Fox refuses to mediate between lion and l. J811.2; friendship between cow and l. A2493.30.2; magic milk of l. D1500.1.33.1.2; penance: l. foregoes meat Q535.2; transformation of lovers to lion and l. for desecrating temple Q551.3.1.

Lip. — Cure for leprosy by drinking from opposite l. of horn from that which caused it D1783.2; giant covers eye with l. F531.1.1.1.1; giant with upper l. reaching heaven and lower, earth F531.1.4.1; moon splits hare's l.: hence hare-lip A2216.3, A2234.4.

Lips cut in laughing contest K87.1; of giant F531.1.4; sewed together as punishment for slander Q451.12. — Honey on infant's l. B147.3.1.2; magic l. *D992.2, (animal) D1011.5; mutilation: l. cut off S166.5; origin and nature of animal's l. A2342; remarkable l. F544.1; revenant with cold l. E422.1.4; roses fall from l. *D1454.2.1; troll stretches neck so long that fire comes from l. G304.2.1.2.

Liquid, see also **Fluid.** — Disenchantment by l. D766; life token: troubled l. E761.6ff.; magic l. *D1242.

Liquids. — Animal "drinks apart" mixed l. B781.

Liquor, see also **Wine;** for betrothal T61.4.1; blessed by saint causes magic sleep D1364.7.1. — Animals discover l., get drunk B299.3; ghost drinks l. E556.1; gods discover l. A154.3; kamas offer l. to gods A1689.5; magic dog vomits any l. required of him B182.1.1; much l. from single grain F815.2.1; parson takes a drink of l. during the sermon X445.1; queen pours l. for champions P29.3.

Liquors. — Acquisition of spirituous l. A1427.

Lisping sisters K1984.1.

Listening tabus C885. — Six dwarfs l. to singing by confirmed children F451.5.21.

Literal following of instructions by one daughter, liberal by other J555.1; fool *J2450—J2499; obedience J2460ff., (to oath) K2312; payment of debt (not real) K236; pleading: letter of law has been met J1161. — Trickery: l. bargain K196.

Literary contest won by deception H507.6. — Origin of l. arts A1464.

Literature known to poets C568.1.

Litter. — Dupe guards "king's l." K1056.

Little, see also **Small;** bird as large bird's mate J1293.1; child drives out giant L311.4; Christmas V72.1; fish in the net kept rather than wait for uncertainty of greater catch J321.2; fishes escape from the net L331; girl bribes prince to marry her T55.4; men preferred to big J493; old men help perform task H971.2; people from the sky F205. — Death of l. hen (cumulative tale) Z32.2; devil a l. gray old man G303.3.1.5; dwarf follows countess around like l. dog F451.5.8.1; dwarfs have l. horses F451.7.5; fool advises buyer that horse is worth l. or his father would not sell it J2088.1; girl who ate so l. K1984.2; help from l. man N821; husband to wife's lover: "keep a l. for me" K1218.10; identification of man by his l. toe H79.2; Socrates builds himself l. house J401.1.

Live (adjective) bird earrings *F827.1; head-dresses F827.2; man thought to be returning corpse K2151.1. — Eyes of l. coals F541.1.3; steaks cut from l. cow who heals herself by magic D2161.2.1; tabu to eat l. animals C221.5.

Liver removed for breaking tabu C948.4. — Cow with tallow l. B15.7.9, H1331.3.2; divination by condition of animal's l. D1812.5.0.5; dragon's l. of thunder H1332.6; heart and l. of murderer torn out Q469.6; human l. as medicine D1248; inexhaustible l. D1652.19; magic bird l. D859.4.2; magic l. D997.3; magic l. of animal D1015.4; magic potion mixed with brains (l., etc.) of deceitful person as remedy for snakebite D1515.4.6; origin of l. A1319.5; return from dead to punish theft of l. from man on gallows E235.4.4; soul (life) in the l. E714.5; victim eats swallower's l. F912.3; why adder's tail tastes like l. A2378.9.4; witch takes man's l. G262.5; woman has l. stolen by bird (cumulative tale) Z41.1.

Livestock. — Killing ogre's l. G614; magic object furnishes l. D1477; question (propounded on quest): why do the l. die? H1292.3; shortsightedness in caring for l. J2172.

Living corpse *E422; man in dead man's shroud E463; mountain F755ff.; person acts as image of saint K1842; person in service of a dead man E596; torn to pieces by dead E267. All l. things from Jesus' spattered blood A1724.3; ass good l. but not dead (riddle) H841.1; cow good l. and dead (riddle) H841.3; culture hero still l. A570ff.; dead husband l. with his wife E321.2; dead and l. go together to gate of heaven E754.2.3; dead try to carry off l. E266; enchanted princess l. with dwarfs F451.5.4.3; fight of revenant with l. person E461; ghosts bestow gifts on l. E373; ghost laid when l. man speaks to it E451.4; god of the l. and the dead in the otherworld A108; gods and men formerly l. together A189.9; hog good dead but not l. (riddle) H841.2; inanimate objects act as if l. F990ff.; island in otherworld garden inhabited half by dead and half by l. F162.1.2.5; king imprisons all l. creatures R9.6; men l. by gods' breath A1394; ogres l. in trees G637; peasants want a l. God J2495.4; people l. in tree nests F811.10; people l. under sea F725.5; people weary of l. A1335.9; quest for the l. harp H1335; revenant overawed by l. person E462; sacrifice for l. 300 years V17.6; stars as l. beings A761.6; two dead men struggle over l. man E467.1; why l. cannot go to land of dead E489.8; why there are more l. than dead (riddle) H773; wolf not good l. or dead (riddle) H841.4.

Lizard defeats leopard L315.11; frightens leopard away K1715.5; got tail from snake A2247, A2378.1.3; in human form D712.9.1; jumps into person's mouth B784.1.7; offspring of the devil G303.10.10; as ogre G354.3; paramour B613.3; transformed to person D397; tries to make himself as long as the snake J512.9; wins contest with toad: why lizard changes skin A2250.2. — Boy reborn as l. E694.3; why l. bobs head up and down A2255.2, A2211.9, A2474.1; burning down house to drive out l. J2516.6; chain tale: l. and eagle involved Z49.10; contest lost by toad, won by l. A1319.12.1; creation of l. A2148; divination by house-l. B147.3.0.1; dragon as modified l. B11.2.1.2; enmity between chameleon and l. A2494.16.2; enmity of bird and l.: latter muddies water A2494.16.4; why giant l. is blind A2332.6.2; how l. got red head A2211.8, A2320.3; helpful l. B491.2; leopard ashamed of l. bite J411.10; man becomes l. D197; man's hand modeled on that of l. A1311.1; marriage to l. B604.4; mountains from accident to primeval l. A961.3; reincarnation as l. E614.2; sun, moon born of l. A715.6; thread sold to l.: treasure reward J1852.1.1; treacherous l. K2295.4; wooden l. kills evil spirits F839.7.

Lizard's language B215.5.1; lungs inflated H522.1.3. — Crushing l. eggs tabu C544.1; toad exchanges daughter for l. K476.5.

Lizards hero's parents A511.1.8.3. — Child born holding l. T552.2.1; god of l. A446.1; king of l. B244.3; why l. change skins A2311.9.

Llama, multicolored B731.3.

Llewellyn and his dog B331.2.

Load. — Ant carries l. as heavy as himself A2251.1; carrying l. up hill to roll it down J2165; compressible l. D631.3.4; contest in flying with l. K25.2; if the horse can pull one l. he can pull two J2213.4; huge l. carried by saint D1691.1; strong man carries giant l. F631ff.; victim killed while l. is being removed K837.

Loads. — Hills are l. from hero's shoulders A962.10.

Loaded. — Magic gun is always l. D1652.4; man in otherworld l. down with wood F171.6.1.

Loading ferocious camels H1154.3.5.

Loadstone draws ship to it *F806.1.

Loaf of bread locates drowned man D1314.6; bursts in oven because sign of cross not made V86.6. — Child divides last l. with fairy (witch) Q42.1.1; great l. of bread (cake) X1811.1; test of strength: breaking heavy glass bottle over a l. of rye bread H1562.3; unlucky man given l. filled with gold exchanges it for another N351.

Loaves and fishes D2106.1. — Large l. need a large oven X434.1; lies about l. of bread X1811; saint restores eaten l. D1652.1.10.1.

Loan. — Fairy grateful for l. F335; giants repay l. with large interest F531.5.5.

Loans refused J1552ff., (by usurer) P435.2.

Loathly bridegroom D733, (carried on back in basket by wife) T216; deed proves Christian virtue H1573.1.2; lady *D732; man father of supernatural boy L112.1.1. — Adulteress chooses l. paramour T232.2.

Loathsome. — Person forced to eat l. animal S183.2; princess's l. disguise to avoid demon-lover T327.6.

Lobster. — Helpful l. B495.2; origin of l. A2171.3; why l. is flat A2305.1.3; why l. is shallow: cattle stepped on it A2213.2.4.

Lobsters mistaken for Norwegians J1762.7. — Stealing l. from shark guardians K341.16.

Local deluges A1011; gods A410ff.; moon J2271.1; winter D2145.1.1.

Location determined by halting of an animal *B155; of fort determined by reading in book D1816.3; of fountain revealed in dream D1816.1; of lost person by magic object D1315; of otherworld F130ff.; of stone determines king's race D931.0.2.1; of sought object learned by eavesdropping N455.9. — Angel reveals l. of object D812.10.0.1, V232.6; extraordinary l. of castle F771.3ff.; extraordinary l. of tree F811.4; magic discovery of desired l. D1816ff.

Lochinvar steals bride K1371.1.

Lock magically opens for saint D1557.1. — Entrance into wine cellar by removing l. D317.2; extraordinary l. F782.4; magic l. *D1164; sun will l. moon in deep ditch A1066.

Locks in house to be shot during childbirth T582.2; marvelously open R121.6.2, D2088; spring open for troll G304.2.3.1. — All l. opened on Christmas Eve D2088.0.1; "keep everyone's l. in your hand" J2489.2; seduction access by removing l. K1349.5; thief burns off l. K317.1; take people by the l. H588.16.

Locked doors open for ghost E599.11. — Fairy enters l. city D2088.1; filling l. pen K1427; husband l. out by adulteress K1511; securing dishes l. in vault H1199.15; tiger l. into house K737.2; witch escapes from l. room G288; wolf almost l. in the stable by the shepherd J2172.2.1.

Locking. — Adulteress l. up husband K1514.6; faithful servant l. up master R53.4; husband's comment to wife on l. up shop J1545.5; jealous husband l. up wife T257.9.

Locksmith. — Prophet not a l. J1289.1.

Locust carries person B557.9; with strong teeth B747.2. — Enmity of starling and l. A2494.13.11.2; magic l.-egg cures D1502.7.1.

Locusts. — Army of l. B268.8.2; helpful l. B486.1; iron-winged l. eat wheat crop B16.6.3; origin of l. A2062; why l. hide in day A2491.5; why l. live in certain towns A2434.3.1.

Lodes. — Knockers show miners richest l. F456.1.2.2.1.

Lodge-Boy and Thrown-Away as joint adventurers Z210.1.

Lodging of bird's feathers built in one night H1104.1. — Troublemaker in night-l. K2138.

Lofty. — Otherworld on l. mountain *F132.

Log-birth slander K2115.2.2; transformed to bear D441.3.2. — Animal seizes hollow l.: heart pulled through it K952.3; escape from descending l. by digging hole K615; fool tries to make l. obey commands J1828; forgetting by stepping over l. D2004.5.1; frogs given l. as king J643.1; ghost becomes l. during day E553; great snake mistaken for l. X1321.1.2; hands in cleft l. as punishment Q469.13; hero drives l. into frozen ground F611.3.2.1; holiday until l. burns out: log soaked K197; magic l. of wood D1401.8; magic hollow-l. boat D1121.1; man in hollow l. fires rifle, scares off Indians K547.3; man transformed to l. D216; meddler gets himself caught in the cleft of a l. K1111; thread made to appear as a large l. carried by a cock D2031.2; wolf thought to be a l. of wood J1761.5.

Logs. — Marking l. by pinching out piece X952; why tortoise lives in l. in stream A2433.6.1.1.

Logger. — Lie: remarkable l. X987, X1081.

Logic. — Absurd lack of l. J2200—J2259.

Logical. — Lies: l. absurdities X1700.

Logician's argument over ghee, saucer J2062.2.

Loin. — First man from maid having licked l. cloth A1211.7; magic l. cloth transforms self D697.1; rainbow as l. cloth F829.1; speaking l. of goat meat D1610.7; wearing of l. cloths A1683.5.

Loins. — Origin and nature of animal's l. A2364.

Loki. — Foal born of L. and mythical stallion T465.2; fetter for L. F864.2; serpent above L. continually drops venom in his face Q501.3; son of L. transformed to wolf Q551.3.2.1.

Lonely creator A73. — Devil met by night in l. spot G303.22.12.

Lonesomeness. — Creation because of creator's l. A832.

Long armed people F516.3; -bearded dwarf F451.2.3.1; day (fifty o'clock) J2466.3; distance sexual intercourse K1391; ears F542.1; hair F555.3, (prized by Irish) P632.5; -legged people F517.0.2; nose F543.1; pregnancy T574; teeth F544.3.5; term of service imposed on suitor H317; span of life for first men A1323; tongue F544.2.2. — Why animal has l. tail A2378.3; animals with l. life B841; cannibal has l. tooth and nail G88; child born with l. hair T551.13.1; devil has a l. nose G303.4.1.4.1; doing thing too l. forbidden C761; fairies have breasts l. enough to throw over their shoulders *F232.2; fairies in l. robes F236.2; giant with l. beard F531.1.6.4; hair robe "not too l., not too short" J1161.8; hero prefers fame to l. life L212.3; how l. to live? frog wins L395; lizard tries to make himself as l. as snake J512.9; magic object makes nose l. D1376.1ff.; man suddenly acquires l. gray beard on scaffold at execution F1044; miraculously l. life as reward Q145; prophecy of l. life M321; sausage for the l. winter K362.1; strong hero's l. nursing F611.2.3; way short yet l. J21.5.3; why animal has l. life A2578; wife of merman not to stay too l. at home C713.3; wild huntsman with l. hair E501.7.7; witch with l. teeth G214.1; worn-out shoes as proof of l. journey *H241.

Longest. — Riddle: what is l. H644.

Longevity of saints V229.2.12. — God of l. A474.2; heroes' l. A564; magic l. D1857; magic object gives l. D1345ff.

Longing in fairyland to visit home F374; of human child of sky-mother to visit father on earth D2006.2.1. — Death from l. F1041.1.4; fairy dies of l. F259.1.3; inordinate l. F1041.15; magic l. D2037; magic object causes l. D1374.

Longings. — Tasks assigned because of l. of pregnant woman *H936.

Look. — Fairy's l. burns mortal F363.4; "have a black l." H588.14, J2489.7;

dupe induced to l. about: seized and killed K832; why animals always l. down A2471.9; why mortal cannot l. at sun A733.2.

Looked. — Hero feigns fear when l. at too much K1777.

Looking in magic object reveals witch G259.1; at saint's corpse punished Q227.2. — Advice on l. about in strange place J21.34.1; why dog is always l. A2471.6; magic sight by l. in certain place D1821.3ff.; magic strength acquired by l. at necklace D1835.1; rejuvenation by l. into mirror D1889.2; separation of persons by l. for water N311; tabu: l. *C300—C399, (around while raising treasure) N553.4, (at supernatural husband) *C32.1, (at supernatural wife) C31.1; transformation by violation of l. tabu D513.

Looking Glass, see Mirror.

Looks. — Man's l. depend on wife's obedience T254.3.

Loom of woman's breasts, vagina F856.1. — Countertask: making a l. from shavings H1021.6.1; countertask: making spindle and l. from one piece of wood H1022.3; making l. from a rod H1022.2.2.

Loon. — Why l. has big beak A2343.1.3; color of l. A2411.2.6.1; why l. holds legs backward A2371.2.9; ugly voice of l. A2423.1.3.

Loop. — Cure by passing patient under l. D2161.4.5.

Loophole. — Leave l. for escape J762.

Loosing ferocious animals against attackers B17.1.1. — Magic results from l. knots D1782.3; wind raised by l. certain knots D2142.1.2.

Loquaciousness. — Man rebuked for l. speaks after thirty-seven days W225.1.

Lord, see also Creator, God; above, lord below K1525; above will provide for child of illicit union K1271.5; has departed J1823.1.3; has risen J1399.1. — Cowardly to leave battle while l. alive W34.3; devil carries away l. on his back G303.9.5.2; rich l. who robs poor widow of her cow chokes on first mouthful Q552.6; sheep helpful to the L.: get wool A2221.10; to have good servants a l. must be good U212; treacherous l. K2247.

Lord's — Man escapes devils by reading L. blessing G303.16.2.3.1; three faiths: L. and his two children's J1262.9; woman shows that the L. Prayer is the best V51.3.

Loris. — Why l. never look at sun A2231.13.

Loser in bride-race must die H331.5.0.1. — Judicial combat interrupted by friends of l. H218.1.

Losing luck as punishment N134.1.3. — Gambler l. everything N9.1; help to l. player in game C746; tabu: l. consecrated wafer *C55.

Loss of all evil, corruption as reward Q150.2; of goods by thief *K420ff.; of invulnerability D1847; of magic object D860ff.; of magic object's power through overuse D877; of magic power D1740; of magic power of stolen flageolet D1651.7.3; of magic sight D1822; of miraculous powers after son born V229.20.1; of property as punishment Q595; of skill D2099.1; of speech as punishment *Q451.3.

— Accidental l. of property M350ff.; choices: little gain, big l. *J340ff.; choice: l. of beauty or speech J213; feeding with l. or gain (slaughtered hen or milk) H583.9; riddle propounded on pain of l. of (property) H541.2, (official position) H541.3; ringing of church bell causes l. of devil's power G303.16.12; tasks to pay gambling l. H942; weight of bodily member chosen rather than its l. J341.

Losses. — Gains and l. J330—J369.

Lost object discovered by magic D1816.2; object (found by holy man) D1810.0.3.2, object (found by throwing spade at ghost) D1816.2.1, object (returns to its owner) N211; parson asks devil's help, dies C12.5.4; person in ogre's power G406; soul in raven feathers E752.4; souls E752; wind found in tree A1122.3. — Absurd searches for the l. J1920ff.; angel reveals l. object V232.6; animal leads l. man B563.4.1; animal retrieves l. object B548; chimpanzee leads l. hunter home B563.1.2; deaf persons: search for the l. animal X111.1; death message l. K978.2; deer l. through premature celebration J2173.4; disenchantment by being found when l. D783; fairies grateful for returning l. child F339.3; fool gets l. playing blind J2387; forgotten name confused with l. treasure J1805.3; ghost returns to hunt l. article E415.1; horses carry l. riders to safety B563.1.1; king marries girl who finds l. object N713; love l. by magic D1908; luck in hunting l. for breaking tabu C933; magic causes person to be l. D1418; magic power to see l. things D1825.4.3; magic powers l. *D1741ff.; magic object locates l. person D1315; magician recovers l. object with the devil's help G303.22.2; mortals keep l. fairy child F329.4.1; person reported l. joins search for self N692; power of prophecy l. D1812.6; quest for l. magic mirror H1346; quest for l. persons H1385; quest to lower world for l. words H1276; recovering l. objects H1132; rescue of abandoned or l. persons R130ff.; vow not to eat until l. son found M151.8; warrior having l. a city claims that he did not wish to sell it for a higher price J875.

Lot on altar chalice indicates guilt H233.1. — Kings chosen by l. P11.1.1; oath concerning l. drawing M187; one's fated l. as paradox answer H1075; sacrificial victim chosen by l. S262.3.

Lot's wife, having had father and mother, is not dead like other mortals (riddle) H815; wife transformed to pillar of salt for breaking tabu C961.1.

Lots cast to determine fate N126. — Casting l. for queen's gown J2060.4; casting l. as truth test H245; incantation over l. H245.1.

Lotus causes forgetfulness D1365.1.1; disappears at plucking attempt D1641.15; flower as chastity index H432.3; flower flourishes in water J97; flowers on cherry tree F811.7.2.3; leaf full of rice as deceptive wage K256.1; leaf raft in primeval sea A813.2; on Vishnu's navel A123.9, H1289.4.1, T541.11; transformed to human hand D451.4.1. — Birth from l. T543.2.1; earth from l. seed placed on water A814.8; elephant becomes l. D421.3.1; golden l. F814.4.1; instruments of torture transformed to l. flowers D454.16; magic l.-flower *D975.1; magic l. plant *D965.6; magic stick kills l. guardians D1402.10.1; quest for l. flower H1333.5.1; reincarnation as l. E631.1.3; soul as l. E745.4.1; stealing golden l. H1151.1.1; voyage to Land of L. Eaters *F111.3; woman becomes l. D212.3.

Lotuses shower at hero's birth F960.1.2.1.1.

Loudest mourners not greatest sorrowers J261.

Louse on eyelash mistaken for game J1759.2; fattened *F983.2; and flea wish to marry (cumulative tale) Z31.2; neither man nor jinn nor beast nor bird (riddle) H862. — Altar casts away host with l. baked in it V31.4; conception from eating l. T511.5.3; cormorant's tongue pulled out by putting l. on it K825.1; creation of l. A2051; cumulative tale: l. eats crow Z33.4.1; flea bites man and jumps away, but bed is searched and l. killed J2137.1; friendship between l. and crow A2493.23, M246.1.2; giant l. B873.1; magic l. answers for fugitive D1611.13; as obstinate wife sinks she makes a sign of cracking l. T255.3; picking the l. and the flea J2415.2; pricking l. to release curse M429.5; why l. has mark on back A2412.3.1.

Lice banned by magic D2176.2; become gems D475.4.2; as cleanliness test H1585; made smaller A2302.6. — Battle between l. of Strassburg and of Hungary X651; cleanest girl to be eaten: one pretends to have l. K619.1.1; earth transformed to l. D442.2.1; foxes as giant's l. F531.4.11.2; hunter throws away what he catches (l.) and what he does not catch he carries with him H583.3; lies about l. X1296; philosopher nourishing large population of l. J1452; seat covered with l. skins F894.

Lousing as task set by ogre *G466. — Daughter reveals secret while l. mother N466; deception by pretended l. K874; escape by pretended l. *K611.1; goddess discovered by l. A475.1.1.1; magic sleep by l. *D1962.2; tabu: l. supernatural wife C31.7; theft by putting owner to sleep by l. K331.2.1.1; transformation by l. D583; witch's horn discovered by l. her *G253.

Lousy. — Witch makes person l. G263.8.

Love *T0—T99; among giants, other supernatural beings F531.6.15.2; between foster sister and brother P274.1; charm put in princess's food K1831.2.1; detected by quickening pulse J1142.2; falsely pledged for wooer's benefit K2094; image grants man wife D1595.1; induced by magic *D1900ff.; letter hidden in apple K1872.3; like salt H592.1; like wind in hot sun H592.1.1; -longing produced by elf F301.2.1; lost by magic D1908; -mad queen kills husband K2213.2.1; -making in otherworld F181; -producing magic objects *D1355ff.; purified by magic D1900.0.1; rewarded Q56; -sickness T24.1, (cured by bath of beloved's blood) T82, (produced by magic) D1355.0.1, D2064.0.1; -songs A1554; -spot D1355.13; wagered N2.7; -working stone B722.1. — Adulterous l. changed into chaste T372; all women fall in l. with man at sight N202.1; angel kills man because of too much l. for his child J225.5;

animal helps person to success in l. *B582; boy falls in l. with first woman he sees after mother T371.1; bride to suitor giving greatest l. token H315.2; brothers' great l. for sister P253.10; brotherly l. and patience both dead J1633; castle warmed by l. F771.13; choice between l., wisdom J231.2; clerical vows after disappointment in l. V472; conversion through l. V331.5; courtier shields king's l. affair J1211.3; disguised husband wins faithless wife's l. K1813.1; dwarfs in l. with supernatural beings F451.10.3; dwarf's magic l. seduces girl K1672; fairy abducts those with whom in l. F302.3.1.4; false message of l. causes trouble K2132; father unwittingly in l. with daughter N365.2.1; fiancée falls in l. with another man, elopes T157; fidelity in l. tested H1556.4; first man falls in l. with fairy A1275.9; giant in l. with giantess F531.6.8.1; girl masked as man wins princess's l. K1322; girl to be perfect in l. but die of it M365.2; girl frightened by l. becomes insatiable K2052.2; gods, goddesses in l. with men A188; god of l. A475; hero may win lady's l. but die early M366; injunction: to forsake woman who arouses l. C686; innocent girl sells her l. and later receives it back K1362; insanity from l. T24.3; judgment by testing l. J1171; magic object acquired by gaining l. of owner D856; making princess fall in l. H315.1; man in l. with own sister learns her identity N681.3.2; man unwittingly in l. with mother N365.1.1; mother l. P231.3, (dearer than gold) H662, (in animal) F989.8; mountain in l. stretches leg out to meet beloved A965.1; peasant preaches about bishop's l. J1211.1; prince to fall in l. with witch's daughter M436; prince prefers first l. to princess he later marries J414.2; prophecies concerning l. M369.2; queen in l. with own brother K2213.3.4; quest assigned by wife through appeal to husband's l. for her H1212.2; relative pleasure of l. taught by parable J99.1; return from dead to ask back l. tokens E311; sham magician promises to induce l. K1963.2; stepmother in l. with stepson P282.3; suitor with only l. to offer wins L393; tabu: boasting of l.-conquest C453; test of mother's and father's l. for children H491; tragic l. T80ff.; two men in l. with one girl strike bargain M296; what is most pleasant? l. H659.13.1; woman in picture arouses l. H1381.3.1.2.1; woman tricked into giving poison to her husband: thinks it a l.-philtre K945; youth in court for kissing prince's daughter pleads his l. for her J1174.1.

Loved. — Least l. friend truest H1558.1.1.

Lovely. — Hateful or l. child to be born first? T548.1.1.

Lover, see also **Paramour, Suitor;** allowed to sleep with bride few nights after marriage to another T161.1; arrives home just as mistress is to marry another *N681; asks girl to kill her father S56.1; with ass's head G269.22; away too long, returns, finds fiancée married N391; as bird visits mistress D641.1; commits suicide on finding beloved dead N343.4; dies beside dying sweetheart F1041.1.2.1; disguised in enemy's clothes K1810.1.2; disguised as fool K1818.3.2; disguised as monk K1826.1.1; has head cut off at girl's desire H333.1; identified by scratches H58.2;

identifies mistress by chalk marks H58.1; imposes tabu C901.1.3; kills fool for disclosing adultery J2365; kills self believing his mistress dead (Pyramus and Thisbe) N343; made ridiculous K1213ff.; masks as doctor to reach his sweetheart K1825.1.1; only one can lift woman D1651.13; put off till girl bathes and dresses K1227.1; refuses to take back unfaithful paramour Q241.2; rescues his lady R161; slow to follow advantage J2166; stays awake by washing eyes H1484.1; taken to fairyland F302.3.4.4.; transported to girl in fortress by spirit F414.1; unloads wood on door to keep husband out K1514.9; wins gamble as girl distracts opponent K92.3. — Adulteress has l. killed K2231.1; arrogant mistress repaid in kind by her l. L431; avoiding wife's l. by going home slowly J2523.2; brothers persecute sister's l. P253.7; clandestine l. identified by paint marks left on his skin by his mistress H58; clandestine l. recognized by tokens H81; chaste woman promises herself to her l. when rocks leave coast *M261; color formula for girl's l. Z65.1.1; conqueror must be called "l." W11.5.11.1; cure by seeing lost l. F950.8; curse on wife's l. M414.14; dead girl frightens father and l. J2621; dead l. haunts sweetheart E214; dead l. sets tasks E212; death feigned to meet l. K1862; demon l. F471.2.0.1; devil in guise of girl's l. G303.12.5.7; disenchantment of girl only by her l. D791.2.1; disenchantment from tree form by embrace of l. D735.3; drawing l. out of wall with single thread rope H412.6; dwarf l. of mortal girl F451.5.18; escape from undesired l. *T320ff.; fairy l. F301, (abducts wife) F301.6; fairy avenges herself on inconstant l. F302.3.3.1; foolish l. ignorant of mistress's flaws J1737; which was most generous, husband, robber, or l.? H1552.1; generosity enables impoverished l. to entertain his lady W11.7; ghost of tragic l. E334.2.3; girl falsely accused of murdering l. K2116.1.3; girl goes to fairy l. F301.7; girl has monster as l. T118; girl has unworthy l. T232; girl masks as doctor to find departed l. K1825.1.4; god as giantess's l. A164.6; goldsmith as l. P447.7; heart breaks when girl hears l. kiss another F1041.2; humiliated l. in repartee J125.1.1; husband and l. fight for wife T243; husband tricks poet into slaying wife's l. K863.1; importunate l. put asleep in street Q473.4; impoverished l. falsely accused of theft K401.3; lamia devours her l. G262.0.1.1; magic object draws l. to woman D1425; magic object protects from unwelcome l. *D1386ff.; magic view of future l. D1825.1.2; maiden sent to rendezvous to capture l. K787; man kills wife's l. Q411.0.1.2; marriage tokens identifying l. H82.2; menial disguise of l. of princess K1816.0.3; mistress expecting l. accidentally changes places with maidservant N391.1; one l. disguised and carried out of house by other K1517.1.1; princess's clandestine l. punished Q256; prostitute's favorite l. T450.4; quest for vanished l. H1385.5; repulsed l. kills woman's child S322.5; riddle of murdered l. H805; ring springs asunder when faithlessness of l. is learned *D1318.9.1; sandhill surrounds l. F969.6; scorned l. poses as rich man and cheats his scornful mistress L431.2; seduction by bearing false order from l.

K1354.4; spells to recall dead l. E218; tests for true l. H421; transformation combat between l. and maid D615.3; transformation to escape l. D652.3; treacherous l. K2232, (rival) K2221; wife tricks husband into freeing l. K2213.10; witch causes maiden to hate l. G263.6; woman punished for preferring mortal l. Q255; wraith stays in room where l. died E723.5.

Lover's fidelity tested in bed H1556.4.1; joke frightens mistress to death N384.9; magic sleep at rendezvous D1972; place in bed usurped by another *K1317ff.; spur catches in sheet, prevents escape N386.1; wound breaks while he is in bed with mistress N386; — Apparently happy woman discloses l. skeleton U115.1; dead l. friendly return E310ff.; dead l. malevolent return *E210ff.; dream reveals l. death D1813.1.5; flood from l. tears A1012.1.2; girl in disguise at l. court K1816.0.2; son killed at l. instigation S303; transformation to l. form to seduce woman *D658.2.

Lovers abducted by pirates R12.3; buried apart found in one grave E419.6; fleeing slavery recaptured R352; give each other up when they learn that they are brother and sister T415.4; identical in appearance F577.4; involved in adultery K1500ff.; are man's son not his wife's and wife's daughter not her husband's T491; meet in their dreams T11.3.1; not destined to meet in life, faithful after death M369.2.2; as pursuer and fugitive K1517.1; ransomed from prison R121.7; reared as brother and sister learn to their joy that they are not related T415.3; on stile bewitched G269.23; visit while guardian sleeps D1965; vow to marry only each other M149.1. — Accidental meeting of l. N710ff.; accidental reunion of l. N737; accidental separation of l. N318; baffled l. *K1210ff.; dead l. become stones together E642.1; parts of dragon identification between l. H105.6; false guardian betrays fleeing l. K2093; forest as refuge of eloping l. R312.1; forgotten fiancée reawakens husband's memory by detaining l. through magic D2006.1.1; humiliated l. *K1210ff.; mermaids tear mortal l. to pieces B81.2.2; mountain-men as herding-girls' l. F460.4.1.1; origin of rainbow: souls of l. A791.9; predestined l. T22, (born simultaneously) T22.4; prophecy: girl shall have a hundred l. M345.1; stars as transformed l. A761.3; sun and moon as l. A736.3; three l. mourning dead girl T29.14; tokens between l. H82.3; tops of trees from graves of l. show shapes of their heads E631.0.1.1; treacherous l. K2230ff.; twining branches grow from graves of l. E631.0.1; Virgin Mary as protectress of illicit l. *T401; witch transforms her l. into animals G263.1.0.1; woman entertains two l. on alternate nights T72.4.

Lovers' assignation by symbolic messages Z175.2; tragedy re-enacted E337.3. — Bird carries off veil, causes l. separation N352.1; cliff from l. leap A968.2; message falsified to bring about l. death K1087.1; news of l. death breaks heart F1041.1.1.4; smoke from l. funerals mingles E643.1.

Loving. — Curse: not l. same woman long M455.2; foster children l. foster father P271.6; man on Island of Fair Women overcome by l. women *F112.1; mother not l. children of forced marriage P230.2; polygamist l. all wives T145.6.

Loving-cup at betrothal T61.4.2.

Lower lip hangs down to neck F544.1.1. — Consorting with l. class punished Q243.5; giant with l. lip reaching earth F531.1.4.1.

Lower world, see also **Hell, Underworld;** *F80—F109. — Adventure from following animal to l. N773; captivity in l. R47; descent to l. F81; eating in l. forbidden C211.8; emergence of tribe from l. A1631; expressing surprise in l. forbidden C413; goddess divides time between upper and l. A316; impostors abandon hero in l. *K1931.2; journey to l. *F80ff.; land of dead in l. *E481.1; life-lights in l. E765.1.3; nature of l. A670ff.; parents rescue son from l. on rope R153.1.1; princess(es) rescued from l. R111.2.1; quest to l. H1270ff.; series of l. A651.2; tear from upper world of mortals falls on departed in l. E361.1.

Lowlands. — Dwarfs undermine l. for homes F451.4.1.6.

Lowly animal tries to move among his superiors J952; hero L100, (marries princess) L161; heroine marries prince (king) L162; person in love with royalty T91.6.1; tries in vain to be greater than he is J955. — God brings low the proud and exalts the l. H797.1; great refuse to associate with l. J411; presumption of the l. *J950ff.; princess declares her love for l. hero T55.1; queen rewards l. man's love Q56.3; self-deception of the l. J953.

Loyal. — Fairies l. to mortal who owns their knoll F336.

Loyalty, see also **Fidelity,** W34; rewarded Q72. — When debt is due trickster offers creditor his l. K231.5.1.

Luchrupain, see **Leprechauns.**

Lucifer, see also **Devil;** appointed chief for demons A1187; causes fall of man A63.5; as serpent D191.1. — Mouse created by L. A1751.1; saints battle L. at world's end A1082.6.

Luck in gambling N6; in hunting lost for breaking tabu C933; lost by leaving fairy wife F302.5.3; only with honest money N143; personified N112. — Bad l. put into a sack N112.1; casket with Good L. in it given to men by Zeus N113.1.1; devil gives l. with fishing and hunting G303.10.7; escape by prophesying ill l. K573; fishing l. lost C933.2; food left on magic stone brings good l. thereafter D1561.1.6; goddess of good l. A482.2; knockers bring ill l. F456.1.2.1.1; magic object brings good l. D1561ff., (to gambler) D1407; magic brings bad l. D1409.1; nature of l. and fate N100ff.; one not to wish hunter good l. C493.1; princess brings ill l. to bridegroom K443.12; quest for l. H1376.9; speaking of good l. forbidden C424; spilling oil good l. J2214.7; spirit of ill l. A482.1.1; sudden love gives bad l. T10.3; ways of l. and fate N100—N299; why spider brings good l. A2536.3; youngest son always has good l. L11.

Lucky accidents *N400—N699; bargain *N421; person N203. — Foolish imitation of l. man J2415; yellow l. color Z148.

Lucretia seduced by threat K1397.

Lugaid. — Seven sons all named L. T586.1.2.2.

Luggage. — Man carries extraordinary l. F1016.

Lulling to sleep by "sleepy" stories (songs) D1962.4.1.

Lumber. — Squaring l. on stone H1199.13; witch breaks up l. pound G283.1.2.6; wraith selects coffin l. E723.7.5.

Luminous, see also **Bright, Gleaming, Glowing;** face as sign of royalty H71.6.1; ghosts *E421.3; god A124ff.; jewel in animal's head B722.3; person F574ff.; spirits F401.2; witch-boat G222.2; witches G222. — Cat's l. eye *B721; following l. tree in the desert K1886.1.1; hero l. F574.3.3; men originally self-l. A1281.4; men with l. arms F574.2; saint's l. tooth F544.3.2.1; self-l. objects *D1645ff.; wild huntsmen l. *E501.7.6.

Lump on forehead identifies fool P192.7.

Lumps. — Little l. of sugar are sweeter but servant takes large ones J1341.8.

Lunatics. — Jokes on l. X541.

Lunch with Christ J1261.3. — Farmer's hot l.: mustard sandwich W152.12.2.

Lungs cut out for breaking tabu C948.5. — Guessing origin of animal l. H522.1.3.

Lured. — Fairy l. away from house by treasure which he claims F381.5; hunters l. by magic birds B172.6; victim l. by (gingerbread house) G412, (ogre in animal form) G403, (ogre's disguised voice) G413.

Luring hunters by transformation D659.10. — Devil as woman l. man G303.3.1.12; murder by l. to feast, then suffocating S113.2.3; music l. to otherworld F175.

Lust personified Z127.2. — Repression of l. T317, (by magic object) *D1356, (by observation of dying people for year) J62.

Lustful, see also **Lecherous;** stepmother T418. — Conception through l. glance T515.1.

Lute. — Listening to l. tabu C885.3; magic l. D1232; recognition by unique manner of playing l. H35.1; playing l. at funerals A1547.2.

Luxury of dwarfs' underground palace F451.4.1.3; of host rebuked J1566. — Abbot's l. and cardinal's J1263.4.1; repartee concerning clerical l. J1263.4.

Lye. — Milk becomes l. D476.2.3.2.

Lying (telling falsehood), see also **Liar, Lies;** goat K1151, (punished by being half-shorn) Q488.1; incurable U235; punished *Q263. — Contest in l. X905; lawyer who tries to practice without l. fails X314; origin of l. A1343; ruler wants l. confessor J1263.6; tabu broken by l. K1076.

Lying (reclining) on ancestors' bones tabu C541.4. — Capture by l. in wait for enemy K782; girl summons fairy lover by l. under tree *F301.1.1.3; Thumbling l. by sleeping man is blown to window by man's breath F535.1.1.3; trickster blackmails princess after l. with her K443.6.2.

Lynx. — Enmity of l. and rabbit A2494.6.1; face of l. mashed in A2213.2.1; how l. got his squint A2211.1, A2330.2; man transformed to l. D112.3; wedding of l. B281.4; why l. has short, blunt nose A2335.2.2.

Lyra. — Origin of L. A776.

Lyre. — Ass tries in vain to play l. J512.4; man transformed to ass plays the l. *D693; magic l. D1231.1, (charms stones into their place in building) D1565.2; origin of l. (from tortoise) A1461.2.

Mac Con, man suckled by dog T611.10.

Mace-bearer attacked, throws away mace J1166.2.

Machinery. — Ghost causes m. to run unattended E299.1; lie: remarkable m. X1025.

Machines of war P552.4.

Mackerel's creation A2121.

Mad elephant F628.1.6, H1155.4; fisherman as hero L113.1.3; patients cured in pit J1434. — Bite of wild huntsman's dogs drives other dogs m. E501.15.6.3; devil drives cow m. G303.7.8; lawyer's m. client *K1655; remedy for m. dog bite D1515.5; sham m. man H599.2; usurer prays rich sons will go m. P435.1; woman who drives those who see her m. F581.

Mädchen ohne Hände Q451.1.

Made. — Objects m. by magic *D2178ff., (boat) *D1121.0.1, (bridge) *D1258.1, (fort) D1136.1, (iron chain) D1251.1, (water-hole) D928.1.

Madman disguise K1818.3, (tests bride) H384.1.2; may not bring law suit P523.2. — Clever m. J1116.1; disguise as m. to enter girl's room K1349.1.2; escape from m. K611.21; princess unwittingly promised to m. S241.3; saint subdues m. V221.4; woman gives m. food, falsely accused K2112.5.2.

Madman's contract void P525.1.

Madmen P192. — Jokes on m. X540.

Madness cured (by coition) F950.4, (by magic object's recovery) D880.0.1; feigned to escape unwelcome marriage K523.0.1; from fright N384.0.1; from grief F1041.8.2; from loss of fortune F1041.8.11; from loss of magic D860.0.2; from love T24.3; miraculously cured F959.1; as punishment Q555; from seeing beautiful woman *F1041.8.1; from strange sight F1041.8; from spirit leaving body E721.3.1. — Cannibalism brings m. G91; escape by shamming m. K523.1; feigned m. catches thieves F439.9; feigned m. unmasked by threatening man's child J1149.1; jackal-tooth as cure for m. D1508.3; meeting ghost causes m. E265.2; nudity as sign of m. Z181.1.

Madonna, see also **Virgin Mary.** — Pagan sybil draws picture of M. and Child in sand V341; reward for offering food to M. Q32.

Maelstrom. — Prayer saves mariners from m. V52.6.

Magellanic. — Origin of M. Clouds A778.0.1.

Maggots multiply inside girl B784.1.6; squirm from god's mouth A123.2.2.1. — Creation of m. A2053; dwarfs originate from m. in flesh of giant F451.1.1; punishment: m. fill food Q501.2.2; sun from transformed m. A718.4; saint changes m. into jewels V222.15.

Magi. — Youngest of M. becomes senior D1897.

Magic D (entire chapter); aids to witches' flight G242.6; animal supplies treasure B100.2; animals B100—B199; boat to fairyland F213.1; change of color D57; change of size D55; contains life essence E765.3.5; cup tests truth H251.3.13; drink gives immortality to gods A154.1; enables hero to drink sea dry H1142.2.1; fluid takes away magic powers D1410.3; folding mule D491.1.2; food gives immortality to gods A153.2; flight D670ff.; flower opens dwarf home F451.4.3.7; holds mortals in otherworld F182; herb protects from witch G272.2; illusion prevents raising treasure N564; manifestation required as proof in test of saintliness H1573.2.1; manifestation as omen D1812.5.0.13; manifestation at execution proves innocence H215; manifestations as punishments Q551; object (aids task) H987, (guards treasure) N581, (lost, person dies) E765.3.0.1, (reveals witch) G259.1, (sinks into earth) F948.3; objects *D800—D1699, (characteristics of) D1600—D1699, (as decoy for pursuer) D672.1, (functions of) D1300—D1599, (kinds of) D900—D1299, (in otherworld) F166.4, (ownership of) D800—D899, (powerful against fairies) F384, (received from animal) B505; perils threaten bridal couple T175; phantom army F585.2; power from animal *B500ff.; pig heals wound its skin touches B511.2.1; power lost by breaking tabu C947; powers and manifestations D1700—D2199; prevention of childbirth T572.1; protection (against pestilence) F493.3.3, (against revenants) *E434ff.; remedies for barrenness or impotence T591.1; rescue of prisoner from mound R112; as saintliness test H1573.2.1; shirt as reward Q53.2; spells control witch G272.15; stick chosen over money L222.3; tree F979.16. — Animals made by m. exchanged for real K139.1; ascent to sky by sticking to m. feather *F61.2.1; ascent to upper world by m. F68; attention drawn by m. objects: recognition follows H151.1; barrenness or impotence induced by m. T591; birth obtained through m. or prayer T548; bridegroom driven from bridal chamber by m. T171; building m. castle (task) H1133.1; capturing m. pig carrying scissors, comb, and razors between its ears (task) H1154.1; chastity test by m. objects or ordeals H410ff.; childbirth assisted by m. T584.0.1; children given for being taught m. S233; compressible m. animals D491.1; conception from contact with m. object T532.1; contest (in m.) D1719.1, (won by m.) K1; copper as defence against ghosts and m. D1385.5.1; coughing up m. object K331.4; daughter pulls out father's m. life-containing hair K976; deception into m. bag which closes on prisoner K711.1; deceptive exchange: useless given for m. object K140.1; destructive m. object tried out on something inanimate K525.8; destructive m. powers D2050—D2099; devil cheated by religious or m. means K218; devil's m. power turned on himself K214; disenchantment (by m. contest) D785, (by use of m. object) D771; dwarf's m. love seduces girl K1672; dwarfs steal m. objects F451.5.2.2.1; employment of m. powers D1760ff.; escape from lower world by m. F101.4; escape by playing m. music K606.1.1; fairy defeated by druid's m. F389.5; fairy gives m. cloak F343.5.1; fairy mother gives son m. powers F305.1.1; fairy offers mortal m. objects F343.0.1; fairy smith gives knight m. sword F343.3; fairies made visible through use of m. object F235.4; fairyland quest for m. object H1286.2; familiar spirit brings news with m. speed F403.2.3.4; fool loses m. objects by talking about them J2355.1; foolish imitation of m. J2411; ghost laid when tells m. secrets E451.1.1; giant killed with m. knife G512.1.1; giants' m. gifts return to original form in hands of men F531.5.6.1; god made by m. A119.1; god has m. vision only from his throne A199.2; herd of cattle put into m. cup D491.1.1; husband's m. gift returns to him N212.1; identification by m. hand H145; journey to otherworld for m. object H1254; lasting m. qualities D1800—D1949; life bound up with m. object E765.3.0.1; lover caught on m. basin *K1217; magic object teaches m. D1302; maiden in m. (garden) N711.3, (castle) N711.2; manifestations of m. power D1800—D2199; miraculous or m. rewards *Q140ff.; ogre tied so he may learn m. K713.1.5; owner of m. object chosen king P11.3; possession of m. powers D1710—D1799; pursuit of m. arrow H1226.2; pursuit revealed by m. D1813.2; quest for m. objects or animals H1320ff.; quest to other world for samples of m. animals' food H1251; quest as payment for m. object H1219.1.1; reading m. book H31.7.2; recognition by unique ability to perform m. act H31.7; resuscitation by m. *E50ff., (object) E64, (root) E104.1; rocks leave coast by m. *M261; river issues from m. nut F715.1.1; source of witch's m. G224; stealing during alleged m. spell K341.22; stolen objects powerful in m. D838.1; suitor task: cutting open m. gourd H335.2; sympathetic m. for exorcism G271.4; tabu: eating m. catch before mother C231.3.1; tabu imposed by m. C901.3; tests of m. power H1576; temporary m. characteristics D1950—D2049; test of truth by m. object H251ff.; thief rendered helpless by m. *K422; treasure discovered by m. object *N533; unfaithful husband loses m. wife C31.12; unique ability to perform m. H31.7; unpromising m. object chosen *L215; using m. power too often forbidden *C762.1; using m. tabu after sunset C752.1.6; weaving m. cloth H383.2.2; woman must relight m. fires as punishment Q492.

Magically conceived children M146.3. — Corpse is m. killed and laid E446.1; cows m. multiply Q141; cutting down huge tree which m. regrows H1115.1; journey to otherworld by clinging m. to an object *F155; stolen object m. returns to owner K423.

Magician *D1711; able to cast mountains upon enemies D2152.2; assigned three places at table confesses to carrying two persons in his body J1141.2; becomes paddybird D169.2; as beggar frees prisoners D2031.4.3:

carries mistress with him (in his body) *F1034.2, (in glass coffin)
*D2185; who causes plague punished Q392; claims he can make dogs
grey K1677; controls winds D2142.0.1; fights as dragon D199.2.1; as
foster father P271.1; in generosity contest H1552.1.1; and giant contest over dog's tail D1719.1.3; of the gods A165.8; as helper N845;
helps exposed woman S45.3; loses contest with saint V351.3; makes
people lift garments to avoid wetting in imaginary river D2031.1; rebukes
usury D1810.0.2.1; recovers lost object with devil's help G303.22.2; sells
self to devil, coffin bursts E411.9; shoots arrow of each finger D2091.14;
teacher D1810.4; transforms self to seduce queen D2031.4.2. — Abduction by m. R39.1; advice from m. *D1814.1; agar-tree a transformed
m. A2731.4; animal as m. B191; child sold to m. S212; contest with m.
won by deception K5; druid as m. D1711.4; dwarf as m. F451.3.3ff.;
hero as m. A527.3; imitation of m. unsuccessful J2411.4; magic knowledge of m. D1810.0.2; magic power from m. *D1721; princess rescued
from m. R111.1.7; pupil surpasses m. L142.2; resuscitation by m. E121.7;
seduction by posing as m. K1315.3; seventh daughter to be m. N121.4;
sham m. K1963ff., (causes simpleton's death) N384.6, (has paramour fall
in trap) D1574.1, (identifies enemies as dishonest) K1956.10; sick crew
accused as m. K2129.2; test of gratitude: m. makes pupil believe himself superior H1565.1; theft by posing as m. K353; transformation by
m. D683; trickster as sham m. makes adulteress produce hidden food
for her husband K1571.1; wolf from man transformed by m. A1833.2.
Magician's familiar animal G225.7.1; gifts D812.13. — Anchorite immune
to m. powers V228.2; conception by m. power T513.1.1; false bride
fails m. test K1911.3.3.2; familiar in m. cellar G225.0.5; magic from
fish fed on m. flesh D1721.2; magic power when m. feet on ground
D1719.10.1.
Magicians. — Family of m. D1711.11; giants as m. F531.6.5; transforma-
tion contest between m. D615.1.
Magistrate. — Deduction: m. is a bastard J1661.1.2.1.
Magistrates. — Jokes on X330ff.
Magnetic mountain F754; stone F806.
Magnificent. — King seeks one more m. than himself H1311.1.
Magpie is hybrid of dove and raven: not baptized during flood A2382.1;
leads other magpies into master's net K2032; refuses to get into ark, sits
around outside jabbering, is unlucky A2542.1.1; as suitor B623.3. —
Color of m. A2411.2.1.10; creation of m. A1922; why m. is cursed
A2542.1; dove and m. exchange eggs (dove's seven for magpie's two:
why dove has two eggs) A2247.4; feathers of m. A2247, A2313.2; helpful m. B451.6; prophetic m. B143.0.2; soul in form of m. E732.4; how
m. got long tail A2236.4, A2378.3.1; why m. is bald A2317.6; why m.
has no tongue A2236.4, A2344.2.6; why m. has long neck A2351.4.2.
Magpie's wedding B282.14. — Punishment for slitting m. tongue
Q285.1.1.1; why m. tail is like chisel A2378.7.2.

Mahadeo turns wood chips into insects A2002.1. — Animals created while M. quarrels with wife A1758.

Mahogany ship F841.1.3.

Mahrtenehe, die gestörte C31ff.

Maic Milid A1611.5.4.2, invade Ireland F211.0.2.1.

Maid behind statue of Virgin advises mistress to give servants better food K1971.3.1; cuts off breast to heal man's serpent wound D1515.4.1; given to lover's companion as bed-partner T484; impersonates wife K1843.4; rebukes pilgrim for eating too much J1346; substitutes for princess in conquering king's bed K1223.5; substituted in mistress's bed H1556.4.3, N391.1. — Bride has m. sleep in husband's bed to conceal pregnancy *K1843.1; clever m. J1111.6; devil dances with a m. till she dies G303.10.4.1; devil impersonates woman's m. at toilette Q331.2.1.1; hen put in witch's hair to scratch while m. escapes G276.1; king advised to marry m. rather than widow J482; making love to m. fidelity test H1556.4.2; mistress's m. saves paramour K675.1; mistress sends m. out for man T271.1.1; ogre's m. as helper G530.6; old m. promises devil her first born S223.3; priest's fifty-year old m.: one 20, one 30 J2212.1.1; queen and m. conceive from eating same food T511.0.1; recognition of m. as substitute bride H38.2.3; tasks set m. by elfin knight before she can marry him F301.4; transformation combat between lover and m. D615.3; treacherous m.-servant K2252; wife dismisses m., husband's mistress J1112.2; woman jealous of a fair m. in her house T257.1.

Maid's confederate comes out of woman's room K2112.2.3. — Man takes m. place in mistress's bed K1347; old m. plea: "Anybody, Lord" J1811.1.1.

Maids. — Faithless men-servants corrupt m. in household P365.1; jokes on old m. X750ff.; reincarnation of old m. as birds E613.0.3; wife's m. disguised as saints K1827.1.

Maiden abducted R10.1, (by monster) *R11.1, (by pirates) R12.1, (by transformed hero) R16.1; at bridge to hell A672.2; in castle gives quest directions H1232.3; daughter of giantess and prince F531.5.7.1.3; queen offers hand as reward Q53.3; queen sets hero tasks H933.2; sent to rendezvous to capture lover K787. — Allegorical game of witch, devil, m., church Z178; burial alive of m. to keep her from rival S123.5; cat transformed to m. runs after mouse J1908.2; darkness comes in daytime in order to save life of m. about to be executed F965.1; disenchantment by m. sitting at head of enchanted king's bed D759.7; falsely accused m. dies of sorrow F1041.1.3.1; giant rescues m. R164.1; gull a transformed ravished m. A1945.2; magic from celestial m. D1726.1; magic from m. walking naked in public *D1796; magic object received from m. D825; magic object from m.-spirit D812.15; magic object from otherworld m. D813.3; man hunting honey encounters lost m. N785.1; snake heals mutilated m. B511.1.2;

well rises for m. F933.1.3.1; winner of m. queen becomes king H1574.3.2; witch causes m. to hate lover G263.6.

Maiden's — Animal tamed by m. beauty B771.1.

Maidens slain in revenge Q411.12; take mortal to heaven F63.1. — Disenchantment by m. walking with lighted candles in procession D759.6; four m. as earth-supports A841.2; holy m. invulnerable to glowing embers D1841.3.2.4.

Maidservant, see Maid.

Maimed victims at ogre's house G691.3. — Broken oaths cause of m. people M101.2; dupe's animals m. K1440ff.; king must resign if m. P16.2; ogre m. *G510ff.

Maiming, see also Mutilation; animal exorcises witch G271; by deception K800; by magic D2062. — Magic object m. D1403; witch m. animals G265.5.

Maina. — Friendship between parrot and m. A2493.26.

Maine. — Seven sons all named M. T586.1.2.1.

Maize. — Man becomes m. D214.2.

Majority. — Ruler should follow advice of m. J21.35.

Make-believe eating, make-believe work J1511.1.

Make-up. — Woman vowing not to use m. rewarded V39.5; women as painters in m. art H659.16.

Male children killed (by Amazons) F565.1.2, (for fear that they will overcome parent) M375.1; Cinderella L101; from deity's body by his mere thinking A1211.0.1; and female creators A12.1; and female waters A918; rabbit bears young B754.4; sungod while ascending, female while setting A227.1; transformed in womb to female T577.1; witch G207. — Adam names m. animals, Eve, female A2571.0.2; adulteress pretends shame before m. statue K2051.1; beef neither m. nor female H1074; cloud on m. mountain bows to female mountain A969.2; ghost in m. dress E422.4.5; god presides over all m. spirits A161.4; origin of m. sex organs A1313.1; princess not to see m. person C313.0.1; tabu: m. presence in girl's puberty-hut C132; women blush in presence of m. statue (fish) F647.4.

Males. — All new-born m. slaughtered S302.1.

Malediction. — Execution escaped by threats of m. J1189.2.

Maledictions. — Old woman's m. inform abandoned hero of his parentage and future S375.

Malevolent dwarf F451.5.2ff.; fairies F360ff.; mountain-men F460.4.4ff.; return from the dead E200—E299. — Tabu: uttering name of m. creature C433.

Malice. — Baffling m. with ready answers J1251.

Malicious wife reports her husband as famous doctor H916.1.1.

Mallet. — Saint's m. cures D1500.1.14.

Mammal transformed to person D310—D349. — Domestic m. transformed (to another animal) D412, (to object) D422, (to person) D330ff.; man transformed to wild m. D110ff.; soul in form of m. E731ff.; wild m. transformed (to another animal) D411, (to object) D421.

Mammals magically called D2074.1.1. — Creation of m. A1800—A1899; cries of m. A2426.1; food of m. A2435.3ff.; gait or walk of m. A2441.1; haunts of various animals: m. A2433.3; lies about m. X1210; markings of m. *A2412.1ff.; origin of color of m. A2411.1.

Man, see also **Person;** acts as statue of saint in order to enter convent K1842.1; admitted into heaven but must not find fault *F13; as animal's servant, supplies their food J2214.5; calls wife "my swallow": she becomes swallow D511.1; -cat B29.4; controls rising, setting of sun A725; by day, animal by night D621.1.1; in every house killed to punish king Q411.8; excels woman A1376; -goat B24.2; with horse's mouth B21.3; honored above God: the dead hen J2215.3; -killing flower H1333.5.0.4; lacking money better than money lacking a man J482.2.1; lion, and bear in pit J685.1; looks at copulating snakes: transformed to woman D513.1; made to appear to pursuers as woman carrying babe D2031.6.1; made to believe that he is someone else J2013; in moon A751, (lets himself down) X1851; in otherworld loaded down with wood F171.6.1; not to be present at childbirth C151; poses as bride for beggar K1911.4; proof against weapons D1841.5.1; reincarnated as god E605.3; rescues his wife from fairyland F322.2; scorned by his beloved T75; magically becomes smaller D55.2; magically stretches himself D55.1; transformed (to animal) D100—D199, (to ass plays lyre) *D693, (to cannibal) D91, (to different man) D10—D99, (to beast leads herd) B241.3, (to green knight) D57.1, (to insect) D180ff., (to person of different social class) D20ff., (to woman) D12, (to woman has children) D695; and tiger in contest: winner to live in town A2250.1.1; undertakes disastrously to do his wife's work J2431; unharmed in den of animals B848; as weapon F628.2.7; will not do woman's bidding W214. — Animals created to serve m. A1705; animal by day, m. by night D621.1; automatic statue of m. D1620.1; creation of ant: avaricious m. transformed A2011.2; devil developed from m G303.1.3.1; devil fights with m. G303.9.6.1; devil helps ugly m. win wife G303.22.7; devil in place of dead m. in shroud G303.18.2; disguise as m. to escape lover K1236; disguise of m. in woman's dress *K1836; dragon from transformed m. lying on his treasures B11.1.3; enmity between tiger and m. A2494.10.1; fairy entices m. into fairyland F302.3.1; falling in love with m. disguised as woman T28; friendship between m. and dog A2493.4; giant obtains treasure from m. F531.6.7.2; giant's skull holds a m. seated F531.2.3; giant swallows m. F911.5; girl masked as m. wins princess's love K1322; girl transformed into m. G263.3.2; god reborn as m. E605.2; god as part m., part fish A131.1; hare and m. contest in watching for leaf to fall off tree A2256.1; headless m. lives four years E783.7; killing certain m. as task H1162; lie: the large m. X920; madness from seeing beautiful m. F1041.8.1.1; magic changes in m. D50ff.; magic change of size in m.

D55; magic object received from old m. D822; marriage to beast by day and m. by night *B640.1; mermaid swallows m. B81.10; mistress sends out for m. T271.1.1; Norse m.-horses "fingalkn" B21.1; old m. contented till forbidden to leave city H1557.3; old m. nods "yes" J1521.2; old m. of the sea G311; one m. for worship, two for cultivation, three for journey Z64.1; precept of lion to his sons: beware of m. J22.1; pregnant m. T578; punishment: m. reborn as girl Q551.5.1.1; punishment: m. to do woman's work Q482.6; reincarnation of m. as (animal) E610.1, (nature spirit) E653, (objects) E648, E671; revenant as m. E425.2; serpent swallows m. F911.7; sun is m. during day B722.13; sun as m. who left earth A711; sun and moon as m. and woman A736.1; transformation: m. to baby at will D55.2.5; transformed m. as hostile dog B17.1.2.3; transformation of m. to animal as punishment Q584.2; treacherous dark m. K2260.1; tree by day, m. by night D621.2; why animals serve m. A2513; wild m. as king of animals B240.3; wisdom from old m. J151ff.; witch transforms m. to object G263.2; woman not to look at m. C313; woman reborn as m. E605.1.1; woman transformed to m. D11; woman dies at seeing naked m. F1041.1.13.2; woman disguises as m. to enter enemy camp K2357.6.

Man's Fall A63.5, A1420.5, A2236ff., A2631.1.1, A2721.8. — Dead m. tooth as cure for toothache D1502.2.1; disguise of woman in m. clothes *K1837; soul leaves m. body and enters animal's E725.1; universe from parts of m. body A614.1.

Men deceived into killing each other K929.7; as God's advisers A41; previously menstruated A1355.3; swallow men F911.1. — Adulteress feigns disdain of m. K2051.3; animal learns through experience to fear m. J17; animals that live with m. A2433.2.4; are there more m. or women? H708; beast-m. in lower world B20.2; council of fishes decide to get rid of m. B233.1; first m. without beards A1597.1; giants and m. F531.5ff.; why goat lives with m. A2433.3.8; god lived among m. A151.9; journey to Land of M. of Heads Only F129.1; land of m. F113; land where women live separate from m. F566.2; soldiers of fairy king are trees by day, m. by night F252.3.1; stars are m. peering through holes in sky A761.5; strong man kills m. F628.2.5; tabus on m. C182ff.; trolls and m. F455.6; village of m. only F566.1; Virgin tests m. with hot iron H221.2.1; why m. become old A2861; wise m. J191; young sparrows have learned to avoid m. J13.

Man-eating ants B16.6.1; birds B33; cattle B16.1.5; giantess D429.2.2.1; god A123.2.2.1, A135; humans, see **Cannibals;** mice B16.2.8; monster B16.0.3; sea-monster B16.5.1.2; sow H1155.3; tree F811.24, H1163; woman G11.6.

Mandrake. — Magic charm uproots m. D1599.5; magic m. *D965.1; origin of m. A2611.5, A2664.

Mandrakes. — Elephants have sexual desire only after eating m. B754.2.

Mane. — Bells on horse's m. P651.2; child born with hairy m. T585.5.1;

dog-headed man with horse's m. B25.1.1; eel with fiery m. B15.7.12; horse with golden m. B19.5; origin of goat's m. A2322.4.1; origin of hair and m. A2322ff.

Manes. — Fairies plait horses' m. F366.2.1; sea waves are m. of sea horses A1116.1.

Mange. — Magic object cures m. D1502.5.

Manger. — Dog in the m. W156.

Mangling. — Murder by m. with axe S139.4.

Mango. — Conception from m. T511.1.3; covering m. tree grove with fruit overnight H1103.3; half child born to queen eating half m. T550.6; hero gets into m. seed D55.2.6; magic m. returns to tree D868.1; man becomes m. D211.4, D215.8; rajah to marry when cut m. blooms M261.1.1; white m. tree F811.3.2.

Mangoes. — Dying woman requests m.: priests claim them J1511.18.

Maniac's. — Casting of image of Buddha delayed until m. mite is thrown into the furnace V125.

Manifestation. — Magic m. as omen D1812.5.0.13.

Manifestations of magic power D1800—D2199.

Manioc. — Acquisition of m. A1423.4; origin of m. A2685.5; transformation by eating m. D551.2.7.

Maniplies. — Cow swallows book: cause of m. in stomach A2219.2.

Mankind. — Witches at emergence of m. F203.2.

Mankind's journeyings A1630ff.

Manna D1031.0.1; does not fall on Sabbath D1676.1, V71.2; tastes bitter to gentiles D1665.4. — Shower of m. F962.6.2.

Manner. — Recognition by unique m. of performing an act H35; tabu: doing thing in certain m. C854; unusual m. of life F560ff.

Mannikin. — Magic sack furnishes m. who cudgels owner's enemies D1401.2; soul as m. E747.

Mansion. — Hat becomes m. D1867.1.

Mansions. — Golden m. of gods A151.4.3.

Mantis transformed to another animal D415.1. — Origin of m. A2093; vulva hair becomes m. F547.5.9.

Mantle, see also **Cloak;** ever new D1652.12; will not fit unchaste woman H411.7. — Beautiful m. F821.4; drunken officer's stolen m. J1211.2.1; escape under invisibility m. K532; escape, only m. injured K525.5; magic m. *D1053, (changes color) D682.4.1; night from deity wrapping self in dark m. A1174.4; recognition from gold wrapped in m. H91.2; servant by using master's m. deceives his master's lady K1317.1; sleeping under same m. transforms D592; saint's m. determines land grant K185.4.2; weaving m. from single sheep's wool H1022.4.2.

Mantles. — Custom of wearing m. A1683.3.

Manufactured object transformed D454, (to animal) D444, (to person) D436. — Man transformed to m. object D250ff.

Manure, see also **Dung, Excrement.** — Why beetles live in m. A2433.5.4;

cleaning m.-filled barn H1102.2; clearing out m. K1424; devil's money m. G303.21.2; filling the yard with m. (task) H1129.1; footsteps in m. show dead man walked H264; murdered person's corpse put in m. heap S139.2.2.8; nest made of m. not for nightingale U144; sensitivity to food raised in m. F647.5.2; witch power from standing on m. pile G224.6.

Manuscript. — Law involving ownership of m. P526.1; penitent's m. of sins V29.6; resuscitation by m. E64.7.1.

Many admit theft: real thief concealed K415.1; children at a birth T586.1; -eyed antelope B15.4.1.1; -headed animal *B15.1.2; -horned animal B15.3.1. — Animals with m. legs B15.6.3; father makes m. out of few (sows grain) H583.2.2; finding how m. people are in dark, closed room as test of resourcefulness H506.2; hare with m. friends H1558.4; invulnerability bestowed by m.-headed monster D1846.2; people with m. (arms) F516.2, (eyes) F512.2, (feet) F517.1.2, (hands) F515.0.2; person with m. (ears) F511.2.3, (teeth) F513.1.2; same reward promised to m. K2034; strong man kills m. men at once F628.2.1.

Marauder pretends beggary K2369.1.

Marble cup becomes crystal D475.5. — Acquisition of m. A1439.1; fortress of m. in otherworld F163.5.4; man transformed to m. column D231.2.

Marbles. — Devil plays m. in church G303.9.9.19; playing m. with jewel H151.1.1.

March. — Tabu: going to certain place in M. C755.4.

Marching. — Swine m. like soldiers B290.1.

Marcolf and Solomon H561.3, H1595.1.

Mare, see also **Horse;** brings hero back from land of no return F129.5.1; with foal left behind finds road home B151.1.1.1; not to pull corpse C181.11; from water world disappears when scolded C918. — Adulteress transformed to m. and stirruped Q493.1; contest in lifelike painting: m. and curtain H504.1.2; dancing m. rescues persecuted boy in belly K551.3.6.2; fairies milk mortal's m. F366.1.1; god as m. seduces stallion D658.3.1.2; grooming unruly m. H1155.1.1; helpful m. cools boiling bath for master B526.2; man-eating m. B16.1.3.1; outstripping wild m. F681.6.1; paramour unties m. K1514.14; revenant as m. E423.1.3.2; seduction on promise to transform woman into m. K1315.3.2; strong man son of man and m. F611.1.6; which m. colt's mother? real one swims to it J1171.4; white m. thought to be church J1761.2.

Mare's egg J1772.1. — Crows reveal m. killing B131.1; guessing sex of m. offspring H528.1.

Mares. — Riddle about catching m., walking sticks H586.8.

Marienkind C611, K2116.1, Q451.3.

Marine counterpart to land F133.1; lamb B95.2.

Mariners saved by prayer V52.6.

Marital, see also **Marriage;** experiences of the devil G303.12ff.; impostors K1910ff. — Refusal of m. relations punished Q257.

Mark of Cain (as curse on murderer) Q556.2; of mother's hand on moon
A751.5.3; of tiger's paw on moon A751.5.4; of wandering soul seen on
body E721.0.1. — Ghostly fingers leave m. on man's hand E542.1.1;
holy water removes m. made by devil V132.2.1; indelible m. D1654.3.1;
magic m. on forehead renders invisible D1361.43.

Marks from ghost's strike E542.1.4.2; of royalty H7. — Animal pressed:
hence facial or bodily m. A2213.2; battle m. in rock F1084.0.4; dead
returns to replace boundary m. he has removed E345.1; lucky m. on
body N135.4; recognition by bodily m. or physical attributes H50ff.;
why women have m. on belly A1310.4.

Market. — Numskull buys water at m. J2478; princess must sell goods
on m. as punishment Q483; queen exposed in m. place Q483.1; witches
steal m. goods G266.1.

Marking coveted object with name: claiming it later K448; the place
J1922; way in unfamiliar country J765. — Appearance of animal from
m. or painting A2217ff.; devil m. person he touches G303.4.8.10; groom
m. bride's forehead at wedding T135.4; marked culprit m. everyone else,
escapes detection K415.

Markings on bark of plant A2751.3. — Origin of animal m. A2221.3,
*A2412ff.

Marko (king asleep in mountain) *D1960.2.

Marksman. — Fairy's skill as m. F273.1; lie: great m. X1120; skillful
m. F661ff.

Marksmanship. — Lie: remarkable m. X1122.

Marmot. — Man transformed to m. D117.4; why m. has short tail
A2378.4.3.

Marooned man reaches home and outwits marooner K1616; person in
ogre's power G406. — Pleiades are hunters m. in sky A773.5.

Marooning as punishment Q467.5.

Marplot at creation A60ff. — Food at first comes without effort: m.
changes plan so that man must labor A1346.2, A1420.4.

Marriage, see also **Wedding;** *T100—T199; to avoid shame at undress
J2521.3; of beautiful woman and hideous man T268; of child of demon
king to mortal F402.2.3; of clerics V465.1.1.2; compared to drowning
J1442.12; customs T130ff.; destroys friendship T201; of earth and sky
A702.5; with equal or with unequal J414; with fairy *F300ff.; forbidden outside the parish X751; -god A475.0.2; of the gods A164; into
house full of wild animals J347.5; of kings P18; of lowly hero to
princess L161; of lowly heroine to prince (king) L162; of man to girl
who guesses his riddles H552; of mountain-girl to mortal man F460.4.1;
of person to animal *B600—B699; to person in animal form *B640ff.;
of poor boy, rich girl L161.1; of prince, princess prophesied M331;
promise induces fight between foster brothers P273.2.1; promised to
save life M268; prophecy for newborn princesses H41.6; of queen P28;
ring protects from devil D1385.3; tests H300—H499; tokens identifying

lover H82.2. — Angel warns against forcing girl into m. V231.5; brother-sister m. T415.5; consummation of m. J1306, N681.3.1, T160ff.;
continence in m. T315; covenant confirmed by m. M201.5; dead man
seeks m. E353; dead wife haunts husband on second m. E221.1; death
feigned to escape unwelcome m. K522.0.1; death to come same year as m.
E765.4.4; disenchantment depends on m. D791.2.2.1; death prophecies
connected with m. M341.1.1.1ff.; dream of m. with another's wife
T11.3.2; elopement to prevent undesired m. R225.2; erecting m. hall
overnight H1104.4; eyes burst for urging saint's m. Q551.8.4; faithfulness in m. T210ff.; faithlessness in m. T230ff.; father will die at
daughter's m. E766.4.1; foolish m. of old man, young girl J445.2; friendship covenant concerning m. of children M246.2; ghostly m. E495; how
m. was consummated J1306; human-dragon m. B11.12.3.1; humiliating
m. as punishment Q499.7; ignorance of m. relations J1744; infant's
m. to twelve-year-old to avoid death prophecy M341.0.3; Jews protesting
against m. of Jewess and Christian are struck dumb V343; joke on Jewish m. ceremony X613; king must have m. P13.4; life long penance for
brother-sister m. Q520.3; love kept up despite m. to another T88.1;
mankind from human-animal m. A1224.0.1; marathon m. F1073; monkey
saved from trap by feigning m. K579.4; mother tries to prevent
daughter's m. P232.1; murder for m. against family's wishes K959.2.1;
origin of customs of courtship and m. A1550ff.; origin of m. A1555;
prince's m. to common woman prophesied M359.2; princess humiliated for
loathly m. S322.1.4; promise to dying father on m. M258.2; prophecies
concerning m. M369.2; races from offspring of animal m. A1610.3;
sacrificing self for m. T24.8; seasons produced by m. of North and South
A1153; seduction upon false promise of m. K1315.8; tabu: m. with certain person C162; tabu connected with m. C160ff.; treasure to be found
by man after his m. to the daughter of the original owner N543.3;
trickster exacts promise of m. as price of silence after having seen a
princess naked *K443.6; trickster falsely announces m. celebration and
distracts owner's attention K341.12; unusual m. T110ff.; unwitting m.
to cannibal *G81; vow concerning m. M134ff.; wealthy m. foretold for
poor boy M312.1; woman promises m. for earrings K233.8; woman
refuses second m. (if husband is good she will fear to lose him, if bad
she will repent) J482.1.

Marriages. — Relationship riddles arising from unusual m. of relatives
H795; riddle about no sons after three m. H585.2.

Married life *T200—T299. — Devil m. to widow who maltreats him
G303.12.2; foolish m. couples J1713; girl in fairyland m. to fairy F301.3;
maiden m. to merman B82.1; man disguised as woman m. by another man
K1321.3; man m. to spirit of willow tree F441.2.3.1.1; mermaid m. to
man *B81.2; moon m. to woman A753.1.4; moon m. to sky-god's son
A753.1.4.1; mortal man m. to fairy woman F302ff.; numskull believes
that he is m. to a man J2323; parents made to believe that they are

dead and are m. to each other again J2311.8; sun and moon m. A736.1.4; tailor m. to princess betrays trade by calling for needle and thread H38.2.1; witches m. to fairies G287; wolf punished by being m. K583.

Marrow. — Bath of m. F872.4; corpses' m. used in sorcery D1278.2; obtaining wild pig's m. H1154.11; wounds healed by m. bath F959.3.3.

Marry. — Counsel to m. new wife every week (not to see your wife too much) H588.3; disenchantment by promise to m. D741ff.; father casts daughter forth when she will not m. him S322.1.2; giants m. human beings F531.5.7; how girl thus far avoided by suitors can m. H1292.5; husband (lover) arrives home just as wife (mistress) is to m. another *N681; king advised to m. maid rather than widow J482; moon wants to m. his sister the sun A751.5.2.1; magic plant bears fruit to indicate that heroine is ready to m. D1310.4.2; mother wishes lazy daughter may m. devil C12.4.1; not to m. a girl from abroad J21.4; prince agrees to m. a servant girl if she will help him on a quest H1239.1; punishment for refusal to m. after girl is pregnant Q245; quest undertaken before hero will m. H1227; tasks set maid by elfin knight before she can m. him F301.4; trickster concealed in sacred·tree advises that he is to m. princess K1971.10; vow not to m. till iron shoes wear out M136; why brothers and sisters do not m. A1552.1; youth lamed by man whose daughter he refuses to m. Q451.2.1.

Marrying first woman met C664; person to die same year E765.4.4. — Advice against m. more than one woman J21.32; condemned woman may be freed by m. a rogue P512; demons m. among selves G302.7.2; devil m. G302.12.5; fairy punished for m. mortal F386.2; first man m. a fairy A1275.9; girl m. man on whom fly lights B152.2; girl complains about m. stranger J2463.2; girl m. lover who thought her dead K1839.2; king does not want daughter m. T50.2; man m. fairy F302.3.1.3; man m. often: always looking for good wife T251.0.3; man m. tree maiden F441.2.3.1; mortal m. otherworld king F167.12.1; oath concerning m. king M192; parson with bad eyes m. wrong couples X413; returning home after m. fairy tabu C644; sun m. woman A736.7.1; tabu: m. until hero chooses husband C566.4; witch m. man G264.4.

Mars lies on moon A759.7.

Marshall P50.2. — Treacherous m. K2245.

Marshsnipe's enmity with raven A2494.13.6.

Marsyas flayed Q457.1.

Marten. — Color of m. A2411.2.1.17; enmity between m. and squirrel A2494.12.6; man transformed to m. D124.3; origin of m. A1824; wedding of m. B281.5.

Martens recover magic ring from kite B548.1.1.

Martin, St. — Jesus appears to M. V411.8; nun refuses to see M. T362.1.

Martyr with Sign of Cross on his heart V86.2. — "Live confessor better than dead m." J1261.9.

Martyrdom to preserve virginity T326.3. — Colors symbolizing m.

Z141.2ff.; place of saint's m. perpetually green V229.2.5; religious m. V463.

Martyrology. — Reciting m. prevents body's decomposition V52.14.

Marvel as sign of royalty H71.10. — King questions six doctors: what must you most m. at on earth? J171.2.4ff.; respite given to witness m. K551.28; sign of cross enables relating of m. D1766.6.3; tabu: expressing astonishment at m. C491; transformation by expressing astonishment at m. D512.

Marvels *F (entire chapter); seen in dreams D1731.2. — Recognition by ability to perform m. H151.1.3; seventeen m. at Christ's birth V211.0.3; tabu: asking about m. which one sees C411.

Marvelous creatures *F200—F699; manifestations at death of witch G278.1; objects as prince's marriage price T55.4; occurrences F900—F1099; otherworld journeys F0—F199; places and things F700—F899. — King's quest for m. object H1218; quest for m. objects or animals H1320ff.; quest for m. thing seen in dream H1229.3; quest for m. water H1321; quest for most m. thing: needed to save life H355.0.1; tabu: revealing the m. C423; wager on second m. object N72.

Mary, see also **Virgin Mary;** "of the Gael" V250.1. — Girl named M. has virginity spared by knight who has bought her T321.2.

Mary's — Origin of M. "bed straw" (thymus serpyllum) A2654.

Maries. — Three M. Z71.1.7.

Mashed. — How wildcat got his m. face A2330.1.

Mask disguise for disfigured warrior K521.2.3; mistaken for face J1793. — Abduction with m. rendering invisible R23; magic m. D1067.4, (renders invisible) D1361.32.

Masks' origin A1465.6.

Masking as ghost in graveyard forbidden C94.5. — Capture by m. as another K755; girl m. as man wins princess's love K1322; lowly m. as great J951; ogre's secret overheard by m. as bird G661.2; peasant boy m. as prince betrays self by answers H38.2.2; seduction by m. as woman's husband *K1311; test of sex of girl m. as man H1578.1; Thor m. as woman kills giant K235.2; women learn witchcraft by m. as men G286.1; wound m. another wound K1872.4.

Mason P455. — Why m.-wasp looks for fireplace A2471.8.

Masons mutilated to prevent duplication S161.0.1.

Mass V40ff.; of the dead *E492. — Chaplain searches the prayer-book for hunter's m. J2474; color symbolism in m. vestments Z140.3; dead man asks for m. E443.2.1.1; death respite until m. said K551.1.2; devil is cheated of his reward when priest dismisses m. early G303.16.16; devil interrupts m. by pretended battle G303.9.9.2; disenchantment by m. of Pope D781; ghosts punish intruders into m. of ghosts *E242; holy man has his own m. (hangs coat on sunbeam) V43; holy water and m. prevent demons alighting on grave D1385.15; knockers' midnight m. in mines F456.1.2.3.1; magic articles made during m. D1766.5.2; magic produced by saying m. D1766.5; parson and sexton at m. X441; penance: holding midnight m. until someone will make responses Q521.6; priest may use his own mother's m. money J1261.6; priest who never reads m. J1263.1.3; priest's rushing through m. J1263.1.3.1; punishment for neglect of m. Q223.7; snakes have m. B253.1; stay at church till m. is finished (delay saves youth from death) J21.17; symbolism of m. Z176; treacherous priests prolong m. to let enemy destroy city K2354; Virgin's private m. for lady unable to attend V255.2; well floods until m. said F933.7.

Masses used along with magic for cursing D1766.5.1; work miracles V41. — Charity rewarded above prayer or hearing of m. V410.1; ghost laid by saying m. E433.2.1; ghost of priest failing to say m. E415.3; seven m. to free soul from hell Z71.5.6.6; sons break promise to have m. for father M256.1.

Massacre. — Punishment for wholesale m. Q211.11.

Massacring prisoner R51.4. — Jealous king m. handsome captives T257.6.

Mast. — Climbing the m. (bluff) K1762; gold (silver) m. F841.2.1; human sacrifice carried on m. S264.1.1; riding up m. as suitor contest H331.1.3; witch sits atop m. D2142.0.1.2.

Masts transformed to serpents D444.11.

Master, see also **Servant;** asked to help in theft J2136.5.6.1; as magician tricks servant K1963.3; rescues disciple R167; and servant *P360ff.; takes serving man's place in woman's bed K1317.1.1; tests disciple by river plunge H1561.10; thief *K301ff. — Animal cares for wounded m. B536; animal recognizes returned m. H173.1, H173.3; animals help imprisoned m. B544.1; ass tries to caress his m. like the dog J2413.1; boat transforms self at will of m. D632; choice between bad m., bad official, or bad neighbor J229.5; contentment with evil m. for fear of worse successor J229.8; contest in lying: m. brought to say "You lie" X905.1; cumulative tale: m. goes to kill animals Z32.4; dog wants most powerful m.: stays with man A2513.1.1; faithful horse follows dead m. to grave B301.4; fool releases bear while m. is away J2191; horse's devotion to m. B301.4ff; magic object from m. D829.1; man blames m. for not correcting him in youth J142.2; only m. able to bend bow D1651.1; pupil returns from dead to warn m. of futility of his studies E368; pupil surpasses m. L142; servant boasts where the m. cannot hear K1776; servant plans to deceive his m. by refusing to eat J2064; servant repays stingy m. J1561.4; servant saves m. from death H187; skillful smith calls self m. of all masters F663.0.1; Solomon as m. of magicians D1711.1.1; stag found by m. when overlooked by servants J1032; strong hero overawes m. F615.3; transformation contest between m. and pupil D615.2; tree as m. of ceremonies F979.22; trickster sends m. running

after the paramour K1573; which is servant, which m.? J1141.1.6; why
a woman is m. of her husband A1557.

Master's. — Boat obeys m. will D1523.2.4; faithful animal at m. grave
dies of hunger B301.1; follow your m. likes and dislikes U42; helpful
cat borrows measure for his m. money K1954.1; pupils think dog's tail
their m. J2015.

Masters. — Cobolds furnish supplies to their m. F481.2; hard-hearted m.
punished Q291.2.

Masterful. — Magic object makes woman m. D1359.1.

Mastery. — Husband in armor establishes m. of house T251.2.2.

Masturbation. — Mankind from m. of creator A1216.1; universe from
m. of creator A615.1.

Mat. — Man transformed to m. D265; sleeping m. on head J1819.3.

Mats over holes as pitfall K735.1. — Eating off new m. forbidden C219.3.

Match. — Creation m. between god, goddess A85; cursing m. M401;
magic m. D1175; three on a m. D1273.1.1.1; tobacco, pipe, and m.
debate usefulness to smoker J461.3.

Matches. — Striking all m. to try them J1849.3.

Matching. — Identification by m. (parts of divided token) H100ff.,
(weapon wound) H101.1; quest for m. ornament H1317.

Matchmaker T53; passes off fool as eligible K1372.2. — Bee as m.
B582.2.4; swan as m. B582.2.3.

Mate. — Animal grateful for rescue of its m. B365.1; creation of first
man's (woman's) m. A1275; willingness to die for m. disappears at death
H1556.4.5.

Mated. — Lovers m. before birth T22.1.

Material of bridge to otherworld F152.1; rewards Q110ff. — Construction
from impossible amount of m. (task) H1022; construction from impossible kind of m. (task) H1021; extraordinary m. of (bridge) F842.1,
(castle) F771.1, (dress) F821.1, (ship) F841.1, (trees) F811.1ff.; transformation: m. of object changed D470ff.

Materialization. — Creation as m. of creator's thinking A612.

Maternity test: producing baby within year H494.

Mating. — Animals from m. of sun and moon A1771; creation of animals
from unusual primeval m. A1770; lions not m. with their fellows, prefer
leopards B754.3; mankind from unusual primeval m. A1221.

Matins. — Cardinal's decision on monks sounding m. J1179.13.

Matriarchy T148; among gods A164.4.

Matricide punished Q21.1.2.

Matron of Ephesus K2213.1. — Fortune personified as m. Z134.1.

Mattress. — Ear used as m. F542.2.

Maturity. — Man's growth and m. A1360ff.; changeling plays on a pipe
and thus betrays his m. F321.1.1.2; vegetables reach m. miraculously
quickly F815.1.

Maundy Thursday. — Eating flesh on M. tabu C235.

Maxims for law court J1131.

May Day V70.1.1. — Golden plow (throne, crown, palace) is worth a rain in M. H713.1; month of M. is greenest H646.1; tabu for Monday after M. Day C751.4.

Mayor. — The ass as m. J1882.2.

Mead. — Bog becomes flowery m. D479.1; life spared in return for poetic m. M234.1; rivers of m. in otherworld F162.2.4; stealing m. of poetry H1151.16; Virgin Mary supplies m. for unprepared hostess of the king V262; water becomes m. D478.6.

Meadow. — Tabu: staying too long in otherworld m. C761.4.2.

Meadow-lark. — Enmity between coyote and m. A2494.12.4.

Meal. — Accidental meeting of seeker of exiled prince with prince at m. N745; cannibal's gigantic m. G94; commemorative religious m. A1549.1; feeding army from one measure of m. H1022.5; feeding pigs wet m. J2465.1; fool tries to dry up spilt wine with m. J2176.1; frightful m. S183, (as leadership test) H1567.1, (as punishment) Q478; how much m. is in sack J2062.1; magic m. of fishes D1032.1; mill-ground m. blood color E761.1.12; rider takes the m.-sack on his shoulder to relieve the ass of his burden J1874.1; widow's m. J355.1.

Meals. — Children search for stolen m. J124; origin of time for m. A1511.

Mean person reborn as hyena E692.2.

Meander-pursuit (fugitive's doublings cause a river's windings) A931.

Meanings. — Symbolic m. H600ff., (of numbers) H602, (of playing cards) H603.

Measure. — Feeding an army from one m. of meal H1022.5; helpful cat borrows m. for his master's money K1954.1; if you don't believe it, go m. it yourself (center of earth) H681.3.1, (water in sea) H696.1.2, (width of heaven) H682.2.1; inexhaustible m. D1652.5.3; magic iron m. D1470.1.47, L222.4; riddles of m. H696.

Measures. — Origin of weights and m. A1471.2; putting empty m. into pot J2461.1.4.2; use of false m. punished Q274.3.

Measured. — Sky m. by bird A702.6.

Measurement. — Magic m. *D1273.4, (protects against devil) D1385.17, (protects against sudden death) D1389.10.

Measuring fairy gifts tabu F348.6; ocean (task) H1144; sick as means of cure F950.3; time by worn iron shoes *H1583.1; wild boar H1154.3.3.1; the world A1186; worm rescues from a height B542.1.3. — Attempts at m. sky's height, sea's depth L414.1; difficult m. tasks H1145.

Meat changed to toad as punishment for ungrateful son D444.2; disguised as butter during Lent K498; distributed according to rank P632.2; fed to cabbages J1856.1; irresistible H659.20; transformed D476.3, (to roses) D457.5.1 — Bird's red eye cooks m. F989.2; chain tale: animals killing each other in man's field, provide m. Z43.6; children eat m. of luck-bringing animal, becomes fortunate N251.6; cooked m. changed to raw D476.2.2; conception from eating m. T511.7.3; diamond in m. carried to eagle's nest N527.1; dog drops m. for reflection J1791.4; dog waits to be hit with m. J2066.6; "eat m." J21.29; eaten m. of bear lover causes unborn son to have bear characteristics *B635.1.1; eating m. forbidden C221; fairy gift of inexhaustible m. F348.5.1.1; fairies eat m. F243.3; grace before m. X434.2; guessing nature of devil's roast m. H523.4; hungry student cleverly obtains m. J1341.10; why Indians cache their m. A1526; lioness foregoes m. as penance Q535.2; magic m. *D1032; man made from m.-ball A1266.1; man transformed to m. D271; marvelous sensitiveness (m. is dog's flesh) F647.5.1, (m. tastes of corpse) F647.1; message of chastity: uncooked m. left behind T386; modest choice: bones preferred to m. L222.2; mouse dying in m. tub is happy that he has eaten to satisfaction J861.3; murder by slipping coins into m. K929.5; origin of tribes from m. they choose A1616.4.1; people pelt each other with whale m. J2195; quest for best m. H1305.1; secret m.-eating betrayed by greasy mouth N478.1; sending m. home by bird: bird eats it J2124.1; sick queen under red satin mistaken for m. N335.2.1; skillful marksman shoots m. from giant's hands F661.1; stolen m. and the weighed cat J1611; stolen m. handed about K475.1; tabu to eat m. with milk C229.5; tender m. of cocks kept from intercourse B754.5; thief advises that slaughtered m. be hung up over night K343.2; transformed animal refuses to touch m. of that animal D686; transformation: stolen m. to roses D457.5.1; trickster steals m.: blind men accuse each other and fight K1081.2; wolf scorns salt m. in vain expectation of other booty J2066.4; woman has m. stolen by bird (cumulative tale) Z41.1.

Mecca. — Mosque magically turns toward M. D2136.2.1; pilgrimage to M. V532.

Medallion. — Recognition by m. H94.8.

Meddling punished *Q340ff. — Animal characteristics: punishment for m. A2237; queen m. in state affairs P25.

Mediator. — Fox as m. B239.1, (between lion and lioness) J811.2.

Medical books A1487.2.

Medicinal properties of trees A2783. — Charm renders m. herbs efficacious D1577.1.

Medicine, see also **Drug;** changes voice F556.3; against quarreling T256.2; shown by animal *B512; used to abduct woman K1364. — Blowing m. disenchants D778.2; disenchantment by m. D771.6; dwarfs give m. F451.5.1.10; evil spirit exorcised by burning m. D2176.3.1.1; fatal overdose of m. J2115; gold in m. D1500.1.31; healed with his own m. J1513; layman's ignorance of m. J1734; magic m. *D1240ff., (causes loss of memory) D1365.8, (charm) *D1241, (fluid) *D1242ff., (pill) *D1243, (powder) *D1246, (salve) *D1244; magic speed by eating magic m. D2122.1; St. Peter's grass as m. for snake-bite A2623; sham physician refuses to take his own m. K1955.7.

Medicines kill hero G347. — Conception from eating m. T511.8.2; origin of m. A1438; resuscitation by m. *E100ff.; trickster eats m. that physic him J2134.2.

Medicine-man. — Supernatural m. as helper N819.4.

Medicus F956.2.

Meditation as clerical virtue V461.5. — Magic power obtained by m. D1732.

Medusa. — Origin of Pegasus from neck of slain M. E783.2.1.

Meek. — Who are really m.? Cows, daughters H659.21.

Meeting certain persons (animals) as omen D1812.5.1.7, D1812.5.2.2; ghost causes sickness (madness) E265; old woman with water good omen D1812.5.2.2.1; to take place only after death M396. — Accidental m. with person involved in overcoming curse N718; giants m. larger giants F531.6.8.7; hero misses m. man he seeks N187; lovers' m. *T30ff.; men m. in narrow passage; rude retorts J1369.3; sham illness to escape m. K523.0.2; tabu to hold m. in certain place C853.1; women m. when bathing P611.

Meetings of the dead E490ff.; of witches in which church services are burlesqued G243. — Accidental m. N700—N799; devil appears at m. of witches G303.6.2.2.

Melody. — Leaves of tree make m. for saints F979.3; magic m. D1275.2.

Melon in murderer's hand turns to murdered man's head Q551.3.3.1. — Bringing m. 12 cubits long H1047; getting m. out of jar as resourcefulness test H506.8; great m. (lie) X1411.1; thanks for being hit by nut, not m. J2571; tribes emerge from m. A1236.2.

Melons. — Origin of m. A2687.2; ripe m. symbolic of marriageable girls H611.1; vegetable lamb born from m. (as from eggs) B95.1.

Melting. — Bull m. away after evil spirit has issued from him F981.2; flood from ice m. A1016.3; heat m. enemies D2091.10; magic m. of ice D2144.5.2; magically m. snow D2143.6.4; magic poem causes man's m. D1402.15.1; person m. away from heat F1041.4; sword m. from battle heat F1084.0.1; stars m. chariots F961.2.6; sun m. glue on artificial wings F1021.2.1; witch's body m. stone G229.6.

Melusine *C31.1.2.

Member, see also **Genitals, Penis.** — Bodily m. sacrificed to save life J351; disenchantment with missing m. D702.1; loss of one m. after fairy abduction F329.3; missing bodily m. E419.7; recognition by missing m. H57; resuscitation with missing m. *E33; trickster with painted m. K1398.

Members. — Belly and the m. A1391, J461.1; bodily m. as advisers D1312.1; bodily m. wagered in gambling N2.3; disenchantment by cutting off and reversing bodily m. D712.1; magic bodily m. (animal) *D1010ff., (human) D990ff; inability to find own m. J2020ff.; resuscitation by arrangement of m. *E30ff.; vital bodily m. E780ff.; witch with iron m. G219.1.

Memory test H1595. — Lost m. recovered in battle N645; magic object causes m. *D1366; magic m. D1910ff.; magic reawakening of m. D2006ff.; remarkable m. F692.

Mended. — Head of beheaded witch m. by rubbing with salt G223; object miraculously m. F1098.

Mendicant. See **Beggar.**

Menial hero L113.1. — Attention attracted by hints dropped by heroine as m. H151.5; disguise as m. *K1816; god serves as m. on earth *A181; heroine in m. disguise discovered in her beautiful clothes H151.6; punishment: noble person must do m. service *Q482; thief disguised as m. K311.12.

Menstrual period of 12 years claimed K1227.10.1. — Alleging m. pain to escape lover K1227.10; disease caused by m. blood A1337.0.4; ignorance at first m. period J1745.2; magic m. blood D1003.1; moon's waning caused by m. period A755.7.

Menstruation of men F569.2. — Couvade during wife's m. T583.1.0.2; origin of m. A1355; tabu connected with m. C140ff.

Mental. — Origin of m. and moral characteristics A1370ff.; dwarfs make promises with m. reservations F451.5.10.8; sun's m. powers A738.2.

Mentality. — Lie: remarkable m. X1010.

Mention. — Devil leaves at m. of God's name G303.16.8; love from mere m. or description T11.1.

Mentioning, see also **Speaking;** origin of supernatural wife forbidden C31.2; tabus *C400—C499. — Oath against m. secret M188.

Mentula loquens D1610.6.2.

Mercenary soldier (princess's lover) L161.3, (unsuitable as husband) T65.2 .

Merchant P431; as helper N851; rescues abandoned child R131.7. — Clever m. J1115.7; daughter of m. intimate with slave T91.5.1.1; devil as m. G303.3.1.19; disguise as m. to enter enemy's camp K2357.10; fortune from trifling sum sent abroad with m. N412; king in disguise of m. K1812.14.1; monk outwits m. depriving him of fowl J1638; paramour disguised as cloth m. K1517.9; prince in disguise as m. K1812.14; rich m. poor in happiness J347.4; seduction by posing as m. K1315.12; swindling m. suffocated Q274.2; thief disguised as m. K311.14; treacherous m. K2249.4; wife makes m. turn out queen S463.

Merchants try honesty for a year and find that it pays J23.

Merciful. — Christians have a m. God J1263.3; husband (wife) more m. than blood relations P212, P213.

Mercy. — God consults m. on his right A42.2; god of m. A483; olive branch laid on altar of M. as sacrifice V15.

Merit. — Officers praised in reverse from their real m. (trouble for them and their master) K2136.

Mermaid *B81ff.; rescues hero from shipwreck R138.1; rescues heroine who has been thrown overboard R137. — Child promised to m. S214;

giant son of king and m. F531.6.1.4; sight of m. bad omen D1812.5.1.9; siren in m. form B53.0.1; strong hero suckled by m. F611.2.2.

Mermaid's magic power D1719.7. — Possession of m. belt gives power over her D1410.4.

Mermaids give stones to fairies D2066.1.

Merman *B82ff.; forsaken by human wife C713; transformed to horse D131.1.

Message after a week J2192.1; of chastity: uncooked meat left behind T386; from Christ V211.10; of death fatal to sender *K1612; falsified to bring about lovers' death K1087.1; rewarded Q91.4. — Arrow as man's m. shows lion how terrible man himself must be J32; captive sends out secret m. R82; carrying m. to king's father in otherworld H1252.4; carrying his own m. J2242; consoling m. from the dead E361.2; death m. softened by equivocations K2313; false m. of love causes trouble K2132; false m. from otherworld causes man to go on pyre K929.12; falsified m. *K1851; foolish messenger muddles m. J2671.4; girl sends sign m. to prince H611.2; mealtimes from m. from God A1511.1; messenger without the m. J2192; miscarried m. of immortality as reincarnation origin E600.1; misunderstood m. causes messenger to be killed or accused N341; queen's m. on stone H1229.2; spirit delivers false m. F402.1.9; symbolic m. Z174; tabu: failing to heed m. of god C63.

Messenger of Death imprisoned R6; of the gods A165.2; to harem poses as singer K1323.1; sent away as only battle survivor N693; without the message J2192. —Animal as m. *B291ff.; animal sold as m. K131; bluff: trickster as deity's m. K1715.9; court m. P14.15.2; deity's m. can assume any guise A165.2.0.1; devil as m. to adulterers G303.9.4.5.2; earl throws water at m. F1041.16.11; fairy as m. F234.2.6; faithless widow ready to marry m. who brings news of husband's death T231.3; foolish m. muddles message J2671.4; identifying tokens sent with m. H82; king disguised as own m. K1812.15; lightning as God's m. A1141.5; no thanks to the m. J1358; origin of death: wrong m. goes to God A1335.1.1; pestilence brought to man by m. from Creator A1337.0.1.1; pretending to be m. from enemy's relative K477.3; proof that m. comes from certain person H242; provisions provided by m. from heaven D2105.2; rainbow spirit as m. F439.1.3; river as m. F932.5; why snipe m. for warriors A2261.6.

Messengers announce successive misfortunes N252. — Animals compete as m. to call father of newborn child H483; animals mistaken for m. J1762.0.1; death's m. J1051, Z111.6; discourtesy to Gods' m. punished Q221.1.1; enemy's m. mutilated Q451.1.6; four m. sent with four winds Z71.2.8; undesired suitor's m. imprisoned Q433.11.

Messiah. — Jewess makes parents believe that she is to give birth to the M. J2336.

Messiah's coming prophesied M363.2. — Tabus concerning time of M. advent C428, C897.3.

Messianic men beautiful F575.2.2. — Diseases cured in M. era D2161.6.2.
Metal tower F772.2; as defense against spirits D1385.5. — Animals of
precious m. B101; breast broad and made of glittering m. F546.1; fairy
chariot of precious m. F242.1.3; fence of m. or crystal in otherworld
F169.5; flow of molten m. at end of world A1069; magic m. *D1252ff.;
magic multiplication of m. D2106.1.3; men of m. F521.3; ogre killed by
throwing hot m. into his throat G512.3.1; origin of m. ornaments
A1465.3.3; origin of m.-working A1447; otherworld fortress of m.
F163.5.1; punishment for burying m. E419.11; recognition through prec-
ious m. H91; tree with m. leaves F811.2.1.
Metals. — Acquisition of m. A1432; city of precious m. and stones F761;
god of m. A492; mankind originates from m. A1247.
Metamorphosis, see also **Transformation;** brought about by baptism
V813.
Metaphors literally interpreted J2470ff., J2489.
Metaphorical riddles H720ff. — Fire announced in m. language J1269.12.
Meteor. — Cannibal m. G11.8; god as m. A137.16; reincarnation as m.
E646.
Meteors. — Origin of m. A788.
Mewing. — Cat's m. aids thieves K341.7.2; monster m. G346.1; witch
causes person's m. G269.21.2.
Mice. See after **Mouse.**
Michael creates cat to destroy mouse A1751.1; and Gabriel drive Satan
from heaven G303.8.1.2. — Angel M. created from fire A52.1.2;
archangel M. as porter of heaven A661.0.1.3.
Michelangelo. — Presumptuous man's comment on M. J957.
Midas with ass's ears *F511.2.2, (secret discovered by barber) N465;
with golden touch D565.1.
Midday. — Bigger fool in m. heat J1552.1.1.1; four legs in morning, two
at m., three in evening (riddle) H761; ghosts walk at m. E587.1.
Middle. — Castle at m. point of earth F771.3.4; each of two wants to
sleep in the m. J221.3.1; one eye in m. of forehead *F512.1.1, *F531.1.1.1,
G303.4.1.2.1; wager: turning somersault in m. of square N56.
Midgard Serpent surrounds the earth *A876. — Thor battles M. serpent
at end of world A1082.3.
Midge. — Skillful surgeon removes speck from eye of m. F668.2.
Midnight. — Between m. and cockcrow best time for unearthing treasure
N555.1; burial at m. E431.19; cows kneel at m. on Christmas Eve
B251.1.2.3; devil appears at m. G303.6.1.1; disenchantment at m. D791.1.8;
disenchantment by naked virgin undergoing frightful journey at m.
D759.3; disenchantment by taking key from serpent's mouth at m.
D759.1; in dwarf land sunrise is at m. F451.4.6; flower found only at m.
F814.3; ghost laid at m. E459.5; ghosts seen by those born at m.
E421.1.1.1; ghosts walk at m. E587.5; mermaid appears at m. B81.3.1,
B81.12.1; penance: holding m. mass until someone will make responses

Q521.6; stone moves at m. D1641.2.4; treasure reveals itself only on Christmas at m. N541.1; tree blossoms at m. F971.5.2.1; tree maidens bathe at m. F441.2.1.4; wild hunt appears at m. E501.11.1.1.

Midocean. — Tree in m. F811.4.1.

Midsummer V70.3.

Midsummer's Eve. — Sleeping with wife on M. tabu C751.2.

Midway. — Ghost lives m. between heaven and earth E481.5.

Midwife substitutes child for king's stillborn K1923.5. — Brownie rides for m. F482.5.4.1; devil is employed as a m. G303.9.3.2; fairies take human m. to attend fairy woman *F372.1; fool seeks a m. J2661.2; husband acts as m. when no woman is available T584.0.2; lover masks as pregnant woman to meet m. K1514.16; riddle about mother as m. H583.4.5; wolf offers to act as m. for sow K2061.6; woman assists tigress as m. B387.

Mightiest. — What is m.? Rain H631.6.

Migration of animals A2482ff. — Unusual m. of birds at Doomsday A1002.4, A1091.4.

Mild. — Priest who gives m. penances succeeds where others fail L361.

Mildness triumphs over violence L350ff.

Miles. — Carpet sixty m. square F783.1; man can hear ant leave nest fifty m. away F641.2; skillful marksman shoots left eye of fly at two m. F661.5.3; tree with coiling leaves three thousand m. high F811.2.3.1; tunnel of crystal four m. long F721.1.1.

Milesians foster Tuatha Dé Danann's children P273.4; invade Ireland F211.0.2.1.

Milestone. — Fairies assemble at m. F217.2.

Military affairs P550ff.; strategy K2350ff. — Absurdity of giving bishop m. mission J1536.1; quest to king for m. aid H1224.

Milk agitates at death E761.6.6; bath as poison antidote D1515.3; becomes bloody E761.1.10; bought on credit poured into one container K231.6.1; of "cow of plenty" tabu C241.1; dropping from woman's breast reveals her hiding R351.1; drunk from hero's skull gives strength M316; from finger F552.1.5; of the gods A154.4; goes long distance into child's mouth H495.2; gushes from cows in deity's presence H45.2; and honey flow in land F701.1; from the hornless cow J1512.1; as magic drink *D1043; magically appears in woman for orphan T611.6; in man's breast F546.6; overheated to break cat's taste for it K499.4; poured on tree roots D1658.1.5.2; -producing bird B36; sack transformed D454.5; from saint's cows forms lake F989.9; of special cow drunk by man to make wife fruitful T591.1.2; stays in overturned pail D2171.8; in stream as signal H135.2; suddenly appears in woman's dry breast T592; tasting of wine, honey F1094; transformed to blood D457.2; transformed into other substance D476.2.3; transformed to stone D471.4.1; turns dark E761.4.5; of two king's children protects hero in dragon fight D1385.14. — Air castle: pail of m. to be sold J2061.2; animal gives treasure as

m. B103.3; bath in magic m. rejuvenates D1338.4; bath of m. F872.1; bathing hair in buffalo m. makes it unusually long D1337.1.3.1; blow recalls mother's m. Z61.4; bird gives m. B735; boiling m. thought to be overflowing J1813.2; blood turns to m. D457.1.2; brewing ale from m. H1021.10; brotherhood through partaking of m. from same woman P313; carrying m. without spilling makes man forget God J94; charm makes cows give plenty of m. D1449.1; communication by pouring m. into stream K1549.5; cow gives marvelous m. through saint's virtue B597; cow's m. flows by itself B155.2.2; cows made to give bloody m. D2083.2; cow with inexhaustible m. D1652.3.1; cup full of m. symbolic offering to unwanted saint H607.4; cure by bathing in m. *D2161.4.14.1; cure by m. of Virgin Mary D2161.5.2.3; curse: cow will give red m. M471.1; disenchantment by bathing in m. D766.4; disenchantment from bird when queen milks own m. into bird's beak D759.2; disenchantment by drinking m. of queen who has borne two boys D764.1; doe furnishes man m. B292.3; does magically give m. D2156.1; dragon fed m. to keep him pacified B11.12.4.1; dragon likes m. B11.12.4; drinking m. tabu C271; dropping m. pregnancy sign T579.8.3.; dwarfs bewitch cows to give no m. *F451.3.3.5; eating thick m. forbidden C229.1; fairies m. cows F271.1; fairies m. mortal's cows dry F366.1; faithful woman must milk cow for saint's m. V229.2.3; flow of cow's m. increased by licking saint's garment D2182; flowers float on river of m. F814.6; fool takes wife's m., starves baby J2214.4; fountain gives m. on Sunday F716.1; god in sea of m. A151.8; horse fed with worms' m. B710.2.1; how banyan got its m. A2791.3; idol drinks m. D1633.1; infant bathed in m. T601; jester takes cow tells king people have m. U67; king demands m. from all hornless cows: given poison from wooden K839.4; king persuaded ocean of m. has curdled J811.5; lake of m. D921.3.1, (by tree of life) A878.2, (from saint's virtue) A920.1.13; lie about cow's rich m. X1235.2; life token: m. becomes red E761.6.2; living only on fairy cow m. F241.2.5; location of settlement at place a cow stops and where m. flows by itself B155.2.2; magic bag sucks m. from cows D1605.2; magic cow gives red m. *B182.1; magic cow gives extraordinary m. B184.2.1.1ff.; magic m. of animal *D1018; magic cure by bathing in m. D2161.4.14.1; magic healing m. D1500.1.33.1; magic m. produces immunity from hunger and thirst D1349.1.3; magic m. heals wounds D1503.7.1; man recognizes m. of stolen cows F647.5.3; martyrs' wounds emit m. V229.2.6; men fond of m. previously calves J2214.6; Milky Way as m. from breast of a woman A778.5; miraculous increase of cow's m. D2156.2; numskull puts the m. back into goat J1903.2; ocean of m. J2349.3; old woman gives m. F598; plant characteristics from Virgin Mary's m. A2731.2.1.1; plant from mother's m. A2615.2; pond of m. F713.4; pouring water instead of m. into large container K231.6.1.1; prayers believed to stop m. boiling over J1813.2.1; quest for lion's m. H1361; rain of m. J1151.1.3; recognition of son by gushing up of m. in mother's breasts H175.1; rejuvenation by burning and throwing bones into tub of m. D1886.1; resuscitation by bathing in m. E80.1.1; resuscitation by magic m. E102.1; rock becomes m. D476.1.7; river of m. F715.2.3; rivers of oil, m., wine, and honey in otherworld F162.2.6; saint makes lake of m. V229.16; sea of m. F711.2.1; snake eats bread and m. with child B765.6; snake sucks woman's m. A2435.6.2.1, B765.4.1; spring augments mothers' m. D927.3; strength from drinking mother's m. F611.2.0.1; strong man sent to m. lions: brings lions back with him F615.2.1; tabu to eat m. with meat C229.5; test of mother by weighing m. J1142.1; water turns to m. D478.1; watered m. sold K287; well of m. D925.0.2; wife offers starving husband m. from her breasts T215.2; wise men and fool pour m. into tank J1149.12; witch curdles m. D2083.2.2; witch snared by setting out m. G274.1; woman created from sour m. A1275.5.

Milk-bottle. — Child feeds snake from its m. B391.1.

Milk-cup. — Thistle serves as m. for Virgin Mary A2711.4.2.

Milked. — Cow comes to be m. for infant saint B251.2.10.1; cow grateful for being m. B294; cows m. dry by vampire E251.3.2; cows m. at night by snake B765.4; magic bull can be m. B184.2.3.2.

Milker. — Skillful m. F678.

Milking into mouth directly J2173.8; unruly cow H1155.2. — Absurd ignorance about m. animals J1905; husband m. cow blindfolded K1516.5; task: m. a bull H1024.1; transformation to aid m. buffaloes D659.13; unusual m. animal B531.2.

Milkmaid. — Forgotten fiancée reawakens husband's memory by serving as m. and talking to calf *D2006.1.2; proud m. tosses her head (air castle) J2061.2.

Milky Way. — God's palace on M. A151.6.1; origin of M. A778; water monster becomes M. D429.1.

Mill gives birth to horse J1531.1.1; made to turn backwards D2089.4; -mouse told field mouse is dead F405.7.1; slaying scene, grinds red wheat Z141.2.2; as symbol of saint Z185. — Ass jealous of horse but sees horse later working in a m. L452.1; automatic m. D1601.21; crushing in rice m. as punishment Q414.3.1; devil as builder of m. G303.9.1.3; dwarf king (lives in a m.) F451.4.2.5, (turns m. which produces gold) F451.5.1.5.1; earth swallows m. which refused saint's grain Q552.2.3.2.1; fright at m. noise J2615.1; fugitive slave takes refuge in m. house, where he must work harder than ever N255.4; gigantic m. in otherworld F163.4; greyhounds drag m. out of water (lie) X1215.12; grinding up in a m. as punishment Q469.3; magic m. *D1263; murder by grinding in m. S116.1; spirits keep m. from working F416.1; self-grinding salt-m. *D1601.21.1; strong man drags m. F631.1; strong man sent to devil's m. F615.1; wild hunt appears at old m. E501.12.10; youths grind in m. of underworldlings F106.

Mill's clatter thought to be pursuers J1789.3.

Miller P443; of hell A677.2; rescues abandoned child R131.2; rescues

princess R131.2.1; refuses to sell house to king P411.1; his son, and
the ass try to please everyone J1041.2. — Double-cheating m. K486;
fairies lame m. F361.17.1.

Miller's tale (Chaucer) K1225, K1522, K1577.

Millers. — Jokes about m. X210ff.

Millet. — Bear husks m. B571.4; why m. is red on top A2793.8.

Milliner P452.

Milling. — Origin of m. A1442.

Millipede. — Fight between snake and m. B264.4.

Millstone among best of stones H659.3.1; dropped on guilty person Q412;
hung around neck Q469.4; kills giantess F451.10.2.1; preferred to jewels
J245.1. — Baby drags m. F611.3.2.2; dwarfs suspend large m on a thin
thread F451.5.4.2; magic m. D1262.1; magic m. guards treasure N581.1;
man transformed to m. D231.1; numskull sticks his head into the hole
of a m. J2131.5.4; self-grinding m. D1601.20; stealing m. J2461.1.7;
strong man lifts m. F624.2.1; strong man attacked with m. puts it on as
collar F615.3.1; task: sewing together a broken m. H1023.7.

Millstones said to be pearls of the hero's mother K1718.2. — Waters
dissolve m. F930.7.

Mill-wheel. — Giant with m. as shield F531.4.1.

Mimicking. — Fool thinks goat m. him J1835.

Minaret. — Bathroom in the m. J2237; scorned lover plunges from m.
top T75.6.

Mind. — Discontented ass longs for death but changes m. when he sees
skins of dead asses at fair J217.2; partial transformation: animal with
human m. D682.3; power of m. over body U240ff.; strength of m. wins
contest H1562.14.

Minding. — Reward for m. own business H1554.2.

Mine ghosts E336; spirits F456. — "All of these are m." K1917; difference
between "m." and "thine" J179.1; ghost haunts m. E275.1; rich m.
discovered N596; voice warns of danger in m. V542; whistling in m.
tabu C480.1.1; wraith before m. disaster E723.8.1.

Mines found where balls fall N533.5.

Miner. — Imprisoned m. kept alive by masses performed by his wife
V41.1.

Miner's. — Dwarf king has silver m. torch bright as the sun F451.7.4.

Miners. — Devil compels two m. to follow him G303.9.5.3; ghosts annoy
m. E336.2; knockers aid m. F456.1.2.2; knockers hide m. tools
F456.1.2.1.2; knockers' malicious action against m. F456.1.2.1; knockers
as spirits of dead m. F456.1.1.3.

Mineral. — Birth from m. T544; dwarf cave has ceiling of m. white as
snow F451.4.3.3; man made from m. substance A1240ff.; man transformed to a m. form D230ff.; reincarnation as m. E645; transformation:
m. form to person D432.

Minerals. — Origin of m. A978.

Mining. — Origin of m. A1448.

Minister aids woman escape devil G303.12.5.4; in generosity contest H1552.2; makes gardener king: king decides against him in law case M13.3; taught obeisance to king J80.2; tells king to do what seems good J814.5. — Choir imitates apologizing m. J2498.1; clever m. J1115.10.2; falsely accused m. reinstates himself by his cleverness K2101; ghost laid by m. E443.2.4; housemaid disguised as m. K1839.10; king asks m. for new trick H1182.2; king propounds riddles and questions to his clever m. *H561.5; king's enigmatic order to m. H587; prime m. leaves king in anger H1385.12; royal m. rescues abandoned queen R169.7; treacherous m. K2248; washerman failure as m. U129.3; woman in disguise made m. K1837.8.1.

Minister's daughter to marry first arriving bachelor T62.2; son recovers prince's lost wife R131.11.5. — Clever m. daughter J1111.5; devil visible to one who walks in m. holy shoes G303.6.2.4; treacherous m. son K2248.1.

Ministers. — Royal m. P110ff.

Minivet. — Why tail of m. is red A2378.8.5.

Mink as culture hero A522.1.5. — Burnt smell of m. A2416.2; cat sold as m. skin K261.1; color of m. A2411.1.2.5; enmity between raven and m. A2494.13.7, A2494.12.5.

Minotaur B23.1.

Minstrel repays cobbler for stealing songs J1632. — Clever m. gets new robe J1115.5.1; fairy m. F262.3; fairy m. asks admission to heaven as reward Q172.0.1; fairy m. learns mortals' heroic deeds F393.1; lover masks as m. K1371.4.2; prince disguised as m. R24.2.

Miracle attests fact that man does not need to confess V29.3; manifested to nonbelievers *V340ff.; must wait till one man is sacrificed K1785; to permit confession V23; saves saint from unjust censure V229.2.11; wrought for animal B255. — Conversion to Christianity through m. V331.1; corpse exclaims over m. E545.10; escape from undesired lover by m. T321; foolish imitation of m. J2411; masses work m. V41; seduction on threat of performing m. K1315.6.2; sham m.: may the grass grow up K1975; tabu to use m. for trifling purpose C96.

Miracles F900; performed under Virgin's protection V268; at shrine V113.0.1. — Saint asked to perform m. as test H257; saint performs m. while yet unborn T579.5; sham m. K1970ff.; sham relics perform m. V142.1.

Miraculous birth *T540ff.; blindness as punishment Q451.7.0.2; conception T510ff.; manifestation (acclaims saint) *V222, (at birth of holy person) *F960.1, (at confession) V24, (during act of charity) V412, (to scoffers of the Cross) V86.4; power of prayer *V52; powers of relics V144; punishments Q550ff.; rescue R122; rescue of children R131.0.2; reward Q140ff., (for charities) V411; working of the host V34. — Flame as m. index *F1061; holy person loses m. powers after son born

V229.20.1; incredulity as to sacredness of host confounded by m. appearance V33.1; imitation of m. horse-shoeing unsuccessful J2411.2; Jews bribe woman to steal host for them: m. manifestation V35.1; magic object confers m. powers D1561ff.; recognition by m. sight of seer H184; tasks requiring m. speed H1090ff.

Miraculously. — Host m. given when it is refused a man by the priest V32; sacred image m. appears on stolen sacrament V35.1.2.

Mirage K1886.1.

Miriam's. — Miracles cease at M. death F900.3.1.

Mirror begrimed by snail J451.4; held up to show whom he loves T91.6.1.1; -reflection makes dupe think he is captive K1883.7; transformed to mountain D454.12. — Breaking m. as evil omen D1812.5.1.3; bridal couple look in m., heads knocked together T135.13; clairvoyant m. *D1323.1; devil appears when woman looks at herself in m. after sunset G303.6.1.4; dragon attacks own image in m. K1052; girl borrows m. from fairy F324.1; image in m. mistaken for picture J1795; life token: m. becomes black E761.4.3; love through sight in magic m. T11.7; magic m. *D1163, (as chastity index) H411.15, (kills enemy soldiers) D1400.1.13, (quest for lost) H1346; magic wishing m. D1470.1.38; numskull steals m. J2461.1.7.1; peacock admires self in m. W116.4; standing before m. with eyes shut to see how one looks in his sleep J1936; sword as m. F833.3.1; taking m. to bed to see if he sleeps with mouth open J1936.1; transformation by looking in m. D579; treasure found by clairvoyant m. N533.2.

Mirrors. — Guardian beast overcome by m. K335.1.7; sun and moon metal m. in sky A714.4.

Misappropriation of goods K254, K361, punished M368.

Miscarriage. — Charm prevents m. D1501.1; child born from m. T549.4.

Mischief maker, see also **Trickster.** — Friar Rush as m. maker F470.0.1.

Misconstruction. — Literal m. of order to get revenge J2516.0.1.

Misdeed. — Man unable to persuade wife to confess m. to priest succeeds when he makes her drunk U181.

Misdeeds. — Parents' m. innocently betrayed by children J125.

Misdirected kiss K1225. — Accidental death through m. weapon N337; pursuer m. by animal R243.1; pursuer m. by tree to help fugitive D1393.4.

Misdirecting. — Confederate m. pursuer K646.

Miser breaks legs to retrieve single grain J2146.1; enticed by "money tree" report K341.28; goes to mass before committing usury K2097; induced to enter bag, caught K711.2.1; picks up everything H614.1; tricks thieves into digging field K2316; tries to eat money, chokes to death Q272.3. — Bad choice between poor man and m. J229.6; devil marries old maid who proves to be m. G303.12.3; gold causes man to become m. G303.9.8.5; spirit transports m. to treasure F414.2; thief robs blind m. K2096.2; trickster feigns deafness and gets hospitality from m. K1981.1.

Miser's treasure stolen (advised to imagine his treasure still there) J1061.4.

Miserliness *W153.

Misfortune with oneself to blame the hardest U160ff. — Cloud symbol of m. Z156; consolation in m. J850—J899; distance from happiness to m. (riddle) H685; escape from one m. into worse N255; faithfulness of married couple in m. T215; ghost haunts place of great m. E275; man pursued by m. N251; prophecy of general m. M340.3; prophecy of great m. M340.6.

Misfortunes. — Equanimity despite m. W25.1; poor man consoles self by thinking of m. of rich J883.

Misgovernment. — Ruler diverts attention from m. by beginning war K2381.

Misguiding. — Devil m. people G303.9.9.6.

Misinforming. — Man m. competitors on quest H1239.4.

Misleading. — Devil m. travelers G303.9.9.7; ghost m. traveler E272.5.

Mismanagement of king's treasury a mortal offense P13.2.

Misplaced genitalia A1313.3. — Resuscitation with m. head *E34.

Misreported remarks K1775, message A1335.1, K1851.

Misrepresentation. — Unique weapon obtained by m. K362.0.1.

Misshapen child from brother-sister incest T550.3.

Missile thrown among enemy causes them to fight one another K1982.1. — Disenchantment by striking with a m. D712.3.1; magic m. *D1093; suitor contest: aiming with m. H331.7; weapon (m.) miraculously removed F959.3.4.

Missing. — Disenchantment with m. member *D702.1; druid finds m. person D1816.5; person with m. member cannot rest in grave E419.9; quest for m. ring H1386.2; recognition by m. hair H75.6; resuscitation with m. member *E33.

Mission. — Falsely accused hero sent on dangerous m. K2102; tabus for men on m. C833.9.

Missionary. — Disguise as m. K1826.4.

Mist as barrier to otherworld F141.2; on mirror as life token E761.4.3. Deity arises from m. A115.3; egg transformed to m. D469.1; extraordinary m. F962.10; fairy m. mistaken for enemy smoke K2369.9; fairies's magic m. F278.2; giant disappears in m. F531.6.12.1.1; land of m. F704; magic m. D902.1, (aids fugitive) R236.1, (battle defense) D2163.4, (causes person to become lost) D1418.1, (of invisibility) D1361.1, K532.1, (protects against attack) D1381.22, (separates person from his companions) D1361.1.1; man shoots into wreath of m. and brings down fairy *F302.4; origin of m. A1134; saints create concealing m. V229.8; soul as m. E744.1; transportation from heaven in m. F61.3; trying to swim in m. J1821.1; universe created from m. A623.

Mists which lead astray K1886.2.

Mistake. — Servant refused payment because of single m. K231.9.

Mistakes. — Account-book of m. J1371.

Mistaken identity J1485; hasty killing or condemnation N340ff. — Animal or person m. for something else J1760; giant's glove m. for house F531.5.2; objects with m. identity J1770ff.; one thing m. for another J1750—J1809.

Mistletoe prevents barrenness D1501.1.1. — Magic m. *D965.4; prophecy: death by m. *M341.2.1.

Mistreated orphan hero L111.4.4. — Devil promises to help m. apprentice G303.22.12.

Mistreatment by poltergeist F473.3; of prisoners R51.

Mistress aids task H974.1; deceives lover with a substitute *K1223; disguised as wife K1843.1.1; identified by chalk marks H58.1; who saves lover H592.3; summoned by wish D2074.2.3.1. — Arrogant m. repaid in kind by her lover L431; bower for fairy's m. D2185.1; choice of friend over m. J496; disguise as m. enables murder D40.2.1; fairy m. F302ff., (insists man leave wife) F302.5.4, (strikes human lover) F361.17.9, (surrenders man to mortal wife) F302.5.1; foolish lover sees no flaws in m. J1737; former m. as sons' foster mother P272.3; incognito m. T476, (overhears lover, leaves him) J2364; lover arrives home just as m. is to marry another *N681; maid behind statue of Virgin advises m. to give servants better food K1971.3.1; magician carries m. with him in his body *F1034.2; moon mutilates earth m. S160.5; otherworld m. helps hero H335.0.1.1; priest gives up parish and immediately loses fickle m. J705.1; quest for vanished m. H1385.3; Rakshasa's m. decapitated G369.1.7; servant repays stingy m. J1561.4; sham illness to escape m. K523.0.1.1; sister as robber's m. K2212.0.2; taking friend's m. K2297.2; treacherous m. K2231; wife has been m. of servant, knight, fool, and priest J1545.2; wife dismisses maid, husband's m. J1112.2; wife sends disguised m. to husband K1843.1.1; wife substitutes for m. K1223.3; wife takes place of m. in husband's bed K1843.2; wife transformed to m. D659.7; winning m. hard on heart J2572.

Mistress's descendant to serve handmaid's M369.2.5; nose cut off for faithlessness Q451.5.1.1. — Exposing m. person to public Q476; thief steals m. ornaments K346.6.

Misunderstanding. — Animal m. remark flees victim K547.5; criminal confesses because of m. of a dialect N275.2; helpful animal killed through m. B331ff.; task assigned from m. H946.

Misunderstandings due to language difference J2496.2. — Absurd m. J1750—J1849.

Misunderstood message causes messenger to be killed (accused) N341; wife banished by husband S411.1; words lead to comic results X111.7. — Criminal confesses because of m. animal cries N275.1; physical phenomena m. J1810ff.

Mite. — Casting of image of Buddha delayed until maniac's m. is thrown into furnace V125.

Mithian. — Village founded where m. bellows B155.2.1.

Mitten transformed to dog D444.10.2.

Mixed. — All joys m. with sorrow J171.2.2; blood of contractors m. to seal bargain M201.1.1; society, like a dish, must be m. J81.1.

Moaning ghost E402.1.1.2; waves F931.4.2.

Moccasins. — Magic m. *D1065.4; man with fire m. G345; ogre's own m. burned K1615.

Mock, see also **Sham;** battle to scare enemy K2368.2; sunrise K1886.3.

Mockers. — Wild hunt harmful to m. E501.18.1.1.

Mocking punished Q288. — Birds m. ascetic B787; ghost punishes person for m. him E235.1; tabu: m. animal C94.3.

Models. — Tribes from clay m. A1610.6.

Moderate request rewarded; immoderate punished *Q3.

Modest choice best L210ff.; woman forced to disrobe, outwits robber K551.4.3. — Absurdly m. wish J2076.

Modesty brings reward L200—L299; of God A102.15; personified Z139.6. —Bride's false m.: wears clothes to bed K2052.1; false m. *W136; king's m. P12.14; parable on M. having no address J91; Zeus gives man m., but it leaves when love enters T1.

Modus Liebinc J1532.1.

Mogli flower. — Why the m. is cursed A2721.6.

Mohammed goes to the mountain J831; lures doves to ears, claims God sends them K1962.1.

Mohammedan. — Riddle: what is the best religion, Christian or M. H659.5.

Moistest. — What is m.? H659.8.

Mole pretends that he sees, smells, and hears J958; struck on head while stealing fire: hence flat head A2213.5.1; as trickster killed in his own tunnel K1642. — Why m. is blind A2332.6.5, A2239.8, A2378.1.4; why m. burrows underground A2491.3; burying the m. as punishment K581.3; creation of m. A1893; why m. has hand like man A2375.2.6; giant's soul in m. E714.9; helpful m. B449.2; why m. lives underground A2433.3.20; where m. got tail A2332.6.5, A2378.1.4.

Mole's. — Why m. "hands" are turned backward A2375.2.7.

Moles. — Golden wagon drawn by m. F861.1.1.

Molten. — Devil holds m. coin in mouth G303.4.8.2; flow of m. metal at world's end A1069.

Moly (magic plant) *D965.5.

Moments thought years D2012. — Years seem m. to creator D2011.3; years seem m. while man listens to song of bird D2011.1.

Monarch, see **King.**

Monastery site magically indicated D1314.4.0.1. — Accepting blow from m. superior H1553.4; anchor catching in submarine m. N786; bell from

underwater m. F725.6; burning m. for monks' incontinence Q414.0.3.1;
quest to submarine m. H1287; saint's m. to be persecuted M364.1; submarine m. F133.3; thief as monk robs m. K311.4; Virgin becomes m.
abbot K1837.7; witch lives in m. G235; woman disguised as monk enters m. P425.3.3.

Monasteries V118.

Monday after May Day tabu C751.4; unlucky day N128.2. — Judgment
day on M. E751.7.

Money, see also **Treasure;** borrowed from fairies F358; from broken
statue J1853.1.1; cannot be kept from where it is destined to go N212;
given by dwarfs F451.5.1.5; does not always bring happiness J1085;
of the hardhearted transformed to scorpions D444.1; hidden where object
jumps E539.1f.; hung on tree stolen K331.6; left on hill to repay helpful mountain-men F460.4.2.2; loss as punishment Q595.4; from offertory
as cure *D1500.1.10.3; received from ghosts as reward for bravery
E373.1; in the stick J1161.4; spent for vanity W116.2; tempts anchorite
V475.5; tests friendship H1558.7; tested by throwing it into stream to
see if it will swim J1931; thrown to frogs J1851.1.1; tied on corpse
thrown overboard from ship in order to secure burial V64; to be
taken from chest only twice C762.5; transformed to ashes D475.2.3;
transformed to pewter D475.2.4; turns to counterfeit C939.2;
vanishes after saint ransoms prince K236.3.1; will grow if buried
J2348. — Accidental acquisition of m. N630ff.; "Agnus dei"
as a prayer for m. J1741.2; alchemist steals m., claims he made it
K1966.1; animal earns m. for master B579.7; animal handles m. B294.2;
blind men duped into fighting: m. to be divided K1081.1; borrowing m.
from fairy F342.2; carrying off huge quantity of m. (task) H1127;
Chapperbands coin false m. A1689.8; child proves his innocence by
choosing apple rather than m. H256; child sold for m. S221ff.; children
envious of m. given by deceased father to bishop V415; city without
provisions but with much m. starves J712.1; coin left in m. scales betrays
secret wealth N478; dead dog transformed to m. D422.2.1; dead husband
protests wife's spending his m. E221.4; dead returns to repay m. debt
E351; dead supplies tribe with m. E373.4; deposit m. secured by false
order to banker's wife K362.6; devil's m. G303.21ff.; devils carry away
stones of church built with ill-gotten m. Q274.1; "don't travel without
m." J21.39; dwarf promises m. to mortal father for hand of daughter
F451.5.18.1; eavesdropping sexton duped into giving suppliant m. K464;
escape by throwing m. for guards to fight over K626.1; fairies give
mortal m. F342; feeding stolen m. in flour to animal K366.0.1; fool
stops hole with m. J1851.3.1; fools send m. by rabbit J1881.2.2; ghost
demands stolen m. E236.5; ghost rebukes those withholding church's
m. E415.2; ghost seeks return of stolen m. E236.8; ghosts laid by giving
beggars m. E451.5.1; half m. paid for half-milk, half-water J1551.9;
heller thrown into others' m. K446; helpful cat borrows measure for

his master's m. K1954.1; horse-headed men become m.-lenders E605.8;
inexhaustible purse furnishes m. D1451ff.; judge's ruse to obtain m.
from rich J1192.1.2; king caught trying to steal man's m. M205.4; king
fleeing without m. L410.2; labor contract: as much m. as my companion
(strong man) can carry F613.2.1; luck only with honestly earned m.
N143; man divides m. into three (four) parts H585.1, W11.3; man eats
up m. before dying W151.7; man lacking m. better than money lacking
a man J482.2.1; miser enticed by "m. tree" report K341.28; miser trying
to eat m. chokes to death Q272.3; numskull gives away old water bag in
which m. is hid J2093.1; numskull puts m. into exchange so as to
participate in business J2428; object transformed to m. D475.2; origin of
m. A1433; payment with the clink of the m. J1172.2; penniless wooer:
m. in hand K1917.2; planting m. in hole J2489.12; possession of m.
brings luck N135.2; pseudo-magic m.-dropping ass K249.3; putting m.
in sheep's anus J1851.4; quest for m. in hell H1275; recovering m. owed
by a foreign king (task) H1182.1; return from dead to demand m.
stolen from corpse E236.5; ruler settles quarrel between loser, finder
of m. W11.6; secret wealth betrayed by m. left in borrowed m.-scales
N478; selling a sheep and bringing it back along with the m. H1152.1;
sending back by venal judge for rest of the m. J2662; shower of silver
(m.) F962.8.1; sons given equal amounts of m. H501.3; speaking of lost
m. tabu C401.3.1; spirits give m. to mortal F403.1; star drops from
heaven: is m. F962.3; stealing m. while kissing it K378; stick with m. in
it breaks and betrays thief H251.3.4; stingy man forced to share his
m. when he lies and says he has none W152.4; tabu: giving certain m.
away C783.1; tabu: misuse of m. in alms box C51.1.4; taking m. instead
of revenge J229.11; thief hides in m. bag K307.1; tree gives m. to good
brother D1663.6; transformation: water to m. D475.2.2; theft of m. from
fairies F351; trickster reports lost m.: searchers leave him in possession of
premises K341.1; unknown prince reared by fisher spends m. for princely
tastes H41.5.1; unlucky man given a loaf filled with m. exchanges it
N351; Virgin Mary returns borrowed m. and reveals cheat V252.1; vow
never to touch m. M172.1; wife keeps half of m. for shrine W152.17.

Money-lender. — Stones turn to gold for charitable m. V411.4.

Money-stick. — Robber's m. K437.4.

Mongoose with golden hair, silver ears B101.9; leads to witch's house
G402.2. — Creation of m. A1857; enmity of m. and snake A2494.12.2;
helpful m. B433.4; reincarnation as m. E612.7; woman slays m. which
has saved her child B331.2.1.

Mongooses. — King of m. B241.2.14.

Monk, see also **Cleric, Priest;** appropriates girl's dowry K361.4; who did
not ask for the position made abbot Q61.1; avoids flattery V461.6; becomes husband at night K1915.1; confesses intention to rob monastery
V21.3; who dies without his cowl cannot rest in grave E411.7; discouraged by large amount of work to be done persuaded to undertake
but a small amount each day J557.1; escapes sin by living alone J495;

fails to escape work J215.4; falsely accuses novice of laziness K2129.1; forces devil to sing hymn G303.8.1.2.1; goes into desert to avoid women T334.1; learns about temptation U231.1; leaves monastery after seeing devil: sees scores in world U230.0.1; who has left his order (forgiven and miraculously reinstated) V475.2, (punished) V475.1; loses temper at cup W185.4; loses temper at overturned cup H1553.5; neglecting to prostrate self punished Q223.13.1; obedient only as long as work is agreeable W126.1; outwits merchant depriving him of fowl J1638; under pressure from abbot forgives the crucifix which has fallen and hurt him U221; resists woman he formerly loved T331.8; says that he is a stallion J1361; seduces girl afloat in box K1367; tells parable of modesty J91; unsuccessfully tempted in nunnery T331.1. — Angel shows m. value of work, prayer H605; devil blamed by m. who takes what does not belong to him G303.25.10; devil comes out of man when m. recognizes the devil's voice in man G303.16.19.7; devil as old woman seduces m. G303.3.1.12.4; devils cause m. to perspire and stay away from church service V5.3; dissatisfied m. admonished W128.5; doves show m. treasure B562.1.3; feigned ignorance to keep hero as m. K1792.2; disappointed lover becomes m. T93.2; first m. A1546.3.2; hospitality to m. rewarded Q45.3.1; incognito princess travels as m. K1812.8.2; incontinent m. V465.1.1; layman made to believe that he is a m. J2314; lion disguised as m. K1822.1; lover disguised as m. or friar meets sweetheart K1826.1.1; paramour disguised as m. K1517.6; peasant exchanges places with m. U119.2; penance: adulteress masks as m. and lives chastely in monastery Q537.1; reward to almsgiving m. Q44.1; self-righteous m. rebuked by abbot L435.1.1; stupid m. recovers stolen flocks L141.1; thief becomes m. to rob monastery K311.4; truthful m. refuses to cheat even for his order V461.2; Virgin Mary has dissolute m. buried in consecrated ground (his only mass is that of the Virgin) V255; Virgin Mary reproves m. who sleeps at altar V5.1; Virgin pardons overworked m. for neglecting prayers V276.2; vow to become m. if execution escaped M183.4; woman kicks lecherous m. down stairs T322.1; woman has husband made m. while he is drunk K1536; devil disguised as m. K1961.3.

Monk's enemies quarrel and thus save him J581.3; cordon saving him from hell J1261.8; curse M411.15; lust conquered by cruelty T317.6; prayers weave garment for Virgin V276.1.

Monks P426.3; sacrifice themselves S263.5.2; sharing with poor receive supplies Q141.1; shrive selves clean under threat of complete exposure of their sins by brother possessed of fiend V29.2. — Animal m. B252.1; bishop wishes all m. were castrated X457.1; cardinal's decision on m. sounding matins J1179.13; chastity tests of m. H426; twenty-four nuns for twelve m. J1264.9; two m. renew their appetites (locked up for a day) J1606.

Monks' bread given to poor inexhaustible V412.2; revenge on millers X214. — Monastery burned for m. incontinence Q414.0.3.1.

Monkey as animals' king B240.12; attracts attention of mowers until young
birds can fly away from the harvest field K644; borrows deer's tail
A2241.11; buys liquor B294.2.2; causes girl to cry: eats her food K461.2;
cheats fox of bananas K171.9; cuts throat in imitating cobbler J2413.4.3;
cut in two becomes two D1652.9; in danger on bridge of crocodiles pretends that king has ordered them counted K579.2; destroys nest of
bird who has made sport of him Q295; as domestic servant B292.2.1;
dresses in dead mistress's gown K1839.3; gives tiger sore-producing ointment K1043.1; gives wrong answer to princess H343.2; a god A132.2;
instead of girl in floating basket K1625; jumps into water after a butterfly J2133.10; jumps over a ravine with his sword girded on and falls to
his death J2133.2; jumps through body of tiger F916.1; killed by
girls pretending to wash it K831.2; -like people F529.8; and lost lentil
J344.1; lures tiger into tree, sets it afire K812.3; mistaken for nobleman
J1762.6; paramour B611.6; plays chess B298.1; released: grateful B375.5;
safe in tree insults gorilla *W121.2.6; saved from trap by feigning
marriage K579.4; shows husband how to rule T252.2.2; sneezes in king's
presence: killed J2413.6; terrified by tiger attacking his shadow J1790.3;
tricked into drowning self K891.3; transformed to other animal D411.5ff.;
transformed to person D318.1. — Abduction by m. R13.1.7; buying m.
instead of cow J2081.4; charm to catch hare and m. D1444.2; color of
m. A2411.1.5.1; crocodile opens mouth, m. escapes K561.3; disease to be
cured by heart of m. K961.1; enmity of m. and (leopard) A2494.2.7,
(lion) A2494.7.1; escape in m. skin K521.1.3; fakir returns to m. friends
W34.4; friendships of m. A2493.14; ghost as man-m. E423.2.9; hair
transformed to m. D447.1.1; helpful m. B441.1; how m. got its tail
A2378.1.8; man given members by m. A1225.2.1; man transformed to m. D118.2; man tries to kill m. rescuer W154.5.1.2;
marriage to m. B601.7; marriage to person in m. form B641.7; patient
laughs at m., cures self N641.1; pay for teaching m. to talk K491.1;
person plans to marry m. B601.7.1; pet m. in sheet frightens owner
K1682.1; prince married to m. fairy F302.11; rebirth as m. prophesied
M354.1; reincarnation as m. E612.12; speaking m. B211.2.10; transformation into m. Q551.3.2.4; transformation: handkerchief to golden m.
D454.3.2.2; wedding of m. B281.10; why m. lives in tree A2433.3.19;
why m. has first fruits of harvest A2433.3.19.1; woman bears m. T554.4.

Monkey's money stolen B294.2.1. — Cause of m. walk A2441.1.1; snake's
brain as only cure for m. disease K961.2.1; thorn removed from m. tail
B381.2; why m. buttocks red A2362.1; why m. face black A2330.3; why
m. tail is short A2378.4.6.

Monkeys attack by throwing coconuts B762; carry off tortoise's salt
K343.4; construct bridge across the ocean B846; copy men B786; plan to
found city but desist J648.1. — Birhors eat m. A1422.2; devils in form
of m. G303.3.3.2.7; king of m. B241.2.2; kingdom of m. B221.1; man
carried off by m. steals magic cups K311.6.2; man descended from m.

A1224.5; men as m. without tails A1224.5.1; merchant traps robbing m. J1115.7.1; promise to return m. to their human form T68.5; war of m. and grasshoppers B263.6; why m. do not fall from trees A2576.

Monogamy among animals A2497.

Monopoly. — Fee from two persons for the same m. K441.3.

Monotony of one favorite food: compared to marriage J81.0.1.

Monsoon's origin A1129.2.

Monster born because of hasty wish of parents *C758.1; disguises and wins girl K1918; guards door of habitable hill F721.2.2; as hero L112.1; killed from within K952; with life in neck E714.8; turning over causes lake overflow F713.3; ungrateful for rescue W154.2. — Abduction by m. R11; all-swallowing m. F911.6; bride's m.-father T172.3; daughter promised to m. as bride to secure flower (bird) she has asked for S228; devastating m. G346; devil puts convert's body on sea m. M219.2.6; disenchantment of m. when prince promises to marry the monster's mother D741; earthquakes (from movements of subterranean m.) A1145.1; (from sea m.) A1145.2; earth rocks at m. fight F969.4.2; eclipse caused by m. devouring sun or moon A737.1; fairy becomes ape-headed m. D49.3; fettered m. A1070ff.; four-headed m. B15.1.2.3.1; giant sea m. B877.1ff.; girl married to (enamored of) m. T118; god reincarnated as m. E652; grateful m. helpful to hero N812.5; hero conquers sea m. A531.4; hero as sacrifice to m., kills him K1853.2.1; hero shoots m. and follows it into lower world F102.1; insects from body of slain m. *A2001; invulnerability bestowed by many-headed m. D1846.2; killing m. as suitor test H1174; magic adhesion to m. *D2171.2; magic object received from m. D826; magic object vomited by m. D826.1; magic power of m. child D1717.1; periodic sacrifices to m. S262; person transformed to m. D494; plague as m. F493.0.1.1; sea m. G308; severed heads of m. become birds E613.0.5; skull transformed to water m. D447.2; snake from blood of slain m. A2145.1; strong man slays m. F628.1.0.1; tabu: finding age of m. C821; tabu to tell children about lake m. C423.6; transformation to m. D47; watch for devastating m. H1471; water m. becomes Milky Way D429.1; water m. dragged to house by horse K1022.2.1; youngest daughter to marry m. L54.1.

Monster's arm token of dog's innocence H105.3; blood makes tree poisonous D1563.2.2; returning head G635.1. — Dying m. request and promise M257; fettered m. chains renewed A1074.7; magic from reversing m. orders D1783.4.

Monsters *G301; kill each other off A1087. — Battle of gods and m. at end of world A1082; cannibal m. G11.16; culture hero overcomes m. *A531; entrance to otherworld guarded by m. F150.2; killing m. as suitor task H335.3.7; magic spring guarded by demons (m.) D927.2; path between m. G333; saint's bachall keeps off m. D1385.8; stepbrothers kill m. P283.1; saint overcomes m. V229.4; valley full of m. F756.5.1; youths, maidens yearly tribute to m. S262.2.1.

Monsters' birth at world's end A1070.1. — Flood from m. conflict A1015.1.1.

Monstrous births *T550ff., (from incest) A1337.0.7, (as punishment for girl's pride) Q552.5; child exposed S325.0.1; creatures in otherworld F167.11; gods A123; offspring from animal marriage B634; persons F510ff. — Cannibal with m. features G11.11; curse: m. birth M437; god m. as to body A123.1ff.; ogres with m. features G360ff.; woman deserts husband for m. lover T232.

Mont Saint Michel built by devil G303.9.1.11.

Month of May is greenest (riddle) H646.1. — Fasting the first m. J2135.1; full moon and thirtieth of m. (enigma) H582.1.1; tree bears fruit each m. F811.18.1; woman bears child every m. T586.5.1.

Months. — Determination of m. A1160ff.; twelve m. as youths seated about fire Z122.3.

Monuments. — Origin of erection of m. to mark boundaries A1599.2; priest uses fortune dishonestly made to erect m. to himself W157.1.

Moon A740—A759; blessed for beautiful light L351.2; bloody at Crucifixion V211.2.3.2; -boat A757; brings murder to light N271.1.1; answers questions D1311.6.1; captured R9.1.2; as creator A19.1; curses son A736.9; as deity A121.1; doesn't shine during deluge A1010.1; eats wife's corpse G27; at end of world A1053; on forehead royalty sign H71.1.1; falls into sea, causes flood A1016.6; from fish's belly A713.1; forged by smith A700.5; -god A240ff., (threatens to withhold rain) A182.3.6; as god's child A700.8; as gods' home A151.6.2; keeps star children in hiding A764.1.2; kills sun's children A736.1.4.1.1; as land of dead E481.8.2; from light A712.1; magically provides D1470.1.49; mutilates earth mistress S160.5; as next world A695; nourished on fire A700.7; as omen D1812.5.1.5; punishes for tabu breach C905.2; purchased A700.6; as real traveller H726; shines on God's forehead A123.10; splits hare's lip with hatchet A2216.3; steals food from gods A153.3.1; steals tree of life E90.1; tied to sun, when sun sinks, moon dragged up A735.1; transformed to person D439.5.1. — Absurd theories concerning the m. J2271; animals think m. shines for them J953.15; animals from mating of sun and m. A1771; banished devil appears on earth only on day of dark m. A106.2.1.1; barking to dog in m. K1735; bride like m. Z62.2; castle east of sun and west of m. F771.3.2; chest of murdered child becomes m. A1277.3; deity departs for m. A192.2.1.1; directions on quest given by m. H1232; color of sun, m., and stars F821.1.5; drinking the m. J1791.1; eating the m. (task) H1035; escape to m. R321.2; extraordinary behavior of m. F961.3; feast of the new m. V70.7; falling stars as pieces of m. A788.1; full m. and thirtieth of the month (enigma) H582.1.1; ghosts walk at full m. E587.6; gold m. F793.1; half-m. indicates treasure N532.1; handkerchief color of sun, m., and stars F822.1; hare as ambassador of the m. K1716; how much the m. weighs (riddle) H691.1; jewel-box in tank floats at new m. N513.6;

local m. J2271.1; looking at m. when shooting game forbidden C315.2.1; magic objects received from sun, m., and stars D814; making m. shine in north H1023.16; man in the m. A751; man put in m. for cursing Q235.1; marriage of mortal and m. T111.2.2; moonmakers make new m. F675.2; new m. with old moon in her arms a sign of storm D1812.5.1.5.1; origin of eclipse of m. A737.0.1; original m. becomes the sun, sun the moon A736.8; prophecy: man will make m. stand still M312.8; pursuit of sun by m. A736; quest to m. for answers to questions H1283; rescuing the m. J1791.2; stars as pieces of the m. A764; sun and m. (from cave) A713, (kept in pots) A721.0.1, (as man and woman) A736.1, (placed for eyes in sky) A714.1, (placed in top of tree) A714.2, (as uncle and nephew who ascended to sky) A711.1; sun, m., and stars (bring forth first parents) A1271.1, (are highest) H642.1; sun-god couples with m. A220.0.2; sun as offspring of m. A715.5; sun will lock m. in ditch A1066; tabu to offend m. C75.1; thunder from crashing of stones in m. A1142.5.1.1; tide inquires whether m. is up J1292; tower reaches m. F772.1.2; treasure nearest to surface at full m. N555.2; vision of m. entering husband's mouth V515.1.2; visit to land of m. *F16.

Moon's. — Diving for m. reflection in water J1791.3.3; marvelous sensitiveness: ulcer from m. rays F647.7; stars as drops of m. blood A764.2; stars as m. children A764.3; stars are m. spittle A764.4.

Moons. — Sovereigns compared to new, full m. H599.3.

Moonbeam. — Robber persuaded to climb down the m. *K1054.

Moonbeams. — Partridge subsists on m. B768.1.

Moonlight. — Brownies sew by m. F482.5.2; conception from m. T521.1; crabs eaten on m. walks K772.1; dwarfs play in the m. F451.6.3.5; hedge to keep in m. J1796.1; why sunlight stronger than m. A733.1.

Moorish girl substituted for mistress K1317.8. — Virgin Mary destroys M. army V268.3.

Moors free great painter Q88.1. — Friends ransom selves from M. P319.1.

Moose mistaken for mouse J1759.1. — Body of m. made larger A2301.1; creation of m. A1876; man becomes m. D114.1.7; why m. eat willows A2435.3.6.

Morass. — Frogs reprove ass for lamenting when he falls into m. J2211.1.

More. — Greedy man keeps demanding m. J514.3.

Morning. — Bed-partner to receive payment from first man she meets in m. T456; fairies leave at m. star's rise F383.4.2; four legs in the m., two at midday, and three in evening (riddle) H761; god of m. star A251; origin of birds' m. songs A2425.2; origin of m. star A781.1; quest to m. star for answers to questions H1282; sun eats all children except m. star A764.1.2.

Morning-glory. — Origin of wild m. A2665.

Mortal, see also **Human, Man, Person;** abandons world for fairyland

*F373; as ally of gods A189.1ff.; characteristics of fairies F254; in deity guise D43; man marries or lives with fairy woman F302ff.; marries star-girl A762.2; rules fairyland F252.1.0.1; as servant in fairyland F376; son of giant F531.5.7.1; as umpire of quarrel between gods A187.2; visited by angel V235; woman seduced by a god K1301. — Angel carries m. V232.2; angel and m. struggle V230.3; angel punishes m. V245; child of demon king marries m. F402.2.3; divinity becomes m. A192.4; fairy becomes m. F259.1.2, (for husband) F302.6.2.2; fairy causes m. husband's death C435.1.1.1; fairy lover entices m. girl F301.2; fairy mistress surrenders man to his m. wife F302.5.1; god in guise of m. D42; god half m. A122; horse used by m. under fairy spell changes to gray cat F234.4.1; magic spear always inflicts m. wounds D1402.7.2.1; marriage of m. and supernatural being *T111ff.; salt renders fairy m. F384.1.1; transformation by offspring of fairy and m. D683.7.1; twin gods: one m., other immortal A116.1; Virgin Mary substitutes for a m. K1841; wedding of m. and fairy F303; why m. cannot look at sun A733.2.

Mortal's attempt to defile goddess punished Q246. — Tasks test m. prowess before gods H927.1.

Mortals become gods A117; as captives in fairyland *F375; help fairies F394; unable to cross river F141.1.2; unable to endure God's glory A182.0.1. — Demigods fight as allies of m. A536; dwarfs direct m. to treasure F451.5.1.9; dwarfs serve m. F451.5.1.7; fairy living among m. F393.0.1; fairies and m. F300—F399; fairies borrow from m. F391; fairies call out to m. F276; fairies heal m. F344; gods in relation to m. *A180ff.; gods (saints) in disguise visit m. K1811; hero assists m. A581.1; tear from upper world of m. falls on departed in lower world E361.1.

Mortality of fairies *F259.1.

Mortar transformed to tigress D444.8. — Carrying heavy m. as punishment J2044; found m. taken to king reveals peasant girl's wisdom H561.1.2; ogre carrying m. and pestle G676; tigress becomes m. D421.4.1.

Mortgage. — Hogs as m. collateral K231.5.2.

Moses L111.2.1; as prophet M301.7.1; rescued by princess R131.11.1. — Cure by M. D2161.5.4; God's radiance upon face of M. A124.4; God speaks to M. A182.3.0.1; what kind of man was M.? He was a day laborer X435.1; wisdom gates open to M. J182.1.

Moses's staff (tree that became flesh) H823, (has drunk water for its sustenance and eaten after death) H824. — Lions tamed by M. rod B771.2.3; miracles cease at M. death F900.3.1.

Moslem. — Moving away from M. land to escape Allah J1823.4.

Mosque magically turns towards Mecca D2136.2.1.

Mosques V112.2.

Mosquito advises hero B569.3. — Bringing quantity of m. bones H1022.9; serpent transformed to m. D418.1.3.

Mosquito's buzz A2426.3.5.

Mosquitoes prick king, show they are stronger L392.1. — Bumblebees crossbreeding with m. X1280.1.1; deity's wife creates m. to drive husband from jungle A2034.1; fireflies as lantern-carrying m. J1759.3; gods' m. A155.4; lies about m. X1286; numskulls try to kill m. with bows and arrows J2131.0.1; origin of m. A2034; why certain district free of m. A2584.1.

Moss grows overnight F971.1.3. — Dwarfs grown over with m. F451.2.0.2; face covered with m. F545.4; origin of m. rose A2656.1; resuscitation by smelling of m. E72; why rocks at river are covered with m. A976; sieve filled with m. so as to carry water H1023.2.0.1.

Mossynoikoi. — Voyage to Land of M. F129.2.

Mote. — Man can put head through m. in sunbeam F535.2.4.

Moth. — Fairy as m. F234.1.16.2.

Moths. — Souls feed on night m. E752.7.1.

Mother ape burns bear L315.4; and daughter P232, (rivals in love) T92.6; who devours her children when they grow up (riddle) H734; dies from joy at son's return F1041.1.5.3; does for another what the latter cannot do for her (enigma) H583.4; does not love children of forced marriage P230.2; falsely accuses son of incest K2111.5; guilty of incest with son whose honor she is testing T412.3; of the gods A111.1; will die when daughter is wooed E765.4.2; guards girl T50.1.1; -incest prophecy M344; kills husband for daughter's murder P211.2; -love in animal F989.8; -love dearer than gold (riddle) H662; of men A1282; prefers son P230.1; as procuress for son T452.1; recognizes child's flesh when served G61.2; rescues son R153.4; resuscitated by breaking nuts on head E181.1.1; of saint admitted to heaven Q172.8; sends son to find unknown father H1216; shown what would have been evil fates of her dead children N121.2; and son *P231; -son incest T412; -son marriage of the gods A164.1.1; sought in upper world F15.1; test H495; of Time F118, H1285, Z122.2; treats changeling well, own child returned F321.1.4.8; tricked by forcing child's cry D2034; of unbaptized child cannot rest in grave E412.2.2; of world bears three sons A1282.1. — Abandoned child cared for by m. secretly S351; Adam and Eve, having neither father nor m., are dead H813; adopted child reproaches foster m., returned to real one T672; accidental meeting of m. and daughter N736; accidental meeting of m. and son N735; animal m. of man helps him B631.1; backbone of ogre's m. broken G512.7; bird prevents m. from killing babe B524.4; boy unwittingly commits incest with his m. N365.1; chaste m. of wife J482.3; child does not recognize m. in new skin A1335.4; child mystically recognizes m. H175.2; child seeks unknown m. H1381.2.2.2; children rescue m. from lion's den R154.0.1; colt's real m. will swim to it J1171.4; creative m. source of everything A3; cruel m. *S12; dead m. appears and makes disobedient child eat fatal serpent Q593; dead son tells m. death inevitable E361.3; devil's m. G303.11.3; devils carry off girl who abuses her m. Q281.1.1; disenchantment of

monster when prince promises to marry monster's m. D741; earth as
virgin m. of Adam A1234.1; Elias, having had father and m. is not
dead H814; fairy foster m. F311.3; fairy m. bestows magic powers
on son F305.1.1; father hides children from murderous m. R153.2.1;
foolish m. does not understand how babies cry J1911.2; formerly I was
daughter, now I am m. H807; foster m. summoned D2074.2.4.1; girl
hidden in skin of her dead m. R318; goddess as m. of Pacific Ocean
A109.2; grandmother as foster m. P292.1; gullible m. J2303; help
from ogre's m. G530.3; hero licked by deer m. B635.3.1; infant picks
out unknown m. H482; jealous m. casts daughter forth S322.2; journey
to hell to retrieve soul of m. F81.4; killing m. by overfeeding J2465.3.2;
kissing the m. (earth) J1652; in large family father unwilling but m.
willing to sell children H491.1; lazy m. given shoes of cotton W111.5.1;
Lot's wife, having had father and m., is not dead like other mortals
H815; magic object received from m. D815.1; magic power from m.
D1737.1; magic object from foster m. D815.7.1; master's m. killed by
wood on head K1466; moon's m. A745.2; mortal m. ignores changeling
F321.1.4.7; moon stays with his m. under earth during day A753.3.3;
naïve remark of child: "You forgot to strike m." J122; origin of relation
of m. and children A1575; prophecy: either youth or m. will die M341.5;
prophecy: m. will be killed by children M343.0.2; rescue by captor's m.
*R162; river flows from corpse of hero's m. A511.1.1.1; St. Peter's m.
dropped from heaven because of hard-heartedness Q291.1; seduction
by bearing false order from m. K1354.3; son buries aged m. alive S21.1;
son chastizes father for scorning m. P233.9; son must not see m. in
intercourse C114.1; son warns animal m. B631.0.1; stolen m. returns
from fairy land each Sunday to minister to her children *F322.3;
strong man son of bear who has stolen his m. F611.1.1; succession by m.
right P17.6; tabu: eating magic catch before m. C231.3.1; task for virgin
wife to accomplish: have by departing husband a son whose real m.
she is H1187; tasks assigned by jealous m. H913.1; test of m. by weighing
milk J1142.1; to every son belongs his m. P526.2; transformed m. called
by her child D792; transformed m. suckles child D688; transformed m.
as helper N819.2.1; trickster leads m. into sham murder K522.7; trickster
secures man's help against m. K2384; vision of m. in hell leads to good
life V511.2.3; will-o-the-wisp is girl cursed by her m. A2817.2; woman
pretends to be m. of future king K1923.4; youth made lame: had kicked
his m. J225.1.

Mother's bosom is softest H652.2; breast is sweetest H633.3; brothers
P293.1; curse on son causes eclipse A737.2; eyes are brightest H651.2;
weeping for thief made plausible J1142.4.1. — Child betrays m. adultery
J125.2.1; dead m. friendly return *E323ff.; dead m. malevolent return
E222; disregarding m. warning J1054; false bride makes child demand m.
clothes K1911.1.8.1; girl avoids eating m. flesh G61.1.1; magic object
found on m. grave D842.1; man dies over m. death F1041.1.3.8; mark

of m. hand on moon's shoulder A751.5.3; plant from m. milk A2615.2; recognition of son by gushing up of milk in m. breasts H175.1; retrieving m. soul F81.4; son on gallows bites his m. nose off Q586; son returns on day of m. marriage N681.4; tabu: listening to m. counsel C815; tasks assigned because of m. foolish boasting H914; unborn son's soul issues from m. mouth E726.2; using m. corpse to get presents K2321.1.

Mothers exchange children S216, K1921.2; of saints give curing milk D1500.1.33.1.1. — Birth from nine m. T541.12; child with several m. T589.9; city of married m. X1563; six imprisoned m. eat own children, seventh refuses Z215.

Mother Earth *401. — First humans from womb of M. A1234.1.1; marriage of M. and ogre T126.1; sun, moon from breasts of M. A715.4.

Mother-in-law *P262; casts woman's children forth S322.6; humiliated as cure for daughter-in-law's malady K1945.1.1; seduces son-in-law T417.1; tabu C171. — Cruel m. S51; devil frightened by threatening to bring m. K2325; man unwittingly lies with m. N365.4; treacherous m. K2218.1.

Motionless. — Hero has lain m. since birth F583.

Motley. — Dwarfs clad in m. F451.2.7.10; wife orders m. wear for husband J1112.1.1.

Mould put on table for the dead E433.1; thrown on corpse to prevent return E431.3. — Magic churchyard m. *D1278.1; wild huntsman released from wandering by m. from Christ's grave *E501.17.7.1.

Mound, see also **Grave-mound.** — Captivity in m. R45; fairy m. destroyed R121.8; magic rescue of prisoner from m. R112; man becomes m. D287; task: removing m. in one night H1101; witch lives in fairy m. G233.

Mounds from horns cast by cattle A967.1. — Burial m. fairy dwellings F211.0.1; habitable caves and m. in otherworld F164; origin of m. A967; pagans flee into fairy m. P426.0.1; sitting on sepulchral m. tabu in autumn C755.5.

Mount Meru. — Moon travels around M. A759.4.

Mount Sinai. — Tora given on M. F960.10.

Mountain, see also **Hill;** at borders of otherworld F145; at center of earth A875.1.1; of cheese (lie) X1528.1; -climber's rope cut, murdered K963.1; of fair-haired women F131.1.1; god A499; of grain to be eaten through on way to Schlaraffenland X1503.4; in human shape prophesies M301.15; in labor brings forth mouse U114; moved by prayer D1641.2.2, D2136.3.1; pass to otherworld F151.2; reaches to sky F55; -sheep A2326.3.5; -spirits *F460ff.; where sun goes through A722.7; supports sky A665.3; of Venus F131.1. — Abandonment on m. S147; abode of dead in m. *E481.3; bird carries a grain of sand from a m. each century H701.1; brush becomes m. D454.7; carrying m. on head H1146; climbing glass m. D753.4, H1114; cloak becomes m. D454.3.4.1; covering m. with killed birds H1109.3; creator's giant servant makes valley and m. A857.2; culture hero asleep in m. *A571; deity of particular m. A418;

demon looks like m. F531.2.11; dragon's home at top of m. B11.3.2; dwarf moves mortal's castle from one m. to another F451.5.1.12; dwarfs seen on a m. F451.4.2.6; dwarf serves king sleeping in m. F451.5.1.8; eating m. of bread (task) H1141.1; entrance to lower world through m. F92.4; escape from deluge on m. A1022; false judgment of distance of m. J2214.12.1; gate as huge as m. F776.1; giant bestrides m. F531.3.5.1; girl having been stolen by m.-folk must be baptised anew V81.1; glass m. from mirror D454.12; god speaks from m. A182.3.0.5; holy m. free from plague D2162.4; home of gods on high m. *A151.1; house inside m. F771.3.5.1; illusory m. K1886.7; king asleep in m. *D1960.2; lifting m., placing it on shoulders H1149.9; magic leveling of m. D2152.1; magic m. *D932; man becomes m. D291; man kicks down m. F626.2; mankind emerges from m. A1234.2; marriage of m. and cockle-shell T126.2; Mohammed goes to the m. J831; mortal transformed to god on m. top A117.4; Old Man of the M. K1889.3; otherworld in hollow m. *F131; otherworld on lofty m. *F132; quest for m. of gold H1359.4; remaining on m. as punishment C983; removing m. in one night (task) H1101; rescue of princess from m. R111.2.2; rock transformed to m. D452.1.2; saint causes m. to melt D2149.2; saint's bachall (brings down m. on heads of enemies) D1549.4, (leads stream through m.) D1549.3.2; slamming door on exit from m. otherworld *F91.1; stream bursts from side of m. A934.9; strong man throws m. F624.2.0.1.1; strong man holds up m. F623; submarine castle on a m. F725.3.1; suitor contest: riding up glass m. H331.1.1; tails fall off m. spirits when they are baptized V81.2; touching sacred m. tabu C526; stones of m. for church D1552.7; transformation to m. ridge C961.4; treasure buried on top of m. N511.1.11; trolls' riches inside m. F455.4.1.1; upper world (heaven) as a m. A662; weighing m. as task H1149.8; wild hunt appears by m. E501.12.5; witch dwells on glass m. G232; wrestler boasts he can carry m. K1741.4.

Mountains, see also **Hills;** fall together at end of world A1062; magically transported D2136.3; open and close *D1552ff.; in otherworld F162.9; push water westward A914; seem to be fighting D2031.14. — Clouds in sky to shade m. A1133.2; creation of m. A960ff.; dwarfs live in hills, m. F451.4.1.11; extraordinary m. *F750ff.; extraordinary activity of m. F1006; failure to bless m. gives mountain-men power F460.4.6; flood from m. made of flat earth A1016.5; giant hurls m. F531.3.2.4; giants live in m. F531.6.2.1; giants sit on m. and wash feet in stream below F531.3.9; god's voice shatters m. A139.5.1; icy m. in hell A671.3.2; lies about m. X1520; magician casts m. upon enemies D2152.2; man born from m. A1245.5; piling up m. to reach heaven forbidden C771.2; why porcupine lives in high places in m. A2433.3.11; ship becomes m. D454.10.1; Sion appointed chief of m. A1187; strong man pulls down m. F626; valleys created by stamping down m. F756.2.2; why dinner time comes soon in m. J2276.1; wings cut from flying m. A1185.

Mountaineer. — King disguised as m. K1812.16.

Mountebank cures incurables F958.

Mounting tower takes year F772.1.1. — Mutilated master m. prone horse B301.4.5.

Mourners. — Loudest m. not greatest sorrowers J261.

Mournful. — Sea's m. sound A925.5.

Mourning customs P681; dead ass: cumulative tale Z32.5; dead lover T85; tabus C898. — Bride's constancy tested by seven years' m. over supposed dead lover H387.1; failure to observe m. punished Q223.12; fairy music causes m. F262.3.5; forgetfulness by m. D2004.8; heavenly bodies m. Adam F961.0.3.1; hens in m. J1886; king m. on wife's grave P27.2; loud noise of m. F1051.2; magic object causes m. D1359.2; objects m. saint's death V229.19; pigeon cheated out of chick: always m. A2275.4.1; professional m. V65.4; sister is m. last year's laughter H583.5; stepmother m. stepson's death P282.2; sun smears face in m., hence eclipse A737.8; swallows put on m. at crucifixion: have never taken it off A2221.2.4.1; three lovers m. dead girl T92.14; what shall be his m.? J1301.

Mouse as beast of ill-omen B147.1.2.3; bird, and sausage keep house together J512.7; bursts open when crossing a stream (cumulative tale) Z41.4.1; and cat's association over when danger ends J426.1; causes thief's hair to fall out Q557.4; created by Lucifer, cat by Michael to destroy mouse A1751.1; destroying elephant H1161.3.1; dying in meat tub is happy that he has eaten to satisfaction J861.3; in jug (test of curiosity) H1554.1; gathers rice for man: may eat a little of his rice daily A2223.3; on lion's mane J411.8; regains its tail (cumulative tale) Z41.4; stronger than wall, wind, mountain L392; teaches her child to fear quiet cats but not noisy cocks J132; torments bull who cannot catch him L315.2; trampled to death by his lion bride B363.1; transformed to (cat) D411.6.2, (person) D315.2, (another animal) D411.6. — Cat transformed to maiden runs after m. J1908.2; chain tale: fat m. cannot get into hole Z49.2.1; creation of m. A1853; devil as a m. G303.3.3.2.4; dying person's soul as m. B766.1.1; elephant poisoned by m. L315.5.1; enmity between m. (and cat) A2494.1.1, (and dog) A2494.4.3, (and owl) A2494.13.4; enticing cat and fortune with m. K2.1; how m. got his eyes A2332.1.1; friendship between m. and butterfly A2493.28; friendship of cat and m. A2493.9; ghost as m. E423.2.11; giant tricked into becoming m. K722; gold, silver m. H151.1.2; helpful m. B437.2; husband transformed to m. to rescue wife R115.1; improvident m. eats grain stored for famine J711.2; lawsuit between owl and m. B270.2; lion spares m.: m. grateful B371.1; magic m. B183.1; magic m.-skin bears person aloft D1532.1.1; man transformed to m. D117.1; marriage to m. B601.3.1; mill-m. told field-m. dead F405.7.1; moose mistaken for m. J1759.1; mountain in labor brings forth m. U114; singing m. B214.1.9; speaking m. B211.2.8; soul in form of m. E731.3; swallowing m. without vomiting

H1567.1.1; tabu to eat m. C221.1.1.7; thumbling hides in m. hole
F535.1.1.10.2; town m. and country m. J211.2; transformation to m.
C962.1; wedding of m. and (cockroach) B281.2.2, (frog) B284.1.1, (weasel)
B281.2.1; why m. does not defend self against cat A2462.3; why m.
crushed in crossing road: elephant's curse A2239.9; witch in form of m.
G211.2.5.

Mouse's body made smaller A2302.1; food A2435.3.7; magic skin
*D1025.3; nose pulled out long A2213.4.3; prayer granted D1766.1.6;
tail causes person to cough up magic object K331.4, K431. — Chain
tale: m. acquisitions Z39.9; why elephant hurts self in grass: m. curse
A2239.10.

Mice army saves kingdom from invasion K632.1; consecrate bishop (lie)
X1226.1; cursed M414.8.1; dying of hunger since priest receives only
forty florins a year J1269.10; escape into their holes where weasels
cannot follow them L332; engendered after flood from rottenness: no
mice on ark A1853.1.1; gnaw enemies' bowstrings and prevent pursuit
K632; gnaw through metal B747.3; gnawing garments bad omen
D1812.5.1.12.4; hitched to wagon B558.5; and hogs let loose put elephant
cavalry to flight K2351.3; overcome camel L315.10; win war with
woodcutters L318. — Army of m. B268.6; bargain with king of m.
M244.1; cat hangs on wall pretending to be dead but m. detect plan
K2061.9; cat makes truce with m. then eats them K815.13; clock ticking
thought to be gnawing of m. J1789.2; why m. eat grease and salmon
A2435.3.7.1; exterminating m. infesting city H1109.4; giant man-eating
m. B16.2.8; giant m. B871.2.7; how m. can rid themselves of cats
H1292.10; iron-eating m. J1531.2; king of m. B241.2.5; land of m. B221.5;
lies about m. X1226; troll has team of m. G304.3.2.1; weasel paints self
to deceive m. J951.4.

Mouse-trap, trying to catch light in J1961.1.

Moustache becomes grass D457.10; pulled out as punishment Q497.1.
— Being swung by m. without crying H328.2; god with white m. A137.18;
golden m. F545.1.1.2; lighting lamp with king's m. P672.4; transformation
by m. D537.3.

Mouth bleeding as death omen J2311.1.2; crooked from ghost's strike
E542.1.3; expanded for breaking tabu C948.1; full: cheeks cut open to
find abscess J1842.2; -less people F513.0.3. — Adulteress's m. loyal to
husband K1595; animal captor persuaded to talk and release victim from
m. K561.1; animal impregnated through m. B754.6.1.1; why animals move
m. A2476; birth from m. T541.4.1; boy throws ball into hostile dog's
m. N623.2; burning wood in m. tests sham dead H248.4; child born without m. T551.6; coin placed in m. of dead to prevent return E431.11;
consecrated bread kept in m. (and fed to toad produces love) D1355.10.1,
(in order to be witch) G281; curse: toads from m. M431.2; death respite
until m. washed K551.4.6; devil holds molten coin in m. G303.4.8.2;
disenchantment by taking key from serpent's m. at midnight D759.1;

dupe opens m.; hot stones thrown in K721.1; dupe's m. smeared with butter brings accusation of theft K401.1; earthquake spirit's long m. F438.2; fish with coin in m. B105.4.1; flame issuing from m. as sign of royalty H41.4; flames issue from corpse's m. E421.3.7; flounder's crooked m. A2231.1.2, A2252.4; ghost's blow makes m. crooked E265.1.3; god's unusual m. A123.2.2ff.; headless person with m. on breast F511.0.1.1; husband proves intrigue by secretly blacking paramour's m. K1504; lily issues from buried devotee's m. V255.1; man with horse's m. B21.3; "a measured m." as health secret H596.1.1; mirror in bed to see if sleeping with m. open J1936.1; moon enters husband's m., star enters wife's V515.1.2; murder by throwing hot stones in m. K951.1; ogre monstrous as to m. G363; opening m. makes door open D1782.1.1; origin and nature of animal's m. A2341ff.; peasant opens his m. at dinner for his wife J2473; penance: carrying water in m. from a distance and watering dry staff until it blooms Q521.1.2; person swearing oath places hand in m. of image H251.1; person unusual as to his m. F513; remarkable m. F544; river flows from man's m. F715.1.5; saint silent by holding stone in m. V73.6.2; silver and gold run from cod's m. B103.4.1.1; sinner in hell falls into devil's m. Q569.3; skillful marksman shoots pipe from man's m. F661.2; snake crawls into sleeper's m. B765.5; snake creeps into man's m. and heals him B511.1.1; sore m. as punishment C941.3.1; stolen fig in m. leads to cheek lancing W111.5.8, J1842.2; spear pins animal's m. shut N623.1; stopping up m. to keep wisdom in J1977; thundergod's long m. A284.3.1; transformation by placing pill in m. D551.6.1; treasure falls from m. *D1454.2; unborn soul issues from mother's m. E726.2; what princess puts in m. prophesies marriage H41.6; why animal's m. is closed A2341.3; witch recognized by seeing wasp enter m. while asleep *G251.1; wood-spirit without m. F441.4.2; yawning person cannot close m. D2072.0.5.2.

Mouths. — Animal with many m. B15.2ff.; cannibal with seven m. G11.17; contest in making m. water H509.2; flowers grow from m. of saints in graves V229.2.7; husband and wife burn their m. J1478.

Mouth-harp left by bed H142. — Magic m. D1225.1; quest for gold m. H1335.1.

Move. — Enchanted person cannot m. D5.1; ghost light indicates impending m. E530.1.4; giants by night m. buildings built by men in day F531.6.6.1; horse withheld as sacrifice to a saint refuses to m. K231.3.4; ship refuses to m. with guilty man aboard D1318.10.1; wagon refuses to m. because ghost is sitting in it *D1317.10.

Moved. — Castle m. from one mountain to another by dwarf F451.5.1.12; dead move when cemetery is m. E419.4; murdered body cannot be m. Q559.3; objects magically m. D2136ff.; stone cannot be m. by perjurer H251.2.1.

Movement of leaves A2762. — Auguries from animal m. D1812.5.0.8.1; wild hunt disappears with m. of tree tops E501.16.2.

Movements. — Animal's habitual bodily m. A2470ff.; earthquakes from
m. of subterranean monster A1145.1.

Moving mountain F755.6. — Devil prevents m. of little stone by sitting
on it G303.9.9.1; futile m. to avoid death M382; poor man's m.: putting
out fire, whistling for dog W226; soul of sleeper prevented from
returning by m. the sleeper's body E721.1.2.2; tabu: m. dead cat or
dog C537.3; two fixed, two m., etc. (riddle) H851.

Mower. — Swift m. F681.11.

Mowers sing about bad food J1341.11. — Monkey attracts attention of
m. until young birds can fly away from the harvest field K644.

Mowing contest with household spirit F488.2; contest won by trickery
K42.2; grass: the meadow torn up K1423.

Much. — Gift seems too m.: sign of death W11.13.

Muck. — Food transformed to m. D472.1.

Mucus turns to gold D475.1.13. — Birth from m. from the nose T541.8.3;
sky-rope of m. F51.1.7.

Mud flood injures corn Q552.14.2; sold as butter K144.3. — Adulteress
falls in m. at lover's door K1523; animal grateful for rescue from m.
B364.5; bread made from m. D476.1.1; bringing much m. without buffaloes H1129.1.1; cakes of m. gilded K122; dead walk on m. without
sinking E489.9; earth made by m. shaken off boar A822; lawyer thrown
back into m. when rescuers learn that he is a lawyer X317; lies about
m. X1655; man caused to sink into m. D2092; man in m. too lazy to
take hand extended to help him up W111.5.5; numskulls carrying each
other through m. J2163.1; priest walks in m. J82; seduction access
through fall in m. K1349.6; sinking into m. in duel F943; why pigs
in m. lift their legs A2479.5; woman hidden in m. cabin R53.1; world
is transformed m. parrot A822.1.

Muddy. — Death respite until m. victim dries self K551.12; lizard makes
water m., hence enmity with bird A2494.16.4; magpie tells why sow
was m. J2211.2.

Mudhen's red head A2320.3.1.

Mudpuppy poisonous B776.3.2.

Muffins. — Fire's hissing mistaken for m. cooking J1812.4.

Muirlan removes itself D1641.5. — Magic m. D1256; speaking m.
D1610.23.

Mulatto child's birth explained by adulteress J2338.

Mulberry. — Origin of m. tree A2681.9; transformation to m. tree
D215.6.

Mule, see also **Ass, Donkey;** as descendant of king's warhorse J954.1;
paralyzed by witch D2072.0.2.4. — Access to mistress by riding rival's
m. K1349.3; adulteress kicked to death by m. as punishment Q416.1.1;
Dante beats m. driver J981.1; going wherever his m. wants to J1483.2;
helpful m. B403; magic folding m. D491.1.2; man chooses to remain transformed to m. rather than to live with his shrewish wife T251.1.3; man

transformed to m. D132.2; overloaded m. J1302; selling old m. back to owner K134.3; speaking m. B211.1.3.2; why m. is sterile A2561.1; thumbling drives m. F535.1.1.1.1; three brothers take turns using m. J1914.2; witch as m. G211.1.2.

Mule's bite causes death B766.4; double ancestry L465.

Mules. — Adulterers tricked into riding thirsty m.: drowned K1567; lies about m. X1242; spirit rides, wears out m. at night F473.4.1.

Mullet. — Creation of m. A2112.

Multicolored fires F882.2; llama B731.3. — Fairy's m. dress F236.1.7; fairies m. F233.7.

Multipede. — Origin of m. A2182.5.

Multiple births T586; disguise K1834. — Nimrod's m. throne F785.2.

Multiplication of objects D1652, D2106ff.; of man by fragmentation A1296. — Asking for too great magic m. of coins forbidden C773.1.1; magic m. of cows Q141; magic m. of objects by saints D2106.1; wife's m. of secret J2353.

Multiplying. — Coin m. self D2100.2; magic object m. objects D1599.3; magic ring m. wealth D1456.2.1.

Mummified dog resuscitates E53.1.

Münchhausen tales X900.

Munching grains to keep awake H1483.

Munia. — Why m. wears his crop on back of neck A2351.7.

Murder *S110ff.; avenged in like manner Q581.1; causes dwarf to lose his soul F451.5.9.6; of child to avoid fulfillment of prophecy M371.1; feigned to effect escape K579.6; of homecoming husband by adulteress K1510.1; made known in dream D1810.8.2.3; opportunity presented to assassin H1556.3; will out N271; of pregnant woman to avoid prophecy fulfillment M376.2; punished *Q211; by slaves P176; by sympathetic magic D2061.2.2. — Animal avenges m. B591; bird reveals m. B131.1; blood smeared on innocent person brings accusation of m. K2155.1; child in mother's womb reveals m. T575.1.1.1; daughter's betrothal as m. compensation T69.3.1; dog clears master of m. B134.5; dog betrays m. B134.2; earth from m. of first brother and sister A831.4; earthquake at m. F960.2.5.1; external soul avenges m. E710.2; flame indicates m. site F1061.4; friendship feigned to avenge m. K2010.2; ghostly m. sounds E337.1.1. grass will not grow where m. committed F974.1; horse stops where m. has occurred B151.1.1.0.2; innocent person accused of m. K2116; last moment prevention of m. by burning N657; light where m. is committed D1318.11.1; magic detection of m. D1817.0.3; magic m. D2061; nobleman unpunished for m. E34; origin of m. A1336; origin of penalty for m. A1581.1; prince, princess join in spouse-m. pact S63; prophecy: daughter shall commit m. and incest M345; quest as punishment for m. H1219.2; resuscitation after m. E185; return from dead to reveal m. *E231; speaking blood reveals m. D1318.5.4; speaking bones of murdered person reveal m. E632.1; speaking earth reveals m. D1318.16;

speaking flesh reveals m. D1318.7.0.1; sun refuses to shine where m. is done F961.1.1; trickster's sham m. by mother K522.7; truth-telling dog killed to hide m. B339.1; various kinds of treacherous m. K950ff.; voluntary exile as punishment for m. Q431.1; walling up as punishment for m. of children Q455.1; wild huntswoman wanders for daughter's m. E501.3.10; woman confesses m.: unharmed by execution fire V21.2.

Murdered girl, reincarnated as bird, resumes original form E696.1; person cannot rest in grave E413; person recognized by fingernail H57.2.2; person's request and promise M257.2. — Abandoned or m. children *S300ff.; animal reincarnation of m. child B313.2; animals in wild hunt reincarnation of m. persons E501.4.0.1; bones of m. person tabu C541.3; carrying m. man's blood as ordeal H227; earth from body of m. child A831.5; ghost of m. child E225; ghost of m. person haunts grave E334.2.1; infant eats m. father's corpse G25; insect in m. person simulates snoring K661.3; magic properties of m. man's head D1549.7; object substituted for m. person K525.3; person unwittingly m. N320ff.; reincarnation of m. child as bird *E613.0.1; riddle of the m. lover H805; son of first couple m. by tiger A1277.3; stepfather m. P281.2; tongue as proof that man has been m. H105.2; vulture's chicks will not eat m. hero B159.4.

Murderer cannot rest in grave E411.1; or captor otherwise beguiled *K600ff.; detected by actions of murdered man's dog J1145.1; does penance Q520.1; -emperor abducted by devil R11.2.1.1; escapes on sky rope R323.1; forced to eat victim's flesh, dies G62; makes outcry to accuse innocent K2116.4; refused payment for killing, killed K231.10; tricked into false accusation J1141.12. — Ball of fire haunts m. E530.1.2; Christianized Jewish priest as m. V364; corpse bleeds when m. touches it D1318.5.2; corpse of murdered man sticks to m. Q551.2.4; dead mother curses m. -son E222.3; demand m. restore victim's life J1955; escape by questioning would-be m. on guilt K573.1; faithful servant kills master's m. P361.1.1; ghost causes m. to confess E231.5; ghost reveals m. E231.1ff.; ghost slays own m. E232.1; horse kicks m. to death B591.2; mother m. uses her corpse K2321.1; murdered man's body leads to exposure of m. Q559.3; queen marries fiancé's m. P22; ruler pardons his would-be m. W11.5.2; saint offers m. refuge R325.3; son as pledge for father m. P233.1; test of friendship: substitute as m. H1558.2; victim's son aids m. W15.1; woman shelters m. of her son out of charity W15.

Murderer's children become dwarfs F451.1.2; short hair H75.7; wraith confesses E723.4.2. — God kills m. son Q589.3; grass does not grow on m. grave E631.2; melon in m. hand turns to murdered man's head Q551.3.3.1; punishment: calf's head in m. hand turns to corpse's head Q551.3.3.

Murderers. — Hardhearted person refuses reprieve to m. W155.4.

Murderess forced to leap from cliff Q417.1. — Devil appears to m. who prays over pit where she has thrown the bodies of her babies G303.6.2.7; paramour shuns m. K2213.3.2.2.

Murdering. — Brownie m. travelers for blood F363.2; king m. man after killing his sons M2.1; mother kills husband for m. daughter P211.2; young queen m. old husband K2213.12.

Murderous bird H1161.1; bride T173; witch G262. — Dogs flee from m. master J2211.3; father hides children from m. mother R153.2.1; girl marries m. husband S62.1.

Murmuring against deity tabu C66.

Murrain upon cattle as punishment Q552.3.7.

Muses, nine A465.0.1.

Mush scattered on heroine's body as test H1503.

Mushroom. — Goose boasts superiority to m.: both served at same meal L419.1; great m. X1424; origin of m. A2613.1, A2686.1; "whoever eats this m. is my wife" N365.3.2.

Mushrooms shrink in water J1813.1. — Why m. are slimy A2794.1.

Music attracts bride T56.1; of bird's wing enchants saint D2011.1.1; of heaven A661.0.2; of the spheres A659.1; tabu on sabbath C631.6; teacher charges double for those who have taken music before X351. — Abduction by sleep-giving m. R22.2; acquisition of m. A1461; animal tied to learn m. K713.1.6; animals attracted by m. B767; ascetic avoids m. V462.6; bitches enchanted by fairy m. B182.1.7; boar makes m. for saint B256.6.2; cat lures foxes with m. K815.15; dead make m. on their ribs E548; devil's m. G303.25.16.1; disenchantment by m. D786; dupe persuaded to play m. for wedding party K844; dwarfs emigrate because they dislike peasants' dancing and loud m. F451.9.1.9; dwarfs have m. F451.6.3.3; escape by playing m. K606.1ff.; ethereal m. E402.4; fairies make m. F262; fairy m. evil omen D1812.5.1.13; fairy m. prevents elephant grazing F369.8; fish follow sound of m. B767.1; ghost summoned by m. E384; god of m. A465.2; goddess of m. A112.1.1.1; harp m. makes merman restore stolen bride B82.1.2; heavenly m. caused by columns under Lord's chair A661.0.2.1; hero escapes tiger by playing m. K551.3; magic m. *D1275.1, (lures to otherworld) F175; man pretending to enjoy m. told when to applaud W116.6; merman teaches m. B82.4; recognition by m. H12; respite from death while captor plays m. K551.3.2; resuscitation by m. E55; saint leaves religious order for m. V475.4; sleep-bringing m. in otherworld F156.1; soul leaps from body on hearing heavenly m. E722.2.5; sound of plates and spoons is best m. J1343.1; three strains of m. Z71.1.3; wild hunt heralded by m. E501.13.2; women transformed to bitches enchanted by m. B297.2.1.

Music-box continues playing when it is touched contrary to tabu *C915.1.1; plays by itself at death E761.7.11.

Musical animals B297; fountain F162.8.3, F716.5; pillar F774.3; rock F803. — Ghost plays m. instrument E402.1.3, E554; giant plays m. instrument F531.6.17.4; magic m. branch *D1615.2; magic m. instruments *D1210ff.; magic pipe (m.) *D1224; man becomes m. instrument D254;

34*

reincarnation as m. instrument *E632ff.; test of m. ability H503; three magical m. strains *D1275.1.1; tree with m. branches F811.6.

Musician P428; playing for devil's dances G303.25.17.2; in wolf-trap B848.1. — Disguise as m. to (enter enemy's camp) K2357.1, (escape) K521.4.2; dwarf m. F451.3.3.1; imprisoned m. defends himself J814.1; skillful m. F679.9.

Musicians. — Thieves disguised as m. K311.11.

Musk. — Origin of m. A2812.

Muskox. — Bow shoots m. F836.4; man becomes m. D114.1.5.

Muskrat. — Beaver and m. exchange tails A2247.6; dwelling of m. A2432.5; how m. got long, thin tail A2378.3.2; why m. lives in water A2433.3.10.

Mussel. — Color of m. A2411.5.4; dog mistakes m. for an egg J1772.2; reincarnation of ears into m. shell E649.4.

Musselman. — Contest between Yogi and M. V351.5.

Mustard sandwich as farmer's hot lunch W152.12.2; smeared on bridal couple T135.12. — Counting seeds in m. package H1118.1; peasants in city inn order whole portion of m. J1742.3; thieves deceived into stealing m. J1517.1.

Mustard-seed trail R267. — Magic m. *D971.1, (causes man to turn to ashes) D1402.16; suitor test involving mountain of m. H1091.3.

Mustelidae, creation of A1820ff.

Mute water-maidens F420.1.2.2.

Mutilated god A128; man chased into forest S143.3. — Child m. to avoid prophecy fulfillment M375.4; children m. by father S11.1; false bride's m. feet K1911.3.3.1; girl wants to marry m. lover T99.2; primordial animal m. to produce present form A1727; prisoners m. R51.3; wife carries m. husband on her back so that he may beg T215.1; woman deserts husband for m. lover T232.

Mutilating. — Animal m. self to express sympathy B299.5.1.

Mutilation S160ff.; of children's bodies for identification H56.2; of girls punished Q411.5; as punishment C948, Q451ff.; to repel lover T327; substituted for death K512.2.4. — Beheading punishes m. Q421.0.5; cruel m. punished Q285.3; disguise by m. so as to escape K521.2.2; fairy causes m. F362.4; girl demands suitor's m. H333; magic m. of sexual organs D2062.4; self-m. to remove temptation T333.

Mutinous clerics expelled Q226.2.

Mutton. — Horse meat becomes m. D476.3.3.

Mutually. — Senseless debate of the m. useful J461ff.

Muzzle, see also **Mouth.** — Origin and nature of animal's m. A2335.4; why wolf's m. is black A2335.4.5.

Myna. — Creation of m. A1928.

Myrrh. — Ant collects m. for Christ A2221.4; origin of gum in m. tree A2755.3.2.

Myrtle, magic *D965.10.

Myself K602.

Mysteries. — Revealing sacred m. tabu C423.5.

Mysterious animal punishes penitent Q554.5; death as punishment Q558, (remitted) Q574; ghostlike noises heard E402; housekeeper N831.1; poisoning of food N332.6; punishments in other world F171.6; stranger performs task H976; visitation as punishment Q554ff.; voice announces death of Pan F442.1; voice announces prohibition C601. — Knowledge from m. woman J155.7.

Mystically. — Child m. recognizes mother H175.2.

Mythical animals *B0—B99; beasts B19; being asks for girl to marry T50.3. — Soul in form of a m. animal E738; witch as m. animal G211.9.

Mythological motifs A (entire chapter).

Naboth's vineyard will not be sold to king P411.1.

Nag becomes riding horse D1868.1.

Naga (serpent demon) B91.1; -king B244.2.

Nagas' dance B293.5.

Nagging wife T253; will never make a husband virtuous T253.2.

Naglfar ship F531.6.7.1.2, F841.1.5.

Nail, see also **Fingernail.** — Cannibal has long tooth and n. G88; extraordinary n. F844; devil's chair in hell made from thrown-away n. parings G303.25.5; girl has "wolf's n." T611.10.1; iron n. in witch's head G272.14; murder by driving n. through head S115.2.1; throwing away n. trimmings tabu C726.1; train of troubles from lost horseshoe n. N258; vessel full of n.-scrapings H1129.8.

Nails for Crucifixion made by smith's wife V211.2.3.0.2; driven into grave to lay ghost E442.2; on witch's back G219.9. — Carpenter blames the n. J1891.2; earth from worm scratched by creator's n. A828; fiery n. in hell A671.2.4.10; four earth n. A841.4; ghost with peculiar n. E422.1.8; giant with n. like claws F531.1.6.1; giant's n. grown into earth F531.1.6.9; horse-n. used to bewitch G224.13.1; long n. of beings born in hell A671.6; magic n. D1252.1.2; transformation by sticking n. in feet D582.1; ship with gold n. F841.1.7; witch has long n. G219.3; woman fed human n. G11.6.2.

Nailing horse's head over gate F874.1; to pillar as punishment Q462.1; wolf's tail to tree X1132.1.

Naked, see also **Nude;** ghost asks for shirt E412.3.2; idol considered poor J2216; leper P162.1; man imitates jockey riding himself G269.21.3; person made to believe that he is clothed J2312ff.; servant used to incriminate innocent woman K2112.4; soldier becomes general N684; tribe F568; woman pursued and cut in two by rider E501.5.1.1. — Aphrodisiac given n. woman in stream K1395; brother who conforms to n. people's customs honored J815.2; coming neither n. nor clad (task) H1054; country of the n. F709.1; dandy tailored by devil, n. G303.9.9.11; dead not to be buried n. V68.4.1; disenchantment by n. virgin undergoing frightful journey at midnight D759.3; endurance test: scalding mush scattered on heroine's n. body H1503; fairies n. F238; girl dies at being seen n. F1041.1.13.1; girl has had relations with priest (not n. but with a hood on) J2499.2; girl shows herself n. in return for youth's dancing hogs *K1358; Godiva rides n. through streets to obtain freedom for citizens M235; guilty woman to go n.: accused undresses J1141.1.8; humiliated lover shows women n. to friends K1218.4.1; injured husband will not kill a n. man P641; king boasts of wife, shows her off n. T295; land of n. people F129.7; lazy wife taken n. in bundle of straw to a wedding Q495.1; looking at supernatural wife n. forbidden C31.1.3; loser of shooting wager to go n. into thorns for bird N55.1; magic from maiden walking n. in public *D1796; man at first n. A1281.3; men shamed for their cowardice by woman standing n. before them J87; paramour exposes adulteress n. K1213.1; penance: creeping n. through thorns Q522.3; rebuke for going with a n. head in public J2521.2; revenant as n. woman E425.1.2; seducer led n. through streets Q473; sleeping n. on cold floor H1504; sleeping n. girl: goddess or mortal? H45.5; standing n. in winter river H328.4; trickster exacts promise of marriage as price of silence after having seen a princess n. *K443.6; weakness from seeing n. woman C942.3; woman dies at seeing n. man F1041.1.13.2; women n. in beauty contest H1596.3.

Nakedness for life as punishment for nudity Q589.2. — Origin of shame for n. A1383.

Name on article as ownership token H88; does not alter condition U119.5; tabu *C430ff.; of victorious youngest son L10.1. — Accidental calling on God's n. held to outweigh a life of wickedness V91; Adam's n. from initials of four stars A1281.6.1; bonga girl surrenders man to his mortal wife if he will n. first daughter after her F302.5.1.1; calling sacrificial animal by son's n. K527.5; charm containing God's n. D1273.0.5; criminal's n. accidentally spoken out N611.1.1; dead's n. not on heavenly roll E586.4; deceptive bargain based on an unusual n. K193; devil becomes powerless when called by n. G303.16.19.9; devil leaves at mention of God's n. G303.16.8; devil produces animals only in God's n. A1756; disguise by changing n. K1831.0.1; do not walk half a mile with a man without asking his n. J21.11; dwarf promises mortal much money if he will guess his n. *F451.5.15.1; dwarf suitor desists when unwilling maiden guesses his n. F451.5.15.3; earl's n. preferred to king's P50.1.1; escape by using equivocal n. K602; fairies disappear when some n. of the Christian Church is used F382; fly asks what is her n. Z25; genie called by writing his n. on papers and burning them *D2074.2.4; ghost tells murderer's n. E231.1; ghost laid by using God's n. E443.5; ghosts summoned by n. E386.3; girl with the ugly n. K1984.3; god gives n. to child A182.2; god's ineffable n. A138; guest under false n. P322.2; helper summoned by calling n. D1420.4; hero learns n. at first adventure T617.2; highsounding n. frightens off enemy chief K1951.5; "I don't know" as a n. J2496; ignorance of own n. J1730.1; ineffable n. creates magic D804;

king of Jews' ugly n. A1689.6; knight dismisses devil in n. of cross
G303.16.3.5; luck changing after change of n. N131.4; magic results
produced in n. of deity D1766.7.1; magic from uttering n. D1766.7; man
burns temple so that his n. will be remembered J2162.1; marking
object with n. to claim it later K448; not recognizing own n.: accustomed
to nickname J2016; ogre sings own n. G652; own n. inscribed on stolen
object J1162.3; person accidentally met knows other's n. N762; person
summoned by saying his n. D2074.2.4ff.; prophecy: son of certain n.
to become king M395; prophecy: death at hands of man bearing a
certain n. M341.2.15; rat changes n., wins bride K1371.3; secret n. overheard by eavesdropper *N475; senses regained by hearing n. F959.1.1;
service under false n. K1831; tabu: asking n. of supernatural husband
C32.2.1; tabu: desecration of God's n. C51.3.1; tabu: finding n. of
ghost C824; theft by assuming equivocal n. K359.2; transformation by
breaking n. tabu D511; trip to find n. wife already knows J2241.1;
unusual n. K193, S243; voice from grave answers to pet n. E324.1.

Names applied to devil G303.2ff.; of dogs literally interpreted J2493;
for dwarfs F451.8ff.; of future kings foretold M369.4; of giants have
sinister significance Z100.1; given the soul E700.1. — All things receive
n. A1191; animals with queer n. (henny-penny) Z53; how animals
received their n. A2571; devil writes down n. of men on a hide in
church G303.24.1.3f.; dogs' n. give warning K649.5; extraordinary n.
X1506; friends exchange n. P311.0.1; gods have many n. A139.1; guessing
n. in magic writing H517; Jacob-Israel had two n. (riddle) H817; lands
with extraordinary n. F703; mortal completes fairies' song by adding
the n. of the days of the week F331.3; murder revealed by unusual n.
of boys N271.2; origin of personal n. A1577; princess calls her suitors
ugly n. T76; servant deceives by unusual n. K1399.2; symbolic meaning
of n. H602.3; symbolic n. Z183; trolls may not utter holy n. F455.7.3;
wager involving learned and common n. of trees N51.1.

Named. — Districts n. from first person met in each N125.4; fairy leaves
when he is n. F381.1; king's son n. for king's foster father P271.7;
seven sons all n. the same T586.1.2.2; son n. for mother T148.1.

Nameless. — Adam at first n. A1281.6; hero at first n. Z252.

Namesake. — Bonga's n. first daughter F302.5.1.1; eating animal n. forbidden C221.2.

Naming of children T596; events which have not yet happened H1011;
the stars A765. — Angel n. child V241.4.1; disenchantment by n. D772.

Nandia provides warrior's equipment D2107.1.

Naphtha. — Riddles about n. H886.

Napkin. — Miraculous image of Christ impressed on n. V121; sickness
cured by n. of Veronica F950.1.

Narcissus T11.5.1. — Origin of n. A2665.1.

Narcotic. — Capture by giving n. K776; escape by giving n. to guards

K625; fatal deception by giving n. K873; girl foiled by hero's refusal to take n. K625.1; origin of n. plants A2691ff.

Narcotics. — Theft by giving guard n. K332.1.

Narrow road to heaven F57.1. — Broad and n. road in otherworld F171.2; rude retorts of men meeting in n. passage J1369.3; task: putting a large squash whole into a n.-necked jar H1023.11.

Narwhale's origin A2135.1.

Nasal. — Origin and nature of animals' n. organ A2335.

Nation of thieves K304.

Nations P710ff. — Humor concerning n. X600—X699; number of n. A1601; wise n. J192.

Nativity of Christ V211.1. — All locks opened on N. night D2088.0.1; angels sing at N. V234.2; animals rejoice at N. B251.1; animals speak at N. B211.0.1; children speak in wombs at N. T575.1.5; devil exorcised at N. G303.16.19.10; fetters loosed at N. D1395.8; magic fruit blooms at N. D2145.2.2.1; treasure found at N. N529.1, N541.4; wells break forth at N. A941.5.0.2; whale cast ashore at N. B874.3.2.

Natural child, see **Illegitimate;** is easiest (riddle) H659.14.1; law suspended D2137; laws inoperative at end of world A1091; phenomena accompanying the devil's appearance G303.6.3ff.; son refusing kingship P17.9.1; son succeeds to throne P17.9; underground treasure N511.2. — Absurd disregard of n. laws J1930ff.; establishment of n. order A1100ff.

Nature fruitful during good king's reign Q153; fruitless after false judgment H243; gods A405; transformed every seven years A1103; will show itself U120ff. — Absurd attempt to change animal n. J1908; absurd disregard or ignorance of animal's n. *J1900ff.; animal should not try to change his n. J512; dwarfs are subject to laws of n. F451.3.5; extraordinary n. phenomena F960ff.; fruitfulness of n. proves kingly right H1574.2; recognition by "force of n." H175; reincarnation of man as n. spirit E653; tasks contrary to laws of n. H1020ff.; why powers of n. work on Sabbath A1102.

Naught. — Nix-N.-Nothing S243.

Navel of the earth A875.1. — Child helps mother in severing n. string T584.8; heaven, earth connected by n. string A625.2.1; intercourse by n. A1352.3; long n. F559.2; lotus grows from god's n. A123.9; witch sucks blood from child's n. G262.1.3.

Navigable streams shoot from well F718.11.

Navigators. — Bird conducts n. B563.7.

Nearsighted knight mistakes own servant for enemy X124; man persuaded he can see J2341.

Necessity is strongest (riddle) H631.7; of work J702. — Wisdom (knowledge) taught by n. J100ff.

Neck hard as ivory F559.5.1. — Bird's n. broken, witch dies G252.3; birds hatched from broken eggs repaired by skillful tailor have red line around n. F662.1.1; burial alive up to n. Q456.1; chain around n.

tests truth H251.3.6; child born with chain around n. H71.7; fowl makes another animal believe that he has had his n. cut off J2413.4.2; ghost leaves mark on n. E542.1.2; giant with one eye in n. F531.1.1.1.1; horse breaks n. J21.24; where horse got arched n. A2351.6; lower lip hangs down to n. F544.1.1; man whose n. fits rope to be executed P14.18; millstone hung around n. Q469.4; monster with life in n. E714.8; origin and nature of animal's n. A2351ff.; red thread on n. of person who has been decapitated and resuscitated *E12.1; sea as n.-deep H681.4.2; sexton behind statue tells old maid praying for a husband to raise her foot to her n. K1971.9; snake disenchanted by being allowed to wrap itself three times around person's n. D759.8; transformation to swans by taking chains off n. D536.1; troll stretches n. so long that fire comes from lips G304.2.1.2; why man's n. its present size A1319.13.

Necks. — Contestants tug iron rings, sever n. H1562.7.

Necklace bursts after emotion F1041.6.1; dropped by crow in snake's hole K401.2.2; of human eyes F827.4, S165.5; transformed D454.8.1; of unsuccessful suitors' heads S110.3.1. — Bride's n. to match mother's H355.5; dead anchorite to accept n. M151.5.1; fairy n. stolen F357; gathering ruby n. from sea H1023.21; girl gives suitor n. to pay bride-price T52.6; hawk carries off queen's n. N698; identification by n. H92; magic n. *D1073; magic strength acquired by looking at n. *D1835.1; man becomes n. D263.2; pig swallows n. F989.22.3; princess's n. in hell F102.3; resuscitation by removing n. E155.3; soul in n. E711.4; speaking n. D1610.27.1; stealing Freya's n. H1151.15; stolen n. does not have same scent as defendant uses J1179.7; transportation by n. D1520.34; tree to heaven from goddess's n. A652.1.1.

Necromancy. — Ghost summoned for n. E387.3.

Necrophilism T466.

Nectar in poison H592.3; -yielding cow B19.2. — "Poison in n." H592.2; riddle involving ruby, n., faithless creature H587.1.

Need. — "Friend is known in n." J401.0.1; magic ownership to be used only in extreme n. D805; parson has no n. to preach X452; philosopher in n. J1289.4; spring breaks forth at primitive hero's n. A941.4.2.

Needle falls into the sea: sought the next summer J1921; in garment as sign H119.2; goes on warpath F1025.2.1; kills an elk (slips into his stomach) L391; put in food causes eater to say "Oh my!" H1185; under hearth causes death D2061.2.2.8.1; that pierces anvil F663.2; and thread as symbol of sex J86, Z186; transformed to another object D454.4; as thumbling's sword F535.1.1.12. — Abbot cannot find his n. J1651; blinding by n. in eyes S165.3; chain tale: pulling n. out of seamstress's hand Z41.8; fool sticks n. in haywagon J2129.4; lie: roofs on n. X1743.3; magic n. *D1181, (from heaven) D811.2.1; man so small he can go through eye of n. F535.2.2; man transformed to n. D253; sewing many garments simultaneously with one n. F662.0.1.1; sexton puts n. in sacramental bread (parson sticks his hand) X411.2; shooting n. from long

distance F661.5.5; soul as n. E745.2; squirrel steals dog's n.: enmity
between them A2281.2; in storm on ice, numskull sticks n. into ice to
keep from blowing away J1965; tailor married to princess betrays trade
by calling for n. and thread H38.2.1; thief throws n. containing stolen
cloth K341.13.1; swallowed n. emerges through relative's skin X1739.1;
threading n. by convent guest H509.1; transformation by magic n.
D582.2.

Needles and anchors as fox's excuse J1391.8. — Making n. as devil's
task G303.16.19.3.2; origin of tree's n. A2767; piercing with n. as punishment Q469.9.2; skillful marksman throws n. F661.7; sowing n. (like seed)
J1932.5.

Needlework. — Fairies' n. F271.8; recognition by unique n. H35.3.

Negating. — Curse given n. good wish M416.

Negative penances Q535ff.

Neglect not what four or five say J21.35.1. — Fairy takes revenge for n.
to offer food (drink) F361.1.2; ghost of wife dead from n. E221.5;
penance: seven years' service for seven days' n. of religious duty Q523.7;
punishment for n. of services to gods (God) Q223ff.; tabu: n. of service
to deity C57ff.; untrained colt result of master's n. J143.

Neglected surpasses favorite child L146; wife T271; wife given trifle
boasts of it W117.1. — Dead mother returns to care for n. baby
*E323.1.2; king n. in exile, courted on throne U83; what one has is n.
in search for other things J344.

Neglecting religious exercise V5. — Animal n. its young B751.5; gorilla's
large teeth as punishment for n. possessions A2345.9; tabu: n. sexual
relations in marriage C163.

Negligent. — Devil likes n. men G303.25.3; host rebukes n. servant J1573.

Negro so black that he makes whole garden somber F573; cannibal G11.4;
takes refuge under princess's throne R314; tries in vain to be washed
white J511.1. — Treacherous N. K2261; white man made to believe
that he is a N. J2013.1; white person transformed to N. D31; why the
N. works A1671.1.

Negroes as curse on Ham for laughing at Noah's nakedness A1614.1;
made from leftover scraps at creation A1614.5.

Neigh. — Kite tries to n. like a horse J512.2.

Neighbor. — Choice between bad master, bad official, or bad n. J229.5;
magic object stolen by n. D861.2.

Neighbors. — Precept of the lion to his sons: keep peace with the n.
J22.3; wisdom from n. J179.3.

Neighing of stallion in Assyria impregnates mares in Egypt B741.2. —
Wild hunt heralded by n. of horses E501.13.3.2; witch causes person's n.
G269.21.2.

Nemesis. — Villain n. Q581.

Neophyte impervious to piercing by saint F1041.0.1.

Nephew P297. — Accidental meeting of n. and uncle N738; cruel n.

S74; murder by n. prophesied M343.3; sun and moon as uncle and n. A711.1; treacherous n. K2217.1; uncle poisons n. S71.1.

Nephew's. — Uncle sleeps with n. beloved H1556.4.4.

Nephews. — Giants dissuaded from eating n. K601.2; king lured to kill n. K948.

Nephites. — Three N. Q45.1.1; three N. granted immortality D1856.2.

Nereid F423.1.

Nessus-shirt burns wearer up D1402.5.

Nest built in tree for fish J1904.4; in penitent's hair Q541.5. — Animal destroys bird's n. in revenge B275.4; abandonment near bird n. S147.1.1; birds forced from n. by mother J65; bird n. of salt J171.5; burning wasp n. J2102.5; why crow cannot enter sparrow's n. A2431.3.6.1; why crow's n. is not tightly built A2431.3.6.2; dove rebuilds her n. in the place where she lost former brood J16; eagle carries giant to its n. F531.6.17.3; eagle's n. as refuge R322; escape from n. of giant bird R253; fools see bee's n. reflected in water: try to carry off well J1791.9; fox burns tree in which eagle has his n. E315.3; fox destroys boasting bird's n. L462; hero prevents destruction of n. B365.2; magic bird n. *D1292; man can hear ant leave n. fifty miles away F641.2; man kills n. of ants J96; prince grows up in eagle's n. B535.0.5; punishment for breaking bird's n. Q285.1.2; recognition through gold found in eagle's n. H91.1; train of troubles for destroying bird's n. N261.1; treasure carried by bird to n. N527; trickster pollutes n. and brood of bird K932.

Nests. — Birds' n. A2431ff.; tree in which people live in n. F811.10.

Net. — Animal grateful for rescue from n. B363; animal rescues from n. B545; birds fly away with n. K581.4.1, K687; dead place n. across river to prevent living man from returning to earth F93.1.1; dove helps deity draw wife into n. B582.2.5; doves in n. console selves J869.1; giant's n. hems in forest F531.4.12; girl comes (drawn by horse on n.) H1053.4, (wrapped in n.) H1054.1; hero captured by n. A511.2.1.1; lion freed from n. by mouse B363.1; lion rescued from n. by rat: eats rat W154.3.1; little fish in n. kept rather than wait for uncertainty of greater catch J321.2; little fishes escape from the n. L331; magic n. *D1196; magpie leads other magpies into master's n. K2032; origin of fishing n. A1457.3; owl warns other birds from limed n. B521.3.5; rat gnaws n. B545.2; traveler says he must look after his n. to see if it has taken fish (enigma) H586.2.2; unraveling a n. in a short time (task) H1094.1.

Nets. — Catching huge fish without n. or tackle (task) H1154.4; catching fish with n. A1527; flying n. of battle hair F1084.0.2; strong man destroys fish and n. F614.5.

Nettle. — Milk added to saint's n. pottage K499.2.2; person compared to ungrateful n. W154.22.

Nettles in bag make man cry out H1185.1; on moon A751.6. — Butter made from n. D476.1.5; reincarnation to n. E648.1; thistles and n. are the devil's vegetables G303.10.13.

Never *Z61. — Ghost laid by n.-ending task E454; giant ogre n. crosses water G131; literal fool: something n. experienced J2469.5; person who n. laughs F591; sham threat: something he has n. done before K1771.3.

New creation shouted away A636; race from single pair (or several) after world calamity A1006.1; star for each birth E741.1.1.1; sun after world catastrophe A719.2. — Clothes remain ever n. F821.11; emperor's n. clothes *K445; father's counsel: marry a n. wife every week H588.3; fool in n. clothes does not know himself J2012.4; old chosen rather than the n. L214; person transforms self, is swallowed and reborn in n. form *E607.2.

News. — Alleged n. of absent lover used to seduce K1349.2; clever ways of breaking bad n. to a king J1675.2; familiar spirit brings n. with magic speed F403.2.3.4; magic object tells n. D1310.4; merchants as spreaders of n. P431.1; promise of dying man to bring n. of other world M252; quest for n. of ancestor H1252.1.1; telling only very good n. J2516.3.5; woman who asked for n. from home J2349.4.

New Year's. — Cow disappears N. night D2087.3.1; dwarfs emigrate N. Eve of 1800 to return N. Eve of 1900 F451.9.3; giant eats men on N. Day G15.1.

Newborn babe reveals secret N468; baby's protest saves life S341.1. — Fairy predicts n. child's greatness F317; fairies make good wishes for n. child F312.1.1; innocent woman accused of killing her n. children K2116.1.1; murder of n. children punished Q418.2; woman eats n. child G72.2; woman refuses to eat own n. child L71.

Next. — If I were not your n. of kin E229.1; planting for the n. generation J701.1.

Niche. — Small n. in house brings large price K182.1.

Nicholas, St., brings Christmas gifts N816; drives off fairies F382.5; saves girl from slavery R165.1; steals bread which is later restored V412.1.

Nick, Old *G303ff.

Nickname. — Not recognizing own name: accustomed to n. J2016.

Niece P298. — Aunt kills n. S72.1; intercourse between man and n. tabu C114.2; uncle slanders n. to appropriate patrimony K361.5.

Night controlled by magic D2146.2; as gods' period A189.17; spent in tree F1045; -spirits *F470ff. — Ability to see by n. F642.4; animals in n.-quarters K1161; castle revolving at n. so that entrance cannot be found F771.2.6.2; children by day and by n. J1273; coming neither by day nor by n. H1057; day husband: n. husband T482; day as son of n. and dawn A1171.4; dead man visits wife every n. E321.2.2; devil comes and works with man who continues to work after n. G303.22.9; devil destroys by n. what is built by day G303.14.1; devil takes the place of woman who went to spend n. with priest G303.25.11; devil promises

to help mistreated apprentice if youth will meet him by n. in lonely
spot G303.22.12; devil tries to wall in too large a piece of ground in a
n. and fails G303.13.3; dwarfs heard at n. F451.3.4.0.1; fairies ride mortal's
horses at n. *F366.2; fairies visible only at n. F235.2.1; fear test:
spending n. (in church) H1412, (under gallows) H1415, (by grave) H1416;
felled tree raises itself again at n. *D1602.2; fool locked in dark room
made to believe that it is continuous n. J2332; giants by n. move buildings
built by men in day F531.6.6.1; going out at n. alone tabu C755.8;
illusory n. K1889.5; intercourse at n. tabu C119.1.6; magic power at n.
D1719.9.1; magic stolen at n. D838.13; man attacked on Christmas n.
by dancing ghosts E261.3; man protected from the devil by holding
three-year old child through the n. G303.16.19.6; marriage to beast by
day and man by n. *B640.1; marriage to man alive only at n. T113;
marriage for a n. to evade law T156; marriage to tree by day, man by
n. T117.5.1; numskull plants seed in daytime and takes it out at n.
J2224; object borrowed for one day, one n. retained K232.2; ointment
makes n. seem day D1368.11; one sun-god for n., another for day
A227.2; origin of n. A1174; person dead by day, alive at n. E155.4;
pigeons cover sun, lengthen n. H982.1; prepare for n. camp while it is
still day J21.20; princess speaking all n. H343.0.1; riddle of day and
n. H722ff.; rivers cease flowing in dead of n. F932.6.3; saint banishes n.
for a year *D2146.2.5; size of object transformed at n. D621.4; slaying
king by n. P13.6; soldiers of fairy king are trees by day, men by n.
F252.3.1; sun caught by man, thus causes n. A728.3; sun shining at n.
A1052.2, F961.1.5; sun's n. journey A722; tabu to carry food at n. E751.8;
tabu: feasting by n. at beginning of harvest C237; thieves' n. habits
J1394ff.; things thought at n. to be other frightful object J1789; thinking
it is still n.: mat on head J1819.3; transformation to snakes at n. in
order to sleep D659.1; trolls go about at n. F455.3.6; vow to kill wild
boar alone at n. M155.1; waxing of strength at n. D1836.3; why animal
howls at n. A2427; wife in heaven by day, with husband by n. E322.3;
wild hunt appears at n. E501.11.1; witch rides person all n. G269.3.2;
witch scatters tools at n. G265.1; woman alive by day, dead at n.
E155.4.1; work of day magically overthrown at n. *D2192.
Night's steeds A1172.3.
Nights. — Tabu: staying two n. in one place C761.4.1; why more days
than n. (riddle) H772.
Nightcap. — Disguised man wears wife's n. K521.4.1.4.
Nightfall. — Witch's familiar comes at n. G225.0.6.
Nightingale borrows blindworm's eye A2241.5; cannot live in manure nest
U144; hears boy call oxen: learns her song A2272.1.1. — Creation of n.
A1912.2; helpful n. B451.2; jealous husband kills n. which his wife gets
up to hear T257.5; man transformed to n. D151.3; wedding of n. B282.3.1.
Night-jar. — Friendship of leopard-cat and n. A2493.7.
Nightly resuscitation of same man E155.3. — Ghost visits earth n.

E585.3.1; island with n. noise of drums F745; slain warriors revive n.
E155.1; tree blooms and grows ripe fruit n. F811.13.

Nightmare F471.1.

Nightmares. — Curse: to be plagued by n. F431.10.

Night-spirits *F470ff.

Night-swallow. — How n. got voice A2421.1.

Nimrod's multiple throne F785.2. — Hill as unfinished tower built like
N. tower A963.8

Nine children at a birth T586.1.3; days' fall from heaven to earth A658.1;
-headed dragon B11.2.3.4; -headed giant F531.1.2.2.5; heavens A651.1.6;
-horned sheep B15.3.1.2; hundred ninety-nine gold pieces J1473.1; as
magic number D1273.1.3.1; magic waves D911.1.1; nights' riding from
heaven to hell A658.1.1; ranks of heaven A651.1.6.1; -tailed fox B15.7.7.1;
-tailed leopard B15.7.7; thousand nine hundred ninety-nine as magic
number D1273.1.7.2; worlds A651.0.1; worlds tremble at rebirth F960.1.5.
— Are there n. or ten geese? J2032; birth from n. mothers T541.12; boar
with n. tusks in each jaw B15.7.8; cauldron warmed by breath of n.
maidens F686.1; child born with n. faces, arms, feet T551.10; descendants
of n. robbers never to exceed n. M461; devil's n. daughters G303.11.5.1;
formulistic number: n. (99, 999, 99,999, etc.) Z71.6; ghost will vanish if
walked around n. times E439.8; giant occupies space of thrice n. men
F531.2.9; god as son of n. giantesses A112.5; hydra: n.-headed monster
B15.1.2.8.1; knights drink from a n.-gallon cup F531.4.3; pygmies n.
inches tall F535.2.1; man can breathe n. days under water F691; resuscitation by n.-day dance E63.2; ten for the price of n. J2083.4; witch's n.
rows of teeth G214.3.

Ninth. — Leaving capital n. night tabu C751.6.

Ninety. — Getting n. pigs and horses H1154.2.1.

Ninety-nine wise men J1149.12. — Devil has n. heads G303.4.1.1.1; formulistic number: 99,999 Z71.6.

Nine-hundred horses draw strong man's chariot F639.12. — Disenchantment after n. years D791.1.5.

Niobe boasts of her children C452.

Nipple from brother's caress J1833.1.1.

Nipples. — Black n. reveal virginity loss T494; thorns around n. F546.4.

Nisser (brownies) F482; in form of cows D133.1.1.

Nit lives at edge of hair A2236.6, A2433.5.1.

Nix-Naught-Nothing S243.

Nkundak's. — Origin of n. (crest) A2223.2, A2321.6, (feathers) A2313.4,
(voice) A2421.5.

"No" C495.2.2.1. — Answering only "Yes" and "N." J1255; princess
must answer all questions by "N." K1331; witness always to answer
"N." J1141.13.

Noah saves a giant on the ark F531.5.9. — Dove returns to ark in
obedience to N. A2221.7; raven does not return to N. A2234.1ff.

Noah's curse admits devil to ark C12.5.1; secret betrayed by his wife K2213.4.2. — Father of N. sons J2713; helpful animal stops leak in N. Ark *B527.2; devil gets into ark by hiding in shadow of N. wife G303.23.1; persons excluded from N. ark build another A1021.0.1.

Nobility of character of kings P12.9. — Animal granted patent of n. A2546; prohibition on intercourse with girls of n. C110.1; royalty and n. *P0—P99; tokens of n. left with exposed child S334.

Noble lady P60ff.; in love with lowly T91.6; person must do menial service as punishment *Q482; poets refuse to associate with lowly born J411.3.1. — Disguised n. recognized by habitual speech H38.1; special food of n. girl tabu C246.2; tests for n. blood H1574.1.

Nobles ruin peasant's crops U35.2. — Riddle: the king is surrounded by his n. H825.

Nobleman P50; after death must serve as menial Q482.3; marries, abandons poor girl T72.2; rescues lady R111.5; unpunished for murder U34; as wild huntsman E501.1.2. — Conflict between peasant and n. decided so that each must answer riddles H561.1.1; deaf man and proud n. X111.6; dwarf conducts shepherd to hell to collect debt from n. F451.5.1.14; impoverished n. offers wife to ruler W11.7.1; perseverance wins place for n. Q81.1; seduction by posing as n. K1315.5; sham n. K1952.

Nobleman's. — Troubled n. request not to be refused P95.

Noblemen who quarreled over a device J552.1. — Origin of n. A1656.

Noblewoman weds shepherd T121.2.

Nocturnal, see also **Night.** — Deceptive n. noises K1887.2; thieves' n. habits J1394ff.; vow against n. assault M163.

Nod. — Son obeys aged father's n. J1521.2.

Nodding. — Dwarfs appear n. F451.2.0.4.

Nodes. — Why bamboo has n. A2756.

Noise heard before death D1827.1.3; in house as ghost J1782.3. — Capture by causing animal to make n. K756.2.1; catching a n. (task) H1023.12; devil goes through stove with great n. G303.17.2.3; flute makes more n. J1541.2; foolishness of n.-making when enemies overhear J581; giants' shouts are storms or great n. F531.3.8; great n. from bass-viol (lie) X1866; husband deceived by paramour's n. K1549.7; island with nightly n. of drums F745; making n. tabu on way to otherworld C715.2; marvelous sensitiveness: fainting from n. of wooden pestle and mortar F647.8; wild hunt disappears with loud n. E501.16.1; wild hunt heralded by n. E501.13.1.

Noises. — Deceptive nocturnal n. K1887.2; mysterious ghostlike n. E402; poltergeist makes n. F473.5.

Noisy things often empty J262. — Mouse teaches her child to fear quiet cats but not n. cocks J132; ogre kills n. children G478.

"Noman" *K602.

Non-believers. — Miracle manifested to n. *V340ff.

None. — "Let n. in" J2516.6; riddles with "n." as answer H881.

Nonsense. — Cumulative n. tales Z20.1.

Noodle. — Strong hero born from n. F611.1.11.1.

Noonday. — Fairies visible only at n. F235.2.2.

Noose changed, ogre's daughter killed K1611.4; used by suicide as protection from accident D1384.2. — Capture in n. K743; hangman's n. cures scrofula D1502.2.3.1; hangman's n. gives luck in gambling D1407.2; ogre caught in n. and killed G514.3.

Norns prophesy at childbirth M301.12.

Norse custom of vow taking M119.3.

North as abode of evil spirits G633; forbidden direction C614.1.1; wind tempers fury of south wind A1127.1.1. — God of N. Star A253; hero goes n. to trolls H945.2; hell located to the n. A671.0.1; land of dead in n. E481.6.1; making sun, moon shine in n. H1023.16; origin of N. Star A774; saint's body laid n. and south E411.0.8; sky supported by N. Star A702.3.

Northern. — Origin of the N. Lights A795.

Northwest. — Giants live in n. F531.6.2.4; otherworld in n. F136.3.

Norwegians. — Lobsters mistaken for N. J1762.7.

Nose cut off (to get it out of the light) J2119.1, (as punishment) Q451.5ff., (for breaking tabu) C948.2, (to fulfill wish) J2072.6, (for not paying tax) P536.1; -flute A1461.7; made from clay from previous man A1316.1.1; mutilated S172; wagered N2.3.4. — Animal unusual as to his n. B15.5; why animals move n. A2476ff.; birth from mucus from the n. T541.8.3; child born through n. T541.8.3.1; contest in life-like painting: fly on saint's n. H504.1.1; corpse bites off woman's n. E259.1; cut-off n. K1512; devil's n. G303.4.1.4; "follow your n.": fool climbs tree J2461.6; fool and visitor's large n. J2512; giant with peculiar n. F531.1.6.6; huldra's long n. F460.1.6; husband believes he has cut off wife's n. J2315.2; improving the wife's face by cutting off her n. J2119.1.1; killing fly on judge's n. J1193.1; law: n. for a nose P522.1.1; magic object makes n. long (restores it) D1376.1ff.; man too lazy to wipe n.: loses bride W111.1.4; nature of animal's n. A2335.2ff.; ogre monstrous as to n. G362; person unusual as to his n. F514; remarkable n. F543; resuscitation by powder in n. E108.1; rubbing n. on hot griddle as punishment Q499.8; ruby appears as charitable king is blowing n. V411.7; sharp instrument as n. deceives ogre G572.2; son on gallows bites his mother's (father's) n. off Q586; treasure from n. D1454.9; why tapir has long n. A2335.3.2; wife's n. cut off, husband resuscitated E165.2.

Noses. — Convention of all with long n. X133; distribution of n. A1316.1; ears, fingers and n. of demons cut off as proof of killing them H105.5; noseless man persuades others to cut off n. J758.1.1; numskulls count selves by sticking their n. in the sand J2031.1; robbers' n. cut off K912.0.1; scavenger eats human n. G63; thousand-faced goddess blowing her n. J1261.10.

Nosebleed. — Amulet cures n. D1504.2; devil dies of n. G303.17.3.1.

Noseless man persuades others to cut off noses J758.1.1; ogre G362.1; pygmies F535.4.3; person F514.1.

Nose-ring. — Shooting jewels from n. F661.10; spear shot through n. F661.3.1.

Nostril. — Devil has only one n. G303.4.1.4.2; upper lip curls over n. F544.1.1.

Nostrils. — Creation of cat: sneezed from lion's n. A1811.2; devil drives carriage drawn by horses whose n. shoot fire G303.7.3.2; devil without n. G303.4.1.4.2; greedy one stuffs food in n. W151.10; remarkable n. F543.4.

Notary collects invented debts K441.2.1. — Ignorant n. incompetent J1749.2.

Notches in elder twigs reveal witch G257.6. — Cutting n. in table reveals witch G257.3; game of putting heads in n. K865.

Noteriety. — Burning the temple to attain n. J2162.1.

Nothing. — Boy who worked for n. at all demands it J2496.1; Christ, not having married, knew n. about suffering T251.0.2; first man created from n. A1275.7; getting n. H1045.1; lazy man spoiling materials, makes n. W111.5.9; lazy wife's defence: has done n. W111.3.4; Nix-Naught-N. S243; poor husband has n. to give guest P336.2; to get "n." and show it K1218.1.8.

Notice. — Death feigned in order to leave without n. K1864; transformation to escape n. D642.5.

Nourished. — Men n. by animals B530ff.; starving wife n. with husband's flesh and blood T215.3; sun, moon and stars n. on fire A700.7.

Nourishing. — Transformation for n. animal D518; wood of sixty trees n. three hundred men apiece F812.2.

Nucleus. — Creator sends crow to scout for earth n. A812.3.

Nude, see also **Naked;** woman clothed in own hair F555.3.1. — Certain peoples go n. A1683.4; small-pox deity rides n. on ass A137.8.

Nudes' sex unknown since no clothes on J1745.1.

Nudity a sign of anger Z181. — Hair protection against n. F555.3.4; magic power of n. D1796.1; princess brought to laughter by n. of old woman in quarrel at well H341.3.1.

Number of animals' eyes A2332.2ff. — Extraordinary n. of children in family T586.2; feet with unusual n. of toes F551.2; hands with unusual n. of fingers F552.1.1; test of resourcefulness: finding n. of people in dark, closed room H506.2; thirteen as unlucky n. N135.1.

Numbers. — Chains based on n. Z21; formulistic n. Z71ff.; illogical use of n. J2213; in n. there is strength J1279.4; lies about n. X1710; magic n. *D1273.1; riddles of n. H700ff.; symbolic meaning of n. H602ff.

Numskull, see also **Fool;** bribed to keep silent in elephant sale N613; injured J2131; talks to himself and frightens robbers away N612.

Numskull's outcry overawes tiger N691.1.

Numskulls go a-travelling J1711; quarrel over a greeting J1712.

Nun aids capture of ravisher Q244.2; asked why she did not call for help when raped says it was during the silent period J1264.4; claims her child is by the Holy Ghost J1264.6; eating unblessed lettuce eats a demon G303.16.2.3.4; falsely accused of adultery K2112; forgets to hail Mary and goes into the world to sin V254.5; leaving convent wounded by Jesus's image V122.1; refuses to look at man T362; sees Jesus after prayer D1766.1.2; tells friar to castrate self J1919.5.2; turned to stone Q551.3.4.3; who saw the world K1841.1. — Disappointed sweetheart becomes n. T93.2.1; image bars way of n. trying to escape convent to join lover V122; incontinent n. *V465.1.2; long-suffering n. rewarded Q87.3; maiden banished because she wants to become a n. Q431.3; obedient and industrious n. worthiest in the convent V461.1; owl (ghost of n.) in wild hunt E501.4.5; prophecy: unborn child to be n. M364.7.4; tabu for n. to ring church bell C94.7; Virgin appears to n. V277.1; Virgin miraculously prevents n. from deserting convent V265; woman continent in two marriages becomes n. T315.3; youth says he is associating with a pious person (n. as mistress) J1264.5.

Nun's illegitimate child T640.1. — Maggots in n. sores become jewels V222.15; pregnant n. virginity restored T313.1.1; wager on n. chastity N15.2.

Nuns fondled infant Christ V211.1.8.2; seduced by men in disguise K1321.4. — Abbess has 24 n. for 12 monks (12 n. left for guests) J1264.9; devil brings about seduction of n. Q220.1.1; devil seduces impious n. G303.3.1.12.1; priest impregnates five n. J1264.7.

Nunnery, see **Convent.**

Nuptial tabu C117.

Nurse begs alms to feed child R131.0.1; exchanges children so favorite will be wealthy K1923.1; rescues child R169.1.3. — Absent-minded n. puts child down well J2175.3; animal n. *B535; divine n. T605; fairy n. as helper N815.1; fairies take human n. to attend fairy child F372; faithful n. exposes own baby instead of tyrant's P361.4; identification by n. H183; prince stolen while n. dances K341.17.1; repentant n. disguises as hermit K1837.3; sham n. kills enemy's children K931; wolf waits in vain for n. to throw away child J2066.5.

Nurse's eye covered to conceal lover K1516.2; false plea admitted: child demanded J1162.1.

Nurses. — Diabolical child kills his wet-n. T614.

Nursing of Christ by saint V211.1.8.1; of hero A511.2.2; mothers' milk augmented by spring D927.3. — Baby saint not n. on fast days V229.2.3.1; strong hero's long n. F611.2.3; why bears have no breasts for n. A2353.3.

Nurture and growth of children *T610ff.

Nut clarifies waters F930.8; falls and wakes man about to be bitten by snake N652; hits cock in head: he thinks world is coming to an end X43.3; transformed to another object D451.7; transformed to person

D431.11. — Antelope transformed to n. D421.2.1; ape throws away n. because of its bitter rind J369.2; boy follows n. into lower world F102.4; creation of man from n. A1253.2; deceptive n. and olive division: inside and outside K171.3; earth from n. in devil's mouth A835; extraordinary n. F813.3; fairy's share of feast a n. F263.1; giant thinks hammer blow on head is n. falling F531.5.4; magic n. *D985ff.; magic n. tree D950.16; man becomes n. D222; ungrateful wanderer pulls n. tree to pieces to get the nuts W154.6; why lightning spares n. tree A2791.2.

Nuts held by curly hair F555.9. — Devil in woods to gather n. on Christmas Eve G303.8.13.3; fairies eat n. F243.2; girl eats only kola n. and tobacco F561.5; girl summons fairy lover by pulling n. F301.1.1.4; girls looking for n. have adventures N771.2; god blamed for small n. J2215.6; men from long n., women from short ones A1253.2.2; men wait in vain for n. to fall from tree J2066.3; picking all n. from tall tree as task H1121; pulling n. forbidden C517; resuscitation by breaking n. on head E181.1.1; sexton hears thieves in cemetery cracking n. X424; test of sex of girl masking as man: n. and apples offered H1578.1.5.

Nutshell. — Dress so fine that it goes in n. F821.2; wagon of n. F861.4.2.

Nutshells. — Boat made of n. F841.1.4.

Nymph of Luck and Ill-Luck N141.3; wives make hero sleep with fingers in mouth K521.4.6. — Magic object received from river-n. D813.1.

Nymphs of Paradise F499.2. — Man sees celestial n. F642.5.

Oak smell maddens swine B783. — Bashful suitor woos o. T69.4; fairies dance under o. tree F261.3.1.2; fettering to o. Q434.2; last leaf never falls from o. K222; magic o. tree *D950.2; numskulls try to get pears from an o. J1944.1; origin of o. A2681.2; sacred o. V1.7.1.1; why o. leaves are indented A2761.1.1.

Oaks. — Talking to o. to warn sons K649.6.

Oar. — Ferryman puts o. into king's hand and he must remain ferryman P413.1.1; golden o. F841.2.4; magic o. *D1124; silver o. F841.2.3.

Oars and masts transformed to serpents D444.11. — Boat with many o. mistaken for animal J1772.14; goose wings as witch's o. G241.4.1.

Oarsman. — Lie: remarkable o. X971.

Oasis. — Unexpected encounter in o. N761.

Oath to break oaths J1458; on boiling oil as chastity test H412.4.2; that devil may whet scythe C12.3; of friendship between cat and rat A2493.9.1; on the iron K1115; literally obeyed K2312; taken on boy's head: boy dies if false H252.4; taken before image H251.3.5. — Animal makes religious o. B251.7; attitudes of animals toward o. B279.2; escape by equivocal o. K550.1; false and profane swearing of o. forbidden C94.2; fruit falls if o. false H252.3; faithless wife's o. to be faithful J2301.1; impostor forces o. of secrecy *K1933; magic o. *D1273.5; magic o. stops killer D1400.1.11.1; unjust o. countered by another J1521.4; wife's equivocal o. K1513.

Oaths and vows *M100—M199; before gods as test of truth H253; drive ogres away G571. — Goddess of o. A484.1.

Oatmeal. — Miller disturbs fairies' o. F361.17.1.

Oats transformed to wheat D451.2.3.

Obedience W31; to bride as suitor test H313. — Animal blessed for o. to deity A2221.6; bride test: o. *H386; disenchantment by o. and kindness D731; intemperance in o. J555; literal o. J2460ff.; test of wife's o. *H473ff.; tests of o. *H1557.

Obedient husband: the leave of absence J2523; and industrious nun the worthiest in the convent V461.1; woman's pestle magically suspended J2411.9. — Boat o. to master's will D1523.2.4; magic object o. to master alone *D1651ff.; wager on the most o. wife *N12.

Obeisance to devil at witch's sabbath G243.1; to king taught J80.2.

Object-birth slander K2115.2; bleeds F991; magically attaches itself to a person D2171.1; magically made hideous D1873; sent to go by itself J1881.1; sinks into earth F948; thought to be animal J1771; transformed to animal D440ff.; transformed to another object D450—D499; transformed to person D430ff.; of wild hunt's pursuit E501.5ff. — Animal characteristics from transformation of o. A2262; animal or o. indicates election of ruler H171; animal retrieves lost o. B548; animal thought to be o. J1761ff.; animal transformed to o. D420ff.; child born bearing an o. T552; disenchantment by use of magic o. D771; earth from o. thrown on primeval water A814; escape by use of substituted o. *K525ff.; fairy in form of o. F234.3; fairies made visible through use of magic o. F235.4; food given to o. J1856; forbidden o. C620; gift or sale to o. J1850ff.; inability to find o. one is carrying J2025; life dependent on external o. *E765ff.; looking at certain o. forbidden C315; magic o. received from animal B505; magician recovers lost o. with the devil's help G303.22.2; man made from o. A1240—A1269; man transformed to o. *D200—D299; marriage of person and o. T117; moon from o. thrown into sky A741; object transformed to o. D450—D499; one o. thought to be another J1772; partaking of one particular o. forbidden C620ff.; person enamored of an o. T461; pestilence in form of o. F493.0.3; quest for lost o. H1386; reincarnation in o. *E630ff.; resuscitation by magic o. E64; size of o. changed at will D631.3; soul as o. E745ff.; soul kept in o. E711; soul of o. E701ff.; suitor test: finding o. hidden by princess H322.1; sun from o. thrown into sky A714; test of truth by magic o. H251ff.; transformation to o. for breaking tabu C961; transformation by magic o. D685; transformation: pig to o. D422.3; treasure discovered by magic o. *N533; troll in form of o. G304.1.2; witch in form of o. G212.

Objects attacked under illusion that they are men K1883.2; effect change of luck N135; go journeying together F1025; with mistaken identity J1770ff.; as part of wild hunt E501.10ff.; thought to be devils, ghosts J1780ff.; of worship V1ff. — Absurd sympathy for animals or o.

J1870ff.; animals or o. treated as human J1850—J1899; attention drawn by magic o.: recognition follows H151.1; capture by hiding in disguised o. K753; chastity test by magic o. H410ff.; devil in form of inanimate o. G303.3.4; fool loses magic o. by talking about them J2355.1; furniture and o. in otherworld F166; ghosts of o. E530ff.; heavenly bodies from o. thrown into sky *A700.1; invisible o. D1982; magic o. D800—D1699, (acquisition) D810ff., (characteristics) D1600—D1699, (function) D1300—D1599, (kinds) D900—D1299, (loss of) D860ff., (in otherworld) F166.4, (ownership) D800—D899; mountain with marvelous o. at top F759.1; princess defeated in repartee by means of o. accidentally picked up H507.1.0.1; quest to devil for o. H1273; recognition by overheard conversation with o. H13.2; recovering lost o. from the sea (task) H1132; religious edifices and o. *V100—V199; stars from o. thrown into sky A763; tasks contrary to nature of o. H1023; vital o. E770ff.

Obligation. — Return from dead to repay o. E340ff.

Obliterated. — Sin o. by saying of "Aves" *V254.1; sincere confession miraculously o. as sign of forgiveness V21.1.

Oblong. — How the earth became o. A851.

Obscene language tabu C496; pseudo-magic letters K115.1.3; tricks played on simpleton wishing to marry K1218.9. — Giantess in o. skirt F531.4.7.1.2; man seduced by woman's o. trick K1386.

Observation of dying people for a year takes man's thoughts from lust J62. — Deductions from o. J1661.1; imitation of diagnosis by o.: ass's flesh J2412.4; tasks performed by close o. *H962; wisdom (knowledge) acquired from o. *J50ff.

Observer insists on sharing love intrigue K1271.1.4.2.

Obstacle flight *D672, (Atalanta type) *R231, (reversed) D673; race between deer and hare K11.9.

Obstacles. — Magic object removes o. D1562ff.; remove o. from path J753.

Obstinate wife *T255ff.

Obvious. — Futility of trying to hide an o. deed J1082.

Occasion. — Identity tested by demanding that person say again what he said on former o. H15.1; tabu: looking at supernatural wife on certain o. *C31.1.2.

Occasions. — Prayer on special o. V57.3.

Occult. — Contours of land from o. hero harrowing A951.3; studying o. tabu C825.

Occupation. — Hero (heroine) of unpromising o. L113.

Occupational tricks on new employees J2347.

Ocean, see also **Sea;** from creator's sweat A923; of milk J2349.3; the son of Earth and Heaven A921; under this world A816.2. — Catching o. foam in cloth H1049.1; devil piles sand in o. so that vessels may run aground G303.9.9.5; ditch is really o. F1071.2; drunk wagers he can

drink o. dry J1161.9; extraordinary descent into o. F1022; giant wades
o. F531.3.1; riddle of o. and rivers H734; task: measuring o. H1144;
witch in bed gets o. water G259.5.

Octopus grows inside girl B784.1.4; holds sky against earth A665.5; transformed to stone D426.2. — Demigod conquers great o. A531.4.1; demon-
o. G308.9; enmity of o. and rat A2494.16.7; helpful o. B477; mythical o.
B63; rat defecates upon rescuing o. K952.1.2, (origin of tubercles on
head) A2211.14; thieving o. K366.8.

Odd number strokes in beating the devil G303.16.19.19; numbers (formulistic) Z71.0.1.

Odes. — Marriage o. T136.3.2.

Odin *A128.2; battles Fenris Wolf at end of world A1082.2; as falcon
D152.4.1; as magician D1711.6.1. —Going to bed with O. H1199.11.

Odor, see also **Smell;** reveals witch G259.2; of wine cask J34. — Animals ask for goddess's perfume: punishment, bad o. A2232.5; devil has
a sulphurous o. G303.4.8.1, G303.6.3.4; foul o. in hell A689.2; marvelous
sensitiveness: woman has o. of goat's milk F647.5; person's remarkable
o. F687; sea's unpleasant o. A925.3, A1119.3; sweet o. in heaven A661.0.8;
why herrings have bad o. A2416.7.

Odors. — Soul sustained on pleasant o. E708.

Odysseus, see also **Ulysses;** bends his bow H31.2; and Polyphemus K521.1,
K602, K603, K1011; recognized by his dog H173; returns in humble
disguise K1815.1; and Sirens J672.1.

Oedipus exposed and reared at strange king's court S354; fulfills prophecies (parricide) M343, (mother-incest) M344; solves riddle of Sphinx
*H541.1.1.

Offending the gods C50ff., (punished) *Q221; spirits tabu C40ff.; supernatural husband forbidden *C32ff. — Christianity o. dwarfs F451.9.1.6.

Offense to skull *C13. — Magic knowledge of o. to deity K1810.0.12;
smallness of o. no excuse when hunter prepares to kill lark U32.

Offensive. — Curses because of o. answer to saint M411.8.3.

Offering. — Base money in the o. J1582; merman demands cattle as o.
B82.2; sexton's own wife brings her o. K1541; punishment for failure to
give o. to gods Q223.14; theft of cup from fairies o. mortal drink
F352.1.

Offerings to holy wells V134.2. — Tabu: eating from o. to gods C57.1.3;
trickster shams death and eats grave o. K1867.2.

Offertory. — Money from o. as cure D1500.1.10.3.

Office. — Robber promised larger sum at o. D439.7; Virgin designates
favorite for election for o. V261; Virgin restores o. to ignorant man
V261.1.

Offices. — Animals perform o. of church B253; largest burdens laid on
smallest asses, best o. to most ignorant men U12.

Officer accidentally finds fugitive N618. — Common man transformed
to grand o. D22.1; rescuer disguised as o. saves prisoner K649.2.

Officer's. — Drunken o. stolen mantle J1211.2.1.

Officers praised in reverse from their real merit K2136. — Treacherous o. and tradesmen K2240ff.

Official. — Choice between bad master, bad o., or bad neighbor J229.5; clever o. J1115.10; riddle propounded on pain of loss of o. position H541.3; symbolic interpretation of o. robes H608; theft by disguising as palace o. K311.10.

Officials. — Presumptuous o. disregarded J982.

Officiousness rebuked J1300ff.

Offspring, see also **Children, Descendants;** of fairy and mortal F305; of first parents A1277; of human and animal intercourse B636; of living and dead person E474.1; of marriage to animal *B630ff.; of water-spirit and mortal F420.6.1.6. — Charm for begetting o. K115.1.4; first parents devour o. A1277.1; horses as o. of the devil G303.10.8; lizards are o. of the devil G303.10.10; man as o. of creator A1216; monstrous o. from animal marriage B634; quality of o. preferred to quantity J281; sun as o. of moon A715.5; universe as o. of creator A615.

Often. — Tabu: doing thing too o. C762.

Ogam inscription on shield misreported K511.2. — Origin of o. inscriptions A1484.1; recognition by o. carving H35.4.1; till o. and pillar be blent Z61.1.

Ogre, see also **Giant;** allows self to be tied to learn magic K713.1.5; appeased by being called uncle Q41.1; assumes form of widow's husband K1919.2; bribes boy not to cut tree N699.5; defeated G500—G599; disguised as holy man K1827.0.1; frightened into rolling self in mat K711.3; frightened at rustling K2345; as helper *N812; helps tortoise who catches him K1111.3; keeps girl in drum R49.3; overawed K1710ff.; poses as mother, kills child K2011.1.1; produces water for caravan N812.6; released in return for magic girdle M242.3; sees beautiful woman reflected in water and attempts to drink lake dry J1791.6.2; suitor persuaded to bury woman's murdered lover K912.3; tars hero's boat, thinking to injure him J2171.1.2; tempts fugitive with ring R231.1; vulnerable only if face turned away Z315. — Abduction by o. R11; adventure from following o. to cave N773.1; ants' nest thrown on o. K621.1; bringing an o. to court (task) H1172; calling on o. forbidden C20ff.; centipede kills o. B524.1.10; child sold (promised) to o. *S211; flight on a tree, which o. tries to cut down *R251; giant o. can be killed only with own club Z312.2; giant o. guards tree D950.0.1.1; girl promised by parents to o. S240.1; grateful o. resuscitates benefactor G513.1; madness from seeing o. F1041.8.3; magic adhesion to o. *D2171.2; magic fish talk so that o. thinks hero has many brothers with him D1613.1; magic tree guarded by giant o. D950.0.1.1; man becomes o. D94; ornament compels woman to follow o. D1427.2; prophecy of o.-child so pregnant woman will be killed K2115.3; rescue from o. G550ff., R111.1.1; secret of killing o. N476.3; sex exchanged with o. D593;

sham doctor kills o. K824.1; skillful marksman shoots both eyes of o. F661.5.4; strong man serves o. as punishment for stealing food F613.4; sultan's daughter as bribe to o. S222.4; sun, moon born from an o. A715.3; tasks assigned o. H932; treacherous mother marries o. and plots against son S12.1; troll as o. *G304ff.; youth sells himself to an o. in settlement of a gambling debt S221.2.

Ogre's beard caught fast K1111.1; exchange of sex D10.1; life in feather in pocket E715.1.3.1; magic invisibility D1981.4; separable soul in many objects E718; son guards treasure N571.1; soul in spot below ear E714.10. — Falling into o. power G400—G499; magic object taken from o. house D838.2; man married to o. daughter T115; noose changed, o. daughter killed K1611.4; stealing o. grain H1151.25; substituted string causes o. death K1611.1.

Ogres G (entire chapter); duped into fighting each other K1082; live with men A1101.1.3; overawed by stray objects N691. — Castle guarded by o. F771.5.2; castle inhabited by o. F771.4.1; country ridded of o. A1416; giant o. G100—G199; invulnerable o. D1840.3; men transformed to o. D47.2.

Ogress bathes in pool, beautified G264.0.1; with breasts thrown over her shoulder *G123; captured and reformed R9.3; demands eyes of six raja wives K961.2.2; disguised as queen H919.6; frightened of child with moustache K547.10; in frightening guises H1401.2; puts bride in tree, takes her place K1911.1.7; reincarnated as bramble bush E631.4; transformed to man D11.1; turns child into cannibal G34; whets teeth to kill captive G83.1; -wife orders rajah expel other wives S413.1. — Cannibal o. G86.1; children devoured by o. F913.2; dagger indicates o. dead or alive E761.7.15; escape from o. by substituting pig K525.7; princess becomes o. D47.3; separable soul of o. E710.1; slander: woman an o. K2124; stealing drum of o. H1151.24; tongue of o. becomes surfboard D457.14.1; transformation to escape o. D642.6; winning daughter of o. for bride H305.

Oil, see also **Ointment;** becomes jewels D475.4.9; bursts from ground as saint made bishop V222.5; poured in dog's ear brings rain D1542.1.6; from relics has curative powers V211.0.1.1; sold to iguana J1852.1.2; on tree prevents pursuit K619.2; well driller drills for fifty years W37.1. — Bath of boiling o. F872.2; boiling to death in pitch or o. Q414.1, S112.1; burning o. thrown on ogre G572.1; discovery of edible o. O1429.1; discovery of o. A1426.1; escape from boiling o. R215.2; hot o. poured on guinea fowl's feet A2375.2.10; jar of o. broken before sold J2061.1.4; jinn falls into boiling o. G512.3.4; magic object provides o. D1482; magic o. D1242.4; magic o.-spouting fountain D925.0.1; man becomes o. D242; murder by burning in o. K955.2; oath on boiling o. H412.4.2; ordeal by burning o. H221.3; origin of o. press A1446.5.6; pressing out large quantity of o. F639.7; quest for magic pig's o. H1332.5.1; quest for o. to anoint dying H1265; rivers of o., milk, wine and honey in otherworld F162.2.6; saint unhurt by boiling o. D1841.2.2; saint uninjured by boiling o. D1841.2.2.1; selling old o. wells for post holes X1761.1; shower of o. F962.6.4; spilling o. good luck J2214.7; thieves hidden in o. casks K312; underground o. pools discovered N597; water becomes o. D478.7; well of o. runs into river F932.4; where is o. in sesame flower? J1291.4; why palm o. is red A2877.

Ointment, see also **Oil;** in eye to imitate witch G242.8; makes night seem day D1368.1.1. — Fairies made visible through use of o. F235.4.1; invulnerability by being burned and anointed with magic o. D1846.1; itch-producing o. X34; magic o. *D1244; pepper given as o. for burns K1014; transformation by rubbing with o. D594.

Oisin's poor diet in Patrick's house J1511.13.

Ojibwa. — Origin of the O. A1611.1.1.

Old, see also **Age;** age personified Z114; age must be planned for J761; chosen rather than new L214; devil dies when he is fastened in hell's door by his beard G303.17.3.2; god slain by young A192.1.1; king attacked P16.3.1; maid marries devil G303.12.5.1; man (burns self with gunpowder, then hot water) N255.6, (as creator) A15.3, (contented till forbidden to leave city) H1557.3, (and Death) C11, (desires human flesh) G95, (as godfather to underground folk) F372.2.1, (helper) N825.2, (in love with young woman) J1221, (married to young, unfaithful wife) T237, (of the sea) G311, (from sky as creator) A21.2; Nick *G303ff.; ox yoked with young ox J441.1; people killed in famine S110.1; person commits suicide when strength fails P674; person helps perform task H971; person helper on quest H1233.1; shoes patched with new J2129.5; sweetheart chosen in preference to new J491; teacher wants to marry young girl T91.4.1.1; warrior longs for more adventure H1221.1; wine chosen (must honor old age) J1313; woman (beautiful as in youth) F575.1.2, (has control over frost) D2143.5.1, (doesn't want to die for daughter) H1556.4.5.1, (gives chickens to devils) G303.25.6, (as guardian of gods' islands) A955.12, (helper) *N825.3, (intercepts letter and takes girl's place in man's bed) K1317.2.1, (has lived for ages) D1857.1, (in ogre's house) G530.5, (and her pig: cumulative story) Z41ff., (as prophet) M301.2, (ruler of dead in lower world) E481.1.1, (by spring as helper) N825.3.2, (substituted for bride) K1911.1.5, (substitutes for wife in bed) K1843.3, (suckling babies to prove child hers) H495.3, (and tiger flee each other) K2323.3; woman's (curse) M411.5, (maledictions inform abandoned hero of his parentage and future) S375, (pleas tabu) C745.1. — Abduction by o. woman R39.2; angel in form of o. man V231.6; association of young and o. J440ff.; bedridden o. man hanged, guilty youth spared J2233.1.1; conception in o. age T538; creation of monkeys from o. woman thrown into fire A1861.2; deity disguised as o. person K1811.2; defeating certain o. woman (task) H1149.3; demon as o. woman G302.3.3; devil a little, gray, o. man G303.3.1.5; devil marries o. maid who proves to be a termagent and miser G303.12.3; disguise as o. man

K1821.8; disguise as o. man to enter enemy's camp K2357.3; diving into lake makes person o. K1072; dwarfs have o. faces F451.2.5.1; escape in o. woman's skin K521.1.4; extremely o. person F571; foolish youth in love with ugly o. mistress J445.1; Fortune as o. woman N114; in o. age spirits become gods A117.3; jokes on o. maids X750ff.; king killed when o. P16.3; king seizes o. woman's cow U35.1; king too o. goes himself into grave P16.3.2; magic object makes person o. *D1341ff.; magic object received from o. (man) D822, (woman) D821; new bags for o. K266; not to go where o. man has young wife J21.3; ogre so o. that his eyelids must be propped up G631; owl advises o. man of gods' visit B569.1; princess brought to laughter by indecent show made in quarrel with o. woman at well H341.3.1; prophecies from o. man who writes in a book M301.4; revenant as o. man E425.2.1; resourcefulness test: finding how o. three horses are H506.11; Satan as o. man G303.3.1.24; selling three o. women (task) H1153; sexton behind crucifix tells o. maid she will have no husband K1971.8.1; supplies from toe of o. woman D1470.2.4; tasks performed with help of o. woman H971; thief disguised as o. woman K311.16.1; three hundred year o. man has had intercourse only every two years T317.0.1; transformation to o. man to escape recognition D1891; transformation: prince to o. man D93; treacherous o. woman K2293; what becomes of the o. moon J2271.2; where the devil can't reach, he sends an o. woman G303.10.5; why men become o. A2861; wild hunt appears at o. (battlefield) E501.12.6.1, (mill) E501.12.10; wine very o. but small serving J1316; wisdom from o. man J151ff.; women o. from their birth T615.2.

Older, see also **Age, Elder.** — "Ass of twenty o. than man of seventy" J1352.2; enigmatic counsels of o. brother H596.1.1; inquirer always sent to o. person *F571.2; transformation to o. person *D56.1.

Oldest son responsible for others' welfare P233.5; warrior preferred as suitor T92.13. — What is o. (riddle) H659.1.

Olive branch (insures fidelity of husband) D1355.8, (laid on altar as sacrifice) V15, (makes woman master in household) D1359.1.1, (symbol of peace) Z157. — Athena chooses o. tree because of its fruitfulness J241.1; deceptive nut and o. division: inside and outside K171.3; laurel and o. tree scorn thornbush as umpire J411.7; magic o. tree D950.9; why o. is bitter A2771.8.1.

Ollamhs sacred V291.

Olympus A151.1.

Omen, see also **Divination.** — Animals of good o. A2536; ghost as death o. E574; ghost light as death o. E530.1.6; magic spear gives o. of victory D1311.17.1; mermaid appears as o. of catastrophe B81.13.7; priest makes the o. come true J1624; stars as o. D1291.2.1; wild hunt as o. E501.20ff.; wraith as calamity o. E723.8.

Omens in love affairs T3. — Beasts furnish o. B147.1ff.; fool believing in o. refuses to prepare for death J2285.1; foolish interpretation of o.

J2285; future learned through o. *D1812.5ff.; house where o. work by contraries X1505.1.

Omnipotent god A102.4.

Omnipresent god A102.5.

Omniscience of a god A102.1, D1810.0.1; not possessed by fairies F254.2. — God's o. J1617; magic seat gives o. D1310.1.

Once. — Door to fairyland opens o. a year F211.1.1; fairies can set down an object o. but cannot raise it again F255.2; magic effective when struck o. D806.1; strong man kills many men at o. F628.2.1.

One, see also **Unique**; bull, one cow survive plague F989.6; day from happiness to misfortune H685.1; day and one night taken as forever K2314; -eyed (see heading following this); -footed animal B15.6.0.1; forbidden thing C600—C649; -horned (cows) A2286.2.3, (ox) B15.3.0.2; hundred brothers seek 100 sisters as wives T69.1; hundred one as magic number D1273.1.7.1; killed none and yet killed twelve H802; lie a year X901; -legged horse F241.1.3.1; man disappears each night S262.0.1; -sided man F525.1; wish granted D1761.0.2.2; wrong and five hundred good deeds J1605. — Bluff: only o. tiger, you promised ten K1715.2; calf of o. color the property of the devil G303.10.9; can drink only o. kind of wine at a time J1511.15; cat's o. trick J1662; chaste woman can blow out candle with o. puff and relight it with another H413.1; devil builds road for farmer in o. day G303.9.2.2; devils have only o. leg G303.4.5.1; disenchantment by only o. person D791.2; dwarfs must return to spirit world by o. o'clock a.m. F451.3.2.2; fairies visible to o. person alone F235.3; formulistic numbers: a number plus o. Z71.0.2; fox had rather meet o. hen than fifty woman J488; ghost visible to o. person alone E421.1.1; giant with o. (hand, foot) F531.1.6.12, (arm) F631.1.6.7, (foot) F531.1.3.3, (leg) F531.1.3.3.1; if the horse can pull o. load he can pull two J2213.4; invulnerability for o. day D1845.1; image of horse will be vivified only for o. person D445.1.1; island inhabited by only o. species F743; making the beard golden: such a o. *K1013.1; making many kinds of food from o. small bird (task) H1022.6; making many shirts from o. hank of flax (task) H1022.2; man can stand still all day on o. foot F682; man to have wishes if he can repeat them in o. breath D1761.0.2.1; more than o. swallow to make a summer J731.1; objects on o. side of palisade in otherworld garden black, on other white F162.1.2.3; only o., but a lion J281.1; only o. oath binding M115; only o. person can help secure magic object D827; only o. person possesses power to heal certain wound D2161.4.10.0.1; only o. present to be asked for at home of spirit son-in-law C714.1; person with o. leg F517.0.1; person using only o. leg, hand, eye F682.0.1; pledge to say but o. phrase M175; pretended exchange of confidence as to the o. thing that can kill K975.1; riddle about turning o. into two (split peas) H583.4.6; suitor test: to get imprisoned princess in o. year's time H322.2; tabu: putting house in order for o. man C743; three women have among them but o. (eye)

*F512.1.2, (tooth) F513.1.1; treasure found by going with o.-night old
colt onto o.-night old ice N542.1; two for the price of o. J2083.2; two
giants with o. axe G151; weaver prefers master with o. hedgehog
J229.8; witch known by hose unbound on o. leg G255; woman with
horseshoe on o. foot F551.1.2.1; youth sees o. and one-half men and
a horse's head H583.1.

One-eyed child T551.11; demon G369.7; giant F531.1.1.1, G511.1; god
*A128.2, (transforms islands) A955.5; king J1675.4; man as appraiser
of horse X122; monster, the Antichrist A1075; one-footed, one-handed
men F525.3; parson X413; person *F512.1; pig B15.4.5; sow in wild
hunt E501.4.3.1; villain K2273; witch G213.1. — Deduction: the o. camel
J1661.1.1; king will not permit a o. man in his presence P14.2; why o.
soldiers good J1494; why women o. A1316.3.2.

One hundred. — Crow refuses to marry o. year old titmouse B282.22.1;
eating o. carcasses H331.17; getting o. oxen H1154.2.1; valley of o.
giants G105; person wandering for o. and fifty years F1032.1.

One-third for the price of one-fourth J2083.1.

One thousand men to string bow F836.3.1.

Oneself. — Counting wrong by not counting o. J2031; curse by o.
M411.0.1; quest for bride for o. H1381.3.1.2.

Onion. — Hot o. to the eye as cure J2412.1; origin of o. growing A1441.5;
wedding of o. and garlic B286.1.

Onions. — To eat a hundred o. J2095; transformation by eating o.
D551.2.5.

Only, see also **Once, One, Unique.** — Cat's o. trick J1662; otherworld
dwellings open o. at certain times F165.2.

Onyx offered in innocence test H256.1. — City of o. F761.3.

Opaque. — Ability to see through o. objects F642.3.

Open Sesame D1552.2, N455.3. — Genie sleeps with eyes o. G634; king
demands o. gate to vassals' castle P50.0.1.1; man claims to sleep with o.
eyes and beguiles ogre K331.1; mouth o. for forty days F544.0.4; sleeping
with eye, ear o. F564.4; temple rises where ground bursts o. A992.3.

Opened. — Dwarf home o. by magic flower F451.4.3.7; locks o. by magic
D2088.

Opening bottle tabu C625; box forbidden C321ff.; gift prematurely tabu
C321.2; mouth makes door open wider D1782.1.1. — Disenchantment
by o. fruit D721.5; door to fairyland o. once a year F211.1.1; earth o.
at command F942.3; earth o. for fugitive R327; ghosts summoned by o.
sacred book E383; ground o. swallows up person F942.1; hair from
fox's tail o. all doors D1562.2; idol o. to grant refuge R325.2; images
o. eyes D1632; kingship for o. palace door P11.4.1; magic escape o. in
house D2165.4; magic object miraculously o. and closing *D1550ff.;
otherworld dwellings o. only at certain times F165.2; tabu: o. gourd
where starwife kept C31.1.5; treasure o. itself N552; tree leaves o.
to give saint passage F979.2; visit to lower world through o. rocks

*F92.3; well-trained kid not o. for wolf J144; wife o. forbidden chest, killed T254.4; witches o. doors, windows G249.8.

Operation. — Caesarean o. a custom T584.3; doctor performs useless o. X372.4.

Operations. — Lies about surgical o. X1721.

Opium produces reincarnation qualities A2733; substituted for tobacco in pipe K873.3. — Origin of o. A2691.4.

Opium-smoker lost on journey J2027.

Opossum. — Deer, o., and snake each render indispensable aid to man J461.4; marriage to person in o. form B641.8; why o. has bare tail A2317.12; why o. has large mouth A2341.2.1; why o. plays dead when caught A2466.1.

Opponent. — Boasting scares o. from contest K1766; vow not to be killed by single o. M162.

Opponents agree not to fight, remain undefeated M237.1; humble selves, become friends J917. — Creator's o. A50—A69.

Opposite of present A633, A855. — Girl must do o. of commands H580.1; land where all is o. from the usual X1505; power over monster obtained by reversing orders: hero does exact o. of the command D1783.4; witch's charm o. of Christian *G224.1.

Opposites. — Dream interpreted by o. D1812.3.3.10.

Opposition of dead to return of living from land of the dead F105 (cf. F93.1.1); of good and evil gods A106. — Animals created through o. of devil to God A1750ff.; man's miraculous death for o. to dogma of Immaculate Conception V312.2; punishment for o. to holy person Q227.

Oppression. — Famine as punishment for o. Q552.3.2; magic stone protects church from o. D1389.1.

Optimist becomes pessimist when money stolen U68.

Oracle, see also **Divination;** D1712; tells whether eunuch to be father J1271; that the first of three sons to kiss his mother will be king J1652. — Ambiguous o. M305; fatal deception: changed message from o. *K981.

Oracles from holy well V134.1.

Oracular animal *B150ff.; fish D925.2; images occupied by spirits or priests who give the answers K1972; object used for divination *D1311ff. — Pseudo-magic o. object sold K114.

Orange thrown indicates the princess's choice H316.1. — Birth from o. T543.3.1; conception from eating o. T511.1.4; magic o. *D981.3; transformation to o. D211.1.

Oranges grow on tree-limb knives F811.7.2.2.

Oratory. — Submarine o. V118.2.1.

Orchard. — Fairies dance in o. F261.3.3; magic chain renders o. barren D1563.2.1; tearing up the o. K1416.

Orchestra of ghosts E499.2.

Ordaining the future M (entire chapter). — God o. ceremonies A176.

Ordeal substantiates unjust claim J1521.4. — "Bear the o. in peace" K1354.2.2; chastity tested by o. H412ff.; substitute in o. K528; thief betrays self in o. J1141.16; trial by o. subverted by carrying magic object D1394.1.

Ordeals *H220ff.

Order, see also **Command;** for spirit's help left on card D2074.2.4.4. — Culture hero establishes law and o. A530ff.; death o. evaded K510ff.; God reduces elements to o. A175; establishment of natural o. A1100ff.; islands by o. of deity A955.0.1; king's enigmatic o. to minister H587; literal misconstruction of o. to get revenge J2516.0.1; marriage by royal o. T122; seduction by bearing false o. from husband or father K1354; theft by presenting false o. to guardian K362.

Orders. — Dwarfs give o. to mortals F451.5.20; punishment for leaving holy o. Q226; religious o. *V450—V499; sun, moon under God's direct o. A726.1.

Ordering of human life A1300—A1399.

Orderly. — Battle between God's o. and plague A1626; giant as gods' o. A133.3.

Ordination. — Forced o. of ignorant priest U41.

Oreads F450ff., F460ff.

Organ. — Bird rewarded for moving woman's o. to its present position A2229.6; combat with horse's sex o. F998; dead arise when one plays o. for first time in church E419.5; ghost plays o. E554.1; horse's o. provides treasure D1469.5; monk recognized by o. H79.7; origin of o. A1461.3; wants the o. to come and play for her J1888; woman lends female o. to boy D11.2.

Organs, see also **Genitals;** exchanged with animal E789.1. — Child with all o. displaced T551.14; cutting off sex o. in madness Q555.4; enemy's sex o. prove slaying H105.7; magic animal sex o. D1029.4; magic mutilation of sex o. D2062.4; man's o. replaced with animal's X1721.2; remarkable physical o. F540ff.; remarkable sex o. F547ff.; removable o. F557; sex o. mutilated S176; skillful surgeon removes and replaces vital o. F668.1.

Orient. — Dwarfs emigrate to the O. F451.9.2.2.

Origin. — Hero (heroine) of unpromising o. L111; prohibition against mention of o. of person or thing *C440ff.; sword of magic o. *D1081.1; test: guessing o. of certain skin H522.1.

Origins A (entire chapter).

Original creator followed by transformers A72. — Giants' magic gifts return to o. form in hands of men F531.5.6.1; person returns to o. form when tabu is broken C963ff.; quest for o. of picture H1213.1.2; reflection in water thought to be the o. of the thing reflected J1791; treasure to be found by man who marries o. owner's daughter N543.3.

Orion's origin A772.

Ornament as chastity index H433; transformed to other object D454.8.
— Fairy's o. snatched F354; magic o. provides treasure D1456ff.; man
becomes o. D263; quest for matching o. H1317; stolen o. presented to
owner as gift N347.4.

Ornaments bride wore in former birth H1371.4; buried with hero V67.1.
— Animal with jeweled o. F826.1; clouds as sky's o. A1133.2; devil
as helper of robber refuses to let woman's o. be stolen M212.1; extraordinary o. F827ff.; identification by o. H90ff.; magic o. *D1070ff.;
origin of metal o. A1465.3; recognition by o. under skin H61; serpent's
bite produces o. and clothes B103.6.1; thief steals mistress's o. K346.6;
trickster promises to turn gold into o. K283; trickster tries on o., steals
them K351.3.

Ornamental. — Choice between useful and o. J240ff.

Ornamented. — Sky o. with clouds A1133.2.

Orphan deprived of inheritance S322.0.1; gets wife because swollen
creek prevents other marriage N699.4; hero L111.4; inquires about
parents T621. — Bird must bring o. to king H901.0.2; marriage of
dragon and o. T118.2; milk magically appears in woman for o. T611.6.

Orphans. — Inhospitality to o. punished Q292.2; kindness to o. repaid
by dead parents Q47.

Orpheus journeys to land of dead to bring back wife F81.1.

Orthoptera. — Origin of o. A2060ff.

Osprey. — Magic o. produces lightning B172.8; man becomes o. D152.5.

Ostrich. — How o. lost beautiful feathers A2252.3, A2402.2; kite fails
to secure o. at wedding B282.2.1.

Other. — Devils leave hermit who turns o. cheek when struck G303.16.15;
sinful person spoken of as "the o." C433.1.

Others. — Consolation by thought of o. worse placed J880ff.; fortune-
teller shows o. how to get rich but remains poor himself X461.1.

Otherworld journeys *F0—F199; mistress helps hero H335.0.1.1. —
Answers found in o. to riddles propounded on way H544; arrow shot
to o. F638.4; birds in o. sing religious songs B251.3.1; birds show way
to o. B151.2.0.2; flower from o. F979.10; food appears, disappears in o.
D1982.4; hero sees guarded maiden in o. T381.1.1; home of Fortuna
in o. N111.1.1; huge oxen on o. island K1784.2; immediate return to o.
because of broken tabu C952; journey to o. foretold M358.2; journey
to o. with magic speed D2122.0.1; magic aging by contact with earth
after o. journey D1896; magic knowledge from queen of o. D1810.1;
magic object from o. D813.3; magic received from o. D859.2.1; magic
sight of earthly object from o. D1825.2.1; malevolent beings in o.
F360.0.1; person carried off to o. for breaking tabu C954; person must
remain in o. because of broken tabu C953; quests to the o. H1250--
H1299; rejuvenation by going to o. and having digestive tract removed
D1889.5; sight of old home reawakens memory and brings about return
from o. *D2006.2; slamming door on exit from mountain o. *F91.1;

tabu: staying too long in o. meadow C761.4.2; tabu to touch fire in o. C542.2; tabus connected with o. journeys *C710ff.; telling adventure in o. tabu C757.2; transformation to go to o. D641.4; visions of the o. V511.

Otter becomes person D327.1; carries flaming wood in mouth B193; persuaded to rob K1022.5.1; retrieves magic object B548.3. — Blood of o. venomous B776.5.4; color of o. A2411.1.2.3; creation of sea o. A1821.1; dog becomes o. D412.5.3; foolish seller of fox skins mixes o. skins with them J2083.3; helpful o. B443.1; man transformed to o. D127.2; reincarnation as o. E612.14; water-spirit as o. F420.1.3.12.

Otters recover magic ring B548.1.2; supply man with fish, wood B292.7.

Outcast builds castle like king's, is recognized H153. — Prophecy of luck for o. child M312.7.

Outcry. — Murderer makes o. to accuse innocent R2116.4; robbers frightened from goods by man's o. K335.1.3.

Outcries. — Abducted woman's o. drowned by thieves wailing K419.8.

Outdoors. — Chief going o. tabu C564.9.

Outhouse. — Paramour trapped in o. K1574.2.

Outlaws. — Fairies o. in hiding F251.14.

Outlets. — Riddle: dam up o. H588.9.

Outside. — Ghost haunts o. E279.1; marriage o. the group T131.5.

Outstripping. — Marvelous runner o. March wind F681.2.

Outweighing. — Magic jewel o. many heavy objects in the scale D1682.

Outwitted. — Adulteress and paramour o. by (husband) *K1550ff., (trickster) K1570ff.; husband o. by adulteress K1510ff.; husband o. by wife J1545; wife o. by husband J1541.

Outwitting. — Suitor test: o. princess *H342.

Oven door jumps into room E539.1; heats without fire D1601.6. — Captivity in o. R49.2; cure by putting children into o. D2161.4.11; dwarf has o. F451.7.2; father throws son in o. H165; ghost drives priest into o. E264; Jewish child thrown into o. by father for baking eucharist preserved by Virgin Mary V363; large loaves need a large o. X434.1; murder by roasting in o. S112.6; ogre burned in his own o. G512.3.2; ogress makes o. blaze with foot G345.1; wife not to go into o. while husband is away H473.2; woman in moon's o. seen on clear night A751.8.4.

Overawed. — Captor o. with help of magic object D1613; master o. by strong hero F615.3; ogre o. *G570ff., K1710ff.; revenant o. by living person E462.

Overawing. — Escape by o. captor *K540ff.; son o. father P236.6.

Overbearing husband loses fortune J1545.6; wife T252.

Overboard. — King brings victory by leaping horse o. W32.1; passenger brings ship bad luck: cast o. N134.1.5; person thrown o. (and abandoned) S142, (by faithless wife and paramour) K2213.2, (by impostors) *K1931.1.

(to placate storm) S264.1; throwing shipboard rivals o. when food gone K527.4.

Overcome. — Contest in enduring cold: frost o. by wind H1541.2; devil o. by man G303.9.6.1.1; fairy's curse partially o. by another fairy's amendment F316.1; magic sight o. by incantation D1822.1; man on Island of Fair Women o. by loving women F112.1; man's adversary o. by animal B524; person o. by magic object D1400ff.; robber o. K437; strong o. by weak in conflict L310ff.; vampire's power o. E251.1; witch o. or escaped *G270ff.

Overcoming robbers as suitor task H335.4.2. — Amazon o. enemies in forest K778.1; cannibal disenchanted by o. it G33.1; disenchantment by o. enchanted person in fight (contest) D716; enduring and o. curses M420ff.; hero o. devastating animal G510.4; lowly hero o. rivals L156.1; suitor test: o. princess in strength *H345; youngest animal o. adversary L72.

Overdose. — Fatal o. of medicine J2115.

Overdressed. — Spilling dirty water on o. youths X32.

Overeaten. — Girl claims having o. on bird thigh K1984.2.1; madness from having o. F1041.8.5.

Overestimating. — Enemy o. opponents retreats K2368.

Overflowing river D2151.2.2, F932.8; well F718.6, *F933.6.1.

Overhasty man kills his rescuing twin brother N342.3.

Overheard secret tabu C420.3; wish realized N699.6. — False accusation o. causes hasty killing N342.4; magic power from o. talk D1739.1; ogre's secret o. G661ff.; recognition by o. conversation with animals or objects H13ff.; remedy learned from o. animal meeting *B513; secrets o. N450ff.; sham wise man utilizes o. conversation K1956.7; tasks performed by means of secrets o. from tree *H963.

Overhearing. — Deception by o. prearranged conversation J1517.

Overheating. — Devil dies of nosebleed resulting from o. G303.17.3.1.

Overleapt. — Garden wall that cannot be o. D1675.

Overlooking. — Beggar o. money N351.2.

Overlord. — Death for slaying o. Q411.4.1; riddle about o. H853.

Overnight. — Food baked o. tabu C152.3.1.

Overpopulation. — Death from world's o. A1335.8; diseases to combat o. P721; flood from o. A1019.3.

Overpowered. — Bird o. by stepping on his shadow D2072.0.4; female o. when caught in tree cleft K1384.

Oversalting food of giant so that he must go outside for water K337.

Oversight of the thievish tailor X221.

Overtaking. — Only one person o. hero Z313.1.

Overthrown. — "He who throws himself against wave is o." J21.52.9; walls o. by magic D2093; work of day magically o. at night *D2192.

Overuse. — Magic object loses power by o. D877.

Overwary. — Game animals magically made o. D2085.

Overweening ambition punished *L420ff.; conceit punished Q330ff.; pride forbidden *C770ff.

Overworked. — Virgin pardons o. monk for neglecting prayers V276.2.

Overzealous. — Emperor rebukes o. servant J554.

Owl advises old man of gods' visit B569.1; advises where to plant crops B569.2; is baker's daughter punished for stinginess to Jesus A1958.0.1; as bird of ill-omen B147.2.2.4; birds' king B242.1.8; ends elephant and ape's dispute J461.8; (ghost of nun) in wild hunt E501.4.5; invites cricket to share his nectar K815.5; likes own children best T681; made bird king over peacock J515; proud of son's feet T681.1; reveals deity's secret: power of speech removed A2239.3.1; saves man from cliff B521.5; saves man from drowning B527.3; as suitor B623.2; thinks hoot's echoes praise J953.16; warns other birds from limed net B521.3.5. — When one learns age of o. he kills it K1985; why o. avoids daylight A2491.2; why o. is blind by day A2233.3, A2332.6.6; color of o. A2411.2.4.2; creation of o. A1958; devil as o. G303.3.3.3.6; disenchantment as o. hoots D791.1.8; enmity between o. (and crow) A2494.13.1, (and mouse) A2494.13.4; fools attack o. J1736.2; friendship of o. (and bat) A2493.2, (and prairie-dog) A2493.1; helpful o. B461.2; lawsuit between o. and kite B270.1; lawsuit between o. and mouse B270.2; lazy o. punished Q5.2; man transformed to o. D153.2; why o. lives where he does A2229.3, A2433.4.1; priest throws chalice at o. J1261.2.7; prophetic o. B143.0.3; reincarnation as o. E613.2; revenant as o. E423.3.5; truth-telling o. B131.0.1; wedding of o. B282.4; weeping man turned to o.: still bewails A2261.5; where o. got his eyes A2332.1.5; why o. hoots at night A2427.3; why o. shakes head A2474.3; wise o. B122.0.3; witch as o. G211.4.4.

Owl's food A2435.4.9; hoot misunderstood by lost simpleton J1811.1; hooting bad omen D1812.5.1.27.1; wings borrowed from rat (or other animal) A2241.2. — Crow accepts o. hospitality, then kills him K2026; origin of o. cries A2426.2.17.

Owls and crows dispute over day, night vision B299.2.1. — Crow learns secret of o., defeats them K2042; enmity of o. and fowls A2494.13.4.1; god of o. A433.2.1; vampire with eyes of o. E251.4.3; war between crows and o. B263.3.

Own. — Adopted child deserted when o. child born T674; falling in love with one's o. reflection T11.5.1; king in disguise as one of o. men K1812.19; one's o. kind preferred to strangers J416; person eats o. flesh G51.

Owner assists thief J1392; disguised as monk enters own captured castle K2357.0.2; of magic object chosen king P11.3; resolves to sell swearing ram B211.1.1.1.1. — Lost object returns to his o. N211; magic birds die when o. is killed B192.0.1; magic harp plays only for o. D1651.7.1; magic object acquired by gaining love of o. D856; magic ring permits o. to learn person's secret thoughts D1316.4; means of hoodwinking the guardian or

o. *K330ff.; object stops or dies when o. dies E766; ring to be cut in two: real o. laments J1171.11; stolen property sold to its o. K258; thief accuses o. of having stolen property K401.5; trickster reports treasure's o. dead: gets it K482.2; well rises only for sheep's rightful o. H251.3.9.2; witch punishes o. by killing animals G265.4.0.1.

Owner's. — Foolish thief asks o. help J2136.5.6; magic object comes at o. call D1649.2.

Ownership of magic objects D800—D899. — Divided o. of cow J1905.3; imagined o. derived from dream J1551.7; name on article as o. token H88; skillful companions create woman: whose is the o. *H621.

Ox bought, buyer also claims wood load J1511.17; curses man M411.19.2; demon F401.3.2, (as magician) B191.2, (transformed to pig) D412.2.2, (transformed to tiger) D412.2.3; and donkey not to plow together C886; with gold and silver in horns B101.8.1; -hide (carried by strong man) F631.5, (saves persons) K515.3; with golden horns B15.3.2.3; head divided according to scripture J1242.1; horns' growth F983.4; to jackal, "dogs are chasing you" K1725.1; lent fairies must not be worked after sunset F391.1.1; likes loving strokes of man: flea fears them U142; with magic wisdom B121.5; as mayor J1882.2; rib as fairy gift F343.16; as sacrifice V12.4.4; transformed to another animal D412.2ff. — Ass who has worked with o. thinks himself his equal J952.4; at the blessing of the grave the parson's o. breaks loose X421; boy lives on o. F562.1; bringing home ten instead of one o. K1741.2.1; complaint about stolen o. J1213.1; cry of giant o. impregnates all fish B741.1; deceptive bargain: o. for five pennies K182; deceptive land purchase: o.-hide measure K185.1; devil as an o. G303.3.3.1.4; why o. is draft animal A2252.2, A2513.5; dragon eats o. each meal B11.6.7; enmity of o. and antelope A2494.12.3; eating o. forbidden C221.1.1.1; exchanging wife with o. J2081.3; in preparation for slaughter feet of o. are cut off the evening before J2168; fool kills himself in despair because o. has been killed J2518.2; four-horned o. B15.3.1.3.1; frog tries in vain to be as big as o. J955.1; giant o. B871.1.1.1, (ancestor of all animals) A1791; giant o.-rib B871.1.1.1.1; gold horn of three-horned o. H1151.7.1; great o. X1237; guests call each other o., ass: given appropriate food J1563.4; why o. has no hair on his lips A2342.2; helpful o. B411.2, (wild) B443.7; how o. got horns A2326.1.4; killing o. as task H1161.2.1; lakes from digging of primeval o. A920.1.2; land grant: as far as o. can be heard K185.14; magic o. B184.2.4; man kills o. with flat of hand F628.1.2; man transformed to o. D133.3; monkey transformed to o. D411.5.4; monster o. killed B16.1.5.1; old o. yoked with young one J441.1; one-horned o. B15.3.0.2; oracular o. B154.1; origin of o.-goad A1446.3; origin of race colors from eating of o. A1614.4.1.1; parson rides o. into church X414; race of o. and horse: o. must labor A2252.2; reincarnation as o. E611.2.2; runaway o. leads to Adam and Eve's burial place N774.3.1; speaking o. B211.1.5.1; strong man carries o. F631.4; strong man lifts o. F624.1; three-horned o. B15.3.1.3; thief punishes the escaped o. J1861; treacherous o.-herd K2255.2; why o. is draft animal A2515.1; why o. serves man A2513.5.

Ox's leg as person F988.1; tail in another's mouth K404.2. — Cause of o. walk A2441.1.8; curiosity satisfied: riding the o. horns J2375; escape by reversing o. shoes K534.1; why flies fly around o. eye A2479.9.

Oxen bear dead usurer to gallows to be buried N277; decide not to kill butchers, since inexpert killers might replace them J215.2; protect child B535.0.10; stoop for king H171.4.1. — Devil drives several teams of o. G303.7.5; devil pulls up tree to goad his o. G303.9.2.1; eating three hundred fat o. (task) H1141.2; fool cuts off tails of o. so that they will look like fine steeds J1919.4; getting one hundred o. H1154.2.1; giant guards huge hornless o. in otherworld K1784.2; magic object furnishes o. D1477; nightingale hears boy call o.: learns her song A2272.1.1; nisser have o. F482.4.2; origin of custom of yoking o. A1441.2; saint carried by wild o. B557.2; wild o. plow for man B292.4.1; warriors hidden on o. driven into enemy's camp K2357.15; why not milk idle o.? J1905.4.

Oyster. — Dividing discovered o. K452.1; why o. lives in salt water A2433.6.2.

Oysters. — More small o. to hundred J2213.8.

"P. C." in clouds X459.1.1.

Pacific Ocean's goddess mother A109.2.

Pacified, see **Peaceable.**

Packhorse becomes palfrey D412.4.1.

Package. — Night (darkness) in p. A1174.1.

Packet. — Magic p. D1283.

Pact. — Flying Dutchman sails because of p. with devil E511.1.2; Virgin frees man from p. with devil V264.1.

Pads. — Why rabbits have soft p. on feet A2375.2.4.

Paddle. — Magic p. D1124.1; marvelous p. F841.2.7.

Paddles broken in enemies' boat K636.1.

Paddy as life token E761.7.13. — Exorbitant price for lending p. K255.2; man becomes p.-bird D169.2; man becomes p. sheaf D218.1.

Paddies. — Rice p. controlled by toad D2149.5.

Pagan gods become devils G303.1.3.4; loses dispute with Christian V352.1; otherworld F160.0.3; punished for conversion to Christianity Q232.1. — Punishment for denying p. gods Q225.2; saint's kindness converts p. priest L350.2.

Pagans flee clerics P426.0.1.

Page P50.3; dreams of being king J955.2.1; hides under woman's bed K2112.2.2. — Appointment to p. as reward Q113.2; lovers' meeting: hero as p. in service of heroine T31.

Paid, see **Paying.**

Pail. — Milk stays in overturned p. D2171.8; proud milkmaid tosses her head and spills p. of milk J2061.2.

Pain because men too happy A1346.2.3; preferred to poverty J229.14;

stopped by prayer D1766.1.4; of souls in hell ebbs and flows Q562. — Animal grateful for relief from p. B380ff.; bird indifferent to p. (cumulative tale) Z49.3; magic girdle protects from p. D1389.16; magic relieves p. D1514; man beheads rescuer for leaving him so long in p. W154.17; pulling out the eye so that the p. will cease J2412.2; reward for enduring p. Q84; saint transfers sick man's p. to himself D1500.3.1.1.

Pains of childbirth magically eased D2161.1.3; as punishment Q553.3.6; repeated in person of the man T583.1.1. — Girl promises unborn child to devil if he will suffer p. S223.1; origin of p. A1351.1.

Paine's. — Ghost flits between Thomas P, graves E419.9.

Painless. — Birth of holy person p. T584.0.3.

Paint. — Dead rubbed with red p. V68.5; husband threatens to scrape p. off wife's cheeks Q331.2.1.3; keeping p. on bride's feet J2489.11; man in the moon from p. A751.5.

Painted jackal an outcast J951.4.1. — Doves see p. cups of water and dash into them J1792.1; life story p. on wall H11.1.2; weasel p. to deceive mice J951.4.

Painter can paint from description of a dream F674. — Devil pulls p. from chair P482.1; great p. freed by Moors Q88.1; house-p. P457; image of Virgin saves p. from falling D1639.2.

Painters. — Who are best p.? Women H659.16.

Painting on the haycock K1013.2; the house red (house set on fire) K1412; with a red hot iron K1013.3; on wife's stomach as chastity index H439.1.1. — Appearance of animal from p. A2217ff.; contest in lifelike p. H504.1; creator p. clothes on clay models of men A1453.6; disguise by p. (body) K1821.2, (so as to escape) K521.3; girl p. face because pregnant T579.8.2; lie: realistic p. X1788; thief p. horse different colors K419.5.

Paintings. — Erotic p. reform continent husband T315.2.2.1.

Pair, see also **Couple, Twin(s);** of culture heroes A515. — Capturing p. of every wild animal H1154.9; first human p. from drops of wine A1211.6; primeval human p. A1270ff.

Pairs of animals in ark *A1021.1. — Everything created in p. A610.1.

Pajamas. — Stealing laborer's p. H1151.22.

Palace, see also **Castle;** appears to be floating: actually glass K1889.6; filled with tongues, hands, etc. of sinners Q561.4; of 8760 stones (riddle) H721.4; haunted by Satan G303.15.4.2; in heaven for pious king Q172.4; model brings about recognition of lost brother H16.1; with seven gates F776.3; shakes from man on roof F639.8; turns to gold D475.1.15; underneath tank F725.3.4. — Animal lured into p. by trickster K811.0.1; animals build p. for man B572.1; building p. and city as task H1133.5; building p. of gold H1133.4; child exposed at p. gate S335; constructing p. overnight F675.4; diamond reveals underground p. D1551.7.1; dwarfs live in luxurious underground p. F451.4.1.3; extraordinary p. *F771ff.; fairies' underground p. F222.1; fool thankful that God has built a p. without columns J2565; Good Luck leaves p. night king is to die N113.3;

guarding p. at night H1199.17.1; hawk as sky p. architect J2060.3; hut transformed to p. D479.8; jumping horse over p. H331.1.2.1; magic diamond reveals underground p. D1557.3; magic p. *D1132; mosquitoes with p. in mouth X1286.1.6; mountain-spirits help build p. F460.4.2.1; nut transformed to p. D451.7.1; one hundred doors in p. F165.1.0.1; princess as price for sparing p. T52.7; queen kept in p. of forty doors R41.5.1; serpents' subterranean p. F127.1.1; submarine p. F725.3; sunken p. magically raised D2136.2.2; theft by disguising as p. official K311.10; thieves abduct p. bride K315.3; transformation to lion in order to guard p. D659.4.1; tree branch becomes p. D451.1.0.1; underground p. full of jewels F721.5.1.

Palaces. — Devil as builder of p. G303.9.1.5; gods' p. A151.4.

Palanquin. — Magic p. D1154.3.2; tabu to use p. in temple C93.5.1.

Pale moon as evil omen D1812.5.1.5.2; sun restored by using egg, yellow grass A721.4. — Dwarfs p. F451.2.0.6; why moon is p. A759.3.

Palestine. — Punishment for leaving P. Q232.2.1; world calamity will begin in P. A1007.

Palfrey. — Imagined refusal of p. tests friendship H1558.6; packhorse becomes p. D412.4.1.

Palisade around otherworld F148.3. — Island with rampart of gold and p. of silver F731.3; objects on one side of p. in otherworld garden black, on other white F162.1.2.3.

Palladium D1380.0.1.1.

Palm blooms at Nativity D2145.2.2.1; tree grows on serpent B765.26; trees on moon A751.9.1. — Coat fits in p. of hand F821.2.1; counting p. trees within view of palace H1118.3; drinking p.-drink tabu C272.3; dwarf makes p. wine F451.3.4.9; lake filled with p. wine A920.1.16; like Christ on P. Sunday J1265.1; magic p. tree D950.19; origin of p. tree A2681.12; parents fed, clothed from one p. tree A1420.5; prophecy by reading p. M303; scurf becomes p. tree D457.6; stars on p. of hand royalty sign H71.1.1.; why p. oil is red A2877; why p. is tall A2778.2; why sap comes from top of p. A2791.8.

Palms as reward Q193. — Greasing the judge's p. J2475; origin of p. A2681.5; hairless p. from handling gold J1289.16.

Palm rat pretends deafness, cheats bargain K231.15. — Enmity of dog and p. A2494.4.13; why p. has swollen head A2320.7.

Palmer disguise K1817.2; as helper N846.1; rescues abandoned child R131.13.

Palmetto gives flying power D1531.10.

Palmyra residents (as magicians) D1711.10.5, (have narrow eyes) A1666.2.

Palsy cured by saint V221.1.

Pan *F442. — Mysterious voice announces death of P. F442.1.

Pancake. — Fleeing p. (cumulative tale) Z33.1; hog loses p. in mud: still seeks it A2275.5.1.

Pancakes growing on lime-tree (lie) X1472.1; made of snow D476.1.6.

Pandora not to look into box *C321; sent as temptress F34.

Pangs of childbirth, see **Pains of childbirth.**

Panther devours girl in tree: chain tale Z39.7. — Enmity between p., antelope, and tortoise A2494.12.1; fox and p. contest in beauty J242.3; giant p. B871.2.3; helpful p. B431.4; sweet smell of p. protects him from other beasts B732.

Panthers. — Lies about p. X1213.

Pants. — Stealing p. by pretending to dirty them K344.3.

Pap, see also **Breast.** — Severed p. regrows when woman bears child E788.

Paps. — Saint's two p.: one milk, one honey T611.5.1.

Paper in hand which none but king can remove D1654.11. — As many stars in the heavens as points on p. H702.3; boy with hat of butter, clothes of p. X1854; fairy gifts turn to p. when shown F348.9.1; spirit tears p. off rooms F473.6.1.

Papers. — Genie called by writing his name on p. and burning them *D2074.2.4.

Papiha. — Creation of p. A1997.

Parable. — Pleading in court by p. J1163; wisdom (knowledge) taught by p. J80ff.

Paradise, see also **Heaven;** lost because of one sin *A1331. — Animal characteristics from carrying devil into p. A2236.2; artificial p. and hell F705; bird from p. B39.1; blindfolded emperor seeks p. J2326.3; Christian p. A694; crops' extraordinary growth in p. F815.3; dawn the reflection of roses of p. A1179.2.1; earthly p. on mountain F132.1; false p. K1889.3; fig from p. F813.7.2; four rivers of p. *F162.2.1; four rivers rising in p., water world A871.2; hero taken to p. alive D1856.1; how many exits from p.? H682.3; journey to earthly p. *F111; journey to upper-world p. *F11; nymphs of p. F499.2; plain that is earthly p. F756.2; quest for location of p. H1257; quest to p. for anointing oil H1265; serpent as deceiver in p. B176.1.1; stream of p. from roots of world-tree A878.1; student from p. (Paris) J2326; supernatural lapse of time in p. F377.1; tree blossoms as God arrives in p. F971.9.

Paradises, eight A661.2.

Paradoxical quests H1378; tasks H1050—H1089.

Parakeet. — Helpful p. B469.9.1.

Parakeets. — Land of p. B222.3.

Paralysis for breaking tabu C941.5; from spirit's blow E265.1.1. — Death from p. for breaking tabu C929.2.1; magic p. D1419.2; *D2072ff., (of foe) D2091.9, (as punishment) Q551.7, (as punishment remitted) *Q573.

Paralyzed. — All body p. except tongue saying "Ave" V254.3.1; man fleeing saint p. Q583.3.

Paramour, see also **Lover;** beats husband K1514.4.1; bites off mistress's nose S172.1; carried off in chest, accused of being robber K675.1; hidden in chest frightens off robbers K335.1.6.1; quarreling with mistress about escape caught by her husband J581.2; leaves token with girl to give their son *T645; successfully hidden from husband K1521; threatens to kill hiding husband K1514.4.1. — Adulteress and p. (fettered) Q434.1, (plot against her stepson) S31.1; animal p. B610ff.; death is wife's p. J2349.2; fairy offers gifts to man to be her p. F302.3.2; hidden p. buys freedom from discoverer *K443.1; husband afraid of cornered p. J2626.1; husband frightened by p. in hog pen K1542; husband outwits adulteress and p. *K1550ff.; husband substitutes leaky vessel so that his wife and p. are drowned Q466.1; king may have any woman for p. P19.2; man returning home thinks newborn son sleeping with his wife is p.: restrains himself J21.2; magician's mistress carries p. in her body *F1034.2; mother and p. plan son's death S12.1.1; prospective p. imposes tests H939.2; taking money from wife's p. J229.11; tasks assigned by wife and p. H916.3; terrorizing the p. K1213; theft by wife's p. K365.3; thief steals from wife's p. K341.14; treacherous wife plots with p. K2213.3; trickster outwits adulteress and p. K1570ff.; unknown (clandestine) p. *T475; wife's p. tied to horse's tail and conducted through streets Q473.2.1; woman substitutes figures of p., self in bed: husband attacks them K525.1.1.

Paramours. — Vengeful p. send syphilitic man to substitute in woman's bed K1317.3.

Parapet. — Breaking egg on castle p. H1149.6.

Parasol goddess A499.7.

Parchment. — Devil shows priest long p. roll of sins of congregation G303.24.1.1; identification by fitting together p. pieces H102.1.

Pardon given if hero produces lady about whom he has boasted M55; in return for confession J1198. — Confession brings p. V21; delay in p. allows deserved execution N394; jester wins p. from prince J1181.3.

Pardons. — Seller of p. robbed by man whom he has pardoned beforehand K1684.

Pardoner's tale K1685.

Pardoning of criminal comes too late P515. — King p. person addressing courtier as king P15.1.2; ruler p. his enemies W11.5.1.

Parent rescues child R153; seeks relief from abandoned child H154; will die on same day as daughter E765.4.3.1. — Animal nurses fight real p. for children B535.2; child seeks unknown p. H1381.2.2; curse by p. M411.1; deer foster p. resuscitated E138.1; helpful animal reincarnation of p. *B313.1; like p., like child U121; task assigned by jealous p. H913; unnatural children eat p. G71.

Parent's heart is hardest H637.1. — Fairy p. gift D630.3.

Parents affiance children without their knovledge T69.2; become servants to secure wedding funds T132.2; and children *P230ff.; exchange children K1921; expose son to tiger H105.5.4; of the gods A111; go to hell instead of sons P241; will humble themselves before their son M312.2; killed by abandoned children S366; learn to wean children A1566; meet daughter they tried to drown N732.3; pray to have a child T548.1. — Abandoned child joins p. in game: recognition follows H151.9; bride's p. help suitor H335.0.1.2; children punished for offenses of p. Q402;

children rescue p. R154; cruel p. *S10ff.; daughter unwittingly turns p. out N367; daughters flogged by p. P237; dead child's friendly return to p. E324; eating p. at their deaths G23; fate of p. revealed in dream J157.2; foster p. P270; ghost of unknown child passes over p. H175.5; kind foster p. chosen rather than cruel p. J391; kindness to orphans repaid by dead p. Q47; land where p. marry children as babies X1503.1; marriage against will of p. T131.1.3; married man not to eat in country of his p. C215; noodles push p. over a rock as a favor to them J2119.3; offspring of first p. A1277; origin of first p. A1271; punishment for murder of p. Q211.12; prophecy: death at hands of p. M343.5; quest for unknown p. H1381.1; recognition when p. come to son (priest, pope) to be confessed H151.3; son returning home after long absence unwittingly killed by p. N321; swearing by one's p. M119.8.1; unnatural p. eat children G72.

Parentage, see also **Paternity;** of culture hero A512. — Brothers deem p. unworthy, pose as princes K1952.3; repartee concerning p. of children J1270ff.

Pari. — Love between P. and mortal T93.5.

Parings. — Devil's chair in hell made from thrown-away nail p. G303.25.5.

Paris exposed M371; judges beauty contest H1596.1; returns to father's court N731.1. — Talkativeness of P. fishwives X253.1.

Parish. — Marriage forbidden outside p. X751; priest gives up p. and loses his fickle mistress J705.1.

Parishioner steals alms J1262.5.

Park. — Ghost haunts p. E279.4.

Parka. — Daughter born with p. T552.8.

Parliament of animals B230ff.; of devils G303.25.19; of giants F531.6.8.5.2; of women F565.3.

Parody of church ceremony at witch's sabbath G243.2; sermon *K1961.1.2.1. — Woman warns lover of husband by p. incantation K1546.

Parricide S22; because of love rivalry T92.9.1; prophecy M343, (slaughter or exposure of child to prevent fulfillment of) M371.2, M375.2, (unwittingly fulfilled) N323; punished Q211.1. — Magic spring detects p. H251.3.9.1; wild huntsman wanders because of p. *E501.3.3.

Parrot advises queen playing chess B565; and cat cheat each other at dinner J1565.3; as messenger B291.1.6; prefers cold freedom to luxury in palace L451.4; recovers jewel from sea B548.6; scouts enemy camp B122.8; sold as speaking foreign language K137.2; and sparrow argue right to inherit property left by man B271.1; suggests task H919.3; transacts business of trader B294.5; transformed to person D357; unable to tell husband details as to wife's infidelity J1154.1; warns of sex test H1578.1.6. — Clever p. J1118.1; color of p. A2411.2.6.11; creation of p. A1994; enmity of p. and starling A2494.13.11.3; faithful p. killed by mistake B331.3; friendship between p. (and hare) A2493.13, (and maina) A2493.26; helpful p. B469.9; hungry p. set to guard figs J215.1.1; king

transformed to p. frees captured parrots R115; why p. lives in tree
A2433.4.4; man transformed to p. D157; marriage to p. B602.7; ogre with
life in p. speaks from inside parrot E715.1.3.2; prophesying p. B122.0.4;
raja enters body of dead p. K1175; reincarnation as p. E613.12; why p.
says A2426.2.11; separable soul in p. E715.1.3; seventy tales of a p.
prevent wife's adultery K1591; speaking p. B211.3.4; why tail of West
African grey p. is red A2378.8.2; thief disguised as p. K311.6.3; warning
p. B143.1.3; why p. helps man A2493.36; wife demands p. who has accused her B335.4; witch's soul in p. G251.1.1; world is transformed mud
p. A822.1.

Parrot's cry frightens off robber K1796.—Why p. beak is black A2343.2.1.

Parrots carry couple across the sea B551.2.1; sham death, are released
K522.4; speak of beautiful girl H1214.1. — Image of p. vivified D445.2;
king of p. B242.2.8; land of p. B222.4; seven girls as seven p. D658.3.3;
why p. fly high A2442.1.2.

Parsley. — Dog P. in the soup J2462.1; effects of wild hunt remedied by
asking the huntsmen for p. E501.19.3.

Parson P426.1; deceived into marrying his intended bride to her real lover
K1371.1.1; and sexton at mass X441; tricked into giving up room: afraid
of snake K2335. — Card-playing p. N5; deaf p. praises youth's foolish
answers X111.12; ghost as p. E425.2.3; lost p. asks devil's help, dies
C12.5.4; sham p. K1961.1ff.

Parson's share and sexton's J1269.1.

Parsons. — Jokes on p. *X410ff.

Part. — Animal gives p. of body as talisman for summoning its aid *B501;
birth from unusual p. of person's body T541; coming with p. of body
clothed (neither naked nor clad) H1054.3; effects of wild hunt remedied
by eating p. of flesh thrown down by it E501.19.5; man created from p. of
body A1263; soul kept in special p. of body E714.

Parts of human body furnish treasure D1454; of slain animals as token of
slaying H105. — Animals from different p. of body of slain giant
A1716.1; cannibals cut off p. of children's bodies G86; eating certain p.
of animals forbidden C221.3; gods born from various p. of creator's body
A112.3; quest for marvelous p. of animals H1332; treasure-producing p.
of animals *B110ff.

Partaking in booty of wild hunt E501.19.4. — Not p. of one forbidden
object C620ff.; tabu: p. of certain feast C286.

Partial disenchantment D702ff.; overcoming of fairy's curse F316.1; transformation D682ff. — Buyer refuses more than p. payment K233.7.

Participants in wild hunt E501.2ff.

Particular. — Dwarfs p. as to foods F451.3.7; magic object received
through p. intermediaries *D827; origin of p. stars A770ff.

Partner misappropriates common goods K364. — Hero made business p. of
rich man Q111.1; sham sickness so p. must work K495; treacherous p.
K2296.

Partner's — Smoke prevents p. eating K336.2.

Partners. — Jackal and tiger as business p. A2493.11.3; rabbit and elephant p. as traders B294.6.

Partnership valid after forty years' absence P319.4. — Deceptive p. between man and ogre K170.1; sham physician and the devil in p. K1955.6.

Partridge distracts girls, fox eats their curds K341.26; entices woman from food, jackal eats it K341.5.2; subsists on moonbeams B768.1; too clever for jackal J423.1. — Color of p. *A2411.2.6.8; why p. has pretty feet *A2375.2.1; friendship between p., monkey and elephant A2493.14.5; friendship between jackal and p. A2493.11.4; reincarnation as p. E613.8.1; revenant as p. E423.3.3; striking at p. on another's head J1833.1.2; treacherous p. K2295.1; how p. got voice *A2421.4; witch as p. G211.4.2.

Partridge's — Crow tries to imitate p. walk J512.6.

Partridges. — Kite tries to carry off so many p. that he drops them all J514.1.

Parturition, see also **Childbirth,** *T584. — Unusual p. of animal B754.7.

Pass. — Fairy unable to p. crossroads F383.1; ghosts cannot p. crossroads E434.4; mountain p. magically closes D1552.3; mountain p. to otherworld F151.2; wild huntsman's dogs cannot p. over grave E501.15.6.4.

Passage of time U260ff. — Dwarfs live in underground p. F451.4.1.4; fairies excavate p. F271.2; leaves of tree open and close to give saint p. F979.2; thief enters treasury through secret p. K315; underground p. magically opens D1555; underground p. to paramour's house K1523.

Passages. — Underground p. F721.1.

Passenger. — Ungrateful river p. kills carrier from within K952.1.

Passengers within winged serpent as boat F911.3.2. — Man sacrifices self to save other p. W28.3.

Passer-by — Woman mistakes p. for lover K1317.7.

Passeriform. — Creation of p. A1910ff.; man transformed to p. D151ff.

Passing through hound-guarded door H1423.1; under magic rod as chastity ordeal H412.1. — Physician p. graveyard hides eyes P424.1.

Passion. — Fool as actor in P. Play J2041.1, J2495.3; king overcomes p. for beautiful captives P12.9; moon's p. A753.3.4; queen's illicit p. for diseased man T481.2; sun's p. A738.2.2.

Passions. — Sword vanquishes five evil p. D1389.14.

Passionate. — Devil has p. look in eyes G303.4.1.2.5.

Passover V75.1. — Magic power at P. D1719.9.2; miracles at P. F900.1.2; origin of P. A1541.5.

Password. — Recognition by p. H18.

Past. — Bringing p. time to present H1026.2; consolation by thinking of the p. J866; in planning future, profit by p. J752; present preferred to p. J310ff.; rue not a thing that is p. J21.12; wisdom from continual reminder of foolishness in the p. J167.

Paste turns to gold D475.1.11.

Pastry. — Magic p. D1031ff.; woman cannot find p. which is sticking to her posterior J2025.2.

Pastries. — Thief distracts owner, steals p. K341.15.

Pasturing black sheep until they become white Q521.4; cow which runs all day H1112.2; unusual p. as task H1199.12.

Patches on fairies' coats F236.5.1. — Brown p. on soil where marvelous cow lay A989.1.

Patent. — Animal granted p. of nobility A2546; dog loses his p. right and seeks it: why dogs look at one another under the tail A2275.5.5; place to live given as p. right to dog A2433.1.3.

Paternal aunt as aid P294.1.

Paternity, see also **Parentage.** — Brother duped into killing each other over p. slander K1092; dying mother tells children p. J1279.1; man doubts children's p.: kills them S11.3.1; test of p. H486ff.

Paternoster, see also **Prayer.** — Cheaters examined apart: first made to repeat P. J1141.3; devil unable to take one who has read the P. G303.16.2.1; levity regarding P. J1262.4.1; plowman to get horse for saying P. H1554.3; saint's P. outweighs ox V52.13.

Path, see also **Way;** to heaven *F57; to lower world F95; between monsters G333; to sun on sun's rays (eyelashes) F154; to world of dead F95.0.1. — Father makes evil greater by closing p. H583.2.1; Milky Way as p. (of a bird of passage) A778.7, (of souls) *A778.2.1; remove obstacles from p. J753; quest over p. guarded by hags H1236.3; perilous p. (to hell) *F95.3, (to otherworld) *F151.1, (for soul to world of dead) E750.2, (traversed on quest) H1236; straight p. not always shortest J2119.2.

Paths open in sea for Israel's tribes F931.9.3.

Pathelin (lawyer's mad client) *K1655.

Patience *W26; rewarded Q64. — Brotherly love and p. both dead J1633; children teach p. J124; lack of p. W196; test of p. *H1553; why weavers have p. P445.2.

Patient. — Doctor gives advice after p. dies J756.1; man p. in misfortune finally elected ruler N251.1; quieting p. by killing J2489.5.

Patients frightened from hospital by harshness K1955.1.2. — Repartee concerning doctors and p. J1430ff.

Patriarchs because of long life made the inventions A1440.3.

Patrick (Saint) curses Welsh F251.13; judges Irish souls E751.3. — Angel speaks to P. from bush A182.3.0.1.1; people to live "till coming of P." M300.1, M363.1.2; poor man's hospitality to P. rewarded Q45.1.2; vision of flames as faith brought by P. V515.1.3.

Patrick's — Oisin's poor diet in P. house repayed J1511.13.

Patriotism P711.

Patron. — Serpent as p. of wealth B108.1.

Pattern. — Taking a p. (picture) of conduct J2471; task: making a rope of sand (countertask: first showing the p.) H1021.1.1.

Paunch fat removed as stomach cure F959.4.

Pauper, see **Penniless**.

Paved. — Castle p. with gold and gems F771.1.1.1; city p. with precious seeds F761.5; great road p. in short time H1108; pool p. with gold F717.1.

Pavement. — Extraordinary p. F865; feet magically fixed to p. D2171.7; treasure found while digging p. N534.7.

Pavilion as lovers' rendezvous T35.2.

Pavilions produced by magic D2178.3.

Paw. — Cat with missing p. G252.0.1; cat's p. cut off: woman's hand missing D702.1.1; wolf puts flour on his p. to disguise himself K1839.1.

Paws. — Bear riding horse lets p. fall on horse's flanks J2187; dog's claws as grains under p. A2376.2; dupe puts p. into cleft of tree *K1111; indentions on rock from p. of King Arthur's dog A972.5.3; rat and frog tie p. together to cross marsh J681.1.

Pawn. — Wife's foolish p. J2086.

Pawned. — Stolen cow successively p. K408; stolen pot p. with the real owner K405.2.

Pawning. — Thief finally confesses when p. stolen goods N276.

Pay. — Calamity follows failure of king to p. soldiers C831; counting out p. (hole in hat) K275; helper on quest demands p. H1235.1; monk refuses p. V473.

Paying dwarfs makes them cease help to mortals F451.5.10.9. — Buying things in common, each p. full price J2037; custom of p. soldiers A1596.1; dwarfs buying peas and p. more than they are worth F451.5.10.5; dwarfs p. for being ferried across water F451.5.10.6; suitor p. for bride H318; wife p. paramour T232.5.

Payment with the clink of the money J1172.2; precluded by terms of the bargain K220ff.; with "something or other" J2489.10. — Bed-partner to receive p. from first man she meets in the morning T456; crane pulls bone from wolf's throat: wolf refuses p. W154.3; deception in p. of debt K200—K249; imaginary debt and p. J1551; too large a p. J1559.3; literal p. of debt K236; magic object returned in p. for removal of magic horns D895; quest as p. for gambling loss H1219.1; spiritual p. for misfortune J893.

Pea. — Chain tale: bird's p. stuck Z41.6; sack of earth in giant's hand resembles p. F531.2.15; princess on the p. H41.1; removing p. from ear J1115.2.2.

Peas become pearls D475.4.4; strewn on stairs so that person will slip K1071; transformed to stones D451.9.1. — Cannibal crunching human bone says noise is only eating of p. G87; Christ changes stones to p. D452.1.6.1; dwarfs buy p. from mortals and pay more than they are worth F451.5.10.5; dwarfs turn p. into gold pieces F451.3.3.1; fairy leaves when mortal strews p. in his path F381.2; fool thinks p. will burn walkers' feet J2214.1; God's tears become p. A2612.3; hog won't tell where p. are W151.6; literal numskull cuts p. into four parts J2461.1.4; man compelled to live on p. takes comfort when he sees man once rich eating the hulls J883.1; origin of p. A2612.3, A2686.2; riddle about splitting p. H583.4.6; why p. do not soften in boiling A2721.3.1; sorting a large amount of p. in one night H1091; sweeping, winnowing p. as devil's task G303.16.19.3.1; test of sex of girl masking as man: p. spread on floor H1578.1.1.

Peace among the animals J1421; between sheep and wolves K191; bought for husband M236; in heaven is sweetest (riddle) H633.2; more important than truth in marriage T203; reward for good law Q176. — Angel of p. A467.1; avoid enemies' revenge either by making p. and friendship or by killling them all J647.1; bishop struck for breaking the p. J1823.2; druid as p. emissary P427.2; enemies make p. rather than slay each other *J218; forced p. valueless U220ff.; god establishes p. between mortals A185.15; magic branch of p.: warfare ceases when it is shaken D1351.2; making p. tabu C642; mankind from P. and Quiet fructified by Light A1221.2; olive branch symbol of p. Z157; origin of p. ceremonies A1533; other-world land of p. F173.2; precept of the lion to his sons: keep p. with the neighbors J22.3; prophecy: eternal p. in an early death or long troublesome life M365; reign of p. and justice A1101.1.1; seven year's p. Z71.5.3; sham p. discussion to get reinforcements K2369.7; strengthening self during p. J674.2; tabu: coming to Ireland in p. time C755.3; two groups of animals make p. treaty B260.1; vow to ask nobody for p. M165; wisdom from fool: make p. before rather than after the war J156.1.

Peaceable. — Why elephant is p. A2531.3; fools learn to be p. J24; magic object makes person p. D1351f.; why grizzly bear is p. A2531.2; wild huntsman made p. E501.17.6ff.

Peacefulness W43.

Peacemaker killed in feigned quarrel K929.6 — Dolphin and whale scorn crab as p. J411.6.

Peach branch exorcises devil D2176.6. — Conception from eating p. T511.1.6; magic p. *D981.2, (tree) D950.3; man becomes p. D211.6.

Peaches. — Putting p. back on tree H1023.18; thank God they weren't p. J2563.

Peacock admires self in mirror W116.4; as bird of ill-omen B147.2.2.7; birds' king B242.1.7; and crane in beauty contest J242.5; dissatisfied with her voice W128.4; on golden bowl of sun A724.2; on king's steeple as dowry C655.1; preens too long, loses kingship J515; proves to be bad king J242.4; shows rivers way to valley A934.12; spies on adulterous wife K1591.1; pregnant without intercourse B754.6. — Birds envious of p. point out ugly voice, legs W195.1; color of p. A2411.2.6.7; constructing automatic p. H326.1.1; creation of p. A1996; golden p. B102.1.2; horse with p. tail H1331.4.2; how p. got its tail A2378.1.9; jackal tries to pose as p. J953.14; king makes wooden p. machine F675.1; making p. of silk H1021.11; man carried by p. B552.2; man transformed to p. D166.2; person carried by p. B557.12; quest for golden p. H1331.1.3.2; reincarnation as p. E613.11; star from girl and p. mating A760.2; thrush's hospitality to p. rewarded by being given motley coat of feathers A2222.1; tortoise dances with p. J684.3; warning p. B143.1.2; why p. is vain A2527.2; why p. has ugly (feet) A2232.7, A2236.2.2, A2375.2.1, *A2375.2.2, (voice) A2236.2.2, A2423.1.2; wedding of turkey and p. B282.1.

Peacock's feathers ruffled in presence of poison B131.5. — Fire from p. tail burns enemy army K916.1; jay in p. skin unmasked J951.2; origin of p. feathers A2245, A2313.3, A2411.2.6.7.

Peacocks of gold F855.3.1. — Four p. to sit on four pinnacles of palace H1154.7.3; king of p. B242.2.5; land of p. B222.2.

Peanut — Man becomes p. D222.1; reincarnation as p. plant E631.5.2.

Pear. — Enchanted p. tree K1518; great p. X1411.4; magic p. *D981.6, (tree) *D950.5; man transformed to p. tree D215.2; quest for marvelous p. H1333.3.2; silver p. F813.4; transformation by eating p. D551.1.3.

Pears. — Numskulls try to get p. from an oak tree J1944.1; stealing p. from guarded garden H1151.10.1.

Pearl-dropping cow B103.1.2.1; found in fish N529.2; kingdom F707.4. — Centipede plays with p. B109.2; conception from swallowing p. T511.8.6; dragon's p. stolen B11.6.2.3; magic p. draws storm away D1541.2.2; mountain formed of a p. F752.3.1; pavement of p. F865.1; servant takes p. to wife instead of merchant N351.1; transportation by magic p. D1520.29.1.

Pearls from hair as sign of royalty H71.3; from magic tortoise shell D1469.14; shed for tears H31.7.1. — Animals live on p. F989.22.4; cock prefers single corn to peck of p. J1061.1; death respite until king reaps p. K551.21; deer with p. around neck B105.2; fairy's tears p. F239.6; impossible to eat p. J1191.5.1; island of p. F731.6; magic p. cure disease D1500.1.9.2; millstones as p. of the hero's mother K1718.2; origin of p. A2827; peas become p. D475.4.4; quest for unpierced p. H1348.2; recognizing p. by their smell F655.1; refusing p. for worthless stones J2093.3.1; saint refuses p. as alms V462.2.2.1; shooting p. from wife's nose-ring F661.10; spider catches p. B109.1; stealing p. from king H1151.13.5; swans live on p. B768.3; tortoise gives p. B103.1.6.

Peasant *P411; always busy producing food A1655.1; ashamed of being thrown off by ass J411.4; asks to be knighted J955.3.1; betrays fox by pointing K2315; boy masking as prince betrays self by his answers H38.2.2; exchanges place with monk U119.2; girl married to king longs for old food U135.3.1; girl betrays her hiding place to nobleman W136.1; girl outwits prince L151; as helper N854; hero L113.4; leaves honey tree standing J241.2; opens his mouth J2473; preaches about bishop's amour J1211.1; as priest preaches on the troubles of laymen K1961.1.1; rescues abandoned child R131.6. — Clever p. J1115.6; clever p. daughter J1111.4; clever p. girl asked riddles by king H561.1; devil as a p. G303.3.1.10; disguise as p. K1816.9; disguised king punished by p. P15.1f.; dying p. summons bishop who dies D1715.2; king disguised as p. flees battle

K1812.10; king and p. vie in riddling questions and answers H561.6; knight weds p. girl T121.1; mountain-folk steal from p. F460.4.4.5; mountain-men chain captive p. F460.4.4.2; prince substitutes p. girl for father's bride K1911.1.9; son ashamed of p. father who brings him money W165; stupid p. J1705.1; treacherous p. K2258; wife banished for p. origin S412.1; wounded hero restored by p. R169.14.

Peasant's enigmatic conversation with king H585; share is the chicken J1562.2. — Spirits tangle up p. cows F402.1.3; trolls' horses water at p. well F241.1.2.1.

Peasants in city inn order whole portion of mustard J1742.3; fed white bread demand the rye bread to which they are accustomed U135; as foster parents for king's son P270.1; give quest directions H1232.1; persecuted by one-eyed, dog-headed savages B25.1.2; want a living God J2495.4. — Wise men disguised as p. debate J31.1.

Peasants' — Dwarfs emigrate because they dislike p. dancing and loud music F451.9.1.9.

Peasantry. — Origin of p. A1655.

Peau d'âne K1815.

Pebble, see also **Stone;** for each sin J2466.1; put in box for each mass heard V46. — Abandoned children find way back by p. clue R135ff.; magic p. D931.2, (prevents burning) D1382.1, (splits wood) D1564.1; swallowed p. grows into snake B784.1.2.

Pebbles. — Animal attacks by throwing p. B762.1; crow drops p. into the water jug so as to be able to drink J101; quails become p. D423.2.

Peccary. — Man transformed to p. D114.3.1; origin of p. 1871.2; why p. has spots A2412.1.6.

Peck. — Deceptive bargain: p. of grain for each stack K181.

Pecking. — Bird eaten by king escapes by p. on his stomach F915.1; bird p. hole in sky F56.2.

Peddler causes delay in starting, not dog J1475. — Defeated king as p. L410.4; disguise as p. K1817.4.1, (to enter woman's room) K1349.1.3.

Peddler's. — Child born with claws from p. curse T551.9.

Pedestal supports island F736.2. — Otherworld door in p. F156.2.

Pedestrian. — Ghost chases p. E272.4.

Peeling. — Thrifty p. of apple as bride test H381.2.1.

Peeping at sacred font forbidden C51.1.7; Tom C312.1.2, C943.

Peewit. — Voice of p. A2421.7.

Pegasus B41.1; from neck of slain Medusa E783.2.1.

Pegs driven into backs of baboons become tails A2262.2. — Sitting on p. to make anus F529.2.1.

Pegged. — Bonga p. to ground F386.3; ogress p. to boulder G514.5.1.

Pelican as birds' king B242.1.4; kills young and revives them with own blood B751.2. — Rejuvenation by song of p. D1889.3.

Pelt. — Woman draws a p. to her instead of her husband K1281.

Pelts. — Ear tips become p. D457.19.

Pen. — Birds drop quill for man's p. B159.1; creator distributes p. A1440.1; filling locked p. K1427; fish recovers p. from sea B548.2.4; recovering p. from sea (task) H1132.1.4; saint confines self in p. V262.8.1.

Penalty. — Judge reducing p. when accused his son U21.5; origin of p. for murder A1581.1; riddle propounded with p. for failure H541.

Penalties. — Origin of special p. A1581.

Penance magically concluded by confession V27; for sin A1549.4. — Admission to heaven as reward for p. Q172.3; condemned soul saved by p. E754.1.3; devils appear to knight to try to call him from doing p. G303.9.4.5; failure to do p. punished Q223.8; fox fasts as p. B253.3; ghost laid when p. is done E451.2; husband duped into doing p. while rascal enjoys the wife K1514.2; imagined p. for imagined sin J1551.2; literal p.: boy outwits pope J1161.5; origin of p. for sins A2835; otherworld journey as p. F5; priest's p. saves soul from devil K218.6; return from dead to do p. E411.0.2.1; robber gives priest double his p. and then takes his horse J1635; self-righteous hermit must do p. L435.1; true p. effective J557.1.1.

Penances Q520ff. — Priest who gives mild p. succeeds where others fail L361; wife undertakes man's p. for him: also to go to heaven for him? M292.

Peninsula's — origin A956.

Penis, see also **Genitals, Member.** — Dwarf splits wood with p. F451.3.4.10; extraordinary p. F547.3; man threatens to cleave bear's skull with p. K1755.1; nature of animal's p. A2365.2; sham-dead tiger betrayed by live p. K607.3.1; why animal's p. is large A2365.2.1.

Penitent worries over little sins, belittles big U11.1.1.2.

Penitent's manuscript of sins V29.6. — Barrel filled miraculously with p. tears F1051.1.

Penniless, see also **Poor;** bridegroom pretends to wealth K1917; hero L123. — Man robbed and p. entertained by wealthy widow and enriched N225.

Penny from bad man, two from good J1672; baked in the wafer J1582.1. — Anger bargain: may God give you a p. K172.1; blessing not worth a p. J1261.4; buying p-worth of wit J163.1; pretence of taking trip to return p. debt K2054.1.

Pennies. — Deceptive bargain: an ox for five p. K182.

Pension. — Double p. falsely received K441.1.

Pent cuckoo flies over the hedge J1904.2.

Pentecost's origin A1541.6.

People, see also **Human beings, Men, Persons;** created by magic D2178.5; to whom devil appears G303.6.2. — City of extraordinary p. F768; city of petrified p. F768.1; fairies carry p. away to fairyland *F320ff.; trees in which p. live in nests F811.10; ways in which the devil kills p. G303.20ff.; wild huntsman makes p. carry him on their backs *E501.15.3.

Peoples, see also **Nations, Races, Tribes.** — Characteristics of various p.

(in industry and warfare) A1670ff., (in personal appearance) A1660ff.; distribution and differentiation of p.: general A1600ff.; treacherous p. K2299.2.

Pepper eaten instead of cooking it J1813.6; given as ointment for burns K1014; plant from body of slain person A2611.4; as remedy K1014; as sham doctor's remedy K1955.2.1. — Dirt becomes p. D452.4.1; dupe persuaded to put too much p. in food K1045; red p. for the slow ass: man tries it on himself X11; spitting p. into opponent's face K11.7; theft by blinding with p. K333.5; witch killed by putting p. inside skin G229.11.

Peppers. — Horse with p. sent against enemy K2351.6.1.

Peppercorn. — Conception from eating a p. T511.3.1.

Peppercorns. — Armies like seeds and p. J1625.

Perception. — Extraordinary powers of p. F640ff.

Perch. — Color of p. A2218, A2411.4.2; magic birds keep falling off p. D1649.1.2.

Percival must ask meaning of strange sights he sees *C651.

Percute hic (inscription on stone) N535.

Perfect god A102.7.

Perfume, see also **Fragrance.** — Garments emitting p. F821.10; girl lives on p. F647.12; herbs as p. F817.3; magic p. *D1245, (produces immunity from hunger and thirst) D1349.1.2; recognition by p. H44.

Perfumed mountain F759.4.

Peri. — Raja refuses to marry a p. F302.3.0.2.

Peris in sky-world F215.2.

Peril. — Animals grateful for rescue from p. of death B360ff.; sword which will break in only one p. Z314.

Perils of the soul *E750ff. — Magic p. threaten bridal couple *T175.

Perilous bed F846.1; falling gate *F776.2; path (to hell) *F95.3, (to otherworld) *F151.1, (for soul to world of dead) E750.2, (traversed on quest) H1236; river as barrier to otherworld F141.1.1; river in otherworld F162.2.11; seat H31.4; trap bridge *F842.2.1.

Periodic habits of animals A2480ff.; resuscitation *E155; sacrifices to a monster S262; transformation D620ff; weakness D1837.1. — Origin of p. sowing A1441.4.1.

Periodically. — Dead person visits earth p. E585; wild hunt appears p. E501.11.3.

Perjurer cannot rest in grave E411.3; dismembered by magic lion H251.1.1; stricken dead Q558.2. — Magic paralyzes p. D1419.2.1.

Perjurers. — Devil and his servants live where p. dwell G303.8.6.

Perjury punished *Q263. — Tree tests p. H251.3.1.

Permanent. — Command would become p. J1521.3; disenchantment made p. D793.

Permission to pull lion suitor's teeth J642.1. — Chaste woman refers lover to her husband for p. K1231; demon given p. to be on earth four times a year A106.2.1.2; discovery of abbot's incontinence brings p. to monks to do likewise K1274; entering castle without p. angers king P14.11; execution escaped by use of special p. granted the condemned *J1181; fraudulent p. sold K157; tabu: entering assembly without p. C864.1; tabu: stranger to play with someone without asking p. C892.

Perpetual summer in otherworld F161.1. — Tree in p. fruit F162.3.3.

Persecuted queen meanly clothed and set where all are commanded to spit on her Q471.1; wife *S410ff. — Brother faithful to p. sister P253.2.1; dead mother returns to aid p. children *E323.2; quest for p. woman H1381.3.6.

Persecution by bad luck N250.2; of wife punished Q421.0.8.

Persecutions. — Cruel p. *S400—S499.

Perseus fights dragon B11.10; seeks Gorgon's head H1332.3.

Perseverance rewarded Q81.

Person, see also **Human being, Man;** comes to life E1; changes size at will D631.1; disenchanted D700ff.; mistaken for object J1763; mistaken for something else J1760ff.; swallowed without killing F911; thought to be animal J1765; transformed to object D200—D299. — Animal as guard of p. B576.1; animal thought to be p. J1762ff.; animal transformed to p. D300ff.; certain p. to find treasure N543; deity takes form of particular p. K1811.4; escape by substituting another p. in place of the intended victim *K527; extraordinary nature phenomena at birth of holy p. F960.1; fairy in form of p. F234.2; fairies visible to one p. alone F235.3; invisibility conferred on a p. D1983; living p. becomes God A104.1; lucky p. N203; magic cure by certain p. D2161.5; magic object rescues p. *D1390ff.; man in moon is p. thrown or sent there as punishment A751.1; marriage to p. in animal form *B640ff.; moon as a p. A753; not to look at certain p. or thing C310ff.; object transformed to p. D430ff.; prophecy: death by certain p. M341.2.9; remarkable p. F500—F599; spirit leads p. astray F402.1.1; swallowed p. alive in animal X1723.1; tabu imposed by p. C999.1.1; transformed p. sleeps before girl's door, at foot of bed, in bed K1361.1; vulnerability only by one p. Z313; witch rides on p. G241.2; wound healed only by p. who gave it, D2161.4.10.2.

Persons, see also **Men, People;** with extraordinary powers F600—F699; magically stick together D2171.5. — Clever p. *J1100—J1129; curses on p. M430ff.; magic objects effect changes in p. D1300—D1379; sacred p. *V200—V299; wild hunt harmful to certain p. E501.18.1.

Personal appearance of wild huntsman E501.7ff.; offenses against gods punished *Q221. — Foolish disregard of p. danger J2130ff.; unfavorable traits of character: p. W110ff.; vows concerning p. appearance M120ff.

Personification of (death) Z111, (luck and fate) N110, (time) Z122, (truth) Z121, (wind) Z115; prophesies M301.8.

Personifications Z110. — Giants as p. F531.6.1.5.

Perspiration, see also **Sweat,** in winter from emotion F1041.12. — Boy drinks p. F561.7; transformation by eating rice mixed with p. D551.6.2.

Perspire. — Devils cause monk to p. and stay away from church service V5.3.

37*

Persuaded. — Ogre p. to go into hole and buried alive G512.4; woman p. by trick *K1350ff.

Persuading persons to intercourse A1352.2. — Wife only one p. husband P216.

Persuasive person or thing not to be heeded *C810ff.

Perversions, sexual T460ff.

Pessimist. — Optimist becomes p. when money stolen U68.

Pests. — Ridding country of p. Q512.3; why white ants are p. A2522.3.

Pestilence, see also **Plague;** F493ff.; brought to man A1337.0.1.1;magically sent D2094. — Fast to prevent p. V73.1; goddess of p. A478.1; locality sanctified against p. *D2162.3; magic p. D2064.0.3; priest keeps in container relic which when kissed renders people immune from p. J762.1; spirit of p. F493; saint's shrine suppresses p. V221.0.1.3; wild hunt as omen of p. E501.20.1.2.

Pestle to frighten away guests J1563.5.1. — Fainting from noise of wooden p. and mortar F647.8; fencer's opponent picks up p. J676; magic p. D1254.3, (draws storm away) D1541.2; obedient woman's p. magically suspended J2411.9; origin of p. A1446.5.2; sky struck by p. A625.2.2.

Pet. — King's wives jealous of p. animal T257.1.1; man transformed to animal kept as p. by heroine T33; snake wants to act like p. J512.14; transformation to child or p. to be adopted *D646.2; visible sun is p. of real sun A722.12.

Pets. — Lions as king's p. P14.22.

Petals. — Flower sheds p. when husband thinks of wife H1556.4.6.

Peter (Saint) acts as God for a day: tires of bargain L423; addressed in throwing contest K18.1.2; called fool for enduring poverty J1263.4.2; creates grass as medicine for snake-bite A2623; drives devil out of a man G303.16.11.1; lets key of heaven fall: origin of "Heaven Key" (primrose) A2622; as porter of heaven A661.0.1.2; receives the blows twice K1132; reminded of his denial of Christ admits soldiers to heaven J1616; rules air, rain A287.2. — Angel helps P. escape prison V232.8.

Peter's contest with Simon Magus V351.3.1; fingerprints on fish A2217.3.1; mother dropped from heaven because of hard-heartedness Q291.1; wife meets him with a broomhandle T251.3. — Heaven entered by trick: sitting on P. chair K2371.1.4.

Peter Ox J1882.2.

Petition. — One-word p. J1618.

Petrification as curse M458; by glance D581; on hearing woman's voice D529.1; by magic *D231; by magic formula D573.2; of suitors D581.1.

Petrified. — Approachers p. by magic bird B172.1; city of p. people F768.1; gravity p. in p. forest X1741.3; passersby p. by river F715.7; wood p. by lake F934.3.

Petulance W127.

Pewter. — Money transformed to p. D475.2.4.

Phaëton drives sun's chariot A724.1.1.

Phalanx P552.3.

Phantom army attacked K1883.1; hosts E500ff.; house disappears at dawn F771.6; sailors E510ff. — Sight of p. ship a bad omen D1812.5.1.10.

Phantoms F585ff.

Pharaoh as magician D1711.7.1.

Pharaoh's drowned army origin of (animals) A1715.1, (birds) A1901, A1944.1, (mermaids) B81.1.

Phases. — Causes of moon's p. A755.

Pheasant. — Color of p. A2411.2.6.9; friendship between ant and p. A2493.29; helpful p. B469.10. — Why cheeks of p. are red A2330.6.

Phenomenon. — Enigmatic p. explained H614.

Phenomena at appearance of wild hunt E501.13ff.; at disappearance of wild hunt E501.16ff. — Natural p. accompanying the devil's appearance G303.6.3ff.; natural p. associated with gods A139.11; physical p. misunderstood J1810ff.

Philandering god A188.1; man's wife has affair K1510.2.

Philanthropist will give his spurs if someone will drive his horse for him W11.1.

Philemon and Baucis entertain Zeus Q1.1.

Philistines. — Riddle about P. H831.

Philosopher, see also **Sage;** P485; advises on life J152.3ff.; brings king to sense of duty by feigned conversation of birds J816.1; chooses poverty with freedom J211.1; conquers evil fate M137; forgets Charon's fee E489.3; instructs king on domestic harmony J816.1.1; keeps silent J1074.1.1; laughs at world's sins, vanities U15.1; loses all wealth, thankful to be out of business J2569; spits in king's beard J1566.1; teaches son to beg from stone statue H1553.1; tells king to seek harmony at home J1289.9. — Cynical p. lives in tub J152.1; holy man tells p. wisdom before learning J1217.2; needy p. asks king for money J1289.4; wealthy girl marries penniless p. T121.5.

Philosopher's sham threat to break head K1771.5; stone from cocoanut D451.3.2. — Drunk p. foolish wager J1161.9.

Philosophical watchman J2377.

Philosophy. — Suitor task: to study p. H335.0.2.1.

Philosophies. — Aristotle drinks both red and white wine to show that all p. are good J462.2.

Philtre. — Magic love-p. D1355.2; mutual love through accidental drinking of love p. *T21.

Phoenix B32; creator's companion A36.

Phorcides F512.1.2, K333.2.

Phrase. — Using only one p. C495, J2516.3.3.

Phylactery. — Magic p. D1282.1.2.

Physical characteristics of culture hero (demigod) A526; characteristics of giant ogres G120ff.; circumstances of devil's disappearance G303.17.2; features of underworld F80.1; phenomena misunderstood J1810ff.; requirements for suitors H312. — Devil's p. characteristics G303.4ff.; extraordinary p. reactions of persons F1041ff.; fanciful p. qualities of animal B720—B749; humor of p. disability X100—X199; magic cure of p. defect *D2161.3; magic object works p. change D1330ff.; recognition by p. attributes H50ff.; remarkable p. organs F540ff.

Physician, see also **Doctor;** *P424; cures by imitation F957; dupes patient, entertains mistress K1516.1.1; of the gods A144; removes animal from patient's stomach B784.2.4; tells who inflicted wound F956.4; willing to believe in four persons J817.2. — Animal p. B299.6; clever p. J1115.2; double dealing p. K2041; druid as p. P427.5; fairy p. F274, (abducted to heal mortals) R33, (has healing powers) F344.2; illness feigned to call p. paramour K1514.11; no p. at all J1432; poor girl masks as a doctor and is made court p. K1825.1.2; sham p. *K1955; skillful p. F668.0.1; treacherous p. K2292.

Physicians. — Hero refuses to slay p. W11.5.12; origin of p. A1594.1.

Physics. — Eating p. by mistake J2134.2.1.

Pice. — Riddle involving p. H587.1.

Pick. — Dripping water as ghost with p. J1782.2.1; man transformed to p.-handle D266.

Picked. — First objects p. up bring fortune N222; guilty man p. out by magic object D1318.0.1; transformation to be p. up D646; unknown father p. out by infant H481.

Picking all nuts from tall tree (task) H1121; things up only when master gives the signal J2516.2; up everything in path indicates miser H614.1. — Magic statue of archer put into action by p. up precious object from ground D1620.1.5.1.

Pickpockets strike man so he takes hand off purse K357.

Pickpocketing while confederate in pillory K341.24.

Picture as chastity index H439.1; comes to life D435.2.1; falls from sky F962.12.3; magically made hideous D1873.1; mistaken for original J1792; burns black (life token) E761.4.2; of a voice H1013. — Eye with p. in the pupil F541.2; ghost-like p. E532; hero ransoms saint's p. N848.1; hoodwink: "cuckold can't see this p." J1492; image in mirror mistaken for p. J1795; imagining other half of p. J1551.11; king seeks bride like p. H1381.3.1.1.1.; love through sight of p. T11.2; magic p. *D1266.2. (causes bed-wetting) D1379.4; marvelous p. falls from sky in storm F962.13.3; pagan sybil draws p. of Madonna and Child in sand V341; recognition through p. H21; stone turns red when saint's p. removed V229.23; taking a p. of conduct J2471; tiger-p. comes to life, kills M341.2.10.2; Virgin Mary's p. (appears to devotee) V263, (saves priest) K218.5; vow to starve until original of p. found M151.2.1; wizard shows p. of thief D1817.0.1.4; woman in p. arouses man's love H1381.3.1.2.1.

Pictures of creator A18; of gods A137ff. — Bridegroom chosen from p. T131.1.2.2; match arranged by p. T51.3.

Pie deceptively goes to clerks K362.8. — Cat eats p. instead of mouse J2103.1.1.

Pieces taken from flags serve to identify H103. — Fixing the two p. of a broken sword together (task) H1923.8; magic needle makes everything fall to p. D1562.4; murder by slicing person into p. S139.7; stars as p. of the moon A764.

Piecemeal mutilation as punishment Q451.11. — Creator creates earth p. A837. — Murder by p. destruction of separable soul K956.1.

Pied Piper of Hamelin D1427.1.

Piercer-of-souls G322.

Piercing magic object D1404. — Frog p. metals F989.23; ghost laid by p. grave with stake S442; murder by p. with pins, needles S115.3.

Piety, see also **Pious;** renders magic ineffective D1745.2; rewarded Q20ff. — Magic power from p. D1736; paramour pretends p. by attending matins after visiting mistress K2059.3; pretended p. K2058; wager over mortal's p. G303.9.8.7.

Pif Paf Poltrie Z31.1.

Pig, see also **Hog, Sow, Swine;** attempts to imitate goat's tricks J2415.6; big as mountain H1149.8; boiling only after true stories H251.3.11; born with man's head after bestiality T465.5; cooked when true story is told D1316.10; dedicated to St. Anthony tramples would-be slayer Q228; and dog's plowing contest K41.2; -fairy transformed to fish D412.3.1; as healer B511.2; impersonates plague, owner flees K335.0.2.1; licks sleeping man who thinks it is a kiss X31.2; as magician's familiar G225.7.1; in pit as unknown animal J1736.3; as sacrifice V12.4.3; as suitor B621.6; swallows necklace F989.22.3; theft exposed by child's curiosity K433; transformed to object D422.3; transformed to person D336.1; with venomous bristles B776.4.1. — Beggar's ghost laid by p. E451.6; cart as back legs for crippled p. X1202.1; eating magic p. prevents disease D1500.2.5; escape from ogress by substituting p. K525.7; fattening the p. J1903.3; god's urine used to make p. A1871.0.1; greedy p. looks up into tree, killed J514.4; happiness from eating magic p. D1359.3.2; hare and p. in race H625; how p. is domesticated A2513.3; hunting p. tabu C841.4; husband wishes wife into p. J2075.4; inexhaustible p. D1652.1.9.1; industrious p. rewarded Q5.1; imitation and real p. J2232; killing giant p. as suitor task H335.3.5; killing golden p. H1161.4; literal numskull kisses a p. J2461.2.1; magic p. B184.3.2ff., (burned to prevent resuscitation) B192.1, (carrying scissors, comb, and razors between its ears) H1154.1, (dead) D1281.1, (invisible) B184.3.2.1, (heals wound its skin touches) B511.2.1; monster cat born of a p. B16.1.1.1; oil of magic p. H1332.5.1; old woman and her p. Z41; one-eyed p. B15.4.5; ox-demon transformed to p. D412.2.2; quest for marvelous p. H1331.2; thief disguised as p. K311.6.5; venomous p. B776.4; stingy parson and slaughtered p. K343.2.1; woman meets a p. (cumulative tale) Z33.3; wedding of p. B281.6.

Pig's blood disenchants D766.2.1; bones become pig D447.7; flesh magic *D1032.4; food A2435.3.14. — Counting hairs in p. back (task) H1118; devil has p. foot G303.4.5.5; divination from p. liver D1311.10.2; goddess with p. head A131.3.2; goddess with p. teeth A131.8; obtaining wild p. marrow H1154.11; sham all-knowing p. head K1956.10.

Pigs become other animals D412.3ff.; bewitched G265.6.1.1; cursed M414.8.2; cut from sow's body: raised T584.4; paralyzed by witch D2072.0.2.5. — Acorns alleged to protect p. K119.2; curse: p. to be lean M471.2; deceptive division of p.: curly and straight tails K171.4; demigod keeps wild p. B845.1; devil payed when p. walk, not run, home K226; feeding p. wet meal J2465.1; getting ninety p. H1154.2.1; making p. dance (task) H1186; miser killing his own p. W153.9; planting hog in order to grow p. J1932.4; resuscitation of dismembered p. E32.3; roast p. run around ready for eating X1208.1; St Anthony's p. B256.2; slain p. revive nightly *E155.5; slaughter of wild p. in vengeance J1866.1; sow saves p. from wolf coming to baptize them K1121.2; spirit owns herd of p. F241.3.1; why the p. shriek J1733; trickster shears sheep, dupe p. K171.5; why p. in mud lift their legs A2473.2, A2479.5; why p. are plentiful A2582.1; why wild p. ravage rice-fields A2545.5; wolves, wild p. condemned to death for killing sheep B275.1.3.2; woman bears three p. T554.9.

Pigskin. — Magic p. *D1025.1; quest for magic p. H1332.5; stealing p. from a king H1151.13.1.

Pigsty abode for unpromising hero (heroine) L132. — In duel with long poles the ogre is forced into the p. K785; suitor locked in p. K1218.2.

Pigeon god A132.6.5; hastily kills his mate for stealing wheat N346; as messenger B291.1.12. — Creation of p. A1947; creation of sea p. A1947.1; crow befriends p. to steal from his household K359.4; green p. cheated out of chick: mourns A2275.4.1; helpful p. B457.2; how was p. killed? J2133.14.1; jay in p. skin unmasked J951.2; man becomes p. D154.2; marriage to p. B602.3; reincarnation as p. E613.6.1; tabu to eat p. C221.1.2.2.

Pigeon's entrails fetch lover D1355.3.4; wedding B282.3.4, B282.20. — Heroine with p. head L112.11.

Pigeons cover sun with wings to aid hero H982.1. — Breaking p. egg on castle parapet H1149.6; king of p. B242.2.4; land of p. B222.1; racing p. tabu C865.1.

Pike helps Christ: made king of fishes A2223.4. — Creation of p. A2111; enmity between white fish and p. A2494.15.1; devil cannot change into p. G303.3.6.1; friendship between p. and crawfish A2493.33; helpful p. B475; man becomes p. D179.2; woman tricks lover with p. head K1222.

Pilate appears periodically at Mt. Pilatus and washes his hands E411.8. — Bittern from P. transformed A1965.1; Christ's coat of mercy protects P. D1381.4.1.

Pilav. — Father's counsel: let p. be your daily food H588.2.

Pilgrim rebuked for eating too much J1346. — Devil in form of p. G303.3.1.9; disguise as p. to enter enemy's camp (castle) K2357.2; first p. A1546.3.2; pious p. dies unknown in father's house K1815.1.1; woman disguised as p. questions lover K1837.2.

Pilgrimage with hands and loins weighted with iron as penance Q522.4; as penance Q526. — Girl vows not to marry until p. K1227.7; reward for p. Q28; stubbornness loses woman chance for p. W167.2.

Pilgrimages V530. — Religious p. V85.

Pill transformed to white rabbit D444.3. — Alleged oracular p. sold K114.3; disenchantment by removal of enchanting p. from mouth D765.1.1; magic p. *D1243; transformation by placing p. in mouth D551.6.1.

Pills. — Magic p. bring twin sons D1347.3.1; snake gives away magic p. J621.1.1; throwing away p.: sores result J2075.3.

Pillar of fire *F964.0.1, (guides person to church) D1314.10, (from heaven to earth) F962.2.2, (rises over woman pregnant with saint) V222.0.1.1; -stone as weapon F614.2.1; supporting sky A665.2. — Captivity in p. R41.6; castle stands on a p. F771.2.5; demon as fiery p. G302.3.1; fiery p. sign of Christ's visit V211.2.1; god flies in p. of floating clouds A171.3; quest for silver p. H1322.1; rice in hands joined around p. J2119.6; river issues from p. F715.1.2; soul hidden in p. E712.5; standing on p. as penance for incest Q541.3; till ogam and p. be blent Z61.1; transformation to p. of salt for breaking tabu C961.1.

Pillars of dead chief's bones A151.4.4; of Hercules at Gibraltar set up by Hercules A984; magically dance D1599.1; of silver and glass in other-world *F169.1; of smoke, light lead to heaven E754.6; supporting sky A665.2.0.1. — Castle on golden p. F771.2.5.1; extraordinary p. F774ff.; gold p. in otherworld F169.1.2; habitable hill raised on four p. F721.2.1; sky extended by p. A665.2.1.3; twelve iron p. steady the earth A841.3.

Pillory. — Man stands in p.; confederate picks pockets K341.24.

Pillow causes magic sleep D1364.11. — Horse's skull as p. F874.2.1; magic p. *D1154.5; one feather makes hard p. J2213.9; stone becomes p. D452.1.9; treasure hidden in p. under dead man's head N522.

Pillows as chastity test H411.10.

Pilot. — Saint's staff as sea p. D1313.5.1.

Pin pricks which do not bleed reveal witch G259.3. — Disenchantment by removal of enchanting p. D765.1.2; lost p. found in fish N211.1.1; magic p. *D1182; pricking with p. to keep awake H1484; swallowed p. emerges through relative's skin X1739.1.

Pins in horse's heart release curse M429.2; stuck in soles of dead man's feet to prevent return E431.12. — Murder by feeding with bread full of p. K951.2; murder by piercing with p. S115.3; object pierced with p. as love charm D1355.3.2, D1355.3.3; witch sticks victim with p. G269.17.

Pincers. — Tearing off flesh with p. Q469.9.1.

Pincher. — Remarkable p. X952.

Pinching. — Fairies p. as revenge F361.17.3; shell-fish p. trickster J2136.4; witches p. victim G269.19.

Pine bender G314; and thornbush dispute as to their usefulness J242.2. — Discontented p. tree: cause of p. needles A2723.1, A2767.1; fairy's back like p. cones F232.1.2; floors in dwarf home covered with p. twigs F451.4.3.5.

Pining. — Animal p. away with grief B773.2; fairy child p. away F329.4.2.

Pink. — Person with p. fluid in place of blood F554.1.

Pious, see also **Piety;** child able to carry water in sieve H1023.2.0.2; die on birthday F1099.7; woman rescues child R131.18. — Angels as souls of p. A52.0.4; animal characteristics reward for p. act *A2221; animals leave wicked, go to p. master B292.0.2; devil prevented from revenge by p. priest G303.16.11.2; living with ordinary vs. p. man J417; oath uttered by p. against temptation M110.3; souls of p. advise creator A45; souls of p. as angels E754.7; tree supports p. family F979.19; youth associating with a p. person (nun as mistress) J1264.5.

Pipal protection against witch D1385.2.4. — Why p. leaves tremble A2762.3.

Pipe. — Changeling plays on a p. and thus betrays his maturity F321.1.1.2; dead man smokes p. E555; devil's p. G303.25.16.1; gun as tobacco p. K1057; magic p. (musical) *D1224, (causes magic sleep) D1364.25.3; opium substituted for tobacco in p. K873.3; recognition by tobacco p. H147; skillful marksman shoots p. from man's mouth F661.2; tobacco, p., and match debate usefulness to smoker J461.3; wind raised by blowing into tobacco p. D2142.1.6.1.

Pipes. — Fairy tobacco p. F246.

Piper. — Ghost as p. E425.2.5.

Piracy. — Brothers help each other in p. P251.5.1.

Pirate excommunicated V84.3.

Pirates. — Abduction by p. R12; escape from p. R211.4; man patiently undergoes cruelty of p. N251.1; partner abducted by p. P319.4.

Pisāca drink blood and eat human flesh G312.1.

Pistol. — Magic p. *D1096.2.

Pit entrance to (lower world) F92, (otherworld) F158; placed under bed K735.4.1. — Abandonment in p. *S146; animals grateful for rescue from p. B361; blind leading blind falls into p. J2133.9; burning p. will close only for rider F1061.3; devil appears to girl who prays over p. where she has thrown the bodies of her babies G303.6.2.7; dupe tricked in race into falling into a p. K1171; dupe takes prisoner's place in p. K842.2; escape from snake p. R211.7; fox climbs from p. on wolf's back K652; jackals enter p. to escape storm, killed K811.2; jumping over p. chastity test H412.7.2; jumping over p. proves sex H1578.1.4.2; man, lion, and bear in p. J685.1; mankind emerges from p. A1232.31; moon buried in p. A754.1; moon falls into p. A754.1.1; pig in p. as unknown J1736.3; riding across p. as suitor contest H331.1.4; sun shut up in p. A721.0.2; throwing into p. as punishment Q465; traitor thrown into p. Q417.2; traveler saves monkey, snake, tiger, and jeweler from p. W154.8; warriors hidden in battlefield p. K2369.2; witch kicks helper into p. G269.1.1.

Pitch becomes cold water D478.14; shower as punishment Q475.2; smeared on threshold to trap fleeing girl J1146.1. — Boiling to death in p. S112.1; saint unhurt by boiling p. D1841.2.2.

Pitcher magically sticks to ground D2171.4.1. — Identification by ring dropped in p. of wine H94.3; magic p. *D1171.4; water drowns girl filling p. D1432.1.

Pitchfork. — Devil with p. G303.4.8.7.

Pitchforks wrench souls in hell E755.2.1.1.

Pitfall. — Capture in p. K735; deceiver arranges p. but is himself caught K1601; husband catches the paramour in a p. K1562; mats over holes as p. K735.1; origin of p. A1458.1; victim escapes p. K1601.1.

Pittance. — Man dismissed after years of service with a p. W154.1.

Pity. — Calf's p. for draft-ox ill-placed L456.

Pitying. — God p. mortal A185.16.

Pixies F200.1; in dancing contest F302.3.4.2.1.

Placard. — Importunate lover wears humiliating p. K1218.6.

Placating ghosts by sacrifices E433; ruler with soft words J811.4.

Place of bad omen D1812.5.1.30; and conditions of childbirth T581; of giving curse M413. — Absurd ignorance concerning p. for animal to be kept J1904; animal council assigns p. and work to all B238; compulsion to go to certain p. C666; devil helps man p. cart wheel when it becomes unfastened G303.22.4; devil in p. of dead man in shroud G303.18.2; devil takes p. of woman who went to spend night with a priest G303.25.11; fear test: staying in frightful p. H1410ff.; forbidden p. C610ff., (for bathing) C721.2, (for drinking) C260ff., (for eating) C210ff., (for sleeping) C735.2; forgetfulness caused by p. D2004.9; fortune-telling dream induced by sleeping in extraordinary p. D1812.3.3.2; husband takes p. of paramour K1569.4; magic discovery of desired p. D1816ff.; magic object causes things to seek their proper p. D1565ff.; magic object indicates desired p. *D1314ff.; marking the p. J1922; Nero has reserved p. in hell for lawyers X316; origin of p.-name A1617; princess rescued from p. of captivity R111.2; prophecy: death in particular p. M341.3; sea rises and changes p. F931.1; tabu: being in certain p. at sunrise C751.7.1; tabu: staying too long in certain p. C761.4; thief persuades owner to take his p., robs him K341.9.1; transformation to reach difficult p. D641.

Places changed in bed with ogre's children *K1611; and conditions of captivity R40ff.; haunted by the devil G303.15ff. — Avoiding p. which have been fatal to others J644; congregating p. of fairies F217; curses on p. M411.8.2; extraordinary p. F700ff.; origin of particular p. A980ff.; quest for unknown objects or p. H1382; saints in several p. at once V225.

Placenta covering as escape disguise K522.1.1. — Child born from p. T549.4.1; motifs associated with p. T588; origin of p. A1313.5; plant from transformed human p. A2611.0.3.

Placidas pursued by misfortune N251.

Plague, see also **Pestilence;** as bad omen D1812.5.1.19; banished by burying girl alive S266; for breaking tabu C941.4; ceases after pestilence spirit destroyed F493.3.1; from Jews' poisoning wells V362; magically invoked D2061.1.5; as punishment Q552.10; strikes down boasting usurer Q558.3; talk frightens away guests J1563.8. — Battle between God's orderly and p. A162.6; bull, cow survive p. F989.6; cannibalism during p. G78; end of p. as reward Q146; enemy tricked into fleeing p. K2368.3; "flame of fire" p. to destroy Ireland M356.2; holy mountain free from p. D2162.4; magic incense protects against p. D1389.15; magic p. of frogs drawn down on foe D2091.2; magic object relieves from p. D1586; proclamation of dogma of Immaculate Conception stops p. V312.1; pseudo-magic letter against p. K115.1.3; punishment of magician who causes p. Q392; recognition by p. H94.8; spirit of p. F493; woman stricken by p. dies in lover's arms T88.

Plagues. — Animals from frogs sent as one of Egypt's p. A1734; ten p. Z71.16.2.1.

Plain at borders of otherworld F144; that is earthly paradise F756.2; people put on vain display W116.3; sinks to become lake bottom F944.4. — Crossing p. after sunset tabu C752.1.2; hero crosses impassible p. in path of magic object D1562.5; magic p. *D937, (to which one sticks) D1413.19; otherworld as p. F160.1; quest to P. of Wonders H1288; sea appears like flowery p. D2151.1.4; strong man clears p. F614.9.

Plains of heaven A663. — Burning p. in hell A671.2.4.4; extraordinary valleys and p. F756; god clears p. A181.1; heroes clear p. A537.

Plainness. — Choice between p. with safety or grandeur with danger J212; magic needle transforms a room from p. to beauty D1337.1.7.

Plaintiff assigns impossible task H919.4. — Animal as p. B271; judgment as rebuke to unjust p. J1172.

Plaiting — Fairies p. horse's manes F366.2.1.

Plaits. — Hair p. cut off to escape lover T327.7.

Plan. — All aspects of a p. must be foreseen J755.

Plans. — Absurd p. J2060ff.; forethought in prevention of others' p. J620ff.; modest business p. best L250ff.; swindler's p. foiled J1521.

Plane-tree blamed for not bearing fruit W154.7; tests perjury H251.3.1.

Planet. — Sun, moon pursued by dark p. in black chariot A735.2.

Planets A780ff.

Plank test H1534.

Planks. — Skillful tailor sews together scattered p. in capsizing boat F662.2.

Planning for greater office J703. — Father p. child's death S11.4; in p. future, profit by the past J752; servant p. to possess his master's goods P365.2; woman p. to eat her children G72.1.

Plant from blood of slain person E631.0.3; grows to sky F54.2; from scrapings of princesses' bodies H522.2; shrieks when uprooted F992; transformed into animal D441.4; transformed to other object D451.2;

transformed to person D431.6; wife T117.10.—Animal languages learned from eating p. B217.2; birth from p. T543; cockscomb p. used to kill sun A1156; conception from eating p. T511.2; creator sent down insects to p. plants A2601; deceptive land purchase: to raise certain p. K185.11; disenchantment by eating p. D764.6; guessing nature of p. H522.2; girl persuaded to sit on certain p.: seduced K1315.2.1; grateful p. D1658.2.3; guessing unknown p. (test) H522ff.; hand becomes p. D457.9.1; heavens created after p. world A700.4; magic p. *D965ff., (furnishes treasure) D1463ff., (bears fruit to indicate that heroine is ready to marry) D1310.4.2, (heals broken bone) D1518.4.1, (heals wounds) D1503.10; man made from p. A1255; one p. transformed into another A2616; origin of p. names A2781; owl advises where to p. crops B569.2; quest for extraordinary p. H1333.2; quest for p. of immortality H1333.2.1; recognition by overheard conversation with p. H13.2.3; reincarnation as p. E631.5; reincarnation in p. growing from grave *E631ff.; sickness from drying, shriveling p. D2064.8; soul in p. E711.2; touching p. forbidden C510ff.; vampire p. E251.5; wild hunt avoided by holding certain p. E501.17.5.7; why leaves of p. are flat A2741.3, A2761.3; woman gives birth to p. T555.

Plants as gods' bodies D210.1; grow after sky lifted A625.2.5; magically shriek D2091.12; and trees miraculously unbent F973. — Creator p. tree on moon A751.6.1; creator sent down insects to plant p. A2601; devil plows and p. for farmer in one day G303.9.2.3; extraordinary behavior of trees and p. F970ff.; extraordinary p. F815; God p. fields A432.0.1; goddess of forest p. A431.1.2; hoarded p. released A1423.0.1; lies about p. X1400; magic flower pot bears p. with gold letters on leaves D1469.1; magic gardens and p. D960ff.; magic object makes p. grow D1487; origin of trees and p. A2600—A2699; procuring food p. as bride contest H375.3; quest for extraordinary p. H1333; strong man as gardener destroys p. F614.3; sun's power over p. A738.4; tabu to eat certain p. C226; why leaves of p. are flat A2741.3, A2761.3; why p. no longer reach sky A2775.0.1.

Plantain. — Bringing p. leaf without tearing it H1041; magic p. *D965.11; man becomes p. stalk D213.6; why p. bears but one stalk A2722.1, A2771.2.

Plantains. — Green p. sold as matured K147.1.

Planted — Why wheat must be p. one year, harvested next A2793.2.1.

Planting animal's tail to produce more animals J1932.4.1; beautiful garden H1199.1; cooked food K496; the earth A2602; for the next generation J701.1; a hog in order to grow pigs J1932.4. — Origin of p. A1441.4; snow taken away by p. certain root D2143.6.1.

Plate. — Guessing nature of devil's p. H523.7; magic p. *D1172.1; stolen church p. E236.7; turning the p. around J1562.1.

Plates. — Dogs with eyes like p. B15.4.3; leaves become gold p. D475.1.19.

Plated. — Deceptive sale of p. ware K123.

Platform. — Magic p. *D1157.

Platter. — Stealing silver p. K362.3.1.

Play. Why great man joins in children's p. J25; prince will not join p. of common children J411.3; sun's p. with moon A722.9; unknown prince chosen chief of children in p. *P35.

Players. — Card p. scared by ghost E293.2.

Playful fairies F399.4; ghost E599.10.

Playing cards with devil in church (fear test) H1421; flute forbidden C844; game with reassembled dead man (fear test) H1433; at marriage tabu C167.1; poison K439.4. — Animal with men in its belly p. cards F911.3.3; captive escapes by p. further and further from watchman K622; changeling p. on a pipe betrays his maturity F321.1.1.2; dead persons p. games E577; devil p. fiddle at wedding G303.9.8.2; dwarfs p. in moonlight F451.6.3.5; dupe p. for wedding K844; fox feigns to be p. with sheep K2061.2; giants p. with men's lives F531.3.15; mortal wins fairies' gratitude by p. for their dance F331.4; mountain-men p. games F460.3.2; recognition by unique manner of p. lute H35.1; resuscitation by p. music E551ff.; recognition by unique manner of p. lute H35.1; serpents p. with precious green stone B11.6.2.2; symbolic interpretation of p. cards H603; tabu: stranger p. without asking permission C892.

Playmates. — Strong man kills p. F612.2; unknown prince shows his kingly qualities in dealing with his p. H41.5.

Plea by admitting accusation and discomfiting accuser J1162. — Escape by false p. *K550ff.

Pleas. — Tabu: heeding p. of old woman for food and warmth C745.

Pleading. — Clever p. J1160ff.; princess skillful in p. J1111.1.1.

Pleasant women A1372.7. — What is most p.? Love H659.13.1.

Pleasing. — Animal's p. voice A2423.2; impossibility of p. everyone J1041.

Pleasure. — Bringing greatest p. giver H1065; comfort in the contemplation of impossible p. J864; otherworld land of p. F173.1; relative p. of sexes in love J99.1, T2.

Pledge with enemy P557.2. — Drinking blood as covenant p. T312.1; host as p. to keep one's word V39.6; mother of illegitimate child given as p. for his crime T640.2; parting lovers p. not to marry for seven years T61.2; son as p. for father murderer P233.1; tabu to give arms in p. C835.2.6.

Pledged, see also **Promised.** — Love falsely p. K2094; maid p. to celibacy is given beard T321.1; princess secretly p. to many K2034.1; Virgin Mary substitutes for woman whom husband has p. to the devil K1841.3.

Pleiades. — Origin of the P. A773.

Plentiful. — Why certain animals are p. A2582.1; wild hunt as omen of p. year E501.20.2.

Plenty. — Horn of p. D1470.2.3; land of p. F701; in time of p. provide for want J711; wolf prefers liberty and hunger to dog's servitude and p. L451.

Plot. — Man knowing of murder p. against his friend disguises and is killed in his place P316.1; faithless wife and paramour p. against husband's life K2213.3; sham stupidity to overhear p. K1818.3.3; treacherous mother and ogre p. against her son S12.1; triangle p. and its solutions T92.1.

Plotting. — Angel kills man p. murder J225.4.

Plover. — Creation of p. A1941.

Plow without horse or wheels (lie) X1855. — Bluff: p. as hero's hoe K1718.5; cow and bullock yoked to p. A1689.1; creator distributes p. A1440.1; cutting at p.: fool cuts bullock's legs J2465.8; elephant draws p. to mark empire's boundaries B599.3; extraordinary p. F887.1; furnishing p. animals determines crop share J1179.11; golden p. D1620.2.7, F858; magic p. D1209.3; ogre harnessed to p. G675; saint yokes wild animals to his p. B558.6; stags p. for man *B292.4; strong man lifts p. F624.4; tiger injured by p. K547.9; tilling with gold p. D1620.2.7.

Plow's — Heating p. colter to release curse M429.4.

Plowboy. — Fairies' revenge on p. F361.17.3.

Plowed. — Fairy unable to cross p. ground F383.3; island p. out by goddess A955.4; lake bursts forth where island is p. out A920.1.9; land purchase: as much as can be p. in a certain time K185.8; magic song causes p. ground to become unplowed D1565.3; men formerly p. with cattle as their masters A1101.2.1.

Plowing in certain place forbidden C522; contest K41; enormous amount of land in one day (task) H1103.2; the field K1411; field of vipers (task) H1188; above tree: numskull hauls plow into tree J2465.12; with donkey and ox tabu C886; by magic servants D1719.8.; swiftly F681.10; as test for bishop H1573.2.3. — Boy shows foolishness of p. up crop J92; brother is running back and forth (p.) H583.3.1; contours of land caused by p. of goddess A951; devil p. and planting for farmer G303.9.2.3; dog p. for man B292.4.3; extraordinary p. F1099.6; god implored to delay p. season J713.1; letters in clouds seen by man p. corn X459.1.1; origin of p. A1441.1; rain produced by p. D2143.1.5; stags p. for saint B256.9; tiger p. for man B292.4.2; treasure to be found by man p. with cock and harrowing with hen N543.2; wild oxen p. for man B292.4.1.

Plowman god A432.0.2; promised horse for saying paternoster H1554.3.

Plowshare frightens tiger K547.11.

Plucked. — Bird's feathers p. out by another bird K2382.1; flower p. from grave becomes a girl E251.2.2; king and peasant: the p. fowl H561.6.1.

Plucking fairy flowers tabu F378.5; flowers forbidden *C515; fruits as unique ability H31.12. — Conception from p. flower T532.1.1; disenchantment from flower by p. it D711.4.1; disenchantment from fruit by p. it D711.6; girl summons fairy lover by p. flowers F301.1.1.2; raven p. out men's eyes B17.2.3.1; transformation by p. flowers in enchanted garden D515.

Plum. — Magic p. D981.7; why the p. tree so hardy A2711.6.

Plumage. Goddess in bird's p. A136.1.8.

Plumed serpent B91.2.

Plunging into stream suitor test H353.

Pluto's. — Ability to see P. messengers D1825.3.4.2.

Plutus in bad company J451.3.

Plymouth. — Devil and Drake carry waters of English Channel from Dartmoor to P. G303.9.2.4.

Poaching. — Attempt to chastise devil for p. C12.5.6.

Pocket. — Elephant put in p. to show friends X941.3; giant carries man in his p. F531.5.1.1; magic p. *D1064; thumbling carried in p. F535.1.1.13; tortoise escapes from p. with hole K563.2.

Poem for poem: all for all J1581.1. — Beggar rewarded for p. P163; dead poet teaches p. E377.1; ghost laid when p. cited E451.10; king rewards p. Q91.3; kingdom as reward for p. Q112.0.1.2; magic p. *D1275.4, (causes king to waste away) D1402.15, (causes man to melt) D1402.15.1, (kills animals) D1445.4, (makes land sterile) D1563.2.3, (raises blotches on face) D1403.1, (causes man to die) D1402.15.2; quest for unknown lines of p. H1382.2.1; unrequited love expressed in p. T75.3.

Poems, see also **Poetry;** as presents to king J2415.1.2. — Magic p. protect D1380.14.

Poet P427.7; calls king baker's son J816.2; cursed M414.6; leaps to death with woman in arms Q411.0.1.3; may not act as legal security P524.1; as prophet M301.18; puts others out of countenance J1224; rescues child R131.19; as satirist P427.4; silent until fourteen L124.1.1; sings after death E371.3; uses confounding words J1684. — Blind p. unintentionally kills friend N337.1; contest in making p. ridiculous H509.4.1.1; dead p. teaches poem E377.1; disguise as p. K1817.3.1; dwarf p. F451.3.3.1; dwarf p. swims in human drinking-horn X142.2; female p. traced through poetry H12.1; future p. chants in womb T575.1.4; hero as p. A527.4; husband tricks p. into slaying wife's lover K863.1; king honors p. and critic J811.3; magic knowledge of p. D1810.0.11; princess kisses ugly p. Q88.2; sight restored while p. writes hymn F952.0.1; turning away from p. tabu C872; ugly child becomes great p. L112.9; waters react to words of p. F996.

Poet's curse M411.18; slayer eaten by wolves Q415.7.1; story brings reparation for destruction J1675.6.

Poets carry on obscure discussion H607.2; interpret dreams D1812.3.3.0.2; lose ability as punishment Q559.6; as sacred persons V291. — King must procure whatever p. ask P19.3; noble-born p. refuse to associate with lowly-born J411.3.1; seven orders of p. Z71.5.6.7; tabus of p. C568.

Poetic ability (tested) H509.4, (uncovers missing female poet) H12.1; mead M234.1.

Poetry, see also **Poems;** personified Z117. — Acquisition of p. A1464.1; first p. composed in imitation of tones of hammer on anvil A1464.1.1; god of p. A465.1; "spirit of p." as hideous youth beautified D682.4.2; stealing mead of p. H1151.16.

Poignard. — Magic p. *D1083.1.

Point. — Castle at middle p. of earth F771.3.4; god dwells at particular p. on earth A151.10; justice depends on the p. of view U21.

Points. — As many stars in heavens as p. on paper H702.3; quest over path bristling with sharp p. H1236.1; symbolic interpretation of p. on a bishop's hat H608.1.

Pointed leg F548.0.1. — Deity p. out by insect settling where he is H162.1; demon with p. head G342; direction p. out by lazy man with his foot W111.5.3; magic object p. out by bird D849.2; road p. out by magic object D1313ff.; treasure p. out by supernatural creature (fairy, etc.) N538; unchaste woman p. out by magic object H411.

Pointing at door causes fall D2069.1.1; forbidden C843. — Animal with horn p. to sky B15.3.5; death by p. D2061.2.3; image with p. finger F855.1; peasant betrays fox by p. K2315; where is tail p.? (toward rear) J1305.

Poison damsel F582; flows out of ale vessel F1092; of hydra corrodes the skin F1041.5; in nectar H592.2; magically separated from drink D2168.1; pool F717.2; transformed to stone D471.7. — Animal warns against p. *B521.1; bath in milk of white, hornless cows as antidote for p. D1515.3; doctor who can cure can also p. P424.2; drinking p. prepared for victim Q582.8; eating lover's heart with p. Q478.1.1; elephant eats p. man intended for self N627; god of p. A499,6; husband shows his wife p. to avoid: she takes it and died T254.1; immunity to p. by eating poison F959.6.2; lover at tomb takes p.: beloved revives, shares fate T37.1; magic antidote for p. *D1515ff.; magic detection of p. D1817.0.2; magic object detects p. *D1317.0.1; magic object protects from p. *D1383ff.; magic ring warns of p. *D1317.5.1; magic used against p. D2168; man proof against p. D1841.8; marvelous cure for p. F959.6; nectar in p. H592.3; one man's food is another man's p. U140ff.; ordeal by p. H223; peacock's feathers ruffled in presence of p. B131.5; poisoner poisoned with his own p. K1613; prophecy: death by p. M341.2.8; resuscitation by removal of p. E21ff.; rivers of p. in hell A671.2.2.1; saint invulnerable to p. D1840.1.2, H1573.3.1; serpent feeds other serpents p. A2219.3; sign of cross protects against p. D1766.6.4; sleeping potion substituted for p. K512.4, K1856, K2111.1; snake created to suck p. from earth A2145.3; substitute bridegroom to save husband from p. maiden K1844.2; transformation: p. to stone D471.7; vessel of poisoned ale inverted: only p. flows out F1092; why water snake has no p. A2532.1.1; woman tricked into giving p. to her husband K945.

Poisoned arrows F831.3; cakes intended for husband eaten by thieves N659.1; clothing test H1516; food (drink) fed to animal instead of to intended victim K527.1; food sent to enemy camp K2369.11; weapons P553.1; woman revives T37.0.1. — Attempt to kill hero by feeding him p. food H1515; boar with p. bristles K898; centipede's p. sting A1335.13; cup said to be p. by friend P317.1; enemy tricked into thinking self p., retreats K2351.6.1.1; enemies invited to feast, p. K811.1.2; falcon saves master from p. water B143.1.4; greedy animal eats p. fruit W125.1; hus-

band believes he is p. and lies down for dead J2311.2; murder by
leaving p. wine K929.1; murder by throwing p. bread into mouth K951.3;
queen sells p. cheese K1817.4.1.1.1; resuscitation by removal of p. apple
*E21.1; robbers fed p. food K439.6; saint makes p. food harmless
D1840.1.2.1; sword with p. edge F833.6; thief leaves food untouched when
owner pretends to be p. by it K439.4; victim pounded up with p. fish
K838; woman sells p. curds to man A1335.12.

Poisoner. — Double-dealing p. K2041.1.

Poisoning fish causes storm C41.4; by magic D2061.1.3. — Accidental p.
N332; adulteress p. husband T232.3; disappointed lover attempts p. girl
T93.4; disguise as physician for p. K1825.1.6; husband p. wife to avoid
her being ravished T471.3; murder by p. S111ff.; plague from Jews' p.
wells V362; punishment by p. Q418; queen falsely accused of p. husband
K2116.1.2; saint immune to p. V228.1; sister p. brother K2212.0.1; uncle
p. nephew S71.1; wife p. husband for paramour K2213.3.2; woman p.
rival K2221.1.

Poisonous, see also **Venomous;** eyebrow causes death to beholder F555.7;
toad sits on food of undutiful children Q557.1; water cures man N646.
— Birds with p. spells on wings B33.1.4; monster's blood makes tree and
surroundings p. D1563.2.2; origin of p. plants A2692; person with p.
teeth F513.1.4; rebel god authors all p. things A63.7.

Poker. — Long nose used as p. F543.1.1; reversing p. protects from witch
G272.9.

Pole for coffin-rests appears at door at death E767.1; through horse's body
pulls fairy chariot F241.1.6. — How did the cow get on the p.? J2382.

Poles. — In duel with long p. ogre is forced into pigsty K785.

Policeman. — Don't make friends with p. J21.46; trickster dupes jewels
from p. and his wife K714.1.1.

Policy in dealing with the great J810ff. — Truth the best p. J751.1.

Polished. — Magic sight by looking at p. object D1821.3.7.

Polishing. — Origin of p. stone A1465.4; resuscitation by p. sword E142.

Polite rescuers J2516.3.2; travelers miss train J2183.2.

Politeness rewarded Q41.

Political visions V515.2.

Polluted. — Brahmin decides that dog has p. clothes by walking under
them J2184; Brahmins p. fish K344.1.1; house p. so that trickster is left in
possession K355; nest and brood of bird p. K932; water-spirits revenge
for p. water F420.5.2.6.6; well p. by (battle blood) D1563.2.2.1, (ogre)
G585.

Poltergeister *F470ff.

Polyandry T146; among gods A164.5.

Polychromatic dogs B731.6.0.1.

Polycrates *N211.1.

Polygamy T145; of the gods A164.3. — Advice against p. J21.32; parents'
code towards children of p. A1576.

Polygonum persicaria (heartsease) has red stripes A2772.3.
Polyphemus F512.1.1.
Pomegranate and apple tree dispute as to which is worth most J466.1. — Demon imprisoned in p. D2177.2; eating p. without letting seed fall H326.2; eating p. seed forbidden C225.1; extraordinary p. F813.8; magic p. D981.12; soul in p. E711.2.4; transformation to p. D211.2.
Pond, see also **Pool;** always clear for deity's bath F713.5; of milk B531.2.1. — Bailing out a p. (task) H1113; bringing a p. to king (task) H1023.25; digging a p. quickly (task) H1105; enigmatic statement: the tank (p.) does not belong to you H594.2; extraordinary p. F713; killing eels with snakes in p. J2114; large p. emptying into smaller ones (parable on spending) H614.2; lies about p. X1546; magic control of p. D2151.5; magic p. D921, (causes disease) D1500.4.3; ogre persuaded to drink p. dry bursts G522; otherworld at bottom of p. F133.4; "soak me in the p." K553.5; victim persuaded to look into p.: pushed in K832.1.1; wild hunt goes thrice around p. E501.14.3; world at bottom of p. F725.8.
Ponds. — Giant's eyes like p. F531.1.1.2.2; origin of fish p. A1457.6.
Pontius Pilate. See **Pilate.**
Pool fills with sand in answer to prayer D1766.1.5. — Attire for certain p. C61.15.5; blind wives fall into p., bear children there T581.2.2; bottom-less p. F713.2; extraordinary p. F717; ice forms while fish leaps from p. F935.2; looking in p. to see if it is raining J2716.1; man looking at birds pulled into p. K832.6; transformation to p. of water D283.1; woman becomes p. of water A920.1.11.
Poor, see also **Impoverished, Poverty;** boy finds treasure in deserted city N534.5; boy marries rich girl L161.1; boy said by helpful cat to be dispossessed prince K1952.1; boy's boast of building palace comes true N234; bride pretends to wealth K1911.5; girl chosen rather than the rich L213; girl masks as doctor and is made court physician K1825.1.2; man consoles self by thinking of misfortunes of rich J883; man surpasses rich L143; man happier than king J1085.3; man banishes bad luck, becomes rich N250.4; man deceives rich, causes his death K890.1; man imitates rich J2416; man presented rich robe jailed as thief N347.5; man rejects wealth J1085.4; man wants high office: made cook L427; people given alms, recognized H152.1; person's great effort to entertain guests P336; prince overcomes king L311.3; son-in-law preferred to rich J247.1; suitor served good supper J1561.3.1. — Bad choice between p. and miserly man J229.6; daughter punished by marriage to p. man T69.5; difference between a p. man and a rich (riches) H875; excessive hospitality makes chieftain p. Q42.1.3; fortunes of rich and p. man N181; grass pleasant couch for p. U65.1; judge favors p. defendent J1192.1.2; king seizes p. man's lamb U35.1.1; man so p. all he does to move is put out fire W226; marriage between rich and p. T121; naked idol considered p. J2216; nobleman marries, abandons p. girl T72.2; prophecy: rich man's son to marry p. girl M359.7; prophecy of future greatness for p. youth M312;

prophecy of wealthy marriage for p. girl M312.1.1; rich girl in love with p. boy T91.5.1; rich man made p. to punish pride L412; rich and p. in love T91.5; Satan at feast where p. are absent G303.15.4.3; sun as caretaker of the p. A739.8; water-spirits help p. F420.5.1.2; when p. man eats H659.17; why the p., being in the majority, do not kill off the rich J2371.4.

Poorest. — Quest for bride richest and p. H1311.2.

Poorly dressed woman chosen as wife L213.1.

Pope V294, (Boniface VIII) K2282.1, (Clement V) K2282.1, (Joan) K1961.2.1; calls persistent courtier a fool J1289.3; disguised as caulker K1816.2; guilty of simony V466.1; overawes captor, escapes K546, reconciles estranged couple N741.3; selected by chair moving towards him H171.6; tests women's disobedience: not to look into box H1557.4. — Audience secured with the p. by rudeness D477.1; bells sounds to designate p. D1311.12.1; bird indicates election of p. H171.2; disenchantment by prayer of p. D781; magic knowledge of the p. D1810.0.9; man magically made to believe himself bishop, archbishop, and p. D2031.5; mother guilty of incest with son forgiven by p. T412.1; pretender as p. K1961.2; priests stamp on stone to prove truth of p. A972.1.2; seduction to engender a p. K1315.1.2.1; recognition when parents come to son as p. to be confessed H151.3; test of p.: his candle lights itself H41.3; uncharitable p. wanders after death V425; wine gives courage to face p. J1318; woman in disguise becomes p. K1961.2.1.

Pope's decision on priest's wife J1179.10. — Devil flees at p. blessing G303.16.2.3.2; magic wind blows open church door for p. body Q147.2; rich man shakes ducats into p. lap J1263.2.2; wind aids p. burial F963.3.

Poplar cursed for serving as cross A2721.2.1.2; leaves tremble A2762.2.

Poplars from weeping maidens transformed by god A2681.3.

Poppy characteristics from reincarnations A2733; seeds poured into ghost's mouth E439.4.

Popularizing. — Dream advises against p. science J157.3.

Population P720. — Differences in p. sizes A1621; over-p. A1019.3, A1335.8, P721.

Porcupine as controller of cold D2144.1.1; crawls inside buffalo and kills him K952.1; duped into leaving food K335.0.4.2; pricks rabbit host P332. — Beaver and p. trick each other K896.1; broom, transformed into p., drives away would-be ravisher B524.5; creation of p. A1858; enmity of p. and snail A2494.12.10; why p. lives underground A2433.3.22; why p. has only four claws A2376.3; why p. lives in high places in mountains A2433.3.11; wrestling between p. and deer K12.5.

Porcupine's dwelling A2432.4; skin A2311.5.

Porcupines absent from Cape Breton Island A2434.2.1.

Pork. — Tabu to eat p. C221.1.1.5; why Jews do not eat p. A1681.2; women not to eat p. C181.8.

Porpoise helper on quest H1233.6.3. — Man transformed to p. D127.6.

Porridge eaten in different rooms J2167; in the ice hole J1938. — Complaint of p. pot J1875.2; fool spits in the hot p. J2421; hot p. in the ogre's throat K1033; hungry parson and p.-pot X431; magic p.-pot keeps cooking *C916.3; substituted p. K471; speaking p. D1610.31.1.

Portent, see Omen.

Porter rescues abandoned child R131.9. — Disguise as p. K1816.7; (to enter girl's room) K1349.1.1; lost soul to serve as p. in hell for seven years E755.2.3; Saint Peter as p. of heaven A661.0.1.2; treacherous p. K2244.

Porter's revenge for three wise counsels J1511.6.

Porters. — Man robbed by p. who carry his treasure J2092.

Portia masks as lawyer K1825.2.

Portrait, see also Picture; of the Virgin appears to devotee V263.

Portraits exude oil V128.2. — Devils dwell in p. G303.8.14.

Portrayal. — Punishment for foul p. of Jesus Q222.3.

Posing *K2000ff. — Escape by p. as member of murderer's family or tribe K601; hare (jackal) with horns of wax p. as horned animal K1991; seduction by p. *K1310ff.; theft by p. as doctor K352; trickster p. as helper eats women's stored provisions K1983.

Position. — Deception into humiliating p. *K1200—K1299; fortune-telling dream induced by sleeping in extraordinary p. D1812.3.3.2; high p. as reward Q113.3; loss of social p. Q494; riddle propounded on pain of loss of official p. H541.3; tabu: sleeping in certain p. during certain time C735.1.0.1; tests of social. p. H1574; shape and p. of animals' eyes A2332.4ff.; wife gets would-be seducer's p. for husband K443.2.1.

Possessed. — Devil cast out of p. man D2176.3.4; people p. by trolls F455.6.10.

Possession of magic powers D1710ff.; by spirit of dead person gives second sight D1821.8; of wisdom J180ff.; of woman disputed by skillful creators *H621. — Acquisition and p. of wisdom (knowledge) J0—J199; demoniacal p. K2385; exiled wife's dearest p. J1545.4; fairy gift not to leave p. of mortal's family F348.3; lovers flee, leave hidden man in p. K1271.1.4.2; madness from demonic p. D2065.1; monk's most valuable p., virtue T331.9; test of valor worthy for kingship: taking p. of royal insignia H1561.5.

Possessions, see also Belongings; of brownies F482.4; buried with the dead E433.2; of dwarfs F451.7ff.; of fairies F240ff.; of giant ogre G110ff.; not to be counted C776. — Allies and p. of the devil G303.10ff.; gigantic p. of giant F531.4ff.; great p. bring great risks U81; guessing nature of devil's p. H523ff.; lie: remarkable p. X1020; not to touch p. of god C51; present p. preferred to future possibilities J321; soul leaves p. on road to resting place E750.4; troll's p. G304.3ff.

Post falls when owners lose estate E766.3; hole murder K959.6; wears down from top D1688. — Earth supported on p. A843; ghost transfers boil to a p. D2161.4.2.1; insects from devil's p.-hole A2004; origin of sacred p. A992.1; vows taken by placing foot on certain p. M119.4.

Posterior. — Why man's p. large A1319.4.

Posthumous child exposed S312.3. — Hero a p. child A511.1.6, T682.

Postponing death *D1855, T211.1; demanding of promised boon M204; payment to gather reinforcements K2369.4; wedding by hiding girl R53.3. — Constant p. tests suitor H317.4; penance: always p. sentence Q520.4.

Pot breaks (life token) E761.5.1; of Basil T85.3; cannot be lifted D1654.16; calls kettle black J1063; of flour broken before sold J2061.1.3; has a child and dies J1531.3; on head after command not to show head J2489.13; jumps, indicates hidden money E539.2; too heavy with ghosts to lift E499.3; transformed D454.6; -tilter G331. — Alleged soup-making p. sold K112.2.1; animals help repair p. B579.4; bluff: huge cauldron called hero's kitchen p. K1718.3; boiling p. seen as threat, broken J1813.10; boiling p. thought to be self-cooking J1813.4; breaking p. with sword to show new sight J2469.5.2; child born in p. T561.4; cock under p. crows for guilt H235; damages for broken p.: pay for elephant K251.5; dividing eggs in p. J1241.5; dwarf falls into porridge p. X142.1; escape from deluge in p. A1029.3; filled milk p. shows city full of fakirs J1293.4; filling p. with dew H1129.4; getting the calf's head out of the p. J2113; great cabbage and great p. to put it in X1423.1; hare in p. escapes tiger K521.11; magic flower p. bears plants with gold letters on leaves D1469.1; magic p. *D1171.1, (with demons who beat owner's enemy) D1401.4; man transformed to p. D252; numskull licks out p. and gets it caught on his head J2131.5.2; only one man can lift p. H31.4; poisoned p. J2311.2; reckoning in the p. J2466.2; spring made to flow into p. D2151.6.2; stolen p. pawned with real owner K405.2; tabued p. broken: town appears C917.1; thief uses p. in hole as feeler K315.2; three-legged p. sent to walk home J1881.1.3; universe created from clay p. A617.1; wife bangs p. on husband's head while guest is present T252.7; woman thinks boiling p. is complaining J1875.2.

Pots symbolic of sons' inheritances J99.2. — Ass in potter's shop breaks p. J973; banishment for breaking water p. Q431.16; earthen and brazen p. in river J425.1; eating from fine p. forbidden C219.1; filling p. with subterranean outlets H1023.2.5; looking into the p. in hell forbidden *C325; man smells p. boiling far away F652.2; old woman's maledictions because of broken p. inform abandoned hero of his parentage and future S375; sun and moon kept in p. when they do not shine A721.0.1.

Potatoes as "eggs of the earth" J1772.1.2. — Lies about p. X1435; lazy man digs three p. in one day W111.5.12; plowing p. out of ground J2465.13; why p. are hard A2793.4; witch steals p. D2087.8.

Potion, see also **Drink, Medicine.** — Magic p. *D1242.2, (heals wounds) D1503.13, (remedies impotence) T591.1.1; sleeping p. *D1364.7, (given suitors) H347.

Potiphar's wife K2111.

Potlatch. — Origin of p. A1535.1.

Potsherd. — Transformation: handkerchief with three knots to clod, p., and charcoal D454.3.2.1.

Pottage. — Conception from eating p. T511.8.3; milk surreptitiously added to saint's p. K499.2.2.

Potter as creator A15.4.1. — Disguise as p. K1816.4; king formerly p. retains earthenware J913; treacherous p. K2249.1, K2259.3.

Potter's. — Ass in p. shop J973.

Pottery. — Goddess of p. A451.4; origin of p. A1451; piling up p. by breaking pots into fragments J2465.2.

Pottle of brains like clever girl J163.2.1.

Pouch transformed to ptarmigen D444.9.

Pouka-herb speaks D1610.3.3.

Poultry. — Fairy p. F241.8.

Pound. — Literal pleading frees man from p. of flesh contract J1161.2; moon weighs p., for it has four quarters H691.1.1; people in otherworld stand on heads and p. yams with their heads F167.4.1; witch breaks up lumber p. G283.1.2.6.

Pounded, see also **Beaten.** — Devil p. in knapsack until he releases man K213; king to have head p. M369.9; victim p. up with poisoned fish K838.

Poured. — Water p. into tub full of holes in otherworld *F171.6.2.

Pourer. — Remarkable p. of water F636.3.

Pouring water instead of milk: each member cheats K231.6.1.1; water on fire as witch protection G272.8. — Fire p. on earth A1031.4.1; ghost summoned by p. blood of sacrifices into trench E382; rain produced by p. water *D2143.1.1.

Poverty, see also **Poor;** to be no bar to marriage of friends' children M246.2; personified Z133; as saintly virtue V461.8. — Angel of p. A473.0.1; blackmail about p. K443.10; choice between free p. or enslaved wealth J211; former p. chosen over new riches L217.1; magic prevents p. D1389.9; outcast wife and son live in p. S442; pain preferred to p. J229.14; prophecy: p. from birth M359.5; seven causes of p. Z71.5.6.1; saints called fools for enduring p. J1263.4.2; wealth and p. U60ff.

Powder. — Captor's p. removed, gun doesn't work K633; magic p. *D1246, (transforms) D572.6; resuscitation by magic p. E108; sham physician using the flea p. K1955.4.

Powders. — Transformation by smelling p. D564.3.

Powdered skull as remedy D1500.1.7.1.

Power of habit U130ff.; of mind over body U240ff.; of dwarf in his belt F451.3.1; to which sacrifice is made V11; of self-transformation received from (a god) D630.2, (wood-spirit) D630.1; in words, herbs, and stones J1581.2. — Aspiring to too much p. forbidden C773; avoidance of others' p. J640ff.; changeling shows supernatural p. to work and thus betrays maturity F321.1.1.4; devil's magic p. turned on himself K214; not to disclose source of magic p. C423.1; failure to bless mountain gives mountain-men p. F460.4.6; fairy comes into man's p. when he steals her wings

*F302.4.2; falling into ogre's p. G400—G499; fatal deception into trickster's p. K810ff.; girl tricked into man's p. K1330ff.; hero's p. to transform girl to carnation brings about recognition H151.7; how devil's p. may be escaped or avoided G303.16ff.; husband attracted by wife's p. of healing: recognition follows H151.8; magic journey through p. of imagination D2121.3; magic object gives p. (over animals) D1440ff., (of flying) *D1531ff., (over other persons) D1400—D1439; magic object loses p. by overuse D877; magic p. (from animal) *B500ff., (of prophecy) *D1812ff., (lost by breaking tabu) C947; magic results from p. of thought *D1777; magic smoke carries p. of saint D1572; man given p. of wishing *D1720.1; man obtains p. over fairy mistress F302.4; miraculous p. of prayer *V52; silence under punishment breaks p. of enchantment *D1741.3; tests of p. to survive *H1510ff.; not to use magic p. too often *C762.1; vampire's p. overcome E251.1f; why one people superior in p. to another A1689.11; wild hunt's p. evaded E501.17.4ff.; wisdom of concession to p. J811ff.; witch sells p. to control winds D2142.0.1.1; witch's hair has p. to bind or to transform G221.1.1.

Powers of dragon B11.5ff.; of nature as God's messengers A165.2.4. — Abnormally born child has unusual p. T550.2; extraordinary p. (of deduction) H505, (of perception) F640ff.; extraordinary physical p. of fairies F253; fairy mother bestows magic p. upon half-mortal son F305.1.1; falsely claiming the p. of a god forbidden C51.6; fluid takes away magic p. D1410.3; kingly p. P19.4; magic object confers miraculous p. D1561ff.; magic p. *D1700—D2199; persons with extraordinary p. *F600—F699; special p. of (chaste women) D413, (troll) G304.2.3; unpromising hero given great p. L103.

Powerful man as helper N835. — Angels p. V230.2; king show he is less p. than God L418; magic objects p. against fairies F384; prophecy: son to be more p. than father M312.2.1.

Powerless. — Demons p. over souls commended to God before sleep E754.1.1.1; dwarf rendered p. F451.3.2; fairy rendered p. F383; magic horse becomes p. because of broken tabu C942.2; ogre p. to cross stream G638; ogres p. after cockcrow G636; wild hunt p. E501.17ff.; witch rendered p. G273ff.

Practical and impractical defenses J671. — Clever p. retorts *J1500—J1649.

Prairie-dog. — Enmity between crow and p. A2494.13.5; friendship of p. and owl A2493.1.

Praised. — Object grateful for being p. D1658.1.1ff.

Praising. — Animals p. B251ff.; husband p. suitor causes wife's love T13.

Pranks played by (devil) G303.9.9ff., (dwarfs) F451.5.2.7.

Prattlers. — Why women are p. A1372.1.

Prawn. — Chain tale: man bitten by p. Z49.6.3.

Prawns. — Creation of p. A2132.

Prayer, see also **Paternoster;** *V50ff.; -contest to prove which religion better V351.4; creates house D1133.1.1; either to keep friend from death or for both to die E165.1; over the underdone hen J1342; by the soul E757. — Adam's p. that he father mankind A1285.1.1; Agnus Dei as a p. for money J1741.2; angel answers mortal's p. V243; angel shows value of work with p. H605; animal tamed by saint's p. B771.2.2; barrenness removed by p. D1925.3; beautification by p. D1864; birth obtained through p. T548; boon granted after p. R123; charity rewarded above p. or hearing of masses V410.1; child as reward for p. Q192; claim that a trap is a p. house K730.1.1; conception by p. T526; condemned soul saved by p. E754.1.1; deity answers p. and aids task H975.0.1; devil's power over one avoided by p. G303.16.2; disenchantment by p. of pope D781; efficacy of p. V316; flood caused by p. A1017.2; food supplied by p. D1030.1.1; ghost laid by p. E443.2; holy man's p. reforms rich man J153.1; magic house made by p. D1133.1.1; magic results produced by p. *D1766.1; mountain moved by p. D2136.3.1; neglect of p. punished Q223.1; one saved from the devil by p. to Virgin G303.16.2.2; pain stopped by p. D1766.1.4; provisions in answer to p. D2105.1; repression of lust through p. T317.2; respite from death granted until p. is finished *K551.1; resuscitation by p. E63; river answers desert travelers' p. D2151.2.5.1; rivers from saint's p. during drought A934.5; saint changes boat's course in answer to p. T321.6; saint's p. causes wolf to bring back child B256.8; saint's p. wins battle D2163.5ff.; sea calmed by p. D2151.1.3; storm produced by p. D2141.0.7.1; summoning by p. D2074.2.5; sun turned from one hour to another through the p. of Moses alone F961.1.7; vampire's power overcome by endurance and p. E251.1.1.

Prayers for cruel tyrant J215.2.1. — Adulteress pretends going to say p. K1514.12; animal tamed by saint's p. B771.2.2; ceremonies and p. used at unearthing of treasure N554; church spared in flood because of p. D2143.2.1; control of weather by saint's p. D2140.1; dead grateful for p. E341.3; devil appears among youths who jest while they say their evening p. G303.6.2.3; loud reproofs during p. J2254; magic spells mixed with Christian p. *D1273.0.2; monk's p. weave garment for Virgin V276.1; origin of p. A1546.0.2; resuscitation by holy man's p. E121.5.2; reward for saying p. Q33; seven p. of saint Z71.5.6.10; sinner saved through p. of confessor V52.9; wife's p. save usurer J155.5.

Prayerbook. — Ghost cannot pass cross or p. E434.8.

Praying with arms forming cross V86.5; before the King of Kings J1269.7; over corpse saves soul from devil K218.7; ship sink since prayers are never answered J1467.1. — Animals p. B251.4; cat is really p. when it purrs A1811.3; escape from p. captor K562.1; long p. as test H1508; man murdered while p. K918; Satan p. to God G303.9.8.8; Satan stops p. G303.9.4.5.3; sexton behind statue tells old maid p. for a husband to raise her foot to her neck K1971.9; unnecessary choice between p. or reading J465.

Preach. — Footprints still visible where holy man stood to p. A972.1.3;

numskull tries to p. while the priest is preaching J2131.1.1; parson has no need to p. X452; return from dead to p. repentance E367.

Preacher. — Bear on haywagon thought to be p. J1762.2; saint's follower miraculously becomes p. F660.21.

Preaching, see also **Sermon.** — Fish come to hear saint p. B251.2.7.1; repression of lust through p. T317.3; saint p. three days F1086; time flies as saint is p. D2011.1.2.

Prearranged answers fail J1741.3; conversation brings comic results C495.2, J1741.3, X111.9.

Precedence shown by shield's position P632.4.1. — Strangers to be given p. over man at home P631.

Preceptor, see **Teacher.**

Precepts, see also **Counsels;** of the lion to his sons J22ff. — Reward for fulfilling p. Q20.2.

Precious properties of the gods A156. — City of p. metals F761; magic statue of archer put into action by picking up p. object from ground D1620.1.5.1; recognition through p. metal H91; sacrament too p. to be bought J1261.2.4.

Precious stones, see also **Jewels;** in heaven produce music A661.0.2.2; in otherworld F162.0.1.2. — City of p. F761; doors of p. F782.2; fourteen daughters find p. N231; pillars of p. F774.1; snakes play with p. B765.12.

Precipice. — Disrobing woman pushes robber off p. K551.4.3; dupe induced to jump over p. K891.4.5; fools make a boat go over a p. J2129.1; hero is pushed over a p. H1535; lark causes elephant to fall over p. L315.5; wife throws husband down p. K1514.8.

Precipitation, see also **Rain;** produced by magic D2143ff. — Extraordinary p. F962ff.; lies about p. X1650.

Precocious hero A527.1, (leaves cradle for war) T585.7, (as mighty slayer) F628.0.1; infant T585; speech T615.1; strength F611.3.2.

Precociousness T615.

Predestined husband T22.3; lovers T22; rescuer R169.8; slayer D1812.4.1; wife T22.2.

Predicted. — Birth of child p. by fairy *F315; saint's birth p. V222.0.1; sex of unborn child p. by sham physician K1955.3.

Predicting. — Dead p. death E545.2; dead p. war E545.16.1; dwarf p. F451.3.3.7; fairy p. death F361.17.9; fairy p. newborn child's greatness F317; sea ghost p. death E271.2.

Pre-existing world of gods above A631.

Prefect dies of fish bone in throat N339.12.

Preferring one's own children T681; one's own kind to strangers J416; ugly to pretty sister L145.

Pregnancy, see also **Impregnation;** T570ff. — Bride has maid sleep in husband's bed to conceal p. *K1843.1; girl punished for p. Q254; origin of medical treatment during p. A1562; pseudomagic potion for p. K115.3; premarital p. among sisters H507.4; tabus during p. C152ff.

Pregnant abbess secretly delivered of her child by Virgin Mary T401.1; nun's virginity restored T313.1.1; wife left in friend's charge H1558.9; woman abandoned S414; woman crushed beneath chariot S116.2; woman dreams of unborn child's fate D1812.3.3.8; woman ordered to kill child S324; woman vitiates snake's power D1837.4; **woman's longings assign quest** H1212.4. — Adulteress's p. belly pierced Q451.14; cruelty to p. woman S185; deduction: camel ridden by p. woman J1661.1.1.1; dog indicates p. woman B152.1; king with seven wives, seven mares, all p. seven years Z71.5.7; lover masks as p. woman to meet midwife K1514.16; man made to believe that he is p. J2321; Mother Earth p. with Adam A401.1; numskull praises his daughter as being p. J2427; paramour disguised as p. woman K1517.7; peacock p. from eating male's semen B754.6; punishment for refusal to marry after girl is p. Q245; seducer disguised as p. woman K1321.1.1; prophecy of ogre-child so p. woman will be killed K2115.3; snake p. seven years B765.25; stars descend to earth, make woman p. A788.3; tasks assigned because of longings of p. woman *H936.

Premature aging as punishment Q551.12; darkness F965. — Deer lost through p. celebration J2173.4; failure to resuscitate because of p. disturbance of members to be left in cask for nine days E37.1; foolishness of p. coming out of hiding J582; sitting on stone to prevent p. birth T572.1.1.

Prematurely dead man sent back to earth E121.1.3. — Child speaks p. T585.2.2; god born p. A112.7.4.

Prenatal influences T576, (of magic object) D1352.

Prepared. — Punishments being p. in hell Q561; royal children p. for life's hazards J702.2.

Preparing the food "Oh my" H1185; of food taught by gods A1420.2; large quantity of grain as task H1122.

Prescription. — Fool eats paper with p. on it J2469.2; imitation of the p. J2412.3; sham physician hands out p. K1955.9.1.

Prescriptions. — Drawing p. by lot K1955.9.

Presence of cursed person brings disaster to land M491. — Flame indicates p. of beautiful woman F1061.1; marvelous sensitiveness: women blush in the p. of male statue F647.4; not to be in p. of god *C52.

Present evil preferred to change for worse J215; or retaining fee J1559.1; starts quarrel for its possession K1083; values chosen J300—J329. — Absent person seems to be p. K1881; bringing past to p. H1026.2; coming neither with nor without a p. H1056; devil's p. haunts G303.8ff.; devotee of Virgin Mary given p. by her V281; food as marriage p. H335.5; green figs as p. to king thrown in fool's face J2563; modest request: p. from the journey L221; one p. from spirit son-in-law C714.1; why former days better than p.? J311.2; wisdom from fool: the p. returned J156.3; Zeus refuses wedding p. from snake J411.2.

Presents, see also **Gifts.** — Ceremonial p. produced by magic D2178.6; dividing the winnings: p. from man's own wife M241.2; parting p. L222,

T136.4.2; sun and moon divine hero's wedding p. A759.2; two p. to the king: beet and horse J2415.1; wedding p. T136.4.2.

Presentiment. — Future revealed by p. D1812.4.

Preservation of life during world calamity A1005. — Magic p. D2167ff.

Preserved. — Fig magically p. F813.7.1; best types of men, animals p. in inclosure during calamity A1005.2; snake p. in ark to stop hole with tail A2145.2.

Presiding. — Fairy p. at child's birth F312.

Pressed. — Mountains p. together by God A962.4.

Pressing. — Man's feat at p. out oil F639.7.

Presumption of the lowly *J950ff.

Presumptuous man's comment on Michelangelo J957; officials disregarded J982.

Pretence K2000ff.; of adulteress to unusual sensitiveness K2051; of penniless bridegroom to wealth K1917; of sham physician to diagnose entirely from urinalysis K1955.2; of sham teacher K1958. — Absurd p. allowed puts pretender out of countenance J1214; adulteress refuses to admit husband under p. that he is a stranger K1511.1; captured animal's p. to help captor bring more desirable victim K553.1; maid vexes suitor by p. T77; thief leaves food untouched because of owner's p. to being poisoned by it K439.4.

Pretended, see also **Feigned;** abduction R10.2; virtue K2050ff. — Devil interrupts mass by p. battle G303.9.9.2; girl escapes from robber through p. combing of her hair K551.5; punishment: death p. becomes real Q591.1; sham cure by p. extracting of object from patient's body K1871.2.

Pretender as pope K1961.2.

Pretending. — Blind man p. he can see X128; cat hangs on wall p. to be dead K2061.9; consolation by p. that one does not want the thing he cannot have J870ff.; enemy induced to give up siege by p. to have plenty of food K2365.1; escape by p. to dance and thus be untied K571; hypocrite p. friendship attacks K2010ff.; man behind statue p. to be God K1971; repentant thief p. to have found stolen cow upbraids owner for not guarding her better K416; temporary advantage by p. to yield in a combat K2378.

Pretty feet F551.3; white hands F552.3. — Better send ugly woman to devil than p. one J229.4; fairies' p. room F221.3; ugly preferred to p. sister L145.

Prevented. — Animal p. from straying by magic object D1446; attack p. by druid's hedge D1381.1; child p. from being stolen from cradle by sign of cross V86.1.1; children magically p. from nursing T611.4; devil p. from revenge by pious priest G303.16.11.2; disease p. by magic object D1500.2ff.; escape p. by magic circle D1417.1; father p. from shooting his son by dwarf king F451.5.1.16; man p. from committing incest with his daughter by holy water *V132.1; moving of little stone p. by devil sitting on it G303.9.9.1; nun miraculously p. by Virgin from deserting convent V265; person p. from rising from chair by ring D1413.2; soul of sleeper p. from returning to his body E721.1.2; woman who has p. birth of children casts no shadow Q552.9.

Preventing burial of corpse E273.1. — Banishment till rose grows from table for p. childbirth Q431.4; dead p. living man from returning to earth F93.1.1; murderer's penance complete when he kills a greater murderer, p. a crime Q545.

Prevention of childbirth T572; of marriage by excessive demands H301; of hostility by inspiring fear in enemy J623; of witchcraft by burning cut hair D2176.50. — Forethought in p. of others' plans J620ff.

Preying.—Animals p. on one another teach of death J52.1; vulture p. on fettered monster A1074.4.

Price of consecration (ova or oves) J1263.2.1; depends on where object for sale U84; set on one's head M208. — Bride-p. T52; city where everything sold at one p. J21.52.1; every woman has her p. U66.1; exorbitant p. demanded, received K255; fairy leaves goats as girl's purchase p. F343.8; half p. for half a shave J1522.1; land where everything sold for same p. X1503.3; large p. for curing ogre G682; large p. for corpses: wives killed K941.1.1; town of one p. F769.1.

Prices. — Escape by reporting high p. elsewhere K576; reduced p. but false weights K286; trickster's false report of high p. causes dupe to destroy his property K941.

Pricks. — Ass foolish to kick against the p. J833.

Pricking feet exposes thief posing as corpse J1149.7; with pin to keep awake H1484. — Sham dead tested by p. H248.3.

Pride, see also **Proud;** brought low *L400—L499; punished Q331. — Dead brother reproves sister's p. E226.1; dove's p. in her large brood linked with fear for their loss U81.1; false p. W165; iron created to punish cedar's p. A978.2; magic destroys p. D1359.6; monstrous births as punishment for girl's p. Q552.5; overweening p. forbidden *C770ff.; owl's p. in son's feet T681.1; rich man made poor to punish p. L412; teacher dies of p. over success of pupil P341.

Priest, see also **Cleric, Monk;** P426.1; buys worthless glass as diamond K451.4; carries host across stream J1261.2.8; catches bishop in incontinence J1211.1.1; catches thief at dying man's house J1261.2.6; caught in lasso by rival lover K1218.1.6; chases devil away G303.16.14.1; claims lent only counterfeit money to Jew J1511.10; commends the poor miller X212.1; dies from being duped F1041.1.3.4; dies fleeing girl's corpse N384.8; disguised as layman K1824; disguises as devil to haunt house K1838; drags heavy sack, symbol of sin H606; draws sow instead of woman K1281.1; exorcises witch G271.2.4; exorcising demon taken for demon, killed J1786.4; frightens away guests, tells of plague J1563.8; has no friends until he becomes bishop U63; as helper N846.2; who gives mild penances succeeds where others fail L361; joins devils after death because he let woman die without confessional Q223.4.1; keeps in container relic which when kissed renders people immune from pestilence J762.1; with large hat mistaken for hat J1763.1; makes the omen come true J1624; multiplying his talents: impregnates nuns J1264.7; must give up his charge or his mistress J705.1; punished for refusal to bury dead unless paid in advance Q286.2; refuses to lend but donates grain J1552.4; saves own promised soul from devil M216.1; seduces man's wife J652.3; sells distracting donkey J357; separates girl from devil G303.16.14.1.1; shows absurdity of being forbidden female servant J1539.1; shows host through window, told to imagine payment J1551.10; shows power of excommunication over host V84.2; of snakes B252.3; stamps on stone to prove truth of pope A972.1.2; as surety K455.5; throws chalice at owl J1261.2.7; trapped as lover in chest, enacts Lazarus K1218.1.4; trapped in window, humiliated K1243; told that he is unfit offers to exchange places with bishop J1265.2; uses fortune dishonestly made to erect monuments to himself W157.1; walks in the mud J82; will sell self only for large sum J1263.2.3. — Appointment of p. as reward Q113.4; bishop forced to ordain ignorant p. U41; boy disguises as woman to embarrass incontinent p. K1836.2; at child's funeral real father, p., sings U119.1.1; Christianized Jew becomes p., murders V364; church door magically opens for innocent p. H216.3; devil carries off hunt-loving p. M219.2.4; devil bargains to help man become p. M216; devil is cheated of his reward when p. dismisses mass early G303.16.16; devil cheated when his victim becomes a p. K218.3; devil in form of p. G303.3.1.8; devil prevented from revenge by pious p. G303.16.11.2; devil shows p. long parchment roll of sins of congregation G303.24.1.1; devil and sinful p. disappear amid blaze of fire in the river G303.17.2.4; devil takes the place of woman who went to spend night with a p. G303.25.11; devils disappear when p. blesses bread G303.16.2.3.3; discourtesy toward p. tabu C94.1.3; discussion between p. and Jew carried on by symbols H607.1; disguise as p. K1826.5; father calls p. son a thief H581.4; fig tree is chief p. of trees A2777.1.; frightening off parasite p. K2338; ghost drives p. into oven E264; ghost laid by p. E443.2.4; ghost of p. failing to say masses E415.3; ghost steals book from p. E593.2; ghost steals collar of p. E593.1; ghosts attack bishop who has suspended p. for singing for all Christian souls E243; god as p. A137.13; greedy p. reincarnated as feeding insect Q551.5.1.3; host taken away from sinful p. V31.1; ignorant p. forces rolls of cloth instead of sacrament down dying man's throat J1738.1; incontinent p. V465.1.1; numskull tries to preach while p. is preaching J2131.1.1; recognition when parents come to son as p. to be confessed H151.3; renegade p. punished by death Q222.1.1; resuscitation by p. E121.5; ruler in disguise to frighten uxorious p. K1812.6; scolding p. merely trying to get even for all scolding he must undergo J1269.4; seduction by p. during confession K1339.6; sham p. K1961.1ff.; sharing wife with p. J1919.6; suspected p. detected by husbands J1141.11; thief frightens p., confederate steals from him K335.0.5.2; treacherous p. K2284; trickster tells p. chicken owner a heretic K455.4.1; unquiet dead sinner taken to p. for absolution E411.0.2.

Priest's concubine cannot rest in grave *E411.2.1; curse M411.14; dead wife found alive J1179.11; fifty-year-old maid: two young ones J2212.1.1; guest and eaten chickens *K2137; penance saves him from devil K218.6; words repeated by fool J2498.2. — Abbot escapes in p. disguise K521.6; disregarding p. warning J1055; girl disguised as friar gets into p. bed K1315.6.3; king no p. son J1827.

Priests claim they are entitled to dying woman's last wish: get burned J1511.18; compete in rushing through mass J1263.1.3.1; drinking only one wine at a time J1511.15; ignorant of Latin J1741; outwitted in dream interpretation J1527; substitute gilded images for gold K476.4.1. — Bad year for p.: few funerals X427; devils created from sinful p. G303.1.6; druids as p. P427.1.2; ghost as p. E425.2.3; how many p. one should have in one place J1291.3; why ignorant p. are favored J1263.1.1; magic invisibility of p. D1981.5; negligent p. buried under bags filled with words omitted from service V5.2; oracular images occupied by p. who give the answers K1972; origin of p. A1654.1; tabus of p. C573; treacherous p. prolong mass to let enemy destroy city K2354.

Priesthood — Origin of p. A1654; removal from p. as punishment Q494.2; selling soul to obtain p. M216.1.

Primary elements of universe A654.

Primata. — Creation of p. A1860ff.

Primeval chaos *A605; human pair A1270ff.; water A810ff.

Primitive. — King prefers p. to civilized culture J245.2; topographical features caused by experiences of p. hero (demigod, deity) A901.

Primrose. — Origin of p. A2622, A2653.

Prince abducted by giantess F531.5.7.1.3; accidentally finds maiden and marries her N711; adopts exposed child S354.3; agrees to marry a servant girl if she will help him on a quest H1239.1; avoids misfortune prophecy M391.1.1; awakened by fly, saved from enemy B521.3.3.1; born with gold bow H71.7.2; can feel hair on bedding F647.9.1; chooses dangerous road H1561.9; chooses exile with honor J347.3; disguised as holy man abducts princess R24.1; disguised as madman tests bride H384.1.2; disguises as another prince K1812.3; donates all, including tooth W11.9; of democratic tastes chosen J412.1; escapes home to see world R213.1; to give up life in exchange for learning a secret M232; grows up in eagle's nest B535.0.5; a-hunting enters on quest H1222; identifies disguised horse H62.3; to learn trade as suitor task H335.0.2.2; lost on hunt has adventures N771; in love with lowly girl T91.6.2; and low caste man exchange appearances D22.2; who never laughs F591.1; married to monkey F302.11; must rule five years before receiving all keys C611.1.1; offered as prize T67; overrules king's decisions J123.1; plans to kill wicked father S22.2; penalizes cursing, although he himself curses W133.1; pleads with giant not to eat him K567.1; plucks from grave of

vampire a flower which later becomes a girl E251.2.2; refuses to play
with common children J411.3; regains eyesight: steals other's eyes
E781.1.1; reincarnated as common man E605.5; rescues abandoned child
R131.11.3; as riddle-solver H561.9; steals magic from bathing fairy
D838.10; stolen while nurse dances K341.17.1; substitutes peasant girl
for father's bride K1911.1.9; sulks until quest is accomplished H1212.3;
transformed to old man D93; will want me back: hero spared K512.0.2.
— Angels help boy p. slay uncle V232.1.1; bishop and p. J1289.2; blinded
p. regains sight F952.0.2; common man reincarnated as p. E605.6; day-
light renders fairy p. mortal F383.4.1; disenchantment of monster when p.
promises to marry the monster's mother D741; disguised p. seduces queen
K1814.1; fairies charm p. into deathlike sleep F302.3.4.5; father brings
daughter P. Sobur H946.1, J1805.2.1; flute-player thinks song meant for
the p. is sung to him J953.3; friendship between p. and common man
P311.8; girl sends sign message to p. H611.2; have you seen my p.?
H1292.13; how p. can be cured H1292.4; incognito p. beaten by gamblers
K1812.2.2; incognito p. beaten, realizes folly J18; king's family from
fairy p. A1653.2; little girl bribes p. to marry her T55.4; lowly heroine
marries p. L162; magic spindle brings back p. for heroine D1425.1; man
who unwittingly kills p. is exiled N324; peasant boy masking as p. betrays self by his answers H38.2.2; plant droops when p. in trouble
D1310.4.3; poor boy said by helpful cat to be dispossessed p. K1952.1;
poor p. overcomes king L311.3; quarreling p. and princess vow to
maltreat each other if married M149.4; quest for lost p. H1385.10; repartee between king and p. accused of rape J1289.6; search for p. named
Sabr H946.1, J1805.2.1; sham p. K1952; slander: p. is bastard K2128;
sluggish p. reformed by falling in love T10.1; snake cannot kill p. until
princess bears sons J1173.1.1; taming wild p. grown up among animals
K1399.1; treacherous p. K2246; unknown p. shows his kingly qualities
in dealing with his playmates H41.5; wax p. comes to life D435.1.4; why
p. plays with children J1661.1.7; young p. sent to his uncle P293.4.

Prince's lost wife rescued R131.11.5; marriage to common woman prophesied M359.2; motto on charity V410.2; pulse beats violently as beloved passes H175.3; spouse-murder pact with princess S63. — Human
sacrifice to prolong p. life S268.1.1; princess from p. body A1275.1.1;
protecting p. slumber by shooting frogs all night J2105; secret of p.
father learned by eavesdropper N455.7; servant entrusted with crown p.
care P362; youth in court for kissing p. daughter pleads his love for her
J1174.1.

Princes *P30ff.; asked what they most desire: answers determine who
shall rule P17.3; banished for lewd conduct Q431.5.3; tested for throne
H1574.3.0.1. — Seven p. seek seven princesses T69.1.2.

Princess abducted *R10.1, (through underground passage) R25.1; becomes
ogress D47.3; brings ill luck to bridegroom K443.12; builds tower of
skulls of unsuccessful suitors *S110.3; calls suitors ugly names T76; can

not marry anyone weighing more than she T69.2.2; catches robber K434.2; compelled to keep an inn *Q481; cured by seeing lover F950.8; declares her love for lowly hero T55.1; declares love in sign language H607.3; discovers hero's disguised hair H151.13; disenchanted by seven year old boys D759.10; in disguise aids impoverished man N227; disguised as man accused of adultery with queen K2113; elects husband T55.8; escapes captor by cutting hair K538; falls in love with lowly boy T91.6.4; feigns sickness to woo hero T55.5; follows jeweled mouse, recognized H151.1.2; gives self away to save people T455.7; hangs up weapons of dead lover as continual reminder T85.2; hides in straw R313; humiliated because of loathly marriage S322.1.4; in love with knight T91.6.4.1.1; loves man disguised as woman T28; lured into forest K788.1; married to wounded prince, both left in jungle T89.1.1; marries clever thief Q91.1; to marry first man who asks for her T62; must never see male person C313.0.1; must sell goods on market as punishment Q483; offered as prize *T68f.; on the pea H41.1; price for sparing palace T52.7; from prince's body A1275.1.1; punished by displaying self Q473.6; rescues abandoned child R131.11.1; sacrificed to dragon H335.3.1; secretly pledged to many K2034.1; serves as menial Q482.1; sets hero tasks H933; sick because toad has swallowed her consecrated wafer *V34.2; skillful in argument J1111.1; so lovely everyone loves her T15.1; in tank makes serpent release water F914.1; threatens to kill amorous king T322.2; transforming self to woo T55.11; tricked into engagement K1372.1; has unrestricted choice of husband T131.0.1; will marry whoever gives her all she wishes H313.1; wins wrestling match with suitor by revealing her breast H331.6.1.1. — Abandoned p. raised by herdsmen S351.2.1; abducted p. gives birth R35; abducted p. wishes self with rejected suitor, is N425; altered letter of execution gives p. to hero *K1355; animals help hero win p. B582.2; brothers having extraordinary skill rescue p. R166; calumniated p. corpse of fails to rot H251.3.14; captive p. causes giant's death G527; cast-out p. prospers N145; choosing p. from others identically clad H324; clandestine visit of p. to hero betrayed by token H81.2; crane recognizes p. H188; decapitated p. resuscitated by hero E149.2; demon seduces bathing p. F402.1.15.1; disguised p. recognized by bull H162.3; dragon fight to free p. B11.11.4; dumb p. is brought to speech by tale ending with a question to be solved F954.2.1; enchanted p. lives with dwarfs F451.5.4.3; enchanted p. in castle F771.4.7; fairy p. with golden hair F232.4.2; fairies' gifts to p. F340.1; flea makes p. speak F954.4.1; fruit with p. inside H1333.3.0.2; gardener's son to marry p. H317.3; goose brings sleeping p. B582.1.1.1; grateful dead man helps hero win p. *T66.1; hero directed on journey by p. J155.1; hero substitutes for p. sacrificed to monster K1853.2.1; hero wins p. by magic D1426.0.1; illness spirit enters body of p. F493.0.1.2; incognito p. K1812.8; insanity of p. dependent on height of fire *D2065.4; impostors steal rescued p. K1935; light weight p. F584.1; look of beautiful p. kills F574.1.3; love through

sight of hair of unknown p. T11.4.1; lowly hero marries p. L161; making
p. fall in love H315.1; man slandered as having deflowered p. K2121;
menial disguise of lover of p. K1816.0.3; merman demands p. B82.1.1;
mighty blower slows down racing p. F622.1; newcomers forced to sleep
with p. P616; not to look at p. on public appearance C312.2.1; ogre
guesses correctly and gets p. G463; overly choosy p. marries idiot J2183.5;
Pleiades a p. and six suitors A773.1; prince prefers first love to p. he
later marries J414.2; prophecy: p. will marry bastard M369.2.1.2; prophecy: p. to marry prince M331; prophecy: p. will wed physician, fisherman, prince all in one M306.3; quest for faraway p. H1301.1.2; quest for
Glass P. H1381.3.2; quest for hidden p. H1381.3.7; quest for p. caused
by sight of one of her hairs (dropped by a bird) H1213.1, (stolen) H1385.1,
(transformed into skein of silk) H1381.3.4; race with p. for her hand
H331.5.1; recognition of disguised p. by bee lighting on her H162; rescue
of captive p. *R111; reward for finding abducted p. Q112.0.1.3; robbers
show p. how to treat husband J178; sad-faced p. F591.2; silent p. F569.3.1;
sleeping p. not watched long enough D759.9; sleeping by p. three nights
without looking at her or disturbing her H1472; sneering p. impregnated
by magic L431.3; tailor married to p. betrays trade by calling for needle
and thread H38.2.1; tigers abduct p. to be their ward's wife R13.1.4.2.1;
token taken from sleeping p. H81.1.1; transformed p. as dragon
B11.1.3.0.1; treacherous p. K2246.0.1; trickster concealed in sacred tree
advises that he is to marry the p. K1971.10; trickster exacts promise of
marriage as price of silence after having seen a p. naked *K443.6; tricky
animal secures treasury keys from p. K341.18; trickster blackmails p.
after lying with her K443.6.2; weighing p. against flower H455; whirlwind carries p. away R17.1; question on quest (where is the lost p.?)
H1292.7, (how can p. be cured?) H1292.4.1; winner of most skillful p.
to be king P11.2.3.

Princess's necklace left in hell F102.3; secret sickness from breaking tabu
*C940.1; speech sweeter than sugar H633.5. — Grateful dead man kills
p. monster husband T172.2.1; guessing p. birthmarks *H525; identification by p. garment H118; impostor claims to be father of p. child K1936;
listening to p. counsel tabu C815.1; man disguised as woman carried into
p. room K1343.2; negro takes refuge under p. throne R314; phenomena at
p. birth F960.1.6.

Princesses *P40ff. — Marriage prophecy for newborn p. H41.6; ogress
keeps p. in cave G334.1; plant from scrapings of bodies of p. H522.2;
seven p. compete for hero H375.1; seven p. sought by seven princes
T69.1.2; seventy p. in love with hero T27.2; suitor tests for p. H300ff.;
tabus of p. C567.

Printer P459.1.

Prints. — Indentions on rocks from p. left by man (beast) A972.

Prior pardons sinning friar V21.4.

Prioress's Tale V254.7; V361.

Prison, see also **Captives, Imprisoned;** door opened by prayer D1766.1.7. — Captivity in p. R41ff.; god speaks to saint in p. A182.3.0.2; long p. term leads to marrying princess H317.3; lovers meet in heroine's father's p. T32.1; magic object frees person from p. D1395; man in cold consoles himself thinking of rich man in hell or p. J883.2; means of rescue from p. *R121; saint opens p. door with prayer D1766.1.7; victim tricked into p. and kept there K714.1; wife swims to husband in p. T215.6; witches vanish from p. G249.9; woman sacrifices her honor to free her husband (brother) from p. *T455.2.

Prisoner assigns quest H1219.5; recognized by smile H79.4; to be released after he uses up charmed shoes M202.1.1. — Bishop exchanges places with p. W16; competition in friendship between p. and jailor P315.1; escaping p. falls onto tiger's back N392.1; escaping p. forced to accept hospitality, aided P322.1; king on hunt taken p. N771.1; prayers of family comfort p. V53; rescuer disguised as officer gains custody of p. K649.2; tasks assigned p. so that he may escape punishment H924.

Prisoner's miraculous release F960.5. — Wind blowing flag causes p. execution N394.1.

Prisoners choose between emasculation and blinding J229.12; promise not to escape secretly, ask leave K475.2; released as celebration of king's success P14.1; sacrificed to goddess S260.1.3; starved in corpse-filled pit Q465.2; use up hour of grace in dispute J2183.4; of war hanged S113.1.2. — Magician as beggar frees p. D2031.4.3; mistreatment of p. R51; ogre keeps human p. G334; ogre tricked into carrying his p. home in bag on his own back G561.

Privacy of God not to be betrayed C51.4.1.

Private parts, see **Genitals.**

Privation as curse M448.

Prize — Arrow accidentally makes p. shot N621.1; golden apple as p. in beauty contest H1596.1; ham as p. for husband who rules his wife T252.4; impostors claim p. earned by hero K1932; largest part of a p. to go to the guilty man J1141.1.1; prince offered as p. T67ff.; princess offered as p. *T68; suitor contest: p. to one whose staff blooms H331.3.

Problem. — Easy p. made hard J2700—J2749; solution to p. in dream D1810.8.4; unsolved p. as ending of tale H620ff.

Problems. — Ghost answers person's p. E557.1.

Proboscis. — Origin and nature of animal's p. A2335.3.

Procession of the dead E491. — Disenchantment by maidens walking with lighted candles in p. D759.6; funeral p. of the hen (cumulative tale) Z32.1; ghosts punish intruders into p. of ghosts *E242.

Processions. — Bad omen for two bridal p. to meet D1812.5.1.8.

Proclamation of dogma of Immaculate Conception stops plague V312.1. — Angel's p. V249.1; ceremony of the p. of a Buddha V88.

Procrastination, see also **Laziness,** — Result of labor lost in moment of p. J1071.

Procrustes makes men fit his bed G313.

Procurator. — Devil follows corpse of a p. G303.25.8.1; serpent as p. of rats B221.2.1.

Procuress. — Mother as p. for son T452.1; tables turned on p. by chaste wife K1683.

Procuring. — Hospitality repaid by magic p. of provisions Q45.6.

Prodigal as favorite of fortune N172; son returns P233.8.

Prodigious jump F1071; weeping F1051. — Giant eats p. amount F531.3.4ff.; giant steps p. distance F531.3.5.

Prodigy, see also **Marvel**; as evil omen D1812.5.1.1; as punishment Q552.

Prodigy's rude retort to sarcastic oldster J1369.2.

Production. — Fifth of land's p. belongs to king P13.9.2; unsuccessful imitation of magic p. of food J2411.3.

Profane calling up of spirit forbidden *C10ff.; swearing of oath forbidden C94.2.

Profaning sacred day forbidden *C58; shrine forbidden C51.1.

Professional fool P192.1. — Disguise as p. man K1825; origin of different social and p. classes A1650ff.; transformation into p. man D25.

Professions. — Assignment of p. by Creator A1440.1; clever p. J1115; god of p. A450ff.; how God distributed p. A1650.3.2; humor dealing with p. X300—X499; learned p. P420ff.; trades and p. P400—P499.

Professor examines by signs H607.2.1.—Student enjoys wife of p. K1594.

Proficiency rewarded Q88.

Profit from past in planning future J752.

Profits. — Deceptive division of p. K171; losing chance for future p. J1493.

Profitable association of (great and lowly) J412, (of young and old) F441.

Profligacy *W131ff.

Prognostications from weather *D900.0.1.

Prognosticator — Saint as p. V223.6.

Progress in school J1487. — Ladder as symbol of p. Z139.7.

Progressive purchase of woman's favors K1361.2; type of foolish bargain J2081.

Progressively lucky bargains N421.1.

Prohibitions. — Unique p. *C600ff.

Prolific grain F815.6. — Inexhaustibly p. plant F815.6.1.

Prometheus chained to mountain Q501.4.

Promiscuity. — Fruit-picking time of sexual p. T485.

Promise to return from death E374.1. — Breaking p. to fairy tabu C46.1; disenchantment by p. to marry D742; dwarfs exact p. from mortals F451.5.13; dwarfs p. to emigrate if captured dwarfs are released F451.9.1.5; god's p. not to destroy world by water A1011.3; Land of P. inhabitants F211.0.2; punishment for breaking p. Q266; singer repaid with p. of reward J1551.3; voyage to Land of P. F111.2.

Promises. — Bargains and p. *M200—M299; dwarfs make p. with mental reservations F451.5.10.8; god makes p. A182.3.4; quest to fulfill p. H1229.1.

Promised. — Children sold or p. S210—S259; city falsely p. to enemy K2366; daughter p. to animal suitor *B620.1; that which was p. him J1615; to divide what he has been p. (blows) K187; youth p. to ogre visits ogre's home G461.

Promising. — Devil p. to help mistreated apprentice if youth will meet him by night in lonely spot G303.22.12; disenchantment of monster after prince p. to marry the monster's mother D741; dwarf p. money for girl F451.5.18.1; man p. more to church than he can provide Q266.1; wife p. to die with husband T211.2.2.

Pronouns. — Tale avoiding all p. Z15.

Proof. — Disenchantment as p. of truth: prodigy convinces judge that witness is speaking truth D797; dragon-tongue p. H105.1; dry branches on innocent man's grave blossom as p. of innocence E631.0.5.1; false p. of storm K1894; garment p. against all but man's own sword D1381.3.1; priest stamps on stones as p. A972.1.2; tale-bearer killed for lack of p. S461; worn-out shoes as p. of long journey *H241.

Prop. — Earth supported by p. A849.3.

Props. — Clouds as p. of the sky A702.7; hero removes world p. A1058.

Proper names for dwarfs F451.8.2. — Dead without p. funeral rites cannot rest in grave E412.3; ghost returns to demand p. burial E235.2; lack of p. education regretted J142.

Property acquired by prayer V52.12; claim based on lie X905.3; disposal rouses sham dead J2511.1.1. — Accidental loss of p. N350ff.; all-red, all-black, or all-white calf the p. of the devil G303.10.9; all p. as wager N2.5; corpse who has left good p. not entirely dead H586.5; dividing p.: man keeps house, gives wife road J1541.4; dupe's p. destroyed K1400—K1499; dwarf promises money and p. for hand of girl F451.5.18.1; fire from heaven destroys p. Q552.13.2; fitting destruction of p. as punishment Q585; folly of father's giving all p. to children before his death P236.1; gift of p. silences criticism U21.2; half of p. as reward Q112.0.2; laws on p. division within family A1585; loss or destruction of p. as punishment Q595; magic used against p. D2080ff.; man offers all his p. to daughter's rescuer R111.0.1; misdeed concerning p. punished Q270ff.; mortal confiscates p. of dwarfs F451.5.10.7; original fire p. of one person A1415.0.2; punishment for misappropriation of p. M368; quarreling heirs destroy the entire p. J2129.2; return from dead to demand stolen p. E236; riddle propounded on pain of loss of p. H541.2; Satan causes p. destroying storm G303.9.4.0.1; thunder destroys p. as punishment Q552.1.0.1; transformation to destroy enemy's p. D651.3; vow not to pass into other's p. M186; witch abuses p. *G265ff.; younger brother's clever p. division J242.8.

Prophecy of future greatness (causes banishment) L425, (fulfilled when hero returns home) N682; of ogre-child so pregnant woman will be

killed K2115.3; personified Z139.8. — Animals distribute body according
to p. F989.10; crow tries to make p. like raven J951.3; escape by false
p. K575; gift of p. from fairyland sojourn F329.1; god of p. A471; goddess
of p. A471.1; love through p. that prince shall marry the fairest T12;
magic object gives power of p. D1305.1; magic power of p. *D1812ff.;
marriage p. for newborn princesses H41.6; misfortune from mistaken
interpretation of p. N398; parricide p. unwittingly fulfilled N323; power
of p. induced D1812.2; speaking tree gives p. D1311.4.2; suicide from
evil p. F1041.1.11.3.

Prophecies *M300—M399. — Identical p. for fated lovers T22.4.

Prophesying. — Dead p. Christ's coming E367.3; devil p. in enchanted
castle H1411.3; fairy p. future greatness of (newborn) child F317; fairy
p. lover's fate F302.7; mermaid p. B81.7.1; man's spirit p. own death
E489.4.

Prophet aids quest H1233.3.3; gives prophetic gift M300.3; as helper
N847; locates lost child D1825.4.3.1. — Abandoned person in woods
comforted by p. and birds S465; animal as p. *B140ff.; asking p. for signs
tabu C415; Christ as p. V211.0.4; god as p. A178; incognito p. as matchmaker T53.1; false p. K1962; magic power from p. D1722.1; prophecy:
unborn child to be p. M311.6; resuscitation by p. E121.5.3; water saves
p. from drowning F930.3.

Prophet's curse M411.8; humility J903. — Judge agrees to be p. first
disciple J1169.8; madness on hearing p. voice F1041.8.8.

Prophets M301. — Water-spirits as p. F420.4.10.

Prophylactic. — Magic p. fruit D1500.2.7.

Proposal tests wife H467.2. — Reductio ad absurdum of p. *J1290ff.

Prosperity forever or for a day? L291. — Fairies control p. F366.4; god
promises mortal p. A182.3.4.2; goddess of p. A473.1.1; possession of
relic brings p. V141; prophecy of p. for a people M325; sacrifice to secure
p. S263.3.1; sister honors brother only in p. W175.1; wren helps restore
p. to world A1348.1.

Prosperous. — Men too p.: life becomes difficult L482.

Prostitute, see also **Concubine, Courtesan;** claims to be victim's daughter,
robs him K347.1; frightens lover, calls "Thief!" K1213.2; paid with
counterfeit K1581.11; poses as noble woman K1315.5.1; with venereal
disease sent to king Q244.3; weeps at leaving lover his coat W151.1; will
always deceive lover U129.2. — Clever p. J1115.8; devil causes girl to
become p. T451; father kills daughter lest she become p. T314; go to p.
early in the morning H588.17; man robbed by p.: swallows her pearls
K306.3; wife born to be p. T450.1; wisdom from p. J155.8; woman
slandered as p. K2112.

Prostitutes pursued in wild hunt E501.5.1.2. — Disguised p. take wife to
"convent" K1592; jokes concerning p. X520ff.; women call each other
p. J1351.

Prostitution *T450ff.; punished Q243.1.

Prostrating. — Neglect of p. self punished Q223.13.1; stones p. selves D1648.3.

Prostration. — Prolonged religious p. causes death V383.1.

Protean beggar D611; sale D612.

Protected son has bad luck, unprotected son makes fortune N171. — Child p. all night against demon G442.2; forest p. by dwarfs F451.5.1.17.

Protecting hedge surrounds sleeper K1967.1. — Deity p. mortal A185.2; ghost p. friends E379.3; ghost p. the living E363.2; helpful snake p. man from attack B524.3; person in magic sleep surrounded by p. fire *D1967; reward for p. fugitive Q46; spirit p. each animal species F419.3.

Protection against (Nightmare, Alp) F471.1.2, (pestilence-spirit) F493.3, (witches) G272ff.; during ghost-laying E443.0.2; of sinners by confession V20.1. — Beast invokes saint's p. B251.4.1; church bell rung as p. against storm D2141.1.1; dwarfs flee to caves for p. F451.6.14; extraordinary p. for animal F984; goddess of p. A489.1; giants, heroes for dwarfs' p. F451.10.1; magic illusion as p. D2031.6ff.; magic object as p. *D1380ff., (against wild animals) D1447; magic p. against revenants *E434ff.; mortals under fairies' p. F396; panther's sweet smell as p. from other beasts B732; punishment for slaying king under holy p. Q227.1; sacrifice as p. against disease S276; seduction by offering unneeded p. K1315.9; Sign of Cross as p. from injury V86.1; transformation for hero's p. D651.6; warrior disgraced by slaying of those under his p. P557.5.

Protector. — God as p. of Israel A184; fox with lion p. goes hunting alone and is killed J684.1; supernatural bird as p. of children B524.4.

Protectress. — Virgin Mary as p. of illicit lovers *T401.

Protruding eye F541.5.

Proud, see also **Pride**; animal less fortunate than humble *L450ff.; hide humbled J1476. — Creation of ass from p. horse A1882.1; God brings low the p. and exalts the lowly (riddle) H797.1; lowly hero overcomes p. rivals L156.1; men are too p.: snakes created L482.3; why snakes are p. A2523.2.

Proving, see **Proof.**

Proverbs Z64.

Proverbial wisdom (counsels) J171ff.

Providence. — Escape by intervention of P. R341; ways of P. inscrutable J225.0.3.

Provider. — Magic object as p. D1470ff.

Providing. — Man in tree p. for child of illicit lovers K1271.5; waiting for God's p.: starving J2215.4.

Provision saving tabu C785. — Forethought in p. for life J700—J749; ghosts punish failure of p. for their wants E245; king for year makes p. for future J711.3.

Provisions for the swimming match (bluff) K1761; magically furnished D2105; received from magic object D1470.2ff. — City without p. but with much money starves J712.1; fairy-wife furnishes p. F343.7; hospitality repaid by magic procuring of p. Q45.6; trickster poses as helper and eats woman's stored p. K1983.

Provost's purse stolen K311.9.

Prowess. — Recognition by extraordinary p. H32; sham p. *K1950ff.; tests of p. H900—H1399; vow to perform act of p. M155.

Proxy wedding T135.3.

Prudence J500—J599; in demands J530ff. — Extreme p. W215.

Prudery. — Extreme p. J2521.

Pruning. — Father doing good and bad when p. vines H583.2.

Psalms. — Seven penitential p. Z71.5.6.9.

Psalter. — Thief detected by p. and key H251.3.2.

Psyche. — Venus jealous of P. and Cupid's love W181.6.

Ptarmigan. — Man becomes p. D166.4; pouch transformed to p. D444.9; why p. lives in country A2250.1, A2433.4.3.

Puberty. — Good inclinations enter body at p. W2; why a lad at p. is energetic A1365; tabu connected with p. C130ff.

Pubic hair mistaken for calf's tail J1772.4.1; thought to tell lies, pulled out J1842.1. — Goddess scatters p. on fish A2211.15; magic p. D991.2; origin of p. A1315.5; remarkable p. F547.6.

Public. — Everything on highway belongs to p. J1511.14; king shows self in p. only once a year P14.21; knight feigns murder of p. enemy K579.6; magic from maiden walking naked in p. *D1796.

Publicity. — Love of p. W161.

Publishing. — Advice against p. sin J21.52.4.

Pudding. — Devil descends chimney, spoils p. C12.5.5.

Puddle. — Devil disappears in p. G303.17.2.6; God in the p. J1262.2.

Puddles. — Dark p. in hell A689.1; ghost leaves water p. E544.1.3; sinners in hell sit in dark p. Q569.1.

Puff. — Chaste woman can blow out candle with one p. and relight it with another H413.1.

Puffing. — Bird p. itself up, dies J955.1.2.

Pug-nosed ogre G362.2.

Pugilist. — Mighty p. F616.

Pugnacious. — Why animal is p. A2524ff.

Pugnacity. — Intemperate p. J552.

Pulled. — Bedclothes p. off by spirits F470.1; dead find no rest since grass is p. on grave E419.3; giant's arm p. off G512.6.1; girl p. about by hair S182.2; man looking at birds p. into pool K832.6; mountains p. down by strong man F626; shortsighted wish: all p. on to follow J2072.3; tree to goad oxen p. up by devil G303.9.2.1.

Puller. — Lie: strong p. X953.

Pulling iron bars as strength test H1562.11; nuts forbidden C517. — Deceptive contest in p. fingers K74; girl summons fairy lover by p. nuts F301.1.1.4; life token: dogs p. on leash E761.7.5; magic by p. through a hole *D1795; magic object p. person into it D1412ff.; test of strength: p. up tree by roots H1562.1.

Pulpit sawed almost through by sham parson K1961.1.3. — Hiding from ghosts in p. E434.2.

Pulpits *V117.

Pulse beats violently as loved one passes H175.3. — Cattle formerly ate p. A1101.2.2; detailed diagnosis by feeling p. F956.1; feeling p.: doctor severs arteries instead K1017; let them eat p. J2227.1; love detected by quickening p.J1142.2.

Pumice. — Man becomes p. D244; sea of p. F711.2.3.

Pumping out a leaky ship as task H1023.5.

Pumpkin thought to be an ass's egg J1772.1; tied to another's leg J2013.3; transformed to carriage D451.3.3. — Boiling p. thought to be talking J1813.3; carriage from p. F861.4.3; dog becomes p. D422.2.2; escape in p. shell K521.5; god blamed for large p. fruit J2215.6; lie: large p. X1411.2; magic p. D981.11, (furnishes treasure) D1463.2.1, (yields year's supply of rice) D1472.2.6; man thinks he is dead, p. falls on him J2311.1.3.1; origin of p. A2687.4; silver coins from p. A1433.21; transformed golden p. J1531.1; woman bears p. T555.1.1.

Punctual surpassed by tardy L147.

Punctured. — Persons with p. bodies F529.1.

Pundits. — Foolish p. J1705.3; silly p. as two-footed cattle J1717.

Punish. — Decision not to p. a jealous husband: he already suffers enough T261.1; dwarfs p. F451.5.2.6; ghosts p. failure to provide for their wants E245; iron created to p. cedar's pride A978.2; return from dead to p. indignities to corpse or ghost E235; rich man made poor to p. pride L412; trickster makes woman believe that her husband is coming to p. her adultery *K1572; witches p. lazy spinning women G282.

Punished. — Animal or object absurdly p. J1860ff.; animal p. B275; broken promise p. by animal M205.1; cheaters p. by trickster as sham doctor K1825.1.3; children p. for fathers' sins P242; confession without giving up sin p. V25.2; disguised king p. by peasant P15.1; deeds p. Q200—Q399; fairy p. F386; incredulity as to sacredness of host p. V33; inhospitable misdeed p. by king in anger on Easter day J571.3; monk who has left order p. V475.1; ravisher of his daughter p. by fairy king F304.1; Satan p. in hell G303.17.3.5; scorn of unloved suitor p. T75.1; tailor p. in hell P441.3; usurer p. in hell Q473.1; witches p. in hell G275.11.

Punishing daughter by marrying her to poor man T69.5. — Angel p. mortal V245; fairies punish mortal who needs p. F361.16; ghost p. injury received in life E234ff.; ghost p. molesting person E279.6; god p. man by killing his child A1335.15; god p. many for one sinner J225.0.2; long delay in p. nobleman U34.1; witch p. person G269.10.

Punishment for broken (oaths) M101, (tabu) *C900—C999; for failure to pay tax P536; for profane use of the cross V86.3; and remission Q570ff. — Animal characteristics as p. A2230ff.; any p. except having two wives T251.1.6; automatic p. by fetish-medicine D1601.19; avoid hasty p. J571.4; calamity as p. A1003; city sinks in sea as p. F944.1; clever means of avoiding legal p. J1180ff.; creation of animals as p. A1730ff.; Christ's coat of mercy protects Pilate from p. D1381.4.1; deaf and dumb man can see soul taken to happiness or p. D1821.7; death as p. for scorning deity A1335.6; disease as p. A1337.0.5; disenchantment by three nights' silence under p. D758.1; eclipse as p. by deity A737.9; flood as p. A1018; immunity from p. for sin as reward Q171; kinds of p. *Q400—Q599; losing luck as p. N134.1.3; man must work as p. for theft of fire A1346.1; miraculous p. through animals Q557; moon's phases as p. A755.6; mountains as p. A969.7; origin of death as p. for scorning deity A1335.6; origin of plant as p. A2631ff.; origin of stones: p. for discourtesy A973; plant characteristics as p. A2720ff.; quest assigned as p. for murder H1219.2; rainy weather sent by saint as p. A1131.2; reason for Flying Dutchman's p. E511.1ff.; reincarnation as p. E692; reincarnation as p. for sin E606.1; return from dead to inflict p. E230ff.; saint shares sinner's p. V414; silence under p. breaks power of enchantment *D1741.3; stone's p. for injuring holy person's foot A975.1.1; strong man serves ogre as p. for stealing food F613.4; tasks assigned prisoner so that he may escape p. H924; transformation as p. *D661, Q551.3; vampire brought to life through endurance of p. by her victim E251.2.1; waters created as p. A910.2; wife saves husband from adultery p. K1596; world-fire as p. for Irish A1031.1.

Punishments paid in next reincarnation E601.3. — Chain of p. Q401; account of p. prepared in hell brings about repentance J172; mysterious p. in otherworld F171.6; rewards and p. Q (entire chapter).

Pupil, see also **Student**; returns from dead to warn master of futility of studies E368; surpasses master L142. — Architect kills p. surpassing him V181.2.1; early p. finds the gold N633; eye with picture in the p. F541.2; lazy p. reformed by watching home builder J67.1; magician makes p. believe himself superior so as to test gratitude H1565.1; teacher and p. P340ff.; teacher seduces p. K1399.5; transformation contest between master and p. D615.2; wizard makes p. think himself emperor W154.28.

Pupils all clap their hands when man sneezes and he falls back into the water J2516.3.2. — Eye with several p. F541.3.

Puppet. — Compassionate executioner: substituted p. drowned K512.2.3.

Puppy, see also **Dog**. — Girl transformed to p. D141.1.1; quest for unknown p. H1383.1.

Puppies born of woman D601; tested by gripping hide H1588.1.

Purchases. — Destroying festive p. by mistake J1846.

Purchased, see also **Bought**; cobold F481.0.1.2. — Bride p. T52; helpful animal p. B312.4; hero wakened from magic sleep by wife who has p. place in his bed from false wife *D1978.4; good counsels p. J163.4;

magic object p. D851.1; night p. A1174.3; sun and moon p. A700.6; wisdom p. J163.

Purchaser. — Unwitting p. of stolen ornament jailed as thief N347.4.

Purchasing lover's worthless goods K1581.9. — Custom of p. wives A1555.2; progressive p. of woman's favors K1361.2.

Purgatory. — Deceased husband chooses to remain in p. rather than to return to his shrewish wife T251.1.2; husband duped into believing he is in p. K1514.3; letter from soul in p. E755.3.1; lion sent to kill man frees him from possibility of sinning and sojourn in p. J225.2; masses release souls from p. V42; souls in p. E755.3; visions of p. V511.3.

Purging not needed by heavy drinker J1115.2.1.

Purified. — Love p. by magic D1900.0.1.

Purifying in kettle of boiling oil as preparation for marriage to fairy F303.1. — Saint p. monk V221.5; saint p. poisoned ale V229.6.2; sea bath as p. rite V81.5.

Purity of God A102.11.

Purple as royalty symbol Z147.1; tree F811.3.1. — Casting lots for royal p. J2060.4; nut's p. juice F813.3.3; royal p. P13.3; angry warrior becomes red and p. F1041.16.6.5.

Purpose. — Man's p. greater than God H674.

Purring. — Origin of cat's p. A2236.8.

Purse-cutting knife K341.8.3; found by gravedigger J21.48; lost in bath house J21.33. — "A close p." health secret H596.1.1; bluff in court: the stone in the p. K1765; envy punished: the found p. Q302.1; escape from prison by use of magic p. D1395.3; guessing nature of devil's p. H523.8; magic p. *D1192; man to bring wife a p.-full of sense *J163.2; not the same p. as was lost J1172.1; prophecy: one son p. cutter M306.2; trickster fills found p. with lead K1696.

Pursued animal indicates building site B155.2.4; sweetheart becomes tree D642.3.1. — Attendant p. by dead when shroud bursts E261.2; giant women p. by giants F531.6.8.2; man p. by witches G267; unbaptized children p. by fairies F360.1; woman p. by wild hunter E501.5.1.

Pursuer felled by rock D2153.2; persuaded to sing while captive escapes K606.0.1. — Animal saves man from p. B523; lovers as p. and fugitive K1517.1; magic objects as decoy for p. D672.1; shadow mistaken for p. J1790.1.

Pursuers confused by magic D2031.6.1ff. — Beaver sacrifices scrotum to save life from p. *J351.1; escape by pretending to be one of p. K579.3.1; son appears to p. as spinning wheel D2031.6.2; transformation to elude p. D642.7.

Pursuit by animal C986.1; of bird leads to ogre's house G402; of game leads to upper world F59.2; by giantess F531.5.7.0.3; by hatred of the gods M411.4; of magic arrow leads to adventures H1226.2; by magic object *D1430ff.; of man by ghost E261.4; by misfortune N251; revealed by magic D1813.2; by river F932.1; of rolling cake leads to quest H1226;

by spirit F402.1.10; of sun by moon A735; by wandering skull *E261.1.
— Adventures from p. of enchanted animal N774; cumulative p. Z492;
intemperance in p. J561; magic object answers for fugitive and delays p.
*D1611ff.; magic prevents p. D2165.3; river bursts from well in p.
A934.7; shammed p. saves fugitive K649.8.

Pursuits R260ff.

Pus sold as ghee K144.1.

Pushed. — Dupe p. into pond or well K832.1.1; husband p. down mountain
by wife K1641.1; man p. in boat out to sea by companion on shore S141.1;
mistress p. into crocodile hole by slave bathing her back in river K831.1;
victim looks for tree, p. off cliff K832.5; victim p. into fire K925; victim
p. into water K926; true bride p. into water by false K1911.2.2.

Pusher-into-hole G321.1. — Lie: remarkable p. X954.

Pushing. — Murder by p. off cliff K929.9; naked woman p. lover in water
K1645; witch p. man around on floor G269.18.

Puss in boots B582.1.1, K1952.1, K1954.1, K1917.3, N411.1.1; as name for
devil G303.2.1.

Puteus K1511.

Putrefaction of food and drink refused saint Q552.16. — Animal born
from p. B713.2; magic p. D2096, (of food as punishment for opposition to
holy person remitted) Q575; no p. on island F746.

Putrescence becomes gold D475.1.12; flows from forehead F1041.18.

Pygmalion D435.1.1.

Pygmy turns into a giant D55.1.3.

Pygmies F535; from Ham's curse A1614.1.1. — Hermaphrodite p. F547.2.1;
journey to land of p. F123.

Pyramus and Thisbe N343, T41.1.

Pyre. — Animal husband killed, wife throws self into p. B691; chickens
build p. B599.1; dead burned on p. V61.2; dupe tricked into jumping on
funeral p. K891.4; escape from execution p. by means of wings *R215;
extraordinary p. F882.1; false message causes man to jump on p. K929.12;
resuscitation by laying flesh on p. E134; resuscitation through ashes
thrown on p. E132; selling wood for raja's p. W153.13; wife throws herself on husband's p. T211.2.1; woman cast on husband's p. as punishment
Q414.6.

Pyres. — Smoke from p. of brother and sister refuses to mix F1075.

Python becomes gorilla D418.1.1; goddess A499.1. — Marriage to p. in
human form B656.1; recovering object from hole of p. H1132.3; why p.
lacks hands and feet A2241.8.

Quack doctor hero L113.7.

Quadrupeds. — Animal kingdom: q. **B221ff.; king of q. B241; magic q.
B180ff.; war of birds and q. B261; youth sees half of two q. H583.1.1.

Quadruplet heroes T686.

Quail as food for Israelites F989.16.1. — Creation of q. A1946; flesh of

Artemis eaten as q. V30.1.1; fools frightened at flight of q. J2614.2; friendship of squirrel and q. A2493.6; how q. got voice A2421.4.1; reincarnation as q. E613.8; transmutation of the q. J1269.5; why q. has no tail A2378.2.1; wedding of q. B282.17.

Quails caught in net rise up in a body and escape J1024; transformed for safety D666.1; transformed to sticks and pebbles D423.2. — Army of q. B268.5.1; king of q. B242.2.6.

Quaking of earth (by magic) D2148, (as punishment) Q552.2.0.1.

Quality preferred to quantity J280ff.

Qualities. — Contrasting q. found in otherworld garden F162.1.2; eaten heart gives one the owner's q. *E714.4.1; fanciful q. of snakes B765; human foster child with animal q. B635; man to be judged by his own q., not his clothes J1072.

Quantity. — Carrying off huge q. of money as task H1127; quality preferred to q. J280ff.

Quarrel of dead and living E481.0.2; between earth and waters A917; and fight over details of air-castles J2060.1. — Animal characteristics as result of q. A2258; attention of ruler turned to abuses by starting q. with unjust official *K1657; eclipse from q. of sun and moon A737.7; enmity between animals from original q. A2281ff.; habitat of animals result of ancient q. A2282; interference in strong's q. fatal to weak J2143.3; king settling q. tabu C563.4; mortal as umpire of q. between gods A187.2; murder by feigned q. K929.6; numskulls q. over a greeting J1712; present starts q. for its possession K1083; princess brought to laughter by indecent show made in q. with old woman at well H341.3.1; profitable league made with both parties to a q. K253; ruler generously settles q. W11.6; sun-moon q. when sun eats up all their children A736.1.4.1; tabu: settling q. among thralls C560.1; twins q. before birth in mother's womb T575.1.3; why some married people q. A1375.1; wise man before entering a q. considers how it will end J611.

Quarrels among family of deaf X113; introduced among animals A2575. — Origin of q. A1341.3, A1599.10; ruler too lazy to stop q. W111.5.7; wise judgments settle village q. J1170.1.

Quarreling couple were previously tiger and dog T256.0.1; heirs destroy entire property involved J2129.2; prince and princess vow to maltreat each other if married M149.4; sons and bundle of twigs J1021; tabu to men on mission C833.9; tabu in house (presence) of king C873; wife T256. — Gods and demons q. A106.0.1; joint rescuers q. R111.7; murderers q. and reveal crime N271.11; noblemen q. over a device J552.1; origin of q. A1342; paramour who insists in q. with mistress about escape caught by her husband J581.2; soldiers q. over possessing girl T321.4; while thieves q. over booty, owner comes W151.8.

Quarrelsomeness punished Q306.

Quarter. — One door for each world q. F782.1.1.

Quarters. — Colors corresponding to the four world q. Z140.2; determination of world q. *A1182; earth square with four q. *A871; four stars in q. of heavens A1281.6.1; gods of the q. *A417; moon divided into q. A755.4.2; moon weighs a pound for it has four q. H691.1.1.; own q. need it more J1269.11; tabu on entering woman's q. C182.2; winds of the four q. established *A1127.

Quartered thief's body sewed together K414.

Quartering in effigy Q596.1; by horse as punishment for breaking betrothal Q416.0.1.

Queen banished for defeating king in argument S416; banished for remark on man's condition S411.2.1; begets son while king away T481.6; burned at stake: innocent of husband's death K2116.1.2; changes own twins for slave's son K1921.3; chosen to live rather than king P17.2; compelled to keep an inn *Q481; of demons F402.2.2.; dies of fright from evil prophecy N384.5; disguised as peddler K1817.4.1.1; does not care for son unlike her P230.3; driven from palace, garden withers F975.2; expelled for poisoning stepson Q211.4.1; exposed in leather in market place Q483.1; of fairies F252.2; finds, adopts abandoned child S354.1; flogs jewel-thief suspects J1141.1.10; forced to become courtesan L410.7; gives away a sleeve of her dress: miraculously restored V411.1; gives quest directions H1232.2; of the gods A161.3; as helper N837; hesitates over high bid for her favors U66.1.1; hides her child and accuses wolf of eating it S332; instigates tasks H919.6; kept in palace of forty doors R41.5.1; in love with own brother kills husband K2213.3.4; aids lover dispossess king K2213.8; Mab F252.2; and maidservant conceive from eating same food T511.0.1; makes all men copulate with her T492; passes off girl child as boy K1923.6; placed in kitchen and abused by butcher Q482.2; propounds riddles H540.2f.; promises self to healer H346.1; rescued from slavery R111.1.6.1; of Sea sets tasks H933.5; shames cowards for weeping W121.4; stabs self, accuses princess K2103; takes husband's place in battle F565.1.3; transforms self to defeat death god D651.1.3; transformed to menial D24.2; of watersnakes B244.1.1; writes message on stone: hero searches for her H1229.2. — Abandoned q. blinded S438; abandoned q. entertains in forest, is recognized H155; burial service for fairy q. F268.1; courtier in love with q. T91.6.1.1; devil as insatiable q. G303.3.1.12.5; disenchantment from bird when q. milks own milk into bird's beak D759.2; disenchantment by drinking milk of q. who has borne two boys D764.1; fairy visits q., begets son K1844.4; fairies aid q. in childbirth F312.3; giants' q. F531.6.8.5.1; he who wins maiden q. is king H1574.3.2; incognito prince seducing q. K1814.1; incognito q. K1812.8; incognito q. accused of killing child K2116.1.4; innocent q. burned at stake Q414.0.7; jealous q. dupes child-bearing one K2115.0.1; king overhears girl's boast of what she would do if she were q. N455.4; lady answers q. straightforwardly J751.1.1; love-mad q. pushes husband into well K2213.2.1; magic knowledge from q. of otherworld D1810.1; magician's transformations to seduce q. D2031.4.2; maiden q. offers hand as reward Q53.3; maiden q. prefers fighting to marriage T311.4; maiden q. sets hero tasks H933.2; monkey as fairy q. F302.1; otherworld q. F185; parrot advises q. playing chess B565; persecuted q. meanly clothed and set where all are commanded to spit on her Q471.1; pregnant q. chained to king T579.7; prophecy: girl will be q. M314.0.1; prophecy: one more q. will give rajah son M311.0.3.2; quest for fairy q. H1381.3.8; quest for saree for q. H1355.2; royal minister rescues abandoned q. R169.7; servant falsely accused of familiarity with q. K2121.2; shrewish q. reformed by cobbler T251.2.4; sparrows enact tragedy prophecy before dying q. M369.2.1.1; statue left instead of abducted q. K661.4; stealing belt from q. as task H1151.5; tabu to marry q. C162.1; treacherous q. K2213.8ff.; treacherous q. kills brother K2212.0.3; tricky q. gets kingdom for her son K2213.11; vow to marry q. of fairies M146.1; wisdom from dying q. J155.6; witch disguised as q. eats horses G264.3.1.

Queen's illicit passion for diseased man T481.2; quarters searched before king enters J634.2; royal purple J2060.4. — Fairy q. beauty temporarily destroyed by intercourse with mortal F304.2; girl disguised as doctor exposes q. paramour K1825.1.1.1; king abdicates after q. adultery P16.1.2; leper (beggar) laid in q. bed K2112.2; man with unfaithful wife comforted when he sees q. unfaithfulness J882.1; thief lies by q. bed, steals jewelry K331.7; token betrays q. lover H81.3.

Queens P20ff.

Queer, see also **Extraordinary.** — Animals with q. names (cumulative tale) Z53.

Quenched. — Execution fire q. by helpful animals *B526.1; fire q. by magic (object) D1566.2ff., (stream) D1382.8; heavenly fire cannot be q. F962.2.3; mountain-men cannot enter house till light is q. F460.2.3.

Quenching the burning boat J2162.3; world-fire A1035.

Quest, see also **Search;** H1200ff.; for beauty as king's bride T11.1.1; to hell for magic objects D859.2; imposed for breaking tabu C991. — Beast on a q. N774; couple reunited after q. N741.4; curse: undertaking dangerous q. M446; daughter succeeds on q. son failed L152; fool's q. J2346; host sends guests on q. J1563.2; maiden to marry after q. accomplished T151.0.1; object of q. stolen K2036; servant follows on dangerous q. P361.1.2; substitute on q. K1848.3; vow not to marry until q. concluded M151.2; vow not to see friends until q. completed M151.9.

Quests H1200—H1399. — Attendant circumstances of q. H1200—H1249; nature of q. H1250—H1399; suitors assigned q. H336.

Questing beast N774.

Question. — Answer to certain q. (quest) H1388; dumbness cured by q. F954.2; finding answer to certain q. as test H508; manner of telling tale forces hearer to ask particular q. Z13; one compulsory q. *C651; reductio ad absurdum of q. or proposal *J1290ff.; resting until q. answered tabu C735.2.9; tales ending with a q. Z16; voyagers ask landsman first q. P682.2.

Questions asked on way to otherworld H1291; to dead are dangerous E545.5. — Asking q. forbidden C410ff.; children ask too difficult q. J2370.1; Christ looking for stick to beat those who ask foolish q. X435.3; dwarfs give riddles and q. to mortals F451.5.15; fettered monster asks q. of visitor A1074.3; foolish q. rebuked J1300ff.; hero unwilling to answer q. until dressed P644; magic object answers q. D1311ff.; man answers all q. F645.1; not to ask q. about extraordinary things J21.6; princess must answer all q. by "No!" K1331; quest to morning star for answers to q. H1282; reward for asking proper q. Q85; riches the reward of q. solved on quests H1243; single speech answering many q. H501.2; student is helped by the devil when he can answer three q. in rhyme G303.22.3; theological q. answered by propounding simple question in science J1291.2.

Questioned. — Guests fed before being q. P324.2.

Questioning. — Clever youth answers king's q. in riddles H583; tabu: q. supernatural (husband) C32.2, (wife) C31.4.1.

Quibbling answers J1252.

Quick thinking saves jackals J1662.1. — Magic q. growth of crops D2157.2.

Quiescent. — Dead q. during day E452.1.

Quiet. — Magic objects maintain q. so that fugitive may escape D1393.2; mankind from Peace and Q. fructified by Light A1221.2; mouse teaches her child to fear q. cats but not noisy cocks J132.

Quieting patient by killing J2489.5.

Quill. — Birds drop q. for man's pen B159.1.

Quilt. — Magic q. *D1167; washing dirty q. without soap H1023.6.1.

Quiver. — Magic hair draws back q. from which it has been taken D1428.1; magic q. D1092.1.

Quoits. — Devil throws q. on Sunday: stones' origin A977.2.3.

Rabbi feigns death to approach enemy K2357.4; and king exchange riddles H548.1; returns jewel found with bought ass W37.3; tears out eyes to escape temptation T333.3.1. — Resuscitation by r. E121.5.1.

Rabbit, see also **Hare;** burns self under chin when he steals ember A2218.7; as culture hero A522.1.2; eats seed-grain from fields: nose closed during sowing season A2238.1; and elephant partners on trading expedition B294.6; dupes porcupine into leaving food K335.0.4.2; laughs, cause of hare-lip A2211.2; as king of animals B240.2; slays rhinoceros L315.12; sold as letter-carrier *K131; transformed to another animal D411.3; transformed to person D315.5. — Abduction by r. R13.1.8; bird boasts about capturing r. J2173.3; briar-patch punishment for r. K581.2; creation of r. A1856; dead sweetheart as white r. E211.1; enmity of r. (and coyote) A2494.6.2, (and dog) A2494.4.4, (and fisher) A2494.6.3, (and lynx) A2494.6.1; fools send money by r. J1881.2.2; friendship between monkey and r. A2493.14.4; frightened r. puts head in charred tree: hence black ears A2212.1; helpful r. B437.4; male r. bears young:

female drowned in Flood B754.4; man in the moon a r. A751.2; pill transformed to a white r. D444.3; porcupine pricks r. host P332; pursuing the r. who harmed the garden J2103.2; race won by deception: r. as "little son" substitute K11.6; revenant as r. E423.2.2; skillful flayer skins running r. F664.1; soldiers on r. F535.2.8; theft of horses by letting loose a r. so that drivers join in the chase K341.5.1; turnips called bacon, cat called r. J1511.2; why r. continually moves mouth A2476.1; why r. has long ears A2325.1.

Rabbits afraid of waves J1812.2; freeze feet fast to ice at night (lie) X1115.1. — Herding r. (task) H1112; magic production of r. D2178.4.1; why r. have soft pads on feet A2375.2.4; servant sent to bring in cows is found chasing r. J1757.

Rabbit-herd. — Hero as r. P412.3.

Raccoon. — Witch as r. G211.2.8.

Raccoons. — Hunter bags frozen r. X1115.

Race (= speed contest) with fairies N775; as suitor contest H331.5; won by deception K11; between wooden horses D1719.1.4. — Angels run r. before saint V241.3; animal characteristics determined by r. A2252ff.; animal haunt established by r. A2433.1.1; deceptive land purchase: bounds fixed by a r. K185.5; despised boy wins r. L176; demons hold horse r. F419.1; devil in r. with man G303.9.9.12; dupe tricked in r. into falling into a pit K1171; earth darkened because of sun's defeat in r. against coyote D2146.2.4; escape during r. K624; ghost horse wins race E521.1.3; hag runs r., loser to be beheaded M221.1; hero fattened for r. with cannibals K553.0.1; little man defeats giant in r. L312; mighty blower slows down princess with his breath and causes her to lose r. F622.1; Milky Way as r.-track A778.9; running a r. tabu C865; woman bears twins after foot r. T581.5.

Race (= a people) will always have illustrious woman M317. — Continuous winter destroys the r. A1040ff.; culture originated by previous r. of men A1401; curse: couple to wander until they find new seat of r. M455.4; curse: r. to lose sovereignty M462; fairies as descendants of early r. of gods F251.1; first r. perishes when sun rises A1009.1; heroes as fourth r. of men A502; new r. from girl-rat union A1006.4; new r. after world calamity A1006.1; tabu: marrying a queen of certain r. C162.1; transformation to person of different f. D30ff.

Races, see also **Tribes**; P715. — Deity settles disputes between r. M4; humor concerning r. X600—X699; monstrous r. F510.1.

Racehorse. — Old r. in mill laments vanity of youth J14.

Racing. — Abductors r. while captive escapes K624; foot-r. contest H1594; horse-r. A1535.6.

Radiance fills church at saint's death V222.1.1; of saint's face F574.3.1. — God's r. upon Moses' face A124.4.

Raffia cloth's origin A1453.7.

Raft in primeval sea A813. — Flood scattered carpenters on r. everywhere A1445.2.1; lotus-leaf r. in primeval sea A813.2.

Rafter as weapon F614.2.2. — Giant killed by half-cut through r. K959.3.1; girl fastened by hair to r. S182.

Rag in king's wardrobe thinks self ribbon J953.18.

Rags. — Accustomed r. preferred to new garments L217; fairy as bundle of r. F234.3.3; treasure found in bundle of r. N526; wearing r. to avoid vainglory J916.

Rage. — Battle r. *F873.0.1; father kills son in battle r. N349.2; sight of naked women calms r. K774.2.

Ragwort. — Witch rides r. G242.1.2.

Rail (bird). — Origin of red lump on head of r. A2215.4, A2321.8; why r. has red forehead A2330.8.

Railroads. — Crooked r. in mountains X1526.1; lies about r. X1815.

Rain of blood F962.4; does not wet fairy F259.3; drops large as hand F962.13; drops' sound J1812.3; enters contest between wind, sun L351.1; invoked to destroy world-fire A1035.1; as ogre in bull form G372; produced by magic D2143.1; of sausages (figs) J1151.1.3; of stones as punishment Q552.14.4; -withholding deer B192.2. — Buddhists become slaves of Taoists because they cannot produce r. V355; conception from falling r. T522; elephants bring r. B791; extraordinary r. F962; giant's snoring as r. F531.3.8.2; king's beard worth a May r. H712.2; lazy boy calls dog from r. to feel paws W111.2.4; leaky roof over woman's bed: in r. she beds with seducer K1339.8; lies about r. X1654; magic fountain causes r. D1541.1.3; magic object controls r. *D1542ff.; magic r. *D902; man proof against wet from r. D1841.4.1; man's laughter brings r. H1194.1; numskulls take out clothing and cover trunks to keep r. out J2129.6; origin of r. A1131; owl's knowledge of r.-fall distribution B569.2; peasant and boy sleep during r. in hay barn W111.2.7; protecting from r. as stork does J2442; regulation of r. A1131.0.1; reward for bringing r. Q93.1; saint controls fall of r. D1841.4.4; skillful fencer keeps sword dry in r. F667.1; wise man and r. of fools J1714.2; sun thrown on fire: period of darkness, r. A1068; witch produces r. G283.3.

Rains withheld to punish king Q553.7. — Gold, silver r. at royal birth F960.1.1.2.

Rain-god A287; blamed for heavy rain J2215.5; causes rainfall D2143.1.0.1; discovers liquor A1427.0.2; drags waterskin along sky A1142.8; threatens withhold r. A182.3.6. — Contest between fire-god and r. A975.2.1; rain from r. A1131.5; sea-god and r. conflict A1015.1.

Rain-god's. — Rainbow as r. horse A791.7.

Rain-goddess A287.1.

Rain-spirit. — Dragon as r. B11.7.

Rainbow bridge to otherworld *F152.1.1; -goddess A288; at hero's death F960.2.2; of honey F162.7; as loincloth F829.1; as an ogre G306. — Cloud in r. form F967.4; conception from r. T521.2; god descends on r.

A171.0.3.1; looking at r. tabu C315.2.3; magic control of r. D2149.7; no r. before Judgment Day A1002.3; origin of the r. A791; pointing at r. forbidden C843.1; prophecy of r. at saint's death M364.6; reincarnation as r. E644; snow makes r. behind runner F681.13; treasure at end of r. N516.

Raining. — How to find if it is r. J2716.

Raised. — Habitable hill r. on four pillars F721.2.1; king r. from dead P19.5; object magically r. in air D2135.0.2.

Raising a buried treasure (task) H1181; fallen elephant power of chaste women H413.4; of the sky A625.2; the sun A727; sunken church bell V115.1.2. — Ghost laid by r. a. cross E443.4; mermaid prevents r. of sunken churchbell B81.13.10; return from dead as punishment for attempted r. of ghost E235.3.

Raja betroths daughter as murder compensation T69.3.1; enters body of dead parrot K1175; magically protected from hurled stones D1400.1.22; to marry when cut mango blooms M261.1.1; offends goddesses A189.10; outwits priests in dream interpretation J1527; to prosper by marriage M369.2.4; refuses to marry peri F302.3.0.2; sacrifices entire family to purify lake S263.3.3; substitutes self for condemned man K842.4; warned in dream stranger is son D1810.8.2.5. — Doctor accidentally saves r. N688.1; infertile r. marries beggar T121.8.1; land where every r. dies H1289.5, P16.8; ogress demands eyes of six r. wives K961.2.2; poison sucked out from bitten r. B511.1.3; recognizing r. by his generosity F655.1; wazir fulfills prophecy, murders r. M370.1.1.

Raja's blindness magically healed D1505.14.1; favorite exposed: makes king laughingstock K1678. — Barber reveals r. secret D2161.4.19.1; hero r. neglected grandson L111.9; ogress-wife turns out r. other wives S413.1; prophecy on r. having son M311.0.3.2; wager: r. daughter to bring servant dinner N12.1.

Rajas. — Hundred r. in love with one woman T27.3.

Rake. — Surrender to r. J2613.

Rakshasa G369.1; devours everyone around her G262.3; dies after bird's neck broken G252.3. — King decides son is r. N349.3; maiden rescued from r. R111.1.11; magic power from r. D1721.1.4.

Rakshasas. — Quest to world of r. H1289.6.

Ram blesses plum tree A2711.6; carries off girl D13.2.1; -god A132.14; with green feet and horns B731.9.1; promises to jump into wolf's belly K553.3. — Devil as r. G303.3.3.1.7; dwarf waits for r. K553.2.1; dividing two sheep and a r. J1241.1; dragon as modified r. B11.2.1.9; entrance to woman's room in golden r. K1341.1; escape on r. with golden fleece R175.1; gold-producing r. B103.0.3; lie: great Darby r. X1243.1; revenant as r. E423.1.7; thief forced to buy wethers from r. K439.5; why r. smells bad A2416.5; speaking r. B211.1.1.1; wolf poses as r. K828.3.

Ram's — Escape under r. belly *K603; god with r. head A131.3.3; Satan entangles r. horns on altar G303.9.9.20.

Rams. — Why r. live at home A2433.3.7.

Rama. — Sun, moon as eyes of R. A714.7.

Rammer. — Killing with r. F628.2.6.

Rampart. — Fiery r. around otherworld F148.1; island with r. of gold and palisade of silver F731.3.

Rancher unrecognizable after he cleans up W115.3.

Ranis suspected of eating child G369.1.4.

Rank betrayed by habitual conversation H38ff.; of the gods in Hades A318. — Customs concerning r. P632; high-born alone recognizes one of equal r. J814.2; tests of social r. H1574.

Ransom disappears when prisoner retained Q552.18.3. — Animal grateful for r. from captivity B366; captor contributes to captive's r. W11.5.8; captured animals arrange own r. B278; friends pool r. money P319.1; magic as captive's r. D859.8; miser held for r. W153.12; no r. if captured without arms P557.1; saint's r. bursts into flames Q552.18.1.1; tasks assigned as r. H924.1; wife sells self for husband's r. R152.2.

Ransomed. — Dead grateful for having corpse r. *E341.1; lovers r. R121.7.

Ransoming. — Fairy r. self F341.2; hero r. saint's picture N848.1; saint r. prince, money vanishes K236.3.1.

Rape T471. — Clever decisions concerning kissing and r. J1174; king who intends r. killed P12.4; law against r. A1556.1; lightning strikes woman accusing saint of r. Q552.1.7; magic sickness prevents r. T321.5; no r. during king's reign C563.3; punishment for attempted r. Q244.1; repartee between king and son accused of r. J1289.6; ruler beheads son for r. M13.1; torn garment proves man innocent of r. J1174.5.

Raped, see also **Ravished.** — River r. F932.10; water-spirit r. by mortal F420.6.1.7; women r. by ogre G477.

Raphael. — Angel R. created from water A52.1.4.

Rapids. — Ogre's ashes cast on stream cause r. to stop G655.

Rapping. — Ghost r. E402.1.5; magic object acquired by r. on tree D859.1.

Rascal, see **Trickster.**

Rat changes name, wins bride K1371.3; cures man B511.4; defecates on octopus's head: origin of tubercles on head A2211.14; defecates upon rescuing octopus K952.1.2; digs passage to girl's chamber for hero B582.2.2.; and frog tie paws together to cross marsh J681.1; gives magic medicine B191.4; gnaws net B545.2; imagines self camel's owner J953.17; leaves serpent behind, though spared to rescue him K1182; paramour B611.7; persuades cat to wash face before eating: escapes K562; released: grateful B375.6; releases deer from snare K642.1; servants cut jungle down, till soil B292.9.3; -skin shoes F823.3; as suitor B621.4; trained to aid gambling N7; transformed to another animal D411.2; transformed to person D315.1. — Association of r. with cat ceases as soon as mutual danger has passed J426; cat chooses r. meat at feast J135.1; cat kills attacking r. B524.1.3; color of r. A2411.1.4.3; creation of r. A1854; dwarf as r. reincarnation F451.1.5.1; enmity of bird and r. A2494.13.9; enmity of octopus and r. A2494.16.7; enmity between cat and r.

A2494.1.4; food of r. A2435.3.10; friendship of cat and r. A2493.9.1; ghost as r. E423.2.8; helpful r. B437.1; huge r. borrows into enemy city K2351.8; lion rescued from net by r.: eats r. W154.3.1; man transformed to r. D117.3; marriage to r. B601.3; owl's wings borrowed from r. A2241.2; palm r. pretends deafness, cheats in bargain K231.15; race from union of girl and r. A1006.4; reincarnation as r. E612.13; speaking r. B211.2.9; where r. got tail A2378.1.2; wedding of r. and cockroach B281.11.1, B285.8; witch as r. G211.2.6.

Rat's. — Why r. snout long A2335.4.6; why r. tail looks like folded leaf A2378.9.5; why r. tail round and hairless A2317.12.3.

Rats cause cats to be killed K2172; devour hard-hearted man Q415.2; gnaw king's saddle girths L316; leave sinking ship B757; playing with fire, house burns W111.1.1.2. — Ability to see unborn r. within mother F642.33; Agaria eat r. A1681.4; enmity of r. and spiders A2494.12.8; house burned to get rid of r. J2103.3; jackal feigns holiness to seize r. K815.16; king of r. B241.2.4; kingdom of r. B221.2; lies about r. X1227; procurator of r. B221.2.1; why r. do not stick their eyes out in the straw J2371.3; why we have r.; one escapes slaughter A1854.1.

Rath. — Druids as r.-builders P427.8; god as r.-builder A179.1; magic r. always seems distant D2031.13; smith as r.-builder P447.2.

Raths marked out with brooch A1435.2.1. — Hero builds r. A538; origin of r. A1435.2.

Rattle. — Coyote wears fox's r.: caught in brush and injured J2136.1; devil disappears amid terrible r. G303.17.2.7; fox's heart becomes r. D457.15.1; magic r. D1212; origin of the use of the r. A1461.4; wild hunt heralded by r. of chains E501.13.1.2.

Rattlesnake. — Capturing squirrel and r. (task) H1154.6; copperhead guides r. to prey B765.13; death from r. bite because of breaking tabu C925; enmity of earthworm and r. A2494.16.6; why r. is dangerous A2523.2.1; why r. harmful: earthworm feeds him chili pepper A2211.11.

Rattlesnakes. — Female r. mate with black snakes B754.3.1.

Raven, see also **Crow;** as bird of good omen B147.2.1.1; as bird of ill omen B147.2.1.1; carries off souls of damned E752.3; with cheese in his mouth K334.1; as creator A13.2.1; as culture hero A522.2.2; does not return to ark: black color as punishment A2234.1.1; and dove fight over man's soul E756.3; drowns young, saves one refusing to help him in old age J267.1; on horns thinks he has led bull J953.10.1; inside whale F911.2.1; jealous of partridge's way of flying W181.5; killed by apes who will not receive his teaching J1064.1; as messenger B291.1.1; plucks out men's eyes B17.2.3.1; rescues man from pit B547.2; singes feet: why its wings clap when it flies A2218.6; steals the robes of Red Willow Men and finds them useless J2194; tries to imitate dove's step J2413.9; tries to imitate dove: punished with awkward feet A2232.10; transformed to water bird D413.2; wants to be as white as a swan W181.3. —Alliance of r. and crow B267.2; why r. is bald A2317.5; why r. is black A2411.2.1.5; burial learned from watching r. bury its dead A1591.1; why r. claps wings in flying A2218.6, A2442.2.1; creation of r. A1919; croaking of r. A2426.2.7; crow tries to prophesy like r. J951.3; devil in form of r. G303.3.3.3.1; dog asks raven why he sacrifices to Athena, since she hates r. because of his powers of augury J821.1; why r. lays eggs in March A2251.1, A2486.1; enmity between r. and (marsh-snipe) A2494.13.6, (mink) A2494.13.7, A2494.12.5; helpful r. B451.5; killing r. forbidden *C92.1.1; lost soul in r. feathers E752.4; magpie as hybrid of dove and r. A2382.1; man transformed to r. D151.5; why r. has nose marked as if it had been broken off A2335.2.3; prophetic r. B143.0.4; red as blood, white as snow, black as a r. Z65.1; reincarnation as r. E613.7; revenant as r. E423.3.4; soul as r. E732.8; soul in r. E715.1.6; speaking r. B211.3.6; tabu to kill r. C92.1.1; why r. hops A2441.2.1; why r. cannot talk A2422.6; why r. is thief A2455.3; why r. suffers thirst A2234.1, A2435.4.3; youth shoots r. and takes feather to raven's sister as token H78.1.

Raven's croaking ill omen D1812.5.1.27; wedding B282.16. — Cowardly soldier turns back when he hears r. croak W121.3; dove rewarded with r. sheen by Noah A2221.7; resuscitation by r. blood E113.1.1.

Ravens as attendants of god A165.1.1; carry message to enemies B291.1.1.1; follow wild huntsman E501.4.4; pursue murderer N271.3.1; show Adam how to bury dead: are born with white feathers A2223.7. — Abduction by r. R13.3.1; hero kills horse to feed r. B391.3; giant r. B31.3; why r. have crooked legs and walk lame A2371.2.3; why young r. have white feathers A2313.5.

Ravenous demons F402.4; ogres D47.2. — Feeding r. beast to satisfaction (task) H1123.

Ravine. — Changeling thrown into r. and thus banished F321.1.4.2; monkey jumps over a r. with his sword girded on J2133.2.

Ravines. — Dwarfs live in r. F451.4.2.2.

Ravished, see also **Raped.** — Fairy r. by mortal F304.4.1; girl saved by lion from being r. B549.1; gull a transformed r. maiden A1945.2; husband poisons wife to avoid having her r. T471.3; woman enjoys being r. by enemy T458.

Ravisher unwittingly rapes own sister T471.1. — Chaste maiden vanishes from r. D1714.1.1; fairy king punishes r. of his daughter F304.1; punishment for r. *Q244; woman kills would-be r. T320.2.1.

Ravisher's grave and body miraculously burnt Q414.0.4.1.

Raw. — Dress of r. fur F821.1.3; people who prefer r. flesh F561.1; sham miracle: food turns r. K1975.3.

Rays. — Blindness healed by sun's r. F952.2; conception from dragon r. T521.3; marvelous sensitiveness: ulcer from moon's r. F647.7; path to sun on sun's r. F154.

Razor drips blood (life token) E761.1.7.2; magic *D1173.1; -sharp sword as footbridge (lie) X1817.1.

Razors. — Capturing magic pig carrying scissors, comb, and r. between its ears (task) H1154.1; stairway set with r. H1531.2.

Reach. — Magic objects keep out of r. D1606; man with elastic r. F516.4; never try to r. the unattainable J21.14; transformation to r. difficult place D641.

Reaching. — Burned pillar r. heaven F774.2; magic object obtained by r. in certain cardinal direction D859.3.

Read. — Books in church r. without man's tongue F1055; devil unable to take one who has r. the Paternoster G303.16.2.1; how Jews r. A1689.6; learning to r. by magic D1819.4; man's thoughts r. by fairies F256; teaching ass to r. H1024.4

Reading ability identifies transformed person H62.1.2; inscription unique ability H31.11; magic book H31.7.2; smaller letters than in school J2258. — Divination by r. in book D1816.3; extraordinary r. ability F695; ignorance of r. J1746; man escapes devils by r. Lord's blessing G303.16.2.3.1; origin of r. A1484; rejuvenation by r. in book D1889.1; task: r. Bible: devil unable K211.1; unnecessary choice between praying or r. J465.

Real and apparent values J230—J299; mother preferred to foster mothers T675. — Officers praised in reverse from their r. merit K2136; scarcity of r. friends J401; value depends upon r. use J1061.

Realistic dream F1068; painting H504.1.

Realization. — Man falls dead from sudden r. N383.

Reaping. — Bride as r. contest prize H331.1.7; devil aids farmer in r. contest G303.19.2; prophecy on not r. what thou sowest M306.1; sowing and r. same day F971.7; sowing, r. in one day royalty test H481.8; time for r. A1150.1.

Reared. — Exposed child r. secretly S350.2; human being r. in fairyland F371; hunter discovers girl being r. in cave N724; lovers r. as brother and sister learn to their joy that they are not related T415.3.

Rearing of children taught by hero A1357. — Bad r. causes son to bite parent's nose off Q586; strong man's birth and r. F611ff.

Reason. — Cynic praises power of r. J1442.1.1; magic object restores r. D1508ff.; not to ask for r. of an unusual action C411.1; ruling by r. alone untrustworthy J21.28.

Reassembled. — Fear test: playing game with r. dead man H1433.

Reassembling corpse E422.1.10.1. — Felled tree restored by r. all cut parts E30.1; limbs of dead voluntarily r. E31.

Reassuring. — Dead r. the living E363.4.

Reawakening. — Magic r. of memory D2006ff.

Rebel angels A54 (oppose creation of man) A1217.1; god author of all poisonous things A63.7.

Rebelling. — Created being r. against God A106.3; goddess r. against father A106.1.1; lesser gods r. against chief A162.8; objects r. against owners D1649.6; sons slain in r. against father P17.0.1; stars r. against God A769.2.

Rebirth, see also **Reincarnation.** — Extraordinary occurences at r. F960.1.5; prophecy of r. as monkey M354.1; rejuvenation by r. D1889.7; superior r. as reward Q143.

Reborn. — Culture hero r. A510.2; god r. of human woman A162.5; man r. as girl in punishment Q551.5.1.1; person transforms self, is swallowed and r. in new form *E607.2; rejuvenation by being r.; man in fish form eaten and r. D1889.7; theft of light by being swallowed and r. *A1411.2; woman r. as man E605.1.1.

Rebounding. — Death by r. bow N335.3.

Rebuke for poor, long story J1223. — Judgment as r. to unjust plaintiff J1172.

Rebuked. — Hero r. by father P233.2; miser r. by friend W153.10; officiousness or foolish questions r. J1300ff.

Rebuking absurdities J1536ff. — Father's ghost r. child E327.4; god r. mortal A182.3.2; speaking beans r. wife for misdeed D1619.1.

Reburial. — Angel arranges r. in sanctified ground V244; ghost laid by r. E441.

Recalled. — Banished minister found indispensible and r. P111.

Recalling common experiences brings recognition H15.2; someone else's dream H1042. — Spells for r. dead lover E218.

Recapture of fugitive R350ff.

Receding eye F541.5, (of witch) G213.3.

Receive. — "He that asks shall r." V316.1; transformation to r. food D655.

Received. — Provisions r. from magic tree D1470.2.1; soul r. at birth E726.1.

Receiver of stolen goods J1169.6.

Receivers. — Inflicters rather than r. of wounds chosen J481.

Receptacle. — Contents of forbidden r. are released C915; not to look into certain r. C320ff.

Recipe. — Thankful that the r. is left J2562.

Reciting. — Captive released after r. beginning of Genesis V151.1; invisibility by r. formula backwards D1985.2; magic object recovered by r. magic formula D886.

Recklessly. — Tabu to eat animals r. killed C221.4.3.

Reckoning of the pot (125th day of month) J2466.2.

Recognition H0—H199; by bodily marks H50ff.; of captive's voice brings about rescue from ogre G556; by child (of devil's tail) G303.4.6.1, (of relative's flesh) G61.1; through common knowledge H10ff.; of devil's voice in a man G303.16.19.7; through personal peculiarities H30ff.; by resemblance H20ff.; by tokens H80—H149; of witches G250ff. — Circumstances of r. H150—H199; disenchantment by r. D772.1; remarkable power of r. F654; sham duel to bring about r. K1791; transformation to old man to escape r. D1891.

Recognized. — Magic horse r. by everyone B184.1.9; son must threaten father to be r. P233.7.

Recognizing trolls F455.10. — Man not r. his own reflection in the water J1791.7; mortal not r. fairy who gives him gift F348.5; not r. own house, family J2014; not r. own house converted to mansion J2316.1; not r. own name J2016.

Recompense, see **Payment.**

Reconciliation of separated couple T298. — Estranged couple pay trickster for r. K441.4; footwashing as r. sign P673; serpent having injured man avoids r. J15.

Recover. — Journey to hell to r. devil's contract F81.2; princess must r. consecrated wafer stolen from her first communion H1292.4.1; transformation to r. stolen goods D659.11.

Recovered. — Condemned soul r. E754.1; falcon and heron eaten by wild boar r. alive from his body X1723.2; lost object r. with devil's help G303.22.2; money lost twice: r. third time N183; stolen flocks r. by stupid monk L141.1; stolen cup r. by fairy posing as beggar F361.2.1.

Recovering lost objects as task H1132ff.; money owed by a foreign king H1182.1.

Recovery of fairy mistress F302.6.2; of lover's gift K1581; of magic object D880ff. — Fainting brings r. of speech F954.3; healer's payment: satisfaction at r. K233.6; magic r. of speech D2025.

Recreated. — Earth r. after world-fire A1036.

Recruiting. — Conflicts with r. officers P551.7.

Recruits. — Drunk r. war on haystack X818; secret where r. are being raised P361.7.

Rectum snakes G328.

Red as blood, white as snow *Z65.1; earth from slain child's blood A1277.3; eye F541.6.2; fairy F233.3; knight F527.1.1; as magic color *D1293.1; as otherworld color F178.1; or pale moon as evil omen D1812.5.1.15.2; plant from blood of slain person E631.0.3.1; Riding Hood and wolf K1822, K2011; river F715.9; sea F711.3.2; as symbolic color Z141; teeth as sign of royalty H71.9; thread on neck of person who has been decapitated and resuscitated *E12.1. — Angry warrior becomes r. and purple F1041.16.6.5; bird's r. eye cooks meat F989.2; bottom of R. Sea has seen the sun only once H822; blue, r., yellow horses in fairyland F241.1.1.3; brownie with r. hair F482.1.1; Canaanites' r. eyes A1666.1; one cheek white, other r. F545.3.1; child born blood-r. T551.15; coins thought to be r. beans J1772.3; creature with single r. hair H1331.7; dead rubbed with r. paint V68.4.1; devil dressed in r. G303.5.3; devil has r. beard G303.4.1.3.1; devil's hair blood r. G303.4.1.8.1; dwarfs wear r. coats F451.2.7.5; dwarfs with r. heads and r. caps F451.2.7.1; fairies have r. cows F241.2.1.1; fairies with r. caps F236.3.2; fairies in r. clothes F236.1.1; ghost in r. cap E422.4.6; giantess in r. dress F531.4.7.3; girl born with r. string around neck T552.1; goddess of war in shape of r.

woman A125.1.1; half-r., half-blue man F527.6; king in r., courtiers in different colors (riddle) H731.3; king in r., courtiers in white (riddle) H731.1; magic cow gives r. milk B184.2.1.1.1; magic r. stone D1383.6, magic r. swine B184.3.0.3; magic r. wind D1408.2; man about to be hanged keeps asking for his r. cap. J2174.1; man wears r. cap after his father's death J1462; milk becomes r. (life token) E761.6.2; mountain-men in r. caps F460.1.4.2; pygmies dressed in r. F535.3.2; quest for r. pear H1333.3.2.1; revenant r. E422.2.1; sick queen under r. satin carried off by bird N335.2.1; swallowing r.-hot stones as test H1511.1; tabu: following three r. men C863; why tail of West African grey parrot is r. A2378.8.2; treacherous r. knight K2265; troops of black, white, and r. soldiers F873.1; turning r., white from love T24.5; warning against stepping on r. cloth T299.2.1; why palm oil is r. A2877; why sun is r. A739.5; wild huntsman dressed in r. E501.8.2; witch with r. eyes G213.2.

Red-bird. — Color of r. A2411.2.1.13.

Redcap (Redcomb) murders for blood F363.2.

Reddened. — Man from earth r. with human blood A1241.4.

Reddening weapons tabu C835.2.5. — Severed head r. E783.3.

Redeemers. — True r. recognized by tokens H80.1.

Redeeming. — Three r. kisses D735.2.

Redoubt. — Bees thrown into r. drive out enemies K2351.2.

Reducing. — Teller r. size of lie X904.1.

Reductio ad absurdum of (judgment) *J1191ff., (question or proposal) *J1290ff., (riddle: stallions of Babylon) H572, (task) H952.

Reed as direction finder D1313.5.2; pricks dog urinating on it L391.1; transformed to person D431.7. — Bride reincarnated as r. K1911.3.4; decision rests on ability to go through r. J1141.1.7; fire stolen in hollow r. A1415.1; magic speaking r. betrays secret *D1316.5; man becomes r. D244.

Reeds bend before wind (flood) J832; make ships seem like island K1872.2. — Addressing field of r. J1883.1; devil owns the r. G303.10.12; dwarfs' house of r. F451.4.3.8; mankind from mating of pairs of r. A1221.3; why certain r. are hollow A2757.

Reef is old, ship new J2212.4. — Goddess as coral r. A139.8.2.

Reel. — Extraordinary r. F867.

Re-enacting the accident injuring self J2133.14. — Ghost r. own life E337ff.

Re-entering. — Dead man r. body E1.2.

Reeve's tale K1345.

Reflection in water thought to be the original of the thing reflected *J1791ff. — Falling in love with r. in water T11.5; fugitive discovered by r. in water R351; lover declares self by showing beloved's r. T57.1; soul as r. E743.2; weak animal shows strong his own r. and frightens him K1715.1.

Reflections. — Effect of r. J1791.

Reforged. — Man to be r. chooses present unhappiness J323.

Reform. — Curse removed with victim's r. M423. — Repartee concerning false r. J1400ff.

Reformed. — Harlot r. by sight of holy fringe on garment V131.1; rich man r. by holy man's prayer J153.1; sinner r. after visit to heaven, hell V522.

Reforming. — Parable on r. world J133.5; wife r. husband J1112.1.

Refound. — Maiden disenchanted, deserted, and r. D795.

Refuge. — Captivity as r. R53; cities of r. P518; dogs rescue fleeing master from tree r. *B524.1.2; gods take r. underground A189.13; guest given r. P322; killing animal in r. tabu C841.0.3; man taking r. in woman's house causes her false accusation K2112.3; tabu: violating r. with saint C51.2.5.

Refuges *R310ff.

Refugee entertained in holy place P322.3.

Refusal to believe that a friend has spoken ill of one P317; of crow to marry titmouse, since she is 100 years old B282.22.1; to fight relatives P205; to grant request punished Q287; of great to associate with lowly J411; to return borrowed goods K232; of sham physician to take his own medicine K1955.7; of ship to move with guilty man aboard D1318.10.1; of wagon to move because ghost is sitting in it *D1317.10. — Debtor's r. to pay his debt *K231; friendship without r. P319.7; imagined r. as friendship test H1558.6; only one r. to weep at hero's death Z351; peasant's r. to sell possessions to king P411.1; punishment for r. to (have children) *Q251, (marry after girl is pregnant) Q245; toad's r. to weep over its dead children: dries up when dead A2231.8; transformed animal's r. to touch meat of that animal D686.

Refused. — Host miraculously given when it is r. a man by the priest V32; loans r. J1552ff.; lover abducts maiden r. him R10.1.2.1; owner has r. to accept it K373; reward r. by hero L225; youth lamed by man whose daughter he has r. to marry Q451.2.1; unconsecrated host r. V31.3; wisdom from fool: heaven r. J156.4.

Refusing combat to anyone forbidden C835.1; larger payment than instructed to take J2461.8; a request tabu C871. — Animal curse for r. to carry holy fugitive across stream A2231.7.2; generous person never r. anything W11.15; girl r. her lover final kiss provokes rival to admit selling kisses K1275.1; person never r. a request M223.1; son r. to marry father's choice T131.1.2.4; sun setting and r. to rise; must be coaxed back from underworld A739.6; tabu: r. to elope with woman who desires it C192; tabu: r. a feast C282; vow against r. food to any man M158; wife r. bring warm water, beaten T254.6.1; wife r. to sleep with husband T288.

Regency. — To test a favorite king offers him r. J1634.

Regeneration, see also **Reincarnation.** — Cauldron of r. E607.5.

Regrets. — King sends r. for man he is executing K2098.

Regretted. — Lack of proper education r. J142; parson has never r. silence J1074.1.

Regrowth of flesh E784; of huge tree when cut down H1115.1; of severed head E783.2.

Reigning. — Vow against r. until picture's original found M151.2.1.

Reincarnated person identifies former weapons H19.1.1. — Bride r. as reed K1911.3.4; deity r. A179.5; giants as r. animals F531.6.1.8; girl r. as river so god may lie in its bed A934.11.1; husband r. as cat H1385.4.1.

Reincarnation, see also **Rebirth;** *E600—E699; in form fitted to crime Q584.3; as punishment Q551.5. — Animals in wild hunt r. of murdered person E501.4.0.1; attempts to kill person in r. S401; dwarf as r. F451.1.5; helpful animal r. of (parent) *B313.1, (murdered child) B313.2; newborn child r. of recently deceased person T589.5; punishment: r. as buffalo Q560.1.1.

Reincarnations. — Poppy characteristics from r. A2733.

Reindeer hose protect D1380.26. — Journey of soul to world of dead on r. E750.3; origin of r. A1875.1; food of r. A2435.3.11; why r. has so many qualities A2510.1; where r. got his small teeth A2345.3.

Reinforcements. — Enemy tricked, think r. arrive K2368.4; magic r. D2163.2; postponing payment to gather r. K2369.4.

Reinstatement of true bride *K1911.3.

Rejected suitor wages war T104.1. — Buried body r. by earth E411.0.6.

Rejoicing at arrival of rich man in heaven E758.

Rejuvenating. — Alleged r. object K116; food r. A153.4; man r. self by changing skin A1319.12; quest for r. fruit H1333.3.0.1.

Rejuvenation by animal *B594ff.; by magic object *D1338ff; of other-world people F167.9.1. — Goddess's self-r. when old A191; imitation of magic r. unsuccessful J2411.1; magic r. *D1880ff.

Relation as helper on quest H1233.2. — "Lean upon no r. when in distress" J21.44; nearest blood r. must avenge slaying P525.3.

Relations, see also **Relatives, Sexual intercourse;** by law P260ff. — Business r. of dwarfs and mortals F451.5.10ff.; illicit sexual r. *T400—T499; intimate r. of dead and living E470ff.; multiple births from r. with several men T586.3; refusal of conjugal r. punished Q257; wife more merciful than blood r. P212.

Relationship. — Trickster's claim of r. causes owner to relax vigilance K347.

Relative substitutes in contest K3.1. — Death of r. as punishment Q411.3; fairy r. slain, revenged F361.8; magic object received from r. D815ff.; master discovers that slave he wants to marry is a r. T410.1; not to offend supernatural r. C30ff.; ogre's r. aids hero G530ff.; quest to other world for r. H1252; race won by deception: r. helpers *K11.1; rescue from ogre by r. G551; resuscitation by r. E125ff.; seduction by posing as r. K1315.4; task imposed or r. dies H901.0.1; uttering name of r. tabu C435ff.; woman suckles imprisoned r. through prison wall R81.

Relative's flesh eaten unwittingly *G61. — Dead r. friendly return E320ff.; dead r. malevolent return *E220ff.

Relatives, see also **Kin, Relations;** of the devil G303.11ff.; killed in revenge for wife's wrongdoing S452; steal magic object D861.8. — Animal r. C37; choices between kind strangers and unkind r. J390ff.; cruel r. S0— S99; cruel r.-in-law S50ff.; difficult choice between r. J226; enigmatic counsels of r. H596; ghost protects wife from r. E236.6; lover opposed to sweetheart's r. T95; marriage between r. A1552; ogre overawed by hero's boast about marvelous r. K1718; person forced to eat hearts of r. S183.1; prince drives r. away S110.4; refusal to fight r. P205; relationship riddles arising from unusual marriages of r. H795; tabu connected with husband's or wife's r. C170ff.; token sent with youth to r. H82.6; treacherous r. K2210ff.; treacherous r.-in-law K2218; trickster gets goods for alleged r. in distress J2326.4; wife's r. kill cannibal G551.5.

Release. — Animal grateful to captor for r. B370ff.; animal grateful for r. of relative B365.3; man gives daughter in return for r. T69.3; prisoner's miraculous r. F960.5; woman deceived into sacrificing honor to r. her brother (husband) K1353.

Released. — Dwarfs promise to emigrate if captured dwarfs are r. F451.9.1.5; when ferryman will be r. from his duty H1292.8; prisoners r. in celebrations of victory P14.1; wild huntsman r. from wandering E501.17.7; wild man r. from captivity aids hero G671.

Releasing. — Ogre deceived into r. prisoner G560ff.

Relic. — Cure by r. of Virgin Mary D2161.5.2.2; death feigned to establish reputation of false r. K1865; false miraculous r. K1976; priest keeps in container r. which when kissed renders people immune from pestilence J762.1; sacred r. as magic object *D1296.

Relics of saint cure disease V221.0.1; sacred V140ff. — Resuscitation by sacred r. E64.12; sacred r. protect against attack D1381.20; saint's r. assume Buddha's form D457.16.1; saint's r. control fires D2158.1.3.1; swearing on sacred r. M114.4; tree releases bag of r. D1648.1.2.2; tree shelters r. F979.7.

Relieving beast of burden J1874; souls in hell forbidden C741.

Relighting. — Chaste woman blowing out candle with one puff and r. it with another H413.1; woman r. magic fires as punishment Q492.

Religion *V (entire chapter). — Different r. as marriage obstacle T131.8; king asks holy man for heart of r. J1289.18; person from hell tells of importance of r. E367.1; practicing one's r. forbidden S466; vow to change r. M177; what is best r. (riddle) H659.5.

Religions. — Conflicts between r. *V350ff.

Religious animals *B250ff.; ceremony exorcises witch G271.2; ceremony as magic cure D2161.4.9.1; ceremonials A1549; edifices and objects V100—V199; orders *V450—V499; person suggests tasks H919.2; personages tested H1573.2; rewards Q170ff.; sacrifices *V10ff.; services *V0—V99; sun and moon A738.2.1; tests H1573; vows M183; words or exercises interpreted with absurd literalness J2495. — Child sacrifice as r. rite S260.1.1; coming of r. leader prophesied M363; curse by head of r. order

M411.22; devil cheated by r. or magic means K218; division between r. and lay activities A1472.1; evil spirit exorcised by r. ceremony D2176.3.3; ignorance of r. matters J1738; magic object acquired as reward for r. austerities D855.2; magic results produced by r. ceremony *D1766; no rain falls on r. man D2143.1.0.2; origin of r. ceremonials A1540ff.; origin of r. images A1544; person under r. ban cannot find rest in the grave E412; test of r. learning H502.1; treasure hidden in r. shrine N514; value of r. exercises V4; witch's power from altering r. ceremony G224.5; witches avoid r. ceremonies G285; worldly man puts r. man out of countenance J1217.

Reliquary. — Saint's bones remove self from broken r. V143.1.

Remains, see Body, Corpse.

Remaining on journey too long forbidden C761.1. — Person r. in otherworld because of broken tabu C953; resuscitation of wife by husband giving up half his r. life *E165.

Remark. — Speculative r. causes ghost's appearance E386.5.

Remarks. — Misreported r. K1775; test: making senseless r. H507.2.

Remarkable, see also Extraordinary, Marvelous, Marvels; persons F500—F599; physical organs F540ff.; skill F660ff. — Lie: r. man X910.

Remarriage. — Cynic's comment on r. J1442.12; dead wife's r. to husband E322.8; vow against r. M135.

Remedy for effects of seeing wild hunt E501.19ff.; learned from overhearing animal meeting *B513. — Animal fetches r. for man B514; blood as r. for barrenness in woman D1347.2; carrying person to the r. instead of opposite J2214.8; magic object as r. D1500.1ff.; magic potion mixed with brains (liver, etc.) of deceitful person as r. for snake-bite D1515.4.6; magic r. learned by magic D1818; quest for marvelous r. H1324; secret r. overheard in conversation of animals (witches) N452; sympathetic helper sent for r. and robbed K345.1.

Remedies for animal in stomach B784.2ff.; worse than the disease J2100ff. — Magic r. for barrenness or impotence T591.1.

Remembering former lives after reincarnation E601. — Man r. all he ever learned D1911; man r. all people he has met F654; medicine of r. D1365.8.1; something for r. always: nose cut off J2072.6.

Reminder. — Unjust judge's skin stretched over a footstool as r. to others to be just J167.

Reminders. — Recognition by r. of what has been said H17.

Remission of punishment Q570ff.

Remorse. — Man cuts out own tongue in r. Q451.4.7.

Removable eyes F541.11; organs F557; vagina F547.5.1.

Removal and replacement of vital organs F668.1. — Dry spring restored by r. of certain stone F933.2; magic object returned in payment for r. of magic horns D895; resuscitation by r. of poisoned apple E21.1; waking from magic sleep by r. of enchanting instrument D1978.3.

Removed. — Birthmark r. at touch of dead man's hand E542.2; dead returns to replace boundary marks he has r. E345.1; girl's heart magically r. and fed to man draws her to him D1905.1; hunchback's hump r. by fairies F344.1; lover's gift regained: the r. article K1581.1; magic weakness never entirely r. D1837.2; obstacles r. by magic object D1562ff.; rejuvenation by going to otherworld and having digestive tract r. D1889.5; temporary growths r. by magic object D1375.

Remover of landmarks cannot rest in grave E416.

Removing mountain (mound) in one night (task) H1101. — Disenchantment by r. cause of enchantment D765.1; disenchantment by r. covering of enchanted person D720ff.; magic forgetting of wife at husband's r. shirt she has given him D2004.6; self-r. object D1641ff.; saint's bones for lack of worship r. themselves from church V143; tabu: r. landmarks C846; transformation by r. chains from neck D536; treasure r. itself N562.

Remuneration, see Payment.

Rendezvous. — Devil comes to r. instead of lover K1317.10; keeping r.: trouble between man and wife K1085.2; lover's magic sleep at r. D1972; lovers' r. T35; maiden sent to r. to capture lover K787; obscene tricks played on lover keeping r. K1218.9.1; sham illness to escape r. K523.0.1.1.

Rending. — Animals r. one another B265; stiff hair r. garments F555.8.1.

Renewal of world after world calamity A1006f., A1038, A1045. — Miraculous r. of saint's objects V224.

Renouncing clerical vows *V475; heaven: companions not there V326. — Heaven as reward for r. life Q172.6.

Rent. — Dragon eats people for r. B11.10.2; king punished for raising old woman's r. Q281.4; stone r. at crucifixion A979.1; tricksters feign father's death, flee with r. K356.

Repaid. — Arrogance r. L430ff.; kindness r. by devil G303.22.1.

Repair. — Animals help r. pot B579.4; dead returns to r. injury E345; living smith must r. wagon belonging to wild hunt E501.15.5.

Repairing the house K1415; the roof (not needed in dry weather, impossible in wet) J2171.2.1. — Mortal r. fairies' utensils F338; person cured by r. image that has same deformity D2161.4.4; water carried in leaky vessel by r. it with clay or gum H1023.2.1.1.

Reparations. — Life bought with promise of r. M234.4.

Repartee J1250—J1499. — Test in r. H507.

Repay. — Giants r. loan with large interest F531.5.5; money left on hill to r. helpful mountain-men F460.4.2.2; numskull throws money to frogs to r. them J1851.1.3; return from dead to r. obligation E340ff.

Repaying deceptive loan J1556. — Chain tale: lending and r. Z41.5; troll r. loan F455.6.2.1.

Repayment with leaves (shavings) that turn to gold *E501.15.4. — Ghost seeks r. of stolen money E236.8.

Repeated impressions penetrate mind J67; reincarnation E670ff.; resuscitation *E151; transformation *D610ff. — Death for r. adultery Q411.0.1.4; fool's r. expressions scare off adulterers J2461.2.2.

Repeatedly. — Animal feigns death r. and then entices owner from goods K341.2.1.

Repeating the ceremony J2498; incantation continuously H1508.1; within stories Z17. — Fool keeps r. his instructions so as to remember them J2671.2; identity test: r. what formely said H15.1; sham parson keeps r. same expression K1961.1.2.

Repelled. — Incestuous sister r. by brother T415.2.

Repentance of devil vexing friars G303.24.3; test H1573.7. — Account of punishments prepared in hell brings about r. J172; conversion through r. V331.4; false r. of the sick U236; power of r. V315.1; return from dead to preach r. E367; reward for r. Q36.

Repentant thief pretends to have found stolen cow K416. — Blood from r. woman F962.4.2; devil tempts r. sinner G303.9.4.9; Virgin aids r. slayer V276.3.

Repenting. — Creator r. of certain creations A74.2; son r. of plot to kill father S22.3.

Repetition. — Magic r. D2172.1.

Replaced. — Bodily members successfully r. *E780ff.; magic object cannot be r. D1661; polygamy so head wife may be quickly r. T145.8.

Replacement. — Beautification by decapitation and r. of head *D1865.1; constant r. of fighters E155.1.1; disenchantment by decapitation and r. of head *D711.1; miraculous r. of objects for saint V224; resuscitation by r. of soul E38.

Replica. — Building wax r. of castle H1133.6; soul as r. of body E747.1.

Replying. — Animals r. to person's remarks B210.1; usurers not r. when called on to rise in church X512.

Repopulated. — Ireland r. after flood A1006.5.

Report. — Birds sit on Odin's shoulder and r. what they see and hear *B122.2; owner frightened from goods by r. of approaching enemy K335.0.1.

Representative. — Moon as sun's r. at night A756.

Representations. — Pictorial r. of creator A18.

Repression of lust T317.

Reprimanded. — Boaster of victory over a weaker person r. J978.

Reproached. — Person r. for having no relatives P202.

Reproduction of life stops in absence of goddess of fertility A431.1.1.

Reproductive energy from god A175.1.

Reproving. — Dead brother r. sister's pride E226.1; dead wife r. husband's second wife *E221.2; father r. son in vision P233.10; tact in r. the great J816.

Reptile, see also **Serpent, Snake;** leaps into unjust bishop's throat V229.2.11.1; -men as magicians D1711.13; as ogre G354; paramour B613; transformed to object D425; transformed to other animal D418; as wooer

B622. — Abduction by r. R13.4; cause of movement of r. A2441.4ff.; devil as r. G303.3.3.6; enemies of r. A2494.16; giant r. B875ff.; magic r. B176; marriage to person in r. form B646; marriage to r. B604ff., (in human form) B656; prophetic r. B145; reincarnation as r. E614; soul in form of r. E733; speaking r. B211.6; wise r. B123.

Reptiles transformed to persons D390ff. — Color of r. A2411.5; creation of r. A2140ff.; devastating r. B16.5; God makes birds, devil r. A1903; haunts of r. A2433.6ff.; king of r. B244ff.; kingdom of r. B225; lies about r. X1320; man swallows r. F929.2; man transformed to r. D190ff.; mythical r. B92; war between birds and r. B263.4.

Repulsing. — Animals r. shipwrecked man B772; ruler marries maiden r. his advances Q87.1; transformation as revenge for r. amorous adventures D661.1.

Repulsive. — Disguised husband shows wife he is not r. K1813.1.1; fairy wife deserts mortal husband for r. lover F302.2.1; woman's r. lover T232.4.

Reputation. — Death preferable to loss of r. for hospitality W12.1; overlooking adultery for sake of r. J221.1.1.

Request, see also **Wish;** for immortality punished by transformation into tree Q338.1. — Condemned man's last r. (red cap left in prison) J2174.1; dwarfs r. that cow stable be moved F451.4.4.3; fallen trees upraised at saint's r. D1602.2.1; fruit produced out of season at saint's r. F971.5.1; immoderate r. punished *Q338; moderate r. rewarded, immoderate punished Q3; modest r. best L220ff.; person never refuses a r. M223.1; refusal to grant r. punished Q287; refusing a r. tabu C871; reward for carrying out dead man's r. Q37; troubled nobleman's r. must not be refused P95.

Requests. — Departed deity grants r. to visitors *A575; tabus concerning r. made in otherworld C714; vow that no bards will make r. M164.

Requiem. — Ghost chooses own r. E545.11.

Rescue *R100—R199; of abandoned or lost person R130ff.; alone from shipwreck chosen over drowning with goods J222; of captive R110ff.; from deluge as reward Q150.1; from fairyland F321.3, F322.2, F322.5; by ghost from drowning E379.1; of hero by dragon B11.6.1.2; from ogre G550ff.; by magic object *D1390ff.; of sister from ogre by another sister G551.2; tokens *H83. — Animals grateful for r. from peril of death B360ff.; bat undertakes r. H1562.2.2; dog is to r. the farmer's child from wolf and receive reward K231.1.3; dogs r. fleeing master from tree refuge *B524.1.2; extraordinary companions r. hero F601.4; magic horn summons army for r. D1421.5.1; magic object received from man in return for r. of child D817.1; monster ungrateful for r. W154.2; prince will marry girl who will r. him from embarrassing position T67.3; reward for r. Q53; tasks assigned before man may r. wife from spirit world H923; transformation to r. D643.

Rescued animal threatens rescuer W154.2.1. — Captive r. by animal

*B544; drowning man r. by siren B53.1; girl r. by companions H621.2; hero captured by man he has formerly r. N763; impostors steal r. princess K1935; incognito king r. in fighting K1812.19; man attacked by the devil r. by Virgin Mary V264; man swallowed by fish and later r. alive (lie) X1723.1.2; moon falls into pit, r. by man A754.1.1; stolen child r. by animal nurse B543.3; victims r. from swallower's belly F913; woman r. from mountain men F460.4.4.1.1.

Rescuer disguised as officer gains custody of prisoner K649.2. — Actual r., not watchers, gets woman J1179.12; animal r. or retriever *B540ff.; bungling r. caught by crab J2675; daughter unwittingly promised to dog r. S247; disguised king rewards r. from robbers Q53.1; enchanted person attracts attention of r. D794; girl leaves r. for younger lover T92.3; man kills r. to collect reward W154.12; man rescued from drowning kills r. W154.9; princess offered as prize to r. T68.1; rescued woman stolen from r. R111.8.2.

Rescuers *R150ff.; polite J2516.3.2. — Escape by reporting approach of r. K545.

Rescuers' Sabbath (Jew fallen into pit) J1613.

Rescuing drowning man forbidden C41.1; the moon (reflected in water) J1791.2. — Animal r. man from dangerous place B547ff.; dog tries to bite man r. him from well W154.5; fairy r. hero from battle F302.9; god r. sleeping man A185.2.1; horse r. children B540.2; husband r. wife's paramour K1544.1; wife r. husband from supernatural H923.1.

Resemblance of children to mother's brothers P293.2.1. — Close r. of unrelated children F1072; recognition by r. H20ff.

Reserved. — Certain objects r. for royalty P93.

Resewoir emptied for crane J758.2.

Resignation of king if he begets natural son P16.2.1; of maimed king compulsory P16.2.

Resin. — Revenant with chip of r. between teeth E422.1.7.

Resisting. — Girl r. devil G303.9.4.7.1; man r. blandishments of leader's fiancée W34.1.

Resources. — Never use your entire r. J1073.

Resourcefulness test. H506ff.

Respect. — Druid inspires r. P427.0.1; foolish trading to gain r. J2096; king's champion enforces r. P14.15.

Respice finem J21.1.

Respite granted dragon in fight B11.11.1. — Deceptive r. in payment obtained K238; definite r. from death granted K551.22; year's r. for unwelcome marriage T151.

Responsible. — Oldest son r. for others P233.5.

Rest. — Bluff: You take one, I can manage the r. K1715.8; dead find no r. because of a sin E411; ghost finds r. when certain thing happens E451; losing all for a r. J356.

Resting forbidden C730ff.; near lake tabu C615.4; tabu until question answered C735.2.9. — Creator r. on tree or stake A813.3; gods make earth for r. feet on A5.1; snake kills men while creator r. A1335.10.

Restlessness as curse M455; of dead E410ff. — Magic r. in bed D2063.2.

Restored. — Broken weapons magically r. D2163.1; dry spring r. by removal of certain stone F933.2; dumb man's speech r. by saint V221.2; magic object voluntarily r. to giver D878; nose r. by magic object D1376.1ff.; reincarnated person r. to original form E696; severed hand magically r. D2161.3.2; stolen sun r. to sky A721.3; treasure given away by saint r. V411.5; unshriven man r. to life in order to confess V23.1.

Restoring life to murder victim J1955.1. — Brownie r. stolen property F482.5.4.2; dead r. stolen goods E352; deity r. city A185.8; herbs r. sight D1505.1; prayer r. shattered vessel V52.5; son r. mother wished into pig J2075.4.

Restrained. — Animal r. by magic object *D1442ff.; hasty judgment r. when man sees someone sleeping with his wife (newborn son) J21.2; man r. from fornication by sight of holy fringe on garment V131.1.

Restrictions, see also **Tabu;** on burial V62. — Betrothal r. T65; marriage r. T131; sexual r. A1556.

Resurrected boys choose to return to heaven E755.0.1. — False daughter accepted as r. child K1926; Jewish child r. after burning V363.1.

Resurrection, see also **Resuscitation;** of gods A193; at Judgment Day E178; as reward Q151.9; on Sunday E751.6. — Christ's r. V211.8; place of saint's r. prophesied M364.4; reward: burial and r. in one place Q175.

Resurrections. — Two r. E751.0.1.

Resuscitated. — Boy r. by lie H252.4.1; death feigned to learn how soldiers r. K1863; faithless r. wife *K2213.5; intercourse with r. wife tabu C117.1; ogre r. to help hero G513; recognition of r. person by missing member H57.0.1.

Resuscitating. — Companions r. girl: to whom does she belong? H621.1; evil spirit cast out of person by killing and r. E728.1.1; faithful animals r. master B301.5; god r. man A185.12.1; lion, bear, and wolf r. master B515; ogre r. benefactor G513.1; ogre r. princess G335; pseudo-magic r. object sold *K113; pupil r. people demon kills K1955.6.1; reward for r. dead Q93.2; wife's constancy r. husband T212.1; Virgin Mary r. man V251.1.

Resuscitation *E0—E199; by animals B515; of unshriven man in order to confess V23.1. — Beautification by death and r. D1865ff.; fatal game: death and r. K856; false death, r., to exploit relic K1865; failure at r. E186; foolish imitation of r. J2411.1.1; magic pig burned to prevent r. B192.1.

Retainers. — Military rights of r. P551.8.

Retaining fee J1559.1.

Retaliation on cheating goldsmith J1511.20. — Bridegroom's r. to bride pleading headache K2052.3; king observes r. among animals and becomes just J52.

Retiring. — Divinity r. to end of the world A567; kings r. from world P16.1.

Retorts. — Clever r. J1250—J1649.

Retreat in return for cessation of attack M263.

Retreating warriors driven back to battle P551.4. — Good king never r. P12.5; treasure hidden by r. army N511.1.7.

Retrieving attempt fatal to jumper J2146; king's falcon H1154.7.1. — Animal r. lost person or object *B540ff.; seduction by alleged r. of lost gem K1315.2.2; wife r. husband's fortune J1545.6.

Return of dead soon after burial E586; from dead E200—E599, (to inflict punishment) E230ff., (to protest against easy-going priest) V25.1, (to repay obligations) E340ff., (to return and ask back love tokens) E311; of hero A516, Z293; home in humble disguise K1815.1; home to one's own funeral N681.0.1; to master of animal who shams death and is sold K366.1.3.1; from lower world F101; from upper world F10.1. — Culture hero's expected r. *A580ff.; dead lover's r. (malevolent) E210ff., (friendly) E310ff.; dead relative's r. from dead (malevolent) E220ff., (friendly) E320ff.; dwarf makes r. of child dependent upon guessing of riddle F451.5.15.2; dwarfs emigrate New Year's Eve of 1800 to r. New Year's Eve of 1900 F451.9.3; dwarfs must r. to spirit world by 1:00 a.m. F451.3.2.2; dwarfs r. what they borrow F451.5.10.4; expected r. of deity A192.3; friendly r. from the dead E300ff.; immediate r. to otherworld because of broken tabu C952; land of no r. F129.5; lover threatens to await husband's r. K1581.5.2; magic object causes things to r. to their proper place D1565ff.; magic object received from man in r. for rescue of child D817.1; magic r. of stolen object to owner K423; malevolent r. from dead E200—E299; quest to devil in hell for r. of contract H1273.1; refusal to r. borrowed goods K232; sacrifice for r. of abducted person V17.7; saint promises r. from heaven V229.2.13; witch recognized by seeing wandering soul r. G251; wizard compels thief to r. stolen property D1817.0.1.3.1.

Returned. — Adopted child r. to real mother T672; box on ears r. (sent around table) K2376; magic sword r. to lake whence it was received D878.1; present r. to giver (to give it to no one who is not a greater fool) J156.3; purchase money r. to suitor T52.2; rescued princess r. to her betrothed R111.4; stolen kiss to be r. *J1174.2.

Returning exile succeeds L111.1; hero marries first love T102; magic object D868. — Culture hero r. A581; dead place net across river to prevent living man from r. to earth F93.1.1; excuse for r. home after leaving wife J1545.3.3; fairies grateful for r. lost child F339.3; food placed out for r. souls of dead *E541.1; husband r. secretly, spies on wife K1551; landing of r. heroes prophesied M369.2; man given ability of r. to life E167; relics r. to original church V143.2; self-r. head *D1602.12; soul of sleeper prevented from r. to his body E721.1.2; treasure r. after it removes itself N562.1.

Reunion of lovers after many adventures T96; of outcast wife with husband and children S451; of soul with body E726.3. — Accidental r. of families N730ff.; accidental r. of lovers N737, of couple N741.

Reveal. — Man persuaded to r. fatal secret C420.1; return from dead to r. (hidden treasure) E371, (murder) *E231, (whereabouts of stolen goods) E371.1; speaking bones of murdered person r. murder E632.1.

Revealed. — Crime r. by laughing statue D1639.4. guilt r. by magic object *D1318ff.; murder r. (by child in mother's womb) T575.1.1, (by unusual names of boys) N271.2; peasant girl's wisdom r. by found mortar taken to king H561.1.2; substitution of false bride r. by animal *K1911.3.1; truth r. by magic object *D1316ff.

Revealing name of god forbidden C51.3; secrets of supernatural wife forbidden C31.9. — God r. himself to mortals A182; princess wins wrestling match with suitor by r. her breast H331.6.1.1; treasure r. itself only at certain times N541.

Revelation of magic secret permits animal to be killed D1445.1. — Animals observe sacred r. B251.8; clerics fast for r. P623.0.1.1; mountains fight to be spot for r. A964.2.1.

Revelations of a satyr U119.1.

Revelry. — Breaking up r. tabu C874; ghostly r. sounds E337.1.3.

Revenant, see also **Ghost.** — Sham r. goes out to get a breath of air J2311.3; wind stopped by r. D2142.2.1.

Revenants E200—E599.

Revenge given up as reward Q45.4; by interrupting feast J1564.2; for killing animal Q211.6; by literally misconstruing order J2516.0.1. — Animal takes r. on man B299.1; avoiding enemy's r. J647; blinded slave's r. K1465; curse in r. of father's murder M411.11; curse: undertaking dangerous r. M446.1; creation of animals as r. A1732; cutting hooks for father's r. H591.3; death and r. preferred to life J494; devil prevented from r. by pious priest G303.16.11.2; fairy's r. F361; ghost laid when r. accomplished E451.9; importunate lover's r. on women humiliating him K1218.4.1; king slain in r. P16.7; maidens slain in r. Q411.12; philanderer's wife has affair in r. K1510.2; porter's r. for three wise counsels J1511.6; queen kills husband in r. K2213.13, P22.1; queen offers son in r. for first husband P23.4; reincarnation for r. E693; rejected suitors' r. T75.2.1; stealing from ogre for r. G610.1; taking money instead of r. J229.11; transformation as r. for repulsing amorous adventures D661.1; vow not to take r. M168; vow on r. or death M161.2; wife's r. for second wife K2213.16; wife prepares r. but prefers to die with husband T211.2.1.1; will-o'-the-wisp's r. F491.5.

Revenged. — Theft charge r. Q411.13.1.

Reverberating waves F931.4.1.

Reversal of fortune L (entire chapter).

Reverse magic *D1783ff. — Officers praised in r. from their real merit K2136; witch's charm r. of Christian G224.1.

Reversed obstacle flight D673; transformation flight D671.1. — Facial features of goddess r. A282.0.1.1; judgments of church r. by Virgin Mary M91; ogre with feet r. G365.1; sun's night journey with r. face A722.2.

Reversing the poker protects from witch G272.9. — Disenchantment by cutting off and r. bodily members D712.1; disenchantment by r. enchantment D765; escape by r. K534ff.; power over monster (wizard, king) obtained by r. order D1783.4; resuscitation by r. wooden blocks E79.2.

Revival by day of pigs killed by night H1331.2.3; of lady found in tomb apparently dead K426, T37; of ogre after limbs are severed G635. — Disenchantment by burial then r. D719.1.1.

Reviving trees by magic object D1571; unconscious man with hot iron J2119.7. — Apparently dead woman r. before burial N694; witch r. dead G263.5.

Revolt of bad gods against good *A106.1; of evil angels against God A106.2.

Revolting devil banished to hell A106.2.1; murders or mutilations S100ff.

Revolver. — Sausage as r. scares off robber K437.3.

Revolving animal's skin B738; bleeding rock F809.4.1; castle F771.2.6, (in otherworld) F163.1.1; door of tent F782.6; fortress D1381.23.

Reward for accomplishment of task deceptively withheld K231.2; for the bag of lead K476.2.2; given for return of animal B343; of helpful animal B320ff.; for information claimed by sham dead J2511.1.2; of the uncharitable V420ff. — Animal characteristics as r. A2220ff.; debtor tells creditor that he has had r. in the hope of payment K231.7; devil is cheated of his r. when priest dismisses mass early G303.16.16; devil to enter girl and sham physician to collect r. for driving the devil out K1955.6; double r. successfully claimed K441ff.; false claim of r. K442; foolish r. offered J2085; forgiveness the r. of successful quest H1244; fugitive returns so family may collect r. T215.5; half of kingdom as r. Q112; helpful animal as r. B319.2; hero refuses r. L225; impostors claim r. earned by hero K1932; king gives own wife as r. P14.13; magic object acquired as r. D855; man kills rescuer to collect r. W154.12; modesty brings r. L200— L299; money received from ghosts as r. for bravery E373.1; mortal chooses to sleep with fairy as r. for saving her life F304.5; origin of plant as r. A2632; plant characteristics as r. A2710ff.; princess offers r. for princely husband T55.10; riches the r. of questions solved on quests H1243; sacrifice equal to r. J2067; same r. promised to many helpers K2034; singer repaid with promise of r. J1551.3; stranger dies from joy on receiving r. from ruler F1041.1.5.2; thief (abductor) returns and enforces r. for stolen object (princess) K442.1; transformation as r. D663; worship of deity brings r. V526.

Rewards and punishments Q (entire chapter). — Dwarfs object to r. F451.5.10.2; nature of r. Q100—Q199; revenant r. its conqueror E465.

Rewarded. — Charity r. V410ff.; deeds r. *Q10—Q99; faithfulness to Virgin Mary, even if not to Christ, r. V253; gift of horse r. with a beet J2415.1; hero claims ancestors want him r. K362.11; liar r. by apes J815.1;

mortal r. by god A185.11; owner r. for discarding cobold F481.0.1.2.1; poet r. P427.7.8; sham wise man hides horse and is r. for finding it K1956.2; to be r. by his kind J1364.

Rheumatism cure X1787.

Rhine. — Expelled dwarfs plan to dig underground bed for R. F451.5.22; refusal to tell of R. treasure K239; wine washed in R. J1312.2.

Rhinoceros carries off man R13.1.3. — Color of r. A2247.3, A2411.1.6.7; rabbit slays r. L315.12; tortoise jumps on, kills r. N622.1.

Rhyme for summoning kite's aid B501.2. — Man interrupted at eating answers in r. X12.1; student is helped by the devil when he can answer three questions in r. G303.22.3.

Rhymes about cakes wife has stolen K435.1. — Formulistic r. Z80ff.; hidden cuckold reveals presence by r. K1556.

Rib. — Creation of first woman from man's r. A1275.1; ox r. as fairy gift F343.16.

Ribs crushed in embrace F639.9. — Dead men make music on their r. E548; mutilation of r. S173; skeleton has all his r., hence Adam story false J1262.8; substituted r. E782.2; why an uneven number of r. A1312.2.

Ribald. — Devil as r. traveler G303.3.1.3.1.

Ribbon long enough to reach from ear to ear K195. — Escape by returning for hair r. K551.4.8; giant slings stones with his hair r. F531.3.2.2; magic blue r. D1078.1; magic strength from blue r. D1835.4.

Rice in boy's hands joined around pillar, saved J2119.6; magically produced D973.1.1; paddies flooding controlled by toad D2149.5; producing million-fold F815.4; with remarkable scent F815.4.1; scent identifies children H49.1; thrown at weddings T136.2; transformed to gold D475.1.6; wheat and dal dispute superiority J461.5. — Acquisition of r. A1423.2; all r. cooked for one meal J1813.9.1; bag with r. for the road K444.3; cattle formerly ate r. A1101.2.2; cooking r. without fire H506.9; cows in r. field made to disgorge K366.1.4; creator made earth like r. cake A836; death from thorns in r. M341.2.16; deceptive wage: r. on leaf K256.1; disenchantment by consecrated r. D771.9; dog to scent r. J1341.3; god of r.-fields A433.1.1; gold, silver traded for r. J2093.5; hiding in r.-bin K515.5; hoarded r. once more made available A1421.0.1; identifying r. in sack H522.3; magic growth of r. D2157.2.0.1; magic pumpkin yields r. D1472.2.6; magic r. D965.8.1, *D1033.1; magic r.-grains *D973.1; magic r. harvest D1563.1.6; man becomes r.-grain D214.1; mouse gathers r. for man: may eat a little of his rice daily A2223.3; origin of r-beer A1426.2; origin of r. growing A1441.3; quest for magic r. H1333.2.4; sand becomes r. D452.3.1, D476.1.11; singing r.-pot D1615.6; sowing and reaping r. in one day royalty test H41.8; sowing r. seed in others' fields J2129.8; tortoise cursed for going under water while ferrying r.-goddess A2231.7.3; tortoise given hard shell for ferrying r.-goddess A2223.6; trail of r. husks R135.0.2.1; transformation by eating r. mixed with perspiration D551.6.2; transformation by throwing r. D571.1; vow to make husband eat boiled r. M149.4; wages: successive harvests from one r. grain Z21.1.1; why rats eat r.: brought original rice-plant A2435.3.10.1; why r. is abundant A2793.7; why r. has ears only at top A2771.4.1; why wild pigs ravage r.-fields A2545.5.

Rich girl in love with poor boy *T91.5.1; man P150ff.; man caught in church door Q551.2.8.1; man dragged from grave E411.0.5.1; man falls into sacrificial grave K1603; man humble, knows he can't take wealth with him J912.3; man ignores poor sister J411.11; man poor in happiness J347.4; man made poor to punish pride L412; man in rags treated as beggar J1072.2; man seizes poor widow's cow U35; man shakes ducats into pope's lap J1263.2.2; man as wild huntsman E501.1.3; man's ghost rebukes children withholding church money E415.2; man's trial in heaven Q172.2.1; and poor in love T91.5; but stingy couple adopt son T673; woman falsely accuses ascetic K2113.2. — Child adopted by r. man in order to get rid of him K2015; devil carries off r. man Q272.1f.; devil marries r. girl G303.12.5.3; eater of magic bird-heart will become r. M312.3; false repentance of sick r. man U236.1; fortunes of the r. man and the poor man N181; hero made business partner of r. man Q111.1; holy man's prayer reforms r. man J153.1; how the r. man paid his servant (cumulative tale) Z23; lowly ascetic wins r. woman's love K1322.1; man fated to be r. N213; marriage to r. master's widow N251.3; marriage between r. and poor T121; men are too r.: gods punish L482; newly-r. enjoy giving to beggars U130.1; philosopher advises rescals to throw at a r. man J1602; why the poor, being in the majority, don't kill off the r. J2371.4; poor girl chosen rather than r. girl L213; poor man deceives r. K890.1; poor man imitates r. J2416; poor man consoles self by thinking of misfortunes of r. J883; poor man surpasses r. man L143; prophecy: r. man's son to marry poor girl M359.7; quest to hell for return of contract from deceased r. man H1273.1.1; rejoicing at arrival of r. man in heaven E758; robber's defense for stealing from r. J1269.8; St. George teaches the poor man, "who steals somewhat and lies somewhat will be r." J556.1; sermon about r. man X435.5; sham r. man K1954; when r. man eats H659.17; widow makes penniless man r. N225.

Riches the difference between poor man and rich (riddle) H875; reward Q111ff., (of questions solved on quests) H1243. — Trolls' r. F455.4.1.

Richer. — Birds seeking r. lands are nearly all killed J513.1.

Richest. — Quest for bride r. and poorest H1311.2; quest for the r. person H1311; riddle: what is the r.? H636ff.

Rid. — Adulteress getting r. of husband while she entertains lover K1514; attempt to get r. of man by selling him as slave P173.4; expensive means of being r. of insects J2102ff.; getting r. of fairies F381; house set on fire to get r. of cat J2101; impossible to r. oneself of cobold F481.3; quests (tasks) assigned in order to get r. of hero H931, H1211.

Ridden. — Images of animals r. D1631; land bargain: land r. around during a sermon K185.7.2; punishment: being r. as horse Q493.

Ridding city of thieves H1199.8; country of ogres A1416; country of pests Q512.3; person of animal in stomach B784.2ff.

Riddle. — Death sentence escaped by propounding r. H542; dwarf makes return of child dependent upon guessing of r. F451.5.15.2; ogre gives r. on pain of death G681; quest to devil for r. answer H1278; smith reveals r. solution despite king's orders J1161.7; solving sphinx's r. fatal to sphinx *C822; son frees father by bringing r. the king cannot solve R154.2.1; thief dupes owner, gets him to solve r. K418; witch travels in r. G241.4.3.

Riddles H530—H899; as poetry tests H509.4.2.—Asking r. to test patience H1553.6; dwarfs give r. and questions to mortals F451.5.15; girl gets answers to devil's r. G303.12.5.5; husband discovers wife's adultery by r. K1557.

Ride. — Ghost asks traveler for r. E332.3; husband forbids wife to r. on the dog (she immediately does so and is bitten) T254.2; vow to r. the forest all night and slay all comers M157; warrior whose horse is cut in two continues to r. on the half-horse (lie) X1864.

Rider exchanges parts of body for food M225.1; on magic horse immune D1381.30; takes the meal-sack on his shoulder to relieve ass J1874.1. — Dead R. (Lenore) E215; ghost with horseback r. E332.3.1; lie: remarkable r. X1004; magic horse renders r. invulnerable D1846.3; man chosen king before whom car without r. stops H171.4; naked woman pursued and cut in two by r. E501.5.1.1; riddle of horse and r. H744; tree grows out of horse and gives r. shade X1130.2.1.

Ridgepole. — Man becomes r. figure D268.2.

Ridicule. — Exposure to r. when wig snatched off X52.1.

Ridiculing. — Children r. drunken father P236.5; each stutterer thinks others r. him X135.1.

Ridiculous. — Fool sent on r. quest J2346; witch makes person r. G269.21.

Riding contest won by substitution K27; dirty on black-heeled horse tabu C891.1; horse kingship task H41.7; speckled horse credential test H242.1; three times around hill to free captive confined within R112.2; through street on bull as punishment Q473.1. — Alp r. horse sweaty at night F471.1.1.1; dead person r. E581; coyote r. with sun A724.1.0.1; deceptive contest in carrying tree (horse): r. K71, K72; devil r. horse G303.7.1ff.; devil's mother r. a goat G303.11.3.1; dwarf r. F451.6.2; fairy r. behind man on horse F366.2.2; fairy r. man's back F339.1; fairies r. (calves) F366.1.3, (mortal's horses) F366.2; flying contest won by deception: r. on the other K25.1; ghost r. (in cart) E272.1, (horse) E272.2, (on man's back) *E262; giant r. church-roof F531.3.3; gods r. through air A171; man r. on ant F535.2.5; mountain folk r. through air on horses F460.2.2; philosopher as r. horse for woman K1215; race won by deception: r. on the back K11.2; revenant as woman r. hog E425.1.5; spirit r. horses at night F473.4.1; suitor contest: difficult r. H331.1; suitor test: r. strong princess's horse H345.2; trickster r. dupe K1241; trolls r. F455.3.3; unusual animal as r.-horse *B557; witch r. G241ff., (horses at night) *G265.3, (man) G269.3.1.

Riesenspielzeug F531.5.3.

Rifle. — Man fires r. in hollow log, scares off Indians K547.3.

Right hands cut off enemy Q451.1.6; hand's power for good *D996.0.1.1. — Fool cannot tell his r. hand in the dark J1735; why God changed r. hand into left A1311.2; lucky r. hand N113.2.1; magic sight by looking over r. shoulder D1821.3.2; ointment cures left cheek, nor r. D1663.2; prayer into r. hand efficacious V52.15; sword can be moved only by r. person D1654.4.1; "that is r." C495.2.2; throbbing of r. eye a favorable omen D1812.5.2.1.

Righteous save sinful city from destruction M294.

Righteousness tested H1573.6.

Righthandwise circumambulation D1791.1.1. — Carrying book r. insures victory D1381.25; turning r. (brings luck) N131.2, (insures safety) D1384.3.1.

Rime. — Cow from dripping r. of universe's creation B715.

Rind. — Ape throws away nut because of its bitter r. J369.2; eating r. first J2178.1; giant pomegranate r. holds thirteen men F813.8.2.

Ring as baptismal token H82.4; broken as token of broken engagement Z151; can make or break a king P13.3.2; as chastity index H433.1; to be cut in two: real owner laments J1171.1.1; divided by selling it, dividing money J1243; of Fastrada T85.4.1; fits only one person Z321; with inscribed names as tokens H86.3; with life in it E771; made of coffin-hinge as remedy D1500.1.15.2; proves theft H84.4; to put on corpse's finger K362.2; rises to water's surface D2149.4.2; tabu at certain time C635; transformed to another object D454.8.2; transforms D572.2; under dead girl's tongue enchants D765.1.1.1. — Animals recover lost wishing r. B548.1; betrothal by gold r. T61.4.5; bird carries off r. which lover has taken from sleeping mistress's finger N352; burying r. raises tank's water D2151.5.1.1; cutting off hand to get r. R231.1; dead husband sends his r. to his wife E321.1; demons in r. H973.2; devil gives suspicious husband r. G303.9.7.3; discovering r. thief H1199.9.1; disenchantment by r. D771.10; disenchantment by removing r. from under dead girl's tongue D765.1.1.1; dolphins seek King Solomon's r. *A2275.5.4; dress to go through r. H355.6; extraordinary r. F825; fairy gives r. F343.12; fairy music from fairy r. F262.10.2; fairies visible through magic r. F235.6; fish recovers r. from sea *B548.2.1; fit of r. measures time H1583.2; getting r. from python's hole H1132.3.1; ghost leaves r. E544.1.2; gold r. as reward Q111.4; groom's mother gives bride-to-be r. T133.6; hero will marry girl possessing certain r. H361; identification by r. *H94ff.; king loses r. while studying art of stealing K341.8.4; king marries girl finding his lost r. N713.2; life token: r. (presses finger) E761.7.1, (rusts) E761.4.4, (bursts asunder) E761.5.3; lost r. found in fish *N211.1; magic r. *D1076, (carried off by bird) D865.1, (protects from attack) D1381.7, (stolen)

D865.1, (summons genie) D1421.1.6, (works by sun) D1662.1.1; magic wishing-r. loses power D877.1; man puts marriage r. on the finger of statue of Venus (Virgin Mary) T376; martens recover magic r. B548.1.1; mortal gives fairy mistress r. F302.1.2; murderer traced through r. N271.8; oath taken on r. M112; otters recover magic r. B548.1.2; person transformed to r. D263.1; quest for missing r. H1386.2; quest for most beautiful r. H1319.4; quest for magic r. *H1352; recognition by means of r. enclosed in wound H61.3; recovering lost r. from sea H1132.1.1; resuscitation by r. E64.13; return from dead to demand stolen r. E236.1.1; saint's image lets golden r. fall as sign of favor to suppliant D1622.3; sight of mistress's r. causes husband to withhold himself from his wife T286; skillful marksman casts lance through a r. F661.8; stealing r. from finger as task H1151.4; touch of r. causes sleep D1364.29; vanishing man leaves r. D2188.2.1; wearing deceased wife's r. as bride test H363.2; witch cannot rise if r. lies under her chair G254.1; woman casts r. into sea boasting L412.1.

Rings exchange places on fingers E761.7.14.— Bringing princess another princess's r. H933.3; fairy r. on grass F261.1; false set of r. offset genuine K476.4; father gives son r. symbolizing religions J462.3.1.1; giving away r. tabu C783.2; gold r. on hands as suitor test H312.4.1.

Ringdove eats man's grain: man may kill him A2238.2. — Why r. brings good luck A2536.2; nest of r. A2431.3.3.

Ringing bell tabu C756.0.1; of churchbell causes devil to lose his power G303.16.12; churchbell as fear test H1412.1; of church bell by nun C94.7; of bells herald wild hunt E501.13.1.4. — Disenchantment by r. bell D789.10; saints curse by r. bells M411.8.1.

Rioting. — Queen incites husband's r. P23.1.

Rip Van Winkle D1960.1.

Ripe. — Saint causes wheat to become r. prematurely D2157.2.2; tree blooms and grows r. fruit nightly F811.13.

Ripping. Disenchantment by r. armor D712.8.

Rise. — Chanticleer believes that his crowing makes the sun r. J2272.1; king vainly forbids tide to r. L414; maids must r. even earlier K1636; magic song causes tree to r. to sky *D1576.1; sun refuses to r. A739.6; witch known by inability to r. from chair with four-leaf clover under it G254; usurers do not r. for special blessing X512.

Rising into air despite gravity X1741.1; and falling sky F791; river F932.8; smoke as omen D1812.5.0.4. — Concubine's r. from stone impossible Q551.2.7; counsel on r. earlier J21.23; earth r. from sea A816; fugitive supernaturally r. into air R324; island r. up in sea (river) F735ff.; man controls r. of sun A725; man r. too early J1394.2; object r. into air F1083; ring prevents person from r. from chair D1413.2; sea r. and changing place F931.1; sun and his brother r. and setting alternately A736.3.3.

Risks. — Great possessions bring great r. U81.

Rite. — Christian child killed to furnish blood for Jewish r. V361.

Rites, see also **Ceremonies.** — Birth r. confer royalty P37; dead man speaks demanding proper funeral r. E235.2.1; dead without proper funeral r. cannot rest in grave E412.3; funeral r. *V60ff.; magic r. for obtaining a child T548.2.

Ritual cannibalism G13.1. — Changing r. tabu C65; devils' wives attempt resuscitation r. K113.0.1; fasting a part of magic r. D1766.8.1; ghost returns to perform in r. E379.5.

Rituals. — Magic from special r. D1799.3.

Rival induces mother to kill children S342. — Burial alive of maiden to keep her from r. S123.5; jealousy of r. wives T257.2ff.; magic object stolen by r. for wife D861.4; man kills all guests, hoping some day to kill r. S110.2; searching for r. to wife's beauty H1301.1.3; successful r. gives lady to friend P319.6; transformation of love r. *D665.1; vow to kill successful r. M149.3; young r. derides old one: oldster's retort J1352.2.

Rivals kills each other over woman T86.1; in love T92ff. — Tasks assigned at suggestion of jealous r. H911; treacherous r. K2220ff.

Rivaling the gods forbidden C65; poets P427.7.10; smiths P447.6.

River, see also **Stream, Water;** as barrier to otherworld F141.1; becomes sea D483.1; bed earth saves soul E754.1.7; carrier throws off passenger to drown S131.1; crossed by magic D1524.5; connecting earth and upper and lower worlds A657; entrance to lower world F93.1; of fire as barrier to otherworld *F142; flows from corpse of hero's mother A511.1.1.1; -god A425; grateful for being given color D1658.1.6; grateful for being praised even when ugly D1658.1.1; in heaven E755.1.2; in hell filled with weapons A672.3; of honey (lie) X1547.2; issuing from cave controlled by race of Amazons D915.5; magically rises against enemy D2091.7.1; never freezes F141.1.3; personified Z118.3; produced by magic *D915.1; rises to drown liars D1318.17; says, "The time has come but not the man" D1311.11.1; -spirit F424; Styx A672, M119.1.1; taken to sky becomes star A761.1; that flows around the world A872; valley licked out by giant beast A951.1; water's heat prevents thieves' crossing D1389.2.2. — Adventures from pursuing object on r. N791; bathing in sacred r. V96.1; besiegers drowned by diverting r. K2369.5; boat sails on dry r. bed X1781.1; bones of dead thrown into r. E607.1.1; bracelet gift from r. goddess N815.0.2.1; bride spinning at bottom of r. K1911.2.2.2; carrying woman across r. without wetting feet H1046; city won by turning r. from course K2369.6; corpse thrown into r. as punishment Q491.8; course of r. deflected for king's burial V67.3.1; crossing r. of fire H1542.1; crossing r. with tree's aid F1071.1; curse on r. M476; curse makes r. barren of fish D2085.1; dead place net across r. to prevent living man from returning to earth F93.1.1; devil and sinful priest disappear amid blaze of fire in r. G303.17.2.4; dogs by r. try to get food in r. by drinking r. dry J1791.3.2; dry r. bed bad omen D1812.5.1.16; epidemic does not cross r. at saint's command D2162.2; exposure astride wood floating down r. S141.3; extraordinary r. *F715ff.; father throws boy into r. S11.3.6; flood from rising r. A1011.2; flowers floating on r. of milk F814.6; fool will not drink from a r. because he cannot drink it all J2525; fox in swollen r. claims to be swimming to distant town J873; giant astride r. F531.3.5.3; giant digs trench for r. course F531.6.6.3; giant drinks up r. F531.3.4.2; giant's foot dams r. F531.3.1.2.1; horse transformed to r. D422.1.1; how much water in r.? H696.1.4; impassable yellow r. surrounds city F767.1; intermittent r. D915.4; island rises up in r. F735.0.1; jumping r. on horseback H331.1.6; jumping into r. after their comrade J1832; legitimacy of children tested by dipping them in r. H222.1; lie: remarkable r. X1547; magic object controls r. D1549.3; magic object received from r.-nymph D813.1; magic r. *D915; magician makes people lift garments to avoid wetting in imaginary r. D2031.1; man leaps over r. F1071.2.1; man lives under r. F725.4; marriage to r. T117.9; measuring r. as task H1149.8; Milky Way as a r. A778.3; numskull waits for r. to run down J1967; object magically lifted from r. bottom D1547.3; oracular r. D1311.11; origin of r. worship A1546.1; pursued animal runs through imaginary r. D2031.3; quest for princess caused by sight of one of her hairs floating on r. H1213.1; reading book causes r. to dry up D1542.3.2; sacrifice to r. V11.2.1; sacrifice to r.-god who has stopped boat S263.4; saint's bachall drives back flooding r. D1549.3.1; soldiers fighting force r. from bed F1084.3; source of r. where earth, sky meet A659.3; spirits put corpse into r. F402.1.8; standing naked in winter r. H328.4; swimming in imaginary r. D2031.1.2; tabu: drinking from certain r. between two darknesses C263; tabu: going with dry feet over certain r. C862; tears become r. D457.18.2; treasure hidden in r. N513.4; ungrateful r. passenger K952.1; warming hands across r. J1945; water shallows so r. can be crossed D1551.0.1; wearing shoes only when crossing r. F1015.2; woman enamored of a r. T461.1; woman sells self for help across r. T455.5.

Rivers of blood in hell A671.2.2; of fire A661.0.1.1.1; in hell A671.2.2ff.; in otherworld F162.2; of wine, rose-water and honey surround palace F771.2.4.1. — Angel of r. A425.0.1; why beaver lives along r. A2433.3.12; countertask: stop all the r. H696.1.1, H1142.3, H1143; creator of r. A930.1; dissatisfied r. complain against sea W128.3; eleven r. spring from well in midst of earth A875.2; extraordinary occurrences connected with r. F932; four r. of Paradise A871.2, *F162.2.1; hero regulates r. A533; magic control of r. D2151.2; magic object makes r. and lakes D1486; origin of r. A930ff.; origin of worship of r. A1546.1; palace surrounded by r. of wine, rosewater, and honey F771.7; riddle of ocean and r. H734; sacrifice to r. and seas S264; serpent king dams r. A1019.2; seven fair r. in Eden Z71.5.6.12; standing in r. as penance Q541.1.1.

Road to heaven *F57; to otherworld F151; from reading magic book D1484.2; runs through house F771.9. — Angels defend r. to heaven V511.1.2; animal determines r. to be taken *B151ff.; animals refuse to help make r. and are punished A2233.1; birds point out r. to hero B563.2; broad and narrow r. in otherworld F171.2; children know local r.; why doesn't stranger? J2212.9; choice of dangerous r. as valor test H1561.9; coming neither on nor off the r. H1051; devil builds r. G303.9.1.7, (for farmer in one day) G303.9.2.2; do not prefer new r. J21.5.1; equivocal inscription telling what will happen if each r. is chosen N122.0.1; escape from robbers by pretending to be going the same r. K579.3; father's counsel: dress up the trunks of trees (cover the r.) H588.6; forbidden r. C614; friendly r. ghosts E332ff.; frog persists in living in puddle on r. J652.1; fugitive slave takes wrong r. and is caught N382; giant and wife build Roman r. F531.6.6.5; haunting ghost deceived so that he cannot find r. to return E432.1; holes in edge of r. J95; lighting the r. (house set on fire) K1412; magic object makes r. D1484; magic object points out r. *D1313ff.; man keeps house; gives wife r. J1541.4; Milky Way a r. A778.2; ogress takes lives along r. G321.2; paving r. in short time H1108; picking wrong r. reveals identity H38.2.5; rice for the r. K444.3; sloth refuses to help make r. A2233.1.4; why snake does not go on the r. A2233.1.2, A2441.4.1; spirit blocks person's r. F402.1.2; squirrel points out r. B563.3; "take side r. rather than main" J21.5.2; wild hunt avoided by keeping on one's r. E501.17.5.1.

Roads appear on Hallowe'en F1099.2; appear at hero's birth F1099.2.1; go over houses X1551.1; marked out by supernatural cows A989.2. — Divination by choice of r. D1812.5.0.17; five great r. of Ireland discovered at king's birth A994; ghosts which haunt r. E272; god of r. A413; lies about mountain r. X1526; magic power at cross-r. *D1786; pilgrimage to r. Christ walked V531.1.

Roar. — Dog following lion flees at his r. J952.3; lion's r. causes havoc at 300 miles B741; river in paradise with terrible r. F162.2.8.

Roaring. — Jackal's attempts at r. like lion J2413.8; magic shield r. when bearer is in danger D1317.13.

Roast cock comes to life and crows E168.1; ducks fly (by magic) D2191. — Ghosts seek firewood to r. man E257; guessing nature of devil's r. meat H523.4.

Roasting. — Ghosts r. girl E251.3.1.1; literal numskull throws water on r. pig J2461.1.3; murder by r. alive S112.6.

Robbed. — Fool's talking causes himself and companions to be r. J2356; girl screams when she is r. but not so loud when she is raped J1174.3; merchant profits by being r. J1115.7.1; rich lord having r. poor widow of her cow chokes on first mouthful Q552.6; thief pretends to have been r. K401.4.

Robber, see also **Highwayman, Thief;** attempting to steal cow at night grabs tiger N392; bridegroom K1916; does penance Q520.2; or dog in church thought to be a ghost J1782.1; frightened off by parrot's cry K1796; helps king N884.1; innocent because he is merely following traditions of his ancestors J1179.4; persuaded to climb down the moon-beam *K1054; -proof house D2072.5.1. — Coward gloats over r. slain by another person W121.2.5; which was most generous, husband, r., or lover? H1552.1; giant r. with club G102; he who steals much called king: he who steals little called r. U11.2; king punishes r. violating safe conduct promise M203.1; man curious as to what a r. is going to do waits to intervene J2378; man scolds his ass and frightens r. away N612.1; meeting with r. band N765; old r. frees his three sons by relating frightful adventures R153.3.3; parable on r. plundering weak J133.6; paramour poses as r. K1517.8; snap of finger kills r. F628.2.8; treacherous r. partner K2296.1; Virgin Mary protects r. calling "Ave" V254.8; Virgin Mary supports r. on gallows V254.1.1; wild man son of woman and r. F611.1.4.

Robber's defense for stealing from rich J1269.8; false plea admitted: counter accusation J1162.2.

Robbers P475; commiserated J1392.2; frightened by dog B576.1.2; frightened from goods so that trickster can steal them K335.1; give hero sword J642.2; kill on new road J21.5.1; leave booty to temple idol K1971.14; mistake man for devil X424.1; share loot with simpleton L141.2; spade up saint's garden V222.16; vow to honor shrine V113.2. — Child abducted by r. R12.2.1; descendants of nine r. never to exceed nine M461; incognito king joins r. K1812.2; indentions on rock from weapons of r. A972.3.1.1; magic swine cause drowning of r. Q428.2; man escapes r. by promising to show treasure K567.2; man takes refuge from r. in an open grave J2311.3; overcoming r. H1162.1; overcoming r. suitor task H335.4.2; person deceives r., gets help K432; princess rescued from r. *R111.1.2; riches for helping against r. Q111.3; servants frighted by ferocious actions of r. K335.0.11; sham wise man accidentally unmasks r. K1956.1; sham wise man declares that r. committed the theft K1956.3; thumbling aids r. F535.1.1.11; wife scares r., says husband home D2031.6.3; wisdom from r. J178.

Robbers' heads cut off one by one as they enter house K912; plans overheard: owner warned N455.2. — Rescue from r. den R116.

Robbery. — Advice against r. of women alone J647.2; overheard boast about hidden money brings about r. N455.1; thief beaten for not giving r. warning J1191.6.

Robberies. — Devil agrees to help man with r. M212; Russians like r. A1674.2.

Robe "not too long or too short" J1161.8; for saint not wet by water F930.1.0.2. — Carrying live coals in r. without harm H221.1.1; clever minstrel gets new r. J1115.5.1; dagger cleaned on inside of r. A1599.7; extraordinary r. F821ff.; lawyer's r. stolen K362.9; magic r. *D1052; murder with poisoned r. S111.6; poor man's rich r. causes his jailing N347.5; resuscitation by magic r. E64.11; not to wear unauthorized sacred r. C51.2.1.

Robes. — Druids' white r. V131.2; fairies in long r. F236.2; raven steals r. of the Red Willow Men and finds them useless J2194; religious r. V131; symbolic interpretation of official r. H608.

Robert the Devil (birth) S223.0.1, (kills his wet-nurses) T614; of Sicily
*L411.

Robin steals fire, has breast scorched A2218.5. — Creation of r. A1914;
why r. has red breast A2221.2.2, A2353.2.

Roc (giant bird) *B31.1.

Rock, see also **Stone;** aflame at hero's death F960.2.3; bridge appears
for fugitives R246.1; changed into milk D476.1.7; of extraordinary
color F807; hurled down hill slays enemy K914.2; made repository of fire
A1414.7.2; produces wine D1472.1.2.2; pursues person D1431.1; refuses
to be moved D1654.1; in sea created by magic D2153.1; substituted for
ham K476.1.1; transformed to another object D452.1. — Adulteress
hurled from high r. escapes injury: she may not be punished again
J1184.1; battle marks in r. F1084.0.4; bear persuaded to slide down r.
wears off tail K1021.3; birth from r. T544.1; bleeding r. F991.5; breaking
huge r. to pieces (task) H1116; breaking off r. unearths mine N596.2;
cutting firewood from r. struck by lightning H1116.1; deer causes r. to
fly asunder D1552.9; dream of r.-casting contest D1731.3; dwarfs' r.-door
F451.4.3.1.1; falling asleep on r. which shoots upwards N314; giant
throws a great r. F531.3.2ff.; giant's hair grows into r. G122; holding
the r. K1251; huge r. columns combat each other, form earth's features
A901.2; magic r. *D931; noodles push parents over a r. as a favor to
them J2119.3; oath so great it splits r. M115.1.1; ogre clothed in r. G371.1;
ogre tied to r. G514.5; offended rolling r. C91.1; penance: staying on r.
in sea Q525.1; rain from striking r. D2143.1.7; refuge on r. in sea R316;
roc drops r. on ship B31.1.2; saint's bachall splits r. D1564.3; speaking r.
D1610.18; spirit-woman in r. G312.2; spring flows where saint smites r.
A941.5.1; stone from wictim's r. kills murderer Q582.3.1; striking certain
r. tabu C546; stroke of staff brings water from r. *D1567.6; strong man
moves enormous r. F624.2.0.2; urine softens r. D562.2.2; why sorrel grows
on certain r. A2771.7.

Rocks that clash together at intervals D1553; of one mountain enter caves
of another mountain F1006.4; falling together suggest intercourse J86;
moved by magic *D2136.1; open and close *D1552ff.; piled up to sky
F55.2. — Chaste woman promises herself to lover when r. leave coast
*M261; clashing r. test H1525; why coney lives among r. A2433.3.5;
extraordinary r. and stones F800ff.; helpful spirit warriors dwell in r.
and hills F450.1.1; origin of fire: children strike r. together A1414.3;
origin of r. A970ff.; saint prevents r. from falling D2149.4.1; saint's curse
splits r. D1792.1; saint's spittle splits r. D1564.2; sharp r. on otherworld path F151.1.6; strong man grinds huge r. F639.11; universe from
pre-existing r. A644; visit to lower world through opening r. *F92.3; water
becomes r. D478.12.

Rocking. — Chain tale: wormwood r. me to sleep Z41.7; chair r. by spirit
F473.2.1; witches r. chairs G249.11.

Rocky mountain F759.7.

Rod with alleged fishing magic K119.1.1; from magic hazel-tree kills snaked immediately D1402.10.2; transformed to serpent D441.7.1; used in saint's birth roots, becomes tree T584.0.5. — Chastity ordeal: passing under magic r. H412.1; divining r. locates hidden treasure D1314.2; doing penance till green leaves grow on dry r. Q521.1; dry r. blossoms F971.1; hunting wolves with r. and line X1124.4; magic r. *D1254.2, (produces love) D1355.16; magic wishing r. D1470.1.25; magic r. swallows other rods D1693; magic r. used for divination *D1311.15; making loom from a r. H1022.2.2; poet's r. P427.7.6; quest for magic iron r. H1342; transformation by touching with r. D565.2.

Rods. — Brass r. bitten, powdered in anger F639.10; silver r. cause magic sleep D1364.26.

Rodent gnaws away ladder to heaven A666.2; transformed to man D315. — Helpful r. B431; man transformed to r. D117.

Rodents. — Creation of r. A1840ff.; expensive extermination of r. J2103.

Rogue married with great pomp and celebration T135.0.1. — Condemned woman may be freed by marrying a r. P512; man called a r. by a nobleman makes a joke of the insult J817.1.

Roll. — Dead's name not on heavenly r. D586.4; devil shows priest long parchment r. of sins of congregation G303.24.1.1.

Rolled. — Stones can be r. up F809.9.

Rolling. — Animal occupation: r. A2457; fatal game: r. down hill on barrel K866; giant r. like wheel F531.6.17.6; god r. back primeval sea A816.3; ogre r. self in mat K711.3; pursuit by r. object R261ff.; pursuit of r. hoop leads to quest H1226.1; pursuit of r. cake leads to quest H1226; snake with tail in mouth r. like wheel B765.1; transformation by r. D561.1.

Roman fails to kill Hannibal P711.5. — Giant and wife build R. road F531.6.6.5.

Romans hate Jesus's poverty V385.

Rome hanging by thread (lie) X1561. — Animal journeys to R. B296.1; crawling to R. on knees as penance Q523.1; his father has been to R. J1274; Scipio saves R. from destruction P711.4.

Romeo and Juliet's self-poisonings T37.1.

Romulus and Remus L111.2.1, B535.

Roncevalles' horn calls aid of waiting soldiers R187.

Roof "has no eaves" H594.1; as refuge R335; spouts run with blood E761.1.11; taken off above sick man who cannot die E722.2.3. — Ass tries to jump on r. like ape J2413.2; captive knocks off prison r. R211.5; castle with silver (golden) r. F771.1.2.1f.; cow taken to r. to graze J1904.1; cure by putting children on r. D2161.4.11; devil in r. of church into which he thrusts voices of loud singers Q554.2; does not need r. when it is fair, cannot put it on when it rains J2171.2.1; fasting fool falls off r. J565.1, fox pretends to be holding up the r. and cannot help the bear K1251.1; lover caught in r. K1211.1; mountain-men throw person over church r.

F460.4.4.3; numskull ties rope to his leg as cow grazes on r. J2132.2; shading r. with carts J1879.1; stone-throw carries away r. F636.4.3; strong man throws trees on r. and breaks it F614.6; strong man's throw of stone carries away timber of r. F639.3; strong man on r. F639.8; stupid woman swims on the r. J1972; thatching r. with feathers H1104.1.2; turf from church r. gives clairvoyance D1323.7; women not to climb on r. C181.4; youth promises to marry old maid if she will sit all night on the r. X753.

Roofs. — Lie: r. on needle X1743.3.

Roofed. — King punished for failing to have monks' huts r. Q553.7.

Roofing over fog X1651.1. — Shortsightedness in r. J2171.2.

Rook. — Color of r. A2411.2.1.7.

Room heating in hell for certain person Q561.3. — Clearing out the r. J2465.5; corpse makes r. in coffin for friend E477; dwarf cave has large square r. with little doors leading to all sides F451.4.3.2; eating r-full of salt H1141.3; entrance into girl's (man's) r. by trick *K1340ff.; fairies' r. in hill F221.3; finding how many people are in dark, closed r. H506.2; ghost haunts r. E281.3; in hell one r. for dead, one for unborn, one for evil spirits A678; lover buys admission to woman's r. T45; magic needle transforms r. from plainness to beauty D1337.1.7; magic object found in underground r. D845; magic r. *D1141; no r. left for the feast J2178; parson tricked into giving up r. K2335; suitor tricked into r.: left alone K1218.13; treasure hidden in secret r. N517.1; washing the r. J2465.6; wild huntsman lives in r. on farm E501.15.8.

Rooms in otherworld dwellings F165.3; prepared in heaven for good man Q172.4.1. — Extraordinary r. *F781ff.; gourds with seven r. F813.5.1; porridge eaten in different r. J2167; seven r. in ascetic's house filled with extraordinary things F771.11.

Roost. — Long nose used as hen r. F543.1.2.

Rooster, see **Cock.**

Root of eternal youth D1338.2.2; transformed to person D431.9. — Why animals r. in ground A2477; conception from eating r. T511.2.0.1; demon lives at tree r. F402.6.1.1; incestuous youth reincarnated as r. E692.6; magic makes r. bitter D479.3; magic r. acquired by trickery D839.1; magic r. reveals truth D1316.12; magic r. snaps bar in two D1562.7; magic storm by pointing tree r. D2141.0.12; snow taken away by planting certain r. D2143.6.1; where is floor's r.? H883; youth asks for branch of tree; promised r. H611.

Roots hold land firm A857.3.1; of world-tree H619.3. — Dragon gnaws tree r. B11.6.9; magic r. *D967; man confined under r. of tree R45.1; numskull to water r. of tree J2126; origin of edible r. A2686.4; spring flows from tree r. F933.1.2; spring from r. of sacred tree shot by arrow A941.7.2; streams from r. of earth-tree A878.1.1; test of strength: pulling up tree by r. H1562.1; three wells under three r. of earth-tree A878.1.2; why banyan's r. hang down A2791.13.

Rooted. — Giant r. to ground, nails and hair grown into earth F531.1.6.9; staying r. to one spot while birds nest in hair Q541.5.

Rooting. — Contours of land from swine's r. A951.2.

Rope bridge to otherworld F152.1.5; cut almost in two so prisoner escapes K647; to lower world *F96; of chaff (sand) X1757; cut and victim dropped *K963; transformed to person D434.2; to upper world F51. — Ants carry silk threads to prisoner, who makes r. and escapes R121.4; bluff: animal shows r. as tail K1715.12; climbing into air on a magic r. D1582; climbing r. of excrement J2133.12; deceptive bargain: as much grain as will go in r. K174.1; drawing lover with single-thread r. H412.6; escape by tying r. to post K638; extraordinary r. F843; gallows r. breaks when innocent hanged H215.2; ghostly r. of suicide E538.2; hero tests r. on which he is to be pulled to upper world K677; magic r. *D1203; magic transportation by r. D1520.31; making a r. (of chaff) H1021.2, (of sand) H1021.1; man drawn up into female apartments on r. K1343; man will not lift knife to cut r. about to hang him W111.1.2; miser refrains from suicide: saves r. W153.7; mountain climber's r. cut K963.1; murderer escapes on sky r. R323.1; numskull catches buffalo by r. and is dragged to death J2132.1; numskull ties the r. to his leg as cow grazes on the roof J2132.2; obtaining bucket of well water without r. H1023.20; ordeal by r.-walking H225; parents rescue son from lower world on r. R153.1.1; ring turns to r. and robber is hanged M212.2; robber tries to pull up confederate on r., caught K434.2; saving by r. succeeds in well, fails from tree J2434; serpent acts as r. to collect wood B579.5; spying parent pulled up chimney on r. K1663; stealing only a small amount (r. with mare on the end of if) K188; threat to haul away the warehouse with r. K1745; threat to pull the lake together with r. K1744; watchman outwitted by having r. stretched across the road while fugitives escape K623.

Roper. — Lie: remarkable r. X1003.

Rosary identifies werwolf H64.2. — Disenchantment by r. D771.7; witch's r. consists of goat dung G243.2.1.

Rose as chastity index H432.1; from grave E631.1.2; grows from table F971.2; sheds petal whenever husband thinks of wife H1556.4.6; transformed to person D431.1.1; -water gives magic beauty D1337.1.8.1; — Adulteress pretends to faint when her husband strikes her with a r. K2051.2; banishment till r. grows from table for preventing childbirth Q431.4; conception from eating a r. T511.4.1; contest between r. and amaranth J242.1; digging r.-tree hole reveals treasure N534.7.1; magic r. *D975.2; man becomes r.-bush D213.2; marvelous sensitiveness (blister on back from lying in r. leaves) F647.9, (injury from r. leaves falling) F647.3; origin of r. A2656; origin of color of r. A2772.1; palace surrounded by rivers of wine, r.-water and honey F771.7; river of r.-water F771.2.4.1; transformation to r. D212.2; white r. the symbol of death Z142.1.

Roses fall from lips D1454.2.1; from lips as sign of royalty H71.4; lose thorns when saint walks on them V222.14. — Bringing r. in winter H1023.3; dawn reflection of r. of paradise A1179.2.1; meat becomes r. D457.5.1.

Rotating. — Circular house r. on cock's claw F771.2.6.1; kingship r. among brothers P17.4.

Rotting. — Calumniated corpse not r. H251.3.14; sea from r. snakes A924.2.

Rough treatment of object injures witch G275.13. — Disenchantment by r. treatment D710ff.; resuscitation by r. treatment *E10ff.; voice made r. by swallowing hot iron F556.1.

Round river: runs in circle X1547.1; well F718.2. — Devil as r. bowl G303.3.4.8; fairies' horses have r. shoes *F241.1.4; going r. and round fire marriage custom T135.10; marvelous runner can run r. earth in five minutes F681.5; why hog has r. snout A2335.4.2.

Rounds (stories which begin over and over again and repeat) Z17.

Round Table. — Finding Holy Grail before returning to R. M183.3; prophecy on end of R. M356.5; symbolism of R. Z162.

Rousing sham-dead with whip J2311.12. — Test of valor: r. servant's anger H1561.4.

Rout. — Soldier dies happy at enemy's r. P461.2.

Route. — Copper horseman indicates r. *D1313.3.

Roving. — Why women are r. A1372.3.

Rowan helps Thor out of river A2711.5; -sticks defeat devil G303.9.9.9, G303.16.4.3; -tree used to lay ghost E442.1; wood protects against witches G272.2.1.

Rower prefers to be stoned by his master rather than remain out in the storm J229.7. — Strong man as r. breaks boat F614.4.

Rowers pull in opposite directions J2164.1.

Rowing boat by magic D1523.2.8; contest won by deception K14. — Escape by r. boat stern foremost K534.4; shortsightedness in r. J2164.

Royal bride conducted by embassy to husband's kingdom T133.2; descendants as reward Q112.0.7; family as sacred V205; marriages with close relatives A1552.2. — Identification by r. garments H111.1; marriage by r. order T122; seating arrangements in r. hall A1539.1; sexual incontinence punished by extinction of r. line Q243.0.1; test of valor worthy for kingship: taking possession of r. insignia H1561.5; wild animal will not attack r. person B771.3.

Royalty, see also **King, Prince, Princess, Queen;** and nobility *P0—P99; unable to endure coarse entertainment U146. — Favor with r. induced by magic D1900.1; lowly person in love with r. T91.6.1; marks of r. H71; origin of r. A1653; phenomena at birth of r. F960.1.1; purple as r. symbol Z147.1; recognition of r. by personal characteristics H41ff.; tokens of r. left with exposed child S334.

Rubbed. — Eye must be r. before it can see F541.4; head of beheaded witch mends if r. with salt G223.

Rubber. — Origin of r. A1439.3.

Rubbing charm provides garments D1473.2. — Blindness cured by r. sand on eyes F952.3; disenchantment by r. D714, (with magic grease) D771.2; magic powers from r. D1734f.; resuscitation by r. bones on ground E29.2.

Rubbings. — Man created from r. of skin A1263.3.

Rubbish magically becomes food, clothing D2105.3.

Rübezahl (mountain and storm spirit) F465.

Ruby appears as charitable king blows nose V411.7; shatters for greedy lapidary D1641.14.1; transformed to person D432.3.1. — Bringing r. in serpent's head H1151.26; cup made of single r. J21.49; picking r. from trayful H1198; riddle involving r., nectar and faithless creature H587.1; speaking r. D1610.27.2; tortoise keeps r. from fowler K439.7.1.

Rubies baked in bread J1655.2; found in whirlpool D1467.2; as ransom for goose J514.6. — Blood transformed to r. D457.1.1; gathering necklace of r. from sea H1023.21; stream of r. flows through building F771.12; village where r. sell cheaply X1564.

Rudder. — Golden boat with copper r. F841.1.8.

Rudderless. — Embarkation in r. boat Q466.0.1; self-guiding r. boat D1523.2.7.1.

Rude retorts J1350ff. — "Never be r. to man of low birth" J21.52.2.

Rudeness to sacred person or thing forbidden C94ff.

Rue from drops of Christ's blood A2611.7; not a thing that is past J21.12; protects against evil D1385.2.2. — Magic r. D965.16.

Rug, see Carpet.

Rule must work both ways J1511. — Man created to r. the earth A1201; quest for lost ecclesiastical r. H1386.4; unsuccessful search for man who can r. his wife T252.1.

Rules. — Monk, merchant sticking to the r. J1638; prize for husband who r. his wife T252.4.

Ruler, see also **King;** angered by evil, placated by soft words J811.4; diverts attention from misgovernment by beginning a war K2381; forbids lovers to marry T87; learns lesson from uncharitable king J56.1; persecutes friends, kind to enemies W154.16; refuses spendthrift's hospitality J1566.2, should follow majority's advice J21.35; sent gems as wisdom test H501.1; too lazy to stop quarrels W111.5.7; vies with minister in generosity H1552.2. — Animal or object indicates election of r. H171; bad r., bad subject U210ff.; do not trust a r. who rules by reason alone J21.28; exiled king teaches r. wisdom J55; lady in love with r. T55.3; man patiently undergoing misfortune finally elected r. N251.1; old woman r. of the dead in lower world E481.1.1; poet puts r. out of countenance J1224.2; shepherd's life as preparation for r. P412.1.1; proud r. humbled L410ff.; repartee with r. *J1280ff.; transformation to likeness of r. D41.1;

treacherous r. delivers city to enemy K2364.3; ungrateful r. deposed
Q281.2; woman asks r. how to bear insults J1284.1.
Ruler's absurdity rebuked J1536. — Prophecy: r. death to insure victory
M362; smith sells secret for 100 crowns with r. likeness J1161.7.
Rulers of inferior character C938.
Ruling by reason alone untrustworthy J21.28. — Animals r. celestial
spheres B7.1; man r. all animals A1421.1.1; stepmother r. realm P282.1.
Rum as man's enemy J1319.1. — Salamander in r. drink G303.9.8.4; water
substituted for r. K231.6.2.1.
Rumination of animals A2472.
Rump. — King induced to kiss horse's r. K1288; lover given r. to kiss
*K1225; stick (leaf) thrown at animal's r.: hence tails A2215.1.
Rumpelstilzchen C432.1.
"Runs" within a tale Z14.
Runaway cavalry hero K1951.2; horse carries bride to her lover N721. —
Repartee concerning r. horses J1483ff.
Runes cause frenzy D1367.5. — Dwarfs cut r. F451.3.12.4; magic r.
*D1266.1.
Runner. — Fairy's skill as r. F273.2; marvelous r. F681ff.
Running from ghost J1495. — Brother is r. back and forth (plowing)
H583.3.1; buying foxes "as they're r." K196.1; cripples r. away from
shrine without crutches V113.1; devil cannot cross r. water G303.16.19.13;
fairy unable to cross r. stream F383.2; fawn, in spite of his horns, r. from
the dog U127; magic by r. through a hole *D1795; skillful barber shaves
r. hare F665.1; skillful flayer skins r. rabbit F664.1; skillful smith shoes
r. horse F663.1.
Rupee. — One r. to charity brings back ten Q44.3.
"Rupees make more rupees" J2489.12. — Magic coin fills bell with r.
D1452.5; sham miracle: r. turn to ashes K1975.2.
Ruse, see also **Trick, Trickery.** — Accidental cure by doctor's r. N648;
confession obtained by a r. J1141; detection through r. J1141.11; woman
won by r. K1302.
Rush transformed to leek C462.1, D451.2.1. — Why end of r. is black
A2721.1, A2772.2; Friar R. as mischief maker F470.0.1.
Rushes transformed to grain D451.2.1.1. — Lake where blind king plucks
r. A920.1.12; skillful marksman throws r. into a curtain F661.7.1; spring
flows where leper pulls out r. A941.5.3; uprooted r. reveal spring F933.5.
Rushing. — Priests r. through the mass J1263.1.3.1.
Russian calendar A1689.7.
Russians like thefts and robberies A1674.2; wear red shirts A1683.1.1. —
Why R. wear their shirts outside their breeches A1683.1.
Rustic. — Scholar disguised as r. K1816.0.4.
Rusting. — Life token: r. of object E761.4ff.
Rustling. — Ogre frightened at r. K2345.
Rusty. — Transformation to person of r. color D57.5.

Rye. — Origin of r. A2685.3; peasants fed white bread demand r. U135; sowing r., getting crop next day H1023.17; strong man lifts ton of r. F624.5; test of strength: breaking heavy glass blottle over a loaf of r. bread H1562.3.

Sabbath *V71ff.; -breaker A751.1.1; -keeping cow B259.2. — Breaking the s. forbidden *C631; devil appears to s. breakers G303.6.2.14; failure to observe s. punished Q223.6; fine for s.-breaking J1289.11; god names animals on first s. A2571.0.3; intercourse on s. night only T310.1.1; intercourse on s. tabu C119.1.2; mill refuses to work on the s. D1676; no punishment in hell on s. Q560.2.1; origin of s. A1541.4; ram swears on s. B211.1.1.1.1; removing silver tabu on s. F752.2.1; rescuers' s. J1613; reward for observing s. Q113.4.1; why powers of nature work on s. A1102; witch's s. G243.

Sabbatical fountain F716.1; river *D915.4.1.

Saber with king's name as token H86.1. — Magic s. *D1082; ring transformed to s. D454.8.2.1.

Sack, see also **Bag;** in giant's hand looks like pea F531.2.15. — Bad luck put into a s. N112.1; bees caught in s. which is opened at home J2131.2.1; casting into water in s. Q467.1; charcoal s. magically multiplies D2106.2; deceptive bargain: a s. of corn as reward K174; devil in church fills his s. with dissolute songs G303.24.1.5; dupe persuaded to take prisoner's place in a s. K842; filling s. full of lies (truths) H1045; heaven entered by trick: "wishing s." thrown in K2371.1.3; how much meal is in the s. J2062.1; inexhaustible wheat s. D1472.1.22.2; magic s. C521.1, *D1193; milk s. transformed D454.5f.; origin of insects: released from s. A2003; pious man hangs s. on sunbeam V29.3; priest drags heavy s., symbol of sin H606; recognition by cup in s. (alleged stolen goods) H151.4; soul in s. E711.5; suitor enticed into s., beaten by husband K1218.1.5; witch gets boy into s. K711.4; woman exchanges a horse for a s. of bones J2099.1.

Sacks. — Gold s. traded for rice s. J2093.5; slaves forced to carry earth in s. A1657.2.

Sackcloth. — Fasting in s. Q523.10.

Sacrament, see also **Eucharist, Host** *V30ff. — Administering s. destroys devil's power G303.16.5; disrespect for the s. J1261.2; friar seduces woman, claims administering s. K1354.2.2; ignorant priest forces rolls of cloth instead of s. down dying man's throat J1738.1; sick men die after they hesitate to take s. V39.8; Virgin Mary withdraws s. from a scoffer Q553.1; willing to receive water from leper, therefore must be willing to receive s. from unworthy priest J157.1.

Sacred animal unwittingly killed N361; animals B811, (branded) H55.2; fire V1.6.3.1; groves V114; healing stone D1500.1.2; persons *V200—V299; prostitution T457; relic as magic object D1296; relics protect against attack D1381.20; tree V1.7.1; wells V134. — Why animal is s. A2541ff.; death excluded from s. grove Z111.4; frog recovers s. Host

B548.5; ghosts summoned by opening s. book E383; oath taken on s. object M114; origin of s. places A992; punishment for harming s. animal Q228; sexual intercourse forbidden in s. precinct C116; trickster concealed in s. tree advises that he is to marry the princess K1971.10; woman hidden in s. place R53.2.

Sacrifice of animals to dragon B11.10.0.1; consumed by heavenly fire F962.2.1; drives devil away G303.16.19.16; equal to the reward J2067; of human being to dragon *B11.10; made to free moon from sickness A755.3.1; mixed with sage's blood K1673; of virginity T301. — Camel induced to offer himself as s. K962; deceptive s. of nuts and dates K171.3.1; earth reddened with blood of human s. A1241.4; earth by s. of son and daughter of first couple A831.3; ghosts punish failure to s. to them E246; man put in moon for disdainful s. A751.1.3; miser reducing promised s. W153.14; monthly human s. to devastating fox B16.2.1; mutual agreement to s. family members in famine K231.1.1; neglect to s. punished Q223.3; refusal to make s. after need is past K231.3; reward for religious s. Q21; self-s. W28; ship moved by s. D2136.8; smoke from s. tabu for chief C564.5; substitute s. K1853; sun, moon as circles animated by human s. A714.8; sun from youth offered in s. A718.1; tabu to kill animals for s. C92.1.0.1; tabu; neglect of s. to deity C57.1; trickster eats s. offerings K254.2; wild huntsman pacified by s. E501.17.6.1; woman drowns herself as s. to water-gods T211.1.1.

Sacrifices *S260ff.; at unearthing of treasure N554.1. — Cruel s. S200—S299; druid performs s. P427.1; funeral s. A1547.1; ghosts killed by s. E433.4.1; ghosts placated by. s. E433; ghost summoned by pouring blood of s. into trench E382; magic results produced by s. *D1766.2; origin of s. A1545; religious s. *V10ff.

Sacrificed. — Animals s. to provide food for dead E433.3; bird allowed to sing before s. K551.3.7; bodily member s. to save life J351; deity saves person to be s. S255; lamb prefers to be s. in temple rather than to be eaten by wolf J216.2; man s. for breaking tabu C929.6; miracle must wait till one man is s. K1785; moon from chest of s. youth A741.2; princess to be s. to dragon H335.3.1; wealth of wife s. N531.5.

Sacrificial. — Escape from s. altar R175.1, rich man falls into s. grave K1603.

Sacrificing animal with son's name K527.5; self to marry beloved T24.8. — Dupe s. animal, gives it to trickster K158; friend s. life for other P316; intemperance in s. J558; magic power from s. D1736.1; power of wild hunt evaded by s. to huntsman's dogs E501.17.4.3; woman s. self to save beloved T89.2; women s. in temple tabu C181.12.

Sad. — Why animal is s. A2521.

Sad-faced princess F591, H341.

Saddle. — Ass deprived of his s. J1862; balancing s. load with rock J1874.2; enemies heads hung on conqueror's s. S139.2.2.1.4; extraordinary s. F868; fortune from informing foreign king of use of s., bridle, and stirrups N411.3; lost ass, s., and bridle offered as reward to the finder J2085.1; magic s. *D1209.2; man freezes to s. (lie) X1606.2.1.

Saddled. — Being s. as punishment Q493; horse must agree to be s. and bridled to secure man's help K192.

Sadhu as helper N844.1; a thief K2058.1.

Sæhrimnir A661.1.0.3.

Safe provision for life not to be lightly surrendered J705. — Belongings s., no white man near J1373; champion grants enemies s. convoy W11.5.10; king carries out s. conduct promise M203.1; soul hidden in s. E712.2.

Safety in shadow of wall N253. — Animal allows himself to be tied to another for s. K713.1.2; captive sends token of s. H85; charm gives s. on journey D1384.3; country mouse prefers poverty with s. J211.2; dream tells of person's s. D1810.8.2.4; plainness with s. or grandeur with danger J212; umpiring dispute in exchange for s. guarantee M222.

Sage aids quest H1233.3.3; curses city M411.24; sees worm in loaf F642.3.2; as villain K2286. — Blood of s. mixed into sacrifice K1672; quest to distant s. for advice H1393; wisdom (knowledge) from s. J152.

Sages. — Couple live with s. in Great Bear A761.2; youth educated by seven s. J141.

Sago palm's abundant sap A2791.10. — Why fruit of s. palm looks like an eye A2791.9; why s. bears fruit from the stem A2771.3.

Sail. — Bronze s. F841.2.5; tin s. F841.2.6.

Sails. — Color of s. on ship as indication of good or bad news Z140.1; ghost s. over sound on bundle of straw E581.7; making s. for ship from one bundle of linen H1022.3.

Sailing against contrary conditions D1520.15.1; in leaky boat without sinking D2121.13. — Demon ship s. against wind F411.3; ghost s. on straw E581.7; man building boat and s. about in giant's belly F911.5.1; selling soul for s. through sky M211.6.

Sailor offers saint a candle as large as a mast K231.3.1; prays ship sink, since gods never answer J1467.1. — Returning s. told fine house and child God's bounty J1279.2; treacherous s. K2259.4.

Sailors rescue abandoned child R131.14; rescue hero R169.12. — Flying Dutchman has dead men as s. E511.2.1; ghost hurts s. E271.1; goddess of s. A456.1; mother sells her child to heathen s. S328; phantom s. E510ff.; Virgin Mary protects s. V282.

Sailors'. — Ship in storm saved because of s. "Ave Maria" V254.2.

Saint *V220ff., V221ff. (see these numbers for many additions to references given here); as ball player F697.2; calls fish from lake D2105.5; causes druids to bless D2076; chooses early death J216.6; controls animals D2156.2.1ff.; cures blind hyenas B384; and devil (binds devil with hair) D1831.3, (battles Lucifer at world's end) A1082.6, (dispels pagan devils) V356.1, (renders pacts with devil ineffective) M218.1; drives chariot over displeasing person Q227.3; effects magic, miracles (magic beautification) D1864, (boat's course changed) T321.6, (boy created from blood-clot)

T541.1.1.1, (canal dug with tree roots) D2121.14, (crime magically detected) D1817.2f., (chant kills animal) D1445.3, (crozier falls from heaven) F962.12.1, (death of person delayed) D1855.3, (demons flee stone) F405.10, (closed doors passed through) F694, (door, lock magically opens) D1557.1, (dumbness cured) F954.2.2, (earth scratched, treasures appear) D2157.1.1, (epidemic ended by fasting) D2162.1, (fluid carried in broken container) F866.7.2, (food leaves clothing unspoiled) F1091, (journey with magic speed) D2122.5, (huge load carried) D1691.1, (magic journey over water, bog) D2125.0.2ff., (poison unharmful) H1573.3.1, (magic sleep induced) D1964.5, (song silences hound) D1442.5, (spearhead removed) F959.3.4.1, (stone set afire) D2158.1.2, (fiery sword comes between enemy king and queen) D2196, (magic thirst caused) D2063.3.1.1, (thunderbolt produced) D2149.1, (pagan tree falls through fasting) P623.0.5, (virtue finds lost articles) N211.1.0.1, (miraculous visions) V513, (water produced from tree) D927.1.1, (well produced) D926.1.1; exposes self to temptation for greater reward in heaven T335; flogs tempting woman T331.6; forced to return to monastery walks in backwards K2312.2; gives calf to wolf W10.2; gives liberally to gambler, little to beggar J225.6; goes to heaven each Thursday A182.3.0.3.1, Q172.8.1; leaves order for music V475.4; as matchmaker T53.3; and nature phenomena (cloud evoked) D2147.3, (cold water warmed) D2144.3.1, (fog dispelled) D2143.3.1, (icicles burn) F962.9, (lake dries up) D2151.7.1, (river brings object) F932.5.1, (river frozen in summer) D2151.2.4, (river ford created) F932.10, (sea doesn't encroach upon grave) F931.3, (sea leaves cowl untouched) F930.1.0.1, (sea rises) F931.1.1, (spring where water spilled) F933.1.1, (spring follows) D927.4, (spring, fountain produced) A941.5ff., F932.3, (much water confined in small ditch) D491.3, (waves don't touch) D2151.3.2, (wells caused to fail) D2151.6.1, (winds controlled) D2142.0.2; offered any gift chooses wisdom L212.1; overpowers sea monster B877.1.2; perceives chest D1810.0.3.1; performs miracles while yet unborn H579.5; plucks out eye to avoid marriage T327.3; possessed by gluttony F496.1; prays with woman, learns she is his sister N734.2; prefers to die in exile Q431.0.1; prevents abduction of fairy F389.2; propounds riddles H540.4; proves power of Christianity (horse miraculously preserved) H1573.3.2, (man unharmed by fiery furnace) H1573.1.4, (by transformation) H1573.3.3, (wizard burned) H1573.3.4; as riddle solver H561.10; silent by holding stone in mouth V73.6.2; sleeps with maidens without sin T331.7; suckled by wolf T611.10.2; and symbolism of full milk cup H607.4; threatens to take homicide's place in hell W28.4; wins soul in dice game E756.4.1; in womb renders woman invisible D1361.39; wrests soul from demons E756.4. — Angel reveals relics to s. V140.1; angels singing for s. V234.1; animal deluded by s. B256.0.1; animals aid s. (fly warns against devil) B483.0.1, (hawk carries off hand of displeasing man) F982.3, (hogs root gold) B562.1.1, (lion protects body) B773.3, (oxen carry) B557.2, B256, (tiger carries wood)

B292.11, (whale fights pursuing monster) B523.2; animals from parts of body of deity or s. A1725; angels entertained unawares (hospitality to disguised s. rewarded) Q45.1; attempt to give s. poison H1515.2; beast invokes protection of s. B251.4.1; benevolence of s. (aids man to sleep with princess) K1915.2, (bestows beauty) D1862.2, (bestows father's goods on poor) V437, (bestows immortality) D1851.3, (bestows invulnerability) D1846.5, (charity shown) V433, (feeds two youths) V73.3, (gives credit for good deeds to another) Q42.8, (has tribute remitted) K2314, (heals enemy) V441.1, (helps gambler) N6.3, (hides fugitive from king underground) K2319.3, (wins over pagan priest with kind words) L350.2, (never drives fly from face) W10.1, (murderer offered refuge) R325.3, (souls asked to be released from hell) Q174.1.1, (sinner's punishment shared) V414, (child suckled) T611.5, (another's danger assumed) P319.8, (sick man's pain assumed) D1500.3.3; cow follows s. B159.3; daily visit to s. C687.1; dead s. (body moves in grave to face north) E411.0.8, (corpse sits up from open grave) E235.8, (exonerates cleric) E376.1, (in grave makes room for pious man) Q147.1, (returns from dead to give blessing) E367.2; (returns from dead to preach of heaven and hell) E367.1; dying s. leaves wise message J154.1; extraordinary phenomena at anger of s. F960.4; flower from land of promise appears to s. F979.10; gate lets s. through D1552.6; God speaks to s. A182.3.0.2, hospitality to s. repaid Q45.1.3; humility before s. in disguise Q66.1; infant s. rebukes mother T585.4; ladder symbol of s. Z139.7.1; magic lime tree distills sustenance for s. D1472.1.3.1; mill symbol of s. Z185; phenomena when remains of s. moved F960.8; princess marries s. T121.5.1; prophecy: unborn child to be s. M311.3; punishment for opposition to saint (for jeering) Q559.5, (beheading for turning back) Q421.2, (transformation for denouncing) D661.2; sacrifice to s. V11.8; salmon caught out of season for s. F986.2; sham s. (bear mistaken for s.) J1762.2.1, (hypocrite acclaimed) U116, (jackal) K1961.1.5.1, (seduction by posing as s.) K1315.6.4, (wife's maids disguised) K1827.1; shame's effect on s. F1041.23; stone on which s. born detects perjury H251.2.3; tabu: violating refuge with s. C51.2.5; test of s. H257; time flies as s. preaches D2011.1.2; marvelous light reveals man hiding from s. F969.3.1.

Saint's *V220ff., *V221ff.; anger produces extraordinary nature phenomena F960.4; birth (dry rod blossoms) F971.1.1, blood covenant with animals P312.0.1; body (blood cures) D1500.1.7.3.2, (blood restores speech) D1507.6, (face radiant) F574.3.1, (breath causes drunkenness, death) D1500.4.2.1f., (head, tears, produce fountain) D925.1.1f., (hand lights darkness) D1478.1, (magic from name) D1766.7.3, (shadow cures) D2161.4.15, (tears effect conception) T512.4, (tooth luminous) F544.3.2.1, (teeth give off sparks) F544.3.2, (voice heard from distance) F556.4; curse M411.8, (stops army) D2091.13, (splits rocks) D1792.1; death (rainbow appears from monastery to heaven) F960.2.2; hymn to free himself from wife T253.3; land bargain: staff touching island wins K185.13; mother admitted to heaven Q172.8; motives maligned on entering brothel N347.2; possessions have magic power (bachall defaces idol) V356.3, (bell gives weakness) D1336.5, (bell carried on floating stone) D1524.3.2, (bell heard, never found) K1887.3, (book brings victory) D1381.25, (cloak reveals rewards of heaven) D1329.1, (cure disease) D1500.1.13, (cowl protects fox) D1447.2.1, (holy water makes fairy vanish) F379.4, (magically transported) D2136.5, (Pater Noster outweighs ox) V52.13, (relics recovered) V140.2, (relics transformed) D457.16.1, (staff determines island's ownership) D1524.1.2.1, (sword sacred) D1400.1.4.1.1, (tunic doesn't burn) F964.2; prayer wins battle D2163.5ff.; prophecy on successor D1812.5.0.7.2; vision of three cities in heaven A661.1.2. — Animal eating s. body stricken Q558.11; contest in lifelike painting: fly on s. nose H504.1.1; corpse leaps at s. passing E597; fasting to enforce s. dues P623.0.6; future greatness if s. will followed M310.1.1.1; gospel hung from s. shoulders F1011.1.1; homage to s. bell C94.8; idols found on faces after s. arrival V347; land purchase: as much as s. hood covers K185.4.1; milk from s. cows forms lake F989.9; oath taken on s. hand M116; prayer at s. flagstone V52.7; punishment for looking at s. corpse Q227.2; sham miracle: s. statue raises arm K1972.1; tree grows through s. bell F979.6; thunderbolt prevents intimacy of s. communities F968.2.

St. Andrew A1372.10.

St. Anthony's pigs B256.2, Q228.

St. Cecilia D1840.1.3.

St. Christopher Q25; and the ass J1269.9.

St. Colum K11, V515.1.3.

St. Eligius J2411.2.

St. Eugenia K1837.7.

St. Francis J1261.8.

St. George's precept to poor man J556.1; wolves K1725.

St. Isaac G303.2.5.2, S263.2.1.

St. John the Baptist compared with St. John the Evangelist J466.2. — Feast of S. A1002.1, V70.3.1.

St. John Damascene V256.3.

St. John the Divine F451.5.9.4.

St. John the Evangelist J466.2.

St. John's night. — Dew falling on S. restores sight D1505.5.2.1; fairies emerge on S. F211.1.1.2; fern blossom on S. D965.14; wild hunt appears on S. E501.11.1.3.

St. Loy J2411.2.

St. Martin. — Jesus appears to S. V411.8; nun refuses see S. T362.1.

St. Nicholas brings Christmas gifts N816; saves girl from slavery R165.1; steals bread V412.1.

St. Nicholas' song drives off fairies F382.5.

St. Oswin D1505.12.

St. Patrick. See under **Patrick.**

St. Peter. See under **Peter.**
St. Theodora Q537.1.
St. Thomas' Day E587.2.1.
St. Valentine B232.1.
St. Veronica's napkin F950.1, V121.
Saints *V220ff., *V221ff.; confirm covenant by cutting off thumbs M201.4; exchange bachalls P311.7; have visions of heaven V511.1.1; as prophets M301.5; sacrifice themselves S263.5.1. — Deceiving the s. K2371; devil tempts s. G303.9.4.6; fasting against s. P623.0.4; Irish s. Z71.1.8ff.; land of the s. A661.0.10, V511.4; prophecy: boys to be fathers of s. M312.6; transformation combat between s. D615.5.
Saja. — Burning s. wood tabu C514; why s. bark is white A2751.4.4; why s. tree has knots A2755.4.1; why s. tree has no sap A2755.2.1.
Salad. — Poisoned s. kills faithless wife Q418.1; woman gives a jewel for a s. J2093.2.
Saladin asks to become Christian V331.7.
Salamander enters barefoot person B784.1.8; in rum drink G303.9.8.4; subsists on fire B768.2. — Creation of s. A2148.2; mythical s. B99.1; riddle about s. H842.2.
Salamander's magic blood D1382.13; blood quenches fire D1566.2.7.
Sale to animal (or object) J1850ff.; of worthless articles K110—K149. — Protean s. D612; sacrament for s. J1261.2.1.
Salesman guarantees sow to bear male, then female, then kid X1233.4.1.
Saliva, see also **Spittle.** — Fairies made visible through use of s. F235.4.5; healing power of saint's s. D1500.1.7.2.1; magic circle of s. kills dragon D1402.14.
Salmon appears every seventh year F986.3; caught out of season for saint F986.2; of knowledge B124.1.1, F162.5.3; as oldest and wisest of animals B124.1; transformed to person D376. — Catching s. proof of virginity H411.16; disenchantment by eating s. D764.3; eating magic s. gives knowledge M315; giant s. B874.4; hawk transformed to s. D413.1; helpful s. B474; king of s. B243.2.1; magic s. carries hero over water *B175.1; man transformed to s. D176; origin of flat body of steel-head s. A2305.1.1; origin of s. A2125; reincarnation as s. E617.1; soul hidden in apple in s. E713.1; stones from transformed s. A977.5.2; how s. swims A2444.3; transformation: hawk to s. D413.1; transformation: s. to child D374; why s. has purple belly A2412.4.2.1; why s. has tapering tail A2378.9.1.1.
Salt bullet kills witch D1385.4.1; under chair prevents witch's rising G254.2; exorcises witch G271.3; food without drink as punishment Q501.7.1; given Death's messengers Z111.6.2; of hospitality P321; to keep people clean A1372.10; powerful against fairies F384.1; protects against witches G272.16; in saltless land sold for fortune N411.4; transformed to stone *D471.5. — Acquisition of s. A1429.4; why animals eat everything without s. A2435.2.1; bird nest of s. J2171.5; burning s. love

charm D1355.3.7; dried snow sold for s. X1653.3; dupe persuaded to over-s. food K1045; dupe rubs s. on wounds K1045.2; dwarfs dislike bread baked without s. F451.3.7.2; eating roomful of s. as task H1141.3; effects of wild hunt remedied by asking the huntsmen for s. E501.19.2; enigma on s. as only food H588.21; fool liking s. decides to eat nothing else J2524; giant turns to s. F531.6.12.3; head of beheaded witch mends if rubbed with s. G223; lazy ass loaded with s. and then with sponges J1612; literal host serves bread and s. J2476; load of s. melts in rain (flying contest) K25.2; love like s. H592.1; magic s. *D1039.2; man becomes s. D241; man says his s. is stones: it becomes so Q591.2; man on sinking ship eats s. J861.2; monkeys steal tortoise's s. K343.4; murder by throwing s. in eyes K957.1; origin of s. springs A942.2; person with animal in stomach fed s. B784.2.1; reincarnation as s. E642.0.1 why sea is s. A1115; why sea stinks when it is full of s. J2371.2; self-grinding s.-mill *D1601.21.1; sleeping on s. gives thirst for a week J1322.2; sowing s. to produce s. J1932.3; spilling s. brings bad luck N131.3; stone becomes s. D452.1.3; tabu to eat s. C229.6; thumb cut and s. put on it in order to remain awake H1481; too much s. in food of giant makes him go outside for water K337; transformation to pillar of s. for breaking tabu C961.1; washing s., it melts away J2173.9; why s. disappeared from forests A1196; witches lack bread and s. G229.3; wolf scorns s. meat in false expectation of other booty J2066.4.

Salting man's flayed back S114.2; skin prevents witch's reentering G229.1.1. — Victim enticed into drinking by over-s. food K839.3.

Salty water turns into fresh D478.10. — Mankind from s. stone licked by cow A1245.4.

Salvatio Romae D1323.4.1.

Salvation *V520ff. — Letter of s. given from grave E373.3; since s. predestined, asceticism useless V462.0.2.

Salve, see also **Ointment.** — Magic s. *D1244; person enchanted by witch's s. so as to be ridden by witch G241.2.2.

Same. — All children born s. day as prince become his companions P32.1; buying s. article several times over K258.2; disease cured by s. thing that caused it D2161.4.10ff.; effects of wild hunt remedied by seeing it a year later in s. place E501.19.1; prophecies about children born at s. time M369.8; sowing and reaping s. day F971.7.

Samhain festival V70.5.

Sample. — Injunction: to give s. of food to dog before eating C685.

Sampo F871.

Samson makes water flow from jawbone D925.1.3. — Feast gives S. riddle clue H565.1; riddle about S. and Philistines H831.

Sanctified — Angel brings about reburial in s. ground V244.

Sanctity of saints V229.2. — Books' s. tested in water H222.4; books' s. tested in fire H221.1.3; long beard and s. J1463; woman dies when spoiled of s. T312.1.

Sanctuary. — Escape by taking s. in church R325; punishment for desecrating s. Q411.11.1; treasure hidden in s. N514.1; tabu: unworthy to enter, see s. C51.1.9.

Sand instead of sandalwood for bathing J1511.2.1; mass advances upon city Q552.14.3; permits walking on water D1524.1.4; transformed to rice D452.3.1, D476.1.11. — Binding together s. and string as punishment Q512.2; bird carries a grain of s. from a mountain each century (illustration of eternity) H701.1; blindness cured by rubbing s. F952.3; canoe of s. J2171.1.3.1; city buried in s. F948.5; cooking in hot s. H506.9; demon eats s. F171.8; devil piles s. in ocean so that vessels may run aground G303.9.9.5; earth from s. strewn on primeval water A814.2; eye sockets filled with s. S165.4; food in s. J1924; fortune told by cutting s. D1812.3.2; God throws s. on lazy shepherds (origin of insects) A2005; magic s. *D935.1; making rope of s. H1021.1; man made from s. sprinkled with water A1241.2; marking place in the s. J1922.3; numskulls count selves by sticking their noses in s. J2031.1; ogre teaches smith how to transform s. in his smithy G651; origin of hill: everybody passing by brings s. A963.7; as many stars in heavens as grains of s. H702.1.

Sandal. — Bill of sale on s. F1015.3; prophecy: death from hands of man with one s. M341.2.9.1.

Sandals. — Magic s. *D1065.5; magic from loosing s. D1782.3.1.

Sandalwood brings high price where it is lacking N411.5; tree guarded by dragon B11.6.10. — House of s. F675.3; origin of s. tree A2681.7; praying for raja's death so s. will be sold W153.13; sand substituted for s.; substitute pay J1511.2.1.

Sandhill surrounds lover F969.6.

Sandpiper. — Creation of s. A1944; why s. fights A2524.2.

Sandpipers' — Annoyance of s. chirp J215.1.4.

Santa Claus, see also **St. Nicholas;** as bringer of Christmas gifts N816.

Santals eat hare's entrails A1422.1.1.

Saora wave weapons, shout while dancing A1689.4; women's earrings C181.9.

Sap. — Earth-tree furnishes health-giving and hunger-satisfying s. A878.4; fig tree rewarded with s. of all other trees A2711.7; magic plant-s. D974; origin of blood-colored s. in trees A2721.2.1, A2755.2; sago palm's abundant s. A2791.10; why s. comes from top of palm A2791.8; why the saja tree has no s. A2755.2.1.

Sapling. — Recognition by unique ability to bend s. H31.5.

Sapphire gives magic sight D1331.1.5.1. — House of s. F771.1.5.2; magic s. cures disease D1500.1.9.1; tremendous s. F826.4.

Sapphires. — Book of s. F883.1.5.

Sarai. — Quest for s. flower H1333.5.2.

Sardine. — Man becomes s. D179.3.

Saree. — Hero climbing up girl's s. killed N339.11; quest for s. for queen H1355.2.

Satan, see also **Devil,** *G303ff.; attempts to create another world A63.8; disguised as deer K1823.5; forks soul from body E722.2.4; jealous of Adam A63.5.1. — Demons help S. G302.9.5; devil in serpent form tempts first woman (S. and Eve) A63.6; dialogue between Christ and S. V211.7.2; fall of S. from heaven A106.2.2; father hides son from S. R153.3.6; God conquers S. at world's end A1082.5.

Satans. — Boy who has newer seen a woman: the S. T371.

Satchels. — Falling of s. evil omen D1812.5.1.26.

Satiated. — Coming neither hungry nor s. H1063.

Satin. — Wearing s. tabu C878.1.

Satire M402; causes face ulcers D1402.15.3; as punishment Q499.4. — Magic s. *D1275.4, (as curse) D2175.3, (causes king to waste away) D1402.15, (causes man to melt) D1402.15.1, (kills animals) D1445.4, (makes land sterile) D1563.2.3, (raises blotches on face) D1403.1; man dies as result of magic s. D1402.15.2; origin of s. A1464.3; punishment for s. Q265.2.

Satirist. — Poet as s. P427.4; saint limits s. V229.6.1; woman s. M402.1.

Satisfaction. — Feeding ravenous beast to s. H1123; fool regrets that he has not eaten seventh cake first since that was the one that brought s. J2213.3.

Satisfied. — Refusing to pay for woman's favors: not s. K1353.1.

Saturday. — Jewish automaton will not work on S. V71.1; knockers refrain from work on S. F456.1.2.3.3; souls released from hell every S. Q560.2.2; why sun shines on S. A1177.

Saturn swallows stone instead of Jove G11.0.1.1.

Satyr B24; reveals woman's infidelity B24.1. — Revelations of a s. U119.1; wild man son of woman and s. who overpowers her F611.1.3.

Saucepan. — Man transformed to s. D251.1.

Saucer. — Devil has s. eyes G303.4.1.2.4; does s. protect the ghee? J2062.2.

Sausage mistaken for animal J1771.2; rain J1151.1.3; as revolver scares off robber K437.3. — Fool unacquainted with s. J1732.1; mountain-men make s. of Christans F460.4.4.4; mouse, bird, and s. keep house together J512.7; sale of a s. filled with blood K141; sending back s. skins for refilling W152.14.2; sexton's dog steals s. from parson's pocket X411.1; thumbling in s. F535.1.1.8.

Save it for the beggar C490.1.1. — Animals s. person's life *B520ff.; darkness comes in daytime in order to s. life of maiden about to be executed F965.1; transformation to s. D666.

Saved by mere luck N141; souls E754ff. — Boy doomed to die miraculously s. Q27; condemned soul s. E754.1ff.; heretic s. from fire by devil G303.22.13; kingdom s. by wisdom of hidden old man J151.1; life s. by accident N650ff.; man promises to built church if he is s. at sea M266; man s. from death sentence by animal B522; man s. by enemy W11.5.7; one s. from the devil by prayer to Virgin G303.16.2.2; stolen woman s. from trolls' dance F455.6.6.1.

Saving girl's life with marvelous things H355.0.1; life by guessing troll's name H516; the promised child S250ff.; provision tabu C785; by rope: succeeds in well, fails from tree J2434; from soldiers by receiving them joyfully rather than fearfully K2361. — Children s. parents from hell P241.1; citizen s. country's honor P711.3; extraordinary companion s. hero F601.4.2; fairy grateful for s. family F337; mortal s. fairy's life, sleeps with her F304.5; princess as prize for s. country T68.3; servant s. master H187; son s. kingdom F611.4; woman sacrifices self s. beloved T89.2; wraith s. person's life E723.1.1.

Savings. — Giving s. away: double return for charity J2489.6.

Savior, see **Christ.**

Saw for coffin-making announces death D1322.1; invented by devil A1446.1; in vagina F547.5.8. — Giant with teeth like those of s. F531.1.6.2; ship built with a wooden s. J2171.1.1.

Sawdust. — Quest for s. H1378.1.

Sawed. — Boat for rowing contest already s. through K14; captive soldier s. in two P461.3; legs of table s. so that it collapses K1431; sham parson: the s. pulpit K1961.1.3.

Sawing iron tree H1115.2; leg off by mistake J2131.3.3; in two as punishment Q469.8.

Sawmill. — Lie: remarkable s. operator X1082.1.

Scab. — Magic s. (from skin) *D1009.1.

Scabbard. — Magic s. D1101.5.

Scaffold. — Man suddenly acquires long gray beard on s. at execution F1044.

Scaffolding. — Builders throw away beams from the s. until it all falls down J2171.3.

Scald-crow. — Tabu to kill s. C92.1.5.

Scald-head disguise K1818.2.

Scalding to make dupe strong K1012.2; as punishment Q469.10. — Dupe s. self to learn languages K1046; endurance test: s. mush scatters on heroine's naked body H1503; making the dupe strong by s. K1012.2; murder by s. K955.1; numskull s. children J2175.5.

Scalds. — Charm for s. D1503.3.1.

Scales of dragon B11.2.10; test of witch H234; with wind as beams, heat as pans H1022.9. — Coin left in money s. betrays secret wealth N478; creator distributes s. A1440.1; fortune's s. to weigh man N111.3.2; giant with dragon s. for feet F531.1.3.1; origin of fish's s. A2315; thief's money s. borrowed J1141.6.

Scandal-mongering punished Q314. — Man never listens to s. W23; marriage to avoid s. K1383.

Scapular. — Disenchantment by s. D771.7.

Scar. — Recognition by s. H51.

Scars. — Hands with s. as suitor test H312.4.1; wounds cured by saint leave no s. V221.8.

"Scar-face" as hero L112.6.

Scarcity of real friends J401.

Scarecrow. — Queen used as s. Q482.5.

Scarification. — Conception from s. T537; invisibility by s. D1985.1.

Scaring. — Fairies s. off treasure seeker F244.4; fools s. one another J2632; ghost s. thief E293.1.

Scarlet thread as death omen J2311.1.4.

Scattered. — Bringing back flour s. by wind (task) H1136.1; mountains from s. parts of serpent's body A961.4; skillful marksman shoots eggs s. over table F661.4; skillful tailor sews together s. planks in capsizing boat F662.2; tools s. at night by witch G265.1.

Scattering. — Bride s. presents T136.4.3.

Scavenger carrying wood bad omen D1812.5.1.29; unwittlingly eats human noses G63.

Scavenger's — Royal couple reborn as s. children Q551.5.1.2.

Scene. — Ghosts haunt s. of crime, sin E334.1.

Scent, see also Odor, Perfume; of flowers from magic laughter D1773.1; of rice identifies children H49.1. — Why animals s. from distance A2475; man's body exudes sweet s. F595; rice with remarkable s. F815.4.1; why some flowers have no s. A2795.1.

Scenting. — Animal useful because of s. power A2512.

Scepters. — God's s. A156.3.

Schlaraffenland *X1503.

Scholar disguised as rustic K1816.0.4; given nonexistent egg he has proved to be there J1539.2. — Devil appears to s. G303.6.2.10; fox disguised as s. K1822.2; many books do not make a s. U111.

Scholars. — Jokes on s. X370ff.

School of animals B234. — Progress in s. (at devil and all his works) J1487; seven years s. course Z72.4.

Schooling. — After one day of s. children to cease associating with unlearned J977.

Schoolmaster. — Ogre s. G11.9.

Schoolmasters ignorant of Latin J1741.

Schrätel und Wasserbär K1728.

Science of reincarnation E600.2. — Dream advises against popularizing s. J157.3; theological questions answered by propounding simple question in s. J1291.2.

Sciences. — Origin of s. A1487.

Scientific. — Absurd s. speculations J2371ff.; absurd s. theories J2260—J2299; pseudo-s. methods of detecting J1142.

Scipio saves Rome P711.4.

Scissors drip blood (life token) E761.1.7.2. — Capturing magic pig carrying s., comb, and razors between its ears H1154.1; magic s. *D1183; obstinate wife: cutting with knife or s. T255.1.

Scoffers turned to stone Q551.3.4.1. — Miraculous manifestations to s. of the Cross V86.4.

Scoffing. — Punishment for s. at church teachings *Q225.

Scolded. — Boys s. to conceal their identity K649.3; dwarf is insulted when s. F451.3.6.1; mortals s. by dwarfs F451.5.2.9.

Scolding contest H507.5; drowning child instead of helping him J2175.2; priest says he is merely trying to get even for all the scolding he must undergo J1269.4; punished Q304; supernatural wife forbidden C31.4.2. — Transformation by s. D527; wild hunt frightened away by s. E501.17.8.1.

Scorching. — Animal s. self while putting out fire A2218.1.1; ghost s. hat E542.4; sinners in hell alternately s. with heat, cold Q562.1.

Scorn of unloved suitor punished T75.1. — Caesar's s. of his wife's advice leads to disaster J155.3; illness from shame of s. F1041.9.3; stag's s. of his legs L461.

Scorned hero saves king L154; lover T70ff.; princess sets task H933.4; suitor consoles self J877. — Fairy avenges self on man who has s. her love F302.3.3; wise man's advice s. J2051.

Scorning. — Death for s. deity A1335.6; giantess's son s. father P233.3.1; prince marries, punishes s. girl T72.2.1; son chastizes father for s. mother P233.9; unpromising hero kills those s. him L156.

Scorpio. — Origin of S. A777.

Scorpion bites as punishment: brings poor man fortune N426; in spite of himself, stings the turtle carrying him across the stream U124; scoops out men's eyes B17.2.4.1. — Giant s. B873.2; origin of s. A2092; reincarnation as s. E629.1; woman reborn as s. E693.3.

Scorpions in hell A671.2.9. — Army of snakes, s. B268.7.1; ascetic sees s. as gold D1825.8; money of hard-hearted transformed to s. D444.1; ornaments of s. F827.3.

Scotland. — One foot in Ireland, one in S. K2319.1.

Scotsman mistakes moose for mouse J1759.1.

Scott. — Michael S. extends river's tide G303.9.2.5.

Scourging. — Angel s. mortal V245.1.

Scout. — Creator sends crow to s. for earth nucleus A812.3; vulture as s. after world-fire A1039.1.

Scouts. — Birds as s. B563.6; bird s. sent out from ark A1021.2; parrots as s. B122.8.

Scraping. — Thrifty s. of tray as bride test H381.2.2.

Scrapings. — Plant from s. of princesses' bodies H522.2.

Scraps. — Negroes made from left-over s. at creation A1614.5.

Scratch. — Deceptive agreement not to s. H1184, H263; hen put in witch's hair to s. while maid escapes G276.1; witch begs man to s. her back *G269.1.

Scratches identify clandestine lover H58.2. — Man in the moon from s. A751.5.

Scratch-berries. — Trickster eats s. J2134.1.

Scratched. — Earth from worm s. by creator's nails A828; man in the moon: moon's face s. by hare A751.5.1.

Scratching. — Contest: s. skin off each other K83.2; deceptive s. contest K83; magic s. D2063.4; strong hero asks that chickens stop s. F615.3.1.1; torturing by s. S187; transformation by s. D565.10; witch s. G269.15.

Screams. — Girl's s. louder when robbed than when raped *J1174.3; stone's s. indicate king's successors D1311.16.1.

Screaming at terrible sight forbidden C491.1; woman summons help against robbers K432.1. — Ghost s. E402.1.1.3; monk s. to repel temptress T331.9; stone s. under king's feet H71.10.6; witches s. G249.2.

Screen. — Paramour hidden behind s. K1521.5.

Scribe can't read own writing P425.1; can't write letter with bad leg J2242.1; of the gods A165.6.

Scripture. — Dividing by s. quoting J1242.

Scriptures. — Neglect of s. punished Q223.10; tabu to disbelieve in s. C61.3.

Scrofula cured by magic object D1502.2.3.

Scroll from heaven F962.12.4. — Sacred s. returns to heaven D1641.11; witch as s. G213.3.

Scrotum. — Beaver sacrifices s. to save life *J351.1; hungry fox waits in vain for horse's s. to fall off J2066.1.

Scullion. — King rewards s. for bon-mot Q91.2.

Scum's origin A2847.

Scurf becomes palm tree D457.6.

Scylla F526.2; and Charybdis G333.

Scythe cuts one man's head off: all have theirs cut off J2422. — Going to store with s. K1162; "May the devil whet my s." (devil does) C12.3; on return to body soul crosses on s.-blade as bridge E721.6.

Scythes. — Hero breaks s. F611.3.3.2.

Scythed chariot F861.2.2.

Sea, see also **Ocean;** animal found inland F989.12; animals magically summoned D2074.1.2; bath as rite V81.5; -bird A165.1.3, B463.1; has burned up (lie) X908; is calm for beautiful woman F575.13; -cat 17.2.1.3, B73; -charm D1523.2.7; cow B72; creatures as goddess's ancestors A111.3.2; dragon transformed to serpent D419.1.1; is on fire: protests colt decision J1191.1.1; foolishly accused of cruelty J1891.3; -fowl B267.4; -ghosts E271; of glass in otherworld *F162.4; -god A421; -god and rain-god conflict A1015.1; -horse B611.3.1, B634.1; of ice in otherworld F162.4.1; makes extraordinary noise, throws out fishes at world's end A1063.1; -mammal F531.1.8.8; otter A1821.1; people give the ogre brandy (tar) G525; personified Z118; produced by magic D2151.1.1; -queen (entices lovers) A421.1.1, (sets tasks) H933.5; -rat B17.2.1.1; rolls in overland as punishment C984.4.1; -scum D469.4; -spell Q467.3.1; turns to ice to permit flight D675; of unusual substance F711.2; turtle B177.3; water made like earth D2031.12; water mixes with fresh at world's end A1063.2. — Angel of s. rebels A54.1; animal drowning if taken from s. H842.1; animal rescues man from s. B541; animals helpless in s.-voyage together J1711.1; bell sunk in s. can be raised only under certain conditions D1654.10.1; binding waves of the s. H1137; birds fill s. with dirt A1028.2; boots carrying owner on s. D1524.2.1; building bridge over land and s. H1131.1; building castle in s. H1133.3; castle built on s. F771.2.4; church and congregation sink to bottom of s. F941.2.2; city sinks in s. F944; dashing s. does not touch saint's cowl F930.1.0.1; dipping out the s. with a spoon H1143; dragon's home in bottom of s. B11.3.1; drinking the s. dry H1142.2; how many drops in the s.? (riddle) H704; earth rises from s. A816; earth sinks into s. at end of world A1061; epidemic does not cross river (s.) at saint's command D2162.2; escape from ship by jumping into s. R216.1; extraordinary occurrences connected with s. F931; extraordinary s. F711; fish brings lost object from bottom of s. B548.2ff.; foolish fight with the s. J1968; giant's leg stops ship at s. F531.3.1.2; giant's spittle transformed to s. D483; giants live under s. F531.6.2.2.1; gods' home under s. A151.3; hero wades across s. F1057; how deep is. s.? H681.4; how much water in s.? H696.1; impostors throw hero overboard into the s. *K1931.1; island rises up in s. F735; king descends to bottom of s. P15.6; land rises from s. A952; why s. does not get larger when it rains in it and nothing flows out J2371.1; magic enables one to stay on s. bottom D1388.0.5; magic formula causes s. to open D1551.9; magic object controls s. D1545; magic s. *D911; magic song drives back s. D1549.8; man falls dead when he realizes that he has been riding over frozen s. N383.1; men living beneath s. A1101.2.4; mermaid gives gold from s. bottom B81.13.4; moon falls into s. A1016.6; needle falls into s.: sought next summer J1921; old man of the s. G311; penance: staying on rock in s. Q525.1; people enabled to walk across s. D1766.1.5; people live under s. F725.5; person submerged by s. F945; quest for bottom of s. H1371.2; rain from s. in upper world A1131.3; recovered articles dropped by rescuing animals into the s. D882.2; recovering lost objects from s. H1132.1; river becomes s. D483.1; rock in s. created by magic D2153.1; sacrifice to s. V11.2; saint's bachall (causes s. to divide) D1551.5, (permits him to walk on s.) D1524.1.2; shipwrecked shepherd distrusts s. J11; sinners' souls under s. water E751.5; strong hero son of woman of s. F611.1.14; torment in s. as respite from hell Q560.2.3; tree under s. F811.4.2; water led to s., ends deluge A1028.1; well located under s. F718.1; why s. is blue A1119.1; why s. is salt A1115; why s. is warm A1119.2.

Sea's unpleasant odor A1119.3. — Attempts at measuring s. depth L414.1.

Seas. — Extraordinary occurrences concerning s. F930ff.; journey beyond seven s. Z71.5.2; magic control of s. D2151.1; origin of the s. A920ff.; sacrifice to rivers and s. S264; seven s. encircle world A872.1; three s. surrounding earth Z71.1.9.

Sea-beast allows voyager to land upon his back B556; causes land disease, kills birds and fish B16.4.1.1.2. — Man sacrifices self to s. S263.5.3, W28.3; speaking s. B211.2.7.

Sea-beasts. — Hostile s. B17.2.1.

Sea-foam. — Birth from s. T546.1; devil created out of s. *G303.1.3.3; goddess born from s. A114.1; man created from s. A1261.1; person becomes s. D283.4.

Seagull. — Ghost as s. E423.3.9; soul in form of s. E723.5.

Seagulls save abandoned child T611.7.

Sea-monster G308; honors saint B251.2.8. — Devastating s. B16.5.1.2; devil puts convert's body on s. M219.2.6; earthquakes from movements of s. A1145.2; giant s. B877.1; tide from breathing of s. A913.2.

Sealand plowed out by goddess A955.4.

Seaserpent B91.5, X1396.1.

Seashore flooded with fish F986.5. — Dwarfs live on high s. F451.4.1.8; future hero found on s. L111.2.2; prophecy: death on s. M341.3.4.

Sea waves, see **Waves.**

Seaweed becomes vegetation A2615.4. — Man becomes s. D225.

Seaweeds. — Magic ring makes s. grow D1487.1.

Seal becomes person D327.2; -god A132.11; in human form B651.8; of humiliation put on rivals' backs L11.1; -man B80.1; transformed to another animal D411.7ff. — Boy with s. flippers F515.4; eating s. meat tabu C221.1.1.3; fisherman dragged through sea by s. escapes F1088.3.2; ghost as s. E423.2.5; god's s. A156.4; helpful s. B435.5; magic s. skin D1025.9; man transformed to s. D127.1, G263.1.2; marriage to s. B601.18; numskulls celebrate their new charter by burning up its s. J2181; reincarnation as s. E612.6; soul in s. E715.4.4; soul in form of s. E732.5; speaking s. B211.2.7.1.

Seal's — Ghost with s. head E425.1.7.

Seals. — Chieftain's vision of s. sucking his breasts V515.2.1; ghosts visible to s. E421.1.5; human beings descended from s. B631.2; origin of s. A1837.

Seam. — Milky Way as a stitched s. in the sky A778.4.

Seamanship. — Acquisition of s. A1459.2.

Seamen. — Hungry s. eat human flesh G70.1.

Seamstress's. — Chain tale: pulling needle out of s. hand Z41.8.

Search, see also **Quest;** for confessor V29.1; for a girl like statue artist has made T11.2.1.1; for prince named Sabr H946.1. — Animal's s. for dead man B546; children left at home s. for brothers and sisters S356; husband will not s. for shrewish wife who has run away from him T251.7; jewels aid in s. for treasure D1314.8; unsuccessful s. for man who can rule his wife T252.1.

Searches. — Absurd s. for the lost J1920ff.

Searching queen's quarters before king enters J634.2. — Children s. for stolen meals J124; dead mother s. for dead child E323.5; not to speak while s. for treasure C401.3; wife s. for lover K2213.3.3.

Season. — Defenses in and out of s. J674; fruit produced out of s. at saint's request F971.5.1; intercourse forbidden at hunting s. C119.1.3; procuring bird out of s. H1024.6; which is coldest s.? J1664.1.

Seasons. — Calculation of the s. A1485; causes of s.: deities move sun A1157; determination of s. A1150ff.; four s. personified Z122.4; god of the s. A496; magic control of s. *D2145ff.; proper s. for crops J713; wild hunt appears at certain s. E501.11.2.

Seasonal. — Variations in sun's s. heat A739.4.

Seasonally. — Why animals crowd together s. A2484; why fish come in s. A2484.1.

Seat covered with lice skins F894; heating in hell for certain person Q561.3; magically sticks to person D2171.1.1; next to king as reward Q112.3; in which only king can sit H31.4; pillars indicate settlement site D1314.11. — Capture in trap s. K735.2; he who fills s. to be king P11.5; king's s. on hills P14.10; king's unique ability to occupy certain s. H41.9; magic s. *D1151; vow not to sit on father's high s. until revenge is had M152.2.

Seats. — Devil moves s. in church G303.9.9.18.

Seating arrangements in royal hall A1539.1.

Second blow resuscitates (first kills) *E11.1; born son successor P17.3.1; sight D1825.1, (from dead) D1821.8; wife orders husband persecute first S413.2; wife saves king K2213.15. — Animals have s. sight B120.0.1; crocodile goes aftes s. child J2173.6; dead return s. day after burial E586.3; dead wife haunts husband on s. marriage E221.1; dead wife returns to reprove husband's s. wife for abusing her stepchildren *E221.2.1; deathbed promise concerning the s. wife M255; foolish attempt of s. man to overhear secrets *N471; husband fondles s. wife in presence of first as punishment for adultery Q484; magic object effective when struck on ground once only: s. blow renders useless D806.1; magic object recovered by using s. magic object D881; no s. punishment for same offense J1184; person's s. nose F514.5; wager on s. marvelous object N72; wife's revenge for s. wife K2213.16.

Seconds. — How many s. in eternity (riddle) H701ff.

Secrecy. — Impostor forces oath of s. *K1933.

Secret of eternal soul deceptively learned K975.2; learned by intoxicating dupe K1165; of vulnerability disclosed by hero's wife K2213.4.1; of strength treacherously discovered *K975. — Alchemist paid for "s." K1966.2; barber cured by revealing s. D2161.4.19.1; bargain to keep s. M295; betrayal of husband's s. by his wife K2213.4; birds tell a s. B122.1.1; curiosity about s. ensnares animal K713.1.4; exposed child brought up in s. S350.2; fairies lose power of invisibility if mortals gain knowledge of their s. F235.8.1; fatal s. revealed C420.1; false accusation of being in s. service K2126.2; finding certain s. forbidden C820ff.; god's abode s. A151.0.2; groom's ruse to hear bride's s. K1844.3; guessing name of devil's s. plant K216.2.1; husband's s. magic object discovered and stolen by wife D861.5; if you can't keep s., you must not expect me to J1482;

illness feigned to learn s. K2091; illness from keeping a s. F1041.9.2; jokes
on s. societies X550ff.; keeping princess's s. suitor test H338.1; magic
ring permits owner to learn person's s. thoughts D1316.4; magic
s. *D1316.5; magic speaking reed (tree) betrays s. *D1316.5; mortal not to
betray fairies' s. F348.5.1; numskull talks about his s. instructions and thus
allows himself to be cheated J2355; ogre's s. overheard G661; no place
s. enough (for fornication) T331.4, (for sin) U232; prince to give up life
in exchange for learning a s. M232; princess's s. sickness from breaking
tabu *C940.1; revelation of magic s. permits animal to be killed D1445.1;
speech magically recovered when third person guesses s. transaction
D2025.3; spying on s. help of angels forbidden C51.4.2; tabu to mention
s. water spring C429.1; tabu to utter overheard s. C420.3; test of wife's
ability to keep s. H472ff.; thief enters treasury through s. passage K315;
treasure hidden in s. room N517.1; vow not to eat until s. learned M151.1;
wife cannot keep s. T274; wife multiplies the s. J2353; witch divulges
s. powers G275.5; woman dies as s. love exposed F1041.1.3.3.

Secrets discussed in animal meeting *B235; forced from monster G510.2;
learned by deception C420.1. — Animals tell hero their s. B561; fairy
escaped by learning and using his s. F381.4; foolish attempt of second
man to overhear s. *N471; ghost laid when tells magic s. E451.1.1; god
reveals s. A182.1; king has amours with great men's wives so as to learn
s. from them J155.2; man betraying s. cursed M414.11; ogre tells power
s. to wife G534; reward for ability to keep s. Q62; not to reveal s. (of god)
C51.4, (of supernatural wife) C31.9; tasks performed by means of s.
overheard from tree *H963; uttering s. forbidden *C420ff.; valuable s.
learned *N440—N499; wife obtains husband's s. J1112.5; wife threatens
husband with death if he will not tell s. T252.3.

Secretions. — Birth from s. of the body T541.8.

Security breeds indifference U270ff. — Dog offered as s. for debt B579.6;
don't go to satirist for s. M402.2; legal s. P524; stag tries to borrow grain
from the sheep with wolf as s. J1383; tabu: giving s. for one excommunicated C95.

Sedan bearers carry master to search for dog: they refused to search
J2163.2. — Choosing sweetheart's s. chair suitor test H324.1.

Sedition. — Knight falsely accused of s. K2126.

Seduced. — Creator's wife s. by his son A32.3.1; dead man asks marriage
with s. girl E353; girl s. by brother becomes cannibal G37; monk having
s. girl kills her and becomes infidel V465.1.1.1; paradise lost because first
woman is s. A1331.2.1; virtuous man s. by woman T338; wife s. by husband's friend H492.2.

Seducer led naked through streets Q473.3. — Dead sweetheart haunts s.
E211.1; mermaid ruins her daughter's s. B81.13.9; youngest daughter avoids
s. L63.

Seducer's. — Deceived fiancé may sleep with s. wife J1174.2.1.

Seducing foster brother's sister P273.2.2; friend's ejected wife K2012. —

Daughters s. father T411.2.1; demon s. princess F402.1.15.1; devil s. nuns G303.3.1.12.1; devil as woman s. man G303.3.1.12.2; disguised prince s. queen K1814.1; friends s. wife likened to dogs H592.4; magician s. queen D2031.4.2; ogre s. girl to devour her G17; ogress s. men G264.3; priest s. man's wife J652.3; repeated attempts at s. innocent maiden T320.1; transformation for s. woman *D658.1ff.; ungrateful law-breaker s. magistrate's wife W154.15; wife s. husband's servant T481.4; woman as leper s. enemies K778.2; woman's wager on s. anchorite T337.

Seduction *K1300ff.; punished Q243.2. — Child's remark prevents mother's s. J122.1; service in disguise for s. K1831.2.1.

Seductions. — Wife warns against women's s. T299.2.2.

Seductive. — Revenant as s. woman E425.1.3.

Seed. — Earth from lotus s. A814.8; extraordinary s. F815.5; god carries s. of gods A111.3.0.1; growing oil s. on stony ground H1049.2; magic s. *D971ff., (produces golden gourd) D1463.3; mustard-s. trail R267; numskull plants s. in daytime and takes it out at night J2224; origin of s. A1425; sowing s. in others' fields J2129.8; suitor test involving mountain of mustard s. H1091.3; traveler to look for s. he sowed in street H586.2; white field, black s. (riddle) H741.

Seeds rattling mistaken for insults J1812.1. — Armies like s. and pepper-corns J1625; "battle s." P551.9; city paved with precious s. F761.5; countertask: sowing cooked s. and harvesting the crop H1023.1.1f.; counting s. in mustard package H1118.1; dwarfs emigrate because mortals put caraway s. into bread F451.9.1.1; eater of fruit s. will drop gems as he laughs M312.3.2; magic bird collects s. B172.3; magic turns s. into insects D1594.1; man created from s. A1254; poppy s. poured into ghost's mouth E439.4; trail of s. R135.0.2.

Seeing, see also **Sight;** ability lost if ears cut off J2721; all earth from upper world F10.2; one's wraith E723.2; tabus C300ff.; trolls F455.5.4; without eyes X1724. — All-s. god A102.2; bad omen: s. unusual sight on road home D1812.5.1.22; contest in s. *K85; giant s. great distance F531.1.1.4; insanity from s. strange sight *D2065.2; madness from s. beautiful woman *F1041.8.1; marvelous cure without s. person F950.7; numskull's attempt at s. abstract quality J2488; only particular persons s. treasure in its true form N543.0.1; suffering from merely s. work done F647.2; tabu: bridal couple s. each other before wedding T134.1; tabu: wife of supernatural husband s. old home C713.2; witches s. in dark G249.10.

Seek. — Gods teach how to s. food A1420.2; magic arrow shot to determine where to s. bride D1314.1.3; transformation to s. person D647.

Seeking. — Animal's s. attitude from ancient loss A2275.5ff.; children left at home s. exposed brothers and sisters S356; dwarf s. to enter church F451.5.9.5; hero just misses man he is s. N186; why animals are continually s. something A2471ff.

Seen. — Deceptive grant: as much land as can be s. K185.12; falling in love with person never s. T11; ghost s. in two places at once E599.9;

jinn s. only by those he wishes G307.2.2; one and one-half men and a horse's head s. by youth H583.1; son next s. to be king M314.2.

Seer D1712; banishes ghost E439.8. — Recognition by miraculous sight of s. H184.

Segregated. — Otherworld inhabitants s. F167.14.

Seizing. — Tree s. person F979.4; witch s. man with snuff G269.2.

Selection of king by elephant's bowing to him H171.1. — Care in s. of creature to carry one J657.

Self, see also **Automatic;** -abnegation rewarded Q61; -boiling kettle D1601.10.3; -chopping axe D1601.14; -cooking vessel D1601.10ff.; -created deity A118; -cutting shears D1601.12; -deception of the lowly J953; -dependence J1030ff.; -digging spade D1601.16; -grinding (mill) D1601.21, (millstone) D1601.20; -growing and self-gathering corn D1601.2; -immolation S125.1; -inflicted wounds to accuse another K2116.3; -luminous object *D1645ff.; -mutilation H160.1; -playing musical instruments D1601.18ff.; -returning (cow) K366.1.3, (dragon's head) *B11.5.5, (magic object) *D1602ff.; -righteous anchorite tempted T332.1; -righteousness punished L435; -ringing bell D1601.18.1; -sacrifice W28; -sewing needle D1601.11; -torture as penance Q522; -tying thread D1601.13. — Accidental s.-injury N397; angel ceases to appear to s.-righteous hermit Q553.2; child born of slain mother cares for s. during infancy T612; deception into s.-injury *K1000—K1199; dupe tricked into killing s. K890ff.; giant's s.-returning head F531.1.2.3; inability to transform s. D502; irrevocable judgment causes s. to suffer first M13; magic s.-moving vehicle D1523ff.; magic s.-propelling vehicle *D1523ff.; magic s.-rejuvenation *D1881; man named "s." K602.1; man stretches s. till he reaches otherworld F59.1; never be rude to s.-made man J21.52.2; ogre deceived into s.-injury *G520ff.; origin of animal characteristics: animal persuaded into s.-injury A2284ff.; person eats s. up G51.1; power of s.-transformation D630ff.; pursuer deceived into s.-injury K533.1; treasure opens s. N552; wife s.-sacrifice A1545.5.1.

Selves. — Persons duped into injuring s. K1080ff.

Selfish quest P332. — Why cock is vain and s. A2527.1.

Selfishness. — Origin of s. A1375.

Sell, see also **Sold.** — In large family father unwilling but mother willing to s. children H491.1; peasant refuses to s. possessions to king P411.1; princess must s. goods on market as punishment Q483.

Seller of fox skins mixes otter skins with them J2083.3. — Buyer and deaf s. X111.11; considerate s. at auction warns prospective buyer J2088.

Selling animal and keeping him (task) H1152; forbidden C782; for four rupees instruction: fool refuses six J2461.7; old mule back to master K134.3; oneself and escaping K252; soul to devil G224.4; what is not his K282; to witch tabu C782.2. — Children s. mother S20.1; dog s. rotten peas B294.3; man s. soul to devil M211; wife s. privilege of sleeping with husband T296; wife s. self to ransom husband R152.2; witch s. power over winds D2142.0.1.1, G283.1.3; woman s. favors for particular purpose *T455ff.; woman s. poisoned curds A1335.12; woman substituting child for her own and s. it *K1922; youth s. himself to an ogre in settlement of a gambling debt S221.2.

Semen bellicosum P551.9; in love philtre D1355.2.3. — Birth from s. thrown on ground T541.10; magic strength in s. D1831.3; mankind from maid having licked s.-stained cloth A1211.7; peacock eats s., impregnated B754.6.

Senate ruler amuses small son J553.2. — Overcurious wife learns of s. deliberations of s. J1546.

Senator. — Old simpleton resolves to become s. J955.4.

Sender. — Message of death fatal to s. K1612.

Sending, see also **Sent;** meat home by bird J2124.1; object by itself J1881; to the older F571.2.

Seneca opens own veins and bleeds to death Q427.

Sense. — King brought to say "what is the s. in that?" H507.2; loss of s. after abduction by fairies F329.3; man to bring wife a purse-full of s. *J163.2.

Senses regained by hearing name F959.1.1. — Druids bereave men of s. D2065.3; fairies cause man to lose s. F361.2.2.

Senseless from grief J1041.21.5; judicial decisions M1. — Spying on holy man renders s. D1410.8.

Seneschal. — Treacherous s. K2243.

Sensitiveness of dwarfs F451.3.6. — Adulteress feigns unusual s. K2051; marvelous s. F647ff.; test of s. H1571.

Sent, see also **Sending.** — Companion s. away so as to steal common food supply K343.3; identifying tokens s. with messenger H82; objects magically s. to certain place D2136.10; objects s. through air D2135.5; strong hero s. from home F612ff.

Sentence. — Animal saves man from death s. B522; death s. escaped by propounding riddle king (judge) cannot solve *H542.

Sentences. — Penance: king must postpone all s. Q520.4.

Sentry. — Devil flies away with s. box G303.9.9.13; officer disarmed by s. J1526.1.

Separable soul *E710ff.

Separate examination of witnesses discredits testimony J1153. — Land where women live s. from men F566.2; line drawn by saint's bachall to s. calves from their mothers D1574; marriage to five women, each with s. duties T145.1.

Separated. — Bridal couple s. on wedding night T165.4; husband and wife kill themselves so as not to be s. T211.3; lions succeed only when bulls are s. J1022; lover searching for lost ring becomes s. from mistress N352; lovers treacherously s. T84; reconciliation of s. couple T298; riddle: what are the two s. by jealousy H851.

Separately. — Serve the water and wine s. J1312.1.

Separation of nations A1600ff.; of sexes in otherworld F112.0.2; of souls for heaven, hell E755.0.2; of sun and moon by creator A736.1.4.3. — Accidental s. N310ff.; girl to die of s. from her love M365.3; loving couple die of s. T212; why s. of a good woman from a bad man is a benefit T287.

September. — King's beard worth months of July, August, and S. H712.1.

Sepulchre. — Girl lives in s. to preserve chastity T328; magic s. *D1299.2; stretching s. D482.5.

Seraphim as creator's advisers A42.1.

Serf made to climb tree, shot as cuckoo K1691.1.

Serfs congratulate master, curse by mistake J1845.

Series, see also **Chain, Cumulative, Succession;** of clever unjust decisions J1173; of creations *A630ff.; of enclosed coffins F852.4; of glass coffins F852.1.1; of helpers on quest *H1235; of husbands try to control adulteress T241; of lucky successes N680.2; of lower worlds A651.2; of quests H1241; of tasks H941; of upper worlds A651.1; of witches with increasing numbers of horns G215.2.1; of world catastrophes A1001. — Man created after s. of unsuccessful experiments A1226; soul hidden in a s. of coverings E713.

Sermon, see also **Preaching.** — Boy applies the s. X435; parody s. K1961.1.2.1; parson put to flight during s. X411; parson refreshes himself during the s. X445ff.; priest's short s.: "You're wicked" J1647; wager: to begin s. with illustration from card-playing N71; witty funeral s. V66; wolf loses interest in the s. when he sees a flock of sheep U125.

Serpent, see also **Reptile, Snake;** above Loki continually drops venom in his face Q501.3; acts as rope to collect wood B579.5; asks victim feed him honey K815.18; brew gives witch power G224.7; bursts asunder F981.1; carried by bird lets poison drop in milk and poisons drinkers N332.3; charmed into helplessness by magic formula D1410.5; as child's nurse B535.0.14; chokes woman's undutiful son Q557.2; cursed M414.8.3; damsel F582.1; -eye F541.1.4; given immortality, renews skin A1335.5; guards treasure N583; -hall F771.5.3; as house-spirit F480.2; having injured man refuses reconciliation J15; with human head B29.2.1; inside man's body G328.1; with jewel in (head) B101.7, (mouth) B103.4.2; king B244.1, (assigns task) H939.4.1, (causes flood) A1019.2, (resides in lake) B244.1.2; kneaded into dough H1407; language B215.5; as magician B191.7; as procurator of rats B221.2.1; produces storm D2141.0.11.1; released: grateful B375.9; releases swallowed-up water supply F914.1; relieved of sand in eyes: grateful B385; as saint's whip B292.12; shows condemned man how to save prince's life B522.1; steals from God's coat a stick for his back A2262.3; steals jewels, person accused of theft N352.3; subsists on dust B768.4; supports earth A842.1; supports sky A665.6; swallows canoe F911.4.1.2; swallows man F911.7; taken for island J1761.1.2; transforms self to staff, picked up, bites enemy K928.1; transformed to person D391; tries to bite a file J522.3; as wooer

B622.1; worship V1.8.6. — Animal languages learned from s. (eaten)
*B217.1.1, (not eaten) *B165.1; ants overcome s. L315.14; automatic
brazen s. D1620.2.9; bird grateful for being saved from s. B364.4; blue
s. B731.11; blowing s. B743; brain becomes s. D447.10; bridal chamber
invaded by magic s. T172.2; child born with figure of s. on body
T563.3; child born with s. in caul T551.8; childless woman adopts a s.
(transformed man) T676.1; corpse transformed to s. D449.2; creation
of s. A2145; dead mother appears and makes disobedient child eat fatal s.
Q593; devastating (man-eating) sea-monster (s.) B16.5.1.2; devil in s.
form tempts first woman A63.6; dragon as modified s. B11.2.1.1; earth
rests on tortoise, s., elephant A844.6; fiery s. B19.4.2; giant s. B16.5.1,
B875.1; giant as s. F531.1.8.2; God makes s. ugly A2286.0.1; going into
bath on return from s. kingdom forbidden C711; gold-producing s.
B103.0.4; golden s. B102.6; hair transformed to s. D447.1.3; helpful s.
*B491; hero unharmed by coiling s. F1088.2; human sacrifice to water s.
S263.3.1; hundred-headed s. B15.1.2.10.2; husband lets s. bite him to
save wife T211.1.2; immortal s. B843.1; journey to s. kingdom F127.1;
lake dangerous from haunting s. G308.4; Lucifer as s. D191.1; magic
s. *B176.1, (head) D1011.0.3, (heart) *D1015.1.3, (statue cures)
D1500.1.12.1, (urine) D1027.1; magic tree guarded by s. *D950.0.1; man
attempts to kill faithful s. at wife's instigation B335.1; man
transformed to s. D191; man warned of s. unwittingly carried in sack
N848.12; men lured into s. pit, killed K912.2; marriage to s. in human
form B656.2; Midgard S. *A876; mist after s. fight F962.10.1; multicolored s. B731.10; mythical s. B91; nine-headed s. B15.1.2.8.2; only one
s. has sting: fed poison to rest A2219.3; origin of enmity between s. and
man A2585.1; origin of death: s. given immortality instead of man
A1335.5; origin of horned s. A2145.0.1; penance: wearing s. Q522.8; rat
leaves s. behind, though spared to rescue him K1182; revenant as s.
E423.5; rod transformed to s. D441.7.1; sacrifice to s. V11.7.1; sea dragon in s. form to accompany hero D659.4.2; sea dragon transformed
to s. D419.1.1; seven-headed s. *B15.1.2.6.1; six-mouthed s. B15.2.1;
skillful marksman shoots s. through left eye F661.5.1; soul in form of s.
E733.1; strong man kills s. F628.1.3; tail and head of s. quarrel as to
usefulness J461.1.1; ten-headed s. B15.1.2.9; thousand-headed s.
B15.1.2.10.3; three-headed s. B15.1.2.2.2; twelve-headed s. B15.1.2.10.1;
two-headed s. B15.1.2.1.1; venomous s. B776.7; why s. has no ears
A2325.8; wax prince animated by s. D435.1.4; winged s. as boat
F911.3.2; wisdom from s. B161; wise s. B123.1; wolf defends master's
child against s. B524.1.4; worm becomes s. D418.2.1.

Serpent's beautiful wife directs journey J155.1.1; bite produces ornaments,
clothes B103.6.1; deaths to predict king, queen's P17.2; jewel covered
with spiked helmet K1058.1; life in its gold crown E712.4. — Bringing ruby
in s. head H1151.26; cause of s. ugliness A2286.0.1, A2402.1; disenchantment by eating s. head D764.8; disenchantment by taking key

from s. mouth at midnight D759.1; earth from s. head A815.1; earthquake at s. slaying F969.4.1; man with s. head B29.2.2; magic s. crown *D1011.3.1; mountains from parts of giant s. body A961.4; origin of s. blood and venom A2367.3.1; person with s. head F511.0.9.3; swallowed person tickles s. throat F912.3.1; sword with s. image F833.7; why s. mouth closed A2341.3.1; wise man destroys s. eggs F622.1.

Serpents in hell A671.2.1; in otherworld F167.11.1. — Blood becomes s. D447.3.1.1; bread transformed to s. D444.4; castle on s. F771.2.7; copulation of s. A2496.2; diamond charms s. D1442.11; husband charmed back from land of s. R152.4; king of s. B244.1; kingdom of s. *B225.1; magic in country of s. D838.4; man kills s., toads, dragons with own hands F628.1.3.1; oars, masts transformed to s. D444.11; ordeal by kissing s. H224.1; quest to land of s. H1289.1.1; silence in land of s. H1506; sorcerer's body becomes s. D447.9; uncharitable knight devoured by s. V422; war between s. and storks B263.7; winged s. pull chariot B558.7; world of s. A696.

Servant, see also **Maid;** allowed anything he can take with teeth J1161.10; asks master for arms of knighthood J955.3; becomes arrogant when rich J1085.2; cheats master boasting of eyes in back of head J1511.9; deceives family by assuming unusual names K1399.2; deceives sons falsifying father's will K1628; exposes liar master X907; falsely accused of familiarity with queen K2121.2; girl helps prince if he will make her his chief wife T55.2; girl lies about fairy, leg broken F361.17.4; girl's industry tested H1569.1.1; given garlic as knighthood arms J955.3; of God beaten J2215.2; impersonates dead master, makes false will K1854; to improve on master's statements J2464; in his master's place K1317.1; inadvertently throws master into stream J2133.5.1.1; kills self at master's death F1041.1.3.2; lays skin of dead dog in the bed of his mistress and master K2134; literally takes "year to do errand" J2461.4; passes self off as prince K1952.0.2; plays at being emperor J955.2; poses as master K1969.3; plans to deceive his master by refusing to eat J2064; refused payment because of single mistake K231.9; repays stingy master (mistress) J1561.4; rescues abandoned child R131.5; rescues king's children R169.4.2; saves master from death H187; steals back magic D882.3; substitutes for husband in bed, deceives him K1844.1.1; takes pearl to wife instead of merchant N351.1; tells of few customers, dismissed J551.7. — Animal as s. of saint B256; awkward s. J2665; bringing best friend, worst enemy, best s. etc. H1065; cat as s. of witch G225.3; clever s. J1114; clever maid s. J1111.6; clothing the s. J2491; creators' giant s. puts trees on earth A857.3; creator's giant s. makes valley and mountains A857.2; devil's s. G303.10.16; disinterested party asked to punish s. J571.4.1; dragon fly as snake's s. B765.24; eavesdropping s. realizes own misery N455.11; enemy's s. as helper N857; fairy punishes s. F361.14; faithful s. locking up master R53.4; faithful s. *P361ff.; forehanded s. throws parson's suit of clothes into tub of water J1614; giant as Creator's s. F531.0.2; giant as man's s. F531.5.10; hero rescued by s. R169.4; hero's s. kills giant pig H335.3.5; host rebukes negligent s. J1573; how rich man paid his s. Z21.3; husband has his strong s. substitute in bed with strong wife K1844.1; husband substituting s. in mistress's bed: wife deceived K1843.2.2; king as s. L410.5; lazy s. W111.2; liquor given to s. giant A1427.0.4; man as animals' s. J2214.5; man as giant's s. F531.6.16.3; master as magician tricks s. K1963.3; master, s. exchange clothes for escape K527.3; master demands that s. tell him of his faults as well as of his good qualities P366; master and s. *P360ff.; mortal as s. in fairyland F376; never dismiss old s. for his first fault J21.52.5; nobleman rescues lady from s. R111.5; person as s. in ogre's house G462; present s. girl preferred to absent mistress J326; prince agrees to marry s. girl if she will help him on a quest H1239.1; rescue of bride from mysterious perils by hidden faithful s. R169.4.1; retort from underfed s. J1341ff.; rich girl marries s. T121.7; ruler's retort to stealing s. J1936; thief disguised as woman s. K311.12.2; treacherous s. K2250.1; unpaid s. refuses to blame master J571.8; wager: rajah's daughter to bring s. dinner N12.1; wager on truthfulness of s. N25; weak son condemned to be brothers' s. M438.5; wife seduces husband's s. T481.4.

Servant's fidelity tested H1556.0.1; head to be cut off J1141.1.6; pact with devil to secure nobleman's daughter M217.1. — Knight disregards s. insult J411.9; test of valor: rousing s. anger H1561.4; wife takes s. place and discovers husband's adultery K1585.

Servants frightened, give food to robbers K335.0.11; tell of wife's adultery, rebuked J221.1.2; touch food, guests depart empty J1563.5.2. — Animals as domestic s. B574; devil and his s. live where perjurers dwell G303.8.6; enchanted persons as witch's s. G263.0.1; magic s. plow, swallowed D1719.8; maid behind statue of Virgin advises the mistress to give s. better food K1971.3.1; parents become s. to earn wedding funds T132.2; stag found by master when overlooked by s. J1032; stingy man and his s. W152.12; stealing s. caught by arising early J21.23; tasks assigned by treacherous s. H919.1; to have good s. a lord must be good U212; treacherous s. K2250ff.; wagers on wives or s. N10ff.

Served. — Hero is s. at table by his unknown son: recognition of his wife follows H151.11.

Service in disguise K1831.2; under false name K1831. — Animal in s. to man B292; burial s. read into hat to prevent dead walking E431.1; dead beggar's stick will not stay until back in beggar's s. D1651.5; death rather than go in enemy's s. M161.5; devil's faithful s. to knight G303.22.10; girl in s. of witch G204; god in s. as menial A181; hero in s. of wild man G672; intemperance in s. J554; life spared in return for life-long s. M234; living person in s. of dead man E596; long term of s. imposed on suitor H317; lovers' meeting: hero in s. of heroine T31f.; man dismissed after years of s. with a pittance W154.1; reward for s. of god Q20.1; strong man in s. to ogre as punishment for stealing food F613.4; warriors enter conqueror's s. R74; wild huntsman wanders for disturbing church s. E501.3.8; youth takes s. with (merman) B82.3, (ogre) G452.

Services of grateful objects D1658.3; of helpful animals B500—B599. — Dwarfs hold church s. F451.6.3.6; magic objects perform other s. for owner D1560ff.; penance: performing all s. asked for by anyone Q523.8; punishment for neglect of s. to gods (God) Q223ff.; religious s. *V0— V99; sale of worthless s. K150ff.

Serving by invisible hands E482. — Animal s. only certain man H172; animals s. men A2513, B570ff.; demon s. girl whose chastity is inviolable G303.16.19.5; disenchantment by s. transformed D754; dwarfs s. mortals F451.5.1.7; fairy s. mortal *F346.0.1, F346.2; forgotten fiancée rea-wakens husband's memory by s. as milkmaid *D2006.1.2; man's de-scendants s. his brother's P251.5.6; ten s.-women carried in bottle *D55.2.4.

Servitude. — Wolf prefers liberty to dog's s. L451.3.

Sesame. — Open s. D1552.2, N455.3; where is oil in s. flower? J1291.4.

Setting out vineyard in one night H1103. — A step-ladder for s. the table J1573.1; fairies s. down an object once cannot raise it again F255.2; man controls s. of sun A725; saint prevents sun's s. for year A725.1.

Settlement. — Ball indicates place for s. D1314.4; divining rod indicates place for s. D1314.2.1; location of s. at place cow stops and where milk flows by itself B155.2.2; why lion stays away from s. A2433.3.16.

Settlements. — Origin of s. A996.

Settling. — Insect points out diety by s. where he is H162.1.

Seven children at a birth T586.1.2; brothers seek seven sisters as wives T69.1.2; daughters of Humility J901; days silence at world's end A1057; demigods A501.1; devils' wives attempt resuscitation ritual K113.0.1; -fold doors to room F782.3; as formulistic number Z71.5; girls appear as seven parrots D658.3.3; -headed (dragon) B11.2.3.1, (ogre) G361.1.4, (serpent) B15.1.2.6.1, (witch) *G215.1; heavens A651.1.4; Irish saints never died V229.2.12.1; -league boots D1521.1; -legged beast B15.6.3.3; lower worlds A651.2.3; as magic number D1273.1.3; -mouthed cannibal G11.17; princesses sought by seven princes T69.1.2; reincarnations E604.1; rivers meet F715.8; rooms in ascetic's house F771.11; seas en-circle world A872.1; seven-years olds save princess D759.10; signif-icances of sign of cross V86.7; Sleepers *D1960.1; stags killed by one shot F679.5.3.1; substances in human body A1260.1.4; suns mark world's end A1052.3; tongues in a head (riddle) H793; walls around otherworld F148.5; week days have passed since the time of Adam H706.1; whistlers are souls of Jews who crucified Christ A1715.3; worlds above and below A651.1.3.1; year old girl has child T579.3; years between feasts Z72.3; years' pregnancy T574.2; years of service imposed on suitor

H317.1; years, seven months, seven days Z72.2; years' service for seven days' neglect of religious duty Q523.7. — Boastful fly-killer: s. at a blow K1951.1; bones in s.-fold cloth D717.1; bridegroom only son of s. children H1381.7; butcher wonders that man who has been buying his meat for s. years can still be alive X231; bride's constancy tested by s. years' mourning over supposed dead lover H387.1; cast-forth wife buried up to waist for s. years and despitefully used Q456.1.1; child born each day for s. days T586.5.2; dead person visits earth every s. years E585.1; disenchantment at end of s. years D791.1.1; evil eye covered with s. veils D2071.0.1; eye with s. pupils F54.3.4; fairy music makes s. years seem one day F262.9; fairy wife for s. years only F302.10; formerly s. (moons) A759.5, (suns) A720.1; gourds with s. rooms A1029.4; guilty of everything connected with the s. senses X331; headless man lives s. years E783.7; hero "son of s. mothers" Z215; hero wins contests with s. demons D785.1; hero's s. pupils in each eye, seven toes on each foot, seven fingers on each hand A526.5; island rises every s. years F735.0.2; island supported on s. feet F736.1.1; laws made in groups of s. P541.1; man lives with fairies s. years F379.3; man requires s. women T145.1.1; men with two faces, three legs, and s. arms F526.5; master of s. liberal arts begs from wagoner X371; mountain of s. lights F759.8; nature transformed every s. years A1103; not to speak during s. days of danger C401.2; palace with s. gates F776.3; parents wooing one of s. daughters T69.2.1; parting lovers pledge not to marry for s. years T61.2; person of remarkable sight finds tracks of swine stolen s. years before his birth F642.2; producing s. pairs of chopsticks in s. plates H1199.16; prophecy: s. days' life for baby M341.1.2.5; rivers formed where s. children place stones A934.2; snake s. years pregnant B765.25; lost soul to serve as porter in hell for s. years E755.2.3; spear thrust through s. iron plates H1149.7; strong hero suckled by s. women F611.2.4; swearing by "S. Things Served" M119.6; train of troubles for s. brothers N261.1; tree inside s. series of forts H1335.5.0.2; water-spirit claims life every s. years F420.5.2.1.6; wild hunt appears every s. years E501.11.3.1; woman's beauty shows through s. veils F574.1.2; youth educated by s. sages J141.

Sevens. — Dwarfs are superstitious about the three s. in 1777 F451.3.15.1, F451.9.1.3.

Sevenfold: formulistic number Z71.5.0.1.

Seventh cake satisfies J2213.3; daughter predestined to be magician N121.4. — Cure by s. son of seventh daughter D2161.5.7; death on s. day of marriage M341.1.1.2; holy day on s. day A1541.4.0.1; punishment comes in s. generation Q404; salmon comes every s. year to certain place F986.3.

Seventeen as formulistic number Z71.16.12; marvels at Christ's birth V211.0.3; -storied heaven A651.1.8.1.

Seventy tales of a parrot prevent a wife's adultery K1591. — Swinging s. girls H506.5.

Seventy-two kinds of wisdom J182.2, (mastered by Adam) D1811.0.1; as formulistic number Z71.14.

Seventy-seven as formulistic number Z71.15. — Devil claims to be 7,777 years old G303.4.8.3.

Seven hundred. — Disenchantment after s. years D791.1.6.

Seven thousand people killed for stoning judges N340.2.

Several, see also **Many.** — Person with s. bodies F524; eye with s. pupils F541.3; wild hunt goes s. times around a hill E501.14.4.

Severed, see also **Cut, Dismembered;** finger as sign of crime H57.2.1; heads of monster become birds E613.0.5; limbs as identification H106; limbs replaced by Virgin Mary D2161.5.2.4. — Magic restoration of s. hand D2161.3.2; oaths taken over s. pieces of horse M111; ogre revives after limbs are s. G635.

Sewed. — Hero s. up in animal hide so as to be carried to height by bird K1861.1; horse s. in buffalo-hides F984.1; man s. in animal's hide carried off by birds K521.1.1; quartered thief's body s. together K414.

Sewing clothes on to boy's skin H1505; contest won by deception K47; each other up (fatal game) K861; magic shirt H383.2.2; a shirt of stone (task) H1021.9; shirts to trees J2465.9; together broken object H1023.7. — Brownies s. by moonlight F482.5.2; disenchantment by s. shirts for enchanted brothers D753.1; dwarf s. F451.3.4.4; empress s. in humility J918; resuscitation by s. body together E35.1; statue of Virgin s. for supplicant D1620.1.4; tailor s. up broken eggs F622.1; unsuccessful imitation of magic s. J2411.8; woman skillful in s. F662.0.1; women punished for not s. Q321.1.

Sex *T (entire chapter); activity tabu for warriors C566.6; hospitality T281; organs, see under **Genitals;** tabu *C100—C199; of unborn child (guessed) H528, (prophesied) M369.7.3; (wagered on) N16.1; of witches G220.0.2. — Animal changes s. periodically B754.1; animal controls s. of offspring F987ff.; curse: change of s. M454; disguise of s. to avoid execution K514; exchange of s. with ogre D593; farmer seeks laborer ignorant of s. K1327; god of double s. A111.3.0.1; humor concerning s. X700—X799; ignorance of s. J1745; killing children of undesired s. S11.4.3; mountain spirits change s. at will F460.2.15; origin of s. differentiations A1313.0.2; origin of s. functions A1350ff.; reincarnation with change of s. E605.1; sham physician predicts the s. of the unborn child K1955.3; simulated change of s. to baffle Evil Eye D2071.1.3; tabu confined to one s. C180ff.; telling s. of unborn goat H1576.1; of ten original men one magically changes s. A1275.3; test to discover person masking as of other s. H1578; transformation to person of different s. *D10ff.; transformation of s. to seduce *D658.3; vows concerning s. M130ff.; yearly transformation of s. D624.3.

Sexes of pygmies distinguished F535.4.1. — Relative pleasures of s. in love J99.1; separation of s. in otherworld F112.0.2; why s. differ A2853.

Sexton behind crucifix tells old maid she will have no husband K1971.8.1.
— Cock crows at church and the s. awakes and begins to sing X451;
eavesdropping s. duped into giving suppliant money K464; parson and
s. at mass X441.

Sexton's — Parson's share and the s. J1269.1.

Sextus seduces Lucretia K1397.

Sexual habits of animals B754; intercourse, see following heading; relation
of man, demons G302.7.1; relations in dog fashion unearth treasure
N551.2; relations with fairy F304; relations with wood-spirit fatal
F441.6.3; restrictions A1556; sins punished Q240ff. — Boasting of s.
prowess P665; devil's s. relations with mortals G303.12.7; doctor pre-
scribes s. intimacy for widow: daughters follow treatment K2052.4.1;
eaten fruit causes s. desire D1355.14; illicit s. relations *T400—T499;
magic ox from unusual s. union B184.2.2.1; magic ring gives s. prowess
D1335.5.1; neglect of s. relations tabu C163; unusual s. union of animals B754.0.1;

Sexual intercourse, see also **Copulation;** of animals A2496; forbidden
*C110ff.; on Friday only T310.1.1; of mountain woman F460.4.1.2; with
woman in childbed S185.2. — Bride refuses s. until court orders it
T166; bridegroom must be taught s. T166.2; cocks kept from s. have
tenderest meat B754.5; conception from (dream of s.) F460.4.1.2.1;
(extraordinary s.) T517; death from s. H182; disenchantment by s. D743;
husband objects to wife's enjoyment of s. T257.8; imagined s., imagined
payment J1551.1; Incubus comes in sleep, has s. F471.2; long-distance s.
K1391; luck changed after s. N131.1; needle and thread symbolize s.
J86, Z186; origin of s. A1352; peacock pregnant without s. B754.6; re-
fraining from s. as penance Q535.3; seduction through ignorance of s.
K1363; suitor test: s. with princess despite sleeping potion H347; tabus
concerning s. C119ff.; transformation by s. D565.5.1; trickster advises s.
K1354.1.1; urinalysis reveals s. as illness cure J1149.4; wife denies s. to
enforce demand T283; witches' s. with devil G243.3.

Shabby hospitality forces guests to leave P334.

Shade. — Clouds in sky to s. mountains A1133.2; fighting in the s. best
J1453; tree grows out of horse and gives rider s. X1130.2.1; wanderers
in s. of plane tree blame it for not bearing fruit W154.7.

Shades. — Land of s. *E482.

Shading roof from sun J1879.1; self with foot sole F551.5.

Shadow freezes X1623.1; mistaken for substance J1790ff.; on water
marks demon's victim G336.1. — Bird overpowered by stepping on his
s. D2072.0.4; bird as s. of god A195.3; cure by lying on saint's s.
D2161.4.15; demons cast no s. G302.4.4; devil gets into ark by hiding
in s. of Noah's wife G303.23.1; devil gets s. instead of man F1038.2;
devil takes farmer's s. G303.19.2; elongated s. swells fox's pride J953.13;
ghost as s. E421.4; ghosts cast no s. E421.2; God creates the devil from
his own s. G303.1.1.1; god hides in cloud's s. A179.8; god whose s. is a

lizard A446.1.1; impregnation by s. T532.8; man steps aside so that only his s. is caught K525.2; ogre without s. G369.3; person without s. F1038; person whose s. pierced, dies D2061.2.2.1; safety in s. of wall N253; soul as s. E743; spell over s. brings death D2061.2.2.2; suit about the ass's s. J1169.7; undesired lover asked not to step on s. K1277.6; woman who has prevented birth of children casts no s. Q552.9; worldly honor like s. J152.6.

Shadows. — Fairies seen as dark s. F235.7.

Shaggy. — Giants with s. hair on their bodies F531.1.6.3.

Shake. — Numskull tries to s. birds from tree like fruit J1909.3; why some animals continually s. head A2474ff.

Shaken. — Apple-tree grateful for being s. D1658.1.5; heavens s. by man's voice F688.1; parable on stones s. in jar J98; tree asks to be s. D1610.2.0.1.

Shaking of staff stuck in ground as life token E761.2.1. — Disenchantment by s. certain tree D789.7; water-spirit s. ship F420.5.2.7.2.

Sham, see also **Bluff, Feigned, Masking, Pretended;** astrologer K1964; blind man throws suspicion on real blind K2165; churchman K1901ff.; dead claim reward for information about their death J2511.1.2; dead deceived into moving K607.3.2; dead man deceived into making gesture K607.3; dead man killed by his intended victim K311.1.1; dead man punished J2311.6; death (to avoid debts) K246, (for copulation with divine maidens) K1325.0.1, (to escape) K522, (to be sold) K366.1.3.1, (to steal) K341.2, (to wound enemies) K911.1; eating K81.1; fight to frighten guests J1563.7; illness, see under **Illness,** feigned; mad man H599.2; magician K1963ff.; miracles K1970ff.; nurse kills enemy's children K931; parson (priest) K1961.1; physician *K1955; prince (nobleman) K1952; prowess *K1950ff.; pursuit saves fugitive K649.8; relics perform miracles V142.1; rich man K1954; sickness, see under **Illness;** sleep to kill enemy K911.3; suicide to soften lover's anger K1232.1; teacher pretends to read document brought as a letter K1958; warrior K1951; wise man K1956. — Foolish imitation of s. death J2411.1.1; money received to bury s. dead person K482; property disposal rouses s. dead J2511.1.1; race won by deception: s. sick trickster K11.5; robbers frightened from goods by s. dead man K335.1.2.2; trickster as s. magician makes adulteress produce hidden food for her husband K1571.1.

Shams. — Deception through s. K1700—K2099.

Shaman sent down by Creator equipped with medicine A1438.1.

Shaman's wife controls weather D2140.2.

Shamanism A1654.

Shame and disgrace for refusing love C929.1; for nakedness A1383.1. — Adulteress pretends s. before male statue K2051.1; death from s. F1041.1.13; effect of s. on saint F1041.23; false s. over trivial sin: little over great V26; illness from s. F1041.9.3; what is greatest? S. H659.7.2.

Shameful. — Riddle: what is most s.? H659.12.

Shaming. — Wife s. adulterous husband into gifts K1271.3.1; wife escapes king's lust by s. him T320.4.

Shampooing. — Servant injures master while s. him J2665.2.

Shape of bee's body A2300.1; of leaves of plant A2761; and position of animals' eyes A2332.4ff. — Detecting man in demon's s. J1141.1.7; devil changes s. G303.3.5; divine beings assume their own s. in sleep D796; dwarf can take s. he wants F451.3.3.0.1; fairy as s.-shifter F234.0.2; god as s.-shifter A120.1; Isle of S. F129.4.3; origin of island's s. A955.3; origin of s. of animal's back A2356.2ff.

Shapes. — Wandering soul assumes various s. E721.5.

Share. — Lion's s. J811.1; man had rather be burned alive than to s. food with a guest W152.2; parson's s. and the sexton's J1269.1; peasant's s. is the chicken J1562.2.

Shared. — Strokes s. K187.

Sharing invitation taken literally J2499.6; his wounds J1621. — Child s. food with toad B391.2; friends s. good and evil P310.1.

Shark bites off god's head A179.4; as king of fishes B243.1.3; -man ogre G308.5. — Fishtail becomes s. D447.4; giant s. B874.5; helpful s. B471; mythical s. B65; man becomes s. D178; reincarnation as s. E617.3; stealing lobsters from s. guardians K341.16; tabu to eat s. C221.1.3.4.

Sharks. — Creation of s. A2137; hero kills s. F628.1.4.2; kingdom of s. B223.1.

Sharp elbowed women G341, (duped into fighting each other) K1082; instrument shown ogre as nose G572.2; knife F838.1. — Dancing on s. instruments H1531.1; dupe induced to eat s. fruit K1043; dupe sits on s. stones K1116; quest over path bristling with s. points H1236.1; shield s. enough to cut hair F839.2.2; sword extraordinarily bright, s. F833.3.

Sharpened. — Knife s. by cannibal to kill captive G83; murder by feeding s. pieces of wood K951.6; ogre with s. leg G341.1; tools magically s. D2199.2.

Sharpening leg J2424. — Crow s. bill lets frog escape K561.1.2.

Shattered. — Pieces of s. god's head as hills A962.8; saint's breath restores s. vessel D1565.4.

Shave. — Half price for half a s. J1522.1; mortal wins fairies' gratitude by letting them s. him F331.2; vow not to s. or cut hair until a certain time M121.

Shaved. — Cast-off wife's head s. S436; chastity ordeal: holding s. and greased tail of bull H412.2; creditor to wait till debtor is s. K238.1; importunate suitor s. and tarred K1218.1.7; madmen's heads s. P192.6; magic object in return for being s. D817.2; numskull wants to be s. (orders wife to cut off his ears) J2426; ride on donkey's back with s. head Q473.5.1; running hare s. by skillful barber F665.1.

Shaving head as killing thousands H599.4; head as punishment Q488.2;

tabu C722.0.1. — Barber's contest in s. H504.2; bearded woman ghost laid by s. E451.7; disenchantment by s. D718; disguise by s. off beard so as to escape K521.2.1; fatal game: s. necks K858; giant s. hero's head F531.5.12; loud sound of s. J1484; **origin of custom of s. A1597.2;** squaring accounts by s. the wife J2082.

Shavings transformed to gold D475.1.2. — Countertask: making a loom from s. H1021.6.1; raised treasure turns into s. N558; wild huntsman repays with s. that turn to gold *E501.15.4.

Shawl. — Deceptive land purchase: as much land as a s. will cover K185.4; making large s.-cloth from one cocoon's silk H1022.4.3; prayer s. V58.5.

Shawls. — Thief guards s., steals them K346.4; women spread s. in enemy's path and entangle them K2352.

She-bear. — Strong man son of man and s. F611.1.5.

She-devil. — Man marries s. G303.12.6.1.

She-dragon B11.2.0.1.

She-fox. — Widowed s. rejects suitors who do not resemble her deceased husband T211.6.

She-goat. — Green s. B731.1; man transformed to s. D134.2.

She-goats. — Herdsman neglects his s. in favor of wild-goats J345.1.

Sheaf. — Devil as s. G303.3.4.7.

Sheaves prostrate selves E761.5.6.

Shearer. — Good s. does not skin sheep J531; sheep and ignorant s. J229.2.

Shearing flock of sheep in one day H1106. — Deceptive division of animals for s. K171.5.

Shears. — Magic s. *D1183, (produce love) D1355.15; mountain-man carries s. at side like sword F460.1.3; thief detected by sieve and s. H251.3.3.

Sheath and knife as analogy for mother and unborn child T579.1.

Sheba. — Queen of S. propounds riddles to Solomon H540.2.1.

Shedding of animals periodically A2483.

Sheep becomes dog at night B182.1.4, D621.5, H1331.9; born with human head as a result of bestiality T465.1; -dogs unite to hunt wolf J624.2; duck, and cock in peril on sea together J1711.1; with fiery collar B19.4.3; helpful to Lord: get wool A2221.10; and ignorant shearer J229.2; with inexhaustible wool D1652.14; jealous of dog because he does nothing W181.1; kill a fox who has licked up the blood they spilled in a fight J624.1; kill wolves F989.5.1; killed by the butcher, who they are persuaded will spare them J2137.5; licking her lamb is envied by the wolf J1909.5; magically disappear D2087.3; makes fox run to hunter K1178; protect child B535.0.10; as sacrifice V12.4.6; sleeps if shoe tied to ear B782; as souls redeemed from hell F81.6; thief confesses in church N275.5.1; thief forced to buy ram wethers K439.5; thinks that his weak legs are the reason for loss of eating contest J2228; thrown in well become crimson F933.3; transformed to grasshoppers D412.7; unharmed by beasts F989.5. — Alliance of s. and dog B267.2; black s. thought to be devil J1785.7; black s. turn white F985.1; calf-s. B14.3; carrying hundreds of s. across stream one at a time (task) H1111; cattle and s. of the sun A732.1; creation of s. A1884; deceptive division of s. K171.7.2; deity gives persecuted child s. S464; destructive s. B16.1.6; devil cannot change into a s. G303.3.6.3.1; devil stands in church door and writes down names of his own people on s. skin G303.24.1.4; dividing two s. and a ram J1241.1; divination by shoulder-bone of s. D1311.10.1; diving for s. K1051; dog caresses sick s. (hopes for his death) K2061.3; eagle warns shepherds that wolf is eating s. J715.1; enmity of leopard and s. A2494.2.6; fairy s. F241.7; fairy as s. F234.1.11; fairies threaten s. watcher F361.11; famished wolf asks s. to bring him water K2061.5; first s. in Ireland A1884.0.1; fox feigns to be playing with s. K2061.2; ghosts visible to s. E421.1.4; giant s. B87.1.3; give s. good care but do not let it fatten (task) H1072; good shepherd shears his s. but does not skin them J531; helpful s. B412; hound by day, s. by night D412.5.4; how s. got horns A2326.1.3; hundreds of s. to be carried over stream one at a time (endless tale) Z11; husband says he'll bear a s. J2321.3; inexhaustible s. D1652.1.9.2; island of s. F743.2; why s. has thin legs A2231.7.2, A2371.2.1; lies about s. X1243; magic s. B184.6; magic sight by looking at shoulder-bone of s. D1821.3.8; making s. laugh and dance: mutilation K1445; man boasts he fears saint no more than hornless s.: killed by them Q582.5; man taken to be s. J1765.2; man transformed to s. D135; nine-horned s. B15.3.1.2; numskulls quarrel as to which way the s. shall return J2062.1; pasturing black s. until they become white (penance) Q521.4; peace between s. and wolves K191; why s. is a good runner A2555.1; selling a s. and bringing it back along with the money (task) H1152.1; shearing a flock of s. in one day (task) H1106; why s. do not speak A2231, A2422.2; speaking s. B211.1.1; stolen s. dressed as person K406.1; thief's excuse: bitten by the s. J1391.3.1; three crimes in killing s. with two unborn lambs J1169.9; trickster gets s. for shearing, the dupe pigs K171.5; wager that s. are hogs K451.2; well rises for s. F933.1.3.2; well rises for s. only for rightful owner H251.3.9.2; white s. comes to upper world, black to lower F67; why s. walk with bowed heads: bowed to God A2221.9; witch as s. G211.1.4; wolf locked up with s. J2172.2.2; wolf proposes abolition of dog guards for s. K2061.1.1; wolf sold as a s. K132; wolves' false truce with s. K2010.3; wolves, wild pigs condemned to death for eating s. B275.1.3.2; why s. may keep wool which grows on his forehead A2255.1, A2322.5.

Sheep's head has eaten dumplings J1813.8. — Casting s. eyes at the bride J2462.2; cause of s. walk A2441.1.12; crow sits on s. back, afraid to sit on dog's W121.2.3; hedge to catch s. wool J2060.2; putting money in s. anus J1851.4; thieves claim to be looking at s. teeth J1391.3; test of wife's ability to keep secret: the buried s. head H472.1; tiger in s. clothing stolen by sheep-thief K1621; weaving mantle from one s. wool H1022.4.2; why s. tongue is black A2344.3.1.

Sheepfold. — Ghost laid in s. E437.7.

Sheepskin. — Fox in s. gains admission to the fold and kills sheep K828.1; magic s. *D1025.8; treasure-producing s. B114.1, D1469.11; white s. used as source of light J1961.

Sheet. — Lover escapes behind s. K1521.5.1; milk sack transformed to s. of water D454.5.1; saint stretches protective s. over followers D2163.9; stealing s. from bed on which person is sleeping (task) H1151.3; witch heals child by covering with s. D2161.3.3.1.

Sheets. — Owner and monkey put on s. to frighten K1682.1.

Sheherezade J1185.1.

Sheldrake. — Reincarnation as s. E613.1.1.

Shell transformed to (boat) D452.2.1, (person) D432.2.1. — Blindness cured by s. F952.3.1.1; carrying s. from which ashes fall forms path K321.1; clam s. lures man into sea G308.7; deity arises from s. of darkness A115.6; discourteous answer: tortoise's s. A2231.1.4; fairy lives in s. F225; foolish bargain: good fish for worthless s. J2081.2; ghost sounds conch s. E402.1.3.1; magic cocoanut s. *D985.1; man transformed to s. D233; mankind originates from s. A1246; origin of animal's s. A2312ff.; origin of dents in crab's s. A2312.3; origin of moon from s. A743.1; origin of s. money A1433.3; origin of snail's s. A2312.2; thread tied to ant who pulls it through coils of snail s. H506.4; thumbling hides in s. F535.1.1.10.2; tortoise given hard s. for ferrying goddess A2223.6; transformation when one expresses astonishment at smith drawing water in egg s. D512.1.

Shells. — Origin of s. A2826; sacred s. V1.6.4.2; trickster sacrifices only s. of nuts and inside of dates K171.3.1.

Shellfish. — Devastating s. B16.5.3; dragon as modified s. B11.2.1.4; origin of black scales of s. A2315.1; trickster pinched by s. J2136.4.

Shelter. — Animals grateful for s. B393; animals provide s. B538; curse: lack of s. M443.1; forethought in provision for s. J740.

Sheltering. — Beard s. men from rain F545.1.4; tree s. abandoned girls D1556.2.

Shepherd *P412; who cried "Wolf" too often J2172.1; frightens tiger by threatening report to ass K547.8; -god A453; in God's service H1199.12.1; as helper *N841; as hero L113.1.4; mistaken for ass J1765.1; in palace sickens for country air U135.2; rescues abandoned child R131.3.1; shuts up the lion in the yard with the livestock J2172.2; transformed to bird still calls sheep A2261.1. — Animal as s. for man B292.1; baboon as s. for man B292.1.1; bittern from transformed s. A2261.1, A1965.2; clever s. J1115.9; disguise as s. K1816.6; dog caresses sick sheep but s. knows that he hopes for sheep's death K2061.3; dumb princess brought to speak by s. who insults her H343.1; dwarf conducts s. to hell to collect debt from nobleman F451.5.1.14; escaped lamb delivers himself to s. rather than to slaughter J217.1; fox as s. K934; good s. shears his sheep, does not skin them J531; hungry s. attracts attention J1341.6; is s. known to God? H1292.17; lion leaves sleeping hare to follow the s. J321.3; noble-woman weds s. T121.2; saint's staff as s. D1446.4; shipwrecked s. distrusts the sea J11; wolf almost locked in the stable by the s. J2172.2.1; wolf offers to act as s. *K2061.1.

Shepherd's consecrated staff keeps cow from straying D1446.3. — Origin of s. pipe A1461.6.

Shepherds. — Angel announces Christ's birth to s. V235.1; eagle warns s. that wolf is eating sheep J715.1; God throws sand on lazy s. A2005.

Shepherdess born of egg T542.1.

Sheriff. — Proud s. has only nine farmers in his jurisdiction J2331.1.

Shield in front of otherworld palace F150.3.1; shrieks in battle F995. — Cast of s. annihilates enemy F639.3; child born with s. T552.5.3; clouds as God's s. A1133.4; devil in dragon's head on a s. G303.8.10; engraving s. with unique pattern H1199.4; extraordinary s. F824.2, F839.2; fairy gives invulnerable s. F343.10.3; flaming s. as life token E761.7.9; giant s. F612.3.2; giant's s. F531.4.5.5; giant with millwheel as s. F531.4.1; god's s. A157.4; inscription on s. misinterpreted K511.2; light from s. of cobra A1412.1; magic s. *D1101.1; sword and s. as proxy at wedding T135.3.1; transformation to s. owner's likeness D40.1; turning left side of s. as challenge P556.1.

Shields. — Capture by being pressed between s. R5.2; castles thatched with golden s. F163.1.3; clashing s. in heavens evil omen D1812.5.1.17.2; falling s. as evil omen D1812.5.1.25; god with clouds as s. A137.14.3; precedence shown by position of s. P632.4.1; roaring of s. evil omen D1812.5.1.17.3; roof of s. P552.3.1.

Shift. — Magic s. *D1058.1.

Shifting blame to another J1166; married couples in bed K1318.

Shillings. — Incognito king joins robbers: to take only six s. K1812.2.1.

Shingling the fog X1651.1.

Shining. — Castle of wax, s. like gold F771.1.8; devil has s. teeth G303.4.1.5.1; magic castle s. from afar D1645.3; magic sight by looking at s. object D1821.3.7ff.; moon made from s. fragments A742; origin of s. patches beneath sea A925.7; sun not s. when murder is done F961.1.1; sun s. at night F961.1.5; sun s. for twelve days, nights F961.1.5.1; sword s. as fire, sun F833.4.1; troll bursts in s. sun G304.2.5; well s. at night F718.5.

Shinny. — Deceptive s. match K23; egg as s. ball F878.

Ship, see also **Boat;** becomes small boat D491.7; builder F671; built with a wooden saw J2171.1.1; with devil aboard sinks G303.25.9; of glass in otherworld *F169.3; held back by otherworld women F402.1.13; held back by magic D2072.0.3; of hell A676; magically sunk D2098; moved by sacrifice D2136.8; sails on fog X1651.2; will sink if murderers aboard

N271.10; -spirits F485; in storm saved because of sailors' "Ave Maria" V254.2; summoned by wish D2074.2.3.2; transformed D454.10, (to stone) D471.3; wrapped with feather-beds and canvass and pitched (so as to save it) F1031. — Bells hung at every corner of s. P651; boat expected to grow into s. J2212.7; box transformed to s. D454.1.2; capture by hiding in disguised s. K753.1; capture by taking aboard s. K775.1; color of sails on s. as indication of good or bad news Z140.1; dead body not to be on s. C541.1; demon s. sails against wind F411.3; escape from s. while captors quarrel R216; escape on s. on wheels K611.3; extraordinary s. *F841ff.; fairies stop s. to entice man F302.3.1.2; fire-s. K2364; fish swallows s. F911.4.1; fish rescues s. B541.5; Flying Dutchman's s. E511.2; ghost s. E535.3; giant blows to prevent s. approaching F531.3.1.4; giant's leg stops s. at sea F531.3.1.2; giants' s. Naglfar F531.6.7.1.2; gold, silver shower on king's s. F960.1.1.2; great s. X1061.1; horse that went like a s. J2481; loadstone draws s. to it *F806.1; magic land and water s. D1533.1.1; magic s. *D1123; magic submarine s. D1525; making sails for s. from one bundle of linen H1022.3; making s. of stone H1021.3; man complains of injustice of gods' wrecking s. because of one man's sin U21.3; man magically appears aboard s. D2121.11; money tied on corpse thrown overboard from s. in order to secure burial V64; mountain opens, s. on wheels comes out D1552.4; passenger brings s. bad luck: cast overboard N134.1.5; phantom s. E535.3; pictures that cannot be removed in s. D1654.8; praying that s. sink since prayers never answered J1467.1; pumping out a leaky s. (task) H1023.5; reef is old, s. is new J2212.4; rivals aboard s. thrown overboard when food is gone K527.4; sacrifice to gods holding s. back S263.4.1; sea is salt because of wrecked salt s. A1115.1; seduction by luring woman to look for s. K1339.2.1; seduction by taking aboard s. to inspect wares K1332; sewing together broken s. H1023.7.2; shipman refuses alms: s. turned to stone V421; sick voyagers on s. accused as magicians D1711.12; sight of phantom s. a bad omen D1812.5.1.10; snake becomes s. D425.1.4; strong man carries s. F624.7; strong man holds back s. F637; travelers mistake brushwood at a distance for a s. K1886.4; treasure buried in sunken s. N513.5; vision prevents taking passage on s. which sinks V541; vow to die before surrendering s. M161.4.1; water-spirit holds back s. F420.5.2.7.4; witch raises wind, keeps s. in port G283.1.2.1.

Ship's course left to winds and fate N118.1. — Fairy mistaken for enemy's s. burning K2369.9; magic prevents s. moving D1419.3.

Ships burned to prevent flight R244. — Defending oneself against many s. H1199.8; detonation hurls s. out to sea F1078; devil piles sand in ocean so that s. may run aground G303.9.9.5; fifty s. promised (49 molded out of earth) K236.1; giant fishes for s. G322.1; reeds make s. appear like island K1872.2; sham war threat holds s. back K1771.7.

Shipwreck to avenge self K815.12; as punishment Q552.12. — Animals from transformed survivors of s. A1715.5; bush loses clothes in s.

A2741.4; couple separated in s. reunited N741.2; extraordinary s. F931.5; magic object protects from s. D1388.1f.; mountain-spirit causes s. F460.4.4.7; rescue alone from s. chosen over drowning with goods J222; rescue from s. R138; runes protect against s. D1388.13; separation by s. N317; sham prophecy of s. to leave vacancy K1771.8; Virgin Mary saves from s. V268.4; water-spirit causes s. F420.5.2.7.3; witch causes s. G269.8.

Shipwrecked given piece of gold for death V64.1; man lands on enemy territory N399.1; man repulsed by animals B772; men use false names K1831.1; shepherd distrusts the sea J11. — Bat, diver, and thornbush s. A2275.5.3; disguised s. men kill king K913.1; seaman who defies God s. Q221.4; water-spirits save s. F420.5.1.1.1.

Shirt as chastity index H431.1; made by woman free from trouble, worry H1195. — At betrothal maid makes s. for her lover T61.3; ghost asks to wash s. E412.3.2.1; in return for magic s. hero stays in Ireland M226; luck-bringing s. N135.3; magic forgetting of wife when husband removes s. she has given him D2004.6; magic s. *D1056, (protects against opposition) D1389.7; making s. from piece of linen three inches square (task) H1022.4; making s. from single flax-seed H1022.4.1; man's head is cut off so that the s. sewed together at the neck can be put on him J2161.2; naked ghost asks for s. E412.3.2; Nessus-s. (burns wearer up) D1402.5; sewing magic s. H383.2.2; sewing s. for bridegroom's father H383.2.3; sewing s. from flower petals H1021.9.1; sewing a s. of stone (task) H1021.9; weaving a silk s. from hair (task) H1021.6; weaving s. from piece of thread H1022.2.2; wife lazy: husband has no s. to die in W111.3.5.

Shirts. — Disenchantment by sewing s. for enchanted brothers D753.1; making many s. from one hank of flax (task) H1022.2; Russians wear red s. A1683.1.1; why Russians wear their s. outside their breeches A1683.1; sewing s. to trees J2465.9.

Shock. — Electric s. scares away treasure diggers N561.

Shod. — Coming neither barefoot nor s. (task) H1055; frog wants to be s. J512.12; running horse s. by skillful smith F663.1; transformation to horse by being s. with horseshoes D535.1; witch as horse s. with horseshoes *G211.1.2.

Shoe beating as bride test H386.1; test H36.1. — Asking haystack to clean dirty s. Z41.7.1; bringing lost s. as suitor test H322.4; captive throws his s. at serpent who chokes while he escapes K672; empty s. follows wild hunt E501.10.1; god with thick s. A128.5.1; girl hacks off her heel to get s. on J2131.3.1; lacing bed-clothes to s. J2161.3; magic s. points out road D1313.13; saint's image lets golden s. fall as sign of favor to supplicant D1622.3; shoeless husband threatens wife with s. J1545.3.2.

Shoes, see also **Boot(s), Moccasin(s), Sandal(s), Slipper(s)**; as adultery fee J761.3; buried with dead V67.2; carried into the tree J1521.1; dropped to distract owner's attention K341.6; enable hero to climb stone D1532.3.1. — Big s. in front of the barn K1717; cobbler rewarded for giving s. to poor boy Q42.9; dancing to death in red-hot s. (punishment) Q414.4; dead man asks for s. E412.3.3; devil visible to one who walks in minister's holy s. G303.6.2.4; devil's s. empty G303.4.5.1.2; escape by reversing s. K534; extraordinary s. F823; extraordinary occurrences connected with s. *F1015ff.; fairies make s. for shoemaker F346.1; fairies' horses have round s. *F241.1.4; fool makes s. for animals as well as men, since he expects a cold winter J1873.1; fortune's s. N135.3; hurting feet to save s. J2199.4.1; inverted s. indicate banishment Z174.1; king asleep in mountain will awake when his horse's s. are worn down D1960.2.1; lazy mother given s. of cotton: son knows that she will not wear them out W111.5.1; magic s. *D1065.2; man with earth from his own land in his s. says he is on his own land J1161.3; man puts on s. only when he wades river H591.1; old s. patched with new J2129.5; prisoner's release dependent on charmed s. M202.1.1; promise to be fulfilled when iron s. wear out M202.1; recognition by s. H36.1.1; riddle about wearing new s. H588.13; silver s. F823.4; sleeping in s. to avoid insect bites P2102.1; stag with iron s. J2335; stingy wear out their feet to save s. W152.11; tabu: wearing s. at shrine C51.1.15; tanning s. with bark from saint's tree Q551.6.2.1; time measured by worn iron s. *H1583.1; traveling till iron s. are worn out H1125; vow not to marry till iron s. wear out M136; wandering till iron s. are worn out (punishment) Q502.2; wearing enemy's s. on shoulders L416; wearing s. on pilgrimage tabu C99.2; why s. worn only wading river H591.1; wolves lick saint's s. B251.2.3; woman sells favors for new s. T455.3.1; worn-out s. as proof of long journey *H241.

Shoemaker, see also **Cobbler** P453. — Devil as s. G303.3.1.18; fairies make shoes for s. F346.1; repartee between s., ruling lord J1289.7.

Shoemaking. — Origin of s. A1454.

Shooting, see also **Shot**; contest *H1591, (with bride) H332.1.5, (on wager) N55, (won by deception) K31; dead antelope until it will come to fool J1909.2; drives away ogre G584; at enemy's reflection in water J1791.5.1; object breaks spell G271.4.8; star (as angel) V231.2, (as good omen) D1812.5.2.6; (origin of) A788.2, (signifies a birth) E741.1.2, (signifies a death) *E741.1.1; through iron with arrow H1562.13. — Bad luck follows man s. stork N250.1; cowboy s. injured wife J1919.9; disarming by a s. test K631.2; disenchantment by s. D712.7; dwarf king prevents a father from s. his son F451.5.1.16; dwarfs resentful of mortals s. at birds above Hibichenstein F451.4.4.1; enemies s. at hat held outside shelter K631.3; fire beams s. from devil's eyes G303.4.1.2.3; island created by s. arrow A955.2; liar's s. boast involves odd number X905; man s. into wreath of mist brings down fairy *F302.4.1; resuscitation by s. arrow E61; revenant forced away by s. E439.1; suitor contests: s. H331.4; tabu: s. at consecrated wafer C55.2; test of paternity: s. at father's corpse *H486.2; wishing by s. star D1761.1.1.

Shop. — Animal guards s. B576.5; ass in potter's s. J973; creator opens s., distributes crafts and professions from it A1440.1.

Shore, see Seashore.

Short, dangerous vs. long, sure road J266; magistrate wears high helmet X142.4; pregnancy T573; -sighted (judgments) M20ff., (wish) J2072. — Absurd s.-sightedness J2050—J2199; why animal has s. (tail) A2378.4, (tongue) A2344.1; hair robe "not too long and not too s." J1161.8.1; why hog has s. snout A2335.4.1; why lynx has s., blunt nose A2335.2.2; magic object causes members to grow long or s. D1376; murderer cursed with s. life Q556.10.1; taking the s.-cut J2119.2.1; time seems s. to those who play, long for those who wait U261; vegetables which mature in miraculously s. time F815.1; "way s. yet long" J21.5.3.

Shortened. — Arm s. for breaking tabu C946; day magically s. D2146.1.2; life s. by incontinence T317.0.1; night magically s. D2146.2.3.

Shortest. — Hunting tabu on s. day C636; straight path not always s. J2119.2.

Shortness of life U250ff.

Shot, see also **Shooting.** — Devil s. with silver gun G303.25.7; giant s. into upper world by means of magic bow *F54; king unwittingly s. by own order K1612.2; lie: hunter's remarkable s. X1122; lucky s. with arrow (foot and ear of deer) N621; monster s. and followed into lower world F102.1; on rainy day when s. will not go man flogs his s. J1864; stars from arrows s. at sky A763.1; thousand at one s. K1741.2; youth having s. raven takes feather to raven's sister H78.2.

Shots. — Spirit throws back s. fired at it F473.6.5.

Shoulder. — Divination by bone from sheep's s. D1311.10; dwarf carries his knocked-off leg on his s. F451.6.13; giantess throws her breasts over her s. *F531.1.5.1; Hercules tells driver to put his s. to wheel J1034; looking back over left s. tabu C331.1; magic sight by looking over right s. D1821.3.2; man searches for axe which he carries on s. J2025.1; mark on moon's s. A751.5.3; mountain-wife has breasts so long that she throws them over her s. *F460.1.2; rider takes the mealsack on his s. to relieve the ass of his burden J1874.1; witch power from looking over s. G224.6; at communion witches spit out wine over s. G285.1.

Shoulders. — Armless people have legs growing from their s. F516.1.1; arms magically fall from s. D1403.3; bird rests on person's s. B575.2; birth from man's s. T541.13; cross between s. as sign of royalty (nobility) H71.5; fairies have breasts long enough to throw over their s. *F232.2; giant three spans between brows and three yards between s. F531.2.2; hills are loads from hero's s. A962.10; placing mountain on s. H1149.9; snakes issue from dragon's s. B11.2.7.

Shout remains in air three days F688.2.

Shouts. — Giants' s. are storms or great noise F531.3.8; throwing contest: trickster s. K18.1; wild hunt heralded by s. of huntsmen E501.13.5.

Shouted. — New creation s. away A636; two person believe other must be s. at X111.3.

Shouting after bathing leads to adventure N784; from forbidden place H1199.3. — Battle-s. A1341.1; mysterious s. in glen F756.5; resuscitation by s. at dead E26.

Shovel. — Magic s. *D1205.

Shoving lazy child with knives, killing him J2465.3.1.

Shower of stones seems snowfall to giant F531.5.4.1. — Extraordinary s. F962; god transformed to s. of gold D235.1; gold, silver s. at royal birth F960.1.1.2; prayer for s. of gold V57.2.

Showers. — Fiery s. in hell A671.2.4.3; why the sea is salt: heavy rain s. on ashes of wood burnt by primeval fire A1115.3.

Showing fairy gifts tabu F348.9.1. — Executioner s. hero how to use gallows K715; king s. self in public once a year P14.21; wine s. through woman's white throat F647.6; woman's beauty s. through seven veils F574.1.2.

Shreds. — Trail of s. of dress R135.0.4.

Shrew blows nose into snout A2211.5. — Why s. dies on road A2233.1.3, A2468.1; taming the s. T251.2.

Shrew-mouse. — Tabu to kill s. C92.1.3.

Shrewish wife T251. — Marrying s. wife as punishment Q599.2.

Shriek. — Dragon's s. makes land barren *B11.12.2; giant's loud s. G158; magic object compels person to s. D1419.1.

Shrieking plants, animals D2091.12; shield F995; sword D1081.4. — Contest in s. or whistling K84.1; magic compels s. D1419.1; plant s. when uprooted F992; spirits hover in air s. over battle F418; three-legged cat s. over grave permits finding of treasure N542.2.

Shrike as birds' king B242.1.5. — Why the s. is disliked A2522.2.

Shrimp. — Color of s. A2411.5.7; man becomes s. D179.4; marriage to s. B603.1; origin of s. A2171.4.

Shrine bleeds F991.4; of saint supresses pestilence V221.0.13. — Begging cripples hurry away from s. lest they be healed and lose their livelihood X531; cure at s. of Blessed Virgin D2161.5.2.1; profaning s. forbidden C51.1; tabu: leaving corpse at s. C51.1.14; tabu: wearing shoes at s. C51.1.15; treasure hidden in religious s. N514; vow to build s. M183.1.

Shrines V113. — Saint dispels devils from s. V356.1.

Shrinking of magic dog D491.1.3. — Lies about s. X1785.

Shroud alone left in grave E411.0.7. — Dead arises when s. bursts and pursues attendant E261.2; devil in place of dead man in s. G303.18.2; drunk man lying under his bed thinks he is lying in his s. X811; living man in dead man's s. E463.

Shrouds. — Corpses laid by s. E456.

Shrubs grow after sky lifted A625.2.5. — Sundry characteristics of s. A2792.

Shutting sun up in pit A721.0.2. — Fowls never s. doors at night A2433.4.6; husband rebukes wife and paramour for not s. door K1569.2.

Shuttle. — Magic s. *D1185; making a boat from splinters of spindle and s. (task) H1022.7.

Siamese twins F523.

Sibyll as prophet M301.21.

Sick crew accused as magicians K2129.2; hero overcomes antagonist L311.1; hung in well to cool off: drown J2412.6; lion K961; man offers deity more bulls than he owns K231.3.5; men hesitate to take sacrament, die V39.8. — Attendance on s. rewarded Q57; cauterizing "s." wheel J2412.7; curse: children to be s. M460.1; cruelty to s. persons punished Q285.2; deaf man visits the s. X111.9; deduction: bread is made by a s. woman J1661.1.3; disguise as s. man *K1818; dog caresses s. sheep K2061.3; dwarfs become s. F451.3.5.2; false repentance of s. U236; healing s. as task H1199.2; helpful animal cares for s. master B536; lion licks s. man J413.1; love-compelling man made s. of bargain D1904; magic sickness from wounding s. person D2064.6; mother is cutting off heads of well to cure s. H583.4.3; numskull makes himself s. J2134; punishment: animals become s. Q551.4.1; race won by deception: sham-s. trickster K11.5; reductio ad absurdum: father is s. from snake-bite in winter H1023.3.1; river from blood of s. F162.2.13; roof taken off above s. man who cannot die E722.2.3; sham s. man aroused by beating K1676; stingy man's wife prays husband become s. W152.16; transformation to s. man D53.1; well man made to believe that he is s. J2317.

Sickening. — Boy s. at mother's death P231.1; shepherd in palace s. for country air U135.2; spouse s. at separation T213.

Sickle bought at great cost given back J2514; with life in it E772; put into water to cure fever J1959.1.1; told to cut by itself J1881.1.6. — Alleged self-operating s. K119.1.2; magic s. D1206.1.

Sickly. — Changeling is s. F321.1.2.3.

Sickness, see also **Disease, Illness, Plague;** ascribed to quarreling wines J1891.1; because men too happy A1346.2.3; from love T24.1; from meeting ghost E265.1; brought on ship causes accusation as magicians D1711.12; or weakness for breaking tabu *C940ff.; personified Z112. — Animal's flesh as cure for s. K961; bringing s. to certain tribe H1199.2.1; devil in God's absence puts s. in Adam's body A1293; feigned s., see under **Illness,** feigned; magic s. *D2064ff., (because of Evil Eye) D2064.4, (as punishment remitted) Q572, (prevents rape) T321.5, (as punishment) Q551.6; magic toad under king's bed causes s. *B177.1.1; moon's waning caused by her s. A755.3; quest for only person curing s. H1319.1; sacrifice frees moon from s. A755.3.1; sham s., see under **Illness,** feigned; theft by reporting relative's s. K343.1.2; wandering soul cause of s. E721.3; witch causes s. G263.4; witch pretending s. and kicking helper into pit G269.1.1; wood-spirits cause s. F441.6.1.

Side made numb by ghost E542.3. — Birth through mother's s. T584.1; boy born with one s. flesh and one iron T551.4; child born beautiful on one s., hairy on other T551.4.1; conception through mother's s. T517.2; culture hero snatched from mother's s. A511.1.1; do not leave my s.

(youth obeys command to absurd lengths) J2516.4; druid ugly on one s.,
beautiful on other D2031.4.1; fairy has one s. green F233.1.1; lips on s.
of face F544.1.3; man with one s. of stone (iron) F525.1.1; man with
only one s. F525.1; objects on one s. of palisade of otherworld garden
black, on other white F162.1.2.3; stitch in s. from being told about
hearing a man chopping wood F647.8.1.1.

Sides. — Tearing out person's s. S187.1.

Siege. — Enemy induced to give up s. K2365; king occupies s. perilous
H41.9.

Sieve protection against witches G272.6. — Formula: as many children
as holes in a s. Z75; mountains from breaking of God's s. *A971.2;
murdered person's ashes put through s. S139.2.2.8; special power of
chaste woman: carrying water in s. *H413.3; task: carrying water in s.
H1023.2; thief detected by s. and shears H251.3.3; witch travels in s.
G241.4.3; witches use s. for a boat G249.3; well like a s. F718.10.

Sighs. — Five s. for our sins Z71.3.1; origin of tears and s. A1344.

Sight, see also **Seeing;** of dead woman spinning drives people insane
E561.1; of fairies fatal F363.3; lost by magic D2062.2ff.; of magic
twigs gives foreknowledge of day's events D1311.4.0.1.1; of magic wheel
causes blindness D1331.2.5; of mermaid bad omen D1812.5.1.9; never
seen before: oil pot broken with sword J2469.5.2; of old home reawakens
memory and brings about return from otherworld *D2066.2; of phantom
ship a bad omen D1812.5.1.10; restored by animal B516; restored by
magic D2161.3.1, F952; restored as reward Q161.1; -shifting caused by
magic D1331.4ff.; tests H1575; of wild hunt renders person insane
*E501.18.6; of woman as source of sin T336. — Animals have second s.
B120.0.1; boy loses his s. (no butter on bread) J1561.4.2; cat with
remarkable s. B181.1.1; contest between runner swift as thought and one
swift as s. F681.3.1; disenchantment by s. of old home D789.3; enemies
caused to lose s. of each other K1886.2.1; frog-woman disenchanted by s.
of water D789.3.1; herbs restore s. D1505.1; love at first s. T15; love
through s. of picture T11.2; loss of s. for breaking tabu C943; insanity
from seeing strange s. *D2065.2; magic object restores s. *D1505ff.;
magic power of long distance s. D1820.2; magic s. *D1820ff., (of blind
man) D1820.1.1; marvelous runner swift as s. F681.4; object gives magic
s. D1331.1; person of remarkable s. F642ff.; poor s. of elephant
A2332.6.7; princess restoring blind man's s. R161.2; prophecy: death at
s. of son H341.1.7.1; recognition by miraculous s. of seer H184; second
s. from spirit of dead D1821.8; shooting test won by deception: proof of
good s. K31.2; speaking of extraordinary s. forbidden C423.2; tiger's short s.
by day, good sight at night A2491.4; unusual s. bad omen D1812.5.1.22.

Sights. — Extraordinary s. in otherworld F171; horrible s. in hell A671.2.

Sign of great plague F493.5; hung out informing brothers whether mother
has borne boy or girl T595; language H607; of the Cross V86. — Conversation by s. language mutually misunderstood J1804; devil made to
disappear by making s. of the cross G303.16.3.4; disenchantment by s. of

cross D788; flame issuing from mouth as s. of royalty H41.4; magic results from s. of the cross *D1766.6; magic s. D1299.1, (assures warriors will not flee from battle) D1359.5; permanent s. of disobedience for breaking tabu *C910ff.; severed finger as s. of crime H57.2.1; stone bursts as s. of unjust judgment *D1318.1.1; touching head s. of accepting bargain P675; unacquainted lovers converse in s. language T42.1; wrong s. put out leads to boys' leaving home N344.1.

Signs before Judgment Day A1002.2; of royalty H71. — Weather s. D1812.5.0.15.

Signal. — Lovers' s. T41.3; mantle used as s. for rendezvous with lady is used by serving-man to deceive her K1317.1; milk in stream as s. H135.2; theft s. given in foreign language K358; wife's pre-arranged s. catches paramour K1569.5.

Signature forged to obtain money K362.7.

Silence in fairyland C405; points to guilt J1141.8; under punishment breaks power of enchantment *D1741.3; wager J2511, (leads to sham death) J2511.1.2; wagerers arrested as thieves J2511.2. — Church bell cannot be raised because s. is broken V115.1.3.1; disenchantment by maintaining s. D758f.; hanging for s. about treasure Q413.7; has never regretted s. but often regretted speech J1074.1; Island of S. F129.4.6; maintaining s. as ascetic practice V462.1; maintaining s. in snake pit H1506; power of wild hunt evaded by s. E501.17.4.4; priest induced to betray secrets of confessional: money then exacted from him for s. K443.8; princess to break s. H343; seven days s. at world's end A1057; trickster exacts promise of marriage as price of s. after having seen a princess naked *K443.6; trickster sells s. after lying with princess K443.6.2; value of s. J1074; wager to s. the washerwomen of Bloys N76; two years' s. imposed on suitor H317.2.

Silent dead E545.0.2; hero L124.2; man asks king what to say to fool J1714.5; person F569.3; wife T272. — Causing s. person to speak H1194.0.1; child s. till seven L124.1; during the s. period (why nun did not call for help) J1264.4; elements s. at Nativity V211.1.5; fool passes as wise man by remaining s. N685; girl who cannot keep s. thereby provokes her rival to admit unchastity K1275; philosopher keeps s. J1074.1.1; quarrelsome wife conquered by s. husband T256.1; saint s. by holding stone in mouth V73.6.2; soldier s. before king as before all stupid persons J1369.5; with a s. person one is alone J817.3.

Silk as battle clothing C878.2.1. — Achieving kingship by bringing s. H1355.4; making large shawl from s. of one cocoon H1022.4.3; making peacock of s. H1021.11; origin of s. A2811; quest for princess transformed into skein of s. H1381.3.4; transformation to skein of s. D264; wearing s. tabu C878.2; weaving a s. shirt from hair (task) H1021.6.

Silkworm's origin A2182.1.

Sill. — Ghost cannot cross new door s. E434.10.

Silver animals B102ff.; apple F813.1.2; boat F841.1.9; bullet (protects against

giants, ghosts, and witches) D1385.4, (injures devil) G303.16.19.14; castle
F771.1.2; chairs F786.1; coffin F852.3; coins from pumpkin A1433.2.1;
-colored fairy F233.2; demanded of saint disappears Q552.18.1; dish becomes wooden D475.3.5; floors in otherworld F165.3.3; in gun releases
curse M429.7; hair F555.2; hairs as sign of royalty H71.2; in chain increases in fire D1671; king and attendants F521.3.4.1; kingdom F707.2;
leaps into magic pitcher D1469.9; magically hides self D1555.3; magically produced D2103; mast F841.2.1; object becomes black (life token)
E761.4.2f.; oar F841.2.3; pear F813.4; pillar H1322.1; seeds pave city
F761.5.2; staff kills E64.1.1.1; statue of animal F855.3; tree F811.1.2;
wall around otherworld F148.2; weapon F830.1. — Animal with s. horn
B15.3.2; animals with s. members B101ff.; bird with gold head, s. wings
B15.7.3, B101.1.1; bow of gold, s., and copper F836.1; castles of s.
F163.1.4; city of s. in heaven A661.1.2; dead usurer fed molten s. by
devil Q273.1.1; dogs of gold and s. F855.3.2; dog vomits gold and s.
B103.4.3; dress of gold, s., color of sun, moon, and stars F821.1.5; dress
of gold, s., and diamond bells F821.3; dwarf king has s. miner's torch
bright as sun F451.7.4; fairies give woman s. spoons F342.1; fish of s.
B102.4.1; floors of s. in otherworld dwelling F165.3.3; fortress of s. in
otherworld F163.5.2; fowls eat s. F989.22.1; gold and s. combed from
hair D1454.1.1; heart breaks at third drink from s. canister F1041.1.1.1;
house of s. F163.3.2; island with rampart of gold and palisade of s.
F731.3; king is worth twenty-nine pieces of s. H711.1; man shoots the
devil with a s. gun G303.25.7; moon is hare covered with s. A759.4;
mountain of s. F752.2; objects transformed to s. D475.3; origin of s.
coins A1433.2; person with s. body F521.3.4; person with s. horns
F511.3.1; pillars of s. and glass in otherworld *F169.1; reincarnation
as s. E645.1; shower of s. F962.8.1; towers of steel, s., and gold F772.2.2;
transformation: objects to s. D475.3; tree with s. branches D1461.0.2;
wall of s. about otherworld F148.2; wattling of s. in otherworld
dwelling F165.3.4.

Silversmith restless until silver mixed with alloy U138.1. — Voice changed
by work of s. F556.2.

Silvery. — Dwarfs have s. white hair F451.2.4.2.

Simian transformed to person D318. — Man transformed to s. D118.

Simile. — Proverbial s. Z62.

Simon Magus a druid P427.0.4. — Contest of St. Peter with S. V351.3.1.

Simony V466.

Simorg B31.5.

Simpleton, see also **Fool, Numskull;** dissuades from suicide J628; fools
robbers into sharing loot L141.2; put to ordeal by holy water H222.2.
— Obscene tricks played on s. wishing to marry K1218.9; owl's hoot
misunderstood by lost s. J1811.1.

Simplicity. — Woman loses magic when s. lost D1749.2.

Simultaneous births T589.7.

Simultaneously. — Father and daughter die s. P234.2; tree bears fruit, flower, leaf s. F811.16.

Sin personified Z127. — Anger is s. J153.2; calamity as punishment for s. A1003; cities of s. F769.2; confession brings forgiveness of s. V21; confession without giving up s. punished V25.2; dead cannot rest because of a s. E411; dream reveals s. to saint D1817.2.1; forgiveness for s. for acts of charity Q171.1; giants cause s. F531.5.15; imagined penance for imagined s. J1551.2; immunity from punishment for s. as reward Q171; magic detection of s. D1817.0.5; magic power of person without s. D1714; monk escapes s. by living alone J495; nature of s. U230ff.; "never publish a man's s." J21.52.4; no carnal s. in otherworld F167.10; only man without s. can see God V510.2; pebble for each s. J2466.1; priest drags heavy sack symbolic of s. H606; penance for s. A1549.4; reincarnation as punishment for s. E606.1; sacrifice after s. V17.2; saying of "Aves" obliterates s. *V254.1; sexual desire as original s. T8; sight or touch of woman as source of s. T336; test of s. H263; wild huntsmen wander because of s. E501.3ff.

Sins determine size of hell fires E755.2.4.1. — All s. since the birth of Christ J1743.1; children punished for fathers' s. P242; confession of s. V20ff.; devil accuses congregation of s. G303.24.1; devil's two books for noting s. G303.24.1.9; eight deadly s. Z71.16.1.1; five sighs for our s. Z71.3.1; fox confesses s. but is immediately ready to steal again K2055; fox and wolf forgive each other's s. but punish ass U11.1.1; hiding s. from God J1738.8; man's s. forgiven when he kills a greater sinner Q545; origin of penance for s. A2835; person obnoxious for his s. unnamed C433.1; saint can reveal hidden s. V223.3; reward for confessing s. Q36.1; Seven Deadly S. Z71.5.6.2; three s. of hermit J485; world fire as punishment for s. A1031.1.

Sincerity. — Suitor's s. tested H314.

Sinful city burnt Q486.1.1. — Devil and s. priest disappear amid blaze of fire in river G303.17.2.4; host taken away from s. priest V31.1.

Singer repaid with promise of reward: words for words J1551.3. — Bad s. thinks he is talented: driven from theatre J953.2.

Singers. — Devil in roof of church into which he thrusts voices of loud s. Q554.2; magic identification of s. D1819.6.

Singing, see also **Song;** animal B214.1; apple D1615.3; blossoms F979.12; bones *E632ff.; at death's approach J2461.1.2.1; like leader: sing his distress call J2417.1; mountain F755.2; raises water from tank D2151.5.1; rice-pot D1615.6; snake brings death K445.2; snowshoes D1615.5; snails rebuked J1885; tabu C481; tree D1615.1; water D1615.4; at wedding T136.3.2; wolf's power over humans Z33.4.2. — Animals s. songs of praise B251.2ff.; automatic s. doll D1620.0.1.2; birds' s. ceases at revelation B251.8.1; bird shows way by s. B151.2.0.3; boy learns s. from spirits F403.2.3.3; camel and ass together captured because of ass's s. J2137.6; choral s. accompanies saint V222.3; contest in s. H503.1; dead s.

45*

E546; death respite while s. K551.3.2.1; deer summoned by s. D2074.1.1.2; devil s. on grave G303.9.8.3; devil vexing friars caused to repent by s. "Te sanctum dominum" G303.24.3; dupe loses booty through s. J2351.3; dupe s. on trickster's body K827.3; dwarfs dislike s. of hymns F451.5.9.2; echo of giantess's s. F531.3.8.4; embryos s. in womb T575.1.5.1; fairies s. F262.1; fool s. in small bathroom J2237; ghost s. E402.1.1.4; huldra s. F460.2.13; humor of bad s. X145; husband s. about adultery K1556.1; magic s. D2173; magic object acquired by s. D858; magic results from s. *D1781; magic s. object *D1615ff.; men rulers s. in their houses T252.5; mermaid's s. causes girl to sleep, drown B81.11; mermaid s. in choir B81.3.2; mermaid s. divinely in church B81.13.6; minstrel's birds s. accompaniment F262.3.2; ogre s. constantly G652; parson's s. reminds woman of goat X436; pet swan saves self by s. death song N651; poet s. after death E371.3; punishment for s. worldly songs Q391; pursuer s. while captive escapes K606.0.1; quest for s. (apple) H1333.3.4, (tree) H1333.1.1, (water) H1321.5; rain produced by s. D2143.1.2; rescue from ogre by means of s. G555; sheep encourage wolf's s. K561.2; six dwarfs listen to s. by confirmed children F451.5.21; stars s. together A767; storm because of bird's s. D2141.0.6; thief hears owner's s., thinks self detected N611.4; waves s. gives information D1310.7; water raised from tank by s. D2151.5.1; wolf s. as dog's guest J581.1.

Singeing. — Animal characteristics from burning or s. *A2218ff.

Single combat (between bird chiefs) B264, (judicial) H218, (to prove valor) H1561.2; person entering house after sunset tabu C752.1.3. — Dogs in s. file in wild hunt E501.4.1.8; invulnerability for s. day D1845.1; pledge to say but a s. phrase brings accusation of crime M175; skillful axe-man cuts down trees with s. stroke F666ff.; tabu: going to assembly in company of s. warrior C864.2; vow not to be killed by s. opponent M162.

Single-handed. — Annihilating army s. (task) H1135.

Sink. — Magic s. hole *D933.

Sinking of bodies of water in primitive abyss A910.3; of church and congregation to bottom of sea F941.2.2; of earth as punishment Q552.2; into earth as curse M448; into earth as punishment C984.7; of ship with devil aboard G303.25.9. — Building s. into earth F941; demons s. in sea D1400.1.23.1; divining rod s. at place where tribe shall settle D1314.2.1; heathen idols s. into earth V356.2.1; island s. in punishment Q552.2.3.2.3; lies about s. X1733; magic object s. if person guilty H251.3.7; magic veil keeps man from s. in water D1388.0.2; man s. (into earth) F942, (into mud) D2092; rats leave s. ship B757; vision prevents taking passage on s. ship V541; witch s. ships G283.1.2.3.

Sinkings. — Extraordinary s. F940ff.

Sinless. — Only s. person may touch dead H1558.12; quest for s. couple's son H1381.4.

Sinner confesses before sinning, pardoned V21.5; reformed by visits to heaven, hell V522; thinking of God saved V525; wanders between earth and heaven E411.0.4. — Angel holds nose when handsome s. passes U119.3; dead man begs s. not be buried atop him E545.9; devil harries repentant s. G303.9.4.9; extraordinary island upon which no s. can die (be buried) F747; hand of s. sticks out of grave E411.0.1; other dead drive s. from graveyard E411.0.5; repentant s. comforted by angel V235.2; unquiet dead s. taken to priest for absolution E411.0.2.

Sinner's grave cursed, rolls M411.14.1; punishment: rain or famine J229.13. — Devil leaves s. body G303.18.0.1; tree from s. grave E631.0.6.

Sinners to be burnt on Doomsday M341.2.7.1; endure hell tortures for one year Q560.3; go to heaven as reward for hymn Q172.5; going to heaven numbered by hairs in saint's chasuble M364.3.1. — Devils tormenting s. in hell E755.2.7; decrying of female s. A1556.3.1; protection of s. by confession V20.1; souls of s. spend seven years under water E751.5.

Sinning. — Eating what is stolen without s. H1151.19; god controls mortals' s. A185.14; lion sent to kill man: frees him from possibility of s. and sojourn in purgatory J225.2.

Sion appointed chief for mountains A1187.

Siren *B53ff.; in mermaid form B53.0.1. — Curse: to be swallowed by a s. M434; woman becomes s. D199.3.

Sirens and Odysseus J672.1.

Sirius as bad omen D1812.5.1.6.1.

Sister Beatrice K1841.1; and brother *P253; -brother incest A1331.2, A1337.0.7, A2006, G37, M365.3, Q520.3, T415; -brother marriage of first parent's children A1552.3; escapes to stars from brother R321.1; faithful to transformed brother P253.2; hidden in thigh F1034.3.1; honors brother only in prosperity W175.1; in-law *P264; is mourning last year's laughter H583.5; rescues brother(s) R158; secures blessing due another K1988.1; as wager N2.6.1. — Abandoned s. rescued by brothers S357; accidental meeting of brother and s. N734; begetting child with s. by earbox J1919.7; blood of brother and s. will not mingle *F1075; brother as deer seeks s. D647.1; brother accused of impregnating s. K2121.1; brother flogs unchaste s to death Q458.2.1; brother and s. arrange marriage of their unborn children M146.4; brothers eat their s. G73.1; cruel brothers forced to beg from abused s. L432.1; dwarfs adopt girl as s. F451.5.1.2; earth from murder of first brother and s. A831.4; girls eat their s. G73; husband, wife disguised as brother, s. K1839.14; insects from brother-s. incest A2006; magic object received from s. D815.4; man in love with own s. learns her identity N631.3.2; man unwittingly ravishes his own s. T471.1; moon, sun are s. and brother A736.1.4.2; only youngest brother helps s. L32; quest for lost s H1385.6; rescue of s. from ogre G551; resuscitation by s. E125.2; rich man ignores poor s.

J411.11; riddle: white brother, black s. H722.1; rivers as offspring of Ocean and his s. A938; sacrifice of s. S260.1.2; seven brothers and one s. Z71.5.1; sun s. and moon brother A736.1.1; sun brother and moon s. A736.2; treacherous s. *K2212; treacherous s.-in-law K2212.2; vow to find vanished s. M155.2; woman drugs s., substitutes for her with lover K1317.6.1.

Sister's — Dead brother reproves s. pride E226.1; dead s. return E325; brother qualifies as s. bridegroom H310.2.

Sisters *P252; and brothers do not marry A1552.1; curse child by Thor M437.2; in love with same man T92.8; rescue sisters R157. — Accidental meeting of s. N743; brothers and s. *P250ff.; guessing which of veiled s. has golden hair H511.2; lisping s. K1984.1; man married to several s. T145.1.3; moon ate up her s. A753.1.4.2; queen sets tasks to disenchant s. H933.2; sun and moon as s. A736.4; seven brothers marry seven s. Z71.5.8; three witch s. G201; wit combat among s. for dowry: their pregnancies H507.4.

Sister-in-law tabu C172. — Advances to s. punished Q242.3; brother-in-law seduces s. T425; cruel s. S55; name of s. tabu C435.2.1.

Sisters-in-law assign tasks H934.2. — Chaste sleeping with six s. T355; guarding six s. as task H1199.17.2; tasks set by s. H939.3.

Sisyphus's punishment Q501.1.

Site. — Building s. for church miraculously indicated V111.3; building s. determined by animal B155.1.0.1.

Sitting on eggs (to finish their hatching) J1902.1, (without breaking them) H962.1; on hero saves him K649.1.3; on mounds tabu C755.5; on pillow-covered egg H1568.1; on a sunbeam *F1011.2; in uncomfortable position as penance Q541; up with corpse as test H1461 — Avoiding s. on foot of couch H506.6; brother s. between heaven and earth (in tree) H583.3.2; devil prevents moving of little stone by s. on it G303.9.9.1; dupe s. on hot stone K1032; dupe s. on sharp stones K1116; dupe tricked into s. on hot iron K1074; fairies kill mortals by s. on them F364.1; for six months bride only s. in husband's house T165.7; future learned by s. on hide D1812.3.1; giants s. on mountains to wash feet in stream below F531.3.9; God finds the devil s. under a tree G303.1.2.1; magic power by s. D1733.4; move stool before s. on it J21.34; repression of lust through s. in water T317.1; mermaid s. on knight's bedpost B81.5; thumbling drives wagon by s. in horse's ear F535.1.1.1; vow against s. on father's seat until revenged M152.2.

Siva. — Brahma takes men to S. F12.3.

Six characteristics of demons G302.4.1; children at a birth T586.1.1.1; dwarfs listen to singing by confirmed children F451.5.21; -headed dragon B11.2.3.3; -headed giant F531.1.2.2.4; -headed man F511.0.2.4; -headed ogre G361.1.3; -headed ogre slain G512.8.3; -legged animal F451.4.3.9; -legged horse B15.6.3.1.1; months' respite from unwelcome marriage T151.1. — Animal with one head, two bodies, s. legs B15.7.11; devil drives s. he-goats G303.7.7; devil has s. wings G303.4.2.1; earthborn men with s. arms F516.2.1; formulistic number: s. Z71.4; giant with s. arms F531.1.6.7.2; giants fifty feet tall with footprints s. feet long F531.2.1.2; god with s. faces A173.2.1.4; incognito king joins robbers: to take only s. shillings K1812.2.1; king questions s. doctors J171.2; mountain-man must die s. times F460.2.12; persons (animals) with s. eyes F512.2.1; prophet speaks s. nights a year M301.0.2; universe created in s. days A601.2; what s. things are not worth doing H871.

Sixteen. — Death at s. M341.1.4.1; fish killed by hero, cut into s. pieces A972.7; formulistic number: s. Z71.10.

Sixth toe cut off K512.2.4.1. — Magic created on s. day D803.1; storms in s. heaven A1130.2; when crows are five years old they start their s. year (riddle) H865.

Sixty. — Carpet s. miles square F783.1; formulistic number: s. Z71.13; giant with s. daughters in big wedding X1071; king with s. thousand sons T586.2.2; prophecy: death at s. M341.1.4.5; wood of s. trees nourishing three hundred men apiece F812.2.

Sixteen hundred as formulistic number Z71.16.7.

Sixty thousand Jewish souls in heaven E755.1.4.

Size of animals' eyes A2332.3ff.; changed at will D631; -changing god A120.2; of giant F531.2ff.; of object transformed D480ff.; of revenant E422.3. — Ancient animal squeezed: hence small s. A2213.1; animal's s. increased by stretching A2213.3; battle fury changes warrior's s. F1041.16.6.2; bride test: s. of feet H365; castle of extraordinary s. F771.8; demons' s. changed at will G302.3.0.1; devil's thumb the s. of two fists G303.4.3.2; doubling the s. of the earth A853.1; effects of age and s. absurdly applied J2212; fairies' s. F239.4; magic change of person's s. D55; magic object changes persons's s. D1377; person the s. of a thumb F535.1; trolls the s. of ten or twelve year old child F455.2.1.

Skating avoided over water when spirits are offended C41.3.1.

Skein. — Quest for princess transformed into s. of silk *H1381.3.4

Skeins. — Traveling till two s. of thread are unwound (task) H1125.1.

Skeleton in closet U115; giant G124. — Bone becomes s. D457.12.2; ghost as s. E422.1.11.4; ghost s. reveals murderer E231.2; lover's s. hung in adulteress's room Q478.1.3; origin of human s. A1312.

Skeletons. — Land of s. E485.1.

Skeptic kicked by sacrificial animal V346.

Skis. — Flight on s.: two on one pair R241.

Skiing. — God of s. A459.1; sacrifice for good s. V17.4.1.

Skill as suitor test H326. — Bride test: domestic s. H383; brothers having extraordinary s. rescue princess R166; fairy's remarkable s. F273; loss of s. D2099.1; magic object gives s. D1343; origin of games of s. A1468; remarkable s. F660ff.; son surpasses father in s. L142.3; test of s. H1563, (in handiwork) H504.

Skills. — Lie: extraordinary s. X960.

Skillful companions F601.0.1; companions create woman: to whom does she belong? *H621. — Fairies as s. smiths F271.3; trolls s. as smiths F455.3.1; winner of most s. princess to be king P11.2.3.

Skin changes color because of broken tabu C985; of magic pig heals wounds B184.3.2.3; of murdered person found in enemy's house S114.1; like snow suitor test H312.5. — Animal jumps out of s. so only s. caught K525.4; animal slips out of s. F1088.4; animal with unusual s. B15.7.10; animal's food-producing s. B531.3; animal's s. revolves, while flesh, bones stay still B738; ass in lion's s. unmasked when he raises his voice J951.1; barber kills child; blames thin s. J1166.1; beautification by s. removal D1866.2; bluff: digging canal instead of bringing water in s. K1741.3.1; boats of s. unsuccessful C841.0.1; boy hidden under s. R318.1; burning s. disenchants D793.2; change of animal's and man's s. A1281.2.1; contest: scratching s. off each other K83.2; dead husband's s. worn to seduce wife K1311.0.2; not to destroy animal s. of enchanted person too soon *C757.1; devil blows s. off man who belongs to him and goes into the s. G303.18.3; devil in place of dead man in dead man's s. G303.18.2; devil stands in church door and writes down names of his own people on sheep s. G303.24.1.4; devil writes faults of man on goat s. G303.24.1.2; devil unpeels woman's s. G303.20.5; disenchantment by hiding s. D721.2; disenchantment by removing s. D721; donning s. makes woman fleet D1936.1; escape by dressing in animal (bird) s. *K521.1; feathered s. magically grafted to bald head D2161.3.4.1; giants dressed in s. F531.4.7.1; girl hidden in s. of her dead mother R318; guessing origin of certain s. H522.1; hedgehog's s. reward for good deed A2220.1; impostor dresses in s. of his victim K1941; jay borrows cuckoo's s. A2241.6; jay in peacock's s. unmasked J951.2; magic bag made from s. of crane (transformed woman) D1193.1; magic s. of animal *D1025ff.; magic transportation by animal s. D1520.5; magic unpierceable s. protects against attack D1381.3.2; man created from rubbings of s. A1263.3; man rejuvenated by changing s. A1319.12; mermaid's s. B81.9.5; mutilation: shoulder s. torn off S166.3; mutilation: s. cut from back S166; origin of animal's s. A2311ff.; origin of man's s. A1319.14; origin of s. color A1614.6; pig's s. heals wounds B511.2.1; poison of hydra corrodes the s. F1041.5; punishment: animal s. grows on man's back Q551.2; recognition of ornaments under s. H61; rejuvenation by changing s. D1889.6; riddle: what is the hardest to s. H659.15; serpent renews s. A1335.5; servant lays s. of dead dog in the bed of his mistress and master K2134; sewing clothes into s., tearing them off together H1505; sky changes s. like snake A702.9; soul absent from witch's s. G251.2; substituted s. E785.1; transformation by putting on s. D531; unchaste woman's s. boiling away H411.11.1; unjust judge's s. stretched over a footstool and kept in the presence of judges J167; vital s. E785; why man doesn't change s. A1319.12.1; why men have s. A1310.3; why snakes and lizards change s. A2250.2; witch killed by placing salt or pepper inside s. while it is laid aside G275.8.1; witch out of s. G229.1.1.

Skins. — Origin of death when early people put on new s. A1335.4; saint wears animals' s. V462.5.1.1; seller of fox s. mixes otter s. with them J2083.3; tribe with double s. F558.1; trolls dressed in s. F455.2.4.

Skin-Sore as hero L112.7.

Skinning buffalo alive, turning them loose to grow new skin X983; farmers J2472; a stone (task) H1023.10. — Skillful flayer s. running rabbit F664.1.

Skirt. — Giantess in obscene s. F531.4.7.1.2; woman trips over s., devil laughs Q331.2.3; woman hoists s. to raise thunderstorm D2141.0.10.

Skittles. — Playing s. with demons H1421.1.

Skull of suicide must roll in dust until it has saved a life Q503.1; transformed to water monster D447.2; used as drinking cup Q491.5; with writing on it F559.4.1. — Adulteress drinking from paramour's s. Q478.1.2; deity born from s. A114.3; ghost's s. thrown in Ganges E459.7; giant's s. holds a man seated F531.2.3; helpful speaking s. N819.3.1; horse's s. as pillow F874.2.1; human s. used for divination D1311.8; identification by s. H79.5; king's gigantic s. F511.0.8; laughing s. advises hero E366.1; magic s. D992.4; man makes drinking water from his own s. (lie) X1739.2; man's fate written on his s. M302.2; milk drunk from hero's s. M316; mistress keeps murdered lover's s. in flower-pot T85.3; numskull does not understand about baby's s.: sticks needle through it J1911.1; offended s. *C13; origin of sky from Ymir's s. A701.2; powdered s. as remedy D1500.1.7.1; return from dead to punish kicking of s. E235.5; return from dead to punish theft of s. E235.4.5; speaking s. E261.1.2; swearing on s. M118; trickster puts on buffalo's s. and gets head caught J2131.5.1; wandering s. fulfills prophecy M391.2; wandering s. pursues man *E261.1; whale becomes s. D421.7.1; wild huntsmen carrying s. under arms E501.7.4.

Skulls as sacrifice V12.3. — Bird carries deity's daughter home from land of s. A2223.2; cup of s. F866.4; fear test: eating and drinking from s. H1434; fear test: fetching s. from charnel house H1435; hearth of human s. F420.2.5; house of s. F771.1.9; land of s. *E485; princess builds tower of s. of unsuccessful suitors *S110.3; water-spirits have hearth made of three human s. F420.2.5.

Skunk. — Bad smell of s. A2416.3; color of s. A2411.1.2.4; walk of s. A2441.1.6; why s. is disliked A2522.4.

Skunks. — Why porcupines and s. do not live on Cape Breton Island A2434.2.1.

Sky afire as plague sign F493.5; asked earth to wrinkle up feet: hence hills A969.4; dwellers must not eat on earth C211.3; as helper N818; lowering on people F791.1; -mother's child longs for earth-father D2006.2.1; ornamented with clouds to shade mountains A1133.2; as overshadowing tree A652.4; -basket F51.2; -father and earth-mother

A625; -god A210ff., A736.4, A753.1.4.1, F12.1; -rope *F51; -spirits E752.8, F499.1; -traveling snake B91.4; window F56. — Absurd theories concerning the s. J2273; attempts to measure height of s. L414.1; bottle-fly finds stolen woman in s. B543.1; children escape to s. and become thunder A1142.3; clay dropped from s. forms hill A963.9; creator in s. beneath us A651.2.0.1; creation of the s. A701; creator goes to s. A81; dragon's visit to s. B11.3.3; earth let down from s. on to primeval ocean A817; extraordinary s. and weather phenomena F790ff.; fairyland in s. F215.1; first man descends from s. A1231; four s.-columns A665.2.1; fox pretends to be guarding s. K1251.1.1; giant reaches to the s. F531.2.1.5; heavenly bodies from objects thrown into s. *A700.1; house neither on ground nor in s. H1077; how many stars in s. (counterquestion) H705.3; journey to land without s. F126; land of dead in s. E481.8; leopard releases victim claiming to be holding up s. K547.14; little people from the s. F205; looking down on earth from s. tabu C335; magic song causes tree to rise to s. D1576.1; marriage of earth and s. T126.3; marvelous picture falls from s. in storm F962.12.3; moon from object thrown into s. A741; mountain reaches to s. F55; murderer escapes to s. R323.1; nature of the s. *A702; old man from s. as creator A21.2; origin of s. from Ymir's skull A701.2; rain from container in s. A1131.4; rain from waterskin in s. A1131.4.1; rain produced by spitting blood toward s. D2143.1.4; raising of the s. A625.2; river taken to s. becomes star A761.1; several suns, moons in s. simultaneously F961.0.1; stars from objects thrown into s. A763; stolen sun restored to s. A721.3; sun a fat woman walking across s. A738.1.2; sun and moon as uncle and nephew who ascended to s. A711.1; sun at edge of s. A739.1; sun from object thrown into s. A714; three suns shine in s. F961.1.3.2; tree hanging from s. A652.2; tree stretches to s. *F54.1; tribe climbs down from s. A1631.2; waterskin dragged along s. floor A1142.8; why plants no longer reach s. A2775.0.1; why tortoise looks towards s.: seeks his wife, a star A2351.5; wife carried up tree to s. in bag in husband's teeth J2133.5.1; woman from s.-world marries mortal man T111.2; woman who fell from s. A21.1.

Skies open, reveal heavenly company F969.1.

Skylight. — Woman flown through s. K786.

Slain, see also **Slaying;** warriors revive nightly E155.1. — Animals from body of s. person A1724.1; fairies cannot be s. F259.1.4.1; giant s. by man F531.6.12.6; girl s. to save virginity T321.4; girl's animal lover s. by spying relatives B610.1; god of the s. A310.2; insects from body of s. monster *A2001; magic object found on grave of s. helpful animal D842.3; men s. for girl F1041.1.3.6; parts of s. animals as token of slaying H105; plant from blood of s. person E631.0.3; plants from body of s. person or animal A2611ff.; tabu: stripping dead and s. C877.

Slamming door to otherworld *F91.1, F156.4; drawbridge to otherworld *F152.2. — Ghost s. door E402.1.7.

Slander K2100—K2199; punished Q297. — Quest assigned by s. H1219.6; undoing s. like picking up water J84.

Slandered queen reunited with husband N741.3; wife locked into tower to be burned R41.2.1. — Champion saves s. wife R41.2.1; man absents self from church because he does not like to hear people s. J1269.2; woman s. as adulteress K2112.

Slanderers kill woman, put her near Buddha K2115.2.

Slandering. — Fire consumes woman s. abbot Q552.13.3; uncle s. niece to appropriate patrimony K361.5.

Slap turns man's face around F1041.24. — Public s. accepted by friend H1558.11.

Slapped. — Child s. to stop crying, accidentally killed N333.1.1.

Slapping. — Ghost s. cheating son E234.1.

Slashing. — Spirit s. clothes F473.6.2.

Slaughter of animals by stampede K927; of innocents to avoid fulfillment of prophecy M375; of the ox J2168; from wheel rolling over Europe M341.2.20. — Blood as s. omen D1812.5.1.1.5; escaped lamb delivers himself to shepherd rather than to s. J217.1.

Slaughtering animals to avenge self J1866. — Conservative but absurd s. method kept U139.2.1; ignorance about s. animals J1906; tabu: s. buffalo in temple C93.5.

Slave, see also **Enslaved;** -driver mysteriously stricken dead Q558.7; -driving punished Q285.4; freed as reward for killing enemy Q42.4.1; hero L113.1.7; killed for following owner's order Q211.13; may not bring lawsuit P523.3; not to go near fetish C561; poses as wealthy man's son to gain wife K1917.8; as princess's helper N863; recognized by habits H38.3; shoots arrow into sun's horse A732.2.1; washing mistress's back in stream pushes her into crocodile hole K831.1. — Allowing self to be sold as s. K365.1; animals with human child as s. B292.0.1; clever s. J1114.0.1; clever s. girl J1111.6.1; deceptive sale of another as s. K252.1; disguise as s. K1816.13; dividing property: cuts s. in two J2469.3.1; former s. sickens for accustomed food U135.3; man rewarded for freeing s. Q42.4; master discovers that s. girl he wants to marry is a near relative T410.1; man lets himself be sold as s. so as to practice generosity W11.4; merchant's daughter intimate with s. T91.5.1.1; princess living in s. quarters Q485.1; princess in love with ex-king as s. T91.6.4.2; revenge of blinded s. K1465; sham dead king kills s. K911.4; treacherous s. K2251.

Slaves P170ff.; freed as reward Q121.1; killed by hanging S113.1.1; ordered married are brother, sister N734.1; spare infant they are ordered to drown K512.0.1. — Buddhists become s. of Taoists because they cannot produce rain V355; magic object furnishes s. D1476; origin of s. A1657; paramours dress selves as s., thinking to humiliate mistress K1234; robbers sold as s. K437.5; two 15-year old s. ordered: fool brings one 30 years old J2212.1.

Slaver. — Snake from devil's s. A2145.4.

Slavery. — Child sold into s. S210.1; criminal's wife and children sold into s. Q437.1; escape from s. R211.4; father unwittingly buys daughter who has been sold into s. N732.1; helper grateful for being bought from s. N801; incognito king sold into s. K1812.11; king sells self and family into s. M203.3; lovers fleeing s. R352; origin of s. A1473; person sold into s. R61; princess ransomed from s. R111.1.6; queen rescued from s. R111.1.6.1; saint saves girl from s. R165.1; sale into s. as punishment Q437; wife sells self into s. to ransom husband R151.1.1; woman escaping from s. kills would-be ravisher T320.2.1.

Slayer returns from dead to kill wicked person E232. — Daughter marries husband's s. to save father P234.1; faithless widow marries husband's s. T231.5; ghost's flying head attacks s. E261.1.1; hero as mighty s. F628.0.1; king's s. marries widow, gets kingdom P17.11; strong man as mighty s. F628ff.; Virgin aids repentant s. V276.3.

Slaying, see also **Killing;** to prevent being slain J675; as task H1150ff.; of person unwittingly done N320ff. — Fairy takes revenge for s. F361.8; ghost s. enemies E232ff.; husband's s. horse tames wife T251.2.3; prophecy: first side s. in battle to be defeated M356.1.3; two soldiers s. each other think they are s. common enemy K1883.3.

Sled thongs cut to prevent pursuit K637.

Sledge. — Bringing moon in s. J2271.4; coming neither on horse nor on foot (on s.) H1053.4; dwarf borrows s. F451.5.10.3.1; table thrown out of s. to go home by itself J1881.1.4; tree-trunks laid crosswise of the s. J1964.

Sledges turned in the direction of the journey (at night turned around by joker) J2333.

Sleep-bringing music F156.1, K606.1.2; charm D1364.22; denied to ogre G585; feigned to kill enemy K911.3; forbidden until quest accomplished H1247; is sweetest (riddle) H633.1; thorn D1364.2; walker thought to be ghost J1782.7; — Beggar buys right to s. near the girl K1361; children not left alone to s. A1579.1; cynic helps robber so both get s. J1392.3; death as punishment for feigning s. Q558.10; death thought s. E175; devil writes names of those who s. in church G303.24.1.7; deception by pretending s. K1868; demons powerless over souls commended to God before s. E754.1.1.1; devil works during God's s. at creation A63.1; disenchantment by proper person waking from magic s. *D762; divine beings assume their own shape in s. D796; endless s. given Endymion M433; fairy music brings s. F262.3.4, (to wounded) F262.6; fairies charm prince into deathlike s. F302.3.4.5; feigning s. in bed with hero H1556.5; goddess of s. A472.1; fairy takes lover back to fairyland in magic s. F302.3.4.4; guardian magically made to s. while girl goes to lover D1965; hero lies by princess in magic s. and begets child T475.2; horse pushes s. thorn from master's head B511.3; hospitality: wife to s. with guest C119.2; indebted merchant enjoys untroubled s. J1081.1; injunction: s. where night overtakes you C683: liquor blessed by saint causes magic s. D1364.7.1; long s., long waking F564.3.1; magic bird's song brings s. B172.2.1; magic birds cause s. by shaking wings B172.9; magic cure during s. D2161.4.12; magic power lost in s. D1741.1; magic s. D1364ff., *D1960ff., (causes lover to miss rendezvous) T35.0.2, (takes lover to fairyland) F302.3.4.4; man disguised as woman beguiles hostile chief and kills him in drunken s. *K1321.3.1; man stands before mirror with his eyes shut to see how he looks in his s. J1936; man walking in s. taken for ghost J1782.7; mermaid's singing causes girl to s., drown B81.11; murder in s. K959.2; origin of s. A1399.2.1; otherworld woman appears to mortal in s. F393.4; owner put to s. and goods stolen K331.2; preciousness of untroubled s. J1081; protecting prince's s. by shooting at frogs all night J2105; riddle involving s. H573.2; riddle solved by listening to talk in s. H573.3; saint takes little s. V462.5.2.1; seduction by feigned s. K1325.1; siren's song causes s. B53.4; soul wanders from body in s. E721.1; talking in s. betrays weaver H38.2.4; transformation during s. D696; transformation to snakes at night in order to s. D659.1; unusual s. habits F564.

Sleeper answers for the dead man J2618; not to be awakened since soul is absent E721.1.1. — Contest in seeing sunrise first: s. wins K52.2; ghost disturbs s. E279.2; ghost pulls blanket off s. E544.2; ghostly horse enters house and puts hoofs on breast of s. E281.2; mighty s. D1960.1.1; soul of s. leaves body as bee E721.1.2.4.

Sleepers. — Magic object does not awaken s. D1575f.; seven s. D1960.1; spirit harpoons s. F402.1.11.3.

Sleepers' hair tied to prevent pursuit K635.

Sleeping army *E502; beauty D1960.3, (found in magic castle) N711.2; with fairy a boon for lifesaving F304.5; ghost E568; with head in wife's lap T299.1; king in mountain as guardian of treasure N573; maiden's hair tied to tree K635.1; naked on cold floor H1504; naked girl: goddess or mortal? H45.5; outside prohibited by mosquitoes A2034.1.1; person grazed by arrow, awakes F661.9; place kept dry by magic D1542.4; potion given newcomers sleeping with princess P616; potion substituted for poison K512.4, K1856, N332.4, T37.0.1, T93.4; on salt J1322.2; potion D1364.7, (given to man who is to pass the night with a girl) K675; on totem-tree bed tabu C848; trickster's feast stolen J2173.1; watchman N396; with wife tabu on Midsummer's Eve C751.2. — Adulteress meets lover while husband s. K1514.17; adventures from s. beneath tree N776.3; advice on s. before suicide J21.2.2; advice against s. in strange circumstances J21.41; chaste s. together T350ff.; children s. in village dormitory T688; consorting with princess without s. H347; devil cheated on s. bargain K216.3; dupe tricked into s., killed K834.1;

dwarf washes, combs and braids hair for s. maids F451.5.1.13; fool s. to avoid idleness J2243; fortune-telling dream induced by s. in extraordinary place K1812.3.3.2; genie s. with eyes open G634; ghost s. with living E472; girl kills man s. with her K872.1; girl sees man s. by wayside N723; girl s. in garden to meet lover discovered next morning T36; god rescues s. man A185.2.1; goods stolen while owner is s. *K331ff.; hero lies by s. girl and leaves identification token with her H81.1; heroes dislike killing s. people K959.2.2; hero s. during first of battle K2378.5; husband tests wife by s. on her hair H476; intercourse with s. girl T475.2.1; king given s. potion K873.1; lengthy s. F564ff.; man assuming lover's form s. with princess K1915.2; man can hear one s. F641.3; paramour unwittingly drinks s. potion K675.1; people s. in same room frighten each other H1194.1; person never s. F564; saint s. with maidens without sinning T331.7; sun s. at woman's house J2272.3; tabu: s. C735, (in saint's bed) C93.1; test: s. by princess three nights without looking at her or disturbing her H1472; transformation to likeness of another by s. with arms about him under the same mantle D592; warrior accused of killing s. adversary K2116.5; wrong man s. with king's daughter K1612.1.

Sleepless dragon B11.4.3; god A102.8; person of diabolical origin F564.1; son of waterspirit and mortal F420.6.1.7; watcher magically put to sleep D1961.

Sleeplessness from breaking tabu C995; secret discovered N465.1.

Sleeve. — Fish in the s. J1604; queen gives away a s. of her dress: miraculously restored V411.1; ghosts seen through s. of fur coat G311.1.1.1.

Sleeveless. — Cutting off arms for s. sweater J2131.3.1.1.

Sleigh, see also **Sledge;** as swift as thought D1521.3; makes person magically hold on D1413.3. — Animals try in vain to repair s. B831; devil invites girls into s. G303.7.1.2.3; magic s. *D1115; standing between summer and winter (between wagon and s.) H1058.

Sleipnir (eight-legged horse of Odin) A136.1.2.1.

Slept. — Hills flat where gods s. A972.5.5.

Slicing. — Murder by s. person into pieces S139.7.

Slide. — Bear persuaded to s. down rock K1021.3.

Slighted. — Fairy takes revenge for being s. F361.1.

Slime. — Sea of s. F711.2.4.

Sling-stick becomes boat D454.9.2; -stones' origin A1459.1.3. — Lucky cast from s. N623.4; magic s. *D1087.

Slinging. — Disenchantment by s. against something D712.2; giant s. stone with his garters F531.3.2.2; resuscitation by s. E27.

Slipper test H36.1. — Love through sight of s. of unknown princess T11.4.2; saint kills lion with s. D2156.11.

Slippers, see also **Shoes.** — King and the cheap s. J829.1; magic s. *D1065.7;

murder with poisoned s. S111.7; resuscitation by removal of poisoned s. E21.4; unavailing attempt to get rid of s. N211.2.

Slippery. — Cannibals enticed to climb s. barricade fall K895; dupe tricked on to s. road lined with knives K897; why animal is s. A2306.

Slipping on floor to imitate leader J2417.2; slipping into heaven along with holy person K2371.1.5.

Slope. — Return from lower world up steep s. F101.1.

Slopes. — Lies about steep s. X1523.

Sloth, see also **Laziness;** personified Z139.1; refuses to help make road: may not look on sun A2233.1.4.

Slovenliness W115ff.

Slow. — Extraordinarily s. person F596; red pepper for the s. ass: man tries it on himself X11; second son heir due to s. message P17.3.1.

Slowing down racer with mighty breath F622.1. — Hero's confederate s. down princess with his breath H331.5.1.1.1.

Slowly. — Walking home s.: wife's lover gone J2523.2.

Slowness surpasses haste L148.

Sluggish prince reformed by falling in love T10.1.

Slumber, see **Sleep.**

Sly. — Why fox is s. A2525.3.

Small, see also **Little;** fruit from big trees A2771.9; hero overcomes large fighter L311; jug of wine filled J1317; men preferred to big J493; trespasses punished: large crimes condoned U11. — Why animal has s. waist A2355.1; beggar with s. bag surpasses the one with the large L251; big piece of cake with my curse or a s. piece with my blessing J229.3; choices: s. inconveniences, large gains J350ff.; devil (troll) makes self s. D55.2.2; dwarfs are s. F451.2.1.1; dwarf has s. body and large head F451.2.1.3; easy escape of the s. *L330ff.; exceptionally large or s. men F530ff.; giants large or s. at will F531.6.5.2; help from s. man N821; humor of s. stature X142; man so s. he can go through eye of needle F535.2.2; monk discouraged by large amount of work to be done persuaded to undertake but a s. amount each day J557.1; ogre made to believe s. hero is large K1711; princess brought to laughter by s. animals H341.2; remarkable s. men F535; revenant as s. man E422.3.1; spirit as s. black man F403.2.2.6; stealing only a s. amount K188; very s. hero L112.2; wine very s. to be so old J1316.

Smaller the evil the better J229.10. — Animal's body made s. A2302ff.; devil becomes s. G303.3.5.2; making the earth s. A852; person becomes magically s. D55.2.

Smallest woman the best bride J1442.13. — Beginning with the s. K1024; quest for the s. of dogs H1307.

Smallpox deity rides nude on ass A137.8. — God of s. A478.2; origin of s. A1337.7.

Smeared. — Blood s. on innocent person brings accusation of murder K2155.1; fat s. on broom in preparation for witch's flight G242.1.1.

Smearing. — Sun s. face in mourning A737.8.

Smell, see also **Odor.** — Animal characteristics: color and s. A2410ff.; aromatic s. of saint's body V222.4.1; conception by s. of cooked dragon heart T532.1.4; headless person cannot s. or hear F511.0.1.2; marvelous sense of s. F652; origin and nature of animal's s. A2416ff.; panther's sweet s. protects him from other beasts B732; peculiar s. of body A1662; recognition by s. of jewels H93.0.1; woman brought up on goat's milk has s. of goat F647.5.

Smells. — Evil s. transformed to sweet D479.7; man soon learns to stand the s. of the tannery U133; ogre carries the sham-dead man (he s. already) K522.2.

Smelling out theft J2355.2. — Cannibal s. human flesh makes exclamation *G84; clever deductions by s. J1661.2; conception from s. (flower) T532.1.1.1, (bone dust) T532.1.4.1; foul s. coat to repel lover T323.2; resuscitation by s. of moss E72; rejuvenation by s. apple D1889.4; transformation by s. D564.

Smelting. — Origin of s. A1447.4.

Smile of child as foundation sacrifice wins freedom S261.1; saves infant's life S350.1. — Bat makes sun s. A1046.1; detection of guilt by s. J1149.5; enigmatical s. reveals secret knowledge N456; recognition by s. H79.4.

Smiling vines F815.7.3. — Ascetic never s. V462.7.

Smith, see also **Blacksmith;** *P447; disturbs fairies at night F361.17.2; exorcises sick child G271.9; forges iron man who helps him D1620.1.3; of the gods *A142; of hell A677.1; hero L113.6; with lantern wanders between heaven and hell known as jack-o'-lantern A2817.1; excessively jealous of wife T257.9; as prophet M301.19; rescues abandoned child R131.8.4; swallowed by monster F913.1. — Disguise as s. K1816.12; fairy s. gives knight magic sword F343.3; fettered monster's weakened chains renewed by stroke of a s. A1074.8; giant as s. *F531.6.10.1; heavenly s. is hammering on the moon A744; helpful s. N855; lie: remarkable s. X982; living s. must repair wagon belonging to wild hunt E501.15.5; magic object forged by s. to order D853; monk becomes s. P426.3.1; ogre teaches s. how to transform sand in his smithy G651; presumptuous s. chants the Divine Comedy J981; skillful s. F663ff.; son of king and son of s. exchanged K1921.1; strong hero struck by s. from iron F611.1.12; sun, moon and stars forged by s. A700.5; supernatural s. under lake *D921.3; tailor and s. as love rivals F92.12.1; transformation when one expresses astonishment at s. drawing water in an egg-shell D512.1; underground spirits instruct a s. F450.1.2; youths tutored by Vulcan, s. of hell F107.

Smith's wife made nails for Crucifixion V211.2.3.0.2. — Beast with human head shape of s. bellows B96.

Smiths. — Dwarfs as s. *F451.3.4.2; fairies as skillful s. F271.3; magic hymn protects against s. D1385.16.2; princess as s. P31.1; king cursed by dwarf s. P15.4; trolls skillful as s. F455.3.1.

Smith-work. — Goddess of s. A451.1.1.

Smithy. — Ghosts blow s. into air E279.7; salvaging anvil from burning s. H1574.3.1.

Smock. — Magic wishing-s. D1470.1.10.

Smoke ladder to upper world F52.2; from funeral pyres of brother and sister refuses to mix F1075; from lovers' funerals mingles in sky E643.1; rises from saint F1041.23; rising shows good health H1582.2; from sacrifice tabu for chief C564.5; test H1511.3; transformed to bridge D469.2. — Ascent to upper world in s. F61.3.1; breath in the cold thought to be tobacco s. J1801; choking with s. as punishment Q469.5; clouds come from s. J2277.1; clouds as s. rising A1133.3; devil detected, goes up chimney in s. G303.17.2.1; diagnosis based on s. F956.3; divination from rising s. D1812.5.0.4.1; dwarfs dislike tobacco s. F451.3.6.3; fairies protect selves with s. F399.2; father not yet born, son already at the top of the house (flame and s.) H763; filling house with s. to prevent partner's eating K336.2; genie in form of s. G369.2; house filled with s. so that owner gives trickster lodging K336; magic s. carries power of saint D1572; magic sword causes fire and s. D1566.1.3; magic transportation on s. D2121.7.3; man transformed to s. D285.1; Milky Way as s. A778.8; origin of s. A2816; raven caught in s.-hole: hence is black A2218.1; recognition of good health by s. rising from chimney H1582.2; rising s. as omen D1812.5.0.4; rising s. shows sacrifice accepted V19.1; reincarnation as s. E643; soul as s. E743.1; wolf overeats in the s.-house K1022.1.

Smoker. — Substitute s. K528.1; tobacco, pipe, and match debate usefulness to s. J461.3.

Smokers' punishment in hell Q569.5.

Smoking test H1511.4. — Dead man s. pipe E555; loss of strength by s. C942.1; person lives by s. tobacco F561.4; repartee on donkeys not s. J1289.20; why men like tobacco but spit when s. A2854.

Smooth. — Voice made s. F556.1.1.

Smothering old woman in grain J2465.7. — Death by s. for breaking tabu *C922; numskull s. children J2175.5.

Snail grows and fills house entirely F983.1; kills lion (lie) X1345.1; transformed to person D398. — Color of s. A2411.5.3; enmity of porcupine and s. A2494.12.16; magic s. body cures D1502.8.2; man becomes s. D198; mirror begrimed by s. J451.4; origin of s. A2181; stag defeated by s. vomits his gall-bladder A2211.13; test of resourcefulness: putting thread through coils of s. shell H506.4; thumbling hides in s. shell F535.1.1.10.2.

Snail's — Origin of s. shell A2312.2; origin of s. voice A2423.1.6.

Snails. — Fool thinks gold is being destroyed when s. crawl over it J1816; lies about s. X1345; enmity of cattle and s. A2494.12.3.1; heron wants no s. in heaven U125.1; singing s. rebuked J1885.

Snake, see also **Reptile, Serpent;** accidentally poisons hidden fruit N332.7;

46

adopts abused bride K1911.3.6; avoids object B765.18ff.; -body, woman's head B29.2.3; cannot die until he gives away treasure E765.4.6; can't kill prince until princess bears as many sons as snake J1173.1.1; carries devil into paradise: loses feet A2236.2.1; carries into fire man who has banned snakes Q597.1; coils self about faggots bundle H1023.19; complains to Zeus that people step on him J623.1; as creator A13.4.1; as creator of rivers and lakes A930.1.1; does not die before sunset B752.2; disenchanted by being allowed to wrap itself three times around person's neck D759.8; disregards warnings to improve his manners: eaten by crab J1053; as follower of the devil G303.10.3; as frog's mount J352.2; gives gold daily B103.0.4.1; gives man antidote for poison B514.3; -god A132.1; grateful to man feeding her young B391.1.2; grateful for milk B391.1.3; gives away magic pills J621.1.1; grows in person's stomach B784.1.2; hard to hold by tail H659.2.1; as healer B511.1; heals mutilated maiden with magic herbs B511.1.2; helps girl after winding self around her Q82.1; as house-spirit B593.1; inside woman comes out for cock B784.2.1.1; keeps house with other animals J512.7.1; killed by knives in animal he is swallowing K897.1; killed by own incantation K1613.5; kingdom under the sea B225.1.1; kills self B752.3; kills ungrateful tamer W154.10; magically enlarged D487.1; as messenger B291.4.2; mistaken for flute J1761.6; mistaken for whip J1761.6.1; in mouth as murder punishment Q418.2; around neck chastity test H412.5; as ogre G354.1; paramour B613.1; in person enticed out by milk B784.2.1.0; preys on mankind A1335.10; promises to do no harm to frog K815.6; protects man B524.3; refuses to help choose road: may not use road A2233.1.2; reincarnated as flowers E691.1; rendered powerless by pregnant woman D1837.4; rids himself of wasps J2102.2; at roots of earth-tree A878.3.1; spits out lump of gold B103.4.2.1; strikes person opposing saint Q557.6; shoots river rapids B748; sucks poison from bite D2161.4.10.2.2; sucks poisonous dew from grass B765.3; sucks woman's milk B765.4.1; swallows young to protect them B751.1; takes fugitives across river R245.2; transformed to object D425.1; transformed to other animal D418.1; transformed to person D391; in troll child's dough F455.10.1; turns to gold in answer to dream N182; and turtle exchange head for fangs A2247.2; vomits jewels B103.4.2.2; wanted by stepmother for daughter J2415.7; wants to act like pet J512.14; wants to eat frog friend J426.2; and weasel stop fighting in order to catch mouse W151.4; -woman as paramour B613.1.1; -woman's magic ashes D1469.10.1. — Abduction by s. R13.4.1; animals from mating of s. and person A1772; bad breath, forked tongue reveal disguised s. king K1822.3; bedstead warns of danger of s. D1317.11; big tree thought to be s. J1771.1; bird kills s. attacking master's family B524.1.6; blindness cured by killing s. K2161.4.10.5; child born with s. around neck T552.2; child feeds s. from its milk-bottle B391.1; child tears s. to pieces F628.1.3.2; crab saves hero from s. B524.1.12, B549.5; creation of s. A2145; crow's revenge on s. K401.2.2; cure for s. bite F959.5; death of s. encircling world A1082.3.1;

deer, opossum, and s. each render indispensable aid to man J461.4; deity's s. children A132.1.1; devil in form of s. G303.3.3.15; dog becomes s. D412.5.7; double s., male and female B726; earthworm thought to be s. J1755; enmity between frog and s. A2494.16.1; enmity of mongoose and s. A2494.12.2; escape from s. pit R211.7; fairy in form of s. F234.1.7; fettered monster as s. A1072.3; fight between s. and millipede B264.4; food of s. A2435.6.2; fox transformed to s. D411.8; friendship between s. and crow A2493.25; frog rescues man from s. kingdom B547.4; why s. does not go on the road A2233.1.2, A2441.4.1; head of killed s. bites king N332.3.1; hedgehog forces s. to suck out poison B511.1.3; helpful bird kills s. attacking master's wife and child B524.1.6; helpful s. protects man from attack B524.3; how to cure s. of blindness? H1292.4.2; why s. has no legs *A2371.3.1; how s. got small head A2213.1, A2320.1; lightning as fiery s. A1141.1; lion thankful rescued by s. B374.1; lizard tries to make himself as long as s. J512.9; magic dust kills s. D1402.27; magic object from redeemed s. D817.1.2; magic pills reduce s. to ashes D1402.25.1; magic rod kills s. D1402.10.2; magic s. compresses, expands B176.1.2; magic s. liver D1500.2.8; magic s.-oil causes illusions D1368.1; magic s. tail D1029.2.3; man cannot die: s. will not bite him N101.3; man fears s.-like rope J11.1; man with s.-like feet F551.1.1; man transformed to s. D191; marriage to five-headed s. B646.1.1; marriage to person in s. form B646.1; marriage to s. B604.1; mistaking own toe for s. J1838; murder by feeding poisonous s. S111.8; murder by wrapping s. around man K953.3; person swallows s. semen B784.1.3; poisonous s. bite test H1517; prophetic s. B145.2; punishment: s. sucks woman's breasts Q452; rainbow as s. A791.2; reductio ad absurdum: father is sick from s.-bite in winter H1023.3.1; reincarnation as s. E614.1; rescue of woman from s.-husband R111.1.5; resuscitation by s. E122.2; resuscitation when s. licks his bite E17.1; riddle about deaths of elephant, s., and jackal H803; revenant as s. E423.5; rod from magic hazel-tree kills s. immediately D1402.10.2; why s. sheds skin A2483.1; singing s. B214.1.10; soul in s. E715.5; spirit as s. F401.3.8; speaking s. B211.6.1; sun-god bitten by s. leaves earth for heaven A222; thrifty man saves even s. W216.1; transformation by eating s. eggs D551.6.3; transformation: handkerchief to s. etc. D454.3.2.2; treasure found in s. hole N511.4; treasure-guarding s. around princess's chamber H335.3.4; underworld s. kingdom F92.7; water s. carries boy across river B551.4; where s. got his fangs A2247.2, A2345.5; whoever hears singing s. must die K445.2; why water s. has no poison A2532.1.1; witch as s. G211.8.1; witch transforms self into s. when she bathes G245.1; woman bears s.-child T554.7; woman promises unborn child to s. S222.2; Zeus refuses wedding present from s. J411.2.

Snake's blood venomous B776.5.3; brain as only cure for monkey's disease K961.2.1; habitat A2433.6.8; human offspring B631.9; qualities B765ff.; strike causes swelling X1205.1; venom poisons tree D1563.2.2.2.

Snakes attend goddess A137.9; banned by magic D2176.1; brought to eat frogs, eat family J2102.8; controlled by saint D2156.5; created to humble proud man L482.3; expelled from human body D2156.5.2; have mass B253.1; issue from dragon's shoulders B11.2.7; put to sleep by music D1962.5. — All s. but one placated by music Z355; army of s. B268.7, D2091.2.1; bonga house filled with s., tigers and lions F221.2; why s. are venomous A2532.1; bridal chamber filled with coiled s. T172.1; culture hero banishes s. *A531.2; fanciful qualities of s. B765; four royal families of s. B244.1.4; god girdled with s. A123.10; goddess's bed of s. A155.6; imaginary s. X1396; king of s. B244.1; lies about s. X1321; man looks at copulating s.: transformed to woman D513.1; Muria eat s. A1681.3; no s. in Ireland A2434.2.3, M318; ornaments of s. F827.3; priest of s. B252.3; prison filled with s. R41.3; punishment: taking s. as foster children Q594; quest to land of s. H1289.1.2; rattlesnakes mate with black s. B754.3.1; reptile-men's power over s. D1711.13; rectum s. G328; saint banishes s. V229.3; saint breaks s. in bare hands D1840.1.1; saint turns s. to stone V229.24; sea from rotting s. A924.2; suckling s. eyeballs T611.11; throwing into pit of s. as punishment Q465.1; transformation to s. at night in order to sleep D659.1; why s. change skin A2250.2, A2311.9; why s. are proud A2523.2; witch gives birth to s. G243.3.1.

Snakebite punishment for breaking tabu C992. — Blindness from s. D2062.2.5; charms as antidote for s. D1515.1.1; frog's bite mistaken for s. F1041.1.11.4; head cut off as s. cure X372.2; prophecy: death from s. M341.2.21; St. Peter's grass as medicine for s. A2623.

Snap of finger kills robber F628.2.8.

Snapping door traps victims K736.

Snare, see also **Trap.** — Birds in s. fly out one by one Z11.2; first man catches woman in his s. A1275.10; frog causes deer to dance into s. K730.2; resuscitation by catching in s. E23; sun caught in s. A728; witch caught in s. G274ff.

Snares. — Sun tied to earth by s. of light A733.4; vision of earth in devil's s. V513.2.

Snaring. — Tabu: s. a being C566.1.

Sneering princess impregnated by magic L431.3.

Sneeze mistaken for gunfire J1809.1.

Sneezer wished long life A1537.1.

Sneezing of ghost in form of bear E552; of lion creates cat A1811.2. — Bear frightened by s. K2345.2; magic object causes continued s. D1372; monkey s. in king's presence J2413.6; omens from s. D1812.5.0.1; origin of s. A1319.9; treasure from s. D1454.9.

Sniff. — Why dogs s. each other A2232.8, A2471.1.1.

Snipe. — Hawk frightened at bill of s. J2616; man becomes s. D154.3; origin of s. A1942; where s. got his long beak A2343.1.2; why s. messenger for warriors A2261.6.

Snoring misunderstood J1812.5. — Ghost s. E402.1.1.5; giant's s. as thunder F531.3.8.1; insect in murdered person simulates s. K661.3; numskull thinks bishop's s. is death rattle J1833.

Snout. — Animal unusual as to s. B15.5; origin and nature of animal's s. A2335.4ff.; person with cat's s. F514.3; troll with s. F455.2.7; why rat's s. long A2335.4.6.

Snow always melts on certain hill F759.3; is devil's grandmother bleaching *G303.11.4.2; -child J1532.1; on house death omen D1812.5.1.18; magically burns D2143.6.4; makes rainbow behind runner F681.13; melts above dwarfs' dwelling F451.4.1.10; produced by magic D2143.6.3; tastes of wine F962.11.1; transformed to dogs D449.4. — Angel created from s. A52.1.3; angels melt s. around saintly babe V238.2; drying s. on the stove J2121; drying s. to make salt J1947; earth created from s. under divine throne A835.1; fairy dances in s.: no tracks left F261.2; lies about s. X1653; lover left standing in s. while his mistress is with another K1212; magic control of s. D2143.6; magic journey in s. whirl D2121.7.2; magic s. D903; man who sold dried s. for salt X1653.3; order for six loads of s. K1661; origin of s. A1135.2; pancakes made of s. D476.1.6; person not wet by s. D1841.4.2; red as blood, white as s. Z65.1; riddle: bird without feathers flies on tree without leaves (s. falls on bare tree) H764; sacrifice for s. V17.4.1; saint controls s. fall D1841.4.4; soul in s. E711.11; tribute paid in enchanted s. K236.3; wall of s. around hut in answer to prayer D2143.6.2; witch produces s. G283.3.

Snowball. — Game: rolling down hill in s. X1130.1; only s. can kill dwarf F451.3.2.4.

Snowbirds. — Why s. are everywhere A2434.1.3.

Snowbunting. — Transformation into s. D151.2.1.

Snowdrop. — Origin of s. A2661.

Snowshoes. — Escape by reversing s. K534.2; magic s. *D1065.3.

Snowstorm. — Child born in s. T581.5.

Snuff. — Cannibals persuaded to take s.: killed K827.2; taking s. with devil G303.9.9.8; witch asks for s. so that she may seize man G269.2.

Soaking. — Death respite for s. to make juicy K553.5.

Soap. — Magic s. *D1195, (gives clairvoyance) *D1323.6, (makes fairies visible) F235.4.2; washing dirty quilt without s. H1023.6.1.

Soapstone. — Man transformed into s. G263.2.1.1.

Sobbing, see **Weeping.**

Sobriety from magic food D1359.4.

Social etiquette A1537. — Beginning of s. relationships A1470ff.; culture hero establishes s. system A546; humor of s. classes X200—X599; loss of s. position as punishment Q494; lovers meet at s. gathering T34; origin of different s. classes A1650ff.; origin of s. ceremonials A1530ff.; transformation to person of different s. class D20ff.; unfavorable s. traits W150f.

Society *P (entire chapter); like a dish, must be mixed J81.1. — Tests of position in s. H1574.

Societies. — Jokes on secret s. X550ff.; why birds don't live in s. A2492.2.

Sock. — Giant carries man in s. F531.5.1.1.1.

Socrates builds himself a little house J401.1; and Xanthippe: "after thunder rain" T251.4.

Sod. — Magic s. *D934.1, (indicates falsehood by turning grassy surface downward, truth by turning it upward) D1316.7, (serves as boat) D1524.7; ordeal by creeping under s. H228.

Sodomist makes sport of confession V29.4. — Wife substitutes for s. husband K1843.2.4.

Sodomy forbidden C113; punished Q253.

Sofa. — Magic s. *D1154.2.

Soft answer turneth away wrath J817; words placate ruler J811.4.

Softening breadcrusts J1341.1.

Softer. — What is s. than swan down H672.

Softest. — What is s. (riddle) H652ff.

Softness. — Coming neither in s. nor in hardness H1054.4.

Sohrab and Rustem N731.2.

Soil dropped to form mountains A963.3. — Carrying s. to cover stony ground H1129.3; lies about s. X1530; magic control of s. and crops D2157; magic s. *D935; magic object controls condition of s. *D1563ff.; patches on s. where cow lay A989.1; poor s. transformed overnight into garden D2157.5; why s. is poor A2871.

Sold, see also **Selling.** — Brothers die at sight of brother they s. N384.13; child s. to fairies F321.0.1; children s. S210ff., S240ff.; city where everything s. at one price J21.52.1; criminal's wife and children s. into slavery Q437.1; girl s. for new church bell V115.2; goods s. to animals J1852ff.; goods s. to object J1853ff.; land where all things s. for same price X1503.3; magic s. object returns to owner D1602.17; person s. into slavery R61; relatives s. to otherworld H1252.3; wife s. unwittingly by husband T292.

Soldier P461; asks enemy to stab him in chest J216.4, W45.1; as helper N852; prefers life to death with revenge J327. — Death imprisoned by s. Z111.1.1; disguise as s. K1825.5; don't make friends with s. J21.46; dwarfs attack s. F451.5.2.11; cowardly s. turns back when he hears raven's croak W121.3; friar disguised as s. steals K1839.5; king disguised as s. killed K1821.7; literal s. breaks woman's oil pot J2469.5.2; lowly s. invites general, humbles him L175.1; magic s.-producing cow B184.2.1.2; mercenary s. unsuitable as husband T65.2; mercenary s. princess's lover L161.3; seduction by masking as s. K1315.13; sleeping s. mistaken for statue J1763.3; **treacherous** s. suggests task H919.5; woman disguised as s. K1837.6.

Soldier's bargain with death K555.2.2; ghost haunts battlefield E334.5; retort to officer J1526.

Soldiers P551; **abduct** girl R10.1.1; of enchanted army tabu C549.2; of fairy king are trees by day and men by night F252.3.1; of magic army constantly revived E155.1.2; in wild hunt E501.2.6. — Animal s. B268; custom of paying s. A1596.1; fighting s. force river from bed F1084.3; grass transformed to s. D431.5.1; king not to fail to pay s. C831; magic mirror kills s. D1400.1.13; magic object furnishes s. *D1475ff.; sham warrior intimidates s. with his boasting K1951.3; stingy king will not hire s.: defeated W152.6; troops of black, white, and red s. F873.1; two s. slay each other thinking that they are slaying a common enemy K1883.3; why lame, one-eyed are good s. J1494; woman saves herself from s. by receiving them joyfully rather than fearfully K2361; women throw ashes in eyes of attacking s. so that they are defeated K2356.

Sole. — Ghost demands soul; given shoe s. E459.1; girl stipulates to be s. wife T131.6; giving devil s. for soul K219.5; origin of s. A2126.1.

Soles. — Foot s. covered with hair F517.1.8; pins stuck in s. of dead men's feet to prevent return E431.12; shading self with foot s. F551.5; thief undetected cuts s. off boots F676.2; unique weapon: spits through s. of feet Z312.1; yellowing feet s. death omen J2311.1.5.

Solomon K1921.1; able to detect truth J1140.1; follows angel's warning J158.1; and Marcolf H561.3; as master of magicians D1711.1.1; in memory test H1595.1; offered any gift chooses wisdom L212.2; refuses water of immortality for himself when he cannot have it for his possessions also J369.1; requests wisdom J231.1; as riddle solver H540.3.1; H561.3.1; as wise man J191.1. — Irish S. J1170.2; magic knowledge of S. D1810.10; queen of Sheba propounds riddles to S. H540.2.1; wind serves S. as horse and carries him everywhere F963.1; wisdom gates open to S. J182.1.

Solomon's golden throne F785.1; judgment: the divided child J1171.1; magic ring D1335.5.2; three thousand parables J80.1. — Dolphins seek King S. ring A2275.5.4.

Solomon Grundy born on Monday Z21.1.3.

Solstices. — Deities push sun back and forth at s. A1157.

Solution to problem discovered in dream D1810.8.4.

Solve. — Death sentence escaped by propounding riddle king (judge) cannot s. *H542.

Solvers of riddles H561ff.

Solving. — Means of s. riddles H561ff.

Soma. — Quest to bring S. to wedding H1285.1.

Somersault. — Transformation by s. D561.2; wager: turning s. in public square N56.

Something or other as payment J2489.10. — Searching for food called "S." J1805.4.

Son avenging father's death H1228.2; to be brave, wise but not remain M365.2; as creator A19.1; called daughter to save him from enemy K649.4; drinks poison he intended for father K1613.4; endures embrace: disenchants animal father D735.4.2; of first couple murdered by tiger

A1277.3; insists on following father's trade P401; killed, mistaken for someone else N338.3; kills father who returns to life as cuckoo A2275.6; killed at lover's instigation S303; of the king and of the smith exchanged K1921.1; must not see mother's intercourse C114.1; of the sun A225; on gallows bites his mother's (father's) nose off Q586; named for mother T148.1; next seen to be king M314.2; refuses to marry father's choice T131.1.2.4; rescues father R154.2; rescues mother R154.1; returning home after long absence unwittingly killed by parents N321; returns on day of mother's marriage N681.4; seeks unknown father H1381.2.2.1; slays father in self-defence J675.1; substitutes false bride for father, then kills father K1094.1; succeeds father as king P17.0.2; surpasses father in skill L142.3; warns animal mother B631.0.1. — Abandoned s. exposed to tiger H105.5.4; accidental meeting of mother and s. N735; boon: to have a s. Q115.3; bridegroom only s. among seven children H1381.7; choice between adopted or long-missing s. J226.1; choice between long-lived blind or short-lived healthy s. J226.2; choice between foolish s., wise daughters J226.3; clever man pretends to be s. of God J1675.8; creator's s. A32.1; cruel foster s. S37; cruel s. *S21; dead mother makes s. strong E323.7; dead s. tells mother death inevitable E361.3; defeated enemy's s. changes allegiance R74.2; devil's s. G303.11.2; devil's s. is with his mother at night in the father's place G303.11.1.1; dead mother called up from grave to give her s. charms E323.3; disenchantment of monster when his mother acknowledges him as s. D741.1; divination which s. to be born first D1812.5.0.17; dog buried instead of foster s. K525.6.1; dream warns raja stranger is s. D1810.8.2.5; dwarf king prevents a father from shooting his s. F451.5.1.16; dwarfs steal s., leave image in his place F451.5.2.3.1; earth from body of s. of deity A831.1; fairy s. pale, dark, ugly F233.4; faithful s. guarding father falsely accused N342.1.1; father demands s. break all relations with beloved T131.1.2.3; father feels s. in danger D1813.0.3; father and s. *P233; father kills s. S11.3.3; father orders unrecognized s. thrown into sea N338.3.1; father and s. as love rivals T92.9; first s. died before father A1335.7; fool didn't know that his s. had a ghost to give up J2482; foster s. P275; ghost slaps cheating s. E234.1; God refuses king a s. on account of his many wars Q553.3.1; help from ogre's s. G530.2; hero fights s. without recognizing him A515.5; hero is served at table by his unknown s.: recognition of his wife follows H151.11; hero s. of half-mortal father A511.1.5; human s. of sun A736.10; hungry s. outwits father, gets cherries J1341.9; judge lenient to own s. J1197; king decides oldest s. is rakshasa N349.3; king assigns tasks to his unknown s. H921; king no priest's s. J1827; king's s. persuaded to woo father's bride: killed K1094; king's third s. sacred V205.1; king unknowingly adopts own s. N731.1.1; man gives bangles for s.: takes them back, son dies M101.3.2; man mourns drowned s. in bed F1041.9.1.1; mermaid has s. by human father B81.2.1; miller, his s., and the ass trying to please everyone J1041.2; mortal

adopted s. of god A189.11; mortal s. of giant F531.5.7.1; mother and s.
*P231; mother-s. marriage A164.1.1; mother dies from joy on greeting
long-absent s. F1041.1.5.3; mother kills s. thinking him a wild beast
N325.3; mother sends s. to find unknown father H1216; murderer's s.
dies as revenge Q589.3; paramour leaves token with girl to give their s.
*T645; parents kill own s. for slaying foster son P270.3; parents rescue
s. R153.1; poisoner's own s. takes stepbrother's drink K1613.3; prodigal s.
favored over faithful N172.1; prophecy: death at sight of s. M341.1.7.1;
prophecy: parents will humble themselves before their s. M312.2; prophecy: s.-to-be will destroy lineage M342.2; prophecy: s. will tie father
to horse's leg, strike him M312.0.5; prophecy: s. to be more powerful
than father M312.2.1; quest for unknown s. H1381.6; quest for vanished
s. H1385.3.1; recognition of s. by gushing up of milk in mother's breasts
H175.1; recognition when parents come to s. to be confessed H151.3;
resuscitation by s. E125.1; sacrifice of one s. to get another J2067.1;
philosopher consoles woman for loss of s. J152.4; senate ruler amuses s.
J553.2; sinless couple's s. H1381.4; sister's s. P253.0.1; slaying king's s. to
prevent father's death H1162.2; strong man s. of unusual parents
F611.1ff.; father who wanted s. exposes (murders) daughter S322.1.1;
stupid s. eavesdrops, learns magic N455.10; sun is s. too hot to hold
A736.5.1; tabu imposed on s. by father C901.1.1; theft by disguise as
owner's s. K311.8; treacherous s. leads revolt against father K2214.3;
unexpected meeting of father and s. N731; ungrateful s. punished by
having a son equally ungrateful Q588; ungrateful s. reproved by naive
action of his own son: preparing for old age J121; victim's s. aids
murderer W15.1; victorious youngest s. *L10ff.; vigil for dead father:
youngest s. alone endures frightful experiences H1462.1; vow concerning
birth of s. to chief's wife M184.1; vow not to eat until lost s. found
M151.8; wild man s. of woman and robber F611.1.4; woman drinks
poison so s. may be king W28.1; woman unwittingly poisons her s.
N332.5; youngest s. refuses to shoot at father's corpse H486.2.
Son's acts of charity save his father's soul V413; voice answers mother
from grave E324.1. — Calling animal by s. name, sacrificing it K527.5;
dead father clears s. name E327.3; death from hearing of s. death
*F1041.1.2.2.4; foreknowledge of s. unhappiness D1812.0.4; friendship
despite s. jealousy H1558.10; mother orders s. death S12.3; queen offers
s. death to revenge first husband P23.4; sword bursts in s. hand when
he is about to kill his father *D1317.6.1; unborn s. soul issues from
mother's mouth E726.2; woman murders s. wives Q211.4.2; wrestling to
test s. legitimacy H218.2.
Sons break promise to have masses for father M256.1; falsifying father's
will, deceived K1628; as helpers N832.2; meet at father's grave after
learning trade M271; rescue father R154.2.3; surrender witch G275.6;
tested for skills H500.1; tested for wisdom by equal amounts of money
H501.3; united make living, separated fail J1021.1. — Creator's two s.

A7.1; faithful servant sacrifices s. to save life of king P361.3; father rescues s. R153.3; fathers dream of bloody s., murder omen D1812.5.1.13; father describes s. in uncomplimentary riddle H581.4; first-born and tenth s. given to church V451; forty of man's s. to die at once M341.0.2; gods as s. of supreme god A112.6; king propounds questions to his s. to determine successor H508.1; king sends s. on fatal quests K948; king's vision of s. changed into animals V515.2.3; king sends man's s. to death, murders man M2.1; king sets s. task to determine heir H921.1; magic pills bring twin s. D1347.3.1; man falls dead when all s. reared in sin killed Q582.9; mother of world bears three s. A1282.1; mountains as s. of gods A962.9; no s. left to rule after father: slain in rebelling against him P17.0.1; obedience of s. tested by offering them apple H1557.1; persecuted s. of co-wife S471; pots symbolic of inheritances of four s. J99.2; recognition from overheard conversation of s. H13.3; riddle about no s. after three marriages H585.2; riddle about four wells as father and three s. H588.8; snake can't kill prince until princess bears s. J1173.1.1; stupid s. learn trades, father killed J2499.7; thiefs' s. frightened by punishment threats K335.1.11; tiger, spirit, and man s. of same mother T554.1; two s. granted: one wise and ugly, other fool and handsome M93; unwitting combat between s. of friends N767; wife incites s. to war on father K2213.9; witch has giant s. G206.

Son-in-law P265; given choice, eats all meal W125.3; seduces mother-in-law T417. — Blind s. X124.2; cruel s. S56; lazy s. W111.5.6; one present from spirit s. C714.1; poor not rich s. chosen J247.1; prophecy: murder by s. M343.1; thief disguised as s. K311.8.2.

Sons-in-law treated as unwelcome guests J1563.6.

Song, see also **Singing;** increases cow's milk D2182.2; as protection on journey D1384.5; causes magic sleep D1364.23; duel H503.1; learned in dream *D1731.1; protects against poison D1383.4; protects from fire D1382.7; warns lover of husband K1546.1. — Beer brewed by means of magic s. D1045.0.1; bird's s. consoles man B292.5; birds captured by imitating their s. K756.1; bird shows way by s. B151.2.0.3; bribed boy sings the wrong s. *K1631; child's s. reveals murder N271.6.1; church sinks: s. heard from underground F941.2.1; confederate's s. delays pursuers so that fugitive escapes K643; disenchantment by s. D786.1; dog sings s. B214.1.4; escape by singing s. K606; flute-player thinks s. meant for prince is sung to him J953.3; funeral s. V65.4.1; goat singing threatening s. K1767; holy s. drives off fairies F382.5; love-producing s. D1355.1.1.; magic bird's s. B172.2ff.; magic s. *D1275, (causes paralysis) D2072.6, (as curse) D2175.3, (received from fish) B505.3; mortal wins fairies' gratitude by joining in their s. and completing it F331.3; one compulsory s. before beer can be brewed C671; origin of particular s. A1464.2.1; paramour encouraged by s. K1546.2; recognition by s. H12; resuscitation by s. E55.1; respite from death gained by long drawn-out s. K555.2; riddle: what is the sweetest s. H634; saint's s. silences hound D1442.5; siren's s. causes sleep B53.4; thrush steals woodcock's s. A2245.1; transformation through s. D523; unrequited love expressed in s. T75.3; water chants s. F930.6; years seem moments while man listens to s. of bird D2011.1.

Songs about bad food, its improvement J1341.11; of the angels V234. — Boat guided by magic s. D1523.2.6; creator gives men s. A1503; devil in church fills his sack with dissolute s. G303.24.1.5; love-s. A1554; lulling to sleep by "sleepy" s. D1962.4.1; magic power from s. D1733.6; magic strength from s. D1835.5; origin of religious s. A1543; two animals learn s. together: one successfully, the other unsuccessfully A2283.

Soon. — Dead person returns s. after burial E586; giant comes to bake too s. and spills dough F531.3.7; not to do thing too s. C757; not to look at supernatural wife too s. C31.1.1; not to open bag too s. C322.2; spirit must speak as s. as addressed F404.1.

Soot. — Magic s. *D931.1.1, (opens mountain) D1552.10; naked lover as devil in s. barrel K1555.2.

Soothsayer D1712. — Animal acts as s. *B154.

Soothsaying learned from god D1726.0.1. — Power of s. from serpents' licking ears B161.1.

Soporific given contest opponent K51.1. — Abduction by giving s. R22.

Sorcerer and books in mountain F721.2.3; loses magic with teeth D1741.8.

Sorcerer's army of magic animals B268.4; body becomes serpents D447.9; magic objects D801.1.

Sorcerers can see ghosts E421.1.1.2; use corpse marrow D1278.2.

Sorceress marries man every day, transforms him in evening T113.1; swallowed by transformed husband D1749.1. — Girl exchanges form with s. D45.4; quest to confines of hell for blood of s. H1277; toes of s. become dogs D447.5; transformation by s. D683.2.

Sorcery. — Acquisition of s. A1459.3; god of s. A499.4; magic circle averts s. D1385.7.

Sore on body prohibits sexual intercourse C110.1; eyes from breaking tabu C943.3; -producing ointment K1043.1.

Sores from breaking tabu C941.3. — Woman raises s. to preserve chastity T327.5.

Sorghum's origin A2684.2.1.

Sorrel. — Why s. grows on certain rock every winter A2771.7.

Sorrow, see also **Grief;** is not eternal C498.1; of captivity in otherworld F165.6.1. — Directions followed literally to the s. of giver J2516; feast for those who have not known s. N135.3.1; going to bed for s. F1041.9.1; heart breaks from s. F1041.1.1.3; inexorable fate: no day without s. N101.1; magic musical horn (bell) relieves hearers of s. D1359.3.1.1; object expresses s. F994; quest for person who has not known s. H1394; woman dies of s. for brother P253.9.

Sorrows. — "Two S. of Heaven" D1856.1.1.

Sorrowers. — Loudest mourners not greatest s. J261.
Sorry. — If you take it you will be s.; if you don't you will also be s. J171.1.
Sorting a large amount of grains in one night H1091.
Soul *E700—E799; absent from witch's skin G251.2; leaves body to point out treasure N538.1; of witch leaves the body *G229.1; wanders and demands that a temple be built for him E419.1. — Ability to see the s. F642.7; animals help man overcome monster with external s. B571.1; container for s. can be split only by man's own sword D1651.10; deaf and dumb man can see s. taken to happiness or punishment D1821.7; debate of body and s. E727.1; deity provides man with s. A185.12; devil appears to claim s. offered to devil by farmer in jest G303.6.1.3; devil cheated of his promised s. K210ff.; devil gets another s. instead of one bargained for K217; dwarf loses s. after murder F451.5.9.6; demons as s. of giants G302.1.1; devil cannot touch man's s. G303.25.18; escape by alleged possession of external s. K544; external s. *E710ff.; familiar spirit equivalent to man's s. F403.2.2.3; four places cleanse the s. Z71.2.4; ghost demands s.; given shoe sole E459.1; god removes mortal's s. A185.12.2; handsome exterior no indication of s. U119.3; hidden s. E712; journey to hell to retrieve s. F81.4; magic ability to see s. D1825.3.3; magic armature protects s. D1389.11; magic sight of s. leaving body D1825.3.3.2; man sells s. to devil M211; murder by destroying s. K956; ogre killed by burning external s. G512.5; person with more than one s. E707; prophecy: child to have external s. M354; resuscitation of man with s. in necklace E155.3; resuscitation by replacement of s. E38; resuscitation by returning s. to body E38.1; secret of location of external s. learned by deception K975.2; seeing s. in living man (repartee) J1262.7; separable s. of witch G251.1.1; witch recognized by seeing wandering s. return G251; witch's s. crushed to forehead G275.4.1.
Souls. — Bridge tests s. H210.1; demons have s. without bodies G302.4.3; devil hunts lost s. G303.7.1.3; fairies as s. of departed *F251.2; food placed out for returning s. of dead *E541.1; four categories of s. at Judgment Z71.2.5; light as s. of dead A1412.2; limited number of s. necessitates reincarnation E603; magic sight of s. after death D1825.3.3.1; masses release s. from hell (purgatory) V42; mountain spirits as s. of dead F460.0.1; not to relieve s. in hell C741; sheep as s. redeemed F81.6.
Sound of drum followed into ghost town F102.2; of ghostly object E402.3; of harp J1626; of magic wheel causes deafness D1332.1.2; of wild hunt avoided by sticking fingers in ears E501.17.5.8. — Divination from s. D1812.5.0.11; ghost sails over s. E581.7; hair emits s. F555.11; insanity from hearing strange s. D2065.2.1; riddle: what is the sweetest s. H635ff.; sea's mournful s. A925.5; thunder as s. of God's gun A1142.5.
Sounds heard before death D1827.1.2; of invisible animal ghost E402.2. — Ghostly s. of re-enacted actions E337.1ff.; illusory s. K1887; lies: animals responding to s. X1206; sunken bell s. *F993; vocal s. of ghost E402.1.1ff.

Soup of dog's head cures madness D1508.4. — Alleged s.-making stone (pot) sold K112.2; black beans, white s. J1291.1; bones in s. mistaken for peas J1772.6; dog Parsley in s. J2462.1; lentil in s. J2469.1; stingy woman will not give s. to man until she spills it W152.5.

Sour fruits made sweet by saint F979.1. — Fathers have eaten s. grapes, children's teeth on edge U18; fox and the s. grapes J871; tamarind fruit s. A2791.5; woman created from s. milk and cream A1275.5.

South forbidden direction C614.1.2; wind is moistest H659.8. — Land of dead in s. E481.6.3; north wind tempers fury of s. wind A1127.1.1; saint's body moves to lie s. E411.0.8.

Southern. — Origin of the S. Cross A771.1.

Sovereigns compared to new, full moons H599.3.

Sovereignty for hour as reward Q112.2; personified Z116. — Curse: race to lose s. M462.

Sow, see also **Pig;** kicks wolf into stream, saves pigs K1121.2; in wild hunt E501.4.3. — Cat brings suspicion between eagle and s. K2131.1; devastating s. B16.1.4.2; feeding man-eating s. H1155.3; ferocious s. G353; ghost of s. E521.5.1; giant devastating s. B16.1.4.2; house-spirit in form of a s. F480.1; priest draws s. instead of woman K1281.1; salesman guarantees s. to bear male, then female, then kid X1233.4.1; why s. was muddy J2211.2; wife's former incarnation as s. E601.1; wolf offers to act as midwife for s. K2061.6.

Sows'. — Piglings cut from s. bodies T584.4.

Sowed. — Cooked grain s. by numskulls J1932.1; hempseed s. to acquire magic sight D1331.1.1; slain father returns as cuckoo, tells where grain to be s. A2275.6; traveler says he is going to the city to see what has become of the seed he s. in the street H586.2.

Sowing cheese to bring forth a cow J1932.2; dragon's teeth (task) H1024.5; grain in unplowed field K1428; impossible amount of land overnight H1103.2.1; needles (like seed) J1932.5; and reaping same day F971.7; reaping, winnowing in one day royalty test H41.8; and not reaping M306.1; rice seed in others' fields J2129.8; rye, getting crop next day H1023.17; salt to produce salt J1932.3; seed, then burning land J2460.1. — Countertask: s. cooked seeds and harvesting the crop H1023.1.1; devil s. stones A975.1; disenchantment by burying victim and s. grain over him D719.1; father is making many out of few (s. grain) H583.2.2; origin of s. A1441.4; sacrifice at s. time A1545.4; time for s. A1150.1.

Sown. — Plants grow without being s. F979.17.

Space. — God of s. upholds sky A665.1; tests of s. H1584.

Spade. — Lost object found by throwing s. at ghost D1816.2.1; magic s. *D1205.1; man buried in earth goes for s. and digs self out X1731.2.1.

Spádísar prophesy victory M301.13.

Spain as land of dead E481.0.2; as otherworld F130.2.

Span. — Determination of s. of life A1320ff.; extraordinary bridge s. F842.2.3; giant reveals life s. to dwarf N484.

Spans. — Giant with three s. between brows F531.2.2.

Spangles. — Sun, moon as s. from creator's forehead A714.6.

Spared. — House of woman who launders clothes for church s. in great fire V137; man he is about to devour s. by animal B525; mother who is suckling children s. by angel of death V233.1; Old Age, Cold, Poverty, and Hunger s. by culture hero A531.1.

Sparing. — Reward for s. life when in animal form Q55; vow not to deceive man s. one's life M168.1.

Spark detonation hurls ships to sea F1078.

Sparks come from man's feet F683. — Devils created from s. produced by Satan's striking two stones together G303.1.4.2; when devil combs witches, s. fly G222.1; teeth giving off s. F544.3.2.

Sparrow carries burning straw to fire desecrated church Q222.5.5; dissatisfied with pond wants to go to sea W128.6; family enact her fate to dying queen M369.2.1.1; intervenes in elephant quarrel J2143.1; taught to sing by lark A2271.2; where are you going? Z39.4.2. — Cat as judge between s. and hare K815.7; chain tale: wormwood rocking s. Z41.7; color of s. A2411.2.1.11; creation of s. A1927; crow crowds s. from nest J684.2; fairy as s. F234.1.15.3; fool kills himself in despair because a s. has taken one grain from his field J2518.1; friendship of hen and s. A2493.34.1; helpful s. B451.7; man becomes s. D151.8; why s. is disliked A2522.1; old wife provokes s. to speak, drop new wife K929.10; parrot and s. argue right to inherit property left by man B271.1; separable soul in crop of s. E715.1.2; speaking s. B211.3.7.

Sparrow's nest A2431.3.7; wedding B282.3.3, B282.10. — Crow appropriates s. nest J684.2, K354.1; train of troubles for s. vengeance N261; why crow cannot enter s. nest A2431.3.6.1.

Sparrows of Cirencester (set fire to a besieged city) K2351.1. — Aphrodite's team of s. (doves) A136.2.1, A155.3; king of s. B242.2.7; young s. have learned to avoid men J13.

Spayed. — Ghosts cannot approach s. bitch E439.6.

Speak. — Animal persuaded to s. and release victim K561.1; causing silent person to s. H1194.0.1; why cormorant cannot s. A2344.2.5, A2422.8; dwarfs appear nodding and anxious to s. F451.2.0.4; mother trains old maid to s. properly X756; penance: not to s. Q535.1; princess made to s. desired words when hero threatens to report (falsely) her amorous conduct K1271.1.2; refusal to s. from grief F1041.21.3.1; spirit must s. as soon as addressed F404.1; suitor test: bringing dumb princess to s. H343; teaching animal to s. H1024.7; think thrice before you s. J2516.1.

Speaker. — Bungling s. J2666; deception into listening to s. K477.2.

Speaking bedlegs overheard N454.1; and bleeding trees (reincarnated persons) E631.0.4; animals B210ff.; bird tells where treasure is buried N537; blood reveals murder D1318.5.4; bones of murdered person reveal murder E632.1; corpses J2311.9; earth reveals murder D1318.16; flesh reveals murder D1318.7.0.1; forest F812.4; grass D1312.3; he-goat saves girl D674; horse-head *B133.3; image of saint V126; lamp prevents murder D1381.29; mountain F755.1; river F932.12; sea F931.11; severed head E783.5; skull E261.1.2; spittle reveals truth D1316.3; stars A769.4, F961.2.4; statue D1620.1.7; tabu *C400—C499; tabu in fairyland C715.1; trees A1101.1.2, D1311.4.2; wraith E723.7.1. — Animals, men s. same language B210.3; animals s. at Christmas B251.1.2; ashes of dead dog s. E521.2.1; child s. at birth T585.2; child s. in mother's womb T575.1ff.; cooked human flesh s. out G64; culture hero s. before birth A511.1.2; dead s. E417, E545; deaf and dumb s. F954, F1041.22; devil s. with voice of a he-goat G303.4.7; ghost laid by living man's s. to it E451.4; disenchantment by s. D762.1, D789.6.1; disfiguration for s. falsely H244; flowers fall from s. saint's mouth V222.11; girl possessed by ghost s. unknown dialect E725.2; god s. to mortals A182ff.; gods s. A182.1.1; helpful s. skull N819.3.1; magic results from s. *D1774; magic s. objects *D1610ff.; magic s. reed (tree) betrays secret *D1316.5; man at grave pretends to be dead s. K1974; men refuse to kill s. beasts B210.3; person s. with pestilence dies F493.2.1; pestilence-spirits s. together F493.2.2; quest for s. bird H1331.1.4; reproving each other for s. at prayers J2254; severed head of saint s. V229.2.2; three persons s. at birth Z71.1.13; victim s. from swallower's body F915; wife's s. privates tell of adultery K1569.7.

Spear becomes tree D454.9.1.1; bends on hero's chest F615.4; can be wielded by only one person D1651.1.1; carried crosswise into house as obedience test H1557.5; -casting contest H1591.1; changes size D631.3.8; driven through iron F625.1; in ground pointed toward ferocious animal protects D1381.17; killing king cast into cataract P16.5; made to appear reed D2031.11; pierces person's shadow D2061.2.2.1; shot through nose-ring F661.3.1; stuck in ground ends deluge A1028.1. — Automatic s. D1601.4.2; drawing s. thrust through iron plates H1149.7; enduring s. blow as test H328.3; extraordinary s. F834; fairy gives magic s. F343.10.2; feat on s. point H1149.5; flaming s. cooled in blood D1645.8.1.1; gate of captured town widened for overlord's s. P555.3; giant's enormous s. F531.4.5.6; gift on unknown helper's s.-shaft Q114.1; god's s. A157.3; hero catches s. hurled at him, kills snake N654; identification by s. H125.2; lips used as s. F544.1.4; lucky cast of s. N623.1; luring man by securing his s. K1399.4; magic s. *D1084, (dries up spring) D2143.2.2, (slays ogre) G512.8.3, (point harmless, shaft inflicts mortal blow) D1402.7.2.3; murder by thrusting s. into mouth K951.1.2; own s. kills murderer Q582.3; performing on s. points F698.2; prophecy: king to be slain by certain s. M341.2.17; quest for magic s. H1345; recognition by unique ability to swing s. H31.3; skillful axe-man makes s.-shafts with three chippings F666.1; spell causes s. to pursue and slay man D1438.1; spring breaks forth where magic s. strikes ground A941.3.1, spring where god throws his s. A941.3.2; stealing king's s. H1151.13.2; strong man's s. -cast F628.4; suitor contest: riding up s. H331.1.3; tabu to slay woman with s. C835.2.4; why tortoise may be killed with iron s. A2231.7.3; woman wins s. contest F610.0.1.1; wound healed by same s. that caused it D2161.4.10.1.

Spears cannot penetrate magic garment D1381.3.3. — Broad-headed s. in Leinster A1459.1.2; god with s. as torches A137.14.2; jumping hedges of s. H331.1.6.1; origin of obsidian-tipped s. A1459.1.2.1.

Spear-head miraculously removed from wound F959.3.4.1; not to touch stone C835.2.2; tabu between teeth C835.2.3. — Charm causes s. to return D1428.2; magic s. *D1084.1, D1564.4.1.

Specimen. — Substitute s. for laboratory test K1858.

Speck. — Skillful surgeon removes s. from midge's eye F668.2.

Speckled. — Devil s. G303.4.8.9; journey in s. garment on s. steed C833.8; riding s. horse credential test H242.1.

Spectacles. — Clergy in no need of s. J1263.5; ignorance of reading s. J1748; magic pair of s. D1299.5.

Spectral ghosts E421.

Spectre as evil omen D1812.5.1.17. — Strong man slays s. F628.3; transformation: man to demon (s.) D95.

Speculations. — Absurd scientific s. J2371ff.

Speech, see also **Speaking.** — Animal understands human s. B212; apology for not answering challenge (has never regretted silence but often regretted s.) J1074.1; choice: loss of beauty or s. J213; dumb man recovers s. in order to confess V23.2; evil s. punished Q393; husband's dangers bring wife to s. T272.1; law student forgets s. J2046; loss of s. as punishment *Q451.3; magic object restores s. *D1507ff.; magic recovery of s. D2025; precocious s. T615.1; princess's s. sweeter than sugar H633.5; respite from death gained by long drawn out s. K555.1; saint deprives enemy of s. Q572.5; saint restores dumb man's s. V221.2; single s. answers many questions H501.2; why dog lost s. A2422.1; why God took power of s. from animals B210.3; why owl's s. removed A2239.3.1.

Speeches. — Abusive s. drive ogres away G571.

Speechless vigil in church as test H1451. — Fly punished by failing to answer question: is s. A2239.2.

Speed. — Giant's prodigious s. G157; journey with magic s. *D2122ff.; lies concerning s. X1796; spirit travels with s. F411.0.1; sun's s. depends on hour, season A728.4; tasks requiring miraculous s. H1090ff.; usefulness better than s. J243.

Spell chanted over person's shadow brings death D2061.2.2.2. — Druids boil s. P427.9; holy water breaks fairy s. F382.2; magic object breaks s. D1396; magic results of reversing a s. D1783.1; magic spear protects against s. D1389.5; magic s. *D1273ff., (causes insanity) D1367.3, (causes birds to roost) D1442.6.2, (causes fortress to revolve, preventing entrance) D1381.23; stealing while owner under alleged magic s. K341.22; tabu to eat food from s. C220.1; transformation by s. D573; trickster works magic s. over food, eats it K353.

Spells to recall dead lover E218. — Birds with poisonous s. on wings B33.1.4; drawing witch's blood annuls her s. D1741.2.1; druid's s. kill enemies D1402.13.1; druid's s. to drive away saint V229.6.4; magic s. control witch G272.15.

Spending money for lover's worthless goods K1581.9. — Parable on s. without return H614.2; rude retort on s. to become known J1369.1; subject s. more than he earns chastised J1566.2.

Spendthrift hero L114.2; knight divides his last penny Q42.1; loses friends when poor H1558.7; wife T275.

Spendthrift's sarcastic advice to thrifty J1363; uncut field already harvested H586.4. — King buys s. bed J1081.1.

Sperm. — Conception from drinking s. T512.6; Milky Way as the s. of the gods A778.6.

Spewing. — Ghost kills by s. water from mouth E268.

Sphere. — Magic clairvoyant s. D1323.4; magic s. D1264, (burns up country) D1408.1.

Spheres. — Music of the s. A659.1.

Sphinx *B51. — Riddle of S. *H761.

Spiced wine becomes bitter D477.0.1.3.

Spices. — Origin of s. A2814.

Spider bite cured by Virgin Mary D2161.5.2.5; as creator A13.3.1; as culture hero A522.7; dropping on front lucky D1812.5.2.11; hands box to ant and refuses to take it back: hence ants carry huge loads A2243.1; has no blood B724; invites wasp (fly) to rest on her "white curtain" K815.2; performs penance B253.4; on person's back ill omen D1821.5.1.12.3; spins web across sky F989.21; in stingy woman's house grows thin W152.7; thinks that it has held back the wind J953.9; transformed to man D381; -web garment H1355.1; -web sky-rope F51.1.1; as witch's familiar G225.1. — Color of s. A2221.2.3, A2411.3.2; cowardly s. W121.5; why s. is cursed A2231.5, A2542.2; devastating s. B16.6.4; devil as a s. G303.3.3.17; dog becomes s. D412.5.6; enmity of s. and (crab) A2494.16.5, (wasp) A2494.14.2, (fly) A2494.14.1, (cat) A2494.1.7; fly steals fire from s.: may eat everywhere A2229.4; ghost as s. E423.8; giant s. B873.3; gnats having overcome lion are in turn killed by s. L478; haunts of s. *A2433.5.3; helpful s. B489.1; magic s. catches pearls B109.1; man so small he dances in s. web F535.2.3; man transformed to s. D181; why s. has markings on back A2356.3.4; mythical s. B93; origin of s. A2091; soul in form of s. E734.3; -web over hole saves fugitive B523.1; why s. has thread in back of body A2231.6, A2356.2.8; why s. has small waist A2355.1.1; why s. brings good luck A2536.3; why s. lives under stones A2433.5.3.1.

Spider's body made larger A2301.2. — Boar in s. web F989.18; bed of s. webs F787.1; earth made by cups placed on s. web A823; escape from lower world by s. thread F101.7.

Spiders. — Abandoned souls feed on s. E752.7.1; enmity of rats and s.

A2494.12.8; islands from webs woven by primeval s. A955.7; wishing to destroy all s. J2079.2.

Spike magically appears D1285.1, (causes death) D2061.2.6. — Magic s. *D1285.

Spikes. — Prison floor with s. in it R41.3.3.

Spiked-cask punishment Q462. — Serpent's jewel covered by s. helmet K1058.1.

Spilled. — Animal has color s. on him: cause of his color *A2219.1; fool tires to dry up s. wine with meal J2176.1; dough s. by giant who comes to bake too soon F531.3.7; making a knot of s. brandy H1021.4.

Spilling dirty water on overdressed youths X32.

Spinach. — Conception from eating s. T511.3.2.

Spindle in well leads to adventures N777.4. — Magic s. *D1186; making a boat from splinters of s. and shuttle (task) H1022.7; making s. and loom from one piece of wood (countertask) H1022.3; old woman with s. in the moon A751.8.1; prophecy: death through s. wound M341.2.13.

Spine test H1531. — Fairy physician can heal anyone whose s. is not severed F344.2; soul fastened to s. E714.13.

Spines. — Dragon combats attack with showers of fiery s. B11.11.3.

Spinner P451.

Spinning as bride test H383.2.1; fairies lured away F381.8; forbidden C832; gold (task) H1021.8; on holy days tabu C631.2; impossible amount in one night (task) H1092; wool still on goat's back H1024.8. — Automatic gold-s. doll D1620.0.1.1; bewitched person s. on bedpost G269.25; bride s. at bottom of river K1911.2.2.2; dead person s. E561; devil s. G303.9.8.1; dwarfs s. F451.3.4.6, F455.3.4; dwarfs help human s. F451.5.1.19; fairies s. F271.4.3; goddess of s. A451.3.1; golden s. equipment H1359.2; Hercules s. for his beloved K1214; hidden husband advises wife on s. K1971.4; magic s. D2183; magic s. rod D1399.1; origin of s. A1453.1; sight of dead woman s. drives people insane E561.1; sight of deformed witches causes man to release his wife from s. duty J51; three witches deformed from much s. *G201.1; wife too lazy for s. W111.3.5; witch s. G244; witches punish lazy s. women G282.

Spinning-wheel continues spinning after tabu broken C916.4; sent home by itself J1881.15. — Golden s. F876; phantom s. E534; son appears to pursuers as s. D2031.6.2; test of sex of girl masking as man: s. brought H1578.1.2.

Spires. — Penance until s. of Benares rebuilt Q521.7.

Spirit causes deluge A1015.2; changes to animal D493; causes flood A1015.2; gives power of exorcising D1721.1.3; host fighting as evil omen D1812.5.1.17.1; huts V112.1; as prophet M301.11; reincarnated as man E605.2.1; takes any form D49.2; takes man's shape D42.2; -woman devours men, cattle G312.2; woman sleeps whole year F564.3.5. — Animals s.-sighted B733; bull melts away after evil s. has issued from him F981.2; dead wife asks husband to accompany her to s. world

E322.2.1; evil s. cast out of person E728.1; evil s. exorcised *D2176.3; female s. of tree F441.2.3; god's s. dwells among mortals A151.11; half-s., half-man A506; magic ring protects from s. D1385.3.1; man behind statue (tree) speaks and pretends to be s. K1971; man carried by s. or devil on magic journey D2121.5; man reincarnated as s. E605.4; mortal as s. D44; order for help of s. left on card D2074.2.4.4; power of self-transformation received from wood-s. D630.1; profanely calling up s. forbidden *C10ff.; soul as black or white s. over coffin E722.1.1; storm from calling on evil s. D2141.0.1; witch's familiar s. G225.

Spirit's curse M411.7.

Spirits become gods A104.4; of disease F493.1; frightened off by threatening to eat them K1715.4.1; guard otherworld F150.2.2; live with men A1101.1.3. — Animal wards off s. B785; avoidance of evil s. at childbirth T582.1; cannibalistic s. G11.10; evil s. conjured away in name of deity *D1766.7.1.1; fighting with s. as fear test D1423; Jesus drives evil s. into hogs: hence short snouts A2287.1.1ff.; journey to world of s. F121; magic control of s. D2198; magic object protects from evil s. *D1385ff.; metal as defence against s. D1385.5; mountain-s. *F460ff.; north as abode of evil s. G633; offending s. of water, mountain, etc. forbidden C40ff.; oracular images occupied by s. who give the answers K1972; sacred s. V202; sacrifice to appease s. S263; stealing from s. forbidden C91; tasks performed by (captive s. of the dead) H972.1, (helpful forest s.) H973; things thought to be s. J1784; thunder-s. A284.3; transformation by evil s. D683.6; uttering secrets heard from s. forbidden C423.4; why s. are invisible A2862.

Spiritual exaltation from eating human flesh *G13; recompense for temporal misfortune J893. — "Eat s. food, not material" J1511.16; marvel that those who speak of s. matters are usually the most depraved J171.2.5; three s. gifts of God Z71.1.12.

Spit. — Adultery detected by s. marks J1142.3; monsoon from divine s. A1129.2; recovering cooking-s. H1132.1.6.

Spits. — Unique weapon: s. through feet soles Z312.1.

Spite. — "In s. of devil" C12.5.8; king saved in s. of himself V523.

Spitter. — Remarkable s. F635, X934.

Spitting in face as punishment Q471ff.; on head of slain enemy S139.2.2.1.3; of men while smoking: Adam spat A2854; of all parties into vessel to seal bargain M201.3; on old castaway brooms gives one to devil G303.16.19.2. — Animal s. treasure B103.4ff.; captor s. out smaller animal K683; enraged man s. fire F1041.16.1; Evil Eye averted by s. D2071.1.1; fool s. in hot porridge in imitation of smith J2421; forgetfulness by s. D2004.4; hero s. twice at wife in recognition H186; high-s. the test of a chief H41.2; magic results from s. *D1776; ordeal by s. on fire H211.5; origin of s. A1399.3; philosopher s. in king's beard J1566.1; power of prophecy lost by s. D1812.6.1; protection from witch by s. G272.5; rain produced by s. blood toward sky D2143.1.4; top man

of human chain s. on his hands J2133.5; trickster s. in wine given it
K355.1; witches s. out communion wine over shoulder G285.1; universe
created by s. A618.2.

Spittle, see also **Saliva;** changes to blood D474.7; images enable escape
K525.10; transformed to person D437.5. — Birth from s. T541.8.2;
blood in s. tests subjection H252.2; conception from licking s. T512.5;
devil originates from God's s. G303.1.1.2; earth from creator's s.
A814.10.1; healing s. of Virgin V256.1; healing s. during pregnancy
T579.4; lesser gods from great god's s. A114.1.1.2; licking s. from
ground in penance Q523.9; magic s. *D1001, (animal) D1029.5, (kills)
D1402.14.1; man created from s. of holy person A1263.4; man becomes
s. D295; plant from s. A2613; stars are moon's s. A764.4; stolen wife
makes trail of speaking s. for husband R135.0.1.

Splinter. — Accidental death from flying s. of bone N335.4; child born
of s. T541.2.1.1.

Splinters. — Making a boat from s. of spindle and shuttle (task) H1022.7.

Split dog put together again X1215.11; lapdog becomes two rocks
A977.5.4. — First man s. in two to form mate A1275.2; why hare's lip
is s. *A2342.1; things s. by magic object D1564ff.

Splitting a hair with a blunt knife H1023.14; wood with penis F451.3.4.10;
wood as suitor contest H331.12. — Earth s. when tabu broken F944.4;
hero s. mother's womb T584.7; man s. into two parts F525.2; punishment
for s. head and eating man's brains Q211.7; suitor contest: s. antlers
H331.8.

Spoil. — Hero divides s. for animals B392.

Spoils. — Giant cheated in division of s. of chase K171.0.1.

Spoiled fish eaten by servant K344.1.2. — Owner persuaded that he has
s. goods K344.

Spoiling the rice-field with dung K344.2. — Animals refrain from s.
consecrated food B259.4.1.

Sponge in dead mouth causes illusory breathing K1885.1. — Men with s.
feet F517.1.3.

Spontaneous creation of universe A620ff.; generation of mankind
A1234.3.

Spoon. — Dipping out the sea with a s. (task) H1143; guessing nature of
devil's s. H523.5; magic s. D1177.

Spoons. — Fairies give woman silver s. F342.1; hostess says that she has
no s. J1561.4.1.

Sport. — King demands s. from guests P337; king wants men engaging
in s. P14.8; mortal wins gratitude by joining in fairies' s. *F331; parts
of corpse used in s. S139.2.2.4; vow against man ignorant of s. M171.

Sporting. — Fairies s. with mortal F399.4.1.

Spot. — Dream of marking s. with his excrements X31; invulnerability
except in one s. Z311; fairies made visible by stepping on certain s.
F235.5; grass refuses to grow in certain s. F974; love-s. D1355.13;

murderers kill all at certain s. S110.5; ogre's soul in pale s. E714.10; yellow, green, blue, purple s. on cheek F545.3.2.

Spots on leopard A2412.1.2.

Spotted. — Children s. like leopards after bestiality T465.4; devil s. G303.4.8.9.

Spouse, see also **Husband, Wife;** murder pact S63. — Cruel s. S60ff.; curse by s. M411.20; future s. foretold M369.2.1; future s. met during magic sleep *D1976.2; loss of s. for breaking tabu C932; tasks imposed by s. H916.

Spouse's. — Dead s. malevolent return *E221; uttering s. name forbidden C435.

Spout. — Filling bottle with s. downward H1023.2.2.

Spouts. — Roof s. run with blood E761.1.11.

Spreading goddess's cloth on spot: water flows A941.5.6. — Girl's hair s. out on ground F555.3.1.1.

Spriggins F456.1.

Spring as refuge R317; is most beautiful H641.1; with water lighter than wood F716.2. — Causing dry s. to flow again (task) H1193; entrance to lower world through s. F92; from wooden s. iron bucket makes stones from which water flows (riddle) H765; ghosts haunt s. E278; god of s. A496.1; gods live in s. A151.3.1; goddess's sacred s. C51.1.11; goddess of splendor of s. A430.1.1; gold-producing s. in otherworld F166.2; lazy girl does not know where the s. is W111.5.2; magic s. *D927, (curing) D1500.1.1.2, (detects perjury) H251.3.9; numskull tries to dig up a s. J1933; ogress tricked into boiling s. G519.1.4; old woman by s. as helper N825.3.2; origin of a particular s. A941.0.1; quest for biggest river's s. H1315; question (propounded on quest): why has s. gone dry H1292.1; saint drives demon from s. D2176.3.3.2; secret water s. C429.1; spear dries up s. D2143.2.2; transformation to s. D283.2; treasure hidden in s. N513.3.

Springs. — Extraordinary occurrences connected with s. F933; flood from s. breaking forth A1011.1; god of s. A427; hot s. arise where Christ bathed his feet A942.1; lies about hot s. X1543; magic control of s. D2151.6; magic s. fertilize or sterilize earth D1563.0.1; origin of s. A941.

Springing. — Identification by ring s. off finger H94.7; murder by s. bent tree S135; ring s. asunder (as life token) E761.5.3, (when faithlessness of lover is learned) *D1318.9.1.

Sprinkling salt on fairy food renders it harmless F384.1.2. — Healing by s. water F950.9; treasure found by s. ground with blood of white cock D2101.1.

Sprites. — Fairies as s. who have been given immortality F251.5.

Sprouting. — Dream of s. tree indicates hero's birth M312.0.4.1.

Spruce. — Indians chew s. gum A1681.1.

Spun. — Riddle: who first s. and when (Eve) H811; cotton already s. A1346.2.1.

Spur. — Lover's s. catches in sheet when he tries to escape N386.1.

Spurs. — Philanthropist will give his s. if someone will drive his horse for him W11.1.

Spurge-laurel as the devil's bush G303.10.11.

Spurned ruler rewards maiden Q87.1.1; woman's attempts at revenge K2111.

Spurring. — Horse transformed by s. D566.3.

Spy. — Bee as God's s. overhears devil's secrets A33.3.1.

Spies listen to defendants J1149.10; report falsely on enemies' weakness K2363.

Spying on animal husband C36.2; on holy cloak renders senseless D1410.8; on magic object D830.1; on secret help of angels forbidden C51.4.2; on secret hoard K322. — Blindness as punishment for s. Q451.7.0.2.5; death for s. on uncanny persons Q411.14; disguise for s. K1835, K2357.0.1; disguised husband s. on wife K1813.2; fairies take revenge on person s. on them F361.3; husband s. on adulteress K1551; king disguised for s. K1812.17; king s. to levy fines K2246.1.1; miserly husband s. on wife to see that she does not eat too much burned in the chimney W153.2; sham dead woman s. on husband killed N384.12; transformation for s. D641.2.1.

Square. — Dwarf cave has large s. room with little doors leading to all sides F451.4.3.2; earth s. with four quarters *A871.

Squaring lumber on stone H1199.13.

Squash. — Putting a large s. whole into a narrow-necked jar (task) H1023.11.

Squatting god A137.6.

Squeal. — Wild boar given permission to s. before wolf eats him K551.3.4.

Squeezer. — Remarkable s. X951.

Squeezing to death as punishment Q429.4. — Animal characteristics from s. or stretching ancient animal A2213ff.; contest in s. water from a stone (cheese or egg used) K62; deceptive contest in s. hands K73; milk transferred from another's cow by s. axe-handle D2083.3.1; murder by s. K953.

Squid. — God of s. A445.1.

Squint. — How lynx got his s. A2330.2; son with s. breaks bottle X121.1.

Squinting as punishment D2062.2.3.

Squirrel becomes person D315.4; in human form B651.10; points out road B563.3; released: grateful B375.4; transformed to a horse D411.1.1; tries to dip out lake with tail J133.5. — Why s. barks when attacked A2462.1.; capturing a s. (task) H1154.6; chattering s. in earth-tree A878.3.3; climbing match won by deception: s. as child K15.1; color of s. A2411.1.4.1; cry of s. A2426.1.2; devil as s. G303.3.3.11; enmity between s. and (dog) A2281.2, A2494.4.1, (marten) A2494.12.6; friendship of s.

and (quail) A2493.6, (leopard-cat) A2493.7; ghost as s. E423.2.12;
helpful s. B437.3; why s. lives in tree A2433.3.9; all nuts to be picked
from tall tree (done by grateful s.) H1121; one woman to catch s.: other
to get cooking pot J2661.3; origin of flea: from s. A2032.3; stripes of s.
A2413.3; wedding of s. B281.8; why s. stays hidden in jungle
A2433.3.9.1; where s. got tail A2241.7, A2242, A2378.1.5.

Squirrel's body made smaller A2213.1, A2302.3; food A2435.3.13; markings and immunity from falling as reward A2221.8. — Origin of s. call:
queries viper A2426.1.2.1.

Stabbing. — Dancer s. spectator K916; murder by s. S115ff.; queen s. self
to accuse princess K2103; sham death for s. brother K911.2; by s. bag
of blood trickster makes dupe think that he is bleeding *K1875; ogre
deceived into s. himself G524.

Stabilizing. — God s. the sky A665.0.1.

Stable. — Abandonment in s. S153; child born in s. T581.4; cleaning
Augean s. in one night (task) H1102; devil in the s. wrapped in horse-
hide G303.8.12; disguise as s.-boy K1816.8; farmer prefers s. smells to
flowers U133.1; dwarf home is underground, beneath cow s. F451.4.1.5;
dwarfs request that cow s. be moved F451.4.4.3; great s. X1037; hero is
s.-boy L113.1.2; man in s. mistakes animals for ghosts J1782.4; prisoners
as s. boys escape during race K475.2; strong man uses s.-roof as flail
F614.7; thief finds tiger in s. *N392; treacherous s.-groom K2256; wolf
almost locked in the s. by the shepherd J2172.2.1.

Stables. — Forbidden s. C611.2; king banishes mother to s. S21.4.

Stack. — Deceptive bargain: a peck of grain for each s. K181; mountain-
man has s. of butter before his door F460.2.4.

Stacking wood from felled forest in one day H1095.2.

Staff of life and death: silver stick kills, golden one restores to life
E64.1.1.1; stuck in ground as life token E761.2. — Angel transports
saint's s. V232.2.0.2; blooming s. as chastity index H432.4; bottom and
top of s. (riddle) H882; creator puts out world-fire with s. A1035.2;
ferule to fit s. H1344; god gives Jesus's s. to saint V227.1; magic s.
*D1254ff., (blossoms) D1673, (gives supernatural information) D1310.5;
moss grows on s. overnight F971.1.3; only one ferule fits certain s. Z322;
origin of plant from s. of holy person A2624; riddles about Moses's s.
H823, H824; rivers where god drags his s. A934.4; saint's s. pierces
man's foot F1041.0.1, V331.1.4; saint's s. as sea pilot D1313.5.1; saint's
s. transformed to spear, wins land grant K185.13; serpent transforms
self to s., picked up, bites enemy K928.1; spring where god throws his
s. A941.3.2; suitor contest: prize to one whose s. blooms H331.3; wild
huntman with black fur cap and white s. E501.8.6.

Stag, see also **Deer;** becomes wind D421.5.1; defeated by snail vomits his
gall-bladder A2211.13; found by master when overlooked by servants
J1032; -god A132.4; with golden antlers, silver feet B101.4.1; killed
by lion into whose den the fox puts him K813; escapes from hunters to be

eaten by lion N255.1; scorns his legs but is proud of his horns L461;
with iron shoes J2335; with stripe of every color B731.7.1; weeps
B736.5. — How s. got antlers *A2241.1, A2326.1.1, A2326.3.2; fairy
in form of s. F234.1.4; helpful s. B443.1; hidden s. discovered when he
begins to eat grapevine too soon J582.2; invulnerable s. D1840.2.2;
speaking s. B211.2.1; visitors of sick s. eat up all his provisions so that
he starves W151.2.1; witch as s. G211.2.4.1.

Stags live one thousand years B841.4; plow for man *B292.4; plow for
saint B256.9. — Seven s. killed by one shot F679.5.3.1; yoking s.
H1154.3.6.

Stagnant. — Enigma on s. water H599.1.

Stair to lower world *F94.

Stairs up giant's body G154; of glass F848.5; to which person sticks
D1413.4; set with razors to trap hero H1531.2. — Adulteress caused to
fall down s. from which steps have been removed Q469.1; earth at foot
of s. to swallow up man M341.2.25; magic s. *D1144; man buried beneath s. V61.3.0.3; man pulled down s. by wives T145.5; penance: living
under s. as mendicant Q523.4; robbers make s. slippery K897.3.

Stake miraculously bent F1093; through body overcomes spirit F405.9;
turns corpse to worm H47. — Disenchantment by driving s. D712.10;
fettered monster vainly loosens his s. A1074.6; ghost is laid by piercing
grave with s. E442; giant rescues woman from burning at s. R164.2;
innocent queen burned at s. K2116.1.2, Q414.0.7; rescue at s. R175ff.; son
rescues mother from burning at s. R154.1.1; speech magically recovered
on execution s. D2025.1; Virgin Mary saves criminal from fire at s.
V252.2.

Stakes thrust through slain warriors S139.2.2.7. — Extraordinary s. at
gambling N2; heads placed on s. for failure in performance of task
H901.1, Q421.1; throwing away fence s. J2516.8; unjust umpire keeps s.
K452.2.

Stalk as sky-rope F51.1.3. — Disenchantment from flower by breaking
s. D711.4; magic s. D977; plantain disobeys mother: hence bears but one
s. A2722.1.

Stalks. — Man from sugar cane s. A1255.1.

Stall. — Stealing twelve horses out of s. (task) H1151.2.

Stallion. — Devil as a white s. G303.3.3.5.3; foal born of Loki and
mythical s. T465.2; god as mare seduces s. D658.3.2; monk says that
he is s. J1361; neighing of s. in Assyria impregnates mares in Egypt
B741.2, H572.

Stampede slaughters animals K927.

Stampeding enemy's horses K2351.6. — Devil s. horses G303.9.9.15; ghost
s. cattle E234.2.

Stamping. — Flood from deity s. on heavens A1015.3; priests s. on stone
to prove pope true A972.1.2; wild hunt heralded by s. of horses
E501.13.3.1.

Stanched. — Blood s. by magic object D1504ff.

Stand. — Magic staff thrown causes wild animals to s. still D1442.4.

Standard. — Extraordinary s. F899.1.

Standing in uncomfortable position (punishment) Q541. — Bewitched person s. on head G269.26; charm chanted s. on one foot with one eye shut, etc. D1273.0.4; child s. at birth T585.8; devil s. in church door writes down names of his own people on sheep skin G303.24.1.4; fairies made visible by s. on another's foot F235.5.1; magic sight by s. (alone) D1821.10, (on certain stone) *D1821.5; man s. all day on one foot F682; people in otherworld s. on their heads F167.4; person buried s. V61.3.0.2; pygmy s. on man's hand F535.2.6; saint s. for seven years without sleep V462.5.2.2; water s. still before prince H71.10.2.

Stanza. — Baby's protesting s. saves life S341.1; supplying missing s. as test H509.4.1.

Star drops from heaven: is money F962.2; on breast F546.3; on forehead as sign of royalty H71.1; -gazer falls into well J2133.8; -girl A762.2; -god A250ff.; indicates location of newborn hero D1314.13; as magic object D1291.2; shines through day at Nativity V211.1.2; signifies hero's birth E741.1.1.2; takes mortal maiden as wife A762.1; transformed to person D439.5.2. — Conception from s. T525; evening s. mistaken for morning s. J1772.7; fairies live in s.-world F215; god descends as shooting s. A171.0.3.2; gold s. F793.1, (on forehead) F545.2.1; goose dives for s., thinking it a fish J1791.8; hero marries s. in girl form T111.2.1; man becomes s. D293; morning s. leads to heaven F63.4; quest to morning s. for answers to questions H1282; remarkable s.-gazer F642.1; shooting s. (as angel) V231.2, (as good omen) D1812.5.2.6, (signifies a birth) E741.1.2, (signifies that someone is dying) E741.1.1; sky supported by north s. A702.3; sky's most distant s. as moon's mother A745.2; soul in form of s. E741.1; tortoise looks towards sky: seeks his wife, a s. A2351.5; transformation into falling s. Q551.3.5.1; vision of s. entering wife's mouth V515.1.2; visit to s.-world F15; wish for s.-husband realized C15.1; wish for s. wife C15.1.1.

Stars A760—A789; answer questions D1311.6.1; as cannibals G11.8.1; as deities A121; fall down at end of world A1051.1; forged by smith A700.5; made from the old moon J2271.2.2; nourished on fire A700.7; as omens D1812.5.1.6; on palm royalty sign H71.1.1. — Absurd theories about s. J2275; Adam's name from initials of four s. A1281.6.1; black s. seen over heads of the bad D1825.3.2; counting s. tabu C897.1; directions on quest given by sun, moon, wind, and s. H1232; dress of gold, silver, color of sun, moon, and s. F821.1.5; end of world when s. in one constellation overtake those in another A1051.2; extraordinary behavior of s. F961.2; fugitives rise in the air and become s. R321; handkerchief color of sun, moon, and s. F822.1; heavenly horses strike hoofs on s. A1141.3; horoscope taken by means of s. M302.4; magic objects received from sun, moon, and s. D814; man deriding faith in s. becomes astrologer N186; rain shed by s. A1131.6; riddle: how many s. are in the heavens H702ff.; sun to eat up s. at world's end A1066; sun, moon, and s. (are highest) H642.1, (bring forth first parents) A1271.1; wishing by s. D1761.1.

Starling. — Color of s. A2411.2.1.16; soul in s. E715.1.5.

Starling's enemies A2494.13.11. — Why s. beak is split A2343.3.1.

Started. — Magic gift: power to continue all day what one has s. D2172.2.

Starting. — "Not s. from here" directions J1648.

Starvation prevented by hymn D2105.1.1. — Murder by s. S132; prostitution to avoid s. T450.3; suicide from s. fright F1041.1.11.1.

Starved. — Lover imprisoned, s. K1218.1.3.1; prisoners s. R51.1; prisoners s. in corpse-filled pit Q465.2.

Starving king in mountain chamber S123.4; parents come to abandoned daughter for food S362; while waiting for God to provide J2215.4; woman eats newborn child G72.2; woman to death for her treasure K2116.2.2. — Bird carries food from deserted child to s. parents S361; child hides food from s. parents S20.2; fat abbot cured by s. K1955.1.1; fool s. self at table, later steals food J2541; lazy man s. to death rather than open mouth W111.5.8.1; lovers s. selves to death T87; numskull s. himself J2135; vow on s. until picture's original found M151.2.1; wife offers s. husband milk from her breasts T215.2; woman sells hair for s. husband T215.8.

Statement. — Clever interpretation of judge's s. J1193; ghost summoned to make s. E387.1.1.

Statements. — Enigmatic s. H580ff.

Statue in cave entrance frightens giantess K1726; comes to life *D435.1.1; inscription gives suitor tasks H335.0.4; left instead of abducted queen K661.4; mistaken for living orignal J1794; mourned and buried in order to account for murdered person K661.2; transformed to drinking vessels D454.15. — Dog becomes s. D422.2.3; fool sells goods to s. J1853.1; God finds that his s. sells at low price L417; gold (silver) s. of animal F855.3; lion and the s. J1454; love through sight of s. T11.2.1; magic s. *D1268, (betrays a thief by indirection) K428; maid behind s. of Virgin advises mistress to give servants better food K1971.3.1; man acts as s. of saint in order to enter convent K1842.1; man behind s. speaks and pretends to be God K1971; marriage to s. T117.11; money from broken s. J1853.1.1; not to steal from holy s. C51.2.4; offended s. carries host off to otherworld *C13; sham miracle: s. raises arm K1972.1; sleeping soldier mistaken for s. J1763.3; tabu: disrespect to goddess's s. C51.1.13; talking s. when destroyed, cannot be replaced for thirty thousand years D1661.1; woman blushes in presence of male s. F647.4, K2051.1; young man betrothed to s. T376; youth makes s. of girl and seeks a girl like the statue T11.2.1.1.

Statues animated by water or wind F855.2. — Origin of calf s. A1546.0.3.

Stature. — Humor of small s. X142.

Staves. — Magic s. D1539.3.

Staying too long in certain place tabu C761.4ff.; too long in otherworld forbidden C712. — Choice: s. at home with loving wife or going to tavern and having unfaithful wife J229.1; fear test: s. in frightful place H1410ff.

Stead. — Foster brother killed in man's s. P273.3.

Steadfastness of love for God tested H1573.5.

Steadying the earth A857.

Steak cut from hero's body G269.9. — Contest: pulling on s. with teeth K64.

Steaks cut from live cow who heals herself by magic D2161.2.1.

Steal, see also **Robbery, Stolen, Theft, Thief.** — Animals sent to s. fire but are lazy and fail A2436; devil helps person to s. G303.22.6; fox confesses sins but is immediately ready to s. again K2055; transformation to s. D657ff.; why Gypsy may s. A1674.1.

Stealing as animal's occupation A2455; from blind beggar's stick K333.4; fairy necklace F357; from fairies F350; with help of trained animal K366; ghosts E593; as greatest villainy H659.7.4; from ogre G610ff.; only a small amount (rope with a mare on the end of it) K188; from sacred booty tabu C51.1.2.1; servants caught by arising early J21.23; as a task H1151; as tribal characteristic A1674; a wife Q252.1. — Beasts s. fruit B16.0.1; bird s. island B172.11; brahmin s. to feed guests W11.4.1; bride s. K1371; child-s. demon G442; devil appears to s. person G303.6.2.15; devil s. Thunder's instruments A162.3.1; dwarfs emigrate because mortals object to their s. F451.9.1.8; dwarfs s. from human beings F451.5.2.2; fairies s. F365, (child from cradle) F321, (man's wife and carrying her off to fairyland) F322; fairies' revenge for s. F361.2; false bride s. true bride's garments K1911.1.8; father kills son for s. S11.3.3.1; fear test: s. clothes from ghosts H1431; giant s. from giant F531.6.8.3.2; giant s. from man F531.6.7.2.1; helper s. object of quest K2036; hanging for s. from church Q411.11.2; impostors s. rescued princess K1935; horse s. tabu C884.2; magic object acquired by s. D838; man put into moon for s. A751.1.4; moon s. food A153.3.1; moon s. from a garden A753.3.2; mountain-folk s. from peasant F460.4.4.5; one s. much called king, little called robber U11.2; parishioner s. alms J1262.5; rabbit s. ember A2218.7; robber's defence for s. from the rich J1269.8; seduction (or wooing) by s. clothes of bathing girl K1335; serpent s. jewels N352.3; servant excuses s.: must support family J1636; strong man serves ogre as punishment for s. food F613.4; tabu: s. (from altar) C51.1.2, (from god or saint) C51.2, (from spirits) C91, (god's wife) C51.2.3; task: s. H1150ff.; trolls s. F455.6.3; witches s. G266.

Stealth. — Wife banished for eating by s. S411.4.

Steam. — Earth from s. made by fire thrown into primeval water A814.5; thumbling carried up chimney by s. of food F535.1.1.2.

Steamship thought to be the devil J1781.1.

Steed, see also **Horse.** — Devil as black s. G303.3.3.5.2; speckled s. tabu C833.8; warrior gives s. to his enemy W11.5.9.

Steeds of night and day A1172.3. — Dwarfs have s. and wagons F451.7.6; fool cuts off tails of oxen so that they will look like fine s. J1919.4.

Steel castle (house) F771.1.4; protects against will-o'-the-wisp F491.3.3; on rock produces fire A975.2. — Casting s. releases troll's treasure F455.6.4.2; dragon must give up treasure when s. is thrown on him B11.6.2.1; lie: remarkable s. worker X1083; merman attacked by putting s. in the water B82.5; magic s. *D1252.1; ship of brass within, s. without F841.1.6; towers of s., silver and gold F772.2.2.

Steep. — Return from lower world up s. slope F101.1.

Steeple. — Cat crawls to s. and tries to fly J2133.3; devil destroys church s. G303.24.4; owl will not betray curate: therefore may live in s. A2229.3; witch marks church s. G241.3.3.

Steer, see also **Bull;** swung round by horns F628.1.2.2. — Helpful s. B411.6; man transformed to s. D133.5.

Stella Maris V282.

Stems. — As many leaves on tree as s. (riddle) H705.1.

Stench. — Devil disappears amid a terrible s. G303.17.2.8; ghost leaves s. behind E588.

Step. — Giant's s. leaves furrows F531.1.3.4; one s. from earth to heaven (riddle) H682.1.9.

Steps to submarine world F725.1. — Death respite for six s. toward God K551.14; giant god goes with three s. through the world A133.2.1; giant s. prodigious distance F531.3.5; grass becomes stone s. D451.5.5.

Stepbrother P283. — Boy accidentally drinks poison intended for s. N332.4. — Cruel s. S33; murder of s. S73.1.0.1; poison for s. drunk by own son K1613.3; treacherous s. K2211.3.

Stepchild. — Transformation of s. D665.2.

Stepchildren. — Banishment of s. demanded S322.4.1; dead wife returns to reprove husband's second wife for abusing her s. *E221.2.1; hen's s. starve: lesson to man J134.1.

Stepdaughter heroine L55. — Cow refuses to help s. B335.7.

Stepfather P281. — Cruel s. S32; lustful s. T418.1.

Stepmother P282; cursed by fire lit under her M431.6; falls into fire from fright N384.3; falsely accuses faithful son N342.1.1; hides heroine from suitor T47; orders stepdaughter killed S322.4.2; wants rich snake for daughter J2415.7. — Cruel s. *S31, (enchants stepdaughter on eve of wedding) T154; curse by s. M411.1.1; death passes by man who fed his s. Q151.2; drowning punishes flight with s. Q552.19.4; evil s. casts boy forth S322.4; hypocritical s. K2056; lustful s. T418; quest for witch s. H1397.1; sparrows enact prophecy of cruel s. M369.2.1.1; supplying food to ungrateful s. rewarded Q65.1; task assigned by s. H913.1.3; witch s. *G205.

Stepping into fairy ring F235.5.2; outside line forbidden C614.1.0.3; stones as sight test H1575.1. — Bird overpowered by s. on his shadow D2072.0.4; conception from s. on an animal T532.2; fairies made visible by s. on certain spot F235.5; islands as deity's s.-stones A955.1;

man as king's s.-stone across fire P116; resuscitation by s. (over) E13, (on corpse) E13.1; tabu: princess s. in water C562; tabu: s. on sacred bread C55.1; transformation by s. in footprint D578; warning against s. on red cloth T299.2.1; one wild goat s. over another J133.1.

Steprelatives P280ff. — Cruel s. S30ff.

Stepsister P284. — Cruel s. S34.

Stepsisters cause flies to collect around girl K2129.3. — Treacherous s. K2112.1.

Stepson cursed to stick in grave mound D5.1.1. — Adulteress and paramour plot against her s. S31.1; queen poisons s. Q211.4.1; stepmother mourns death of s. P282.2; woman spurned by s., attempts to poison him K2111.1.

Stepsons. — Stepmother incites s. to murder S322.4.3.

Sterile, see also **Barren;** land as punishment C934.2; woman's magic power D1716.3. — Why certain animals are s. A2561; druid's curse makes land s. M411.6.1; land made magically s. *D2081; magic medicine makes s. land fertile D1347.3; magic poem (satire) makes land s. D1563.2.3; magic swine make land s. B16.4.

Sterility from breaking tabu C949.3; curse on enemy's wife M431.8; of land as punishment Q552.3.1.1; magically cured D2161.3.10; as punishment Q553.3; among women A1358. — Goddess of s. A431.1.4.

Sterilized. — Earth s. by magic springs D1563.0.1.

Sterilizing. — Son tries s. father S21.5.

Stew. — Canons compared to s. J81.3.

Steward. — Ignorant s. straightens his master's accounts L144.1; treacherous s. K2242.

Stewing. — Resuscitation by s. E15.3.

Stick, see also **Staff, Wand;** with money in it breaks and betrays thief H251.3.4; burns in water F964.4; at corpse's side to chase away scavengers J1442.4.1; for scratching back becomes cobra A1335.14; thrown at animal's rump: hence tail A2215.1; transformed to other object D451.6; under table: imitation diagnosis J2412.4.1. — Alleged rejuvenating s. K116.2; bull's tail becomes s., exterminates army D1400.1.21; coming neither on horse nor on foot (on a s. horse) H1053.5; devil carries a thorn s. G303.4.8.5; flight by vaulting on s. R252; fool puts but one s. of wood in stove J1963; giant with tree for herding-s. G152.1; guilty man's s. will grow J1141.1.4; life in s. E711.6; magic power in s. D1718.1; magic s. D1254, (beats person) D1401.1, (chosen instead of money) L222.3, (transforms) D572.1, (of wood) D956; man becomes s. D217; money stolen from blind beggar's s. K333.4; money in the s. J1161.4; new backbone for horse made from s. X1721.1; serpent steals from God's coat a s. for his back A2262.3; sky black because raised by dirty s. A702.8; sweeping with s. instead of broom J1822; taking a s. from the body (task) H1021.7; tortoise speaks and loses his hold on the s. J2357; transformation by smelling s. D564.1; treasure left in s. N521; wild huntsman's dog when seized becomes s. E501.15.6.7; witch exorcised by burning s. G271.1; word for "s." confused with "stone" A1333.1; woman charms s., hides in it D1393.1.1.

Sticks transformed to animals D441.7. — Fiery s. in hell A671.2.4.8; magic pair of s. D1254.1.1; origin of fire: rubbing s. A1414.1; quails become s. D423.2; quarreling sons and the bundle of s. J1021; resourcefulness test: find relationship among s. H506.10.

Sticking to magic object D1413ff.; object into tracks exorcises witch G271.4.6. — Advice on s. fast: fool seizes ass J2489.9; ascent to sky by s. to magic feather *F61.2.1; captive s. out bone instead of finger G82.1.1; greedy person's hand s. in jar W151.9; hand of sinner s. out of grave E411.0.1; magic knife s. in tree causes wine to flow D1472.2.11; ogre jumping on one's back and s. there magically G311; pitcher magically s. to ground D2171.4.1; princess brought to laughter by people s. together H341.1; staff s. in ground as life token E761.2.

Sticky. — Transformation by eating s. rice D551.6.2.1.

Stifle. — Strong bride tries to s. husband in bed T173.1.

Stile. — Lovers on s. bewitched G269.23.

Still. — Extraordinary s. F891.

Stillborn. — Curse: child s. M441.1; live child substituted for king's s. K1923.5; plants from body of s. child A2611.0.2.

Stilled. — Storm magically s. *D2141.1.

Stilts. — Art of walking on s. A1491.

Sting, see also **Stung.** — Bees pray for s.; punishment, first s. suicidal A2232.2; centipede's poisoned s. A1335.13; cure for insect s. D1517; only one serpent has s. A2219.3; origin and nature of insect's s. A2346ff.

Stinger. — Snake has s. B765.16.

Stinginess *W152ff.; punished Q276. — Amends for s. Q589.4; guests accuse family of s. K2129.4; woodpecker punished for s. A2239.4.

Stinging insects test sham-dead H248.2. — Bees s. opposing army B524.2.1; dupe induced to eat s. fruit K1043; god sends s. bees to punish men A2012.3; resuscitation by s. E16; task: cutting down tree without scratching for s. insects H1184; thorns not s. at night J1819.1.

Stingy almsgiving repaid J1581; innkeeper cured of serving weak beer J1341.7; woman's cloth stolen by tailor K341.13. — Beggar tells s. to go beg J1334; rebuke to the s. J1522ff.; rich but s. couple adopt son T673; servant repays s. master (mistress) J1561.4; woodpecker transformed from s. woman A2261.4.

Stink, see also **Smell.** — Fool has himself buried because of his s. J2193; scientific query: why does the sea s. when it is full of salt J2371.2.

Stirring. — Fool frightened by s. of (animal) J2614, (wind) J2622.

Stirrup leather breaking bad omen D1825.1.28.

Stirrups. — Fortune from informing foreign king of use of saddle, bridle, and s. N411.3; tiny person on horse with long s. X142.3.

Stitch in side from being told about hearing a man chopping wood F647.8.1.1.

Stock, see **Livestock.**

Stocking. — Devil must wait for man to tie his s. before the man comes into his possession K551.4.2.

Stockings. — Magic s. *D1062.

Stolen, see also **Robbed, Steal, Theft, Thief;** bedcover J2672; chickens turn to stone D471.8.1; child rescued by animal nurse B543.3; meat and the weighed cat J1611; mother returns from fairyland each Sunday to minister to her children *F322.3; objects powerful in magic D838.1; property sold to its owner K258; ring proves theft H84.4; sacrament V35; sun restored to sky A721.3; woman rescued from lower world R111.2.1.1. — Animal characteristics: s. from another animal A2245; animal finds s. person B543; animal finds s. goods B543.2; animals s. from saint miraculously replaced V224.3; beast brings back s. child D2156.3; brownie restores s. property F482.5.4.2; child of deity s. F31.1; children s. by witch *G261; complaint about the s. kiss J1174.2; crops s. by magic *D2087.1; dead returns to restore s. goods E352; dog's horns s. by deer A2326.2.2; dragon's pearl s. B11.6.2.3; dream shows where s. girl is hidden D1810.8.2.1; fairy girl returns s. goods for man F302.3.1.1; father rescues son s. by animals R153.3.2; fairy's wings s. bring her into man's power *F302.4.2; fire s. from spider by fly A2229.4; flesh of s. animal cannot be cooked D1318.7.1.1; ghost demands s. money E236.5; ghost reveals whereabouts of s. goods E371.1; girl having been s. by mountain-folk must be baptized anew V81.1; husband rescues s. wife R151.1; king has own gifts s. back P14.12; knight's cloak s. by devil G303.9.9.3; magic object s. back D882ff.; man refuses to eat fifth descendant of s. cow F647.10; magic object raises alarm when s. D1612.5ff.; magic object s. D861; mill will not grind s. wheat D1318.15; moon s. A755.4.2; night s., kept in jar A1174.3.1; priest's collar s. by ghost E593.1; purchaser of s. ornament jailed as thief N347.4; quest for s. princess H1385.1; receiver of s. goods J1169.6; recognition by cup in sack: alleged s. goods H151.4; rescued person s. R111.8; return from dead to demand s. property E236; saint's bell when s. miraculously returned D1602.8; sign of cross prevents child from being s. from cradle V86.1.1; strong man son of bear who has s. his mother F611.1.1; stupid monk recovers s. flocks L141.1; things s. by magic object working for master D1605; transformation to recover s. goods D659.11; wizard locates s. property D1817.0.1.2; wolf returns sheep s. from saint B256.11; woman has meat (liver) s. by bird Z41.1.

Stomach, see also **Belly;** borrowed by animal E787; huge from overeating F559.6.1; removed at man's wish J2072.4. — Animal lives in person's s. B784; child's s. split to cure him of wandering J1842.4; eyedrops prescribed for s. ache X372.3; eye treated for the s. ache J1603; giantess tearing woman's s. F531.1.8.5; magic animal s. D1015.5; magic water cures s. trouble D1502.11; murder by cutting up s. S139.5; needle in elk's s. L391; painting on wife's s. chastity index H439.1.1; paunch fat as s. cure F959.4; person with eyes in s. F512.3; person with mouth in s. F513.0.1; reincarnation of s. into flour vat E649.2; ridding person of animal in s. B784.2ff.; tormenting beast in man's s. B16.0.2; transformation to enter s. D641.3; victim pecks on swallower's s. F915.1; when sad, man lets one lip fall to s. F544.1.2; wood-spirits' teeth on s. F441.4.6.

Stone, see also **Rock;** barrier to otherworld F149.1; becomes silver D475.3.3; beheaded, believed to be enemy K1883.4; bleeds three days before church is plundered D1317.12.1; boat (ship) F841.1.1; breaks: life token E761.5.5; breaks in unchaste presence H411.1.1; canoe D1524.3.1; in church sheds blood in prophecy Q222.0.1; -cast quells burning house F679.6; catches fire F964.3.4; changes color as omen D1812.5.0.14; cross indicates treasure W535.1; of destiny roars out under king *H171.5; emerges from primeval water A816.1; falling from sky kills all but one couple A1009.3; fated to kill, powdered up M377.1; under fertile woman gives milk; under barren, blood H1572.1; fish-hooks tabu C895; giants G371; -headed giant F531.1.2.5; with hole protection against witches G272.13; necklace protects from attack D1381.6; produced by magic D931.0.1; to be protected C665; rolls after saint prays D1654.1.1.1; screams under king's feet H71.10.6; substituted for newly-born babies K2115.2.1; transformed to animal D442.1; transformed to person *D432.1; of truth H251.2; turns red when saint's picture removed V229.23; -spirit F495; transformed to another object D452.1; thrown into greedy dupe's mouth K1035; from victim's rock kills murderer Q582.3.1; as witness against farmer J1141.1.3.1; -woman as creator A1.3. — Adulteress turns man to s. K1535.1; alleged healing s. sold K115.2; angel passes over blessed s. V242.3; ascetic sleeps on s. V462.5.2; bat lifts s. H1562.2.2; boaster throws back flung s. H1562.5; blood drops from s. to indicate girl's innocence D1318.5.5; bluff in court: s. in purse K1765; breaking s. in anger F1041.16.3.2; castle inhabitants turned to s. F771.4.6; child born carrying s. T552.6; cloak given to s. to keep it warm J1873.2; conception from swallowing s. T511.8.1; contest in squeezing water from s. K62; corpse buried under s. so that sun will not shine on him again E431.10; cynic and the bastard s.-thrower J1442.7; deity of s. A498; devil builds bridge minus one s. G303.14.2; devil as s. G303.3.4.6; devil in a s. G303.8.11; devil in each s. of church built with ill-gotten wealth G303.8.4.2; devil prevents moving of little s. by sitting on it G303.9.9.1; devil takes s. away C12.5.2; devil turns object to s. A977.4; disenchantment by throwing s. D712.3.2; dragon becomes s. D429.2.2; dry spring restored by removal of certain s. F933.2; duck becomes precious s. D423.3; dwarfs turn to s. at sunrise F451.3.2.1; earth from s. thrown on primeval water A814.1; earth founded on s. A849.1; eel becomes s. D426.1.1; elephant becomes s. D421.3.2; evil spirits imprisoned in s. D2177.3; fairy music from s. F262.10.1; fairies made visible through use of magic s. on eyes F235.4.3;

fairyland entrance under s. F211.2; flock of geese transformed to s. D423.1.1; food concealed from saint changed to s. Q552.16.1; food left on magic s. brings good luck thereafter D1561.1.6; fool kills chickens by throwing them off balcony against s. J2173.5; fugitive transforms self to s. D671.0.1; ghost laid under s. E437.4; giant with s. heart F531.1.6.10.1; giant's s. boat F531.4.8; giant's s. club F531.4.5.4; giantess becomes s. D429.2.2.1; girl mistaken for s J1763.2; God creates the devil by striking a s. with his whip G303.1.1.4; God finds devil under s. G303.1.2.2; god with s. head A123.4.2; handling heavy s. as unique ability H31.9; horse becomes s. D422.1.2; injunction: protect certain s. from molestation C665; is more of s. above or below ground? H527; lazy woman sees how little bird pecks hole in s. J1011; magic sight by standing on certain s. *D1821.5; magic staff draws water from s. D1549.5; magic s. *D931, (transforms) D572.5; making ship of s. (task) H1021.3; man proof against iron, s., and wood D1841.1; man dies for throwing s. at Virgin's image Q558.5; man lifts large s. F624.2; man sinks into s. F943.1; man with one side of s. F525.1; man transformed to s. *D231; man's bones made of s. A1260.1.5; oath taken on holy s. M114.2; object transformed to s. D471; octopus becomes s. D426.2; oracular s. D1311.16; ordeal by s. from bucket H233; origin of polishing s. A1465.4; persons whose heads are s.-hammers F511.0.3; punishment: carrying corpse of murdered man until s. as long as murdered man is found Q511.1; quest for magic s. H1351; recognition by overheard conversation with s. H13.2.2; reincarnation as s. E642; remarkable s.-thrower F636.4; resuscitation by magic s. E64.17; riddle: what is harder than s. H673; river crossed by means of magic s. D1524.6; rose grows from s. F971.2; sacred s. assists childbirth T584.0.6; sacrifice to s. V11.3; saint sets fire to s. D2158.1.2; saint steps on s., demons flee F405.10; saint's bachall cuts s. D1564.3; salt turns to s. as punishment Q591.2; serpents play with precious green s. B11.6.2.2; sewing a shirt of s. (task) H1021.9; Sisyphus must keep rolling great s. up hill Q501.1; sitting on s. to prevent premature birth T572.1.1; skinning a s. (task) H1023.10; snake becomes s. D425.1.1; soul in s. E711.7; strong man plunges sword into s. F628.4.1; strong man's throw of s. carries away timber of roof F639.3; sunlight turns giant to s. *F531.6.12.2; swearing on a s. M119.5; talking s. as Doomsday sign A1002.2.3, A1091.3; test of strength: lifting s. H1562.2; throwing contest: bird substituted for s. K18.3; throwing s. at own reflection J1791.5.2; transformation: s. to salt C456.3; transformation by striking with s. D566.2; transformation to s. (for breaking tabu) C961.2, (as punishment) Q551.3.4; test of strength: heavy s. flung at boaster H1562.5; treasure hidden in s. N523; treasure under s. N511.6; trolls turn to s. F455.8.1; troublesome bonga (fairy) pegged to ground and placed under s. F386.3; unborn son's soul as s. E726.2; unerring s. missile D1653.1.6; warrior deceived into attacking substituted s. K1845.1; witch melts s. G229.6; witch transforms to s.

G263.2.1; word for "s." confused with stick A1333.1; worship of s. idols
V1.11.2; yearly leap over s. C684.3.

Stone's. — Sea a s. throw deep (riddle) H681.4.1.

Stones become jewels D475.4.1; burn enemies' feet D2091.10.1; cast in
ocean keep dry D1841.4.3.2; for church miraculously supplied V111.2;
erected where enemy falls P557.3; fall on churchyard desecrators
Q222.5.1; falling from tree kill enemies N696.2; join in keen F994.2;
to keep cow from blowing away J2119.8; kill ogre G512.8.2; magically
fly through air D2135.3; from mermaids, fairies, elves, devil D2066.1;
move for king's passage H71.10.5; prostrate selves E761.5.5.1; rained
upon raja hurled back D1400.1.22; reproducing J1896.1; say "Amen"
after saint preaches V229.2.10; in throat to lay ghost E441.2; transformed
to gold coins D475.2.1; turn to gold for charitable money-lender V411.4;
watered to make them grow J1932.7. — Angels from s. stuck against
each other A52.0.8; boy throwing s. killed by them Q582.7; city of
precious metals and s. F761; children said to come from s. T589.6.6;
corpse buried under s. E431.10.1; curse makes s. useless D2089.2; dead
live in s. E481.3.2; dead lovers are now two s. lying together E642.1;
devils are created by sparks produced by Satan's striking two s. together
G303.1.4.2; devils carry away s. of church built with ill-gotten money
Q274.1; digging up certain s. tabu C523.1; doors of precious s. F782.2;
dupe eating s. K1043.2; dwarfs live in s. F451.4.1.12; extraordinary
rocks and s. F800ff.; fairy protects self with s. F278.1; fiery s. in hell
A671.2.4.9; from wooden spring iron bucket makes s. from which water
flows (riddle) H765; gathering all s. from brook or field (task) H1124;
god of s. A499.3; heat test: swallowing red-hot s. H1511.1; hills from s.
cast by giants A963.5; hot s. thrown in dupe's mouth K721.1; invulnerability from hurled s. D1841.5.1.1; island's s. are jewels F731.4; islands
from s. cast by giantess A955.6; magic lyre charms s. into their places
in building D1565.2; magic protective s. from holy well D1382.1.0.1;
man created from s. A1245; mountains from s. dropped A963; murder
by throwing hot s. in the mouth *K951.1; number of s. indicate battle
survivors P554; origin of groups of s. A977; origin of s. A970ff.; palace
consisting of 8760 s.: twelve trees, thirty branches (riddle) H721.4;
parable on s. shaken in jar J98; penance: carrying bag of s. (one for
each murder) on back until it falls off Q521.2; peas transformed to s.
D451.9.1; pillars of precious s. F774.1; rain of s. as punishment
Q552.14.4; rivers formed where certain s. are placed A934.2; sacred s.
V1.6.4.1; self-illuminating precious s. in heaven A661.0.7; shower of
s. seems snowfall to giant F531.5.4.1; stepping s. as sight test H1575.1;
strength in words, in herbs, and in s. J1581.2, T251.5; swindlers given
s. for money K1675; take away all the s. and I will weigh earth
H691.2.1; throwing s. to express love H316.5; thunder from crashing of
s. in moon A1142.5.1.1; trick exchange: s. for bread K149.1; twelve s.
unite in one D491.6, F1009.4; war prisoners shut up between s. Q433.13;

what are best and worst s.? H659.3; when pleading fails man brings thief down from tree with s. J1088; wolf cut open and filled with s. as punishment Q426.

Stoned. — Ogre s. to death G512.2; owner of evil eye s. D2071.0.1.1; rower prefers to be s. by his master rather than remain out in the storm J229.7.

Stoning to death (as punishment) Q422, (for breaking tabu) C929.4. — Seven thousand killed for s. judges N340.2.

Stony. — Carrying soil to cover s. ground H1129.3; growing oil seed on s. ground H1049.2.

Stool. — Gold in s. royalty sign H71.11; magic s. D1620.3.2; move s. before sitting on it J21.34; woman becomes golden s. D235.2.

Stooped. — Dwarfs walk s. F451.2.0.3.

Stopped. — Boat s. by magic D2072.0.3; boiling blood s. E761.1.5.1; emergence of tribe from lower world s. A1631.1; pouring of inexhaustible pitcher s. only at owner's command D1651.4; ship at sea s. by giant's leg F531.3.1.2; wind s. by magic D2142.2.

Stopping. — Attempt at s. dog's mouth with food K2062; countertask: s. all the rivers H1142.3; forgotten fiancée attracts attention by magically s. wedding carriage of new bride D2006.1.5; tabu: s. enroute while carrying image of a god C56.2.

Store produced by magic D1149.1. — Going to s. with scythe K1162.

Stored. — Trickster poses as helper and eats women's s. provisions K1983.

Stork as child's nurse B535.0.7.1; killed along with cranes J451.2; is man while hibernating in Egypt B775. — Bad luck follows man who shoots s. *N250.1; children brought by the s. T589.6.1; color of s. A2411.2.5.3; courtship of s. and crane B282.23; creation of s. A1966; friendship between monkey and s. A2493.14.3; helpful s. B463.4; why s. is holy A2541.2; king sees how male s. kills his unfaithful wife and follows its example T252.2.1; why s. must hunt for living A2452.2; man transformed to s. D155.1; bill and legs of a s. to make him look more like a real bird J1919.1; protecting as s. does J2442; tabu to kill s. C92.1.4; why s. has (black back) A2411.2.5.3.1, (long neck) A2351.4.1; Zeus gives frogs s. as king J643.1.

Storks become men in Egypt in the winter D624.1. — War between serpents and s. B263.7.

Storm appears to be island D2031.17; as barrier to otherworld F141.2.1; from broken tabu C984.2; calmed by wizard D2141.0.8.1; frees marooned tortoise N662; of gigantic hailstones F962.5.1; overturns idol F962.0.2; produced by magic *D2141; as punishment Q552.14, (for profaning temple) Q222.4; at royal birth F960.1.1.3. — Animal allows himself to be tied so as to avoid being carried off by s. K713.1.1; church bell rung as protection against s. D2141.1.1; confession of sins of a pilgrim calms a great s. at sea V24.1; death from magic s. F1041.1.7; devil

48*

fetches soul in s. M219.2.1; electric s. breaks island F962.1; false proof
of s.: cloak dipped in water K1894; father saves self in s. S141.2; Flying
Dutchman sails because he defied the s. E511.1.3; fox persuades bird
to show him how she acts in a s. K827.1; human sacrifice to s. spirit
S264.1.1; laying ghost causes s. E443.0.1; magic object raises s. D1541.1;
magic s. *D905, (produced by animal) D2141.0.11; man scorns the s.:
killed by it L471; man thrown overboard to placate s. S264.1; man
transformed to s. D281; marvelous picture falls from sky in s. F962.12.3;
new moon with old moon in her arm as sign of s. D1812.5.1.5.1;
poisoning fish causes s. C41.4; prophecy: death by s. M341.2.2; Rübezahl
as s. spirit F465; Satan causes property-destroying s. G303.9.4.0.1; thief
escapes in magic s. K532.2; wild hunt (disappears during s.) E501.16.5,
(heralded by s.) E501.13.6.

Storms on land (runaway horse) J1483.3; magically drawn down on foe
D2091.5; when wind-spirit awakes A1128.2. — Ghost causes s. E292;
giants' shouts are s. or great noise F531.3.8; herb protects from s. at sea
D1388.1.2; lies about s. X1610; magic object controls s. *D1541ff.; origin
of s. in sixth heaven A1130.2; phantom condemned to wander through
s. E512; saint controls s. D2140.1.1.

Stormy. — Origin of s. sky A1147; wild hunt appears on s. nights
E501.11.1.4.

Story, see also **Tale;** to king brings reparation J1675.6; restrains king's
hasty judgment J571.5; told to discover thief J1177.1. — Cast-forth
wife must sit at horse-block of palace and tell s. to each newcomer
Q482.4; execution escaped by s.-telling J1185; fool believes realistic s.:
inappropriate action J1849.1; free keep in inn exchanged for good s.
M231; king makes everyone tell him s. P14.14; leaving during s. reveals
guilt J1177.0.1; life s. in ten hours Z24.1.1; magic s. D1266.3, (protects) D1380.13; quest for unknown s. H1382.2; rebuke for poor, long-
winded s. J1223; recognition through s.-telling H11; robbery as s. of
theft told K341.20; tabu: chief being in ale-house when there is no
s.-telling C564.1; telling s. to allay woman's desires K2111.0.1.

Stories creep out of man's belly C672.1. — Lulling to sleep by "sleepy"
s. D1962.4.1; pig boils only after true s. H251.3.11; putting out of
countenance by telling evil s. J1211; refusal to accept help until s.
told P331; telling true s. H252.0.1.

Stove runs over hill D1641.3. — Candle put in the s. to dry J2122;
devil goes through s. with great noise G303.17.2.3; drying snow on the
s. J2121; fool puts but one stick of wood in the s. because several others
have burned up J1963; grateful s. D1658.2.1; heat from s. with no fire
J1976; magic s. *D1161; numskull ties yarn about s. to keep heat from
escaping J1942; recognition by overheard conversation with s. H13.2.7.

Straight. — Forest of s. and tall trees F812.1; those departing from s.
path fall in holes J95; why wolf has s. back A2356.2.2.

Straightened. — Master's accounts s. by ignorant steward L144.1.

Straightening curly hair (task) H1023.4; dog's tail H1023.4.1.

Straightforwardly. — Lady answering queen s. J751.1.1.

Straining stream after bathing C721.3.

Strange. — Animals of s. and varied coloring B731.0.1; aversion to burial in "s. clay" V61.11; don't fall asleep in s. place J21.41; don't require honey from s. country J21.40; in s. place look about you J21.34.1; insanity from seeing s. sight *D2065.2.

Stranger accidentally chosen king because picked up by sacred elephant N683; not interested in you J1087; presented with first fish A1528; playing without permission tabu C892; should not sleep J21.41.2. — Adulteress refuses to admit husband under pretence that he is s. K1511.1; children know local road; why doesn't s.? J2212.9; marrying a s. J2463.2; mysterious s. performs task H976; rescue by s. R169.15; rewarded s. dies from joy F1041.1.5.2.

Stranger's. — Brass statue at city gates blows on trumpet at s. approach *D1317.9.1; magic knowledge of s. identity D1810.0.13.

Strangers to be given precedence over man at home P631; umpire beauty contest H1596.2. — Choices: kind s., unkind relatives J390ff.; entertaining s. tabu C745; man seeks s. for hospitality W12.2; no food for s. until one of them wrestles W213; not to speak to s. C492; sacrifice of s. S265; tabus of s. C576.

Strangled. — Animal s. by victim which he tries to eat K1643.

Strangling hawk inside his shirt J2461.1.5. — Demons s. children G302.9.4; fairies s. child J2415.4; miser s. self after he dreams of spending money W153.6; murder by s. S113; murderer s. companion in bed K951.0.2; punishment: s. Q424; suicide by s. A1599.9.

Strangulation. — Adventures from s. attempt N776.2; hare deceives wolf, fox into s. K713.3.

Strap. — Recovering s. from sea (task) H1132.1.3.

Straps. — Devil unable to endure cross made by s. of knapsack G303.16.3.2.

Strassburg. — Battle between lice of S. and of Hungary X651.

Strategy aids hero L311.2; to escape undesired lover T323. — Animals overcome man's adversary by s. *B524.2; fairies' s. F278; military s. K2350ff.; murder by s. K910ff.

Straw becomes animal D442.1; becomes gold D475.1.20; immobilizes witch G273.7.2; on shoulder to identify self J2012.6; transformed to snake D441.9. — Abandoned child wrapped in s. S336; bean, s., and coal go journeying F1025.1; bridge of s. F842.1.5; burning animal in s. to release curse M429.3; covering house with s.: mother suffocates K1462.2; covering mistress instead of roof with s. J2489.8; dead person sails over sound on bundle of s. E581.7; fairy replaces man's heart with heart of s. F281; ghost sails on s. E581.7; magic s. *D1276; magic from swallowing s. D1735.1; old maid with bundle of s. in bed X752; origin of s. A2685.2; princess hides in s. R313; reincarnation as grass s. E631.2.1; soul as s. E745.3; talkative animals given twice threshed s. as punishment J2362; wife covered with s. J1805.1.1; witch in form of blade of s. G212.1; witch's horse transformed from s. G241.3.1.

Straws protection against witches G272.12.

Straying. — Horse s. tabu C884.2; magic object prevents animal from s. D1446.

Stream, see also **Brook, River, Water;** becomes hot in which saint performs his ascetic devotions F932.3; carries message to prisoner R121.9; changed to egg D476.1.8; as deity's wife A425.1.1; devil's trap, kills drinker G303.16.2.3.5; magically appears D2151.2.5; of paradise from roots of world-tree A878.1; runs through house F715.4. — Aphrodisiac given naked woman in s. K1395; not to bathe in clear s. C721.2.1; burial on far side of s. E442.2; carrying hundreds of sheep across a s. one at a time (task) H1111; communication by milk in s. K1549.5; crossing weed-filled s. H1197; devil as s. G303.3.4.11; do not cross a swollen s. until it has run down J21.21; entering a garden by swimming down a s. K2377; fairies ferried across s. F213.2; fairies live in trees by s. F216.1; fairy unable to cross running s. F383.2; flowing s. forms arc over other-world isle F162.2.9; fresh water s. in sea F711.4.1; ghost frightens people into s. E2; giants carry a church across a s. F531.3.6; hair transformed to s. D457.4.1; why iguana lives in s. A2433.6.4; jackal covers up inability to cross s. J873.1; leaf sent down s. as warning to one below H135; long tongue cut out and used to bridge s. F544.2.2.1; magic book conjured away by throwing it on s. D2176.4; magic s. quenches fire D1382.8; man carried and dropped in mid-s. K1268; man helping another across s. drops him *W155.2; milk in s. as signal H135.2; money tested by throwing it into s. to see if it will swim J1931; numskull bales out the s. with nutshell J1967; oath so heavy it dries up s. M115.1.1; ogre's ashes cast on s. cause rapids to stop G655; plunging into s. suitor test H353; prison with s. of water in it R41.3.2; prophecy: drowning in particular s. M341.3.3; reward for carrying Christ across a s. Q25; saint's bachall leads s. through mountain (or up-hill) D1549.3.2; separation by being on different banks of s. N315; servant accidentally throws master into s. J2133.5.1.1; sun cools off in s. A722.5.2; test of resourcefulness: carrying wolf, goat, and cabbage across s. H506.3; transformation: s. becomes bloody D474.2; trickster carries girl across s., leaves old woman K1339.7; turning low s. to fill high s. H1138.1; witch powerless to cross s. *G273.4.

Streams of battle blood F1084.1; of blood magically drawn down on foe D2091.3; from roots of earth-tree A878.1.1; of sugar, milk and molasses dry up in punishment Q552.3.5; of wisdom flow from magic well D1300.3.1. — Four s. from four corners of earth A871.1; magic medicine causes s. to dry up D1542.3.1; navigable s. from well F718.11; origin of s. *A930ff.

Street. — Fishing in the s. J1149.2, K341.11; test of unknown father: gold on s. H485.

Streets. — Fires burnt in s. to ward off witches G272.4; god of s. A413; punishment: disgraceful journey through s. Q473.

Strength, see also **Strong;** from anger F1041.16.3ff.; preferred to cleverness J246; in unity J1020ff.; of witches G221.3; in words, in herbs, and in stones J1581.2, T251.5. — Appetite of twelve men given with the gift of twelve men's s. M416.1; contest in s. won by deception K70ff.; devil performs deeds of unusual s. *G303.9.2; dwarf-hero of superhuman s. F610.2; fairies' extraordinary s. F253.1.1; fanciful marvelous s. of animal B740ff.; giant's s. in hair F531.1.6.13; god of s. A489.2; hero's precocious s. F611.3.2; king chosen for s. P11.4; lion's great s. A1421.1.1; loss of s. from broken tabu C942; loss of magic s. by smoking C942.1; magic cup prevents s. loss D1389.3; magic object restores s. D1519.1; magic s. *D1830ff.; in numbers there is s. J1279.4; object gives magic s. *D1335ff.; old person commits suicide when s. fails P674; saint's s.: breaks wall V229.14; secret of s. treacherously discovered *K975; strong hero acquires his s. F611.3; strong hero suckled by mermaid given s. of twelve men F611.2.2; suitor test: overcoming princess in s. *H345; sword so heavy that hero must take drink of s. before swinging it F833.1; test of s. H1562; tiger challenged to s. contest K547.9; trial of suitors' s. H331.14; troll's food gives s. G304.2.2.1, F455.4.2.1; witch has extraordinary bodily s. G221.3.

Strengthening. — Defenses by s. one's own weakest spots J672.

Stretching the beam J1964.1; cliff D482.4; mountain F55.1; tree *D482.1, K1113, (refuge for fugitive) R311.4. — Animal characteristics from squeezing or s. ancient animal A2213ff.; animal's size increased by s. A2213.3; lies about s. X1785; magic hair s. after fugitive D1435; magically s. self to overcome opponent in battle D55.1.1.1; magically s. self to sink tent pole D55.1.1.2; man magically s. self (overcomes cliff) D55.1.1, (reaches otherworld) F59.1; mountain in love s. out leg A965.1; troll s. neck so long that fire comes from lips G304.2.1.2; woman enticed to upper world on a s. tree K1339.2.

Strewing. — Fairy driven away by s. peas in his path F381.2; ghost detected by s. ashes *E436.1.

Stride. — Giant's mighty s. F531.3.5; hundred-league s. D2122.2.

Strife. — Supernatural beings associated with s. F400.1.

Strike, see also **Struck.** — Naïve remark of child: you forgot to s. mother J122; not to s. (monster twice) *C742, (supernatural wife) C31.8; people and things that s. one another in otherworld F171.3.

Striker. — Lie: remarkable s. X945.

Striking inquirer to death in re-enacting event J2133.14.1; at reflection in jar J1791.7.1; self blows D2184.1. — Blind men s. each other as they try to kill pigs X125; blindness cured by s. F952.3.1, F952.4; devils are created by sparks produced by Satan's s. two stones together G303.1.4.2; disenchantment by s. D712.3; fairy mistress s. human lover F361.17.9; death by s. head against door lintel N339.13; disenchantment by s.

D712.3; flowers spring up on saint's s. ground F971.6; fox produces fire by s. tail to ground D2158.1.1; girl s. man who tries to kiss her T322; God creates the devil by s. a stone with his whip G303.1.1.4; hills from hero's s. earth A962.7; man s. king saves his life N656; ogre killed by s. G512.8; quack goitre cure: s. J2412.8; transformation by s. D566.

String with thirteen knots in child's mouth G271.10. — Disenchantment by removing neck s. D723.2.1; girl born with red s. around neck T552.1; life token: zither s. breaks E761.5.2; literal numskull drags jar (bacon) on s. J2461.1.1; magic ball of s. to which one sticks D1413.18; magic s. *D1184.2; prince born with silver s. H71.7.2; substituted s. kills ogre K1611.1; transformation by binding with s. around neck D585; unknown paramour discovered by s. clue T475.1.

Strings leading blind men to water removed K1081.3.

Strip. — Maid eloping with pretended lover is forced by him to s. T72.1.

Stripes. — Child of three fathers born with three s. T563.1; origin of animal's s. A2413ff.; why grizzly bears have three s. on inside of stomach A2367.2.1.

Stripping. — Tabu: s. dead and slain C877.

Strokes shared K187. — Odd number s. in beating devil G303.16.19.19.

Stroked. — Magic object works by being s. D1662.

Stroking. — Beautification by s. D1863; magic strength by s. D1835.3.

Strong, see also **Strength;** bride tries to stifle husband in bed T173.1; man as magician D1711.8; women *F565.2. — Association of s. and weak J420ff.; alliances with the s. J684; dead mother makes son s. E323.7; devil as a large, s. man G303.3.1.1; diving to become s. K1051.3; dwarfs are s. F451.3.8; husband has his s. servant substitute in bed with s. wife K1844.1; lie: remarkably s. man X940; making dupe s. K1012; making self s. in peace time J674.2; quest for s. adversary H1225; quest for s. man H1213.2; remarkably s. (hands) F552.2, (man) F610ff.; rights of the s. *U30ff.; subordination of weak to s. J421; suitor test (lifting s. princess's giant weapon) H345.1, (riding s. princess's horse) H345.2; sword only for s. hero D1654.4.1.1; trolls s. F455.2.2; trouble-making s. men G512.0.1; weak fear company of s. J425; why animal is s. A2528; wooing s. and beautiful bride T58.

Stronger and strongest Z42. — Child s. than mother at birth T585.1.1; mouse s. than wall, wind, mountain L392.

Strongest man to punish thieves K335.1.11. — Quest for s. H1316; what is s. (riddle) H631ff.

Stronghold in otherworld F163.6. — Fairy duped, loses s. K232.2.1; fairy s. F222.2; fairy s. as riddle answer H768; king's s. on island P14.17.

Struck, see also **Strike.** — Animal characteristics from being s. A2213.5; magic object s. on ground D806.1; man s. dead with iron bar by devil G303.20.3; strong hero s. by smith from iron F611.1.12.

Structure, see also **Building;** to be finished when king's daughter marries H1292.18. — Not to build too large a s. C771.

Structures. — Giants as builders of great s. F531.6.6.

Stubborn couple J2511. — Vow to get s. girl half-married only M149.6.

Stubbornness *W167ff.

Stucco ears after clipping J1184.2.

Stuck, see **Sticking.**

Student, see also **Pupil;** competes with master P342; enjoys professor's wife K1594; from paradise J2326; is helped by devil when he can answer three questions in rhyme G303.22.3; resuscitates whole family E181.2; returns from dead to warn master of futility of his studies E368. — Devil as s. G303.3.1.14; hungry s. talks to cat, gets served J1341.10.

Study. — Magic learned by s. D1721.6; thief observes night s. J1394.1.

Studying magic arts D1738; occult books tabu C825; philosophy as suitor task H335.0.2.1.

Stumble reveals drinking horn N223; reveals treasure N534.1.

Stumbling over bloody corpse brings accusation of murder N342.2. — Forgetting by s. *D2004.5; man s. on bathing maiden N716.1.

Stump. — Lie about pulling s. X1237.1.1; lie: remarkable extrication from tree s. X1133.1; magic s. supplies drink D1472.1.28; treasure buried under s. N511.1.13.

Stumps. — Fighting on s. of legs after they have been cut off at knee S162.1.

Stung, see also **Sting;** by the goblet J1324. — Numskull s. J2131.2.

Stupid classes J1705; devil *G303.13ff.; fear clever J423; hero L121; house-spirit F488; husband J1702; monk recovers the stolen flocks L141.1; ogre *G501; person surpasses clever L141; sons learn trades, kill off father J2499.7; wife J1701; youngest son becomes clever L21. — Futility of trying to teach s. J1064; moon as sun's s. brother A736.3.2; quest for three persons as s. as his wife H1312.1; riddle: three s. things H871.1; soldier silent before king as before all s. persons J1369.5; why animal is s. A2537.

Stupidity, see also **Fools.** — Child cast out because of his s. S327; man pretends s. before plotters K1818.3.3; seduction by feigned s. K1327.

Stuttering. — Humor of s. X135.

Sty. — Why hog lives in s. A2433.3.6.

Styx A672. — Oath by S. M119.1.1.

Subaqueous monastery V118.2.

Subdivisions. — Origin of tribal s. A1640ff.

Subdued. — Wild animals s. by saint's bachall D1442.3.

Subject. — Origin of s. tribes A1657.

Subjects driving away ruler P15.8. — Men die so god of dead may have s. A1335.11.

Subjection. — Blood in spittle tests s. H252.2.

Submarine home of the gods under the sea A151.3; otherworld *F133; world F725ff. — Deity's s. home A192.2.3; magic s. ship (boat) D1525; quest to s. monastery H1287.

Submerged. — Person gradually s. by sea F945.

Submission as clerical virtue V461.4. — Disenchantment by s. D730ff.

Subordination of weak to strong J421.

Subservient. — Riddle on making people s. H588.16; women s. to men A1372.9.

Subsiding. — Primeval water s. in specified time A810.2.

Substance. — Shadow mistaken for s. J1790ff.

Substitute for candle repaid with substitute for money J1551.5; in contest *K3ff.; for the corpse J1959.2; man killed in friend's place P316; used to save promised child S252.1. — Animal adopted as child s. T676; chaste wife deceives gallant with a s. in bed K1223.4; compassionate execution: s. child K512.2.2; death postponed if s. can be found *D1855.2; devil a s. for (dead man) G303.18.2, (new-born child) T684, (woman who went to spend night with a priest) G303.25.11; fairy steals child from cradle and leaves fairy s. *F321.1; fool's brothers s. a goat for the body of the man he has killed K661.1; ghost as s. for bride E363.1.1; gods furnish s. for child sacrifice S263.2.1; image of child as child s. T677; king as s. for condemned man J1189.3; mistress deceives lover with a s. *K1223; recognition of maidservant s. bride by her habitual conversation H38.2.3; test of friendship: s. as murderer H1558.2; husband as s. for wife receives punishment for her adultery T261.1; old woman as s. for girl in man's bed K1317.2.1; wife as s. for (husband's mistress) T318, (princess jailed with husband) K1814.2, (servant discovers husband's adultery) K1585.

Substituted arrows *K1617; bride *K1911ff.; bridegroom K1915; caps cause ogre to kill his own children *K1611; children K1920ff.; eyes *E781.1; letter *K1851; limbs E782.0.1; weapons win combat K97.2. — Animal s. for child served at meal K512.2.1; animals s. for newborn children K2115; compassionate executioner: s. puppet drowned K512.2.3; calumniated wife: s. letter K2117; escape by use of s. object *K525ff.; girl s. for boy to avoid slaughter by father K514.1; leaky vessel s. by husband so that his wife and paramour are drowned Q466.1; maid s. for mistress in assignation bed H1556.4.3; wooden log s. in cradle for unbaptized child by devil G303.9.9.4; worthless object s. for valuable K331.3.

Substitution of false bride revealed by animal *K1911.3.1; of horses causes angry man to kill his own K942; of low-caste boy for promised child H38.2.5; of self for another condemned to die K528.2; of transformed wife for husband's mistress D659.7. — Cheating by s. of worthless articles K476; deception by s. *K1840ff.; deception into fatal s. K840ff.; riding contest won by s. K27; robber cheated by s. K437.1; seduction by disguise or s. *K1310ff.

Substitutions for penances Q520.0.1.

Subterfuge. — Task evaded by s. H950ff.

Subterranean, see also **Submarine;** castle *F721.5; paradise F111.4; world F721ff. — Captivity in s. palace R41.1.1; earthquake from movements of s. monster A1145.1.

Subverted. — Trial by ordeal s. by carrying magic object D1394.1.

Success in battle wins bride H331.2.1; of returned exile L111.1; in replacing eyes *E781ff.; of unpromising hero (heroine) L160ff.; of youngest brother on quest H1242. — Accidental s. in hunting and fishing N620ff.; animal helps person to s. in love *B582; magic medicine brings s. D1561.1.4; unusual s. in love T27.

Succession, see also **Chain, Cumulative, Series;** of creations and cataclysms A632; of helpers on quest H1235; to the throne M314.2, P17, (lost in gambling) N2.5.1. — Bungling fool has s. of accidents J2661; plot to make king criminal, forfeit s. K1166.

Successive disguises K1834. — Disenchantment by holding enchanted person during s. transformations D757; escape by s. disguises K533; five children at birth for four s. years T586.1.4; god in s. animal forms A132.0.1ff.

Successor. — Do not leave kind deed to your s. J1284; dying king names s. P17.3; king propounds questions to his sons to determine s. H508.1.

Succubus F471.2.1.

Sucker. — Why s. has small bones in body A2367.1.1.

Sucking heals wounds F950.6; monster G332. — Ghost s. people's breath E251.3.4; punishment: snake s. woman's breasts Q452; resuscitation by s. out poison E21.5; serpent s. man's breath B16.5.1.2.1; snake s. milk from woman A2435.6.2.1; snake s. poison from (own bite) B765.8, (bitten raja) B511.1.3; vampire s. blood E251.33; witch s. blood G262.1; witch transforming self to hare, s. cows D655.2.

Suckled. — Child s. by transformed mother D688; imprisoned relative s. by woman through prison wall *R81; man s. by siren B53.2.

Suckling of children *T611. — Adoption by s. T671; angel of death spares mother who is s. children V233.1; baby goes to mother for s. H495.1; dead mother returns for s. child *E323.1.1; strong hero's s. F611.2; woman s. all babies at son's circumcision H495.3.

Sudden love gives bad luck T10.3.

Suddenly. — Man s. acquires long gray beard on scaffold at execution F1044; tabu: coming s. on supernatural creatures C52.2.

Sued. — Father-in-law s. for not dying as predicted W151.5.

Suffering healed by time U262. — Choice: s. in youth or old age J214; dwarfs s. abuses by mortals F451.5.11; girl promises unborn child to devil for s. the birth pangs S223.1; long-s. god A139.12; marvelous sensitiveness: s. from merely seeing work done F647.2.

Sufferings. — Ascetic faster increases his s. by placing food and drink before himself V462.2.1; mother's s. impress undutiful son P236.7.

Suffocation as punishment Q425. — Murder by s. P16.3.1.1, S113.2ff.

Sugar transformed to ashes D476.2.4; turns to earth as punishment Q591.2.1. — Fish thought to be chewed s. cane J1761.4; let them eat s. J2227.1; ogress attracted by s. cane scent G677.

Suggestion. — Assignment of tasks in response to s. H910ff.; birth by s. J2338; magic sleep by hypnotic s. D1962.4.

Suicidal. — Wisdom taught by s. example J173.

Suicide in belief loved one dead N343; cannot rest in grave E411.1.1; to carry out own promise M203.2; from fright of evil prophecy F1041.1.11.3; from fright of starving F1041.1.11.1; ghost E266.1; of lover who believes his mistress dead N343; over hasty condemnation N340.1; to make wife widow J2106; of man falsely accused N347.6; to prevent brother-sister marriage T415.7; punished Q211.5; by strangling *A1599.9; to save virginity T326. — Adulterous wife convicted, commits s. T249.1; architect commits s. when surpassed by pupil W181.2.2; brahmin induced to s. J1181.0.1; burial of s. to prevent walking E431.16ff.; curse of s. M451.1; devil gains two souls through s. K217; devil persuades man to commit s. G303.9.4.2; disappointed lover a s. T93.3; dissuasion from s. J628; dupe tricked into s. K890ff.; earth from body of divine s. A831.7; faithful animal plans s. when it thinks master dead B301.3; father commits s. believing that son is dead N344; future s. weeps in mother's womb T575.1.2; ghost haunts s. spot E334.4; ghostly rope of s. E538.2; girl s. rather than marry unwanted suitor T311.2.1; god of s. A310.4; goddess prevents s. V10.1; husband s. when wife dies T211.3.1; king commits s. P16.3.0.1; lover deceived by false s. agreement K1232; man s. in grief for wife T211.9.2; miser doesn't commit s.: saves rope W153.7; mother commits s. over son's marrying foreigner P231.7; nagging wife drives husband to prepare for s. T253.1; noose used by s. as protection from accident D1384.2; old person commits s. when strength fails P674; outcast wife commits s. when she sees relatives' heads S452; poor host commits s. when unable to entertain P336.1; queen commits s. P26; sacrificial s. S263.5; scorned lover's s. T81.2.1; sham s. to soften lover K1232.1; skull of s. must roll in dust until it has saved a life Q503.1; sleeping before s. J21.2.2; snake s. B752.3; wife commits s. at husband's death P214.1; wife threatens s. to get own way T252.6; wife's s. at husband's death T211.2; wild huntsman wanders because of s. *E501.3.2; witch commits s. G279.1; would-be s. cured by drinking poison N646; would-be s. finds treasure N545.2.

Suicides. — Ghost causes s. E266.2.

Suitor, see also **Lover;** asked to kill child by his first wife S303.1; bathing in boiling water without cooling it H1023.24; brings own lamp, outwits girl's mother J1575.1; finds girl immature: father protests she has children J1279.3; with only love to offer wins L393; sent from one relation to the other for consent to the wedding Z31.1; task: make fairies dance H1177.1; test involving mountain of seed H1091.3; test: threats to his person H1406; tests *H310—H359. — Abduction by rejected s. R18; abducted princess successfully wishes self with rejected s. N425; animal s. B620ff.; bashful s. woos oak T69.4; chief performs s. task, rival steals bride K1371.6; devil as s. assigned building task H1131.2; dwarf a s. of mortal girl F451.5.18; dwarf s. desists when unwilling maiden guesses his name F451.5.15.3; extraordinary companions help hero in s. tests F601.2; fly helps s. pass test B587.2; girl behind tree advises unwilling s. K1971.6; girl promises herself to animal s. S215.1; house-spirit as s. F482.8; husband kills unwelcome s. H1551.1; husband praises s., woman falls in love T13; impudent s. threatened with hanging Q413.5.1; killing monster as s. test H1174; lion s. allows his teeth to be pulled and his claws cut J642.1; magic sleep induced by disappointed s. D1964.2; ogre s. buries woman's murdered lover K912.3; poor s. served good supper prepared for rich one J1561.3.1; princess rescued from s. R111.1.9; scorn of unloved s. punished T75.1; scorned s. consoles self J877; shrewd s. blackmails usurer K443.11; spurned s. rewards girl offered by her mother Q87.13; strong girl mutilates s. Q451.0.3; ugly picture makes girl refuse s. T11.2.0.1; undesired s. killed Q411.2; unsuccessful s. pretends friendship with husband, kills him K2022; woman kills impudent s. Q414.0.12.1.

Suitor's. — Scorned s. testimony on adulteress disbelieved J1151.4; undesired s. messengers imprisoned Q433.11.

Suitors ill-treated T75.0.1; receive enigmatic answers H593. — Commonplace expressions scare off wife's s. J2461.2.2; entrapped s. K1218.1; father kills daughter's s. S11.4.1; girl promised to three s. kills self T92.0.1; girl remains virgin after s. killed T311.3; girl's demon s. F402.1.15; girls keep up appearances to deceive s. K1984; gods attempt to settle dispute among s. N817.1; killing all other s. as suitor task H335.4.3; necklace of unsuccessful s. heads S110.3.1; princess builds tower of skulls of unsuccessful s. *S110.3; widowed she-fox rejects s. who do not resemble her deceased husband T211.6.

Sukasaptati K1591.

Sulking. — King's s. chamber P14.6; prince s. until quest accomplished H1212.3.

Sulphur in the censer J1582.2. — Devil's odor of s. G303.4.8.1, G303.6.3.4.

Sultan as beggar tests friends H1558.7.1; of flies B246.2; frees prisoner recognized by smile H79.4; tries to avoid adversity J2488.2.

Sultan's daughter as bribe to ogre S222.4; daughter in love with captured knight T91.6.4.1.

Summer and winter garden D1664; produced by magic D2145.2. — First day of s. V70.1; genealogy of s. A1154; hedging in cuckoo to keep s. year round J1904.2.1; more than one swallow to make s. J731.1; perpetual s. in otherworld F161.1; standing between s. and winter H1058; tie horse between s. and winter H583.7; winter becomes s. at saint's funeral F960.2.6.

Summers. — Year with two s. X1602.

Summit. — Magic transportation to highest s. D2135.4.

Summoned dead prophesies M301.14. — Animals s. by magic object D1441; ghost s. E380ff.; god s. by weeping A189.2; helper s. by magic object D1421ff.; kite teaches rhyme by which he may be s. for help B501.2; person s. by thinking of him D2074.2.1.

Summoning the devil *G303.6.1.2; fairy lover F301.1; souls punished E380.1. — Animal gives part of body as talisman for s. its aid *B501; means of s. spirits F404.

Sun A710—A739; answers questions D1311.6.3; is brightest H651.1; brings all to light N271.1; brothers each work one month, play other eleven A739.3; captured R9.1; caught in snare A728; cooks for saint D2149.3; is creature that is of all countries, that is loved by all the world, and that has no equal (riddle) H762; cursed by man for burning L351.2; cursed by moon A736.9; darkened at Crucifixion V211.2.3.3; darkened at death of holy person F965.2; as deity A121.2; devoured by monster at end of world A1052.1; does not shine during deluge A1010.1; eats all own children except morning star A764.1.2; at edge of sky A739.1; at end of world A1052; falls, causes world-fire A1031.4; father A221; forged by smith A700.5; gives light to stars A769.5; -god A220ff., (as creator) A1; as god's child A700.8; as gods' home A151.6.2; -god banished rain, wind A287.0.1; -Eod's wife pours fire over earth A1031.4; as helper N818.1; as hero's father A512.4; kills brother sun with cockscomb plant A1156; to lock up moon, eat stars at world's end A1066; made to stand still D2146.1.1; makes magic ring work D1662.1.1; as magic object *D1291.1; as magician D1711.3; moon, and stars bring forth first parents A1271.1; moon, and stars are highest H642.1; nourished on fire A700.7; purchased A700.6; -ray D1291.1.1; as real traveler H726; refuses to shine when murder is done F961.1.1; revives self after death E4; sends heat to cook saint's meat V222.13; sets at noon to hide fugitive R236.2; shines only two hours at hero's death F960.2.6.1; shining at night Doomsday sign A1052.2; smears dung on moon's face A751.5.2: steals tree of life E90.1; is swiftest H632.3; takes mortal to heaven F63.3; thrown on fire A1068; turns fiery face upward: hence cold A1135.1.1; in underworld A681; has woman wife T111.2.3. — Absurd theories concerning the s. J2272; animals from mating of s. and moon A177; bargain: if the s. reverses its course K194; bat makes s. smile, ends eclipse A1046.1; bird running before the s. B7.3; blindness healed by rays of s. F952.2; bottom of the Red Sea has seen the s. only once (riddle) H822; bridegroom like s. Z62.2; castle east of s. and west of moon F771.3.2; cattle of the s. A155.1; cloud magically made to cover s. D2147.1; contest in seeing sunrise first: s. on the trees K52.1; cows of the s. B19.6.1; coyote rides with s. A724.1.0.1; contest of wind and s. L351; corpse buried under stone so that s. will not shine on him again E431.10; creator with s. and moon in hands A18.6; deities push s. back and forth at solstices A1157; devils carry away the s. when they fall from heaven G303.8.2; directions on quest given by s., moon, wind, and stars H1232; dress of gold, silver, color of s., moon, and stars F821.1.5;

druid causes s. to stand still D2146.1.1.1; extraordinary behavior of s. F961.1; first men perish when s. first rises A1009.1; foolish fight with s. J1968.1; frogs fear increase of power of s. which will dry up all their puddles J613.1; god hides from s. A179.8; gold moon, s., star F793.1; handkerchief color of s., moon, and stars F822.1; hat which turns the s. D1546.1.1; head of murdered child becomes s. A1277.3; how much does s. earn for his daily work (riddle) H715; jackal carries s. in bag on back: burns his back black A2218.2; looking at s. tabu C315.2.2; love like wind in hot s. H592.1.1; magic object controls s. *D1546.1; magic objects received from s., moon, and stars D814; making s. shine in north H1023.16; man's desire for s. A1017.1; moon deceives s. A753.3.1; moon as grinder to bring fire from s. A741.3; not to let s. shine on girl before she is thirty years old *C756.2; original moon becomes s., sun, moon A736.8; path to s. on sun's rays F154; pigeons cover s. to aid hero H982.1; prophecy: man will make s. stand still M312.8; quest for place s. rises H1371.1.1; quest to place where s. sets H1284.1; quest to s. for answer to questions H1284; riddle of the course of the s. H725; riddle about s. shining only once in land H822.1; selling ability to influence s. K154; sloth may not look on s. A2233.1.4; stars as children of the s. eaten by their father A764.1.1; setting s. mistaken for fire J1806; tabu to face s. while urinating C99.1; tribes from choices s. offers people A1610.5; troll bursts when s. shines on him G304.2.5; tying s. with stone chain H1023.23; visit to land of the s. *F17; war with the s. A739.2; why loris never looks at s. A2231.13; why s. sets early in autumn A1156; why worm avoids s. A2433.6.9.

Sun's children most brilliant stars A764.3; disposition A738.2. — God's palace with doors for s. journey A151.4.2; moon as s. younger brother A745.3; man's beauty eclipses s. F574.1.4; variations in s. seasonal heat A739.4.

Sunbeam as support *F1011ff. — Catching a s. H1023.22; clothes hung on s. *F1011.1; magic journey on s. D2121.10; man so small he can put his head through mote in s. F535.2.4.

Sunday, see also **Sabbath;** christening of Thursday births brings nightmares F471.1.5. — Devil throws quoits on S. A977.2.3; fortress built on S. destroyed Q552.14.1; fountain gives milk on S. F716.1; man in moon burns brush as punishment for doing so on S. A751.1.1; mill refuses to work on S. D1676; respite in hell on S. Q560.2.1.1; resurrection to take place on S. E751.6; stolen mother returns from fairyland each S. to minister to her children *F322.3; tabu: journeying on S. C631.1; well full on S. F718.7; wild huntsman wanders for hunting on S. *E501.3.6; not to work on S. C631; will-o'-the-wisp is girl cursed for gathering plants on S. A2817.2.

Sundays. — Souls leave hell on S. E755.2.0.1.

Sundial covered to protect it J1943.1. — Examining the s. by candle-light J1943.

Sunfish. — Markings on s. A2217.3, A2412.4.1.

Sunk, see also **Sink.** — King's coffin s. into river P16.9; ship magically s. D2098; sword that is to kill one is weighted and s. so as to avoid prophecy M377.

Sunken bell sounds *F993; church bell cannot be raised V115.1.3; palace magically raised D2136.2.2. — Captivity in s. valley R42; disenchantment of s. castle, town D789.8; mermaid prevents raising of s. church bell B81.13.10; raising s. church bell C401.4; treasure buried in s. ship N513.5.

Sunlight carried into windowless house in baskets J2123; fatal to fairies F383.4.3; ray causes leprosy D1500.4.4; turns giant or troll to stone *F531.6.12.2. — Conception from s. *T521; cynic tells king to get out of his s. J1442.1; not to be exposed to s. C842; transformation by s. D567; why s. stronger than moonlight A733.1.

Sunrise direction tabu C614.1.5; to help sick man F961.1.2.1; tabu C751.7ff. — Cock crows at s. A2489.1.1; contest in seeing s. first K52; dwarfs turn to stone at s. F451.3.2.1; in dwarf land s. is at midnight F451.4.6; mock s. K1886.3; no s. at hero's death F965.2.1; origin of colors at s. A797; prayers at s. V58.1; tabus on action after s. C752.2ff.; tabu for king to sleep after s. C735.2.3; tabu on sleeping at s. C735.1.1; trolls turn to stone at s. F455.8.1.

Sunset direction tabu C614.1.5. — Delayed s. F961.1.5.3.1; devil appears when woman looks at herself in mirror after s. G303.6.1.4; early s. hides fugitive F961.1.10; no s. F961.1.5.3; one must not whistle after s. else the devil will go along with one G303.16.18; origin of colors at s. A797; ox lent by fairies must not be worked after s. F391.1.1; prayers at s. V58.1; sun reappears after s. F961.1.5.2; sun's children take human form at s. A736.5.2; tabu: doing thing after s. C752.1ff.; tabu: sleeping after s. in lighted house C735.2.4; trees disappear at s. F811.11.

Sunshine. — Bird wants s., worm clouds U148.1; father's counsel: walk not in s. from your house to your shop H588.1; regulation of s. A1172.1.

Sunwise circuit for good luck D1791.1.

Superhuman race's magic D1719.3, D1728; tasks H1130ff. — Curse mitigated by s. task M428; devil in s. form G303.3.2ff.; disenchantment when s. task is finished D791.1.2; supplying s. amount of grain H1122.1; wild man of s. strength F610.1.

Superior troops distributed throughout army P552.2. — King is s. to all P12.10; why one people s. in power to another A1689.11.

Superiors. — Lowly animal tries to move among his s. J952.

Superlative. — Many times the s. J2217; riddles of the s. H630ff.

Superman. — Magic knowledge of s. D1810.0.7.

Supernatural adversary in gambling N3; being becomes goat D134.4; bird prevents mother killing babe B524.4; birth of culture hero A511; creature aids quest H1233.4; creatures propound riddles *H540.1; creatures tabu after sunrise C752.2.1; creatures change size at will D631.4; growth T615; helpers *N810ff.; lapse of time in fairyland F377;

lover performs girl's work T91.3; lover's food tabu C243.1; manifestations at death (of pious person) Q147, (of wicked person) Q550.1; origin of hero Z216; person seen in dreams gives advice K2035; person reveals infidelity F345.2; person causes sun to stand still D2146.1.1.2; powers identify God H45.1; substitute for pious warrior K3.2.1; voice points out criminal N278; wife leaves husbands stealing from her R227.3; wife bestows beauty D1862.1; woman promises to return if she bears boy M272. — Abandoned child reared by s. beings S353; affront to s. spirit punished Q552.14.0.1; bargains and promises between mortals and s. beings M242; changeling shows s. power to work and thus betrays maturity F321.1.1.4; child of s. birth exposed S313; dismembered s. woman C312.2.3; drop from magic cauldron gives s. information D1310.2; fairies bestow s. gifts at birth of a child F312.1; hero's s. helpers A528; husband (wife) of s. being longs for old home and visits relatives T294; love of mortal and s. person T91.3; magic object causes both s. sight and blindness D1331.3; magic object gives s. information *D1310ff.; magic object gives s. wisdom *D1300ff.; magic object received from s. being D812; magic wisdom received from s. being D1811.2; man created by s. creature A1291; marriage of mortal and s. being T111; mother reveals son's s. father P231.5; not to offend s. relative C30ff.; observing s. helper tabu C311.1.5; people eating child become s. G55; princess rescued from s. being R111.1.10; recognition by s. manifestation H192; rejuvenation by s. person D1882; resuscitation by s. person S121; not to see s. C311; reward for s. help Q93; tabu: coming suddenly on s. creatures C52.2; tabu connected with s. beings C0—C99; tabu to name s. wife C435.1.1; tests for husband s. wife H310.1; task performed with help of s. wife H974; three s. ogre helpers N812.7; treasure placed in ground by s. beings N511.3; not to utter name of s. creature *C432; wife rescuing husband from s. H923.1; wish for s. husband realized C15.

Supernaturals flee at mock sunrise K1886.3.3; tricked into daylight exposure K839.6.

Supernaturally born boy L112.1.1; impregnated woman bears dragon T554.11.

Supervised. — Planets s. by angels A780.1; stars s. by angels A769.3.

Supper won by trick: the mutual friend K455.1. — Undesired lover kept overlong at s. K1227.9.

Suppliant. — Image blamed by s. for misfortune V123; image indicates favor to s. D1622ff.; hidden man behind image gives unwelcome answer to s.: image blamed K1971.8; statue of Virgin sews for s. D1620.1.4.

Supplication. — Feet seized in s. P676.

Supply. — Spirit drinks water s. dry G346.4; water-spirit controls water s. F420.4.9.

Supplies received from magic box D1470.2.2. — Cobolds furnish s. to their masters F481.2.

Supplying food by magic *D1030.1; objects through prayer V52.4; stones for church V111.2; superhuman amount of grain H1122.1; water in land where it is lacking (task) H1138.

Support of the earth A840ff.; of the sky A665. — Bird thinks that the sky will fall if he does not s. it J2273.1; castle (house) with extraordinary s. F771.2ff.; island with extraordinary s. F736; sunbeam as s. *F1011ff.

Supporting. — Old cobra s. earth A1412.1; precocious boy s. mother, self by wits T615.4.

Suppression of prophecy M300.4.

Supreme god A101.

Surely. — As you s. will J1481.

Surety. — First s. A1586; God as s.: the abbot pays J1559.2; priest as s. K455.5.

Sureties. — Hero slain during absence of his s. K929.8.

Surf. — Origin of s. A925.6; rejuvenation by riding s. D1889.8.

Surfboard. — Ogress's tongue becomes s. D457.14.1.

Surge. — Tidal s. marks death place A913.1.

Surgeon. — Skillful s. F668.

Surgical. — Useless s. operation J1842.

Surly. — Dumbness for s. speech Q583.2.

Surpassing. — Unpromising s. the promising L140ff.

Surprise capture R4. — Not to express s. in lower world of dead C413; woman veils self as expression of s. P671.

Surprised. — Wife s. in adultery feigns death K1549.2.

Surrender to the rake J2613. — Capture of castle by pretending to s. and entering K777.

Surrendering R75. — Foolishness of s. weapons J642; fairy mistress s. man to his mortal wife F302.5.1; vow to die before s. ship M161.4.1.

Surreptitiously. — Butter s. added to broth K499.2.1.

Surrounded. — Deceptive land purchase: as much land as can be s. in a certain time K185.7; palace s. by rivers of wine, rosewater, and honey F771.7; person in magic sleep s. by protecting fire *D1967; wild huntsmen s. by fire E501.7.6.4.

Survive. — Tests of power to s. *H1510ff.

Survivor. — Lone woman s. of doomed city A1006.7; messenger sent away only s. of battle N693; unique s. Z356.

Survivors of flood A1029.6.

Susanna and the elders J1153.1, K2112.

Suspected. — Impostor acting as God in tree s. and tree burned K1971.12; innocent man accidentally s. of crime N347.

Suspended. — Building castle s. between heaven and earth (task) H1036; castle s. on four chains F771.2.1.1; crown s. over king's head F828.1; god's function s. during his absence A173.1; large millstone s. on thread over head F451.5.4.2; pestle magically s. J2411.9; sinners in hell s. Q569.4; woman s. by breasts Q451.9.1.

Suspension between heaven and earth as punishment Q552.23. — Magic s. of weight D1691; self s. on iron hooks under armpits Q541.4.

Suspicion. — Dissension aroused in army by casting s. on general K1088; escape from s. of crime K661; killing or condemnation on s. *N340ff.; sham blind man throws s. on real blind K2165.

Suspicious. — Devil advises s. husband G303.9.7.3; trickster makes two friends each s. of the other's intentions *K2131ff.; youngest daughter s. of impostor L62.

Sustenance. — Prisoner's s. from outside prison R84.

Suttee P16.4.1. — Lifting power of widow ready for s. H479.1; origin of s. A1545.5.1.

Swallow advises hen against hatching out serpent's eggs J622.1.1; and the hemp-seeds J621.1; as messenger B291.1.11. — Association of swan, s. J429.1; why s. brings good luck A2536.1; color of s. A2218, A2219.1, A2411.2.1.4; creation of s. A1917; why s. does not like green trees for nest A2431.3.5.1; why s. has black feathers and only two feathers A2378.8.6; why s. has forked tail A2214.1, A2378.5.1; magic skin of s. *D1025.4; man calls his wife "my s.": she becomes s. D511.1; man transformed to s. D151.1; more than one s. to make a summer J731.1; reincarnation as s. E613.4; why s. is thief A2455.2; why s. has no tongue A2344.2.3.

Swallow's lost voice A2422.9; nest A2221.2.4, A2431.3.5. — Annoyance of s. chirp J215.1.4; meaning of s. song A2426.2.12.

Swallows put on mourning at crucifixion: have never taken it off A2221.2.4.1; warn other birds against roosting in tree with glue J652.2. — Contest in beauty between s. and crows J242.6; why s. migrate A2482.1.

Swallowed person becomes bald F921; person reborn E607.2.1. — Boy s. by fish, escapes K565.1; culture hero s. and recovered from animal A535; curse: to be s. by a siren M434; children s. at birth to avoid prophecy fulfillment M376.3; children s. by earth R142; death by being s. C929.5; fairy transforms self to fly, allows self to be s. by woman and reborn as fairy F392; frog spawn s. by girl B784.1.4; heathen s. by earth H1573.1.1; man to be s. up by earth at foot of stairs M341.2.25; man never knowing want s. up by earth L424; man s. by fish and later rescued alive (lie) X1723.1.2; overweeningly proud man s. up C770.1; person s. up by earth F942.1, (and taken to lower world) F92.2; person transforms self, is s. and reborn in new form *E607.2; pregnant wife s. to prevent birth of son M376; princess sick because toad has s. her consecrated wafer *V34.2; sun s. and spit out A721.2; temple s. by earth F941.2.3; tent-house folded and s. as means of carrying it F923; theft of light by being s. and reborn *A1411.2.

Swallower. — Victim kills s. from within F912; victim rescued from belly of s. F913.

Swallowing hot coals because husband unfaithful T818; prostitute's pearls to avenge theft K306.3; stolen goods to escape detection K417. —

Animal s. another to save him K649.1.1; animals s. thumbling F535.1.1.7; conception from s. a stone T511.8.1; cow s. book: cause of maniplies in stomach A2219.2; curse: ground s. children M448.1; darkness from awk s. sun A721.2.1; deceptive s. contest K82.4; dragon s. arrow intended for hero B529.2; fish bears men-children after s. man's rinsings B631.3; fish s. man to rescue him B541.1.1; fire stolen by s. K382; giant s. men F531.3.11; heat test: s. red-hot stones H1511.1; husband s. sorceress D1479.1; magic gate s. axes D1381.31; magic powers from s. D1735; man s. magic servants D1719.8; mermaid s. man B81.10; person s. animal eggs from brook B784.1.1; person s. pebble, snake grows in stomach B784.1.2; person s. snake semen B784.1.2; rakshasa in deer's head s. men G369.1.6; rod s. other rods D1693; Satan s. victim G303.20.7; star s. others F961.2.7; voice made rough by s. hot iron F556.1; wager on s. egg in one gulp N75.

Swallowings. — Earth s. as punishment Q552.2.3; extraordinary s. *F910ff.

Swamp spirit F494.1.1. — Punishment: drowning in s. Q467.3.

Swan birds' king B242.1.9; blamed when crow drops filth J429.2; as crow's wife absurd J1293.1.1; as chastity test H411.17; maiden *D361.1, (finds her hidden wings and resumes her form) D361.1.1; maidens as guardians of treasure N572.2; as matchmaker B582.2.3; song B752.1; transformed to person D361. — Angel whiter than a s. (riddle) H663; association of s., swallow J429.1; color of s. A2411.2.6.2; crow demands young s. in payment K255.3; fairy as s. F234.1.15.1; god rides s. A136.1.4.1; helpful s. B469.2; killing s. tabu C841.5; magic adhesion to s. D2171.3.2; man transformed to s. D161.1; marriage to s. maiden *B652.1; origin of s. A1981; pet s. saves self by singing death song N651; prophetic s. B143.0.1; revenant as s. E423.3.2; sacred s. B811.5; slow s. lasts longer than speedy crow L394; soul as s. E732.7.

Swans do not suffer harsh weather after conversion to Christianity V331.9; harnessed to chariot B558.2; live on pearls B768.3. — Boat drawn by s. B558.1; divine s. on inaccessible island F134.4; king of s. B242.2.10; transformation to s. by taking chains off neck D536.1.

Swarm. — Charm calls down s. of bees D1441.2.

Swarms. — Extraordinary s. of birds F989.16.

Swastika A137.3.1.1.

Swaying. — Transportation by stretching and s. tree D1520.1.1.

Swearer. — False s. not allowed to approach altar M101.1.

Swearing, see also **Oaths, Vows.** — Person s. oath places hand in mouth of image H251.1; wolf s. by God B251.7.1.

Sweat, see also **Perspiration;** used in medicine D1500.1.36. — God born from another god's s. A114.1.1.1; goddess born from s. of rock washed by sea A114.1.1; horse's s. as water that has neither fallen from heaven nor sprung from earth H1073; man created from s. A1262; man from

s. of creator A1211.2; man to earn bread by s. of his brow A1346; ocean from creator's s. A923; origin of s. A1319.8.

Sweating as punishment for theft Q212.3. — Man s. blood F1041.10; resuscitation by s. E15.2; till front is s. J2499.1.

Sweaty. — Alp rides horse s. at night F471.1.1.1.

Swedes as magicians D1711.10.2.

Sweeping as bride test H383.3; peas as devil's task G303.16.19.3.1; with stick instead of broom J1822. — Old woman s. strikes sky, raises it A625.2.3; tiger s. temple for saint B256.7.

Sweet and bitter fountain in otherworld garden F162.1.2.1; potato's origin A1423.1, A2686.4.1. — Blood of certain animal said to be s. K961.0.1; fruits always s. F813.0.4; honey is s. J2497; man's body exudes s. scent F595; sea flows s. water F931.9.2.1; sour fruits made s. by saint F979.1; when s. fails, try bitter J1088.

Sweets turn into bugs D449.1. — Magic s. D1038.

Sweeter. — What is s. than honey (riddle) H671.

Sweetest. — What creature has s. blood: gnat's tongue torn out A2236.1; what is s. (riddle) H633ff.

Sweetheart, see also **Mistress;** kills self when lover dies N343.4. — Dead lover haunts faithless s. E214; dead man warns youth against visiting s. E366.2; dead s. haunts faithless lover E211; forcing attentions on friend's s. K2297.1; invulnerability lost if man forgets s. D1847.1; lover dies beside s. F1041.1.2.1; man thinks s. an enemy, flees N318.1; old s. chosen in preference to new J491; pursued s. becomes tree D642.3.1; tasks imposed by s. H916; wraith of s. stays in room where lover died E723.5.

Sweetmeats. — Preacher's wife gives s. away J1262.5.1.

Swelling from grief F1041.21.2; of limbs from breaking tabu C941.2. — Animal venom causes s. X1205; sight of wild hunt causes s. of head E501.18.8.

Swift. — Devil carries man through the air as s. as wind (thought) G303.9.5.4; devil is s. G303.4.8.6; giant s. despite size F531.1.3.5; king and jester flee: the king's s. horse J1483.1; magic journey as s. as thought *D2122.3; why certain animals are s. A2555.

Swifter. — Eye s. than bird, wing, or lightning H661; horse s. than the rain K134.2.

Swiftest horse on earth B184.1.1.3. — Riddle: what is the s. H632ff.

Swiftness. — Breaking legs to overcome s. K1013.6.

Swill. — Entrance to dwarf home under s. hole F451.4.1.7.

Swim. — Fish eat other fish: guilty must s. deep A2238.3; learn to s. before going into the water J2226.

Swimmer. — Marvelous s. F695; remarkable s. X964.

Swimming with birds tabu C858; in the flax-field J1821; in imaginary river D2031.1.2; in lake tabu C615.2. — Animal's method of s. A2444ff.; attempt at s. in mist J1821.1; beheaded man s. F1041.14; bluff: provisions for the s. match K1761; dwarf s. in human's drinking-horn X142.2; entering a garden by s. down a stream that flows into it K2377; fatal s. race: spirits drowned K869.4; firewood continually swept away from s. man H1129.5.1; giant s. across rivers as others cling to him F531.3.13.2; magic prevents s. fatigue D1384.4.1; strong man s. as he carries companions F631.3; stupid woman s. on roof J1972; wife s. to imprisoned husband T215.6.

Swindler punished *Q274; takes money for parents in heaven J2326.1.
Swindler's plans foiled J1521.
Swindlers given stones for money K1675.
Swine, see also **Hog, Pig, Sow;** bridegroom disenchanted D733.2; eating certain fish H1199.7; -god A132.7; kick trees for fruit F989.7; maddened by oak forest smell B783; magically kept from fattening D2089.3.1; march like soldiers B290.1; shaking tree bole H1199.6; transformed to (another animal) D412.3, (person) D336; worship V1.8.4. — Burrowing s. heat ground B19.4.1; clerics expelled in shapes of s. Q226.2; devastating s. B16.1.4; devil in form of s. G303.3.3.4; devil's abode is between hoofs of s. G303.8.7; eaters of s. not to enter Venus's temple J1447; fairy as s. F234.13; fat from s. never farrowed H1025; magic harp summons s. D1449.3; magic s. B184.3, (cause robbers' drowning) Q428.2, (blight corn and milk) B16.4.3, (make land sterile) B16.4.4; man reincarnated as s. *E611.3; man transformed to s. D114.3, *D136, (will regain human form) M313; marriage to s. B601.8; red or green s. B731.8; revenant as s. E423.1.5; sitting among s. so as to learn Bavarian language X652; person of remarkable sight finds tracks of s. stolen seven years before his birth F642.2; vow taken on holy s. M114.3; venomous s. B776.4.
Swine's. — Contours of land from s. rooting A951.2; elephants fear s. grunting J2614.3; why s. belly is bare A2317.1.
Swineherd P412.2; finds paradise F111.0.2; as hero L113.1.1; rescues abandoned child R131.3.4. — Chieftain recognized by s. H173.1; disguise as s. K1816.6; transformation into s. D24.3; treacherous s. K2255.1.
Swineherds. — Magician and queen as s. D2031.4.2.
Swing. — Dupe takes fugitive's place in s. K845; golden s. F895; magic s. D1154.3.1; pursuer duped into supposed s. K845; recognition by unique ability to s. spear H31.3.
Swinging by moustache H328.2; ogre G327; seventy girls H506.5; steer by horns F628.1.2.2. — Deceiver in s. contest killed *K1618; Evil Eye averted by s. cat over child's cradle D2071.1.2; fatal s. game K855.
Swollen creek causes orphan's marriage N699.4.
Swooning, see also **Fainting;** from cowardice W121.8.1; from grief

F1041.21.7; for love T24.2. — Magic power by s. D1733.5; rescuers s. on seeing rescued R188; wife s. at husband's death T211.9.1.1.

Sword causes death whenever drawn D1402.7.1.2, D1653.1.1.1; causes magic sleep D1364.27; as chastity index H435.1; bridge to otherworld F152.1.6; can be moved only by right person D1654.4.1; of fire from heaven Q552.13.0.2; hidden by old man N511.1.0.2; hidden under water N513.2; inlay melts in battle F1084.0.1; large or small at will D631.3.3; leaves no trace of blow behind it D1666; left for posthumous son to kill father's murderer T645.1; made magically helpless D2072.0.1; magically changes to wood when executioner is to decapitate innocent person H215.1; magically dulled D2086.1; of chastity T351; of Damocles F833.2; that is to kill one is weighted and sunk so as to avoid the prophecy M377; pierces rock F997; as reward Q114.3; received from dead father E373.2; resuscitates princess E149.2; rusts E761.4.7; and shield as proxy at wedding T135.3.1; splinters arrow with each strike F667.2; spoken to as human F997.1; sticks to magic hand D1413.12; as tongue deceives ogre G572.2; too heavy to lift against friend H1558.8.1; tested F611.3.3; transformed to wood D473.1; threat overcomes witch G275.15.1; which will break in only one peril Z314. — Captor deceived into giving up s. K611.3; choice of two s. sheaths H511.1.1; conqueror's s. between teeth signifies defeat P551.1; curse: s. to fail in danger M441.1; deceptive s. game K867.1; deceptive s. loan J1556.1; demon occupies s. F408.1; devil kills man with fiery s. G303.20.1; disenchantment by s. D771.8; don't draw s. against the innocent J21.2.3; extraordinary s. F833; execution s. turned to wood D2086.1.1; extraordinary s. sinks into earth F948.4; fairy gives magic s. F343.10.1; fairy smith gives knight magic s. F343.3; felling wood with s. F1041.16.3; fiery s. between hostile king, queen D2196; fixing the two pieces of a broken s. (task) H1023.8; garment proof against all but man's own s. D1381.3.1; getting s. to lift cheese J2173.2; ghost summoned for s. E387.2.1; giant s. of culture hero A523.1; god makes s. drop from hand A185.2.3; god's s. A157.5; groom's s. marks bride's forehead T135.4; hero's s. falls, cuts enemy F1087; hills from hero's striking earth with s. A962.7; holding king's s. makes one his inferior K1292; identification by s. H125.1; incandescent s. D1645.4; lifting s. tests strength H1562.2.1; lightning from flashing s. A1141.2; lightning as God's s. A137.14.4; lost s. found in fish N211.1.4; magic sight by looking at polished s.-blade D1821.3.7.4; magic song dulls s. D1414.4; magic s. *D1081, (gives warning) D1317.6, (received in dream) D812.12.1; magic wand breaks enemy's s. D1414.1; magic writings on s. render it harmless D1414.2; man kept alive by consecrated s. E163; man passes s. to captive, killed K818.1; man plunges s. into stone F628.4.1; marriage of girl to a s. T117.2; monkey jumps over a ravine with his s. girded on J2133.2; monster fettered with s. just out of reach A1074.1; mountain-man carries shears at side like s. F460.1.3;

needle as thumbling's s. F535.1.1.12; oath taken on s. M113.1; ogre killed with s G512.1; person lives after s. cutting F1096; quest for person who can withdraw s. H1313; quest for s. of light H1337; quest for Thunder S. H1337.1; recognition by unique ability to dislodge s. from stone or tree H31.1; robbers give hero s.: used to kill them J642.2; rock beaten by s. provides water D1549.5.1; resuscitation by polishing s. E142; sign of cross endows s. with magic D1766.6.2; skillful fencer keeps s. dry in rain F667.1; soul in s. E711.10; spring from striking earth with s. A941.3; stealing s. from giant H1151.14; strong man's mighty blow with s. F628.4; substituted s. of wife's paramour T247.1; testing s. by cutting steer in two F611.3.31; unseen s. decapitates in forest F812.5; unsheathing s. thrice before attack J21.2.1.

Swords sheathed in scabbards as thrown in air F661.7.2. — Lengthening s. by twirling them F679.2; precautionary drawing of s. J2255; wild hunt heralded by clash of s. E501.13.1.3.

Swordfish. — Man becomes s. D179.5.

Sword-thrusts. — Magic fly-whisk stops s. D1381.13.

Swordsmanship. — Mountain-spirit teaches hero s. F460.4.2.3.

Sworn brethren P311; brothers as culture heroes A515.1.2.

Syballine books bought at great price J166.1.

Sybil draws picture of Madonna and Child in sand V341.

Symbol. — Magic s. D1299.1.

Symbolic interpretations H600ff.

Symbolism *Z100—Z199; of worship A1546.0.1.

Sympathetic animals B303; helper robbed K345; magic *D1782.

Sympathy. — Absurd s. for animals or objects J1870ff. — Animal mutilates self to express s. B299.5.1; extraordinary s. with animals F648; leaves shed in s. F979.15; river drying up in s. F932.6.2.

Symplegades D1553.

Synagogues V112.3.

Syphalitic. — Vengeful paramours send s. man to substitute in woman's bed K1317.3.

Tabernacle. — Devil disappears after T. erected G303.17.1.3; dust of T. H411.18.

Table always set in otherworld dwellings F165.4; thrown out of the sledge: to go home by itself J1881.1.4. — Beard grows through t. F545.1.3; browbeaten husband from under the t. T251.6; compressible t. D491.2.2; cutting t. reveals witch G257.3; dead children "invited to eat at God's t." E754.2.4; extraordinary t. F784; fool leaves when placed between two fools at t. J1715; magic t. *D1153; mould put on t. for the dead E433.1; rose grows from t. F971.2; scratching contest with devil: man's wife shows scratches in her oak t. K83.1.1; stepladder for setting the t. J1573.1; trickster saws legs of t. so that it collapses K1431.

Tables in otherworld F166.10.

Tablecloth. — Escape from prison by use of magic t. D1395.2; magic t *D1153.1.

Tablets of trees from lovers' graves unite E631.0.1.2.—Theft of t. of fate A1417.

Tabu, see also **Restrictions;** C (entire chapter); against whistling after sunset G303.16.18; fear of threatening animals while treasure is being raised N553.5; imposed as punishment Q430.1; looking around while raising treasure N553.4; spitting on castaway broom G303.16.19.2. — Blackmail about breach of food t. K443.13; boy breaks t., fairies kidnap him F325.1; death postponed by keeping t. D1855.4; disenchantment by breaking t. D789.4; dupe tricked into breaking t. by lying K1076; earth splits, plain sinks when t. broken F944.4; fairy gift worthless when t. broken F348.0.1; fairy mistress leaves man when he breaks t. F302.6; fighting in fairyland t. F210.1; flood from breaking t. A1018.1; girl summons fairy lover by breaking t. *F301.1.1; lake from violating t. A920.1.8.1; magic mango withdrawn for broken t. D868.1; magic sleep from breaking t. D1962.6; mother forces child to break eating t. S12.2.3; rival prevailed on to break t. K2220.0.1; transformation by breaking t. D510ff.

Tabus connected with fairy gifts F348; connected with trip to fairyland F378; in effect while treasure is being unearthed N553. — Death from violating t. fated N101.2; demons coerced by druid t. G583; origin of eating t. A1517; origin of t. A1587.

Taciturn man W225.

Tact in reproving the great J816.

Tadpoles. — Mankind descended from t. A1224.1.

Tail in ground betrays calf's killing K1686; and head of serpent quarrel as to usefulness J461.1.1; buried (thatched) and dupe attacked K1021.1; of dragon B11.2.8. — Animal puts t. in man's hands, caught X1133.3.1; animal tied to another's t., killed J2132.5; bear bites the seemingly dead horse's t. K1047; bear fishes through ice with t. *A2216.1; bear persuaded to slide down rock wears off t. K1021.3; beaver borrows muskrat's t. and never gives it back A2241.10; bird with t. of fire B15.7.14; bush-rat bites off tortoise's t.: hence tortoise's short t. A2216.4; calf's (fox's) t. from earth to heaven H682.1.7; camel's t. cut off, turns to grass R231.2; chastity ordeal: holding shaven and greased t. of bull H412.2; crow's beak and t. alternately stick on tarred bridge Z39.3; devil's t. G303.4.6; why dogs look at one another under the t. A2275.5.5; dog's t. mistaken for master's J2015; dog's t. mistaken for gun J1772.12; dog's t. wagging raises wind D2142.1.1; dragon encircles city with t. B11.2.8.1; fairy's long t. F232.8; fish struck by coconut: hence flat t. A2213.5.2; fox with eight-forked t. B15.7.4; fox prefers weight of his t. rather than give part of it to ape J341.1; fox produces fire by striking t. to ground D2158.1.1; fox's t. drops and frightens animals K2323.1; fox's t. pulled out long A2213.4.2; giantess with t. F531.1.6.14; god with t. A123.11; hair from fox's t. opens all doors D1562.2; hawk's t. cut in two by sword as he is being transformed A2216.5; herd's spirit in last goat's t. D859.6; huldra with cow's t. F460.1.5; hot tin under horse's t. K1181; if witch grabs horse's t. on bridge, man is safe from her G273.4.1; lighting the cat's t. J2101.1; little child recognizes devil by his t. G303.4.6.1; lion's t. as broom H1151.11; lizard's t. imitated from snake's A2272.2; magic animal t. D1029.2; magic object causes t. to grow D1375.4; magpie tells man he is to die next day: no tongue and long t. A2236.4; man escapes from bee's nest on bear's t. X1133.4; man has head and t. of cat B29.4.1.1; as many hairs in the head as in ass's t. H703.1; miller ties cow's t. to himself J2132.3; monkey borrows deer's t. A2241.11; mouse regains its t. Z41.4; mouse's t. in mouth of sleeping thief causes him to cough up swallowed magic ring K431; nailed wolf's t. X1132.1; ogress with knife t. G510.5; origin and nature of animal's t. *A2378ff.; person formerly animal retains t. H64.3; planting animal's t. to produce young J1932.4.1; pulling hairs from bewitched animal's t. G271.4.9; pursuers hanging on to animal's t. shaken off R231.2.1; punishment: tying to horse's t. Q473.2; pursuer pulls out t. of fugitive's horse R265; resuscitation by animal's t. E64.16; shooting off leader's t. (lie) X1124.1; snake hard to hold by t. H659.2.1; snake preserved in ark: to stop hole with t. A2145.2; squirrel borrows coney's t. A2241.7; straightening dog's t. H1023.4.1; swallow thrown on his t.: cause of split t. A2214.1; task: stealing elephant's t. H1151.6; thief escapes by leaving animal's severed t. and claiming that the animal has escaped and left his t. K404; thief maintains that bird had no t. K402.2; tiger explains t. as boil K2011.2; toad trades his t. for mole's eyes A2247.5; why jackal's t. bare A2317.12.2; why rat's t. round and hairless A2317.12.3; where is t. pointing? toward rear J1305; witches kiss devil's t. G243.1.1; woman created from dog's t. A1224.3.

Tails fall off mountain spirits when they are baptized V81.2; tied together for protection *J681.1. — Beaver and muskrat exchange t. A2247.6; deceptive division of pigs: curly and straight t. K171.4; devil pulls off goats' t.: hence they lack t. A2216.2; drawing by horses' t. as punishment Q416.2.1; fool cuts off t. of oxen so that they will look like fine steeds J1919.4; God changes t. of devil's cows A2286.2.4; leopard with nine t. R15.7.7; men with t. on hands F515.3; men as monkeys without t. A1224.5.1; why men have not long t. A1319.2; pegs driven into backs of baboons become t. A2262.2; persons with t. F518; tailless animal tries in vain to induce foxes to cut off t. J758.1; thief steals animals and sticks severed t. into the ground K404.1; witch with t. G219.8.

Tailless fish G303.25.15.1; fox J758.1; jackal J758.1.2. — Dwarf with body like t. hen F451.2.1.2.

Tailor *P441; hero L113.9; married to princess betrays trade by calling for needle and thread H38.2.1; rests head on royal robe J1289.19; and

smith as love rivals T92.12.1; throws stingy woman's cloth out window
K341.13; work in fairyland F376.1. — Clever t. J1115.4; crab mistaken
for t. J1762.1.2; devil as t. to dandy G303.9.9.11; devil can't learn to
be t. P441.2; goose mistaken for t. J1762.1; self-righteous t. in heaven
expelled L435.3; skillful t. F662ff.; trickster dupes t., steals goods K351.1.

Tailor's dream J1401.

Tailors. — Jokes about t. *X220ff.

Taking of vows and oaths M110ff. — Transformation by t. off clothes
D537; devil t. hindmost G303.19; disenchantment by t. off bridle
*D722; dwarf t. back gifts F451.5.2.12; ghost t. things from people
E593; wife t. away only what she brought S446.

Tale, see also **Story;** of the cradle K1345. — Bearer of t. unjustly killed
S461; dragon deceived into listening to t.: hero cuts off his head K835;
dumb princess is brought to speech by t. ending with question to be
solved F954.2.1; formula-t. saves girl from devil K555.2.1; telling t.
punished A2726; unsolved problem: enigmatic ending of t. H620ff.;
weddings as end of t. T135.8.

Tales. — Exaggerated t. about escapes K657; seventy t. of a parrot
prevent wife's adultery K1591; not to tell t. except at certain time of
year (or day) C755.2.

Talents. — Priest multiplying his t. J1264.7.

Talionis. — Lex t. P522.1.

Talisman found in bird's stomach N527.2. — Animal gives part of body
as t. for summoning its aid *B501; compulsion: taking back t. which
opened treasure mountain C652; ghost laid by t. E444; magic power by
rubbing t. D1734.1.

Talk. — Escape by persuading captor to t. K561; fox persuades cock to
come down and t. to him K815.1; ghost summoned to t. to E387.1;
testimony discredited by inducing witness to t. foolishly J1151.1; why
trees do not t. A2791.1; unlucky encounter causes treasure-seekers to t.
and thus lose treasure N553.2.

Talkative animals incense master J2362; fools *J2350—J2369; thief
caught J2136.5.2; wife discredited J1151.1.1; wife's tongue paralysed
D2072.0.53.

Talkativeness W141; of Parisian fishwives X253.1.

Talker keeps person from eating J1564. — Lover late at rendezvous:
detained by incessant t. *T35.0.1.

Talking animals B210ff.; bed N617; with dead wife E322.9; dragon
B11.4.5; flowers F814.2; formerly was by animals and birds, men dumb
A1101.2.3; to oaks to warn sons K649.6; to oneself misinterpreted
J2671.2.1; private parts betray unchastity H451; in sleep betrays weaver
H38.2.4; in sleep gives away riddle's answer H573.3; stone as Doomsday
sign A1002.2.3, A1091.3. — Animal betrays himself to his enemies by t.
J2351; crocodile betrays self by t. K607.2.1; fool loses magic objects by

t. about them J2355.1; forgotten fiancée reawakens husband's memory by serving as milkmaid and t. to calf *D2006.1.2; numskull's t. to himself frightens robbers away N612; pay for teaching t. monkey K491.1; punishment for t. too much Q393.1.1; resuscitation by t. E67.

Tall trees A2778, F812.1. — Extremely t. giant F531.2.1; giantess twice as t. as man F531.2.1.6; lie: remarkably t. person X921; lower world people t. F108.1; remarkably t. men F533.

Tallow. — Cow with t. liver B15.7.9.

Talos (man of bronze) F521.3.1.

Tamarind. — God cheats birds of t. fruit K499.6; why t. fruit is sour A2791.5; why t. leaves are small A2769.1; why t. bark is black A2751.4.3.

Tame doves close wild ones in trap and thus help common enemies J683.2; dog prefers food basin to fleeing hare J487; elephant not accepted by others B261.1.1.

Taming animal by (holiness of saint) B771.2, (maiden's beauty) B771.1, (magic object) *D1442ff.; horse F618.1; the shrew N12, T251.2; wild animals B771ff., H1155; wild prince K1399.1.

Tangle. — Spirits t. up peasant's cows F402.1.3.

Tank has no water despite rains F935.1. — Beheading in water t. K558.2; beggar to stand in t. all night K231.14; enigma: t. doesn't belong to you H594.2; Indra's t. F964.5, H1359.3; magic control of t. D2151.5; magic diamond opens t. passage D1551.7; magic t. *D921.4, (causes disease) D1500.4.3.1; no water will remain in t. D1542.3.5; palace at bottom of t. F771.3.7; palace underneath t. F725.3.4; sacrifice to t. S264.2; water raised from t. by singing D2151.5.1; waters in t. rise up, engulf boy F420.5.2.2.2.

Tanks. — Human blood makes leaky t. hold water S261.0.1.

Tankard magically sticks to lips D2171.1.2. — Magic t. *D1171.6.1.

Tannery. — Man soon learns to stand t. smells U133.

Tanning shoes with bark from saint's tree Q551.6.2.1.

Tantalus's punishment Q501.2.

Taoists. — Buddhists become slaves of T. because they cannot produce rain V355.

Tapa. — Clouds as t. beaten out by woman in moon A705.1.2; goddess in moon beating t. A751.8.6, A1142.5.1.1.

Taper. — Soul as t. E742.1.

Tapir paramour B611.8. — Creation of t. A1889.1; why t. has long nose A2335.3.2.

Tapping. — Beautification by t. D1863; knockers' t. tests F456.1.2.2.3.

Taprobane at end of world A871.0.1.

Tar and feathers as punishment Q475; slake remains after devil killed G303.16.19.20. — Capture by t. baby K741; covering with t. as punishment Q473.5.1; covering the whole wagon with t. K1425; man sends naked wife on all fours in t. and feathers K31.1, K216.2; man in t., feathers frightens off robbers K335.1.8; ogre captured by t. decoy

G514.7; origin of t. in heart of trees A2734.2, A2755.3; punishment: boiling in t. Q414.1; sea people give the ogre t. G525; woman in t. and feathers does not know herself J2012.3; ogre daubs t. on the hero's boat J2171.1.2.

Tara feast A1535.4; festival V70.5.

Tardiness. — Plant punished for t. A2725.

Tardy surpasses punctual L147.

Target. — Impaled head used as t. S139.2.2.1.2.

Tarnkappe renders invisible D1361.15.

Taro. — Origin of t. A1423.1, A2686.4.2; prolific t. F815.6.1; why t. leaves are hollow A2764.1.

Tarring importunate suitor K1218.1.7. — Capture by t. horse K741.1; man in the moon: t. of the moon A751.4.

Task. — Chief performs suitor t., rival steals bride K1371.6; curse mitigated by superhuman t. M428; devil cheated by imposing impossible t. K211; devil to help gambler in exchange for one t. yearly M214; devil to release man for performing seemingly impossible t. K216; disenchantment when superhuman t. is finished D791.1.2; dwarfs help in performing t. F451.5.1.20; false bride finishes true bride's t. and supplants her K1911.1.4; ghost laid by never-ending t. E454; hero professes to be able to perform much larger t. than that assigned K1741; husband busied with t., paramour escapes K1521.6; lousing as t. set by ogre *G466; magic prevention of performance of t. D2072.5; one is freed if he can set a t. the devil cannot perform G303.16.19.3; punishment: performing impossible t. Q512; reward for accomplishment of t. deceptively withheld K231.2; stealing from ogre as t. G610.3; substitute for t. K1848; tabu: eating before t. is finished C231.2; true husband of woman determined by assigning superhuman t. J1176.5.

Tasks *H900—H1199; assigned to learn future M302.5; assigned suitors *H335ff.; performed by use of magic objects D1581; set maid by elfin knight before she can marry him F301.4. — Animals perform t. for man *B571ff.; bride test: performance of t. *H373; dead lover sets t. E212; disenchantment by accomplishment of t. D753; extraordinary companions perform hero's t. F601.1; impossible t. drive off fairies F381.11; ogre sets impossible t. G465; royal children learn all t. J702.2.

Taste of human flesh leads to cannibalism G36. — Food has t. of any dainty desired D1665; injurious food with sweet t. K1889.4; meat takes on t. desired D476.3.1; well with t. of oil, wine, honey F718.4.

Tastes. — Unknown prince's princely t. H41.5.1.

Tasted. — Every fruit t. by fool before he gives it to his master J2245; man who only t. wine W123.1.

Tattoo on newly born baby tells of former incarnation T563.4; on penis F547.3.4. — Catfish transformed from woman carries her t. A2261.3; moon spots are t. marks A751.5.5; origin of animal markings: deities t. all creatures A2412.0.1; recognition by t. H55.3.

Tattooer in otherworld F167.15.

Tattooing on way to otherworld F151.1.5. — God of t. A465.5.1; origin of t. A1465.1, A1595.

Taught, see also **Teach.** — Animal languages t. by magic object *D1301; arts and crafts t. by culture hero A541; bridegroom must be t. intercourse T166.2; dance-loving maid t. by devil to dance G303.10.4.3; people t. by God to work claim to be self-taught C53.1; swordsmanship t. by mountain-spirit F460.4.2.3.

Taunted. — Dispossessed prince t. P36; heroine t. with her unknown past S412; illegitimate child t. by playmates T646.

Tavern. — Choice: staying at home with loving wife or going to t. and having unfaithful wife J229.1; clerk who enters t. arrested with others for murder N347.1.

Tax. — Banishment for assaulting t. collectors Q431.10; captive released on promise to pay t. R74.3; saint to bring about remission of t. M364.2; triple t. N635; weaver evades doorway t. J1289.13.

Taxes. — Hares carry t. to court B291.3.2.1; usurper imposes burdensome t. P12.3.

Taxation P531.

Tea. — Savory t.: peasant puts in many ingredients J1813.7; serving boiled t. leaves J1732.3.

Teach, see also **Taught.** — Cat omitted to t. tiger all he knew A2581; fairies t. bagpipe-playing F262.2; gods t. how to seek food A1420.2; gods t. people all they know A1404; return from dead to t. living E377; spirits t. boy how to sing F403.2.3.3.

Teacher instructs pupil in love, cuckolded K1692; and pupil P340ff.; seduces pupil K1399.5. — Alleged idol to pay t. for book K1971.13; angel as saint's t. V246.2; escape by posing as tiger's t. K601.1; father calls t. son a beggar H581.4; magician t. D1810.4; old t. wants to marry young girl T91.4.1.1; princess to embrace t. on wedding day M261.2; seduction by posing as t. K1315.7; sham t. K1958.

Teachers. — Jokes on t. X350ff.

Teaching, see also **Instructing;** chickens to talk J1882.1. — Deity t. mortal A185.3; dwarfs t. mortals F451.5.1.18; escape by t. song to watchman K606.0.2; god t. people to work A1403; hero t. women to rear children A1357; respite given for t. animal to speak K551.11.

Teachings. — Punishment for scoffing at church t. *Q225; three t. of the fox (bird) *K604.

Team. — Aphrodite's t. of sparrows (doves) A136.2.1; troll has a t. of mice G304.3.2.1.

Teams. — Devil drives several t. of oxen G303.7.5.

Tear from upper world of mortals falls on departed in lower world *E361.1. — Sinner's t. marks bring about pardon V21.6; waking from magic sleep by letting t. fall on sleeper D1978.2.

Tears become jewels D475.4.5; of blood F541.9, (as evil omen) D1812.5.1.1.1, (from grief) D1041.21, (sign of royalty) H71.8; bring recognition H14.1; change to blood D474.6; falling give away presence H151.14; of gold D1454.4.1; of living save soul E754.1.8; transformed to other object D457.18. — Animal sheds t. B736ff.; barrel filled miraculously with penitent's t. F1051.1; bird sheds t. B736; bird's t. restore sight D1505.5.1; birth from t. T541.3; blindness cured by t. F952.1; bodies of water from t. A911; conception from drinking saint's t. T512.4; creation from creator's t. A613; disenchantment by t. D766.3; disenchantment by weeping jug of t. D753.2; fairy's t. pearls F239.6; flood from t. A1012.1ff.; flowers from t. D1454.4.3; fountain from saint's t. D925.1.1; isle of t. F129.4.1; jewels from t. D1454.4.2; lakes originate from t. A920.1.5; magic t. *D1004; origin of t. and sighs A1344; pearls shed for t. H31.7.1; plant characteristics from t. A2731.2; plants from t. A2612ff.; quest for t. shed into the sea H1371.3; rain from t. A1131.1; resuscitation by t. E58; river from t. F162.2.12; river of t. F715.2.5; saint's t. of blood V229.2.6.1; springs originate from t. A941.2.

Tearing boat apart with hands F639.6; down huge wall H1116.3; garments grief sign P678.1; hair, clothes from grief F1041.21.6; opponent to bits F1041.16.3.3; up the orchard (vineyard) K1416; out person's sides S187.1. — Birds t. ogre to pieces G512.9.2; bringing thorn leaves without t. them H1046.2; child t. snake to pieces F628.1.3.2; hound killed by t. out its heart B17.1.2.2; mermaids t. mortal lovers to pieces B81.2.2.

Teased. — Fairies' revenge for being t. F361.10.

Teasing. — Brownies t. F482.5.3; dwarfs dislike t. F451.3.6.2, F451.9.1.7; dwarfs t. people F451.5.14.

Teats. — Dog rescues cow's t. from fire: origin of his black muzzle A2229.1; origin and nature of animal's t. A2363; saint cuts off cow's t. to feed children T611.5.2.

Tedious penances Q521ff.; punishments Q500ff.; tasks H1110ff.

Teeth, see after **Tooth.**

Tegillus. — Riddle about T. H842.2.

Telegraph. — Articles sent by t. J1935.

Telepathy with animals F648. — Magic t. D1785.

Telescope. — Magic clairvoyant t. D1323.15.

Tell shoots apple from son's head F661.3; -tale hand-mark H58; -tale magic objects D1612ff.

Telling adventure too soon tabu C757.2; of fairy gifts tabu F348.7; only very good news J2516.3.5; true stories as test H252.0.1.

Telltown. — Origin of games at T. A1535.3.

Temaie Festival V70.5.

Temper. — Bad t. punished Q313; monk loses t. at overturned cup H1553.5; violence of t. W185.

Temperate and intemperate zeal J550ff.

Temperature. — Extraordinary body t. F593; fountain of any desired t. F162.8.1, F716.3; saint regulates waters' t. D2151.0.1.

Tempering. — North wind t. fury of south wind A1127.1.1.

Tempermental goddess A139.13.

Tempest-box raises storm D1541.1.5.

Temple about to be taken over by pagans saved by appearance of a sign of the cross (image of the Virgin) V344; cedars bear fruit F811.7.2.1; as God's home A151.10.1; in otherworld F163.2.1; rises where ground bursts open A992.3; swallowed by earth F941.2.3. — Animal sacrificed at edification of t. V12.4.0.1; burning the t. to attain notoriety J2162.1; earth swallows t. vessels F948.1.1; god builds t. in heaven A141.2; god's t. of jewels A151.4.1; imprisoned princess rescued from t. R111.2.4; lamb prefers to be sacrificed in t. than to be eaten by wolf J216.2; lovers meet at t. N711.4.1; magic from t. demons D812.5.1; man hiding in t. gets robbers' booty K1971.14; punishment for profaning t. Q222.4; soul of dead in a t. E755.4.2; soul wanders and demands that a t. be built for him E419.1; tabus in connection with t. C93.5; treasure in t. N514.2.

Temples *V112. — Applying hot iron to man's t. J2119.7; nature laments t. destruction F960.3.2; why Brahma has no t. A162.4.

Temporary advantage gained by pretending to yield in combat K2378; magic characteristics D1950—D2049. — Magic object effects t. change in person D1360ff.

Temptation. — Anchorites under t. *T330ff.; monk learns about t. U231.1; monk wants ever-present t. V462.12; oath uttered by pious against t. M110.3; penance: resisting t. Q537; plea by showing t. to crime J1165; punishment for yielding to t. Q233.

Temptations. — Test of fidelity through submitting hero to t. H1556.2.

Tempted. — Clergyman t. by devil G303.9.4.4; man unsuccessfully t. by woman T331; mother t. by incognito son to see whether all women are wicked T412.2.

Tempter. — Devil as t. G303.9.4ff.

Tempting. — Demons t. men G302.9.2; devil in serpent form t. first woman (Satan and Eve) A63.6; wife t. husband H1556.4.2.1.

Temptress sent by deity F34.

Ten as formulistic number Z71.16.2; heavens A651.1.7; as magic number D1273.1.4; measures of magic in world D1719.11.1; for the price of nine J2083.4; servingwomen carried in bottle D55.2.4. — Are there nine or t. geese (horses) J2031.2, J2032; cannibals eat t. men, women, children G94.2; oath valid only with t. witnesses M110.2; prophecy: death in t. years M341.1.5.1; transformation every t. days D623; twenty commandments better than t. J2213.5.1.

Ten-headed giant F531.1.2.2.6; ogre G361.1.5; serpent B15.1.2.9.

Ten thousand. — Transformation: ox-demon becomes t. feet long D412.2.7.

Tenant advised by landlord to steal J1179.8; -less houses at border of otherworld F147.1.

Tenderness. — Sleeping with head in wife's lap t. sign T299.1.

Tent with revolving door F782.6; house folded and swallowed as means of carrying it F923; torn down, man killed K959.3. — Eager warriors go through t. wall W212.1; extraordinary t. F775, F845; magic t. *D1138; seduction by showing wares in t. K1332.2; sinking of t. pole by magic D55.1.1.2; sky as t. A702.2; taking boy to enemy's t. H1418; twins born in t. T581.10.

Termagent. — Devil marries old maid t. G303.12.3.

Termite. — Helpful t. B481.2.

Terrapin hatching from bedbug eggs J1772.1.1. — Enmity between deer and t. A2494.12.7.

Terrestrial. — Journey to t. otherworlds F110ff.; riddles of t. distance H681ff.

Terrible. — Devil destroys hunting party with t. wind G303.20.2; devil disappears amid t. (rattle) G303.17.2.7, (stench) G303.17.2.8; river in paradise with t. roar F162.2.8.

Terrified. — Ogre (large animal) t. K1710ff.

Terrifying experience on Hallowe'en H1423.2. — Ugly ogre t. women who flee and are drowned G476.

Terror. — Curse of everlasting t. M403; hair turns gray from t. F1041.7.

Test for demons in corpses E431.0.1; of hero before otherworld journey H1250; of legitimacy of children: exposure to asps T642; for troll child F455.10.1. — Animal helps person pass t. B599.2; cannibal cuts captive's finger to t. fatness G82.1; false bride fails magician's t. K1911.3.3.2; fly helps suitor pass t. B587.2; girl as umpire in suitor t. K1227.8; husband transforms himself to t. his wife's faithfulness *T235; substitute specimen for laboratory t. K1858; to t. a favorite, a king says that he is going to retire from the world J1634; transformation to t. heroes D645; vigilance t. H1450ff.

Tests H (entire chapter); of character H1550ff. — Decisions based on experimental t. J1176; extraordinary companions help hero in suitor t. F601.2; false bride fails when husband t. her K1911.3.3; strong hero t. weapons F611.3.3; suitor t. *H310ff.

Testament of the dog J1607; of Virgin Mary V283; willing rewards and punishments (conventional ending of story) Z78. — Forged t. dupes host K455.8.2.

Testicle. — Beaver sacrifices t. to save life J351.1; cobold from boar's t. F481.0.1.1.

Testicles. — Enormous t. F547.7; nature of animal's t. A2365.1; why elephant has t. inside *A2365.1.1.

Testifying. — Heavenly voice t. for accused H216.2.

Testimony of fool J2667; gradually weakened J1151.3; of witness cleverly discredited J1151.

Testing money by throwing it into stream J1931; saint by sham death Q591.1.1; of witches G277. — God t. mortal A185.13; judgment by t. love J1171.

Thanks after eating C283. — All questions to be answered "T." C495.3; punishment for neglecting t. to gods Q223.2.

Thanked. — Fairies leave when t. F381.13.

Thankful fool *J2550—J2599.

Thanking fairy for gift tabu F348.5.2. — Tabu: t. (under certain circumstances) C493.

Thatched. — Castles t. with gold F163.1.3.

Thatching of birds' wings F165.5, F171.6.6; roof with feathers H1104.1.2; tail to roof so as to catch dupe K1021.1. — Burning t. protection against witch G272.17; ineffectual t. of house H619.4.

Theft, see also **Stealing, Thief;** of ambrosia A153.1; to avoid starvation forgiven U25; from fairies F350ff.; of fire *A1415; of light *A1411; by magic D2087; of moon *A758; from ogre G610ff.; punished *Q212; of seasons A1151; of sun *A721.1; as a task H1151; by trained animal K366; from troll F455.6.4; from witch G279.2. — Attention drawn by helpful animal's t. of food from wedding table: recognition follows H151.2; boy boasts, advertises father's t. J2355.2; blame for t. fastened on dupe K401; charms against t. D1389.2; fairy takes revenge for t. F361.2; false accusation of t. K2127; feet cut off as punishment for t. Q451.2.2; jewel present brings false accusation of t. K2104; judge wants to know how the t. was committed J2372; magic detection of t. D1817.0.1; man must labor as punishment for t. of fire A1346.1; master asked to help in the t. J2136.5.6.1; penalty for t. A1581.2; return from dead to punish t. of part of corpse E235.4; riddling answer betrays t. H582.1; ring proves t. H84.4; sham wise man declares who committed the t. (robbers) K1956.3; skill in t. granted after prayer V59.1; spurned woman accuses man of t. K2111.2; wolf punished for t.: kings honored U11.2.1.

Thefts K300—K439; and cheats *K300—K499. — Dupe imitates trickster's t. and is caught K1026; hypocrisy concerning t. K2095; origin of t. A1341.3; retorts concerning t. J1390ff.; Russians like t. A1674.2.

Theodora masks as monk and lives chastely in monastery Q537.1.

Theological questions answered by propounding simple questions in science J1291.2.

Theophilus goes to hell for return of his contract H1273.1.

Theoretical. — Practical vs. t. knowledge J251.

Theories. — Absurd scientific t. J2260—J2299.

Theseus and the bent tree released so as to tear him to pieces H1522.1; and giant robber with club G102.

Thetis F423.1.

Thick hair F555.4. — Armor ordered thin in front and t. in back J673.1.

Thief, see also **Highwayman, Robber;** asks any punishment except having two wives T251.1.6; beaten for not giving robbery warning J1191.6;

believes detective mind reader, confesses J1141.1.9; breaks foot climbing wall, sues owner Z49.11.2; -catcher caught by own club K1605; caught by man hiding in chest K751.2; claims he's taken only gifts J1161.11; coughs, watchmen blinded K2062.2.6; crushed to death by fragments of his boring N339.15; cursed M414.10; detected by feeling beard J1141.1.2; as discoverer J2223; climbing rope discovered and rope cut *K1622; detected (by building straw fire) J1143, (by psalter and key) H251.3.2, (by sieve and shears) H251.3.3, (when he pawns stolen goods) N276; in disguise *K311ff.; hears owner singing, thinks self detected N611.4; imagines is being laughed at, confesses N275.4; kept at sea in magic boat Q559.10; lives with twenty cats B292.6.1; makes a lame excuse J1391; masked as devil bought off by owner K152; mistakes leopard for calf J1758.4; to be pardoned if he can steal without being caught M56; posing as corpse detected by pricking his feet J1149.7; rendered unable to remove stolen goods Q551.2.3; reveals self in church J1141.15; robs own purse J2527; shows up owner's unjust claim J1213; suspected of crawling through hole must take off clothes J1141.7; -tailor cuts piece of own coat X221.1; threatened with divine punishment, confesses J1141.14; tries to feed watch dog and stop his mouth K2062; trusted to guard goods K346; warned what not to steal J2091. — Apparently pious man a t. K2058.1; brownie twitches t. F482.5.4.2; careless t. caught J2136.5; cattle t. struck by lightning Q552.1.8.1; cauldron t. detected J1661.1.10; clever t. may keep booty J1211.2; coward gives purse to t. W121.6; crucified t. in passion play complains of thirst J2041.1; ghost scares t. E293.1; god as t. A177; killed paramour alleged to be t. K1569.9; king plays t. H1557.6; lake bursts forth to drown t. A920.1.3; magic cloth betrays t. D1318.8.1; master t. *K301ff.; numskull convinced that he is a t. J2318; numskull as t. J2461.1.7; one-eyed t. J1661.1.8; owner assists t. J1392; pleading with t. fails, stones succeed J1088; priest shouts at t. J1261.2.6; punishment: devil carries off t. Q554.1; return from dead to capture t. E235.7; return from dead to prevent flight of t. E375; return from dead to warn t. E236.3; ruler protects t. W11.10; shadow mistaken for t. J1790.2; sheep t. confesses in church N275.5.1; skillful t. F676; story told to discover t. J1177; stick with money in it breaks and betrays t. H251.3.4; tabus of t. C572; waiting at the well for the t. J2214.3; waiting for the t. to return for the bolster J2214.3.2; waiting in the graveyard for the t. J2214.3.1; why wolf is t. A2455.1; wizard detects t. D1817.0.1.1ff.

Thief's corpse carried through streets J1142.4; money scales borrowed J1141.6. — Divining rod indicates t. house D1314.2.3; ear of stolen animal protrudes from t. mouth Q552.4; ghost prevents t. flight E375.

Thieves attempting to steal from church rendered powerless Q222.5.4; cannot quit plundering U138.2; claim walls so thin, house too great temptation J1165.1; deceived by overhearing conversation J1517; dig field, drain tank for gold K2316; flee man costumed as devil J1786.1;

make invoice of stolen goods J2214.3.3; magically petrified on entering house D2072.5.1; quarrel over booty: owner comes W151.8; waylay goddess in disguise K1811.0.2. — Ass warns of t. J2413.1.1; country of t. F709.3; dying like Christ: between two t. X313; escape from t. by reporting high prices elsewhere K576; god of t. A457; magic club brings t. D1427.6; millers as t. X211; why millers are t. P443.1; murder revealed to t. climbing into bank N615; numskull bridegroom unwittingly detects t. N611.3; poisoned cakes intended for husband eaten by t. N659.1; pupil surpasses t. in stealing L142.1; ridding city of t. H1199.9; river rises to prevent t. escape F932.8.3; tortoise and dog partners as t. B294.7; water for t. in king's garden H1471.1; wild hunt harmful to t. E501.18.1.2.

Thieves' nocturnal habits J1394.

Thievery, see also **Stealing;** habit can't be broken U138; a predestined lot M359.10. — Death as punishment for t. Q411.13.

Thieving contest K305.1; household spirit F480.3; spirit F419.2. — Magic t. object D1605.

Thigh as hiding place F1034.3. — Birth from man's t. T541.5; child incubated in man's t. T578.1; dirk stuck into t. in order to keep from sleeping H1482; tabu to eat t. vein C221.3.6.

Thimble. — Bailing out pond with t. H1113.1; tailor puts on t. as protection from slug J2623; thumbling hides under t. F535.1.1.10.1.

Thin. — Armor ordered t. in front and thick in back J673.1; lie: remarkably t. person X924.

Thinking, see also **Thought;** of God protects against devil G303.16.2.1.1; of good or evil tabu on magic journey D2121.6. — Consolation by t. of some one good aspect of a situation J865; husband forbids wife's t. J1511.8; man from deity's body from his mere t. A1211.0.1; person summoned by t. of him D2074.2.1; sinner t. of God saved V525.

Third, see also **Three.** — By t. day unusual sight has ceased to attract attention J1075.1; dead returns t. day after burial E586.2; heart breaks at t. drink from silver canister F1041.1.1.1; money lost twice, recovered t. time N183; mother's curse on t. son causes eclipse A737.2; obstinate wife: the t. egg T255.4; speech magically recovered when t. person guesses secret transaction D2025.3.

Thirst from breaking tabu C949.5; magically disappears D2033. — Contest in enduring t. H1544; why crane suffers t. *A2435.4.2; death by t. for breaking tabu C924; drunkard refuses cure of fever if it is to take away his t. J343.1; enemies magically feel t. D2091.6; great t. J1322; great t. of dead E489.11; husband lets wife die of t. S62.4; king's son to die from t. M341.2.26; madness from t. F1041.8.4; magic insatiable t. D2063.3; magic object causes constant t. D1373.0.1; magic object produces immunity from hunger and t. D1349.1; origin of t. A1345.1; patient will take care of own t. J1322.1; unremittent t. as punishment Q501.7; why raven suffers t. *A2435.4.3.

Thirsty cattle fight over well B266.1. — Adulterers tricked into riding t. mules drowned K1567; hanged man t. E422.0.1; pun involving t. and Thursday X111.15.

Thirteen as magic number D1273.1.6; as unlucky number N135.1; as name of victorious youngest son L10.1.1; rivers of balm in otherworld F162.2.7. — Formulistic number: t. Z71.9; string with t. knots in child's mouth G271.10.

Thirtieth. — Full moon and t. of the month H582.1.1.

Thirty days' respite from unwelcome marriage T151.2; girls fall in love with young man T27.1; Years War destroys home of dwarfs F451.4.4.2. — Formulistic number: t. Z71.11; God avenges murder after t. years Q211.0.1; man claims to be t. for many years J1218; prophecy: man hanging himself at t. M341.1.4.4; riddle: tree with twelve branches, each with t. leaves, black and white H721.1; talking statue, when destroyed, cannot be replaced for t. thousand years D1661.1; woman requires t. men T146.2.

Thirty-two as formulistic number Z71.16.5.

Thirty-six as formulistic number Z71.8.7.

Thisbe and Pyramus T41.1.

Thistle serves as milk-cup for Virgin Mary A2711.4.2. — Chain tale: conflict between fowl and t. Z41.3; fright when t. catches clothes J2625.

Thistles and nettles are the devil's vegetables G303.10.13. — Devil loses his grain and gets t. K249.1; origin of t. *A2688.1; punishment for first murder: t. A2631.1.

Thong of leather cut out from back as punishment Q451.8. — Magic t. D1209.6.

Thongs. — Sled t. cut to prevent pursuit K637.

Thor battles Midgard serpent at end of world A1082.3; carries giant across stream F531.3.1.3; slays foster father P271.8. — Luring T. into giants' power H1173; rowan helps T. out of river A2711.5; sisters curse child had by T. M437.2.

Thor's — Magic of T. temple D838.3.

Thorn -brake as refuge R311.1.1; fence surrounds food-plants K1038; growing in wound becomes tree F971.3; removed from cobra's throat N647; removed from lion's paw B381; removed from monkey's tail B381.2; removed from wolf's paws B381.1. — Ass begs wolf to pull t. out of foot before eating him *K566; bringing t. leaves without tearing them H1046.2; charm removes t. D1513; cowl in t.-brake symbol of Christ V124.1; cutting white t. tree fatal C518.2; devil carries a t. stick G303.4.8.5; disenchantment by removal of enchanting t. D765.1.2; feeling t. point through clothes F647.9.2; magic t. *D958, D976, D1393.5; man becomes t. D213.5; origin of t. tree from Joseph's staff A2624.1; saint transfers t. from foot D2161.4.2.3; saint digs canal while riding t. tree D2121.14; sleep t. D1364.2.

Thorns believed not to sting at night J1819.1; around nipples F546.4;

planted to kill birds K959.5; on plants A2736. A2752. — Death from t. in rice M341.2.16; evil spirit in spite puts bark and t. on tree A2736; food with t. hidden as test H1515.3; loser of shooting wager to go naked into t. for a bird N55.1; man put into moon for stealing t. A751.1.4; mountain of t. F759.6; riddle: fencing t. with thorns H583.2.5; roses lose t. for saint V222.14; stepmother feeds children t. S31.4; tongue with t. F544.2.4; trail magically covered with t. D2089.9.1.

Thornbush blamed by fox for wounding him J656.1. — Bat, diver, and t. shipwrecked A2275.5.3; laurel and olive tree scorn t. as umpire in their dispute as to who is most useful J411.7; magic t. points out road D1313.14; origin of t. A2688.1.1; pine and t. dispute as to their usefulness J242.2.

Thought, see also **Thinking**; is swiftest (riddle) H632.1. — Devil carries man through the air as swift as t. G303.9.5.4; magic journey as swift as t. *D2122.3; magic results from power of t. *D1777.

Thoughts must be on fairies in fairyland F378.3. — Devils do not know or understand t. of men G303.13.1; fairies read men's t. F256; friends reading each others' t. P310.9; good t. rewarded, bad punished Q6; journey to upper world by keeping t. continually on heaven *F64; magic knowledge of another's t. D1819.1; magic ring permits owner to learn person's secret t. D1316.4; saint can perceive another's t. V223.3; test: guessing person's t. H524.

Thoughtless. — Transformation through t. wish of father D521.1.

Thousand at one shot K1741.2; -headed serpent B15.1.2.10.3; -year old ogre G631.1. — Giant eats a t. cattle F531.3.4.1; giants live to be eighteen t. years old F531.6.4.2; life prolonged t. years D1855.5; man with t. arms F516.2.3; penance: hanging for a t. years head downward over a fire of chaff Q522.6; phoenix renews youth when a t. years old B32.1.1; talking statue when destroyed cannot be replaced for thirty t. years D1661.1.

Thousand-leg. — Enmity between elephant and t. A2494.11.1.

Thrall cursed to sit on chest, be restless M455.3; as sacrifice V12.6. — Curse of t. M411.13.

Thralls. — King not to settle quarrel of t. C563.4; origin of t. P177.

Thread awarded to disputant who knows what it was wound on J1179.6; bridge to otherworld F152.1.7; as a clue to find way out of labyrinth R121.5; cut by arrow F661.12; entering needle suggests intercourse J86, Z186; from lotus stalks on Vishnu's navel H1289.4.1; made to appear as a large log carried by a cock D2031.2; sold to lizard J1852.1.1; transformed to bridge D454.4.1; under dumb man's tongue cut F954.1. — Daw fleeing from captivity caught in trees by t. around foot N255.5; deception: climbing silk t. tossed upward in air K1871.1; dwarfs suspend large millstone on thin t. F451.5.4.2; goddesses descend by t. A189.10; jumping over magic t. H412.7.1; magic ball of t. indicates road D1313.1.1; magic t. *D1184ff., (gives illusion of drinking from spring, not sea) H1142.2.1, (from heaven) D811.2.1, (from yogi's garment) D1400.1.18; oath by touching sacred t. M114.6; recognition of disenchanted person by t. in his teeth H64.1; red t. on neck of person who has been decapitated and resuscitated *E12.1; Rome hanging by t. (lie) X1561; scarlet t. death omen J2311.1.4; sewing contest won by deception: the long t. K47.1; silk t. stretches to sea F642.6; speaking t. D1610.28; why spider has t. in back of body *A2356.2.8; tailor married to princess betrays trade by calling for needle and t. H38.2.1; test of resourcefulness: putting t. through coils of snail shell H506.4; trail of t. R135.0.5; traveling till two skeins of t. are unwound (task) H1125.1; weaving shirt from piece of t. H1022.2.2.

Threads. — Ants carry silk t. to prisoner, who makes rope and escapes R121.4; cotton already spun into t. A1346.2.1; extraordinary t. F877; self-weaving t. D1601.13.1; weaving cloth from two t. H1022.1.

Threading needle test in convent H509.1.

Threat to throw on fire causes changeling to cry out and betray his nature F321.1.1.6.—Bluffing t. K1771; seduction through t. K1397; ugly cobbler's continual t. to throw his last at people X241.

Threats overcome witch G275.15; to person as suitor test H1406.

Threatened. — Child t. with ogre *C25.1; when changeling is t. with burning, child is returned F321.1.4.5.

Threatening. — Dwarfs t. mortals F451.5.2.8; fairies t. sheep watcher F361.11; goat's t. song K1767; man behind tree t. his debtor K1971.2; princess t. amorous king T322.2; sham-dead t. bier bearers J2311.5.1; sham physician cures people by t. them with death K1955.1; son t. father to be recognized P233.7; sun's intense heat t. all life A727.1; suppliant t. image V123.1.

Three, see also **Third;** blasts on horn before sunrise to rescue prisoner from mound R112.1; blows received for every one given J221.3.2; -bodied goddess A123.1.1; -breasted woman F546.2; brothers contest in wishing H507.3.1; brothers take turns using mule J1914.2; caskets H511.1; creators A2.1; days' tournament R222; deformed witches invited to wedding in exchange for help *M233; -eyed person F512.2.1.1; -faced (god) A123.2.1.1, (person) F511.1.2; first cries to God A1344.1; -fold (magic sleep) *D1971, (oath) M115.1; foolish wishes J2071; giants with one eye *G121.1; gods bring up earth A811.2; Graces A468; -headed (animals) B15.1.2.2, (dragon) B11.2.3.2, (person) F511.0.2.2, (ogre) G361.1.2, (woman) F511.0.2.2; heavens A651.1.1; -horned animals B15.3.1; hunchback brothers drowned K2322; joint depositors may have their money back when all demand it J1161.1; lovers mourn dead girl T92.14; lower worlds A651.2.2; as magic number D1273.1.1; magical musical strains D1275.1.1; -night watch over grave to guard man from devil H1463; reasons for not giving alms J2225; reasons for refusing credit J1552.2; redeeming kisses D735.2; roses fall as sign of unfaithfulness H432.1.1; sevens in 1777 drive dwarfs out of the land F451.9.1.3;

sins of the hermit J485; stupid things: riddle H871.1; suns shine in sky
F961.1.3.2; -tailed turtle B15.7.6; teachings of the fox (bird) *K604;
victims of love T92.2; witch sisters G201; women have but one (eye
among them) F512.1.2, (tooth among them) F513.1.1; worlds of dead
E480.2; wells under t. roots of earth-tree A878.1.2; women humiliate
importunate lover K1218.4.1; year eating tabu C231.6; -year old child
as protection against devil G303.16.19.6; young men arrested tell who
they are H581ff. — Child of t. fathers born with t. stripes T563.1; cup
with two and t. handles J2665.1; dead awaken after t. days to new life
and great wisdom E489.1; death's t. messengers J1051; deceptive bargain:
t. wishes K175; devil as t. gentlemen G303.3.1.11; disenchantment by t.
nights' silence under punishment D758.1; dividing four coins among t.
persons J1241.2; equivocal inscriptions at parting of t. roads N122.0.1;
eye with t. pupils F541.3.2; execution avoided by using t. wishes J1181.1;
fairies give t. gifts F341.1; fairies' t. cornered hats F236.3.1; formulistic number: t. *Z71.1; giant t. spans between brows and t. yards
between shoulders F531.2.2; giant with t. arms F531.1.6.7.1; girl
may remain virgin for t. days after marriage T165; god in t.
forms A132.0.1.2; heroine's t.-fold flight from ball R221; king
given t. wheels to control his anger J571.2; magician assigned t.
places at a table J1141.2; magic fan produces rain when waved t. times
D1542.1.4; making shirt from piece of linen t. inches square (task)
H1022.4; men with two faces, t. legs, and seven arms F526.5; modest
choice: t. casket type L211; mother of world bears t. sons A1282.1; one
eye of the t. giants stolen G612; one of the old maid's t. teeth breaks off
X754; oracle that the first of t. sons to kiss his mother will be king
J1652; person with t. bodies F524.1; porter's revenge for t. wise counsels
J1511.6; prophecy: t.-fold death M341.2.4; prophecy: princess will wed
t. men in one M306.3; person with t. hearts F559.7.1; person with t. rows
of teeth F513.1.2.1; prophecy: death in t. years, three months M341.1.2.4;
quest for t. (feathers of marvelous bird) H1331.1.2, (hairs from devil's
beard) H1273.2, (persons as stupid as his wife) H1312.1; quest in hell
for t. dragon feathers H1274; resuscitation after t. days E162.1; riding
t. times around the hill to free captive confined within R112.2; Schlaraffenland lies t. miles beyond Christmas X1712.1; selling t. old
women (task) H1153; skillful axe-man makes spearshafts with t. chippings F666.1; snake disenchanted by being allowed to wrap itself t. times
around person's neck D759.8; son of t. dogs B635.4.1; student is helped
by the devil when he can answer t. questions in rhyme G303.22.3; suitor
test: winning horse-race t. times H331.5.3; test of cleverness: uttering t.
wise words H505; test: sleeping by princess t. nights without looking
at her or disturbing her H1472; theft from t. old women who have but a
single eye among them *K333.2; transformation by encircling object t.
times D563; beggar in disguise obtains alms t. times from same person
K1982; tree bears fruit t. times yearly F811.18; vanquished ogre grants

hero's t. wishes G665; wager: who can call t. tree names first N51; water-goddess allows body of drowning to come up t. times F420.5.2.1.4; woman becomes clean only after t. washings and the use of t. pounds of soap W115.2; woman ravished by t. brothers bears triplets T586.3.1.

Three hundred. — Cup of t. colors F866.1; eating t. fat oxen H1141.2; mermaid lives for t. years B81.13.12; river piles up to t. miles F932.8.6; man t. years old has infrequent intercourse T317.0.1; sacrifice to live t. years V17.6; woman with t. sixty-five children *L435.2.1; wood of sixty trees nourishing t. men apiece F812.2.

Three hundred sixty-five Z72.6. — House with t. windows and doors F782.1.

Three-legged dogs in wild hunt *E501.4.1.6; ghost of horse E423.1.3.1, *E521.1.2; god A123.6.1; pot sent to walk home J1881.1.3; quadrupeds *B15.6.1. — Fairies ride on t. horses *F241.1.3; treasure is found when t. cat shrieks over a grave N542.2.

Three thousand parables of Solomon J80.1. — Tree coiling leaves t. miles high with golden cock on top F811.2.3.1.

Thresher. — Lie: remarkable t. X1001.

Threshing contest K42.1; grain: granary roof used as t. flail K1422; in heaven H84.3. — Dead person t. E567; extraordinary t.-floor F896; woman t. corn in moon A751.8.2.

Threshold. — Bridal couple put one foot inside t. T137.2.1; father tells son not to drag him past t. J121.2; water from foot-washing sprinkled on t. as protection against witch G272.13.

Thrice killed corpse K2151. — Think t. before you speak J2516.1; wild hunt goes t. around pond E501.14.3.

Thrift W216; as bride test H381ff.; -less wife as accursed H659.18.1.

Throat. — Animal killed by forcing ball into t. K951.5; bone removed from animal's t. B382; frog rises from person's stomach into t. every spring B784.0.1; murder by cutting t. S118.2; ogre killed by throwing hot stones (metal) into his t. G512.3.1; punishment: cutting t. Q421.3; stones in t. to lay ghost E441.2; wine shows through woman's white t. F647.6.

Throbbing of right eye a favorable omen D1812.5.2.1.

Throne. — Answering questions only when on t. J1189.1; crown fits successor to t. H36.2.1; eagle regains t. for king B589.1; earth created from snow under divine t. A835.1; extraordinary t. F785ff.; god on t. A137.15; god's t. A152ff.; goddess' t. shakes when worshipper ill A189.5; heaven as God's t. A133.2.2; impostor's letter authorizes t. for him K1952.6; king forces follower onto t. to be killed K1845.2; lifting of goddess's t. D1654.17; magic t. *D1156; mythical animals surround God's t. B7.2; negro takes refuge under princess's t. R314; son usurps father's t. P236.4; succession to t. lost in gambling N2.5.1; sun sits on t. A731.1; tailor occupies God's t. for a day P441.1.

Thrones in otherworld F166.6. — Fairies' four flying t. F282.3.

Throstle giving all attention to sweet fruits is caught by bird catcher J651.1.

Through. — Chastity ordeal: passing t. fire H412.4; magic sight by looking t. keyhole D1821.3.6; magic sight by looking t. ring D1821.3.5; one animal jumps t. body of another F916; stream runs t. house F715.4; suitor contest: riding t. fire H331.1.5.

Throw at a rich man J1602. — Impostors t. hero into pit K1931.4; mountain-men t. person over church roof F460.4.4.3; ugly cobbler continually threatens to t. his last at people X241; wrestling match won by deception: where to t. the ogre K12.1.

Thrower. — Lie: remarkable t. X943; remarkable stone-t. F636.4.

Throwing ball to princess suitor test H331.16; contest won by deception K18; little stones to express love H316.5; stone at own reflection J1791.5.2; stone, not pebble, at girl J2461.9. — Adulteress t. object out window to distract husband K1514.15; animal characteristics from t. members at ancient animal A2215ff.; captor t. away trickster K649.12; deceptive land purchase: bounds fixed by t. object K185.6; devil t. stones A977.2; disenchantment by t. stone D712.3.2; divination by t. objects into water D1812.5.0.6; escape by t. objects far away K622.2; fatal game: t. from cliff K854; lost object found by t. spade at ghost D1816.2.1; magic book conjured away by t. it on stream D2176.4; magic journey by t. knife into whirlwind *D2121.8; man t. opponent into air F624.8; murder by t. from height S127; ogre killed by t. hot stones (metal) into his throat G512.3.1; poltergeist t. objects F473.1; spirit t. back shots fired at it F473.6.5; strong man t. stone F624.2.0.1; transformation by t. object D571; transformation to fish by t. into sea D586.

Thrown. — Ashes of dead t. on water to prevent return E431.9; dupe t. over precipice K891.5.3; footstool t. from heaven F1037; great rock t. by giant F531.3.2ff.; hat t. into air indicates route D1313.2; hero an abortion t. into the bushes T572.2.3; land t. down from heaven A953; magic object t. ahead carries owner with it D1526; magic staff t. causes wild animals to stand still D1442.4; magic sickness because girl has t. away her consecrated wafer *D2064.1; needles t. so that one enters eye of the other F661.7; object t. into air causes enemies to fight over it K1082.2; one strong man t. by another from walls F628.2.2; person t. to ground by wild hunt E501.18.5; suitor test: apple t. indicates princess's choice H316; true bride's children t. away K1911.2.3; water t. on corpse to prevent return E431.2.

Thrush teaches dove to build nest A2271.1. — Color of t. *A2411.12.1.1; creation of t. A1912.1.

Thrush's beautiful voice *A2423.2.1; wedding B282.12.

Thrushbeard, King T76.

Thugs. — Wisdom from t. J178.

Thumb cut and salt put on it in order to remain awake H1481; of knowledge D1811.1.1. — Child nourished by sucking t. of a god T611.1.1;

devil's t. G303.4.3; elves' half t. F232.7; magic knowledge from touching "knowledge tooth" with t. D1810.3; soul in t. E714.7.1.

Thumbs. — Saints confirm covenant by cutting off t. M201.4; why toad has no t. A2375.2.9.

Thumbling F535.1; born as result of hasty wish of parents T553; frightens off robbers K335.1.6.2; swallowed by animals F911.3.1.

Thunder drums of the dead A1142.9.1; at king's birth F960.1.1.1; said to be the rolling of hero's brother's wagon K1718.1; slays devils A162.3.2; spirits A1142.5.1.2, A284.3; sword sought H1337.1; weapon A157.1, A992.2. — Brother as t., sister as lightning R321.1; creator's voice makes the t. A1142.1; curse: to be stricken by t. M447; deserted children become t. S378; devil retreats into hell amid t. and lightning G303.17.2.5; dragon's liver of t. H1332.6; dupe deceived concerning the t.: finally killed by it K1177; extraordinary t. F968; giant's snoring as t. F531.3.8.1; giants killed by t. F531.6.12.4; god of t. A284; god's voice causes t. A139.5.2; hearing t. on setting forth a good omen D1812.5.2.3; impregnation by t. T528; man becomes t. D281.3; man saves devil from t. Q45.2.1; mountainfolk afraid of t. F460.2.1; not far from heaven to earth for t. there can be heard here H682.1.6; origin of t. A1142; rainbow as bow of t.-god A791.1; Socrates and Xanthippe: "after t. rain" T251.4; turtle holds with jaws till t. sounds B761.

Thunders. — Journey to the Land of the T. F117.

Thunderbird A284.2.

Thunderbolt as gods' weapon A157.1.1; magically produced D2149.1; prevents intimacy of saint's communities F968.2. — Death by t. as punishment Q552.1; dragon swallows t. intended for hero B529.2; origin of t. A1142.0.1; where t. fell sacred A992.2.

Thundergod. — Combat between t., devil A162.3; hammer of t. A157.7; man as helper of t. A189.1.1.

Thunderstorm. — Devil is followed by t. G303.6.3.1; woman hoists skirt to raise t. D2141.0.10.

Thursday birthday turns person into nightmare F471.1.5; as lucky day N127.3. — God speaks to saint each T. A182.3.0.3; Maundy T. tabu C235; pun on T. and thirsty X111.15; saint goes to heaven every T. Q172.8.1, A182.3.0.3.1.

Tick. — Bed-t. full of harp strings H1129.7.

Tickling. — Fairies t. mortals to death F363.6; origin of t. sensation A1319.11; resuscitation by t. E18; swallowed person t. serpent's throat F912.3.1.

Tidal wave (from breaking tabu) C984.4, (marks person's death place) A913.1. — Magic t. wave D2151.3.1.

Tide held back D2151.1.2f.; inquires whether moon is up J1292. — Army drowned by incoming t. N339.7; controlling t. as suitor task H335.6.1; deceptive drinking contest: rising and falling t. K82.1.1; devil extends t. up river G303.9.2.5; king vainly forbids t. to rise L414; spirit of t.-crack F429.1.

Tides. — Magic object controls t. D1545.1; magic object indicates t. D1324; origin of t. A913.

Tidings brought to the king: You said it, not I J1675.2.1.

Tied animal persuades another to take his place K842.3. — Deception into allowing oneself to be t. K713.1; fairies t. together by hair F239.1; importunate lover t. to tree K1218.7; marvelous runner keeps leg t. up F681.1; moon t. to sun A735.1; owner's hair t. while thief escapes with goods K338; rowing in a boat which is t. up J2164.2; sun t. to earth by beams of light A733.4; sun t. to sky A721.5.

Tiens-bon-là D1413.7, K1217.

Tiger as animals' king B240.13; attacks man pulling his thorn W154.3.2; beaten, fears man J17.1; becomes person D312.2; carries person B557.10; carries wood for saint B292.11; as child's nurse B535.0.8; and crane quarrel J428; crossing river with vat K1183; disguises as human being K1822.4; eats cow friend J427; enticed away, victims escape K629.2.1; enticed into coffin K714.2.2; enticed into pit by boar K735.6; flatters crow, kills her K815.9; formerly cooked its food A2435.1.2; frees man on promise to keep secret M295.1; frightened by clashing knives K2345.1; frightened of leak J2633; frightened off from prey K547.7ff.; frightened by wind K1727; gives man food for deer bait K361.3; -god A132.10; as god's messenger A165.2.1.1.2; guides lost man home: hence men do not eat tigers B563.4.1.1; has family of jaguars B672; to help foxes divide their young K579.5.2; hides guests in jar K649.1.2; hides woman from other tigers B525.1; in human form B651.9; -husband disenchanted D789.9; -killing tree K1715.6; lives on self-cooking food F989.22.2; made to frighten men L482.4; as magician B191.3; mistaken for horse, saddled N691.1.2; mistaken for other animal J1758; murders son of first couple A1277.3; persuaded to eat own eyes K1025.2; persuaded to enter house, locked in K737.2; plows for man B292.4.2; pretends to be girls' mother K2011.2; returns rope, tail cut off W154.11; seizes bridal couple Q557.7; settles jackals' argument K555.3; -shaped cake fulfills death prophecy M341.2.10.1; in sheep's clothing stolen by sheep-thief K1621; -slayer recognized by tiger parts H105.5.1; -slayers must not eat plant C226.0.1; son of human mother scratches, licks her U128; spares man returning to be eaten W37.2; spirit and man sons of same mother T554.1; stupid J1706.1; substituted for girl tears lecher Q243.6; substituted for woman in box: kills villain K1674; as suitor B621.3; sweeps temple for saint B256.7; thinks dog's tail a gun J1772.12; thinks water dropping sound of monster K1725.2; trip to underworld F98.1. — Abandoned son exposed to t. H105.5.4; abduction by t. R13.1.4; abduction by t.-man R16.4; axe becomes t. D1594.5; bee vitalizes t. D1594.3; being devoured by t. as punishment Q415.5; blind t. recognizes hypocrite F655.2; boar wins duel with t. K97.1; boys threaten to harness t. K1714; buffalo helps t. quench fire: white mark left on buffalo's neck where tiger held on while being ducked in water A2211.12; buffaloes save hero from t. B524.1.5.1; child borne off by t., which is caught by griffin, which is killed by lioness, who rears child with her whelps N215; coffin to prevent t. ghost E431.20; association of t. and crane J428; association of cow and t.: tiger eats cow as soon as she is hungry J427; cow thief grabs t. by mistake N392; creation of t. A1815; daughter promised to t. S232; devastating t. B16.2.2, G358; dog in disguise to frighten t. K1810.2; duel of buffalo and t. B264.3; enmity of t. and (cat) A2494.1.6, (dog) A2494.4.9, (hen) A2494.13.10.5, (boar) A2494.10.2, (man) A2494.10.1; false ascetic in partnership with t. K2058.2; fool rides t. J1758.1.1; four-eyed t. B15.4.1.2; friendship of t. and (buffalo) A2493.3, (cat) A2493.18, (cow, calf and cub) A2493.24, (deer) A2493.17, (jackal) A2493.11.3, A2493.11.5, A2493.14.1, (lion) A2493.30; ghost as t. E423.2.10; giant t. B871.2.2; girl eaten by t. reincarnated E613.0.6; headless king and tailless t. friends J876; helpful t. B431.3; hero cared for by t. A511.2.2.2; honest brahmin spared by t. Q151.10; horse arches neck to kick t. from rear A2351.6; hostile t. killed B16.2.2.1; husband promises t. a cow, wife frightens t. away K235.1.1; jackal and t. and business partners A2493.11.3; killing t. demons H335.3.6; killing t. by throwing hatchet in mouth K951.1.1.1; kindness to t. rewarded Q51.2; magic t. B181.3; man falling from tree frightens away t. N696.1; man gradually reincarnated as t. E695; man-t. B26; man transformed to t. D112.2; man-killing t. must not touch animals C549.1; man and t. in contest: winner to live in town A2250.1.1; marriage to wer-t. N399.3; marriage to t. B601.9; monkey jumps through body of t. F916.1; monkey gives t. sore-producing ointment K1043.1; monkey lures t. into tree, sets it afire K812.3; mythical t. B19.10; numskull's outcry overawes t. N691.1; old woman, t. flee each other K2323.3; ox- demon transformed to t. D412.2.3; quarreling couple were previously t. and dog T256.0.1; sham-dead t. betrayed by live penis K607.3.1; sham- warrior's boasting scares t. K1951.3.2; stripes of t. A2413.4; speaking t. B211.2.2.1; stick, rope frighten off t. K2336; strong man kills t. F628.1.1.1; tailless t. J876; tortoise escapes t. captor K563.1; treasure from t. B103.0.8; trickster's basket for t. partner K2033; trickster eats food left by t. K372.1; trickster to give t. wings K1013.4; two-headed t. B15.1.2.1.2; unborn child promised to t. S222.3; wer-t. D112.2.1; why t. does not attack wildboar until latter is old: result of duel A2257.1; witch rides on t. G241.1.7; why man and t. enemies A2281.1.1; why t. can't come down tree head foremost A2577; why t. lacks some qualities of cats A2581; why t. lives in jungle A2433.3.21; woman carried off by t. N392.2; woman marries t. G11.6.2.

Tiger's enemies A2494.10; fear of crabs exploited K1715.13; food A2435.3.9; paw mark on moon A751.5.4; short sight in day: good sight at night A2491.4. — Animal's tail tied to t. J2132.5.1; buffalo refuses t. dinner invitation J425.2; cat drives fish into t. mouth X1114.2; crab on t. tail J1762.3; crane pecks out t. eyes S165.2; escape by posing as t.

preceptor K601.1; fox drinks t. milk K362.5.1; fox sleeps with t. wife
K1354.2.3; god in t. skin A131.4; groom called "t. son" H151.15; hedgehog jumps into t. mouth L315.13; jackal escapes t. house K563.1; numskull on t. back injured J2132.4; origin of marks on t. face A2330.4;
quest for t. milk H1361.1; trickster eats all of t. cubs but one K933.

Tigers build bridge B299.8.1; dance B293.3; in hell A671.2.14; not discussed lest tiger-son return C441.1; stand on each other to reach man in
tree X1133.5. — Army of t. B268.9; buffaloes fail god: now killed by t.
A2231.12; divine twins cared for by mother of t. B241.2.8.1; ghosts of
those eaten by t. E419.12; girl rescued from t. R111.1.13; hero exterminates race of t. A531.3; king of t. B241.2.8; land of t. B221.6; man-t.
killed by one arrow F679.5.3; ogre changes men into t. G11.6.1; procuring four t. to guard palace H1154.3.7.1; seeds cast on lions and t.
render them helpless D1410.1; why slayers of t. must not eat certain
plants C226.0.1; why t. don't kill women who run away from husbands
A2499.1.

Tigress bears men-children B631.6; becomes mortar D421.4.1; grateful for
opening of abscess B386; swallows baby F914.3. — Mortar transformed
to t. D444.8; tasks to get t. H939.3; woman assists t. as midwife B387.

Tigress's. — Kid puts t. cub in his place: she eats it K1611.5.

Tile transformed to gold D475.1.7. — Taking t. from her house reveals
witch G257.4.

Tilling. — Magic t. D1620.2.7; rats t. soil for master B292.9.3.

Timber. — Good t. given for useless J2093.4.

Time, see also **When;** of appearance of wild hunt E501.11ff.; of death
postponed D1855; favorable for unearthing treasure N555; of giving
curse M412; personified Z122; renders all things commonplace J1075;
tabu C750ff.; is wisest (riddle) H659.9.1. — Absurd theories concerning
t. J2276; animal characteristic because creator runs short of t.
A2286.1.0.1; calculation of t. A1485; changing course of t. H1026;
compulsion to go to certain place at certain t. C666; disenchantment at
end of specified t. D791.1; no t. for lying today X905.4; lake forbidden
at certain t. C615.1; learning to read in extraordinarily short t. F695.3;
not to eat at certain t. C230ff.; goddess divides t. between upper and
lower worlds A316; invulnerability for limited t. D1845; journey to
Mother of T. F118, H1285; no t., no birth, no death in otherworld F172;
passage of t. U200ff.; primeval water to subside in a specified t. A810.2;
prophecy: death at certain t. M341.1; prophecy: hero's birth at certain
t. M311.0.2; resuscitation after great length of t. E162.0.1; resuscitation
impossible after certain length of t. E162; return from death for definite t. E166; river says, "T. has come but not the man" D1311.11.1;
supernatural lapse of t. in fairyland F377; tabu: doing thing after
certain t. C752; tabu: speaking before certain t. C402; tabu: one forbidden t. C630ff.; test of t. H1583; unlearned person wastes t. J252; women
have no t. to help God A1372.8.

Times. — Fairies visible only at certain t. F235.2; otherworld dwellings open only at certain t. F165.2.

Timid animal consoled when he sees others more timid J881. — Brave soldier and t. cabinet-maker as companions P444.1; dwarfs are bashful or t. F451.3.6.5, F451.5.19; more t. than the hare J881.1; why animal is t. A2534.

Timpan. — Bird plays t. B297.1.1.

Tin becomes silver D475.3.2; sail F841.2.6. — Hot t. under horse's tail K1181.

Tinder. — Magic t. *D1175.1; origin of t. A1414.5.

Tinsa. — Why t. bark is white A2751.4.4; why t. tree has no bark at bottom of trunk A2751.2.3.

Tint. — Gold t. as royalty sign H71.6.2.

Tiny, see also **Little, Small;** bow F836.4; fairy F239.4.3; wood-spirit F441.5.1.

Tir Tairngire Island F111.2.1.

Tired as if he had walked J1946. — Boat gets t. J1884; fighting though t. J356; hero t. of man, sends death A1335.9.1.

Titans. — Winds as children of t. A1123.

Tithes. — Ass insists upon payment of t. B259.1; monks persuade wives that they must pay t. as one tenth the number of times of their marital intimacies J2344.1; payment of t. P531.

Tithing. — Origin of t. A1548.

Tithonus given eternal life without eternal youth M416.2.

Title. — "Aforesaid" as t. J1749.1; his proper t. (swine) J1286.

Titmouse allowed to sing before sacrifice K551.3.7; ruffles feathers to enlarge himself J955.1.2.1; whistles for dogs to frighten fox K869.1. — Creation of t. A1918; crow refuses to marry 100-year-old t. B282.22.1; cumulative tale: t., what are you eating? Z39.4.1; friendship of fox and t. A2493.10; man transformed to t. D151.6; wedding of t. B282.8, (and crow) B282.22; why t. has no tongue A2344.2.4.

Toad, see also **Frog;** asks magpie in tree to throw down a chestnut (cumulative tale) Z43.1; carries man B559.1; carries mortars F982.6; carries tree F982.7; causes eclipses A737.3; considered venomous B776.2; controls rice paddies' flooding D2149.5; exchanges ugly daughter for lizard's K476.5; as follower of the devil G303.10.2; mistaken for food, eaten J1761.7; plays drum B297.1.2; receives water from frog K231.8; refuses to weep over its dead children: dries up when dead *A2231.8; remains still when he hears footsteps (defense) A2461.2; swallows woman's earthenware F911.6.1; trades his tail for mole's eyes A2247.5; transformed to man D396; as witch's familiar B225.4. — Cat transformed to t. D412.1.2; child shares food with t. B391.2; consecrated bread kept in mouth and fed to t. produces love D1355.10.1; contest lost by t., won by lizard A1319.12.1; daydreaming t. run over J2061.4; devil in form of t. G303.3.3.7.1; devil roasts t. G303.25.14.2; why t. dries up when dead A2231.8, A2468.2; dragon as modified t. B11.2.1.5; dying t. comforts his paramour J865; why t. has red eyes A2332.5.4; fairy in form of t. F234.1.5; helpful t. B493.2; laughing t. B214.3.1; lizard wins contest with t. A2250.2; magic t. B177.1; man grateful not hideous as t. W27.1; man transformed to t. D196; marriage to t. B645.1; meat transformed to t. D444.2; origin of t. A2161; ornaments of t. F827.3; over-hasty t. (lie) X1862; poisonous t. sits on food of undutiful children Q557.1; princess sick because t. has swallowed her consecrated wafer *V34.2; soul in form of t. E736.2; soul in t. E715.5.1; speaking t. B211.7.2; how t. lost tail A2378.2.7; undutiful son punished by t. clinging to face Q551.1; weeping t. B214.4.1; whistling t. B214.2.1; why t. has no thumbs A2375.2.9; why t. lives in cold place A2433.6.7; witch bone from t. G224.11.1; witch in form of t. G211.6.1; woman bears t. T554.8.1.

Toad's blood venomous B776.5.1; croak A2426.4.2; wedding B284.2. — Cause of t. hop A2441.4.3.

Toads in hell A671.2.8; suck blood B766.3; on way to otherworld F144.1. — Blood becomes t. D447.3.1; community of t. B226.1; curse: t. from mouth M431.2; during the day dwarfs appear in form of t. or other vermin F451.2.0.5; man kills serpents, t., dragons with own hands F628.1.3.1; war between t. and frogs B263.1; witch gives birth to t. G243.3.1; why t. have warts A2412.5.2.

Toadstools. — Fairy bread turns to t. F343.19.1.

Tobacco from grave of (bad woman) A2611.2, (virgin) A2611.2.1; pipe, and match debate usefulness to smoker J461.3; -spirit F445.1.1. — Dwarfs dislike t. smoke F451.3.6.3; earth from primeval water mixed with seeds of t. A814.7; girl eats only kola nuts and t. F561.5; magic t. plant D965.17, (hides treasure) D1463.4; origin of t. *A2691.2; parson takes a chew of t. during the sermon X445.2; person lives by smoking t. F561.4; quest for magic t. H1333.2.2; recognition by t.-pipe H147; reincarnation as t. plant E631.5.1; why men like t. A2854; wind raised by blowing into t. pipe D2142.1.6.1; woman reborn as t. plant E694.2.

Toboggan test H1536.

Tod des Hühnchens Z32.1.1.

Today. — Origin of t. A1178.

Today's catch traded for tomorrow's J321.1.1. — Is t. sun same as yesterday's? J2272.2.

Toe. — Child's missing t. proves legitimacy T318; feet backward prevent t. stubbing F517.1.5.1; identification of man by his little t. H79.2; magic t. D995.1; mistaking own t. for snake's head J1838; recognition by missing t. H57.3; sixth t. cut off as execution proof K512.2.4.1; stumping t. a bad omen D1812.5.1.31.

Toes mistaken for ghosts, shot off J1782.8. — Backward-pointing t. F441.4.4; devil's footprints without t. G303.4.5.3.2; feet with unusual number of t. F551.2; Jesus drives evil spirits into hogs: hence "t." on back of foreleg A2287.1.1; ladder of t. F848.2; mutilation by cutting off t. S162.3; stepping on t. as reminder of lying X904.1.

Toenail. — Hero creates companion from t. A511.1.4.4; man from creator's t. A1211.5.1.

Toenails. — Cutting t. of cannibal woman G519.1.2.

Toilet. — Girl makes t. and calls help K551.5; respite from death until t. is made permits escape K551.7; tabu: attending t. needs C720ff.

Token. — Betrothal t. sent bridegroom's parents T61.4.4; bride to suitor giving greatest love t. H315.2; disguise by carrying false t. K1839.8; life-t. *E761ff.; object stolen as infidelity t. T247; paramour leaves t. with girl to give their son *T645; victim lured by false t. K839.2.

Tokens from a dream F1068.1; of royalty (nobility) left with exposed child S334. — False t. of woman's unfaithfulness K2112.1; god recognized by t. H45.4; identification by t. *H80—H149; return from dead to return and ask back love t. E311.

Toll fraudulently collected K157.1.

Tollkeeper. — Ass as t. B292.13.

Tom-Tit-Tot *C432.1.

Tom-tom beats out king's news P14.20; frightens off ogre K547.6.

Tomb, see also **Grave;** gate magically enlarged D482.5.2; robbed, man buried alive escapes R212.1.1. — Curative waters touching holy t. D1500.1.18.1.1; deer lick saint's t. daily B251.2.6; friends clasp hands through t. P319.5; king refuses fine t. J912.2; lover finds lady in t. apparently dead T37; lover at t. takes poison T37.1; magic t. D1148, (kills) D1402.32; man buried alive with king escapes from the t. R212.1; numskull objects to unhealthy place for his t. J1937.2; resuscitation by vigil at t. E62; riddle: what was the walking t. with the living tenant H821; test: vigil at t. H1460ff.; words from t. E545.0.1.

Tombs. — Saints' t. distill oil V229.2.9.

Tommy Knockers F456.1.

Tomorrow. — Debt to be paid "t." K231.12; inscription "Come t." rots: devil claims soul K231.12.1.

Tomorrow's — Today's fish catch traded for t. J321.1.1.

Tomtit's. — Hornbill borrows t. bill A2241.9.

Ton. — Strong man lifts t. of rye F624.5.

Tongs. — Automatic fire t. D1601.24; gods wrought t. A1402.

Tongue debates with other bodily members J461.1.3; cut off as punishment Q451.4; of dead lawyer found to be lacking P422.1.1; as path to sky F57.2; as proof that man has been murdered H105.2; protusion for breaking tabu C948.3; transformed to other object D457.14. — "Ave" on the t. V254.3; books in church read without man's t. F1055; camel's t. as "one pound of flesh" payment K255.4; cobra writes letter on prince's t. B165.1.3; crocodile punished for attacking man: has only half t. A2239.7; cut-out t. magically restored D2161.3.6.1; dragon-t. proof H105.1; dupe wishing to learn to play flute puts t. in split bamboo

51

K1111.0.1.1; fools try to use buffalo t. as a knife J1971; forked t. reveals disguised snake K1822.3; goat's t. pierced, so is witch's G252.2; gold under t. restores speech D1507.8; leek under t. of dead protects D1389.12; magic object under dead girl's t. D849.6; magic t. D992.5; magic animal t. D1011.6; magic speaking t. D1610.5.1; magpie tells man he is to die next day: no t. and long tail A2236.4; minstrel throws wife into sea: her t. the heaviest thing on board T251.1.5; mutilation: cutting (tearing) out t. *S163; origin of t. A1316.5; origin and nature of animal's t. A2344; person without t. F513.2; punishment for cutting off bird's t. Q285.1.1; punishment: t. protrudes from sinner's mouth Q551.8.6; remarkable t. F544.2; ring under dead girl's t. D765.1.1.1; saint with t. of fire V229.11; sharp instrument as t. deceives ogre G572.2; stretching t. as punishment Q451.4.10; substituted t. E782.5; symbolic meaning of spiced t. H604; talkative wife's t. paralysed D2072.0.5.3; tempted man bites out his t. and spits it in temptress's face T333.1; thread under dumb man's t. cut F954.1; victim persuaded to hold out his t.: cut off K825; woman's t. swells for lying Q583.4.

Tongues. — Animals duped into turning t. upside down K1064; confusion of t. *A1333; dogs with fiery t. in wild hunt E501.4.1.2; enemies' t. as trophies S139.2.2.1.1; ghosts as dogs with glowing t. and eyes E421.3.6; magic knowledge of strange t. *D1815; riddle: seven t. in a head H793.

Tongue-tied heretic Q551.7.1.1.

Tonsure. — Druidic t. P427.1.4.

Tool for unlawful work sticks to user Q551.2.5.

Tools magically sharpened D2199.2. — Acquisition of t. A1446; fairies borrow t. F391.3; giants throw t. back and forth F531.3.2.3; god fashions t. A1402; iron t. become earth D479.2; lie: remarkable t. X1024; witch scatters t. at night G265.1; worship of t. V1.9.

Toolmaker. — God compared to t. J1262.6.

Tooth falls out if charm is incorrectly applied D1273.0.5; transformed to fox D477.6; transformed to axe head D457.8. — Bed made from t. F787.4; blue t. identifies man H79.8; brake where saint loses t. bursts into flame V222.2; cannibal has long t. and long nail G88; dead man's t. as cure for toothache D1502.2.1; heathen to desert spot where saint lost t. M364.5; knocking out slave's t. entitles him to freedom P178.1; knowledge t. D1810.3, (detects crime) K1817.3, (reveals events in distant place) D1813.3; luck residing in t. N101.4; N113.2.2; magic animal t. D1011.4; magic t. *D1009.2; mortal wound from killed enemy's t. N339.16; prince gives away own t. W11.7; recognition by broken t. H57.1; three women have but one t. among them F513.1.1; why frog lacks t. A2239.8; wife persuades her husband to have good t. pulled J2324.

Teeth blackened for breaking tabu C985.2; of slain cyclops H105.5.2. — Animal's strong t. B747; child born with all t. T585.5; children's t. on edge after fathers eat sour grapes U18; contest: pulling on steak with t. K64; corpse asks golden t. be sold E443.2.1.1; devil's t. G303.4.1.5;

giant with t. like those of saw F531.1.6.2; fairies work with t. F271.0.2; false t. overawe Indians K547.2; filing away chain with t. R121.10; giant polishes t. with tree F621.2.2; god with gold t. A125.3; goddess with pig's t. A131.8; huldra with long t. F460.1.6; lion suitor allows his t. to be pulled and claws cut J642.1; love through seeing marks of lady's t. in fruit which she has bitten T11.4.4; magic lost when t. gone D1741.8; man's t. like axeheads F531.2.12; man created from sown dragon t. A1265; monster with golden t. B101.5; mutilation: knocking out t. S164; no t. as excuse for not drinking J1391.6; ogress whets t. to kill captive G83.1; one of the old maid's three t. breaks off X754; origin and nature of animal's t. A2345; origin of t. A1316.6; person unusual as to his t. F513.1; plowing with t. F1099.6.1; pulling out two t. for price of one J2213.7; recognition of disenchanted person by thread in his t. H64.1; red t. as sign of royalty H71.9; remarkable t. F544.3; return from dead to punish t. theft E235.4.6; revenant with chip of resin between t. E422.1.7; servant allowed anything he can take with t. J1161.10; sheep's t. J1391.3; soldier with severed hands fights with t. P461.1; sorcerer's power lost when his t. are knocked out D1741.8; sowing dragon's t. (task) H1024.5; successful suitor must have gold t. H312.2; sword between t. tokens defeat P555.1; warriors use t. F1084.2; why animal lacks t. A2345.7; wife carried up tree to the sky in bag in husband's t. J2133.5.1; witch drinks boiling oil to beautify t. G525.1; witch with extraordinary t. G214; women's vaginal t. A1313.3.1, F547.1.1; woodspirits' t. on stomachs F441.4.6.

Toothache. — False remedy for t. K1015; magic object cures t. D1502.2; witch causes t. G263.4.1.

Toothed penis F547.3.3; private parts F547.1. — Diamond-t. ogre G363.3.

Top. — Men hang down in a chain until t. man spits on his hands J2133.5; mountain with marvelous objects at t. F759.1; sun and moon placed in t. of tree A714.2.

Topographical features of the earth A900ff.; lies X1500. — Lie: hero responsible for t. features X958.

Topsy-turvy land X1505.

Tora as God's adviser A44. — Creation on condition Israel accept T. A74.1; extraordinary events at T. giving F960.10; neglect of T. punished Q223.10.1; oath by T. M114.1.1; study of T. as religious service V97.

Torch within enemy's camp signal for attack K2369.8. — Dead man wanders with t. E594; dwarf has silver miner's t. bright as the sun F451.7.4; life bound up with burning t. E765.1.2.

Torches. — Eyeballs become t. D457.11.2; god with spears as t. A137.14.2; lightning as t. of invisible dancer A1141.7.1; trickster bluffs old woman with t. K335.0.10.

Tormented. — Bull who cannot catch him t. by mouse L315.2; old man who has laid aside his humility t. by devil Q331.1; spirit t. by exorciser F405.14.

Tormenting by magic D2063.1; woman by chaste sleeping together T354. — Demons t. men G302.9.2; devils t. sinners in hell E755.2.7.

Torn garment proves man innocent of rape J1174.5. — Living t. to pieces by dead E267; murderer t. limb from limb Q469.12.

Tornado sunsets A1148.

Tortoise, see also **Turtle;** as animals' king B240.5; breaks elephant's back N335.7; carried, eaten by eagle J657.2; catches ogre helping him K1111.3; cheats leopard of meat K476.1.2; as creator's companion A36; cursed for going under water while ferrying rice-goddess A2231.7.3; and dog partners and thieves B294.7; escapes tiger captor K563.2; given hard shell for ferrying rice-goddess A2223.6; as God's footstool A139.2; lets self be carried by eagle J657.2; has no liver or teeth B723; jumps on, kills rhinoceros N622.1; leads elephant into trap K730.4; left in tree S143.2.1; outwits fowler, gets ruby K439.7.1; shell dug up, man dies E765.4.7; speaks and loses his hold on the stick J2357; as wooer B622.3. — Captured goose warns t. B143.1.6; creation of t. A2147; earth rests on t., serpent, elephant A844.6; enmity between panther, antelope, and t. A2494.12.1; fight between ape and t. B264.5; food of t. A2435.6.1; friendship between antelope, woodpecker, and t. A2493.32; giant t. B875.4; god as t. A132.15; hare and t. race: sleeping hare K11.3; helpful t. B491.5; why t. has humpy back *A2356.2.9; why t. lives in logs in stream A2433.6.1.1; magic t. fed with salt gives pearls B103.1.6; magic t. shell produces pearls D1469.14; man disguises as t. K1823.1; man transformed to t. D193; marriage to t. B604.2; ogre captured by t. G514.8.1; partridge's voice borrowed from t. A2241.3; prophetic t. B148.1; reincarnation as t. E614.4; storm frees marooned t. N662; why t. is amphibious A2214.5; why t. has short tail A2216.4, A2378.4.4; why t. has no voice A2421.4, A2422.4; woman bears t. T554.5.

Tortoise's foolish association with peacock J684.3. — Markings on t. back A2412.5.1; monkeys steal t. salt K343.4; origin of t. shell *A2312.1; why t. neck is outstretched to sky: is looking for his wife, the star A2351.5.

Torture *S180ff.; feigned K512.3; as punishment Q450.1. — Ascetic's self-t. V462.5; instruments of t. transformed to lotus flowers D454.16; magic objects enable one to withstand inquisitorial t. D1394.2; prisoner kills his watchers who enter to t. him K655; prophecy of t. M359.4; secret learned by t. N482; self-t. to secure holiness V464; servant undergoes t. for master P361.8; unremitting t. as punishment Q501ff.; virginity saved despite t. T320.1.1.

Tortured. — Ogre t. by not being allowed to sleep G585.

Tossing. — God t. created things into air A67.

Totem. — Eating t. animal forbidden C221.2; killing t. animal tabu C841.7; using t. tree for bed tabu C848.

Totems. — Animal t. B2.

Totemistic gods A113.

Toucan. — Man becomes t. D169.3; why beak of t. is black A2343.2.2.

Touch. — Birthmark removed at t. of dead man's hand E542.2; blood springs from corpse at t. of murderer's finger D1318.5.2; child's t. resuscitates E149.3; devil's t. marks G303.4.8.10; disenchantment by t. D782; Midas's golden t. D565.1, J2072.1; not to t. possessions of god C51; sight or t. of woman as source of sin T336; transformed animal refuses to t. meat of that animal D686.

Touched. — Keeping first thing t. K285; living man t. by dead man E542.

Touching corpse before burial E431.15; fruit tabu C621.2; head as acceptance sign P675; supernatural husband C32.2.3. — Devil t. body, not soul G303.25.18; disenchantment by t. water D766.1.2; don't sit on bed without t. it first J21.34.2; giant immortal while t. land of his birth D1854; king never t. earth P14.5; magic cure by t. D2161.4.16; magic knowledge from t. "knowledge tooth" with thumb D1810.3; magic powers from t. D1799.4; magic strength by t. earth *D1833; magic wishing-ring loses power by t. water D877.1; resuscitation by t. body E11.3; strength of witches depends on their t. earth G221.2; tabu: t. *C500—C549; tabu: t. deity's image with dirty hands C51.7; transformation by t. D565; vow against t. certain thing M172.

Tournament, see also **Contest;** with bride H332.1.4. — Devil accompanies knight to t. G303.8.9.1; hearing masses causes triumph in t. V41.2; suitor contest: t. H331.2; test of valor: t. H1561.1; three days' t. R222; Virgin substitutes in t. K1841.2.

Tournaments P561.

Tove's magic ring T85.4.1.

Tow transformed to person D439.1. — Husband made to believe that yarn has changed to t. through his carelessness J2325; paramour burned in barrel of t. K1554.1.

Tower of Babel F772.1, D2004.9.1, F941.3.1, Z71.6.4; neither too large, too high C771.1.1; in otherworld F163.7; to upper world F58. — Birds fly into t. of fire B172.10.1; dwarfs build t. F451.3.4.1.1; not to build too high a t. *C771.1; captivity in t. R41.2; confinement in t. to avoid fulfillment of prophecy M372; extraordinary t. F772; giant breaks from t. prison R211.1; girl's long hair as ladder into t. F848.1; fool gives three explanations of how the t. was built J2711; hill as unfinished t. like Nimrod's A963.8; magic t. D1149.2; measuring the t. by piling up hampers J2133.6.1; moving church t. J2328; princess builds t. of skulls of unsuccessful suitors *S110.3; quest for axe which sticks in beam outside a t. H1338; securing eggs from atop glass t. H1114.1; suitor contest: riding to fourth story of t. H331.1.2; virgin imprisoned in t. to prevent knowledge of men *T381.

Town crier frightened by grave robber K335.0.8; of fools J1703; mouse and country mouse J211.2; people transformed into witches G263.3.1. — Birds indicate building site of t. B155.2.3; why cock lives in t. A2433.4.2; why elephant does not live in t. A2433.3.15; ghosts punish intruders into ghost t. E241; how was t. burned? J2062.3; man and tiger in contest:

winner to live in t. A2250.1.1; punishment: sending out of t. on donkeys Q473.5; tabued pot broken: t. appears C917.1.

Toy. — Giant's t. F531.5.3.

Track. — Bear knows if person looks at his t. D1813.0.1; life token: t. fills with blood E761.1.3; thumbling lost in animal t. F535.1.1.5; transformation by drinking from animal's t. D555.1.

Tracks. — Covering t. immobilizes witch G273.7; fox sees all t. going into lion's den but none coming out J644.1; hunter wants to be shown lion t., not lion himself W121.1; person of remarkable sight finds t. of swine stolen seven years before his birth F642.2; sticking objects into t. pains witch G271.4.6; wild huntsmen leave fiery t. E501.7.6.3.

Tracker. — Skillful t. F677.

Tracking. — Dogs t. down law-breakers B578.

Trade involving eggs, needles and rum W154.26.1. — Devil fails to learn t. G303.13.4; don't be greedy in making a t. J21.26; fairies must t. whenever it is demanded of them F255.1; learning a t. in bed W111.5.9; noble person saves self from difficulties by knowledge of a t. P51; origin of t. between two places A1471.1; prince learning t. H335.0.2.2, P31; son insists on following father's t. P401; sons meet after learning t. M271; tailor married to princess betrays t. by calling for needle and thread H38.2.1; youth learns robbery as a t.: boasts of it K301.1.

Trades and professions P400—P499. — God of t. A450ff.; parents murder sons mentioning lowly t. S311.1; stupid sons use t. to harm father J2499.7.

Trader. — Barber wants to become t. J513.2.

Tradesmen of hell A677. — Humor dealing with t. X200—X299; treacherous officers and t. K2240ff.

Trading magic object away D871; wives T292.1. — Farmer cheated in t. horses with devil G303.25.12.

Traditions. — Christian t. concerning Jews *V360ff.; forgotten t. J1445; robber innocent because he is merely following t. of his ancestors J1179.4.

Tragedy. — Ghost haunts love t. scene E334.2.3; reenactment of t. E337.2; trees wither at t. F979.23.

Tragic love T80ff. — Sun eclipses to avoid t. happenings A737.10.

Trail leads to abandoned person R135; magically closed D2089.9; of stolen goods made to lead to dupe K401.1.1. — Faster one walks, longer the t. D1783.3; tokens left as t. H86; walking backwards leaves misleading t. K534.3.

Train of angels V242.1; leaves overpolite travelers J2183.2; of troubles from (lost horseshoe nail) N258, (sparrow's vengeance) N261. — Devil in woman's t. G303.8.9; phantom t. E535.4.

Traits of character W (entire chapter). — Fanciful t. of animal *B700—B799.

Traitor thrown into pit, chased from country Q417.2. — Burning as punishment for t. Q414.0.5.

Traitor's ashes thrown into lake, wind raised D2142.1.4.1.

Traitors, see **Treachery** *K2200—K2299.

Tramp. — Carrying the plow horse so as not to t. up the field J2163; transformation to t. D24.4, D659.12.

Trampling (kicking) to death by horses as punishment Q416.1. — Murder by t. S116.6.

Trance. — Body in t. while soul is absent E721.2; journey to heaven in t. F11.1; wizard detects thief by t. D1817.0.1.6.

Transferred. — Animal bodily members t. to person E780.2; curse t. to another person or thing M422; disease t. to another person or thing by magic object D1500.3; fish t. from tank to river B375.1.2; milk t. from another's cow by magic D2083.3; sickness t. to animal D2064.3; stolen object t. to innocent person K401.2.3; wish foolishly t. to wife J2075; witch power t. G224.10.

Transferring. — Cure by t. disease (to animal) *D2161.4.1, (to dead) E595.

Transform. — Hero's power to t. girl to carnation brings about recognition H151.7; ogre teaches smith how to t. sand in his smithy G651; witch's hair has power to bind or to t. G221.1.1.

Transformation D0—D699; animal to person D300—D399; and disenchantment at will D630ff.; for breaking tabu C960ff.; combat D615; as fitting punishment Q584; flight D671; of giant into mouse by trickery K722; of man to animal D100—D199, (as punishment) Q584.2; of god to guise of mortal D42; of man to different man D10—D99; of man to object D200—D299; of man to woman D12; of one animal to another D410ff.; in order to eat own kind G12; to old man to escape recognition D1891; of people by dwarfs F451.3.3.3; by saint before druid H1573.3.3; of woman to a man D11; by witch *G263; of witch into snake when she bathes G245.1. — Animal characteristics from t. A2260ff.; animal cries a lament over animal's t. A2275.2; creation of animals through t. *A1710ff.; creation of plants by t. A2610ff.; dragon's power of self-t. B11.5.1; means of t. D500—D599; plants characteristics from t. A2731ff.; murder through t. K928; periodic t. D620ff.; punishment: t. to deer which is devoured by dogs Q415.1.1; punishment: t. of lovers into lion and lioness for desecrating temple Q551.3; repeated t. D610ff.; request for immortality punished by t. into tree Q338.1; river from t. A934.11; rocks from t. of people to stone A974; seduction on promise of magic t. K1315.3.2; self t. (of fairy) F272, (of hero) A527.3.1.

Transformed brother as bird N733.4; fairy F234; golden pumpkin J1531.1; person as helper N819.2; person is swallowed and reborn in new form *E607.2; person sleeps before girl's door, at foot of bed, in bed K1361.1; prince killed N324.1; wife rescues husband R152.5. — Abduction by t. person R16; adulteress t. to mare and stirruped Q493.1; animal t. to man wants to marry woman B650.1; animals t. from other animals B318; animals from men t. for discourtesy to God (Jesus) *A1715.2; animals in otherworld pass in and out of church and are t. to human beings

*F171.5; ashes t. to insects, snakes to protect hero K2351.2.2; bad women from t. hog and goose A1371.3; cat from t. eagle A1811.1; devil's horses are t. men G303.7.1.2; devil's money t. to ashes G303.21.1; dog to avoid seeing husband t. K2371.4; extraordinary companions are t. animals F601.6; fairy t. as punishment F386.4; fairy t. to fly allows self to be swallowed by woman and reborn as fairy F392; ghost t. into animal E453; giant as t. man F531.6.1.2; husband t. (by adulteress) K2213.6, (to get rid of him) K1535; identification by feather taken from hero when he was t. to bird H78.2; Io t. to cow with gadfly ceaselessly pursuing Q501.6; man t. to beast becomes leader of herd B241.3; man had rather remain t. to mule than to live with his shrewish wife T251.1.3; man t. to animal kept as pet by heroine T33; man t. to horse and ridden by witch G241.2.1; male t. in womb to female T577.1; maltreated children t. S365; man's human wife t. by fairy mistress F302.5.2; not to mention original form of t. person C441; ogre captured while t. to animal G514.4; person t. to moon A747; recognition of person t. to animal H62; recognition of t. person among identical companions H161; sister faithful to t. brother P253.2; stolen animal magically t. K406.3; sun and moon beget stones and birds: these t. to first parents A1271.2; tabu: wife seeing t. husband C32.1.1; thief claims to have been t. into an ass K403; true bride t. by false K1911.2.1; wedding party t. into wolves by old beggar T155; woman t. to animal bears animal T554.0.1.

Transformer transformed Q584.1.

Transformers D683.1. — Original creator followed by t. A72.

Transforming monkeys to humans T68.5. — Adulteress t. man to stone K1535.1; dupe t. self into animal, can't change back K1062; fairy t. self F234.0.1; husband tests wife's faithfulness by t. himself *T235; jealous wife t. rival to dog T257.2.2; princess t. self to woo T55.11; sorceress t. new husband each day T113.1; witch t. man to object G263.2; wood-spirits t. men into animals F441.6.2.

Transfusion. — Son sold for blood t. S268.2.

Transition formulas Z10.3.

Translation to otherworld without dying F2.

Transmutation of the quail J1269.5.

Transparent body F529.5, (of pregnant woman) T579.8.1; stone F809.7.

Transplanting feather from one bird to another F668.3.

Transportation during magic sleep D1976.1; to or from upper world F60ff. — Gods with unusual t. A136ff.; magic object affords miraculous t. *D1520ff.; magic t. *D2120ff.; sham magician claims t. by demons K1963.6.

Transporting. — Ghost t. human E599.12; spirit t. people F414.

Trap. — Animal (grateful for rescue from t.) B364.1, (rescues from t.) B545; birds discuss the t. J655.1; chasing a hare into every t. in a high tree (task) H1024.3; contest in jumping into a t. K17.3; deceiver falls into own t. K1600—K1699; getting bait from t. by luring in another animal K1115.1; maiden in t. gives self to rescuer Q53.3.1; man enters girl's room through t.-door concealed in floor K1348.1; musician in wolf t. B848.1; paramour falls in t. K1574.1; perilous (t. bridge) *F842.2.1, (t. gate) F842.2.1.1; pitch-t. for fleeing girl J1146.1; small animals dupe larger into t. L315.15; trickster takes an oath by touching t. K1115; wait till I'm taken from t., then eat me K553.1.1.

Traps. — Origin of fish t. A1457.5.

Trapped. — Ogre t. in box (cage) G514.1; victim t. *K730ff., (by ogre) G421; wife and paramour t. with magic armor K1563.

Trapping contest won by deception K32. — Suitor contest: t. H331.9; wounding by t. with sharp knives (glass) S181.

Trappings. — Ass envies horse in fine t. J212.1.

Trash magically becomes food D2105.3.1. — Treasure box filled with t.: joint owners quarrel K2131.4.

Travel to wedding T133. — Devil and the wind t. together G303.6.3.3; forbidden t. direction C614.1; futility of distant t. J1076; transformation to t. fast D644.

Traveler meets ghost E332.2. — Devil (gentleman) invites t. into his wagon G303.7.1.2.2; devil invites t. to feast G303.25.17.1; devil as ribald t. G303.3.1.3.1; ghost misleads t. E272.5; man helps t. and makes riddling remarks H586.1; sham t. K1969.1; woman entertaining every t. H152.1.1.

Travelers draw swords in advance J2255; find exposed baby, save her S354.2; to other world not to look back C331.2; pursued by misfortune N251.4. — Brownie murders t. F363.2; deaf peasant: t. ask the way X111.2; devil as crow misleads t. G303.9.9.17; fairies lead t. astray F369.7; god of t. A491; hawthorn protects t. D1385.2.3; jokes about t. X583; ogress devours t. from cave G94.1; phantom t. E510; riddle: who are real t.? (sun, moon) H726.

Traveling prolongs life thousand years D1855.5; stones F809.5; till iron shoes are worn out *H1125; tooth F544.3.6. — Curse: woman not t. far M459.1; advice on t. with money J21.39; animal t. extraordinary distance B744; devil's t. G303.7ff.; dragon t. on sea or land B11.4.4; fairies t. through air F282; ghost t. swiftly E599.5; girl rescued by t. through air *R111.3.1; ghost t. under ground E591; magic horse t. on sea or land *B184.1.4; numskulls go t. J1711; riddling remarks of t. companion interpreted by girl at end of journey H586ff.; sunken bell t. on sea bottom V115.1.1; tabu: t. beyond spot where feat of skill was performed before duplicating it C888; wife t. for years seeking husband's cure T215.7.

Tray. — Cannibal with winnowing t. and pestle G11.12; stealing t. from king's bedside H1151.3.1.

Treacherous disposal of true bride by false K1911.2; impostors K1930ff.; murder during hunt K917; persons *K2200—K2299; philosophers P485.1; priests prolong mass to let enemy destroy city K2354; river F932.8.4;

servants assign tasks H919.1; soldier suggests task H919.5. — Counselor killed in own t. game K1626.2; king's son has t. foster brother P273.1.2.
Treachery *K2000ff.; punished *Q261. — Bird reveals t. B131.2; confessing all t. wins bride H331.11; death as punishment for t. Q411.4; demons goad man to t. G302.9.9; detection of t. K2060ff.; elder brothers banished for t. Q431.2; gods' t. brings death to man A1335.14; horse reveals t. B133.2; lovers separated by t. T84.
Treacle. — Lover made to fall into t. pit K1218.1.3.2.
Tread. — Plants from t. of holy person A2621ff.
Treading. — Magic sight by t. on another's foot *D1821.1.
Treason punished Q217. — King's advisor falsely accused of t. K2126.1.
Treasonable. — Innocent man compelled to write t. letter K2156.
Treasure buried with dead V67.3; and jewels in otherworld F166.1; animal *B100ff.; cast down crushes besiegers K2353; chest breaks avaricious man's neck Q272.2; disappears C401.3, D1555.3, N553.2; falls from mouth *D1454.2; -finders who murder one another K1685; given away or sold for trifle J2093; given away by saint restored V411.5; -guarding snake H335.3.4; hidden in tree's roots D2157.3.2; -laying bird B103.2.1; -producing animals B103ff.; as reward Q111.6; reward for selling lizard thread J1852.1.1; struck from phantom's hand F585.4; transformed to ducks D449.3; trove N500—N599. — Accidental acquisition of t. N630ff.; animal gives t. to man B583; animals guard t. B576.2; animal shows man t. B562.1; demon brings t. to benefactors G514.0.1; discovery of t. brings luck N135.2.1; dog indicates hidden t. *B153; doves show monk t. B562.1.3; dream of marking t. X31; dream of t. on the bridge N531.1; drowning in attempt to save t. J2146.2; druid causes t. loss P427.0.2; dupe digging t. from ant hill K1125; dwarfs direct mortals to t. F451.5.1.9; dragon feeds on t. B11.6.3; dragon guards t. *B11.6.2; dwarfs possess t. F451.7.1; eater of magic fish to spit up t. M312.3.1; entrusting t. as honesty test H1555.1; escaping robbers by promising to show them t. K567.2; fairy lured away by t. F381.5; fairies' t. F244; father's counsel: find t. within a foot of the ground H588.7; fool hides t. and leaves sign J2091.1; foolish dog finds t. and dies rather than leave it J1061.3; ghost laid when t. is unearthed E451.5; ghost points out t. E545.12; ghost steals t. E593.5; ghosts protect t. E291; giant's t. F531.6.7; hand-of-glory indicates location of t. D1314.5; hanging for silence about t. Q413.7; helpful animal discovers t. B562.1; hero hides in t. box, secures own share K677.1; hero leaves bedmate keys to t. chamber T645.4; hogs root up t. for saint B562.1.1; inexhaustible t. D2100.1; introducing t. animal into flock K2131.5; island covered with t. F731; jewels aid in search for t. D1314.8; magic object furnishes t. *D1450ff.; magic plant (flower) shows location of t. D1314.7; magic t. D2100ff., (as reward) Q142; magic t. animal killed D876; magic t. gives miraculous powers D1561.2.2; magic wand locates hidden t. *D1314.2; man finds t. he refused as gift N224; mandrake shows location of t. D1314.7.1;

miser transported to t.-wood F414.2; miser's t. stolen J1061.4; money or t. given by dwarfs F451.5.1.5; mountain of t. F752; object transformed to t. D475; pseudo-t.-producing objects sold K111; quest for t. in hell H1275; refusal to tell of Rhine t. K239; return from dead to reveal hidden t. E371; return from dead to seek t. E372; return from dead to uncover t. E415.1.2; robbers' hidden t. stolen K439.10; sacrifice made when t. is found V13; sale of false t. K120ff.; not to speak while searching for t. C401.3; serpent demon guards t. G354.1.1; sham priest claims can discover t. K1961.1.4; snake's hoarded t. E765.4.6; spirit in hornet form guards t. F403.2.3.1; starving woman to death for t. K2116.2.2; storm from calling up spirits to help find buried t. D2141.0.2; swamp spirit guards t. F494.1.1; task: raising a buried t. H1181; tax on t. P531.2; test of honesty: man entrusted with t. H1555.1; thief persuades owner of goods to dive for t. K341.4; troll's t. obtained by casting steel F455.6.4.2; underground t. chambers F721.4.

Treasures. — Dragon from transformed man lying on his t. B11.1.3; dwarfs dig for t. F451.6.9; giants fight about t. F531.6.8.3.1; journey to get lower world t. F81.5; not to touch t. of otherworld C542; preferring princess to t. H511.1.2; saint scratches earth, t. appear D2157.1.1.

Treasurer. — Treacherous t. K2249.2.

Treasury. — Animal gets t. keys K341.18; means of entering house or t. K310ff.; mismanagement of king's t. a mortal offense P13.2.

Treatment of husband's good eye K1516.1. — Cobold avenges uncivil t. F481.1; disenchantment by rough t. D710ff.; resuscitation by rough t. *E10ff.

Treaty. — Making t. tabu C751.5; satirizing as punishment for breaking t. Q499.4.1.

Tree aids escape from lower world F101.5; alleged to produce clothes K118.1; appealed to as arbitrator D1311.4.1; appears to save saint from abyss V222.10; bends to certain person D1648ff.; beside holy well V134.0.1; blooms out of season D2145.2.2.2; bows before prince H71.10.1; of cakes D2106.3; consumed by anchorite's breath D2082.2; cursed for serving as cross A2721.2.1; cut down with axe for which it furnished a handle J162; cut down to get victim in top K983.1; by day, man by night D621.2; from which one cannot descend D1413.1; -destroying monsters G346.3.1; dies when owner dies E766.2; with extraordinary fruit F811.7; feeds abandoned children S376; follows murderer N271.9; grateful D1658.1.5; grows from rod used in saint's birth T584.0.5; grows out of horse and gives rider shade X1130.2.2; guarded by dragon H1333.6; guarded by ghosts H1151.10; half green and half in flame in otherworld garden F162.1.2.4; in hell made of living heads of the dead A671.2.3; of immortality D1346.4; from innocent man's blood E631.0.5; inside seventh series of forts H1333.5.0.2; on which Judas hanged himself cursed A2721.5; of knowledge J165, (eaten by serpent) B123.1.1; of Life *E90ff., (in otherworld) F162.3.1; magically withers D2082.0.2;

opens and conceals fugitive D1393.1; points way to fugitive but mis-
directs enemy D1393.4; produced by magic D951, D2178.8; protects
D1380.2; protects Jesus from rain: is green all year A2711.4; pulled
down in order to give it water to drink J1973; -pulling contest K46;
refuge *R311; as repository of fire A1414.7.1; with silver branches
D1461.0.2; from sinner's grave E631.0.6; -spirits C43.2; springs back to
kill enemies K1112.1; supports sky A665.4; transformed (to animal)
D441.1, (to other object) D451.1, (to person) D431.2, (to stone) D471.6;
-trunks laid crosswise of the sledge J1964; as underworld roadway
F95.5; to upper world *F54; warns of danger *D1317.20; as wife
T461.3. — Abandonment on stretching t. K1113; abandonment in t.
S143.2; all-yielding t. in otherworld F162.1.3.1; animals emerge from t.
A1793; animals in t. cause its breathing X1116; bending the t. K1112;
big t. thought to be snake J1771.1; birth from a t. T543.1; blindness
cured by striking t. F952.4; boy in the hollow t. X1854.1; bonga lives
in t. F216.2; buckeye (or other t.) selected as repository for fire
A1414.7.1; branching t. as roadway for souls E750.2.3; bringing
marvelous t. suitor test H355.3; captivity in t. R49.1; capture between
t. branches K742; capture by hiding in hollow t. K763; caste from
catching t. A1651.2; castle in t. top F771.2.2; chopping down large t.
with blunt (fragile) instrument (task) H1115; child abandoned in hollow
t. S143.1; child born in t. T581.3; city inside a t. F765; climbing t. leads
to adventures N776.1; conception from embracing magic t. T532.1.2;
corpses exposed in t. V61.10; creation of man from t. A1251; creator
rests on t. or stake A813.3; crow seems to have caused t. to fall J953.11;
cure by passing patient under cleft of t. D2161.4.5; cutting down t.
tabu C518; cutting t. branches tabu C513.1; cutting t. with one stroke
H1562.1.1; cutting down t. without scratching for stinging insects (task)
H1184; dead t. comes to life *E2; death magically bound to t. Z111.2;
death respite for hero to climb t.: flies away K551.24; deceptive contest
in carrying a t.: riding K71; deceptive land purchase: as much land as
can be shadowed by a t. K185.10; deity born from t. A114.4; deity
lives in t. A151.7.1; demon imprisoned in t. R181.1; demon lives in t.
F402.6.1; devils haunt t. G303.15.4; disease transferred to t. D2161.4.2.4;
disenchantment by shaking t. D789.7; don't plant thorny t. H588.20;
door falls on robbers from t. K335.1.1.1; deer persuaded to butt head
into t. *K1058; devil pulls up t. to goad his oxen G303.9.2.1; disenchantment from leaf by breaking it from t. D711.5; disenchantment
from t. form by embrace of lover D735.3; dogs rescue fleeing master
from t. refuge *B524.1.2; dragon lives beneath t. B11.3.7; dream of
sprouting t. indicates hero's birth M312.0.4.1; dupe lured into t., killed
K983ff.; dupe induced to stand under falling t. K982; dupe persuaded
to climb tall t. K1113.1; dupe tricked into entering hollow t. K714.3;
dwarf caught by beard in cleft of t. F451.6.1; earth from t. grown in
primeval water A814.4; earth-t. A878; escape by catching hold of t.

limbs K685; escape from deluge on t. A1021.0.4, A1023; escape from deluge in hollow t. A1021.0.5; escape by falling from t. K558.1; escape from lower world on miraculously growing t. F101.5; everlasting t. in otherworld F162.3.3; extraordinary t. F811ff.; fairy harper enclosed in yew t. F386.1; fairy imprisoned in t. F386.1; fairies dance under t. F261.3.1; feather becomes t. D457.7; felled t. (raises itself again) *D1602.2, (restored) C43.3, (restored by reassembling all cut parts) E30.1; felling t. resuscitates incarnated being E29.4.1; fire burns up whole t. H1129.5; female spirit of particular t. (hamadryad) F441.2.3; first woman's mate from t. A1275.6; flight on a t., which ogre tries to cut down *R251; following a luminous t. in the desert K1886.1.1; forbidden t. *C621; fox burns t. in which eagle has his nest E315.3; frog becomes t. D428.1.1; fruit of magic t. exhilarating D1359.3.3; fruitful t. chosen J241; future hero found atop t. L111.2.3; future heroine found in hollow t. L111.2.1.1; getting fruit from the top of a tall t. without cutting the t. (task) H1038; ghost laid under t. E437.5; ghosts haunt t. E276; giant bird alighting on t. causes it to tremble B31.6.2.1; giant bird pulls up oak t. B31.6.2; giant with t. for herding-stick G152.1; girl rescued from t. R111.25; girl with t. carried to moon A751.8.5; girl summons fairy lover by lying under t. F301.1.1.3; god as t. trunk A139.81; God finds devil sitting under t. G303.1.2.1; god's home under t. of life A151.7.1.1; gods emerge from t. A115.7; goddess as t. A139.8.5; gullible husband behind t. K1533; harming t. before burning tabu C519.1; helpful t.-spirit N815.0.1; hero returning with berries sent back for t. H1241.1.1; horse made to appear as t. trunk D2031.7; importunate lover tied to t. K1218.7; impostor acting as God in t. unmasked K1971.12; jealous father sends son to upper world on stretching t. *S11.2; king (prince) finds maiden in t. and marries her N711.1; lecherous trickster seduces women from t. and loses them K1387; life bound up with t. E765.3.3; life recreated from t. A1006.9; lost wind found in hollow t. A1122.3; not to lie under t. *C516; life token (knife stuck in t. rusts) E761.4.1, (t. fades) *E761.3; light seen from t. lodging place at night leads to adventure N776; magic belt carries t. away D1539.2; magic belt destroys t. K525.8.1; magic feather causes chips from t. to return as fast as cut D1565.1; magic formula causes t. to open D1556.1; magic glance reduces t. to ashes D2082.1; magic healing hazel t. D1500.1.3.1; magic knife stuck in t. causes wine to flow D1472.2.11; magic knowledge of t. language D1815.4; magic object acquired by rapping on t. D859.1; magic object causes t. to spring up D1576; magic speaking t. betrays secret *D1316.5; magic spell makes t. grow D1487.3; magic song causes chips from t. to return D1565.1.1; magic t. *D950ff., (supplies food) D1472.1.3; man allowed to pick out t. to be hanged on K558; man behind t. speaks and pretends to be God K1971; man has t. for wife T461.3; man transformed to t. D215ff., G263.2.2; man in t. above illicit lovers comments on their child K1271.5; men in t. sing, clap, fall down and die J2133.5.3; man-devouring t. H1163; mankind from mating of t. and vine A1221.4; marriage with a t. T117.5; men wait in vain for nuts to fall from t. J2066.3; marvelous t. survives deluge A1029.1; miraculous growth of t. D2157.4; why monkey lives in t. A2433.3.19; monster's blood makes t. and surroundings poisonous D1563.2.2; murder by crushing beneath t. S116.5; murder by springing bent t. S135; night spent in t. F1045; numskull cuts off t.-limb on which he sits J2133.4; numskull sticks his head in the branches of a t. J2131.5.3; numskull to water roots of t. J2126; numskull tries to shake birds from t. like fruit J1909.3; objects falling from t. frighten off those below N696; object falls on robbers from t. K335.1.1; ogre bribes boy not to cut down certain t. N699.5; ogre's secret overheard from t. G661.1; oil on t. prevents pursuit K619.2; oracular t. *D1311.4; origin of sacred t. for crucifixion of Christ A2632.2; why parrot lives in t. A2433.4.4; picking all nuts from tall t. (task) H1121; placing frogs in a t. (task) H1024.2; plow in t. J2465.12; plane t. tests perjury H251.3.1; plucking fruits from t. unique ability H31.12; provisions received from magic t. D1470.2.1; pseudo-magic cake t. K112.3; pursued sweetheart becomes t. D642.3.1; quest for marvelous t. H1333.1, H1331.1; quest for singing t. H1333.1.1; question (propounded on quest): why does not a certain t. flourish H1292.2; reading from book makes fallen t. stand D1571.3; reason for withering of t. N452.1.1; recognition by tear falling from t. H151.14.1; reincarnation in t. growing from grave *E631ff.; reincarnation as t. spirit E653.2; rejuvenation by fruit of magic t. D1338.3.3; residence in a t. F562.2; return from lower world by being slung by bent t. F101.2; riddle: how many leaves are on the t. H705; riddle: t. with leaves white on one side and black on other H721.2; riddle: t. with twelve branches, each with thirty leaves, black and white H721.1; sacrifice to t. V11.1; saint's girdle causes t. to fall in right direction D1549.2; saints cause t. worshipped by pagans to fall P623.0.5; sawing iron t. H1115.2; sea released from t.-top A924.3; secrets of animals (demons) accidentally overheard from t. hiding place N451.1; self-opening t.-trunk D1556; shape of t. A2785; shoes carried into the t. J1521.1; singing t. D1615.1; sitting between heaven and earth (in a t.) H583.3.2; snake's venom kills t. B765.11; soul hidden in t. E712.1; soul of t. E701.3; souls of dead imprisoned in t. E755.4.1; speaking t. *D1610.2; spear becomes t. D454.9.1.1; spring from sacred t. shot by arrow A941.7.2; why squirrel lives in t. A2433.3.9; stolen sheep's tails severed and put in t. K404.3; strong man: t.-puller F621; strong man fells t. with one blow of axe F614.8; strong man uproots t. and uses it as a weapon F614.2; sun and moon (made from t.) A717, (placed in top of t.) A714.2; symbolism of World T. H619.3; tabu to cut t. where deity lives C93.6; tabu to steal from sacred t. C91.2; tabu: striking deity's t. C51.1.12; tasks performed by means of secrets overheard from t. *H963; test of strength: pulling up t. by roots H1562.1; thief tells his pursuer that the thief has gone to heaven by way of a t. K341.9; thorn growing in wound becomes a t. F971.3; thorn t. roots used by saint to dig canal D2121.14; tiger-killing t. K1715.6; not to touch t. C510ff.; transformation to t. C961.3.2, (as punishment) Q551.3.5.2; transformation: stretching t. *D482.1; transformation by stretching and swaying t. D1520.1.1; transformation: t. to stone D471.6; treasure buried under t. N511.1.9; tree-spirit persuades man spare t. F441.2.0.1; trickster hides in hollow t. K1971.1.1; trickster in t. advises that t. and fruit belong to him K1971.11; ungrateful wanderer pulls nut t. to pieces to get the nuts W154.6; unique ability to cut t. H31.6; vow not to touch certain t. M172.2; water from cut in t. D927.1.1; wager: who can call three t. names first N51; what is the t. that became flesh H823; wife carried up t. to the sky in bag in husband's teeth J2133.5.1; why certain t. is tall A2778.1; why fruit of t. not eaten? H1292.2.1; wild hunt disappears with movement of t. tops E501.16.2; wisdom acquired by hanging in a t. J162; wish for t. as husband realized C15.2; witch lives in t. G234; witch as t. G212.4; witches ride t. G242.4; withering of t. bad omen D1812.5.1.20; wolf transformed to t. D421.1.1; world t. felled by hunters A773.5.

Trees bear first buds to commemorate reign of primitive hero A2771.5; bewitched G265.10; could speak in golden age A1101.1.2; cut down to gather fruit J2126.1; falling reveals Savior's will D1311.4.0.2; killed by magic D2082; from lovers' graves resemble them E631.0.1.1; magically made fruitless D2082.0.1; prostrate selves E761.3.4; unbent F973.1; wither from breaking tabu C998. — Birth t. *T589.3; blinded trickster directed by t. *D1313.4; bramble chosen king of t. P11.0.2.1; city girl: do turnips grow in the ground or on t.? J1731.1; concurrently blooming, bearing t. in otherworld F162.1.3; counting palm t. within view of palace H1118.3; creator's servant puts t. to hold earth together A857.3; not to cut sacred t. C51.2.2; dead t. blossom at saint's command D2157.3; deceptive bargain with ogre: buying t. K186; why t. do not talk A2791.1; druids can pass through t. D1932; enigma on uprooting old t., planting new H599.5; extraordinary behavior of t. and plants F970ff.; extraordinary t. F810ff.; fairies live in t. by stream F216.1; father's counsel: dress up the trunks of t. H588.6; felled t. return to their places C939.3; five t. of paradise A661.3; flesh-eating spirits live in t. G312.3; giants carry t. F531.3.10; giant lies underground with t. growing all over his body F531.2.6; horse which will not go over t. K134.1; killing t. threaten hero H1522; lies about t. X1470; magic forests and t. D940ff.; magic object revivifies t. D1571; magic results from sacrifices at t. D1766.2.1; magic spear-head cuts down t. D1564.4.1; mother curses self, children into t. D525.1; ogres live in t. G637; origin of t. *A2681ff.; person of remarkable sight can see through hearts of t. F642.3.1; plants and t. miraculously unbent F973; riddle about t. not fading until they wither H852; skillful axe-man cuts down t. with single stroke F666ff.; soldiers of fairy king are t. by day and men by night F252.3.1; speaking and bleeding t. E631.0.4; stars are t. growing on clouds A769.1; strong hero practices up-rooting t. F611.3.1; strong man throws t. on roof and breaks it F614.6; symbolic names of three t. Z183.1; tabu: cutting certain t. C43.2; tears of Adam and Eve leaving paradise become t. A2612.1; why big t. have small fruit A2771.9; why t. remain fixed A2774; worship of t. V1.7.

Trembling mountain F1006.3; of pipal leaves A2762.3. — Earth t. at Crucifixion V211.2.3.1; worlds t. at rebirth F960.1.5.

Trench. — Ghost summoned by pouring blood of sacrifices into t. E382.

Trénther. — King's t. P14.15.

Trespasser's defence: standing on his own land J1161.3.

Trespassers. — Fairies take revenge on t. on ground they claim as theirs F361.4.

Trespassing sacred precincts forbidden C93ff. — Vow against t. M186.

Tresses. — Lai of the T. K1512.

Triad. — God as a t. A109.1.

Triads Z71.1.0.1.

Trial among animals (cumulative tale) Z49.6; by combat H218; by ordeal subverted by carrying magic object D1394.1; rehearsed before stick in the ground as judge J161. — Magic objects help hero in t. D1394ff.; rich man's t. in heaven Q172.2.1.

Triangle plot and its solutions T92.1.

Triangular hailstones F962.5.3. — Why dung of ass is t. A2385.1.

Tribal customs established by diviner A150.1. — Origin of t. subdivisions A1640ff.

Tribe born from fire A1268.1; descended from lone woman-survivor A1006.7; of one-eyed, one-footed, one-handed men F525.3. — Bringing sickness to t. H1199.2.1; cannibal t. G11.18; curse on t. M463; divining rod sinks at place where t. shall settle D1314.2.1; promise not to wed into certain t. M258.2; wandering of t. as punishment Q502.3.

Tribes. — Culture from ancestor of t. A1405; distribution of t. A1620ff.; king evades gift to hostile t. K234.1; origin of various t. A1610ff.; paths open in sea for Israel's t. F931.9.3; treacherous t. K2299.2; wandering of t. A1630ff.

Tribunal of the gods A169.1.

Tribute paid in enchanted snow K236.3; as punishment Q595.4.1; slaves must not know Irish P172; taken from fairies by fiend at stated periods F257; of youths regularly sent to foreign king S262.2. — Every third year t. period Z72.5; paying t. to save life, money J223; payment of t. P531; queen must pay t. to victorious queen P24; remitting t. until Luan K2314.2.1; reward for remitting t. Q42.7; tasks as t. H928.

Trick: cadaver arm placed in person's room N384.0.1.1; overawes ogre G572; solves sleeping problem H573.2. — Answer to riddle found by t. H573; cat's only t. J1662; entrance into girl's (man's) room (bed) by t. K1340ff.; heaven entered by t. K2371.1; king asks for new t. H1182.2; magic object acquired by t. D830ff.; series of t. exchanges Z47; underground monster fettered by t. A1071.1; woman persuaded (or wooed) by t. *K1350ff.

Tricks, see also **Deception.** — Occupational t. J2347; ogre killed through other t. G519; ogre outwitted by t. G501.

Tricked. — Girl t. into man's room (or power) K1330ff.; gods t. into help in escaping one's fate K2371.2; ogre t. into carrying his prisoners home in bag on his own back G561.

Tricking enemy by hiding behind hero F601.4.1. — Fairy t. mortal F369.4; man t. saint stricken dead Q591.1.1; parents t. children into forest S345.

Trickster, see also **Clever persons;** appears as Death J217.0.1.1; chooses his gift J1282; concealed in sacred tree advises that he is to marry the princess K1971.10; eats scratch-berries J2134.1; elopes with girl instead of lover T92.4.3; feigns death and eats ripe fruit from the tree K1867.1; gets caught on a fishhook J2136.2; goes around king, gets gem for going around kingdom J1289.14; joins bulrushes in a dance J1883; leads water to sea, ends flood A1028.1; makes two friends each suspicious of the other's intentions *K2131ff.; masks as doctor and punishes his cheaters K1825.1.3; outwits adulteress and paramour K1570ff.; outwits king, forces expensive gift J1593; pinched by shell-fish (crab) J2136.4; potter reborn as crab E692.3; puts on buffalo skull: gets head caught J2131.5.1; shifts married couples in bed K1318; travels, fish burn up J2173.7. — Animal as t. J1117; blinded t. directed by trees *D1313.4; culture hero as t. A521; god as t. A177.1; husband to wife about t.-seducer: "Let him have what he wants" K1354.2.1; liar outdoes t. X909.2.

Trickster's daughter inherits his skill J1111.2; false creations fail him J2186; greed while hunting causes him to be deserted J2751; interrupted feast revenged J1564.1. — Animals killed by t. breaking wind F981.3; sleeping t. feast stolen J2173.1.

Tricksters persuade women to share intimacy K1315.6.1.

Trident. — Magic t. D1102.

Tried. — Animal t. out as messenger B291.0.1; ghosts t. in court E573.

Trifle. — Consolation by a t. J860ff.; not lying for a t. X905; treasure given away or sold for t. J2093ff.

Trinity. — Names of persons in the T. X435.4; physician willing to believe four persons in T. J817.2.

Trinkets seller discovers true bride H151.15.

Triple tax N635.

Triplet. — Mother hides t. sons R153.4.2.

Triplets exposed S314; as heroes T687; killed by tribe at birth T586.3.2. — Extraordinary companions are t. F605.1; woman ravished by three brothers bears t. T586.3.1.

Tripping. — Bridge t. up bridal party if king is not marrying equal H31.2.1; woman t. over skirt Q331.2.3.

Triumph of the weak L300—L399. — Hearing masses causes t. in tournament V41.2.

Trivial. — Subject exiled for t. remark U38.

Trojans deceived by wooden horse K754.1; warned against attacking Greeks J652.4.1.

Troll lets two goats pass, waiting for biggest K553.2; as mountain-spirit F455; makes self small D55.2.2; as ogre *G304. — Disguise as t. aids escape K649.7.3; fat t. Z33.4; sunlight turns giant or t. to stone *F531.6.12.2; transformation by t. D683.3.

Troll's life in his brother's forehead E714.3.1. — Stealing t. golden horse (task) H1151.9.

Trolls F455ff.; live in range of hills F214. — Fallen angels become t. V236.1; hero fights t. H945.2; curse concerning names of t. M427; guessing names of t. H516; magic horseshoe keeps off t. D1385.9.

Trolls' horses water at peasant's well F241.1.2.1.

Troll-woman with beard G219.2. — Strong hero son of man and t. F611.1.13.

Trophy. — Head of murdered man as t. S139.2.1.1.

Trouble. — Beginnings of t. for man A1330ff.; magic t.-making D2097; makers of t. K2130ff.; quest for t. H1376.5; strong men make t. G512.0.1; task: having a shirt made by a woman free from t. and worry H1195; woman makes t. between man and wife K1085.

Troubles escape when forbidden casket is opened C915.1. — Distress over imagined t. of unborn child J2063; king chooses personal t., saves realm J221.2; peasant as priest preaches on the t. of laymen K1961.1.1; small injustices permitted rather than cause t. of state J221; train of t. from (lost horseshoe nail) N258, (sparrow's vengeance) N261.

Troubled liquid as life token E761.6ff.

Troublesome fairies F399.4.

Trough. — Victim lured into t. K838.

Trousers, see also **Breeches.** — Friar's t. on adulteress's bed K1273, K1526; hiding in plowman's t. J2631; magic t. *D1055, (render invisible) D1361.36, (render invulnerable) D1344.9.2.

Trout shams death, fisherman passes by K522.4.1. — Man becomes t. D179.1; stripes on t. A2413.7.

Truce. — Girl's favors traded for t. T455.4.

True. — Tests for t. lover H421.

Truest dreams at daybreak D1812.3.3.1.

Trumpet blown before house of one sentenced to death P612. — Brass (copper) statue at city gates blows on t. at stranger's approach *D1317.9.1; end of world announced by t. A1093; magic t. *D1221; resuscitation by blowing t. E55.3.

Trumpet-bird. — Color of t. A2411.2.1.15.

Trumpeter's false defense J1465.

Trunk. — Boat of tree t. F841.1.11; elephant killed by cutting off t. K825.2; ogre monstrous as to t. G366; origin of animal's t. A2350ff.; princess sent to beggar in t. N712.1.

Trunks. — Father's counsel: dress up the t. of trees, cover the road H588.6; keeping the rain from the t. J2129.6.

Trust. — Lack of t. in God punished Q221.6; not to t. the over-holy J21.18.

Truth best policy J751.1; in drink U180ff.; given in vision D1810.8.1; personified Z121; -speaking rewarded Q68.1; is strongest H631.5; -telling animals B130ff.; -telling dog killed to hide murder B339.1. — Act of t. H252; bird of t. B131; cleverness in detection of t. J1140ff.; disenchantment proves t. D797; fool given t. on his back J551.2; husband discredited by absurd t. J1151.1.2; intemperate zeal in t.-telling J551; Isle of T. F129.4.2; lies closely resembling t. H509.5.1; magic epistle assures wearer will utter t. D1316.9; magic object reveals t. *D1316ff.; peace more important than t. in marriage T203; quest for Bird of T. H1331.1.1; son tells king t., banished J551.6; speaking spittle reveals t. D1316.3; tests of t. H200—H299; wager that falsehood is better than t. N61; what is most difficult to find, to lose? T. H659.19.

Truths. — Flattering lies vs. unflattering t. J267; quest for bag of t. *H1376.4; unpleasant t. must be withheld from the great J815; uttering three t. cleverness test H505.1.

Truthful monk refuses to cheat even for his order V461.2.

Truthfulness as clerical virtue V461.4.1. — Wager on t. of servant N25.

Tryst. — Husband overhears wife's t., appeased K1533.

Trysting tabu C194.

Tuatha Dé Danann A1611.5.4.3; cause island illusion K1886.7.1; as demons G303.1.7; overcome by invaders F211.0.2.1. — Children of T. fostered by Milesians P273.4; jewels of T. F244.1.

Tub drips at high tide, holds water at low A913.4, D1324.1.1; -full of water in sea H696.1.3. — Abandoned wife hidden under a t. S445; bottomless t. holds water D2199.1; cynical philosopher lives in t. J152.1; dropped t. neither breaks, spills F1081; husband in hanging t. to escape coming flood K1522; magic t. *D1171.14; people in otherworld pour water into t. full of holes *F171.6.2; rejuvenation by burning and throwing bones into t. of milk D1886.1; rejuvenation by magic t. D1338.10.

Tubs. — Putting out t. to see if it is raining J2716.2; witch rides on t. G241.4.1.

Tube. — Magic t. *D1255.

Tuber. — Love charm from t. D1355.21.1.

Tuesday as auspicious day N127.1. — Making war on T. tabu C641.1.

Tug-of-war K22.

Tugging contest, loser's neck severed H1562.7.

Tulip. — Fairies care for t. bed F339.2.

Tumble-bug rolls in dung A2457.1.

Tumbler as monk dances while others chant psalms V92.

Tumor. — Magician's power in t. D1711.0.2.

Tune. — Hail produced by whistling t. D2143.4.1.

Tunic. — Fire spares saint's t. F964.2; magic t. *D1052.

Tunnel entrance to guarded maiden's chamber K1344; of crystal four miles long F721.1.1. — Death in t. to underground world J2137.7; mole as trickster killed in his own t. K1642.

Tunnels. — Mighty digger of t. F639.1.1.

Tunny. — Magic t. saves hero B175.2.

Tupilac G377.

Turban on tree far away H1355.3. — Long t. F821.5; numskull warns prospective buyer that t. is too short J2088; remove t. as last duty J2516.7.

Turf laid on breast of dead to prevent return E431.6. — Magic t. *D934, (from church-roof teaches animal languages) D1301.1.

Turkey envious of peacock W195.1. — Color of t. A2411.2.6.5; disguise as t.-girl K1816.5; why t. has red eyes A2332.5.5; helpful t. B469.7; man becomes t. D166.3; object mistaken for t. J1771.3; speaking t. B211.3.1; treasure-producing t. B103.0.1; wedding of t. and peacock B282.1; why brush t. nests on ground A2431.8.1.

Turkey's gobble misunderstood J1811.3; nest A2431.8.

Turkeys. — Why there are wild t. in a certain Pueblo town A2434.3.2.

Turkish ambassador misunderstands Christian ceremonies J1825.

Turks. — Princess gives self to T. to save people T455.7.

Turmeric smeared on bridal couple T135.12. — Man becomes t. plant D213.3; origin of t. A2686.5.

Turned. — Boneless man t. over to produce seasons A1152; boy t. out of doors by father S322.1.5; dogs t. loose on those whom wild huntsman meets E501.15.6.2; insect on back grateful for being t. over B364.3; magic t. against makers D1784; water t. to blood as life token E761.1.1.

Turning aside tabu C834; back after beginning tabu C833.3; jug wrong side out H1023.9.1; the plate around J1562.1; right-handwise brings luck N131.2; stream's course as task H1138.1. — Fairy spell averted by t. coat F385.1; mill t. backwards D2089.4; princess's t. to suitor indicates her choice H315; tabu: t. away from poets C872; transformation by t. magic hood D568; wife resuscitated by t. her around E181.1.

Turnip. — Carriage of t. F861.4.1; chain tale: pulling up t. Z49.9.

Turnips called bacon: cat called rabbit J1511.2. — City girl thinks t. grow on trees J1731.1; lies about t. X1431.

Turquoise gives miraculous speed D1521.5.1. — House of t. F771.1.5.3.

Turtle, see also **Tortoise;** allowed to pick flowers before death, escapes K551.26; carrying man across stream, threatens him J1172.4; carrying man through water upsets him because of a broken promise M205.1.1; carries person across river B551.5; holds with jaws till it thunders B761; induced to rob in a man's garden K1022.5; king B245.2; persuades an animal to swallow him: causes the animal's death and escapes K582.1; released: grateful B375.8; taken for island J1761.1.1. — Why t. beats with forelegs when caught A2466.2; color of t. A2411.5.1; creation of t. A2147; drowning punishment for t. K581.1; friendship between t. and heron A2493.12; friendship between t. and wallaby A2493.12.1; giant t. B875.3;

hedgehog and crab jump from boat after t. J2133.11; helpful t. B491.5; how t. got snake-like head A2247.2, A2320.2; magic adhesion to t. D2171.3.3; magic sea-t. sucks men to bottom B177.3; man-devouring t. B16.5.4; man transformed to t. D193; marriage to t. B604.2.1; scorpion in spite of himself stings the t. carrying him across stream U124; thieving t. K366.6; three-tailed t. B15.7.6; why t. lays eggs on beach A2433.6.12.

Turtle's war-party F1025.2. — Bowl placed on t. back: hence his shell A2215.3; earth from t. back A815; earth rests on t. back A844.1.

Turtles. — Marriage of jackals and t. J414.3.

Turtledove. — Why t. is sad A2521.1.

Tusita world A697.2.

Tusk. — Earth supported on boar's t. A844.9; magic wishing ivory t.: when struck on ground (only once) provides treasure D1470.1.37.

Tusks in ogre's mouth G363.2. — Boar with nine t. in each jaw B15.7.8; how elephant got its t. A2345.6; man-eater hangs carcasses on t. G88.2; stealing elephant's t. (task) H1151.6; wildboar sharpens t. when no enemy is in sight J674.1; witch with twisted t. G214.4.

Twelfth. — Death prophesied on t. day of life M341.1.2.2; tree blossoms on T. Night F971.5.2.1; wild hunt appears between Christmas and T. Night E501.11.2.2.

Twelve Apostles of Ireland V292.2; berserks F610.3.3; -eyed person F512.2.1.3; -headed dragon B11.2.3.5; -headed serpent B15.1.2.10.1; iron pillars steady the earth A841.3; -legged bird B15.6.3.3.2, (in cow's bag) B15.7.9.1, (symbolizes guilt) H619.5; as magic number D1273.1.5; months' pregnancy T574.1; stones unite in one D491.6; -year-old captures town F611.3.2.6; years' fight suitor test H328.6. — Appetite of t. men given with the gift of t. men's strength M416.1; baby to marry t.-year-old to avoid death prophecy M341.0.3; choice: t. famine years or t. hours' rain J229.13; cow gives t. measures of milk for t. apostles B251.2.10; creator establishes t. winds, each a different color A1129.1.1; devil's t. wings G303.4.2.2; disenchantment if t. men will not leave castle for year D759.4; eagle with t. wings B15.7.16; filling t. bed-ticks with feathers (task) H1129.2; formulistic number: t. Z71.8; hail-storm leaves t. chief rivers in Ireland A934.6; king deflowers all t.-year old girls T161.0.1; moon is wife to t. sun brothers A753.1.4.2; prophecy of marriage when t. years old M369.2.3; riddle: tree with t. branches, each with thirty leaves, black and white H721.1; stealing t. horses out of stall (task) H1151.2; strong hero suckled by mermaid and given strength of t. men F611.2.2; sun shines for t. days and nights after death of holy person F961.1.5.1; walking around grave t. times raises ghost E386.4.

Twenty commandments better than ten J2213.5.1; heavens A651.1.0.1. — Man granted t. years more life K551.22.2; punishment not given those under t. Q403

Twenty-first. — Prophecy: death on t. birthday M341.1.4.3.1.

Twenty-five as formulistic number Z71.16.3; years of chaste love T317.5. — Prophecy: death when t. years old M341.1.4.3.

Twenty-four as formulistic number Z71.8.6. — Magic carving knife serves t. men at meat simultaneously D1583.

Twenty-nine. — King is worth t. pieces of silver H711.1.

Twenty-one as formulistic number Z71.16.13.

Twenty-seven. — Giant takes space of t. men F531.2.9.

Twenty-six as formulistic number Z71.16.4.

Twenty thousand. — Recognition of own cow in herd of t. H163.

Twenty-two as formulistic number Z71.16.14.

Twice the wish to the enemy J2074, X111.6. — Money lost t.: recovered third time N183; not to strike monster t. *C742; take, but only t. C762.5.

Twig, born of a woman, is planted and becomes a girl T543.0.1; bows down, releases relics D1648.1.2.2. — Forest from t. F979.8; magic t. *D953, (locates hidden treasure) D1314.2; not to break t. C513; prince buys t. from her mother T52.1; oracular t. D1311.4.0.1.

Twigs. — Elder t. reveal witch G257.6; floors in dwarf home are covered with pine t. F451.4.3.5; oracular t. work only if man has fasted D1733.3.1.1; quarreling sons and the bundle of t. J1021; sight of magic t. gives foreknowledge of day's events D1311.4.0.1.1.

Twilight. — Coming at t. (neither by day nor by night) H1057; origin of t. A1179.1.

Twin, see also **Pair;** culture heroes A515.1.1; destroyers of monsters Z211; first parents A1273; gods A116; goddesses A116.2. — Cure by surviving t. D2161.5.6; husband's t. brother mistaken by woman for her husband K1311.1; jealous and overhasty man kills his rescuing t. brother N342.3; magic pills bring t. sons D1347.3.1; mother hides t. sons R153.4.2; one t. thrown into river to avoid evils of t. birth M371.0.2; sun and moon as t. brothers A736.3.1.

Twins T685; born at end of footrace T581.8; born in tent T581.10; exposed S314; freed from dead mother's body T584.2.1.1; quarrel before birth in mother's womb T575.1.3. — Albino t. cannibals G11.11.1; birth of t. T587, (prophesied) M369.7.1; divine t. cared for by mother-of-tigers B241.2.8.1; divine t. make bow, arrow A527.1.1; extraordinary companions are t. F601.5; medicine causes t. D1501.8; queen changes own t. for slave's son K1921.3; recognition of t. by golden chain under their skin H61.1; separation of t. through being carried off by beast N312; Siamese t. F523; test: which of t. is elder N255; waters created by divine t. A910.5.

Twine. — Twisting t.: trickster cuts it K1433.

Twining branches grow from graves of lovers E631.0.1.

Twisted witch G219.6. — Dwarf's feet t. backward F451.2.2.1.

Twister. — Remarkable t. X948.

Twisting twine K1433. — Murder by t. out intestines S139.1.

Two beams of fire shoot from devil's eyes G303.4.1.2.3; devils come to a dance-loving maid and play when she bathes G303.10.4.2; -edged knife D1313.8; eggs J1341.4; -faced person F511.1.1, F526.5; -facedness

W171ff.; -fold death F901.2; for the price of one J2083.2; giants with one axe throw it back and forth to each other G151; -headed, see following heading; -legged horse in wild hunt E501.4.2.6; lower worlds A651.21; monks renew their appetites J1606; presents to the king: the beet and the horse J2415.1; ravens follow wild huntsman E501.4.4; sheep kill a fox who has licked up the blood they have spilled in a fight J624.1; suns shine in sky F961.1.3.1. — Bad omen for t. bridal processions to meet D1812.5.1.8; cup with t. and three handles J2665.1; devil's thumb the size of t. fists G303.4.3.2; devil in wagon drawn by t. black horses carries off impious people G303.7.3.1; devil has t. horns G303.4.1.6.1; devil gives Eve t. grains of corn G303.9.4.1; dog between t. castles J2183.1; devil builds t. islands in a lake G303.9.1.9; devil compels t. miners to follow him G303.9.5.3; disenchantment by cutting person in t. D711.2; disenchantment by drinking milk of queen who has borne t. boys D764.1; eye with t. pupils F541.3.1; Fortuna with t. faces N111.2.2; ghost in t. places at once E599.9; god with t. faces A123.2.1.1; why horse has only t. eyes A2332.2.1; man fishes up t. blind women from a well F1065; milk of t. king's children protects hero in dragon fight D1385.14; murder by cutting in t. S118.1; skillful marksman shoots left eye of fly at t. miles F661.5.3; stealing t. horns of a savage bull H1151.7; tabu: staying t. nights in one place until certain event is brought to pass C761.4.1; task: traveling till t. skeins of thread are unwound H1125.1; troll drives t. he-goats G304.3.2.2; weaving cloth from t. threads H1022.1; youth sees half of t. quadrupeds H583.1.1.

Two-headed animal B15.1.2.1; child T551.2; dragon B11.2.3.6; ghost E422.1.1.1; man is only one man J1176.4; ogre G361.1.1; person F511.0.2.1.

Two hundred. — Disenchantment after t. years D791.1.4.

Two million stars in heaven H702.1.1.

Tying sun with stone chain H1023.23. — Escape by t. rope to post K638; jealous wife t. husband to her T257.11.

Types. — Different t. of men from one original type A1227.

Typhon F526.1.

Tyrannizing. — Ogre t. over fairyland G464.

Tyranny. — Care against future t. J643.

Tyrant. — Daughter killed to save her from t. T314.1; fear cruel t. will be succeeded by worse J215.2.1; if I were a t. you would not say so J1281; king as t. P12.2.1; suicide to make t. stop bloodshed J173.

Ubiquitous beggar in disguise obtains alms three times from same person *K1982; person D2031.18.

Ugliest girl chosen as bride L213.2.

Ugliness. — Cause of animal's u. *A2402ff.; extraordinary u. F576; frog as beauty doctor unable to cure his own u. J1062.1; humor of u. X137.

Ugly, see also **Hideous;** child becomes poet L112.9; by day, fair by night D621.3; disguise K1815.2; duckling L140ff.; face doesn't mean ugly soul U119.4; feet F551.4; fish borrows handsome fish's skin K1918.1; god

A139.14; husband's advances repulsed J1541.3; man becomes handsome
D52.2; ogre terrifies women G476; picture makes girl refuse suitor
T11.2.0.1; preferred to pretty sister L145; but wise son M93; woman sees
beautiful woman reflected in water and thinks it is herself J1791.6.1. —
Animal's u. voice A2423.1; better send an u. woman to the devil than a
pretty one J229.4; bride refuses to sleep with u. groom T166.1; devil
appears in the form of a man who is repugnantly u. G303.3.1.4; devil
helps u. man win wife G303.22.7; druid makes self appear u. on one side,
beautiful on other D2031.4.1; dwarfs are u. F451.2.0.1; fairy promises
to make u. man beautiful F341.2.1; fairy son u. F233.4; father with
handsome son and u. daughter J244.1; first wife u. but diligent T145.7;
girl with u. name K1984.3; god with u. bodies A123.1.3; God makes serpent
u. A2286.0.1; hero assumes u. guise A527.3.1.1; holy man embraces man who
calls him u. J921; man does not court u. woman J1074.2; man magically
made u. D1872.1; why peacock has u feet. A2375.2.2; princess calls her
suitors u. names T76; trolls u. F455.2.2; useful and u. preferred to expensive and beautiful J245.

Ulcer from moon's rays F647.7. — Curing incurable u. H1199.2.2; death
by u. for destroying churches Q558.17.

Ulcers. — Magic ointment cures u. D1512.1; origin of u. A1337.1; satire
causes face u. D1402.15.3.

Ulysses, see also **Odysseus;** returns home in humble disguise K1815.1. —
Palamides, having injured U., seeks advice from him J646.1.

Umbilical cord connects heaven and earth A625.2.1; cord not to be cut
with iron C531.1. — Child helps mother in severing u. cord T584.8.

Umbrella. — Earth under u. A653; magic u. D1194; tree as strong man's u.
F621.3; using u. under trees H591.2.

Umbrellas welcome bride A1555.3.

Umpire awards own coat to thief K419.3. — Girl as u. in suitor test
K1227.8; magic object acquired by acting as u. for fighting heirs *D832;
mortal as u. of gods' quarrel A187.2; laurel and olive tree scorn thornbush as u. in their dispute as to who is most useful J411.7; respite while
captor acts as u. between captives K579.5; thief as u. in contest K342;
unjust u. (misappropriates disputed goods) K452, (as trickster's confederate) K451.

Umpiring dispute in exchange for safety guarantee M222. — Strangers u.
beauty contest H1596.2.

Unable, see also **Impossible, Inability;** to rid oneself of cobold F481.3. —
Castle revolving at night so that one is u. to find entrance F771.2.6.2;
cuckold's knife u. to carve boar's head H425.1; death sentence escaped by
propounding riddle king (judge) is u. to solve *H542; demon has to serve
girl whom he is u. to persuade to break vow of chastity G303.16.19.5;
devil u. (to eat in an inn) G303.4.8.4, (to endure cross made by straps of
knapsack) G303.16.3.2, (to enter house with horseshoe over the door)
*G303.16.17, (to take one who has read the Pater Noster) G303.16.2.1;

fairies can set down an object once but are u. to raise it again F255.2; forms into which the devil is u. to change G303.3.6ff.; giant ogre u. to cross water *G131; giant so large that horse is u. to carry him F531.2.7; headless person u. to smell or hear F511.0.1.2; human hands u. to complete devil's unfinished work G303.14; mortals, informed by those benefitted, u. to find abode of dwarf F451.5.12.1; mortals u. to cross river F141.1.2; mountain-men u. to enter house till light is quenched F460.2.3; ogre u. to cross stream *G638; ogre u. to endure daylight G632; ogre u. to work evil after cockcrow G636; one is freed if he can set a task the devil is u. to perform G303.16.19.3; trolls u. to endure church bells *G304.2.4.1; witch u. (to cross stream) *G273.4, (to rise from chair with four-leaf clover under it) G254, (to rise if ring lies under her chair) G254.1.

Unacquainted. — Otherworld people u. with fire F167.8.

Unarmed. — Enemies taken u. spared W11.5.11.

Unattainable. — Never try to reach the u. J21.14.

Unavailing attempt to get rid of slippers N211.2.

Unawares. — Enemies taken u. spared W11.5.11.

Unbalanced. — Not everyone lives in the same place since earth would become u. J2274.1.

Unbaptized child reincarnated as bird E613.0.2; child's mother cannot rest in grave E412.2.2; children (as fairies) *F251.3, (as nightmares) F471.1.3, (in wild hunt) *E501.2.7, (pursued in wild hunt) *E501.5.4; person cannot rest in grave *E412.2. — Devil takes u. child out of cradle and lays wooden log in its place G303.9.9.4; fairies pursue u. children F360.1; fairies steal u. child F321.3.1; reincarnation of u. child as bird E613.0.2.

Unbeliever loses argument with hermit V351.2. — Ghost chides u. E367.5.

Unbent. — Aesop with the u. bow J553.1; plants and trees miraculously u. F973.

Unblessed. — Nun eating u. lettuce eats a demon G303.16.2.3.4; trolls live on u. food F455.4.2.3.

Unborn child affected by mother's broken tabu C993; children promised in marriage T61.5.3; son's soul issues from mother's mouth E726.2. — Abode of u. souls E706; curse on u. child: stillborn M441.1; distress over imagined troubles of u. child J2063; friar adds missing member to u. child K1363.2; heart of u. child renders person invisible D1361.8; journey to the Land of the U. F115; magic blood of u. child D1003.3; magic heart of u. child *D997.1.1; prophecy: future greatness of u. child M311; prophecy: u. child to bring evil on land M356.3; prophecy: u. child to be deformed M355; recognition of man u. child will slay D1812.4.1; riddle of the u. H792; room in hell for souls of u. A678; sham physician predicts sex of u. child K1955.3; three crimes in killing sheep with two u. lambs J1169.9; treasure discovered by hand of u. child N533.3; wagers on u. children N16.

Unbound. — Witch known by hose u. on one leg G255.

Unbreakable chain F863.1.

Uncanny. — Gambling with u. being N4.2; spying on u. persons Q411.14.

Unceasingly. — Person walks u. for year F1032.

Uncertainty about own identity *J2010ff.

Uncharitable king loses power Q494.1.1. — Reward of the u. V420ff.; ruler learns lesson from u. king J56.1.

Uncharitableness punished Q286.

Uncharitably. — Destruction (disappearance) of property u. refused Q585.1.

Unchaste. — Brother flogs u. sister to death Q458.2.1; father kills u. daughter S322.1.3; magic object points out u. woman H411.

Unchastity tests H400—H459.

Unchristened, see Unbaptized.

Uncivil. — Cobold avenges u. answer (or treatment) F481.1.

Uncle P293; slanders niece to appropriate patrimony K361.5; sleeps with nephew's beloved H1556.4.4. — Accidental meeting of nephew and u. N738; boy induces u. to climb tree X905.4.1; cruel u. S71; nephew kills u. S74.1; sending to older u. F571.2.1; sun and moon as u. and nephew A711.1; treacherous u. K2217.

Uncles. — Quest for lost u. H1385.11; throwing cakes into faces of u. H35.5.

Uncleanliness tabu C891.

Unclothed, see also Naked. — Curse: caste to remain u. M464; sight of u. women calms rage K774.2.

Unconfessed person cannot rest in grave E411.0.2.2.

Unconfirmed children can see trolls F455.5.4.2.

Unconscious prophecy M300.2. — Applying hot iron to revive u. man J2119.7.

Unconsecrated host V31.

Uncooked, see also Raw. — Why tigers eat u. food A2435.3.9.2.

Uncut field is already harvested (belongs to spendthrift) H586.4.

Undefeated. — Opponents agree not to fight, remain u. M237.1.

Under. — Chastity ordeal: passing u. magic rod H412.1; fairyland u. (hollow knoll) *F211, (water) F212; ghost travels u. ground E591; God finds the devil u. (stone) G303.1.2.2, (tree) G303.1.2.1; magic sight by looking u. one's (arm) D1821.3.1, (legs) D1821.3.3; magic u.-water journey D2126; man can breathe nine days u. water F691; man lives u. river F725.4; mankind ascends from u. the earth A1232.

Underclothing. — Magic u. D1058.

Underfed warhorse fails in war J1914.1. — Retort from u. servant (child) J1341ff.

Underground city F764; house F771.3.5; otherworld F160.0.1; passage *F721.1, (gives entrance to closed chamber) K315.0.1, (magically opens) D1555, (to paramour's house) K1523; people from children which Eve hid from God *F251.4; spirits *F450ff.; treasure chambers F721.4. — Abduction through u. passage R25; church sinks; song heard from u.

F941.2.1; death from attempt to visit u. world J2137.7; dwarf as u. spirit *F451ff.; dwarfs live u. F451.4.1ff.; dwarfs warm heath by u. fire F451.5.1.15; earthquake spirit lives u. F438.1; escape from execution pyre through u. passage R215.1; escape through u. passage R211.3; expelled dwarfs plan to dig u. bed for Rhine F451.5.22; extraordinary u. disappearance F940ff.; fairies' u. palace F222.1; fettering of u. monster *A1071; giant lies u. with trees growing all over his body F531.2.6; journey to u. animal kingdom *F127; lies about u. channels X1545; magic horse goes u. *B184.1.2; magic object found in u. room D845; magic power of seeing things u. D1825.4.1; magic u. journey *D2131; man falls u. F949.2; why mole lives u. A2433.3.20; rivers with marvelous u. connections F715.3; saint hides fugitive u. K2319.3; treasure in u. chamber N512; why crab lives u. A2433.6.3.3; why gods live u. A189.13; why porcupine lives u. A2433.3.22; wisdom learned in u. J179.2.

Under-king P13.0.1. — Military rights of u. P551.8.1.

Undersea river F715.3.1.

Understand. — Devils do not u. thoughts of men G303.13.1; "I don't u." J1802.1.

Understanding poem test H509.4.3. — Animal u. human speech B212.

Undertaker. — Calling u. with doctor J2516.9.

Undertaking quest H1220ff. — Intemperance in u. labor J557.

Underwater, see also **Submarine;** bridge F842.2.3.2; castle of jewels F771.1.5.4; causeway F842.2.4; entrance to lower world F93.0.2; otherworld F160.0.1.1; tree F811.4.2. — Disenchantment by following enchanted woman through lake to u. castle D759.5; extraordinary u. disappearance F940ff.; golden u. tower F772.2.3; water-goddess's u. home F420.7.1.

Underworld, see also **Hell;** F80—F100. — Children said to come from u. T589.6.3; deity emerges from u. A115.4; god of the u. *A300ff.; goddess of u. A300.1; magic salve from u. causes blindness D1331.2.2.1; mankind from bones of dead brought from u. A1232.1; physical features of u. F80.1; sun coaxed back from u. A739.6; sun, moon remain half time in u. A722.10.

Underworldlings. — Youths grind in mill of u. F106.

Undesirable children exposed, desirable preserved S311; girls keep up appearances to deceive suitors K1984.

Undesired. — Elopement to prevent u. marriage R225.2; escape from u. lover *T320ff.

Undeveloped. — First men u. A1225.

Undiminished. — Fairy food u. by eating F243.4.

Undressing. — Dead u. V68.4; marriage so girl won't be ashamed u. J2521.3; woman u., reveals guilt J1141.1.8.

Undutiful children P236; son punished by toad clinging to face Q551.1. — Poisonous toad sits on food of u. children Q557.1.

Unearthing treasure E451.5, *N550ff.

Unearthly. — Sexual intercourse with u. beings forbidden C112.

Unequal marriage T121; returns: man at lady's funeral has repartee with priest J1264.8. — Marriage with equal or with u. J414.

Unequals in love *T91. — Association of equals and u. J410ff.

Unerring spear D1653.1.2.

Unexpected encounters N700—N799.

Unextinguishable fire at end of earth A871.0.2.

Unfading garlands D1652.7.

Unfaithful, see also **Faithless**; husband (loses magic wife) C31.12, (persecutes wife) S413; wives become edible animals A1422.0.1. — Choice: staying at home with loving wife or going to tavern and having u. wife J229.1; husband refuses to believe wife u. J2342; king sees how male stork kills his u. wife and follows its example T252.2.1; man u. on wedding night T245; man with u. wife comforted J882; shooting stars are u. wives A788.5; swallowing hot coals because husband u. T81.8; wife refuses to become u. even though husband is T217; would-be u. wife T92.1.2.

Unfaithfulness, see also **Adultery**; tokened by ring H94.0.1. — Birth of twins an indication of u. in wife T587.1; dream warns emperor of wife's u. *D1813.1.1; false tokens of woman's u. K2112.1; king overlooks wife's u. rather than to cause troubles of state J221.1; man with unfaithful wife comforted when he sees the queen's u. J882.1; wife shields husband's u. T222.

Unfavorable prophecies M340ff.; traits of character *W100—W199.

Unfinished tales Z12. — Devil's u. work cannot be completed by human hands G303.14; fairies leave work u. when overseen F361.3.1; hill as u. tower A963.8; reincarnation to complete u. work E606.2.

Ungracious. — Plant punished for u. answer to holy person A2721.3.

Ungrateful, see also **Ingratitude**; animal returned to captivity J1172.3; cannibal G85; children punished Q281.1; dwarf F451.5.2.1; hero kills helpful animal B336; river passenger kills carrier from within K952.1; son punished by having a son equally ungrateful Q588; son reproved by naïve action of his own son: preparing for old age (the half-carpet) J121; wife T261. — Grateful animals: u. man W154.8; man u. for rescue by animal W154.2.2; supplying food to u. stepmother rewarded Q65.1.

Ungrowing. — Growing and u. (grass) F817.1, (trees) F811.12.

Ungulata. — Creation of u. A1870ff., A1889.

Ungulate. — Man transformed to u. D114.

Unhappiness. — Foreknowledge of son's u. D1812.0.4; man never knowing u. swallowed by earth L424.

Unhappy. — Why weavers are the most u. of men P445.1.

Unicorn *B13; as creator's companion A36; thrown from ark and drowned: hence they no longer exist A2214.3.

Uniform. — Magic u. *D1052.1; spirit of new born child in u. N121.1.1.

Unimportant. — Choice: important and u. work J370ff.

Uninhabited. — Ghosts banished to glaciers and u. places E437.1.

Unintentional curse or blessing takes effect M404; good deed seen as salvation V512.2; injuries bring unfortunate consequences N385.

Unique exceptions *Z300—Z399; oath binding M115; prohibitions and compulsions *C600—C699; weapon got by misrepresentation K362.0.1. — Disenchantment possible under u. condition D791; engraving shield with u. pattern H1199.4; ghost visible to u. person E421.1.1; quests for the u. H1300ff.; recognition by u. ability H31; recognition by u. manner of performing an act H35.

United. — First couple organically u. A1225.1; outcast wife at last u. with husband and children S451.

Uniting against a common enemy J624.

Unity of God A102.10. — National u. by expelling all foreign elements P711.6; strength in u. J1020ff.

Universality of death learned from watching animals J52.1.

Universe A600ff.; as increasing, decreasing paradox answer H1075. — Earlier u. opposite of present A633; size of u. A658ff.

Unjust, see also **Injustice;** judges punished Q265.1.1; official outwitted by peasant who quarrels with him *K1657; umpire (as trickster's confederate) K451, (misappropriates disputed goods) K452. — Animals' u. decision against man: man always unjust to them J1172.3.2; child in mother's womb reveals u. judgment T575.1.1.3; confession induced by bringing an u. action against accused J1141.4; concealed confederate as u. witness K451.3; judgment as rebuke to u. plaintiff J1172; laughing fish reveals u. judgment *D1318.2.1; series of clever u. decisions: plaintiff voluntarily withdraws J1173; stone bursts as sign of u. judgment *D1318.1.1; thief shows up owner's u. claim J1213.

Unkind. — Choices: king strangers, u. relatives J390ff.

Unkindness punished *Q280ff.

Unknown helper turns out to be known R169.11; knight R222; paramour *T475; prince (chosen chief of children in play) *P35, (shows his kingly qualities in dealing with his playmates) H41.5. — Bringing the devil an u. animal K216.2; combat of u. brothers brings about recognition H151.10; dwarfs emigrate to u. place F451.9.2.1; fools and the u. animal J1736; hero is served at table by his u. son: recognition of his wife follows H151.11; heroine taunted with her u. past S412; infant indicates his u. father by handing him an apple H481.1; king assigns tasks to his u. son H921; love through sight of something belonging to u. princess T11.4; mother sends son to find u. father H1216; object u. in a country sold for a fortune N411; prophecy of future greatness fulfilled when hero returns home u. N682; quest for u. (objects or places) H1382, (person) H1381, (woman) H1381.3; sacrifice to u. god V11.9.1; test: guessing u. propounder's name H521; test as to who is u. father of a child H480ff.

Unloading horse tabu C884.1.

Unlucky accidents *N300—N399; days N128; hunt X1110.1; to look at childless person T591.2. — Magpie sits outside ark jabbering, is u. A2542.1.1; thirteen as u. number N135.1.

Unmasked. — Jay in peacock's (pigeon's) skin u. J951.2; robbers accidentally u. by sham wise man K1956.1.

Unmasking. — Recognition by u. H181.

Unnatural children eat parent G71; cruelty S (entire chapter); parents eat children G72

Unpaid servant refuses to blame master J571.8.

Unpeeling. — Devil u. woman's skin G303.20.5.

Unpierceable. — Magic u. helmet D1381.10.3; magic u. skin protects against attack D1381.3.2.

Unpleasant truths must be withheld from the great J815; women A1372.7. — Ignoring the u. J1086.

Unpromising hero (heroine) L100—L199; hero last to try task H991; hero as rescuer R169.10; hero wins quest H1242.1; magic object chosen *L215.

Unquiet dead sinner taken to priest for absolution E411.0.2; grave *E410ff.

Unraveling in short time (task) H1094.

Unreasonable demands of pregnant women T571. — Not to make u. requests C773.1.

Unremitting torture as punishment Q501ff.

Unrepentent drunkard J1321.

Unrequited. — Death from u. love T81.2.

Unrestrained. — Why animals are u. A2526.

Unrestricted intercourse in marriage A1352.1. — Princess's u. choice of husband T131.0.1.

Unruly hero L114.3.

Unscathed. — Books u. by fire, water F883.1.4; passing through sea u. F931.9.

Unscrupulous business conduct turned against usurer J56.

Unseen hands serve hero in deserted castle H1239.2. — Dwarfs emigrate u. but heard F451.9.6.

Unseparated fingers F552.1.4.

Unshriven man restored to life in order to confess V23.1. — Wild huntsman wanders because of u. death *E501.3.4.

Unsolved problem: enigmatic ending of tale H620ff.

Unsophisticated hero L122.

Unspelling quest H1385.0.1.

Unstable bridge to land of dead E481.2.1.2; security J1383.

Unsuccessful attempt by enemy to kill helpful animal B335.3. — Devil's u. creation produces certain animals A1755; paramour poses as u. K1517.5.

Unthriftiness punished Q323.

Untiring object D1657ff.

Untouchable's contract with hungry god M242.2.

Untouchables C551. — Attitude to u. A1651.0.1.

Untrained colt result of master's neglect J143.

Untroubled. — Preciousness of u. sleep J1081.

Untying. — Disenchantment by u. enchanting knot D765.2; eating food without u. container H506.7; paramour u. horse for husband to chase K1514.14.

Unusual, see also **Extraordinary;** animal as riding-horse *B557; draft-animal B558; manner of life F560ff.; marriage *T110ff. — Abnormally born child has u. powers T550.2; animals with u. limbs or members B15ff.; castle of u. material F771.1; death of the little hen described with u. words Z32.2.1; devil performs deeds of u. strength *G303.9.2; feet with u. number of toes F551.2; hands with u. number of fingers F552.1.1; murder revealed by u. names of boys N271.2; people of u. residence F562ff.; person u. as to his head F511ff.; relationship riddles rising from u. marriages of relatives H795; riddles based on u. circumstances H790ff.; witch rides on u. animal G241.1ff.

Unveiling of Ishtar F85. — Image of Virgin veiling and u. itself D1623.1.

Unwashed. — Coming neither washed nor u. (task) H1062; tabu: touching deity's image with u. hands C51.7.

Unwed mother's drowning of child D1314.2.4.

Unwelcome bird (insect) proves to be messenger B291.0.2. — Hidden man behind image gives u. answer to suppliant: image blamed K1971.8; magic object protects from u. lover *D1386; treatment of u. guests J1563.6; vow to die rather than marry u. suitor M149.2; year's respite from u. marriage T151.

Unwise. — Kindness u. when it imperils one's food supply J715; wise and u. conduct J200—J1099.

Unwitting encounters N700—N799; marriage to cannibal *G81. — Tasks assigned at own u. suggestion H917.

Unwittingly. — Brothers u. fight each other N733.1; children u. promised (sold) S240ff.; father u. buys daughter who has been sold into slavery N732.1; human flesh eaten u. *G60ff.; incest u. committed *N365; magic object eaten u. D859.4; man u. sells soul to devil M211.1; money u. given away N351; "Old Saddle" name of an estate, which the king u. gives away K193.1; person u. killed N320ff.

Unworthy person rewarded, worthy not J1364, U14. — Man considering self u. to receive host given it by God himself V39.1; sacrament effective even from u. priest V39.3; woman deserts husband for u. lover T232.

Unwound. — Traveling till two skeins of thread are u. (task) H1125.1.

Uphill. — Saint's bachall leads stream u. D1549.3.2; unnecessary choice: to go u. or downhill J463.

Upper lip (curls over nostril; lower hangs down to neck) F544.1.1, (reaching heaven; lower, earth) F531.1.4.1; world F10—F79. — Access to u. world *F50ff.; fish carries man to u. world B551.1.0.1; god of the u. world A200ff.; goddess divides time between u. and lower worlds A316; hero returns to u. world A566; inhabitant of u. world visits earth F30ff.; journey to u. world *F10ff.; nature of the u. world *A660ff.; quest to the u. world H1260ff.; refuge in u. world R323; river connecting earth and u. and lower worlds A657; series of u. worlds A651.1; tear from u. world of mortals falls on departed in lower world E361.1; tree in u. world A652.3; where horse got his u. teeth A2345.1; woman enticed to u. world on a stretching tree K1339.2.

Uprightness rewarded Q54.

Uprooted. — Plant shrieks when u. F992; tree u. and used as weapon by strong man F614.2.

Uprooting man-eating tree H1163. — Sky window from digging or u. plant (tree) in upper world *F56.1; strong hero practices u. trees F611.3.1.

Upside-down tree F811.15. — Nose turned u. F543.3.

Upstairs. — Persistent beggar invited u. J1331.

Upstream. — Obstinate wife sought for u. T255.2.

Uriah letter *K978.

Urinalysis reveals coition as illness cure J1149.4; reveals illegitimacy F956.2. — Sham physician pretends to diagnose from u. K1955.2; substitute specimen in u. K1858.1.

Urinary. — Magic object cures u. disease D1502.6.

Urinating on fire tabu C99.1.1, C891.3. — Bull's u. thought to be bleeding J1818.1; child's u. turns gold to ashes J2325.1; donkeys u. when others begin A2495.3; fugitive u. from tree: pursuers think it rain, leave N696; goat u. gold for master K366.5; resuscitation by u. E29.6; tabu to face sun while u. C99.1; witch exorcised by preventing her u. G271.4.7.

Urine diagnosis to tell where a man comes from J1734.1; melting rocks F559.8.1; waters tree F979.14. — Conception from drinking u. T512.2; dupe drinks u. K1044.1; flood from u. A1012.2; god's u. used to make pig A1871.0.1; goddess with red u. A139.9.1; lake from u. of horse A920.1.6; lamps burn with u. F964.3.1; magic u. D1002.1, (of animal) D1027; magician's u. drunk D1721.4; ocean from u. A923.1; origin of u. A1317; rain from u. A1131.1.1; river from u. of goddess (giantess) A933; serpent's u. gives longevity D1345.1; spring from horse's u. A941.1.1; sun, moon as spangles from creator's forehead falling into his u. A714.6; transformation by u. D562.7; why butterflies haunt u.-impregnated place A2433.5.6.

Urn. — Fish recovers u. from sea B548.2.5; magic u. D1171.15, (supplies drink) D1472.1.25; soul hidden in u. E712.3.

Useful. — Choice between u. and ornamental J240ff.; riddle: what is most u.? H659.11; senseless debate of the mutually u. J461ff.

Usurer *P435; blackmailed by daughter's suitor K443.11; cannot rest in grave E411.4; charges for rope cut to save him from hanging W154.1.1; encourages sermons against usury, so that his competitors will cease activity X516; gets plague for boasting Q558.3. — Devil comes for u. Q273.1; oxen bear dead u. to gallows to be buried N277; wife saves u. J155.5.

Usurer's practices turned against him J56. — Ass carries u. body to the gallows instead of to the church *B151.1.1.2.1.

Usurers. — Charity of u. ineffective V431; jokes concerning u. X510ff.; only u. to carry body of usurer to grave V62.2.

Usurper imposes burdensome taxes P12.3.

Usurping. — Impostors abandoning their companion and u. his place K1931; son u. throne P236.4.

Usury punished *Q273. — Going to mass before committing u. K2097; magician rebukes u. D1810.0.2.1.

Utensil transformed to person D434.1.

Utensils. — Magic u. and implements *D1170ff.; mortal repairs fairies' u. F338; punishment for desecrating holy u. Q222.6; recognition by overheard conversation with u. H13.2.5.

Uxorcide punished Q211.3. — Quartering in effigy for u. Q596.1.

Uxorious king (burned to death) N339.5, (neglects duties) P12.11.

Uxoriousness punished Q394.

Vætter F450.0.1.

Vagabonds banished P471.1.

Vagina dentata A1313.3.1, F547.1.1. — Extraordinary v. F547.5, F856.1; river from v. of first woman A933.2; seduction on pretence of repairing v. K1315.2.3; speaking v. D1610.6.1; why lover thinks v. is toothed K1222.

Vain, see also **Vanity;** attempts to (escape fulfillment of prophecy) M370ff., (kill hero) *H1510ff. — Why animal is v. A2527; wisdom found among v. words J263.

Vainglory. — Abbot avoids v. J916.

Valentine's Day for bird assembly B232.1.

Valhalla A661.1. — Souls of warriors go to V. E754.2.0.1.

Valkyries A485.2; ride through air and water A171.1.2.

Valley fills with gold at command D2102.2; of fire F756.1; from which no false lover can escape until it has been entered by true lover H421.1; of giants G105; like paradise F756.2.1. — Creator's giant servant makes v. and mountain A857.2; captivity in sunken v. R42; disenchanted v. rises D799.2; enchanted v. D7; otherworld as v. F160.2; peacock shows rivers way to v. A934.12; perilous v. in land of dead E750.2.2; perilous v. on way to otherworld F151.1.1; river v. licked out by giant beast A951.1.

Valleys. — Extraordinary v. and plains F756; lies about v. X1521; magic knowledge of language of v. D1815.6; origin of v. A983.

Valor personified Z124. — Quest to undertake feats of v. H1223; tests of v. H1561.

Valuable neglected for the interesting J345; object becomes worthless C967. — Worthless object substituted for v. K331.3.

Value depends upon real use J1061; -less oath M110.1; of religious exercises V4. — Riddles of v. H710ff.

Values. — Real and apparent v. J230—J299.

Vampire *E251; goddess A139.4.

Vanish. — Magic journey by making distance v. D2121.4; words of Christian comfort cause devil and his crew to v. G303.16.4.

Vanished. — Animal helps quest for v. wife B543.0.1; quest for v. daughter H1385.2; vow to find v. sister M155.2.

Vanishing ghost E599.8; ghost hitchhiker E332.3.3.1; person D2188.2. — Witches v. from prison G249.9; woman v. on breaking of tabu C926.

Vanity, see also **Vain;** W116; punished Q331.2. — Old racehorse in mill laments v. of youth J14; tar and feathers as punishment for v. Q475.1.

Vanquished king gives daughter to hero T68.4; ogre grants hero's three wishes G665.

Vapor. — Universe from congealed v. A621.

Variance. — Jokers set household at v. K2134.1.

Vasa Mortis B46.

Vase. — Emeralds from broken v. A978.3; magic v. *D1171.7; treasure discovered by clairvoyant v. N533.1.

Vassals' obligations to king P50.0.1.

Vat. — Bottomless v. holds water D2199.1; father's counsel: on wishing to drink wine go to the v. and drink it H588.4; paramour in v.: disguise as vat-buyer K1517.3; tiger crossing river with v. K1183.

Vaticinium M312.2.

Vault. — River arches over saint's body like a v. F932.2; sky as solid v. A702.2.

Vaulting. — Flight by v. on stick R252.

Veal thief set free after sending "Calf" K579.7.

Vegetable comes to life at woman's prayer T549.1; form transformed to (animal) D441, (person) D431; lamb B95ff.; supporting life without other food D1472.1.4. — Birth from v. T543.7; conception from eating v. T511.3; death v. must be eaten C662; eating certain v. tabu C224; lie: great v. X1401; magic knowledge of v. language D1815.5; magic v. *D983, (as food) D1034; man made from v. substance A1250ff.; man transformed to v. form D210ff.; person returns to original v. form when tabu is broken C963.3; transformation by eating v. D551.2.

Vegetables which mature in miraculously short time F815.1. — Acquisition of v. A1423; extraordinary v. F816; lies about v. X1420; magic fruits and v. D980ff.; origin of v. A2686ff.; sundry characteristics of grains and v. A2793; thistles and nettles as devil's v. G303.10.13.

Vegetation. — God of v. A430ff.

Vehicle. — Magic amphibian v. D1533; magic self-moving v. D1523ff.

Vehicles of the gods A156.5. — Acquisition of v. A1436.

Veil as chastity index H431.3. — Angels give pious woman heavenly v. V241.5; bird carries off jeweled v., separates lovers N352.1; birth with v. brings luck T589.4; holy water destroys v. over well D1562.6; identification by v. H115; magic v. *D1061, (renders invisible) D1361.33; saint's v. quells volcano D1549.6.

Veils of fire, ice before door of heaven A661.0.1.1.2. — Evil eye covered with seven v. D2071.0.1; image of Virgin v. and unveils itself D1623.1;

why women wear v. A1599.3; woman's beauty shows through seven v. F574.1.2; woman v. self as expression of surprise P671.

Veiled wife taken to paramour K1583.

Veiling. — Disguise by v. face K1821.3.

Veins. — Man's v. made from vines A1260.1.5; punishment: opening own v. and bleeding to death Q427.

Venality. — Repartee concerning clerical v. J1263.2.

Venereal. — Prostitute with v. disease sent to king Q244.3.

Vengeance, see also **Revenge;** for destroying fairy-mound P17.0.3. — Escape from v. caused by broken oaths M106; ghost demands v. E234.0.1; god's v. A194.2; quest undertaken for v. H1228; train of troubles for sparrow's v. N261.

Venom. — Animal v. causes swelling X1205; dragon spews v. B11.2.11.1; giant made of v. F531.6.1.6; man spews v. F582.2; origin of serpent's v. A2367.3.1; poisonous snakes have no v. B765.9; saint orders serpent to withdraw v. D2156.5.1; snake's v. kills tree B765.11; snake's v. poisons tree D1563.2.2.2.

Venomous, see also **Poisonous;** animals B776; man F582.3; sheep destroy enemy B776.1. — Dragon's blood v. B11.2.13.1; dragon with v. breath guards tree B11.6.10; reward: no v. creature ever to hurt man or posterity Q45.1.3; weapons magically v. D1402.7.0.1; why hairy caterpillar is v. A2532.2; why animals are v. A2532ff.; why water serpents are not v. A2531.1.

Ventures. — Lucky business v. *N410—N439.

Venus (goddess) has girl choose among suitors N817.1; jealous of Psyche, Cupid's love W181.6; as sin personified Z127.1. — Mountain of V. F131.1; sabbath from feast to V. A1541.4.1.

Venus (planet) as land of dead E481.8.3. — Origin of V. A781.

Venusberg F131.1.

Verbal. — Clever v. retorts J1250—J1499.

Vergil in basket K1211; as magician D1711.2.

Verità. — Bocca della V. H251.1.

Veritas. — In vino v. U180ff.

Vermicelli. — Magic v. D1039.1.

Veronica's — Saint V. miraculous napkin F950.1, V121.

Verse, see also **Poetry.** — Changeling addresses woman in v. and thus betrays maturity F321.1.1.3; contest in v. making H509.4.1.1; double-meaning v. aids theft K232.1; recognition by song's v. H12.2.

Versemaker, see also **Poet.** — Devil as v. G303.13.4.

Vessel full of nail-scrapings H1129.8; left under mound in sand, lost J1922.3; to be mended leads to adventure N783. — Alleged inexhaustible v. K117; cloak becomes v. D454.3.4.2; carrying water in a leaky v. (task) H1023.2.1.2; creation in covered v. A1295; deception into v. K717; drinking from v. only with certain tube Z323; embarkation in leaky v. as punishment Q466; extraordinary v. F881; fairy causes v. to remain full

F335.1; giant issues from tiny v. G161; magic spell causes v. to burst D1591; magic twigs from buried v. D953.1.1; magic v. *D1171, (furnishes money) D1452; prayer restores shattered v. V52.5; saint's breath restores shattered v. D1565.4; theft of v. from water-deity F352.2; truth-testing v. H251.3.12; wind raised by troubling v. of water D2142.1.4.

Vessels. — Burial in v. E431.18; copper v. are steaming under earth A857.1; devil piles sand in ocean so that v. may run aground G303.9.9.5; earth swallows temple v. F948.1.1; gigantic v. F881.1; king's earthen v. among gold J913; not to profane hallowed clothes and v. C93.2.

Vestments V131. — Color symbolism of mass v. Z140.3.

Vesuvius. — Skillful bowman shoots crater of V. open F661.6.

Veterinarian becomes doctor: does not have to pay for killing people J1438.

Vexing. — Devil v. friars caused to repent by singing "Te sanctum dominum" G303.24.3; maid v. suitor by pretence T77.

Vices. — Clerical v. *V465ff.; dwarfs dislike human v. F451.5.16.

Victim kills swallower from within F912. — Blood springs from murderer's finger when he touches v. D1318.5.1; cannibal fattens v. *G82ff.; disenchantment by blowing on v. D778; disguised flayer dresses in skin of his v. K1941; gods create earth from their dead v. A831.8; ogre carries v. in bag (basket) G441; ogre in animal form lures v. into captivity G403; tasks assigned at suggestion contained in letter borne by the v. H918; vampire brought to life through endurance of punishment by her v. E251.2.1.

Victim's — Ogre sucks v. finger and drinks all his blood G332.1; resuscitation by biting v. bone E29.1.

Victims. — Bodies of v. in front of ogre's house G691; three v. of love T92.2.

Victor demands defeated's daughter T104.2; forgives vanquished ruler J829.3. — Conquered warrior kills v. K235.4; giant becomes friend of v. G510.3; incognito king in court of v. K1812.5; famine punishes oppression of v. Q552.3.2.

Victorious ally feared J684.4; youngest child *L0. — King to be v. as long as rides muzzled gelding N125.3.

Victory by army leaders' single combat H217.1; personified Z132.1; as reward for piety Q156. — Animals help in military v. K2351; boaster of v. over a weaker person reprimanded J978; charm gives v. in fight D1400.1.10; curse of loss of v. for opposition to holy person remitted Q576.1; eagle as omen of v. B147.2.1.2; general gives king v. credit W11.8; king's presence necessary for v. P19.1; magic belt assures v. D1381.18; magic object gives v. D1400.1; magic spear gives omen of v. D1311.17.1; Norse spirits prophesy v. M301.13; prayer before battle brings v. V52.3; prisoners released in celebration of v. P14.1; prophecy: ruler's death to insure v. M362; prophecy of v. against odds M323; reward for getting v.-

stone Q112.0.4; saint's blessing brings v. D2163.8; warrior flees for future v. K2378.2.

Victuals, see **Food.**

Vidua K2213.1.

Vigil, see also **Watch;** with hands in shape of cross V462.4.2; of husband at wife's grave calls her forth E385. — Continuous prayer sustains man through frightful v. V52.2; magic object acquired as reward for v. D855.1; resuscitation by v. at tomb E62; not to speak during v. C401.1; test: speechless v. in church H1451; vow of v. at frightful place all night M156.

Vigilance. — Dupe persuaded to relax v.: seized K827; man killed on night when fairy guardian relaxes v. F311.2.1; tests of v. H1450—H1499.

Village disappears by magic D2095.1; dormitory A1559.1; of lion-men D112.1.1; of men only F566.1; as part of dowry T52.9; sinks in earth C984.7; of tiger-men D112.2.1.2; under lake F725.5.1; vanishes D2188.3; where cock crows, dog barks, mithian bellows B155.2.1. — Bought behind the v. J1169.2; building v. in one night H1104.2; countryman expects to find persons from his own v. when he travels to another land J1742.1; curse on v.: descendants remain few M461.1; fairy curses v. M411.16; lie: whole v. lifted X941.1; slain enemy's head must not enter v. C845.1; wise judgments settle v. quarrels J1170.1; your child's killer is in the v. M306.5.

Villages in otherworld F168. — Origin of v. A991.

Villain accidentally slain by own order K1612.1; nemesis Q581.

Villains and traitors *K2200—K2299.

Villainy. — What is greatest v.? H659.7.4.

Vindication by champion H218.0.1.

Vine as sky-rope F51.1.2. — Escape from land of dead upon v. R219.2; extraordinary v. F815.7; god of the v. A433.3; man becomes v. D213.4; mankind from mating of tree and v. A1221.4; why v.-leaves are hand-shaped A2761.2.

Vines. — Man's veins made from v. A1260.1.5.

Vinegar. — Life token: wine turns to v. E761.6.5.

Vineyard magically in fruit at Nativity D2145.2.2.1. — Father is in v. doing good and bad H583.2; magic v. D962; setting out v. in one night (task) H1103; tearing up the v. K1416.

Vineyards. — Beasts that destroy v. B16.0.1; dream brings treasure: trade v. with neighbor N531.2.

Vino. — In v. veritas U180ff.

Vintages. — Bluff: the rare v. K1786.

Viol. — The great noise from the bass-v. X1866.

Violated, see also **Raped;** woman's child exposed S312.2. — Groans of woman being v. C885.2.

Violating. — Captain hangs own son for v. order M13.2; mortal v. fairy F304.4; tabu: v. woman C118; transformation for v. vow D661.3.

Violence of temper W185; to woman during pregnancy tabu C152.1. — Disenchantment by v. D712; immunity from death by v. Q154; mildness triumphs over v. L350ff.

Violent treatment exorcises witch G271.5. — Buttons burst as consequence of v. emotion F1041.6; victim of v. death cannot rest in grave E411.10.

Violets. — Water with scent of v. F716.2.

Violin. — Fox stumbles over v. J864.1; magic v. *D1233; origin of v. A1461.1; resuscitation by playing v. E55.4.

Violinist. — Devil abducts v. for hell G303.9.5.8.

Viper eats squirrel's children A2426.1.2.1; as magician's familiar G225.7.2. — Child born with v. in heart T557; enmity between cobra and v. A2494.16.3; ruining garden to get rid of v. J2103.2.1.

Vipers. — Plowing field of v. (task) H1188.

Virgin daughter of culture hero A592.2; in monastery becomes abbot K1837.7; suffers no labor pains V211.1.4; tests men with hot iron H221.2.1. — Birth from v. T547; culture hero incarnated through birth from v. A511.3; decree that hero must wed only a v. M51; disenchantment by naked v. undergoing frightful journey at midnight D759.3; earth as v. mother of Adam A1234.1; false v. K1912; girl may remain v. for three days after marriage T165; girl remains v. after suitors killed T311.3; imprisoned v. to prevent knowledge of men *T381; male v. demigod A504; magic power to see whether girl is v. *D1825.4.2; praying to the nearer v. J2495.1; savage elephant lulled to sleep by v. D1964.1; tobacco from grave of v. A2611.2.1; vow: man will love only a v. M133.

Virgins condemned to wander at death E750.1.1; as guardians of doors of heaven A661.0.15.

Virgin Mary *V250ff.; appears to lady neglecting mass, takes taper Q223.7.1; produces spring A941.5.0.1; shielded in childbirth from on-lookers' gaze Q57.1; shows Jesus to nun D1766.1.2; threatens to leave heaven V254.6. — Contest arranged by V. A1372.7; devil as V. G303.3.2.5; flowers from under feet of V. A2621.1; girl claims she is second V. J1264.6; hazel shelters V. A2711.4.1; image of V. chastises clerk Q552.7; intervention of V. cheats devil G303.16.1, K218.4; Jewess to bear child must entreat V. T580.1; plant named for service to V. A2711.4.3; prayer to V. protects against plague D1586.2; seven joys of V. Z71.5.6.5; sham miracle: painting of V. weeps K1972.2; tears of V. become daisies A2612.2; thistle as milk-cup for V. A2711.4.2.

Virginity personified Z139.8; saved despite torture T320.1.1. — Black nipples reveal v. loss T494; catching salmon proof of v. H411.16; girls must pay for young man's v. J1174.4; girl named Mary has v. spared by knight who has bought her T321.2; girl's v. spared by knight when he sees her surrounded by the Virgin and her train T321.3; girl's v. saved by emissary's kindness T324; ravished girl's v. restored by Virgin Mary T313; sacrifice of v. T301; suicide to save v. T326; vow of v. M132.

Virility test for husband H493. — Substitute in v. test K1848.1.

Virtue personified Z125. — Christian v. brings about conversion V331.10; lake of milk from v. of saint A920.1.13; ordinary rather than pious man brings out v. by comparison J417; pretended v. K2050ff.; saint's v. to save great numbers M364.3.2.

Virtues. — Clerical v. V461; devil instructs saint on v. G303.9.4.6.1.; eight v. Z71.16.1.2.

Virtuous man seduced by woman T338. — Reward for v. life Q112.0.5; woman advised that nagging will never make husband v. T253.2.

Vise. — Dupe puts hand (paws) into v. *K1111.

Vishnu lies in bed of river from reincarnated girl A934.11.1; torments aunt's lover K1578. — Deceptive land purchase: as much land as V. can lie upon K185.2; lotus plants from navel of V. A123.9, H1289.4.1.

Visibility of fairies F235; of trolls F455.5.

Visible sun is pet of real sun A722.12. — Child in mother's womb v. T575.4; devil's house is v. on the way to hell G303.8.3.3; devil v. to one who walks in minister's (or minister's wife's) holy shoes (galoshes) G303.6.2.4; devil made v. by sign of cross G303.16.3.6; ghost v. only to summoner E389.2; otherworld v. from high mountain F132.0.1.

Vision as evil omen D1812.5.1.2.1; of sacrament in form of young child V39.4. — Angel visits mortals in v. V235.0.1; birds dispute over day or night v. B299.2.1; devil produces v. to tempt believers G303.9.4.5.1; dragon's miraculous v. B11.5.3; father in v. reproves son P233.10; god has magic v. only from his throne A199.2; journey to otherworld as v. F1; land grant dependent on v. K185.12; seduction by alleged v. K1375; saint in v. demands prisoner's release R121.6.1; truth given in v. D1810.8.1.

Visions. — Religious v. V510ff.; resuscitated man tells v. of beyond E177.

Visit of angel to mortal V235; to deceased F81.1.2; to fairyland F370ff.; to foreign country suitor task H336.1; to land of the sun *F17; to lower world through hole made by lifting clumps of grass F92.1; to mountain-men F460.4.8; to star-world F15; to otherworld F0—F199; to water-goddess's home F420.7.1. — Adventures motivated by v. N787; clandestine v. of princess to hero betrayed by token H81.2; dead person pays periodic v. to earth E585; death respite for paying v. K551.13; do not v. your friends often: counsel proved wise by experience J21.9; dwarfs v. mortal's house F451.5.7; not to eat while on v. home C234; encounter with clever children (woman) dissuades man from v. J31; gods (saints) in disguise v. mortals K1811; mortal's v. to land of dwarfs F451.5.4; youth promised to ogre makes v. to his home G461; wife's long v. to parents inadvisable J21.47.1.

Visitation. — Mysterious v. as punishment Q554ff.

Visiting friends take everything from house of dying man W151.2. — Fairy v. mortals F393; god v. sick mortal A185.17; soul v. important places of lifetime E722.3.3.

Visitor. — Tabus on feasting v. C616.

Visitor's — Chief reads v. thoughts D1819.1.1; fool and the v. large nose J2512; witch eats up v. bow G269.6.

Visitors of sick stag eat up all his provisions so that he starves W151.2.1. — Saints have divine v. V227.

Vital bodily members E780ff.; heads *E783, N819.3; objects E770ff.; skin E785. — Skillful surgeon removes and replaces v. organs F668.1.

Vitals. — Creator makes clouds from own v. A705.1.1.

Vivification of image of animal D445; of mankind from stone image A1245.2; of picture D435.2.1; of statue *D435.1.1.

Vixen's. — Cat as v. husband B281.9.1.

Vocal. — Deceptive v. contests K84.

Vocation. — Wager: fortune made from capital or from working at v. N66.

Voice of eaten child comes from cannibal G72.4; from grave answers pet name E324.1; from heaven curses city Q556.0.2; from heaven testifies for accused H216.1; petrifies suitors D581.1. — Ass in lion's skin unmasked when he raises his v. J951.1; ass tries to get a cricket's v. J512.8; big v.: little creature (frogs, crickets) U113; devil comes out of man when monk recognizes the devil's v. in man G303.16.19.7; devil speaks with v. of he-goat G303.4.7; disguise by changing v. K1832; divination from sound of v. D1812.5.0.11; divine v. points out magic D849.7; druid's spell drowning fairy's v. F381.6; eye bursts from v. overstrain F1085; falling in love with v. T11.8; ghost's v. scares away treasure-seekers N576.1; god's v. A139.5; quality of animal's v. A2423ff.; hearing v. of God as reward Q144; how animal got v. A2421ff.; how animal lost v. A2422ff.; how far his v. will reach J1941; jackal inside carcass pretends his v. is God's K1973; madness on hearing prophetic v. F1041.8.8; magic carrying power of v. D1921; magic power from heavenly v. D1739.2; man with marvelous v. F688; murderer warned by God's v. that murder will be avenged M348; mysterious v. announces death of Pan F442.1; mysterious v. announces prohibition C601; ogre disguises v. to lure victim G413; peacock dissatisfied with her v. W128.4; peacock has snake carry devil into paradise: cursed with ugly v. and feet A2236.2.2; partridge's v. borrowed from tortoise A2241.3; petrification at woman's v. D529.1; picture of a v. H1013; recognition by v. *H79.3; recognition of captive's v. brings about rescue from ogre G556; recognition of good health by hearing v. H1582.1; remarkable v. F556; resuscitation by heavenly v. E136; supernatural v. points out criminal N278; swallows torment Christ on cross: lose v. A2231.2.2; truth-telling v. warns of poison D1317.4.1; what animal has one v. living, seven, dead? H842.3; where sparrow got v.: taught by lark A2271.2; why women have a treble v. A1372.4; woman's v. as source of sin T336.2.

Voices of dead heard from graveyard E401; from heaven (or from the air) F966; from unhatched eggs J646.2. — Heavenly v. proclaim hero's birth M311.0.4; not to heed persuasive v. C811.

Volcano fire as goddess's head A139.8.3. — Giant cooks on v. crater G171; gods' home in v. A151.1.3; saint's veil quells v. D1549.6; saint stops eruption of v. D2148.3.

Volcanoes' origin A966.

Voluntarily. — Magic object v. restored to giver D878; quests v. undertaken H1220ff.; tasks v. undertaken H945.

Voluntary exile as punishment for murder Q431.1. — Reasons for v. transformation *D640ff.; victim enticed into v. captivity or helplessness K710ff.

Volunteers. — No sinless v. for cremating dead H1558.12.

Völva prophesies at child's birth M301.2.2.

Vomit. — Hero proves himself a cannibal by trick v.-exchange K1721; release from curse by burning v. M429.1.

Vomited, see also **Disgorged;** magic object D826.1. — Animals v. up by creator A1792; gold v. D2102.1; heavenly bodies v. up by creator A700.2; stolen magic object v. up D884; swallowed children v. by earth R142.

Vomiting V229.2.2; iron F1041.20; out heart as punishment Q552.21. — Abortion by v. up embryo T572.2.1; animal v. treasure B103.4ff.; burning bodies v. F1099.5; flood from whale's v. A1013.1; magic dog v. any required liquor B182.1.1; swallowing mouse without v. H1567.1.1; theft detected by enforced v. J1144.1.

Vow, see also **Oath;** to visit shrine V113.0.2. — Demon has to serve girl whom he cannot persuade to break v. of chastity G303.16.19.5; ghost laid when v. is fulfilled E451.3; girl pleads chastity v. to repel lover T322.4; punishment for violating v. D661.3; tabu: not to fulfill v. C68; wife keeps v. not to rewed T291.1.

Vows *M100—M199. — Clerical v. *V470ff.

Voyage, see **Journey.**

Voyagers may ask landsman first question P682.2.

Voyaging. — Christ's message to v. clerics V211.10.1.

Vulcan tutors youth F107.

Vulnerability. — Secret of unique v. disclosed N476, (by hero's wife) K2213.4.1; unique v. Z310ff.

Vulnerable. — Alliances which make both parties more v. J681; hound strikes unique v. spot N335.5.

Vulture as bird of ill omen B147.2.2.6; cures blindness B511.5.1; eats those to be reborn as human beings E697; as messenger B291.1.8; places baby in queen's lap F589.6.1.1; scouts after world-fire A1039.1. — Why v. is bald A2317.7; creation of v. A1931; helpful v. B455.1; lion and wild boar make peace rather than slay each other for benefit of v. J218.1; marriage to v. B602.4; man transformed to v. D152.3; return from lower world on v. F101.3.1; speaking v. B211.3.8.

Vulture's chicks will not eat murdered hero B159.4. — Carrion as v. food A2435.4.5.1; quest for v. egg figured with golden letters H1332.2.

Vultures. — King of v. B242.2.11; why v. are bald A2317.3.1.

Vulva, see also Vagina; hair becomes mantis F547.5.9. — Eye in v. F547.5.3; speaking v. D1610.6.1.

Waberlohe D1380.1.

Wading. — Giant w. the ocean F531.3.1; hero w. across sea F1057.

Wafer. — Consecrated w. kept in mouth in order to be a witch G281; not to lose consecrated w. *C55; penny baked in the w. J1582.1; tabu to shoot at consecrated w. C55.2.

Wafted. — Person w. to sky F61.

Wager, see also **Gambling;** greatest liar to get his supper free K455.7; involves spilling water on fops X32; that sheep are hogs K451.2; who shall rise last? J2511.1. — Bull wins master's w. B587.3; deceptive w. K264; devil helps journeyman win w. with master G303.22.8; guessing with life as w. H512; man and wife w. as to who shall speak first J2511; "never w. more than a groat": counsel proved wise by experience J21.8; wives w. as to who can best fool her husband K1545.

Wagers *N0—N99.

Wagering. — Man w. he can run with his head off J322.1; Satan w. with God over mortal G303.9.8.7; woman w. that she can seduce anchorite T337.

Wages: as much as he can carry K1732; successive harvests from grain of rice Z21.1.1. — Deceptive w. K256; high w. bring expensive living J342; sun earns day's w. for his daily work (riddle) H715.1.

Wagon accompanies wild hunt E501.10.3; bewitched G265.8.3.2; of jewels F861.3; paralyzed by witch D2072.0.2.1.1; refuses to move D1654.5; run back and forth to simulate artillery K2368.1.1; and sleigh figures for summer and winter H1058; stops creaking and fool thinks it is dead J1872.0.1. — Bluff: thunder said to be the rolling of hero's brother's w. K1718.1; carrying w. axle which has broken a wheel (task) H1183; child promised to devil for help on road with broken w. S225; corpse in coffin refuses to be moved in w. D1654.9; covering the whole w. with tar K1425; deer hitched to w. B558.4; devil drives horse and w. G303.7.3ff.; devil invites traveler into his w. G303.7.1.2.2; devil in form of wheel on w. G303.3.4.1; extraordinary w. F861ff.; ghosts in glowing w. E421.3.5; ghostly w. E535.2; grain-thief's w. falls into ditch: duped owner helps him K405.1; hay w. and the gate J1411; hen hitched to w. B558.3; living smith must repair w. belonging to wild hunt E501.15.5; magic w. *D1113; mice hitched to w. B558.5; people in otherworld hitch horses both before and behind w. F171.6.4; spirit makes wheels come off w. F473.6.6; spirit shoves w. into ditch F473.6.7; stretching, shrinking harness pulls w. uphill X1785.1; thumbling drives w. by sitting in horse's ear F535.1.1.1; trickster throws fish off the w. K371.1.

Wagons. — Dwarfs have steeds and w. F451.7.6; ghost upsets farmers' w. E299.3.

Wagtail. — Why w. moves tail up and down A2479.1.

Wailing of the dead E547. — Thieves' w. drowns abducted woman's out-cries K419.8.

Waist. — Ant thrown from heaven: hence narrow w. A2214.2; origin and nature of animal's w. A2355ff.; penance: iron band forged round a man's w. Q522.5; sea as w.-deep H681.4.2.

Wait. — Bravest know how to w. J572.1; curious wife: w. and see T258.

Waiter. — Escape disguise as w. K521.4.4.

Waiting to announce choice of boon M204.1; for God to provide J2215.4; twenty-two years to see a beauty T24.7; at the well for the thief J2214.3; for the thief to return for the bolster J2214.3.2; in the graveyard for the thief J2214.3.1. — Drunk man w. for his house to come to him X815; foolish w. J2066; numskull w. for river to run down J1967.

Wakes, see **Funerals.**

Waking contest *H1450.1; from magic sleep *D1978. — Dead wife w. hus-band E322.2; disenchantment by proper person w. from magic sleep *D762; long w. follows long sleep F564.3.1; nut falls w. man about to be bitten by snake N652; ring w. from magic sleep D1364.0.1.

Walk. — Animal's gait or w. A2441; crow tries to imitate partridge's w. J512.6; do not w. half a mile with a man without asking his name J21.11; first w. by Adam A1392; dwarfs w. stooped F451.2.0.3; ghosts w. at cer-tain times E587; magic power to w. on water *D2125.1; faster the w., longer the trail D1783.3; father's counsel: w. not in sunshine from your house to your shop H588.1; man who does not know how to pray so holy that he can w. on water V51.1; why children learn to w. late A1321.1.

Walked. — As tired as if he had w. J1946.

Walking around grave to raise ghost E386.4; backward around church at midnight G224.8; backward to leave misleading trail K534.3; ghost laid *E440ff.; on grass-blades without bending them F973.2; on head in otherworld F167.4; upon water without getting wet D1841.4.3. — Art of w. on stilts A1491; boy lives on ox never w. on ground F562.1; child at first w. resuscitates E149.2; child w. at birth T585.8; dead w. on grass, mud E489.9; dead w. on water G299.1; fairies teach under-water w. F345.1; fool w. on water P192.3; ghost w. through solids E572; giant's w. contest F531.5.11.1; lazy boy claims not w. W111.2.8; magic from maiden w. naked in public *D1796; magic w. on water *D2125.1; man w. faster than horse F681.9; ordeal by rope-w. H225; ordeals by w. H225; penance: w. on all-fours like beast Q523.2; person w. unceasingly for year F1032; power of w. to nearest water F651; sand enables w. on water D1524.1.4; woman has worn out carriage-load of shoes with w. F1015.1.2.

Walking-sticks. — Riddle about mares and w. H586.8.

Wall about otherworld F148; accuses the crowbar J1966; around grave to keep in ghost E431.14; broken by saint's kick V229.14; of cakes separates enemies D2163.6.2; collapses: who is guilty? Z49.11.1; of fire surrounds island F744; opens, closes to let saint through D1552.6; as path to upper world F57.4; of snow around hut in answer to prayer D2143.6.2; of water magically warded off D2151.0.3. — Burial in church w. cheats devil K219.4; coffin carried through hole in w. to prevent return of dead E431.4; communication of lovers through hole in w. T41.1; devil tries to w. in too large a piece of ground in a night and fails G303.13.3; drawing lover out of w. H412.6; eagle saves man from falling w. B521.2.1; garden w. that cannot be overleapt D1675; going through w. suitor test H312.7; horse jumps over high w. F989.1; life story painted on w. H11.1.2; magic horn blows down w. D1562.3; safety in shadow of w. N253; tearing down huge w. H1116.3; treasure found in ruined w. N511.1.6.1; treasure hidden within w. N517.2; waves form high w. around otherworld isle F141.3; woman suckles imprisoned relative through prison w. R81.

Walls of crystal in otherworld *F169.2; magically enclose enemy D2091.16; overthrown by magic D2093; thrown up by chariot wheels R5.1. — Devil as builder of w. G303.9.1.4; heaven surrounded by w. A661.0.9; house's w. so thin thieves must break in J1165.1; inscription on w. for condensed education J168; jewelled w. F165.3.2; shout makes w. fall F688.4; strong man throws another from w. F628.2.2.

Wallaby. — Friendship between turtle and w. A2493.12.1.

Wallet containing night and day A1172.2; from which one cannot escape D1413.9.1. — Sham miracle: w. changes to wasps K1975.1.

Walling up as a punishment Q455ff.

Wallowing. — Hog w. in mud after bath U123.

Wallpaper. — Spirit tears off w. F473.6.1.

Walrus. — Giant w. B871.2.6; hero kills w. F628.1.4.3; man transformed to w. D127.4; origin of w. A1838; soul in w. E715.4.3; strong man throws w. F624.1.2; where w. got his tusks A2247, A2345.4.

Wampaus as monster with huge dog tracks F401.3.3.1.

Wand transformed to other object D451.6.1; transforms D572.4. — King's w. P19.4.0.1; magic w. *D1254.1, (locates hidden treasure) *D1314.2; quest for magic w. H1342.0.1.

Wands of life and death D1663.1.

Wanderer. — Disguise as w. K1817.

Wanderers in shade of plane tree blame it for not bearing fruit W154.7.

Wandering islands F737; Jew Q502.1; ghost makes attack E261; prostitutes J1351.1; as punishment Q502ff.; of tribes A1630ff. — Child's stomach split to cure w. J1842.4; children w. into ogre's house G401; couple w. until they find new seat of race M455.4; dead man w. with torch E594; first man w. until he finds mate A1275.7; gods w. on earth K1811; person w. for 150 years F1032.1; sinner w. between heaven and earth E411.0.4; soul w. E750.1, (from body in sleep) E721.1, (till corpse decays) E722.3.2; uncharitable pope w. after death V425; wild huntsman's w. E501.17.7, E501.3ff.; witch recognized by seeing w. soul return G251.

Waning. — Magic waxing and w. of strength D1836; moon's w. A755.4, (caused by her sickness) A755.3, (caused by menstrual period) A755.7.

Want. — In time of plenty provide for w. J711; man never knowing w. swallowed by earth L424.

Wanted. — What is w., not what is asked J1311.

War of birds and quadrupeds *B261; -club H125.3; cry F418.1; between fairies F277.0.1; between fairies, giants F364.3; between fairies, mortals F364; horse J954.1, J1914.1; -making punished Q305; personified Z132; prisoners fettered Q434.2; prisoners shut up between stones Q433.13; of pygmies and cranes F535.5.1; of spirits in sky causes thunder A1142.6.1; with the sun Q739.2; between wild and domestic animals *B262. — Ass jealous of w. horse until he sees him wounded L452.2; dead predict w. E545.16.1; fairy incites mortals to w. F369.4.1; foreign king wages w. to enforce demand for princess in marriage T104; god of w. A485; goddess of w. as hag A125.1; hero leaves cradle for w. T585.7; lake to quell fairy w. A920.1.7.1; making w. tabu C641; men report false attack to bring about w. K1087.0.1; mortals aid fairies in w. F394.2; origin of w. A1599.11.1; origin of w. among men A1341; prophecies concerning w. M356.1; queen persuades king to w. so sons may have territory P23; rejected suitor wages w. T104.1; ruler diverts attention from misgovernment by beginning a w. K2381; sham threat of w. holds ships back K1771.7; stolen cows cause w. K300.1; tabu broken, w. lost C936; tabus concerning w. C845; test of sex of man masking as girl: w. trumpet sounded H1578.2; Thirty-Years W. destroys home of dwarfs F451.4.4.2; turtle's w.-party F1025.2; wild hunt as omen of w. E501.20.1.1; wives preventing w. J1112.4.

Warbler's — Garden w. song A2272.1.3, A2426.2.2.

Warding. — Animal w. off spirits B785; fires burnt in streets w. off witches G272.4; magic object w. off disease D1500.2ff.

Wares. — Seduction by showing w. in tent K1332.2.

Warehouse. — Cat in the w. J1175.1; hero threatens to haul away w. with rope K1745; where is the w. (cumulative tale) Z49.5.

Warfare of animals B260ff.; as tribal characteristic A1600ff.

Warm body restored E152. — Animals or objects kept w. J1873; beggar tells the bishop how to stay w. K151; dwarf wants to w. self at fire F451.5.7.1; dwarfs w. heath by underground fire F451.5.1.15; fairies w. themselves *F266; guest who could not keep w. J1563.1; seduction by entering woman's room to get w. K1361.3; why earth becomes w. and wet: underground vessels steaming A857.1; why sea is w. A1119.2.

Warmed. — Castle w. by love F771.13; cauldron w. by breath of nine maidens F686.1.

Warming hands across river J1945; man far away J1191.7; stove with wool J1873.3 — Ghosts w. selves E578.1; resuscitation by w. E133; saint carries fire in hands for w. guests D1841.3.2.3.1.

Warmth. — Magic object furnishes w. D1481; seduction: how to store up w. K1399.3.

Warn. — Devil appears to minister's serving man to w. of impending disaster to house G303.6.2.6; pupil returns from dead to w. master of futility of his studies E368.

Warned. — Boys w. by dogs' names to escape K649.5; buyer w. by fool that turban for sale is too short J2088; hero w. of danger by horse *B133.1; lover w. against husband by wife's parody incantation K1546; murderer w. by God's voice that murder will be avenged M348; thief w. what not to steal J2091.

Warner. — Ghostly w. of wild hunt's approach E501.6.

Warning in dreams D1810.8.3; by talking to trees K649.6. — Animal w. (of fatal danger) B521, (hero of enemy trap) B335.6; bird gives w. B143.1; danger w. restores speech F954.5; death w. prophesied M341.0.1; dog as animal of w. B134.3; dream w. against marriage C168; ghost w. the living E363.3; knockers' appearance as accident w. F456.1.2.2.4; leaf sent down stream as w. to one below H135; magic object w. of danger *D1317ff.; mermaid w. of bad weather B81.7; moon w. of assassin F961.3.3; sister w. brothers P253.6; son w. mother P231.2; son w. animal mother B631.0.1; spirit gives w. F403.2.3.2; sun w. of assassin F961.1.4; token as w. H82.5; wife's wise w. T299.2.

Warnings. — Attention to w. J1050ff.; inattention to w. J652.

Warrant. — Tokens sent to jailor as w. of king's authority H82.1.

Warrior attack as valor test H1561.7; buries oversized armor to prove prowess K1969.2; chieftain of underworld A308; combats when spear consents F834.7; deceived into attacking pillar-stone K1845.1; destroyed for asking princess's hand P41.1; fighting foster brother P273.2.1; flees for sake of future victory K2378.2; gives steed to enemy W11.5.9; having lost a city claims that he did not wish to sell it for a higher price J875; offered long life if he delays battle D1857.2; retires to cloister Q520.6; reveals camping place J2366; of special strength F610.3; will not fight where brother slain P251.2. — Admission test to w. band H1566; conquered w. kills victor K235.4; fairies bear dead w. to fairyland F399.1; fairy gives w. equipment F343.10; girl's favors traded for truce with w. T455.4; mask for w. with ruined face K521.2.3; messengers announce successive misfortunes to w. as he sets out for war N252.1; old w. longs for more adventure H1221.1; oldest w. as preferred suitor T92.13; sham w. K1951; supernatural substitute for pious w. K3.2.1; woman in love with dying w. T89.1; women bind w. by hair K713.1.8; women lure w. for confederate to kill K822; wounded w. continues fighting W33.1; wrestling with giant w. H1166.1.

Warrior's deceptive fight in "single" combat K2319.2; equipment magically furnished D2107; marriage for night to insure heir before being slain next day T156.1. — Fire from w. fingers F683.1.1.

Warriors P551; battle leader as valor test H1561.8; boastfully face strong enemy H945.1; discovered about to murder own chief N657; hidden in battlefield pit K2369.2; hidden on oxen driven into enemy's camp

K2357.15; identically equipped Z210.0.1; surrender after chief's death R75.2; tabu in hero's land C566.5; use teeth F1084.2; whitewash weapons as disguise K1839.6. — Band of professional w. P551.0.1; describing approaching w. by senses J1661.3; eager w. go through tent wall W212.1; ghostly w. recount lives E497; giants as w. F531.6.9; helpful spirit w. dwell in rocks and hills F450.1.1; mad w. fly into clouds F1041.8.7; physical reactions of w. in battle F1041.16.6; professional w. A1658; sex activity tabu for w. C566.6; slain w. revive nightly E155.1; souls of w. go to Valhalla E754.2.0.1; spring aids demigod's w. A941.4.2.1; tailors cowards as w. X223; test for sham-dead w. H248.4; transformed fairy w. F383.5; why snipe messenger for w. A2261.6; women w. F565.

Warts. — Why toads have w. A2412.5.2.

Wart-hog's burrow A2432.7.

Wash. — Ghost asks to w. shirt E412.3.2.1; giants sit on mountain and w. feet in stream below F531.3.9; horse advises hero not to w. B521.1.1; numskull tries to w. black hen white J1909.6; paramour hidden under w. K1521.3.

Washed. — Black wool w. white H1023.6; coming neither w. nor unwashed (task) H1062; dead w. V68.1; death respite until mouth w. K551.4.6; mermaid is w. up on beach B81.13.2; negro tries in vain to be w. white J511.1; sleeping maids w. by dwarf F451.5.1.13; wine w. in the Rhine J1312.2.

Washerman makes foolish minister J677; as minister thinks about washing U129.3; rescues abandoned child R131.8.3. — Escape disguise as w. K521.4.3.1.

Washers at ford disaster omen D1812.5.1.1.6.

Washerwoman. — Brahmin in love with w. T91.7.1; seducer disguised as w. K1321.1.2.

Washing the child (in boiling water) J2465.4; enormous number of clothes (and other articles) in short time (task) H1096; of feet by unseen hands F171.7; grandmother (in boiling water) K1462; hair on sabbath tabu C631.3; hairs from salt J2173.9; Jew as devil's task G303.16.19.3.3; in magic bowl produces immunity from old age D1349.2.2; off ascetic's dirt takes twelve years V462.14; quilt without soap H1023.6.1; room (floods it) J2465.6. — Cure by w. in dew D2161.4.14.3; escape by w. clothes K551.4.5; face wiped dry after w. A1599.4; fairies w. their clothes F271.9; flowers drop on w. hands D2193; guilty detected by w. basin J1149.11; man w. blindfolded F1017; Pilate w. hands on Mt. Pilatus E411.8; princess dupes giant into w. in death water G527; punishment for w. clothes in holy well Q559.9; restrictions on w. murdered body Q559.3; vow against w. M126; water from saint's w. curative D1500.1.18.1.2; why women keep w. themselves A1372.10; wife w. face in dunghill puddle H473.4.

Washings. — Woman becomes clean only after three w. W115.2.

Washington's Birthday: bees washed J1743.3.

Wasp released: grateful B376; seeking fame stings courtiers W116.5; steals yeast from old woman A1429.2; teaches man house-building A1445.2.2; twits butterfly with coming from chrysalis J312.1. — Burning w. nest J2102.5; demon as w. F401.3.4.1; devil as w. G303.3.3.4.3; enmity of spider and w. A2494.14.2; getting honey from w.-nest K1023; why w. has nest A2432.2; sexton arranges w.-nest so that parson sits on it X411.3; soul in form of w. E734.4; spider invites w. to rest on her white curtain K815.2; wedding of w. B285.7; witch recognized by seeing w. enter her mouth while asleep *G251.1.

Wasps as alleged interpreters of foreign language K137.1. — Army of w. B268.8.3; bridegroom driven from bridal chamber by w. T171; ground swallows demoniac w. F949.1.1; helpful w. B481.4; sham miracle: wallet (bee-hive) changes to w. K1975.1; snake rids himself of w. J2102.2.

Waste. — Demons live in w. mound F402.6.2; magic poem (satire) causes king to w. away D1402.15.

Wasted. — Bride test: making dress from w. flax H381.1; entire fortune w. before profligate begins his own adventures W131.1.

Wastefulness of God J2215.1; tabu C851. — Food disappears because of w. Q585.4; God punishes man's w. A2723.2; king reproached for w. J1289.15.

Wasting. — Ghost's body w. away E422.1.9.

Watch, see also **Vigil;** for devastating monster H1471; mistaken for the devil's eye J1781.2; runs indefinitely when lost X1755.1. — Hero keeps w. over earth A572; night w. with magic cats H1411.2.1; tailor asks soldier mount w. in his place P441.4; vow to w. at frightful place all night M156.

Watches. — Princess speaking all w. of night H343.0.1.

Watch-dog enticed away K318. — Dog created as w. for Jesus A1831.1; man in place of w. J1511.12; wild animal sold as w. K133; woman bitten by own w. K1651.

Watcher. — Buttocks as magic w. D1317.1; money exacted from w. who permits theft of wooden cow supposed to be real K443.4; sleepless w. magically put to sleep D1961; trickster entices wolves out of a stable by music: exacts money from their w. for his carelessness K443.5.

Watchers permitting theft blackmailed K443.3. — Actual rescuer, not w., gets woman J1179.12; master thief puts w. to sleep and cuts off their hair K331.2.1; money exacted from w. who permit chest to be stolen K443.3.1; prisoner kills his w. who enter to torture him K655.

Watchful. — Monster with magic w. eye put to sleep D1961.

Watching fairy at work tabu F348.8; fairies makes them leave F381.10. — Animal characteristics from contest in w. A2256; not w. sleeping princess long enough D759.9; tabu: w. game without aiding loser C882.

Watchman asleep as enemy approaches N396; of the gods A165.4. — Escape by teaching song to w. K606.0.2; giant's w. F531.6.16.1; owl as w. goes to sleep: does not see by day A2233.3; philosophical w. J2377; suitor outwits w. to meet lady T46; trickster w. exchanges gold for worthless bag K126.

Watchmen. — Coughing thief blinds w. D2062.2.6; demons as gods' w. A165.4.1; escape by singing w. to sleep K606.1.2.1; images to resemble w. K1883.8.

Water, see also **Fountains, Holy water, River, Springs, Stream, Wells;** barrier to otherworld *F141; becomes bloody D474.2; becomes rocks D471.10; becomes wine D477.1; from belly A1013; is best (riddle) H648.2; -bird A2442.2.6; boils when angry warrior is immersed in it F1041.16.6.6; -bottle H1023.2.2; cannibal G11.5; cannot be drawn to wash murdered body Q559.3; deity Q221.8; demon G424; disturbances at world's end A1063; -dragon D399.1; dripping off person becomes agates D475.4.8; drowns girl filling pitcher D1432.1; entrance to lower world F93; enters into giant's boots from above F531.3.1.1; that has neither fallen from heaven nor sprung from earth (horse's sweat) H1073; fairy (carries off woman) F322.0.1, (dies out of water) F321.1.5, (as foster mother) F311.3.1; fairies F212.0.1; falling on head death omen J2311.1.3; features A910ff.; fowl D169.1; from foot-washing sprinkled on threshold as protection against witch G272.13; freezes to form mountains A969.5; -gods S264.1.2; goddess A420.1, V1.6.2.0.1; gushes where strong man digs F639.1.2; -hen A2332.5.3, A2356.2.5; -hole D928; -horse B401.1; kept by monster so that mankind cannot use it A1111; of life *E80ff., F162.6.2; lighter than wood F716.2; from magic well causes person to dance D1415.1; -miller P443.0.1; -ousel A2411.2.1.2; pot A2320.6; from saint's washing as remedy D1500.1.18.4; -snakes A2531.1, A2532.1.1. B244.1.1, J2137.4; stands still before prince H71.10.2; -supply controlled by water spirit F420.4.9; for thieves in king's garden H1471.1; thrown on corpse to prevent return E431.2; transformed D478, (to milk) D478.1, (to money) D475.2.2; turns to blood as life token E761.1.1; turns into wine on Old Christmas M211.1.1; vanishes when man tries to drink D1647.1; -wheel A1441.3; of youth D1338.1.2; without father or mother (stagnant) H599.1. — Acquisition of w. A1429.3; adventures from seeking w. N785; angel created from w. A52.1.4; angel shows where to dig for w. V232.3.1; animal carries man across w. B551ff.; animals given drinking w. B391.4; animals that inhabit w. A2433.2.2; ashes of dead thrown on w. to prevent return E431.9; attempt to cross w. despite devil C12.5.8; audacious w. and continent husband T315.2.1; axe dropped in w.: modest choice Q3.1; ball falling into w. puts person into ogre's power G423; bathing in boiling w. without cooling it H1023.24; birth from w. T546; bitter w. grateful for being praised D1658.1.3; book dropped in w. by saint not wet F930.1; bringing w. from distant fountain more quickly than witch (task) H1109.1; when calf will not drink, peasant woman throws w. on its back J1903.1; cannibal sent for w. which magically recedes from him: victim escapes K605.1; cannibal sent for w. with vessel full of holes: victim escapes K605; captivity under w. R46; carrying w. jugs suitor test

H331.10; carrying w. in a sieve (task) H1023.2; casting into w. sack (barrel) as punishment Q467.1; cast-off wife thrown into w. S432; changeling thrown into w. and thus banished F321.1.4.1; clothes carry owner over w. D1524.2; cold w. warmed by saint D2144.3.1; collecting all drops of w. H1144.1; conception from drinking w. T512.3; contest in remaining under w. H1543; corpses thrown in w. E431.9.2; creator sent for w.: meantime animals assume their present forms A1713; why crabs live in w. A2433.6.3.1; cricket hears w. hiss on hot iron: learns his song A2272.1.2; dead spirits walk on w. G299.1; deity rewards animal for bringing him w. A2221.11; devil cannot cross running w. G303.16.19.13; devil as stream of w. G303.3.4.11; devil creates devils by casting w. behind himself G303.1.4.1; devil lives in w. G303.8.8; disenchantment by bathing (immersing) in w. D766.1; disenchantment by throwing object into w. D789.5; disenchantment by w. D766.1.1; divination by throwing objects into w. D1812.5.0.6; divination by w. *D1311.3.1.1; dragon controls w. supply B11.7.1; drinking bitter w. as chastity test H411.4.1; drops of w. make hollow in stone J67; druids dry up enemy's w. D2091.8.1; dupe crowded into the w.: drowns K892; dwarfs carry w. F451.3.4.8; earth rises from w. so saint can cross D2125.0.1; enigma on w. as only food H588.21; extraordinary bodies of w. F710ff.; fairies made visible through use of magic w. F235.4.4; fairies teach mortal to walk under w. F345.1; fairies' palace undestroyed by w. F222.1.1; fairyland under w. F212; falcon brings w. of life B172.5; falling in love with reflection in w. T11.5; famished wolf asks sheep to bring him w. K2061.5; fearless hero frightened by being awakened by cold w. H1441; fettered monster kept just out of reach of w. A1074.5; filling bottomless w.-tube H1023.2.4; fire and w. mixed to make sacrifice J1952; fish carries man across w. B551.1; flies try to drink w. from elephant's ears J971; fool can live under w. P192.4; fool can walk on w. P192.3; foot touching w. frees king abducted by fairies N661; fool fills self with w. before feast J2178; forbidden body of w. C615ff.; fountain produced from drop of w. D1567.7; four rivers, rising in paradise, w. world A871.2; frog-woman disenchanted by sight of w. D789.3.1; ghost kills by spewing w. E268; ghost laid in w. E437.2; ghost laid by pushing into w. E446.5; ghost summoned by holy w. E386.1; giant killed by own death w. G527; giants live under w. F531.6.2.2; glass of w. breakfast for farmer's help W152.12.1; god of w. A420ff.; god's promise not to destroy world by w. A1011.3, A1113; going on w. tabu C751.4; head of corpse thrown on w. to prevent return E431.9.1; holy w. *V132; how much w. in river? H696.1.4; identification by hair found floating on w. H75.1; impounded w. A1111; land of dead across w. *E481.2; learn to swim before going into w. J2226; lies about w. features X1540; looking at w. tabu C315.3; not to let ball fall into w. *C41.2; literal numskull throws w. on roasting pig J2461.1.3; magic cow from w. world B184.2.2.2; magic body of w. *D910ff.; magic healing w. *D1500.1.18; magic horse from w. world B184.1.3; magic land and w. vehicle D1533.1; magic name brings w. D1766.7.2; magic object enables person to cross w. *D1524ff.; magic object permits man to walk on w. D1524.1; magic power in w. D1718.1; magic power to walk on w. *D2125.1; magic results from contact with w. D1788.1; magic ring loses power on w. D877.1; magic sight by looking into glass of w. D1821.3.7.1; magic staff draws w. from stone D1549.5; magic w. *D1242.1, (protects) D1380.5; man can breathe nine days under w. F691; man proof against boiling w. D1841.2; man made from w. A1261; man stays under w. for long period X1737; man transformed to w. D283; man who does not know how to pray so holy that he walks on w. V51.1; man will not move in bed when w. drops in his eyes W111.1.3; mankind emerges from w. A1232.2.1; mare from w. world offended, disappears C918; mermaid entices people into w. B81.3.1; milk sack transformed to sheet of w. D494.5.1; monkey jumps into w. after butterfly J2133.10; moon is w. slung into sky A741.1; much w. compressed into small ditch D491.3; why muskrats live in w. A2433.3.10; numskull buys w. at market J2478; ogre draws victims under w. G336; ogre magically produces w. N812.6; ogress lives in w. G639; origin of fresh w. welling up in sea A925.4; origin of scum on stagnant w. A2847; ordeal by w. H222ff.; otherworlds under and beyond w. F141.0.1; oversalting food of giant so that he must go outside for w. K337; why oyster lives in salt w. A2433.6.2; people in otherworld pour w. into tub full of holes *F171.6.2; permission refused to drink from w. tank W155.5; person lives on w. for year F1033.1; person thrown into the w. and abandoned *S142; picking up w. thrown on ground no harder than undoing of slander J84; poisonous w. created by devil A63.7.1; pouring w. into his inkwell J1176.1; pouring w. on fire witch protection G272.8; power to walk to nearest w. F651; primeval w. A810ff.; princess stepping in w. tabu C567.2; prisoner has drunk w. furnished by the king and thus become king's guest J1183.1; quest for marvelous w. H1321; question (on quest): when will a certain w. animal be freed from an annoyance? H1292.9; rain produced by pouring w. *D2143.1.1; reflection in w. thought to be original of thing reflected J1791; reincarnation as w. E636; remarkable pourer of w. F636.3; remarkable power to walk straight to nearest w. F651; remedy for lack of w. in certain place overheard in conversation of animals (demons) N452.1; repression of lust through sitting in w. T317.1; residence in w. F562.3; resuscitation by w. E80.3; riddle: how much w. is in the sea? H696.1; rock becomes w. D452.1.10; sacrifice to secure w. supply S263.3; saint unhurt by boiling w. D1841.2.1; sea w. mixes with fresh at world's end A1063.2; serpent releases swallowed up w. supply *F914.1; sex changes after w. crossing D10.2; separation of persons caused by looking for w. N311; sitting in w. as penance Q541.1; sky consists of w. A702.1; Solomon refuses w. of immortality for himself J369.1; soul of w. E701.2; sound of w. mistaken for monster K1725.2; special power of chaste woman (carrying w. in a sieve) *H413.3; (making ball of w.) H413.2; spirit drinks w. supply dry G346.4; standing in w. for forty days as penance Q541.2; statues animated by w. or wind F855.2; stealing magic healing w. H1151.21; stone sheds w. at perjury H251.2.2; stroke of staff brings w. from rock *D1567.6; supplying w. in land where it is lacking (task) H1138; tabu broken, w. withdrawn from lake C939.1; tabu to enter w. during menses C141.3; tabus on drinking w. C273; task: carrying w. in leaky vessel H1023.2.1; touching w. tabu C532; touching w. in fairyland tabu F378.2; transformation by applying w. D562.1; transformation by crossing w. D574; transformation by touching w. D565.6; transformation to pool of w. D283.1; transformation when one expresses astonishment at smith drawing w. in an eggshell D512.1; transformation: w. to milk C479.7; treasure hidden under w. N513; tree pulled down in order to give it w. to drink J1973; trolls' horses w. at peasant's well F241.1.2.1; troubled w. as life token E761.6.1; true bride pushed into w. by false K1911.2.2; use of w. after call of nature tabu C725.1; vari-colored w. in well F718.2; victim pushed into w. K925.1; walking upon w. without wetting self D1841.4.3; wall of w. controlled D2151.0.3; wild hunt appears by body of w. E501.12.4; wine needs no further w. J125.1; wind raised by troubling vessel of w. D2142.1.4; wisdom from dream: the leper with the cup of w. J157.1; woman with newly-drawn w. good omen D1812.5.2.2.1; woman pushes lover into w. K1645.

Waters follow footsteps of one throwing flower D1547.2; made to dry up D2151.0.2; magically divide and close *D1551ff.; magically pursue man D1432; react to poet's words F996; rise to drown wrongdoer F930.2; turn aside for holy man D1841.4.3.1. — Cupbearer of the gods controls w. A165.3.2; escape from drowning by drying up all w. D2165.2; establishment of present order: w. A1110ff.; extraordinary occurrences concerning seas or w. F930ff.; fairies defile w. F369.2; magic control of w. *D2151ff.; magic w. and medicines *D1240ff.; quest for glass of all w. H1377.1; saint regulates temperature of w. D2151.0.1; wild huntsman w. his horse *E501.15.7; woman created from offerings on the w. A1275.5.

Watercress. — Conception from eating w. T511.2.2.

Waterfall as otherworld barrier F141.4. — Dragon's home beneath w. B11.3.1.2; giant's home beneath w. F531.6.2.2.3; ogre draws girl over w. G426; throwing into w. as punishment Q467.4.

Watermelon. — Lie: large w. X1411.1.1.

Water-monster G308.2; allows saint to place cauldron on head K2314.2.1; attacks man B877.1.1; tries to pull horse into water K1022.2.1. — Horned w. B68.

Water-monsters lick saint's feet B251.2.6.1.

Waternut. — Resuscitation with w. E181.1.1.

Waterskin. — Rain from w. in sky A1131.4.1; thunder from w. dragged along sky A1142.8.

Water-spirit. — Helpful w. N815.0.2; mythical horse belonging to w. B19.3.2; reincarnation as w. E653.1; sacrifice to w. S263.3.

Water-spirits *F420ff. — Magic object summons w. D1421.2; not to offend w. *C41.

Watersprite transformed to flood D283.3.

Watered milk sold K287; wine J1312.

Watering cow by pouring water over it J2465.1.1. — Contest in causing mouth w. H509.2; crawling on knees and w. a dry staff until it blooms Q521.1.1.

Wattle. — Building home w. at a time J67.1; silver w. F163.3.4, (in otherworld dwelling) F165.3.4.

Waumpaus F401.3.3.1.

Wave. — "He who throws himself against w. is overthrown" J21.52.9; homesick w. J1875.3; magic w. D911.1; man becomes ocean w. D283.5; roaring w. good omen D1812.5.2.7; saint rides blessed w. D2125.1.1.1; sand w. advances upon city Q552.14.3; singing of w. gives supernatural information D1310.7; tidal w. C984.4, (marks death place) A913.1.

Waves answer roar of magic shield D1549.10; blown by mighty blower F622.2; break caul of abandoned child N655; as daughters or widows of sea-god A423; form high wall around otherworld isle F141.3; as sea-god's horses Z118.2; as tresses of sea-god's wife Z118.1. — Binding w. of the sea (task) H1137; count only the w. before you J311.1; counting the w. H1144.2; dashing w. don't touch saint D2151.3.2; deformity cured by w. F959.2.1; extraordinary behavior of w. F931.4; fairy chariot rides w. F242.1.2; fiery, then icy w. around Judas E489.7; god drives chariot over w. A171.0.1; homeland sinks beneath w. F944.2; magic control of w. D2151.3; magic transportation by w. D2125.1.1; origin of sea w. A925.1, A1116; rabbits afraid of w. J1812.2; roaring of w. ill omen D1812.5.1.24; Virgin Mary saves devotee from w. V268.2.

Waving. — Resuscitation by w. magic object E74.

Wax figure comes to life D435.1.4; turned into earth D479.6. — Bees build church of w. to contain consecrated host B259.4; building w. replica of castle H1133.6; castle of w., shining like gold F771.1.8; creation of bee to provide w. for candles in church A2012.1; ears stopped with w. to avoid enchanting song J672.1; hare (jackal) makes horns of w. and poses as horned animal K1991; hero rides on w. elephant B557.11.1; resuscitation by w. from deer's ear E115.

Waxing of moon A755.4. — Magic w. and waning of strength D1836; sacrifice allows moon's w. A755.3.1.

Way, see also **Path;** to otherworld hard to find F150.1; short yet long J21.5.3; through the world is longest (riddle) H644.1. — Bird shows w. (by dropping feathers every seven steps) *B151.2.0.1, (by singing) B151.2.0.3; devil's house is visible on the w. to hell G303.8.3.3; false bride takes true bride's place on the w. to the wedding K1911.1.1; marking w. in unfamiliar country J765; short, dangerous vs. long, sure w. J266; women refuse to show God the w. A1372.8.

Wazir fulfills prophecy, murders rajah M370.1.1.

Weak fatally interfere in quarrel J2143; fear company of strong J425; son condemned to be brothers' servant M438.5. — Association of strong and w. J420ff.; dwarfs are w. F451.3.9; foolishness of alliances with w. J682; only w.-minded person may unearth a treasure N551.1; three w. things are strongest Z71.1.14; triumph of w. L300—L399; wise fear of w. for strong J613.

Weakest. — Defences by strengthening one's own w. spot J672.

Weakness from seeing nude woman C942.3. — Clever use of human w. J1672; fairy music causes w. F262.3.7; fairies cause w. F362.3; magic object gives w. *D1336ff.; magic w. *D1837; phantom women cause w. F585.3; sickness or w. for breaking tabu *C940ff.; spies' false report of enemies' w. K2363; spirit causes w. F402.1.6; unique source of w. Z312.3.

Wealth, see also **Treasure;** can't be taken with you after death J912.3; gained by seeming to be in the king's confidence K1782; hidden to keep son from gambling N94; marries weaver to princess N141.4; is most important J707; and poverty U60ff.; is relative: beggar with horse, wife, or dog considered rich by poorer beggar U65; sacrificed for freedom, virtue J347; or wisdom more important? N141.2. — Acquisition of w. J706; animal's advice leads man to w. B562; animal helps man to w. and greatness *B580ff.; not to boast of w. C451; cannibal offers w. to save life G683; choice: free poverty or enslaved w. J211; consecrated bread brings w. D1465.1.1; contest of wisdom, w. J185; devil in each stone of church built with ill-gotten w. G303.8.4.2; diligence and economy bring w. J706.1; dispute of w., wisdom J461.7; enjoyment preferred to w. J484; girl gives up w. to flee lecherous man T320.5; giving away all one's w. J211.1.1; god of w. A473, (in bad company) J451.3; goodness preferred to w. J247; magic object as w. D1470ff.; magic w. D2100ff.; man aspiring to greater w. loses all N251.2; penniless bride pretends to w. K1911.5; pretended w. wins girl's love K1917.5; pseudo-magic w.-providing objects sold K111ff.; reasons for condemning w. Z71.1.16; secret w. betrayed by money left in borrowed money-scales *N478; show of w. induces enemy to surrender city K2365.2; uncharitable king loses w. Q595.3; wife sacrificed to procure w. S263.6.

Wealthy man as helper N835; suitor disguised as beggar tests bride H384.1.1. — Forget God, become w. J556.2; how to become w. J706.1.

Weaning children A1566.

Weapon as chastity index H435; miraculously removed from wound F959.3.4; transformed D454.9. — Accidental death through misdirected w. N337; bringing enemy without w. M234.2; death from falling on own w. N339.8; don't uncover w. in assembly J21.2.4; extraordinary w. F830ff.; father gives son w. to kill him with S22.3; girl asks lover for w., uses it against him K1218.5; god with w. A137.14; identification by broken w. H101; identification by matching w., wound H101.1; immovable w. D1654.4; infallible w. D1653.1ff.; king pays for imaginary w. K499.7; lightning w. of the gods A285.1; magic object renders w. useless

*D1414ff.; magic sickness from w. in head D2064.7; man as w. F628.2.7; man pinned in bed by w. caught in quilt N386.2; prophecy: death by particular w. M341.2.0.1; stick becomes w. D451.6.3; strong man uproots tree and uses it as w. F614.2; suitor test: lifting strong princess's giant w. H345.1; tabu: fire, w., dog together C887; thunder from God beating his w. A1142.5.1; unique deadly w. Z312; unique w. obtained through misrepresentation K362.0.1; vow not to flee from w. M155.3; walking on w. edge F679.3.

Weapons, see also **Arms;** P553; disguised to enter enemy's camp K2357.5; of the gods A157; from horse's bones B338; join in keen F994.2; confined by flying bits of hair in furious battle F1084.0.2; magically blown from hands D2086.3; magically dulled D2086; magically venomous D1402.7.0.1; procured for boy at birth T602. — Acquisition of w. A1459.1; broken w. magically restored D2163.1; concealed w. sent king kill servant K929.11; deception by hiding w. K818.4; destruction of enemy's w. J621; dwarfs make w. for gods F451.10.4; father dies in fire while taking down w. N339.8.1; feigned ignorance of hero's w. K1792.2; foolishness of surrendering w. J642; giant's enormous w. F531.4.5; hero wields many w. at once F628.5; hero's extraordinary w. A524.2; identification by w. H125; indentions on rocks from w. A972.5.4; identions on rock from w. of robbers A972.3.1.1; invisible w. D1655.1; invulnerability from w. D1841.5; iron disappears, w. cannot be made D2089.1; magic w. *D1080ff.; moon's wooden w. A759.1; origin of w. A1459.1; precocious child demands w. T615.5; princess hangs up w. of dead lover as continual reminder T85.2; prophecy: w. killing man to recount deed M359.1; reincarnated person identifies former w. H19.1.1; river in hell filled with w. A671.2.2.2, A672.3; seeing man not killed by w. tabu C319.2; stones become w. D452.1.11; strong hero tests w. F611.3.3; substituted w. win combat K97.2; sun's iron w. A739.9; tabus concerning w. C835.2ff.; thunder from w. of sky warriors A1142.6.1; women not to touch man's w. C181.3; worship of w. V1.9.2.

Wearing apparel for menses C146. — Bride test: w. deceased wife's clothes H363.1; clothes never w. out F821.8; correct w. of clothes suitor test H312.6; magic strength from w. ribbon D1835.4; penance: w. friar's cord on skin Q522.7.

Weary. — Death because people w. of life A1335.9.

Weasel as conjurer B191.1; induces cuckoo to give away secret, kills it K815.10; paints self to deceive mice J951.4. — Enmity of hyena and w. A2494.3.3; fairy as w. F234.1.14; man transformed to w. D124.1; snake and w. stop fighting in order to catch mouse W151.4; tabu to eat w. C221.1.1.6; wedding of mouse and w. B281.2.1; why w. is part black A2411.1.2.1.1; why w. is white with dark tip to tail A2411.1.2.1; soul in form of w. E731.4.

Weasel's. — Why tip of w. tail is black A2378.8.3.

Weather auguries D1812.0.15; changed on confession of deed D2140.3; in otherworld F161; signs D1812.5.0.15; to please one only J1041.1. — Ass

predicts w. B141.3; control of w. by saint's prayers D2140.1; effect of
the four winds on w. A1127.1; establishment of w. phenomena *A1130ff.;
extraordinary sky and w. phenomena F790ff.; farmer as w. predictor
L144.2; fault-finding with God over w. Q312.4; favorable w. reward for
good law Q176; futility of w. prophecies M398; good w. for one foul for
another U148; god of w. A280ff.; hot w. from hole in hell A1137; lies
about w. X1600; liveable w. from rain-god, wind-god A287.0.1; magic
object controls w. D1548; magic w. phenomena *D900ff.; making w.
calm as suitor task H335.6; man who asks for good w. given a box full
of hornets J2327; origin of wintry w. A1135; pursuers aided by magic w.
R236; sacrifice for good w. V17.4; saint as w. prophet V223.6.1; sham
wise man predicting w. K1956.9; shaman's wife controls w. D2140.2;
slight inconvenience in w., large gain J355; soul as w. phenomena E744ff.;
wild hunt as w. omen E501.20.3; witch produces clear w. G283.4; witches
have control over w. G283.

Weaver hero L113.3; laments old poverty L217.1; married to princess
N141.4; married to princess betrays identity H38.2.4; outwits tax
J1289.13; poses as deity K1969.4.1; poses as king to seduce K1315.14;
prefers master with one hedgehog J229.8.1; throws himself into the ranks
and holds them (riddle) H581.3. — Thieves set up w. as prince K1952.7.

Weavers P445. — Fairies as w. F271.4.2; jokes on w. X251.

Weaver-bird. — Enmity of woodpecker and w. A2494.13.8; why head of
w. is small A2320.1.1.

Weaving cloth from two threads (task) H1022.1; of the Fates A463.1.1;
large amount by specified time H1092.0.1; love charms D1355.18.1;
magic cloth H383.2.2; mantle from single sheep's wool H1022.4.2; silk
shirt from hair (task) H1021.6; shirt from piece of thread H1022.2.2;
shoes on pilgrimage tabu C99.2. — Contest in w. A2091.1; dead person
w. E562; dwarfs w. F455.3.4; false bride unable to finish w. H35.3.1;
goddess of w. A451.3.1; husband behind saint's statue advises wife about
w. K1971.4; origin of w. A1453.2; prayers w. garment for Virgin V276.1.

Web. — Extraordinary w. of guts F847; man so small he dances in spider
w. F535.2.3; spider spins w. across sky F989.21; spider-w. sky-rope
F51.1.1; suitors put off till w. is woven K1227.2.

Webs. — Islands from w. woven by primeval spiders A955.7; origin of
floating w. in summer A2815.

Wedding, see also **Bride, Marriage;** ceremony T135; of dead E495; dress to
go through ring H355.6; funeral on same day V65.3; to guard as condition of release K612; of mortal and fairy F303; tabus C117. — Attention
drawn by helpful animal's theft of food from w. table H151.2; big w.
X1071; bridegroom's ignorance on w. night J1744.1; brothers reunited at
w. N733.5; chains involving w. Z31.1; child born on w. night J1276.2.1;
curse on w. night M412.2; dead lover appears at w. E214.1; deaf peasant:
w. invitation X111.4; deity assists at w. A185.5; devil plays fiddle at
w. G303.9.8.2; devil's w. feast for woman who hanged herself

G303.25.17.3; drunk man at w. X813; dupe persuaded to play for w. party K844; dwarfs invisibly attend w. or christening feasts of mortals F451.5.17; escape by deceptive w. preparations K536.1; fairy slighted at son's w. F361.1.2.1; fairy runs away from w. F301.8; fairy w. F264; false bride takes true bride's place on way to w. K1911.1.1; feigned w. feast to deceive cuckold K1527; giant invited to plentiful w. feast F531.6.8.4.1; girl hidden to postpone w. R53.3; groom killed on w. night N339.4; hero in menial disguise at heroine's w. K1816.0.3.1; husband returns home just in time to forestall wife's w. to another N681; invisible troll attends w. F455.5.2; lenders never refuse money for w. V411.4; liquor at first w. feast A1427.0.3; lover steals bride from w. with unwelcome suitor K1371.1; man unfaithful on w. night T245; old beggar transforms w. party into wolves T155; origin of w. ceremony A1555.1; prince invites angel to w. C13.1; prophecy: death on w. day M341.1.1; prophecy of particular perils to prince on w. journey M352; quest to bring Soma to w. H1285.1; son named successor at w. P17.0.2.1; suitor sent from one relation to another for consent to w. Z31.1; sun and moon hero's w. presents A759.2; thief bribed to leave w. J1392.5; three deformed witches invited to w. in exchange for help *M233; transformation of w. party to marble statues D231.2.1.

Weddings. — Animal w. *B280ff.; dwarfs celebrate w. and christenings of their own F451.6.3.2; happenings at w. *T150ff.; matchmakers arrange w. T53.0.1; spirits borrow at w. F417.1.

Wedge test H1532. — Dupe puts hand (paws) in w. K1111; magic cranberry opens w. and frees hero D1564.5.

Wednesday as auspicious day N127.2; unlucky day N128.2. — Pun on Wesley and W. X111.15.

Wednesdays. — Fountain gives water on W. and Fridays F716.1.

Wee. — There was a w. w. woman who had a w. w. cow, etc. Z39.2.

Weed. — Crossing w.-filled stream H1197.

Weeds for divination D1311.13.2; spoil harvest of too rich men L482.2. — Magic w. D965.18; origin of w. A2688ff.

Weeding garden from rocking chair W111.5.13.

Week. — Forgetful man counts days of w. Z24; horse bought for each w. day (one for each day of year) H1117; message after w. J2192.1; mortal wins fairies' gratitude by joining in their song and completing it by adding names of days of w. F331.3; seven w. days have passed since time of Adam (riddle) H706.1; tabu: feasting for a w. C230.1; transformation each w. D622.

Weep. — Crane will not w. at crucifixion A2231.2.1; dwarfs w. F451.6.7; only one person refuses to w. at hero's death Z351; toad refuses to w. over its dead children: dries up when dead A2231.8.

Weeping animal B214.4; bitch K1351; coin J1875.4; dead man E551; of future suicide in mother's womb T575.1.2; ghost E402.1.1.6; horse B301.4.2, B736.2; man turned into owl: still bewails A2261.5; rocks F801;

at sins of the world U15.1; statue D1625; tabus G482; for thief J1142.4; -willow's curse A2776.2. — Animals w. B736ff.; ascetic w. V462.3; birds w. in sympathy B303.1; dead father stops daughter's w. E327.1; disenchantment by w. jug of tears D753.2; disguise as w. woman K1836.4; divinity w. A194.1; ghost summoned by w. E381; god summoned by w. A189.2; hardness of heart prevents w. W155.3; horse w. for saint's death B301.4.1.1; illiterate pretends to be w. over book K1795; magic w. object D1618; parson preaches so that half congregation is w. and half laughing X416; people w. at child's birth P617; prodigious w. of saint F1051; queen shames cowards for w. W121.4; resuscitation by w. E58; return from dead to stop w. *E361; Satan w. G303.9.8.10; sham miracle: w. painting of Virgin K1972.2; soul w. as it leaves body E722.2.7; not too much w. for dead *C762.2.

Weevil. — Reincarnation as w. E616.4.

Weigh. — How much does the moon w. (riddle) H691.1.2.

Weighed. — Souls w. at Judgment Day E751.1; stolen meat and w. cat J1611.

Weighing elephant as test of resourcefulness H506.1; fire H1145.1; mountain as task H1149.8; princess against flower H455; witch against Bible H234. — Fortune w. man's balance N111.3.2; princess can't marry anyone w. more than she T69.2.2.

Weight of bodily member chosen rather than its loss J341. — Castration to put on w. J1919.5.3; great w. of witch's corpse G259.4; light w. person F584; magic suspension of w. D1691; riddles of w. H691ff.; "Time" overpowered when w. is taken from his clock Z122.1; trickster threatens to throw w. into cloud K1746.

Weights. — Handling w. loudly enough to outwit robbers K432.2; origin of w. and measures A1471.2; reduced prices but false w. K286; use of false w. punished Q274.3.

Weighted order-cards J1382.2. — Penance: pilgrimage with hands and loins w. with iron Q522.4.

Weinsberg. — Women of W. J1545.4.1.

Welcome to the clothes J1561.3. — Birds w. saint B251.2.5; enigmatic w. of host H595; fish w. saint B251.2.2; umbrellas w. bride A1555.3.

Welfare. — Wraith investigates w. of absent person E723.4.6.

Well entrance to lower world F93.0.2.1; in hell A671.4; indicates life span D1663.5; of life and death D1663.3; located under sea F718.1; magically transported D2136.7; man made to believe that he is sick J2317; in midst of earth from which rivers spring A875.2; of oil runs into river F932.4; polluted by blood D1563.2.2.1; produced by magic D926.1; as refuge R317; rises to aid holy person F933.1.3; rises for sheep only for rightful owner H251.3.9.2; in sea F711.4.2; shines at night D1645.9. — Abandonment in w. S146.1; animal rescues man from w. B547.1; animals refuse to help dig w. and are punished A2233.1; boy protected by Virgin survives week in w. V268.1; bringing w. to king (task) H1023.25; bringing whole w. K1741.3; captivity in w. R41.3.4; child put down into w. instead of bucket

J2175.3; children said to come from w. T589.6.4; cursing by means of w. D2175.1; demons live in w. F402.6.3; devil drinks church w. dry G303.9.9.14; devil's w. G303.10.19; dragon dips wounds in holy w., is healed B11.12.1.2; drawing bucket of w. water without rope H1023.20; drinking from fairyland w. tabu F378.4; dupe sent to w., pushed in K831.1.1; dupe tricked into w. K735.5, K1078; extraordinary w. F718; fairyland entered through w. F212.1; forbidden w. C623; frogs decide not to jump into w. J752.1; ghost haunts w. E285; girl drowned in w. as river's origin A934.10; goats driven into w. J1959.1; holy water destroys veil over w. D1562.6; inexhaustible w. D1652.15; location of w. indicated by bell D1314.4.1; looking at w. tabu C315.4; magic healing w. D1500.1.1.1; magic stones from holy w. D1382.1.0.1; magic w. *D926; magic wisdom from drinking of w. D1811.1.2; man falling into w. kills cobra N624; man fishes up two blind women from w. F1065; miraculous w. yields milk, beer, wine D925.0.2; mother cuts off heads of w. to cure sick (riddle) H583.4.3; numskull tries to dig up w. J1933; object dropped into w. leads to adventures N777.2; one should let w. enough alone J513; otherworld at bottom of w. F133.5; penance: being locked in w. and key thrown into water Q544; person follows magic receding w. D1420.2; person pushed into w. rescued R131.3.3.1; prophecy inscribed on w. M302.6; pushing into w. as punishment Q465.3; queen pushes husband into w. K2213.2.1; rescue from w. R141; rivers from mythical w. A934.8; saint warns against poisoned w. V223.2; saving self from falling into w. J21.34; sick hung in w. to cool off J2412.6; star-gazer falls into w. J2133.8; swans from fowl fed in Urd's w. A1981.0.1; thief sent into w. by trickster K345.2; trickster cheats rescuers into digging his w. K474; troll's horses water at peasant's w. F241.1.2.1; waiting at w. for thief J2214.3; water cannot be drawn from w. to wash murdered body Q559.3; wethers leap from w. B184.6.1; wolf descends into w. in one bucket and rescues fox in other K651; wolf tries to drink w. dry to get cheese J1791.3.1; world at bottom of w. F725.9.

Wells break forth at Christ's birth A941.5.0.2; in otherworld F162.5. — Cursing w. D1792.2; father's counsel: the four w. H588.8; first w. dug A1429.3.1; magic control of w. D2151.6; magic results from sacrifices at trees and w. D1766.2.1; ogre polluting w. G584; plague from Jews' poisoning w. V362; sacred w. V134; selling old oil w. for post holes X1761.1; three w. under three roots of earth-tree A878.1.2; why water from w. not drunk? H1292.1.1.

Welsh. — Fairies are W. cursed by St. Patrick F251.13.

Wen. — Hero breaking w. causes wall to fall X959.1.

Wench. — Devil as black w. G303.3.1.12.3; rakshasa in form of w. G369.1.5.

Wer-bear D113.2.1.

Wer-crocodile D194.0.1.

Wer-tiger D112.2.1. — Marriage to w. N399.3.

Wer-tigers. — Village of w. B221.6.1.

Werwolf *D113.1.1; recognized by man's clothes H64.2; with thread in teeth H64.1. — Boy saved by w. R169.3; magic axe keeps out w. D1385.5.2; not to look at w. C311.1.4; transformation to w. on Fridays D622.1.

Werwolves hold mass *V49.1.

Wesley. — Pun on W. and Wednesday X111.15.

West forbidden direction C614.13; wind exhausted from fleeing deity A1127.2. — Castle east of sun and w. of moon F771.3.2; divinity's departure for w. A561; female god invoked in w. A183.1; land of dead in w. E481.6.2; otherworld in w. A692.1, F136.2; sun travels from w. to east F961.1.2.

Westward. — Mountains push water w. A914.

Wet. — Ascetic sleeps in w. sheet V462.5.1.2; book dropped in water by saint not w. F930.1; feeding pigs w. meal J2465.1; man proof against w. from rain D1841.4.1; person proof against w. from snow D1841.4.2; resuscitation by w. cloth on corpse E80.2; why earth becomes warm and w.: underground vessels steaming A857.1.

Wet-nurse. — Own mother as exposed child's w. S351.0.1.

Wet-nurses. — Diabolical child kills his w. T614.

Wether. — Purple w. B731.9.

Wethers leap from well B184.6.1.

Wetting. — Adam created five devils by w. five fingers with dew and shaking them behind him G303.1.5; dipping water without w. dipper H1046.1; ferrying across river without w. feet H1046; magic causes bed w. D1379.4.

Whale boat *R245; carrying man shakes him off when struck M205.1.1.1; fights monster pursuing saint B523.2; with golden teeth B101.5; husband makes wife impervious to sea D1841.4.5; as messenger B291.4.3; raises back to help voyaging clerics land B256.12; thought to be an island J1761.1; transformed to skull D421.7.1. — Artificial w. made as strategem K922; disenchantment by eating w. D764.5; dolphin and w. scorn crab as peacemaker J411.6; giant w. B874.3ff.; helpful w. B472; killing sacred w. Q211.6.2; man kills w. which carried him across sea W154.5.1.1; man transformed to w. D127.3; marriage to w. B603; origin of w. A2135; people pelt each other with w. meat J2195; Jonah and the w. the walking tomb with the living tenant H821; raven inside w. F911.2.1; reincarnation as w. E617.4; witch killed as w. G252.1; witch rides on w. G241.1.5; witch as w. G211.7.1.

Whale's — Ascetic lives on w. back V462.10; flood from w. vomit A1013.1; foxes killed in w. house K728; magic object in w. heart D849.5.1.

Whales disgorge gold B583.1; rescue drowning king who planned their death W154.9.1. — Giant eats w. F531.3.4.3; giant fishes w. F531.3.12.2; monster w. of human parentage G308.8; why some w. die on land: first whale did so A2211.4.

What should I have done (said)? J2461.

Wheat dough eaten by bitch becomes nobleman A1656.1; rice and dal dispute superiority J461.5; transformed to barley D451.2.2; undamaged by swift runner F681.12. — Bare hillside becomes w. field at Christ's presence V211.1.8.3; birth from w. T543.6.1; why grain of w. is divided A2793.2; inexhaustible w. D1652.1.3.3, (sack) D1472.1.22.2; magic w. *D1033.2; martyrs called red w. Z141.2.1; mill will not grind stolen w. D1318.15; numskull feeds his w. to frogs J1851.1.2; oats become w. D451.2.3; saint causes w. to ripen prematurely D2157.2.2; shower of w. F962.6.1; why w. must be planted one year, harvested the next A2793.2.1.

Wheel buried in doorstep to prevent deviltry D1385.10; followed to otherworld F159.3; symbol A137.3.1. — Carrying a wagon axle which has broken a w. (task) H1183; celestial bodies attached to w. in heaven A702.3.1; destructive rolling w. D1207.1; devil in form of w. on wagon G303.3.4.1; devil helps man place cart w. when it becomes unfastened G303.22.4; earth w.-shaped and boundless A875; Fortune's w. N111.3; get up and put your shoulder to the w. J1034; ghost as glowing w. E421.3.1; giant rolls like w. F531.6.17.6; glowing w. thought to be devil J1781.3; god with w. A137.3; Ixion lashed to revolving w. Q501.5; magic w. *D1207, (at otherworld door) F165.1.0.2; man transformed to w. D256; origin of water w. A1441.3; punishment: breaking upon a w. Q423; revolving w. at otherworld entrance F156.3; slaughter from w. rolling over Europe M341.2.20; victim bound to bladed w. S181.1.

Wheels. — Divination from sound of chariot w. D1812.5.0.12; dupe waits for rear w. to overtake front w. J2066.7; fiery w. in hell A671.2.4.6; god's throne on w. A152.3; king given three w. to control his anger J571.2; ship on w. F841.3.2; spirit makes w. come off wagon F473.6.6.

Wheelbarrow too large to leave shed J2199.2. — Fright at creaking of w. J2615; mad w. J1887.

Whelp leaps through hound F916.2. — King's vision of w. V515.2.1.1; magic w. kills hound B182.1.3.1.

Whetstone among best of stones (riddle) H659.3.1.

Whetting knife: whole blade whetted away K1418. — Devil's aid invoked in w. scythe C12.3; ogress w. teeth to kill captive G83.1; razor w. itself D1601.8.

Whimbrel sends mate to death in cave K813.1.

Whining. — Father kills sons for w. S11.3.3.2.

Whip. — Caves from w. in ground A2825; ghost beats man with w. E261.5; god creates the devil by striking a stone with his w. G303.1.1.4; lie: remarkable user of w. X1002; lightning as god's w. A1141.4; magic w. *D1208; serpent as saint's w. B292.12; sham-dead roused with w. J2311.12; snake cracks self like w. B765.10; snake mistaken for w. J1761.6.1.

Whips. — Origin of horse-w. A1459.1.5; person beaten by w. for breaking tabu C982.

Whipping causes changeling to betray his nature F321.1.1.7; ogre to death G512.8.4; reproves quarrelsome wife T256.3. — Anticipatory w. by schoolmaster J2175.1; tabu on w. magic horse C762.3.

Whirled. — Prisoner w. away in fire R122.1.

Whirlpool. — Devil disappears in w. G303.17.2.2; ebb-tide goes to great w. A913.3; magic calming of w. D2151.4; rubies in w. D1467.2.

Whirlpools. — Nine w. of world Z71.6.2.

Whirlwind as ghost's vehicle E581.1. — Abduction by w. R17; devil as w. G303.3.4.4.1; devil comes in w. G303.6.3.2; god of w. A282.1; magic journey by throwing knife into w. *D2121.8; man transformed to w. D281.1.1; reincarnation as w. E641; soul as w. E744.3; troll rides in w. *F455.3.3.2; troll as w. F455.2.9; witch flies as w. G242.2.

Whiskers. — Cock's w. (cumulative tale) Z43; husband's w. gone, mistaken for lover J1485.1; wooer strokes w., "All of these are mine" K1917.7.

Whiskey, see also **Liquor, Wine.** — Dead man asks for w. E556.1.1; deceptive contest in drinking w. K82.3; origin of w. A1427.2.

Whispers. — Answering dead in w. E545.23.

Whispering in church attracts devil G303.24.1.8.

Whistle heralds devil's coming G303.6.3.5; for Senate ruler's son J553.2. — Alleged resuscitating w. sold K113.2; ghost summoned by blast on w. E384.3; magic w. *D1225, (vitalizes cockroach) D1594.6; one to blow w. J1382.1; one must not w. after sunset, else devil will go along with one G303.16.18; origin of w. A1461.5; priest, devil quarrel over w. M216.2.

Whistlers. — Seven w. are souls of Jews who crucified Christ A1715.3.

Whistling animals B214.2; at mass X442; in mine brings ill luck F456.1.2.1.1; tabu C480.1, C483.1. — Animal w. B214; fairies w. F262.7; ghost raised by w. E384.2; hail produced by w. tune D2143.4.1; maid w. as she brings in dessert W152.12.3; ogre w. G653; respite from death while captor is w. K551.3.2; snake w. B765.15; wind raised by w. D2142.1.6.

White god A124.2; horse in wild hunt E501.4.2.1; as magic color D1293.3; man made to believe that he is negro J2013.1; mango tree F811.3.2; mare thought to be church J1761.2; rat transformed to white-winged elephant D411.2.1; sea F711.3.1; sheep comes to upper world, black to lower F67; sheep-skin used as source of light J1961; woman as guardian of treasure N572.1; woman bears black child T562. — Black beans, w. soup J1291.1; black sheep turn w. F985.1; creation of w. horse A1881.1; why deer has w. mark on nose A2335.2.1; devil as w. stallion G303.3.3.5.3; devil in shape of w. bull G303.3.3.12; dwarf cave has ceiling of mineral w. as snow F451.4.3.3; dwarfs clad in w. F451.2.7.4; dwarfs have silvery w. hair F451.2.4.2; why end of fox's tail is w.

A2378.8.1; explaining "w." to blind man U173; fairies in w. clothes
F236.1.3; fairies ride w. horses F241.1.1.1; Fortuna half w., half black
N111.2.3; ghost in w. E422.4.3; ghost as w. horse E423.1.3.4; glorified
w. garment F821.6; magic leaves turn w. bird black D1337.2.1; magic
w. cow B184.2.0.1; mermaid's w. skin B81.9.5.1; mountain-men in w.
caps F460.1.4.1; negro tries in vain to be washed w. J511.1; no w. man
near, so belongings safe J1373; objects on one side of palisade in
otherworld garden black, on other w. F162.1.2.3; one cheek w., other
red F545.3.1; origin of w. man A1614.9; peasants fed w. bread demand
rye bread to which they are accustomed U135; person in w. mistaken
for ghost J1782.6; pill transformed to a w. rabbit D444.3; pretty w.
hands F552.3; purely w. boar H1331.2.1; red as blood, w. as snow
Z65.1; revenant as lady in w. E425.1.1; riddle (black and w. horses
chasing each other) H722.2, (king in red: courtiers in w.) H731.1,
(king in w., courtiers in w.) H731.2, (w. field, black seed) H741;
series: w. cock, red cock, black cock Z65.2; son forgets to spread
w. sails, prearranged signal of his safety N344; soul as black or w.
spirit over coffin E722.1.1; soul as w. E722.1.2; symbolic color: w.
Z142; treasure found by sprinkling ground with blood of w. cock
D2101.1; troops of black, w., and red soldiers F873.1; wild huntsman
with black fur cap and w. staff E501.8.6; wild huntsmen dressed in w.
E501.8.3; wish for wife red as blood, w. as snow, black as raven T11.6.
Whiter. — Angel w. than swan (riddle) H663.
Whitest. — Successful suitor must have w. hands H312.4.
Whitefish. — Enmity of w. and pike A2494.15.1.
Whitewashing weapons as disguise K1839.6.
Whitsuntide V70.2.
Whittington's cat N411.1; fortune foretold M312.
Whole. — Animals eaten by fairies become w. again *F243.3.1; build
shelter for the w. year J741; journey to otherworld where people are
made w. F125; with his w. heart: devil carries off judge M215.
Whore, see Prostitute.
Wicked burned in heaven E755.1.2; flatter death J814.4; son blinded
Q451.7.5; son confined on island Q433.9; souls eaten E752.9; woman
unable to endure presence of host at mass V39.2. — Animals leave w.,
go to pious master B292.0.2; devil carries off w. people R11.2.1;
failure of crops during reign of w. king Q552.3; return from dead to
slay w. person E232; supernatural manifestations at death of w. person
*Q550.1; two w. men put to fiery test, ask for third K528.3.
Wicket. — Going through w. gate tabu C614.2.
Widened. — River magically w. D2151.2.6.
Widow in armor routs would-be ravisher T320.3.1; may not remarry
T131.4; of ogre's victim at ogre's house G691.2; refuses second marriage
so her brother can not kill a second husband J482.1.2. — Bridegroom
buys w. cloth for bride Z140.4; buying w. cloth: his wife must be

widow J2301.2; devil marries w. who maltreats him G303.12.2; faithless w. T231; ghost visits w. and new husband E321.4; hypocritical, oversensitive w. K2052.4; killing self to make wife w. J2106; king advised to marry maid rather than w. J482; lifting power of w. prepared for suttee H479.1; marriage to rich master's w. N251.3; rich lord who robs poor w. of her cow chokes on first mouthful Q552.6.

Widow's meal J355.1; son as hero L111.3. — Ogre assumes form of w. husband K1919.2; rich man seizes poor w. cow U35.

Widows. — England must be full of w. J2214.11; why w. do not remarry T291.

Widowed. — Woman w. twenty-two times F1073.

Widower marries wife's sister P263.1; tells of his courtship, marriage, and death of his wife, all in a week Z24.1. — Cynic's comment on w. remarrying J1442.12.

Wife, see also **Adulteress, Marriage, Woman;** accused of plan to escape weeps and threatens suicide so as to allay suspicion and escape K579.1; as adviser J155.4; assigns husband tasks H934.1; banished S411; betraying husband likened to poison H592.2; behind tree advises husband (about his marital duties) K1971.6.1, (against having his wife work) K1971.4.1; brings bad luck N134.1.2; carried up tree to sky in bag in husband's teeth J2133.5.1; chooses father's side in feud P211; chosen instead of fairy mistress J414.1; confesses for husband V29.5; cures self by calling husband F950.2.1; curses husband, devil takes him C12.5.7; dead of neglect torments husband E221.5; demands parrot who has accused her B335.4; deceives husband with substituted bedmate K1843; dies so that husband's death may be postponed T211.1; dies of fright after husband relates her adultery J1147.1; dies on hearing of her husband's death F1041.1.1.2.2; disguised as fakir makes husband do her bidding K1814.3; dismisses maid who is husband's mistress and reforms husband J1112.2; drinks blood of slain husband P214; flees husband R227; follows written instructions J2516.3.1; forces husband to kill faithful dog B335.1.1; in disguise wooed by her faithless husband K1814; hangs self on tree: friends ask for shoot of tree J1442.11; and husband poison each other K1613.2; imprisoned to preserve chastity T381.0.2; makes gift to husband's mistress and reforms wayward husband J1112.1; makes her husband believe that he is dead J2311.0.1; misunderstands husband's remark, confesses N275.3; more merciful than blood relations P212; multiplies secret J2353; must be returned pregnant to first husband J1173.1; persuades husband (that she has returned immediately) J2315, (to have good tooth pulled) J2324; of philanderer gets revenge by having an affair herself K1510.2; purchased T52.5; rescues husband R152; rescuing husband from supernatural H923.1; resuscitated by turning around, placing head on brick E181.1; sacrificed to procure wealth S263.6; scares robbers, says husband is home D2031.6.3; substitutes for mistress K1223.3; substitutes for princess jailed with husband K1814.2; suicide believing husband dead N343.2.1; sold unwillingly by husband T292; surprises husband in adultery K1271.3.1; takes mistress's place in husband's bed K1843.2; takes servant's place and discovers husband's adultery K1585; tells way to otherworld F174.1; tempts husband as another woman H1556.4.2.1; tests H460ff.; ties husband to bed so lover can kill him K713.1.7; transformed to mistress D659.7; who saw double X121; as wager N2.6; your own only when with you J21.47. — Abandoned w. recognized H152.3; abducted w. leaves needle sign H119.2; advice on choosing w. as equal J21.31; animal as confederate of adulterous w. B598; animal helps quest for vanished w. B543.0.1; animal-husband killed, w. throws self into pyre B691; animal-w. eats husband G79.1; animal wins w. for his master B582.1.1; animals created while god Mahadeo quarrels with his w. A1758; bear makes woman his w. B601.1.1; boasting coward shown up by w. who masks as highwayman and robs him K1837.1; burial of living husband or w. with dead spouse S123.2; cast-forth w. (buried up to waist for seven years and despitefully used) Q456.1.1, (must sit at horse-block of palace and tell story to each newcomer and offer to carry him inside) Q482.4; chaste woman refers lover to his w. K1231.1; chaste woman sends man's own w. as substitute K1223.2.1; child promised: "what your w. has under her belt" S242.1; church his w. J1264.1; clever w. J1112, (gets money from those who attempt to seduce her) K443.2, (prevents husband's disinheritance) J1521.2.1; concealed w. N741.1; creator's w. A37.3; criminal's w. and children sold into slavery Q437.1; calumniated w. K2110.1; dead w. (haunts husband on second marriage) *E221.1; death of w. for breaking tabu C920.2; debtor's w. demanded T52.8; deceased w. marriage test H363; deceptive division of shared w. K171.7; deity's w. creates mosquitoes to drive husband from jungle A2034.1; departing husband assigns his w. tasks H922; deposit money secured by false order to banker's w. K362.6; deserted w. chokes departing husband K951.0.1; devil (gets into ark by hiding in shadow of w. of Noah) G303.23.1, (helps ugly man win w.) G303.22.7, (takes man's w.) C12.5.6, (tries to get man to kill his w.) G303.9.4.3; devil's w. G303.11.1; discovery w. is witch G250.1; disguised husband visits his w. K1813; disguised w. makes husband buy kiss K1814.4; disenchantment by w. D791.2.2; don't send w. on visit to parents J21.47.1; dove helps deity draw w. into net B582.2.5; dream of marriage with another's w. T11.3.2; druid discovers abducted w. D1816.5.1; eavesdropping w. hidden in bushes killed unwittingly by husband N322.2; exchanging w. with ox J2081.3; fairy lover abducts fairy w. of mortal F301.6; fairy mistress and mortal w. F302.5; fairy offers to disenchant mortal w. if man will marry her F302.3.2.2; fairy w. (converted into woman) F302.5.2.1, (deserts mortal husband for repulsive lover) F302.2.1; fairies steal man's w. and carry her to fairyland F322; faithful w. T210.1; false w. identified by breasts H79.6; familiar spirit reveals infidelity of man's w.

F403.2.3.5; father's counsel: marry a new w. every week H588.3; first w. insists husband take second T282.1; forcing w. tabu C164; forgotten w. recalled as she gives beggar food D2006.1.10; fortune of lucky w. N251.5; fox brings human w. fox-food H48.2; future w. met during magic sleep D1976.2; future w. revealed in dream D1812.3.3.9; god swallows his pregnant w. to prevent birth of son whom he fears M376; god swallows his w. and incorporates her into his own being F911.1.1; good w. makes domestic life H659.21; help from ogre's w. G530.1; hero hidden and ogre deceived by his w. G532; hero wakened from magic sleep by w. who has purchased place in his bed from false bride *D1978.4; hero's w. rescued by friend R169.5.1; horse lays head in lap of dead master's w. B301.4.3.1; host surrenders his w. to his guest P325; husband eats w. G77; husband magically forgets w. D2003.1; husband refuses to believe w. unfaithful J2342; husband and w. *P210ff., (burn their mouths) J1478, (disguised and brother and sister) K1839.14, (each receive money from different persons to bury the other, who is supposed to be dead) K482.1; husband answers behind statue when w. wants to know how to fool him K1971.1; husband arrives home just as w. is to marry another *N681; husband as God behind tree forces his w. to confess adultery *K1971.5; husband behind saint's statue advises w. to spin and weave K1971.4; husband fondles second w. in presence of first as punishment for adultery Q484; husband refuses to murder his wife for high honors, w. agrees to murder husband H492.1; husband substitutes leaky vessel so that his w. and paramour are drowned Q466.1; impoverished nobleman offers w. to ruler W11.7.1; jealous w. tells sister to look below: pushes her over cliff K832.1; jealous w. of god A164.7; judgment: man belongs to third w. J1171.3.1; king demands subject's w. P15.2; king gives own w. as reward P14.13; knight unsuccessfully tempted by host's w. T331.2; lazy w. W111.3ff.; lazy w. taken naked in bundle of straw to a wedding Q495.1; loss of w. for breaking tabu C932; love for captive w. rewarded Q56.1; love image grants w. D1595.1; lover humiliated after leaving w. T75.4; Lot's w., having had father and mother, is not dead like other mortals (riddle) H815; Lot's w. transformed to pillar of salt for breaking tabu C961.1; magic object stolen (by hero's w.) D861.5, (by rival for w.) D861.4; magic object from w. D815.8; man disregards priest's warning that he will seduce his w. J652.3; man betrayed into killing his w. K940.2; man calls w. "my swallow": she becomes swallow D511.1; man commends w. to devil (devil takes charge seriously) C12.4; man disguised as w. K521.4.1.4; man rescues his w. from fairyland F322.2; man to bring w. purse-full of sense *J163.2; man sends his naked w. on all-fours in tar and feathers K216.2; man with unfaithful w. comforted J882; man wins w. for friend P310.7; mistress sends man's own w. as substitute without his knowledge K1223.2; moon as w. to twelve sun brothers A753.1.4.2; mortal saves fairy's w. F337; mountain with w. F755.5; mountain w. has breasts so long that she throws them over her shoulder *F460.1.2; must surrender w. to sovereign J1511.19; not to offend (animal w.) C35, (supernatural w.) *C31ff.; obtaining w. on otherworld quest H1256; ogre's w. burned in his own oven G512.3.2.1; ogre's w. killed through other tricks G519.1; ogre's w. jealous G674; old w. provokes sparrow to speak, drop new wife K929.10; origin of w. self-sacrifice A1545.5.1; paramour hidden in chest taken to own w. K1216; peasant w. asks king riddles H561.1.0.1; persecuted w. *S410ff.; plant w. T117.10; polygamy so head w. may be quickly replaced T145.8; poor girl chosen as w. L143.1; poorly dressed woman chosen as w. L213.1; pregnant w. left in friend's charge H1558.9; priest's dead w. found alive J1179.10; prince envious of hero's w. assigns hero tasks H931.1; promise to lend w. for a day M267; propounder's w. helps solve riddle H574; punishment for banishing w. at paramour's wish Q248; punishment for stealing a w. Q252.1; punishment: winning as w. and then killing Q411.1; predestined w. T22.2; queen says man's condition dependent on w. S411.2.1; quest accomplished with aid of w. H1233.2.1; quest assigned by w. through appeal to husband's love for her H1212.2; quest for lost w. H1237; quest for three persons as stupid as his w. H1312.1; quest for vanished w. H1385.3; rainbow king's w. A791.5; rescue by captor's w. *R162; resuscitation of w. by husband giving up half his remaining life *E165; retorts between husband and w. J1540ff.; reward: any boon that may be asked: king's w. demanded Q115.1; second w. orders husband to persecute first S413.2; second w. serving as menial Q482.1.1; senior w. ugly but digilent, second beautiful but lazy T145.7; serpent directed by beautiful w. J155.1.1; sight of deformed witches causes man to release his w. from spinning duty J51; speaking beans rebuke w. for misdeed D1619.1; squaring accounts by shaving w. J2082; star-w. gives birth to human T111.2.1.1; not to steal w. of god C51.2.3; stupid w. J1701; sun and moon as husband and w. A736.1.4.2; supernatural w. summoned by bell T111.0.2; tabu: giving garment back to supernatural w. C31.10; tabu: stealing god's w. C51.2.3; talkative w. discredited J1151.1.1; task left by departing husband for w. to accomplish H1187; task performed with help of supernatural w. H974; tasks assigned before man may rescue w. from spirit world H923; tasks assigned by w. and paramour H916.3; thief disguised as owner's w. K311.8.1; treacherous w. abandoned by lover Q261.2.1; treacherous w. *K2213; tree as w. T461.3; trickster exacts beautiful w. from curious spectators K443.6.1; unborn daughter promised to snake as w. S222.2; unrestricted intercourse between husband and w. A1352.1; unexpected meeting of husband and w. N741; vanished w. rescued R133; vow never to be jealous of one's w. M137; why tortoise looks towards sky: seeks his w., a star A2351.5; wild boar once faithless w. A1422.3; wish for star w. C15.1.1; woman given to devastating monster as w. to appease it S262.1.

Wife's absurd actions deceive ghost E432.2; attendants on trip chase wrong man as suspected lover and miss real lover K1549.6; equivocal oath K1513; nose cut off, husband resuscitated E165.2; ring proof of unfaithfulness H94.0.1. — Caesar's scorn of his w. advice leads to disaster J155.3; dead w. friendly return E322ff.; death from hearing of w. death F1041.1.2.2.3; disguised husband wins faithless w. love K1813.1; dream warns emperor of w. faithlessness *D1813.1.1; exiled w. dearest possession J1545.4; ghost protects w. estate E236.6; husband attracted by w. power of healing: recognition follows H151.8; husband concealed in w. ear F1034.1; husband disguised as woman answers w. riddle H582.3; husband learns of w. fidelity N455.6; husband unwittingly instrumental in w. adultery K1544; king overlooks w. unfaithfulness rather than to cause troubles of state J221.1; man attempts to kill faithful serpent at w. instigation B335.1; man murdered at w. side K959.2.3; man undertakes to do his w. work J2431; moon eats w. corpse G27; painting on w. stomach chastity index H439.1.1; putting out w. eyes J2462.3; reward for w. fidelity Q83.1; searching for rival to w. beauty H1301.1.3; talkative w. tongue paralysed D2072.0.5.3; tasks imposed because of w. foolish boast H916.1.

Wives exchanged T141.2; with hair thought to be witches J1786.6; killed for large corpse-price K941.1.1. — Animals tested as w.: none accepted B600.1.1; begging for any punishment except two w. K583.1; characteristics of w. and husbands *T250ff.; common w. of man debate as to which has helped him most J461.2; custom of purchasing w. A1555.2; deceptive agreement to kill w. K944; friends agree to beating w. K1394; gullible wife believes report that each man may have many w. J1546; hero granted free access to men's w. A591; king has amours with great men's w. so as to learn secrets from them J155.2; king's seven w. pregnant seven years Z71.5.7; Krishna's three w. A164.3.1; limited number of w. for king P18.2; man sees w. in their former incarnations E601.1; many w. T145; Pleiades six repudiated w. A773.2; repeated transformations to deceive w. D616; shooting stars are unfaithful w. A788.5; supernatural w. carry off hero F174; unfaithful w. become edible animals A1422.0.1; various animals tried out as w. B600.1; wagers on w. or servants N10ff.; woman murders son's w. Q211.4.2.

Wig. — Exposure to ridicule when w. snatched off X52.1; taking off w. overawes Indians K547.2; transformation by w. D537.4.

Wild animal (finds his liberty better than tame animal's ease) L451, (sold as watch-dog) K133; animals (herded) B845, (lose their ferocity) A2531.0.1; beast transformed to person D310ff.; Hunt *E501ff.; man (captured and tamed) R1, (lives alone in wood like a beast) F567, (of noble birth) P55, (becomes normal) D92, (as king of animals) B240.3, (as prophet) M301.1, (as ravisher of women) T471.2, (released from captivity aids hero) G671, (son of woman and satyr who overpowers her) F611.1.3, (of superhuman strength) F619.1, (as wood spirit) F441.3. — Bridling a w. horse (task) H1154.3.1; devil as w. goose

G303.3.3.8; disappointed lover becomes w. man in woods T93.1; god of w. animals A443; helpful w. (beasts) B430ff., (duck) B469.4.1, (hog, boar) B443.5, (ox) B443.7; hero in service of w. man G672; magic object received from w. man D812.9; magic wisdom possessed by w. man D1719.2; Milky Way is the W. Hunt A778.1.1; man transformed to w. beast (mammal) D110ff.; person keeps w. pigs as if domesticated B845.1; reincarnation as w. animal E612; revenant as w. animal E423.2ff.; saint's bachall subdues w. animals D1442.3; smith promises to make horse w. K1181; strong hero sent for w. animals F615.2; strong man sent for w. horses brings them back F615.2.3; unexpected meeting with w. man N764; war between domestic and w. animals B262; why w. animals lose ferocity A2294.

Wild boar captured in church K731; given permission to squeal before wolf eats him K551.3.4; sharpens tusks when no enemy is in sight J674.1. — Blind w. in wild hunt E501.4.3.2; fairy in form of w. F234.1.3.1; great w. X1233.1.2; haunt of w. tabu C619.2; man reincarnated as w. E611.3.1; vow to kill w. alone at night M155.1; why tiger does not attack w. until latter is old: result of duel A2257.1.

Wildcat. — Enmity of hyena and w. A2494.3.5; how w. got mashed face A2213.2.1, A2330.1.

Wildcats. — Lies about w. X1212; why w. eat chickens A2435.3.15.

Wild goats. — Herdsman neglects his she-goats in favor of w. J345.1.

Wild goose's flight A2442.2.7.

Wilderness full of beasts as fear test H1408. — Garden becomes w. F975; penance in w. Q520.5.

Wilhelm Tell F661.3.

Wiliwili tree's shape A2785.1.

Will. — Against his w. J1285; angels to execute God's w. A52.0.1; choice of kings by divine w. *P11.1; ghost foils counterfeiting of w. E236.4.1; giants large or small at w. F531.6.5.2; hare's last w. U242.1; last w. unfulfilled, ghost returns E236.4; magic comb changes person's size at w. D1377.1; magic runes control person's w. D1379.1.1; rascal in dead man's bed makes dead man's w. K1854.1; servant impersonates dead master, makes false w. K1854; sons falsifying father's w., deceived K1628; transformation and disenchantment at w. D630ff.

Will-o'-the-Wisp F491. — Origin of w. A2817; soul as w. E742.2.

Willow. — Man marries spirit of w. tree F441.2.3.1.1; origin of weeping w. A2632.1, A2681.1; why bark of red w. is thin A2751.2.2; why w. bears fruit when fruit trees bear A2771.6; why w. flowers do not bear fruit A2771.10.

Willow-grouse's. — Origin of w. crest A2321.9.

Wind blows persons into woman's eye X941.4; continually blows from cave F757.2; cursed for hot breath L351.2; drives buffaloes for god A199.4; personified Z115; produced by magic D2142ff.; -spirit A1128.2; sued for damages Z115.1. — Animals killed by trickster's breaking w. F981.3; ass finds hidden w. B133.0.1.1; blowing w. as life token

E761.7.8; bringing back flour scattered by w. (task) H1136.1; cannibal breaks w. as means of attack G93; conception from w. T524; contest in enduring cold: w. overcomes frost H1541.2; contest of w. and sun L351; demon ship sails against the w. F411.3; devil (as w.) G303.3.4.4, (and the w. travel together) G303.6.3.3, (carries man through the air as swift as w.) G303.9.5.4, (destroys hunting party with terrible w.) G303.20.2; directions on quest given by sun, moon, w. and stars H1232; divination from sound of w. D1311.22; divination from w. D1812.5.0.15.1; dragon-king transformed to gust of w. D429.2.1; extraordinary w. at world's end A1067; extraordinary behavior of w. F963; fool frightened by stirring of the w. J2622; forgotten w. J755.1; gathering w. in fists H1136.2; god of w. A139.8.4, A282, A287.0.1, A1126; goddess of w. A282.0.1; great w. because of broken tabu C984.1; jinn appears from w. G307.1.1; lost w. found in hollow tree: has been banished and is needed by men A1122.3; love like w. in hot sun H592.1.1; magic object controls w. *D1543ff.; magic object from w. D814.1; magic w. *D906, (against fugitive) R236.4, (blows open church doors for pope's body) Q147.2, (causes arms to fall from warriors' hands) D1414.3; magic red w. devastates country D1408.2; man can keep together feathers in great w. F673; man turned to stone for cursing w. Q551.3.4.2; man's breath made from w. A1260.1.5; measuring gust of w. H1145.2; marvelous runner outstrips March w. F681.2; man transformed to w. D281.1; primeval earth hardened by w. A856.1; regulation of w. A1128; reeds bend before w. J832; sacrifice to w. V11.5; soul borne away on w. E722.2.2; spider thinks that it has held back the w. J953.9; stag becomes w. D421.5.1; statues animated by water or w. F855.2; strong hero engendered by the w. F611.1.9; sun, moon as offspring of goddess and w. A715.2; thief's excuse: the big w. J1391.1; tiger frightened by w. K1727; what is moistest? South w. H659.8; wild hunt disappears with blast of w. E501.16.3.

Winds guard otherworld F150.2.3. — Bag of w. C322.1; bringing w. from the whole world (task) H1136; culture hero tames w. in caves *A532; establishment of w. A1120ff.; flaming w. in hell A671.2.4.12; Indra separates w. trying to unite A1142.7; lies about w. X1610; regulation of w. A1128; saint controls w. D2140.1.1; witch raises w. G283.1.

Windbreak. — Spear as w. F834.6.

Winding. — Witch w. yarn G244.1.

Windmill thought to be holy cross J1789.1.

Window. — Breaking w. to let cold out J1819.2; couple found "living in darkness", cut w. J1738.6; princess pulled through prison w. by hand and freed R121.1; sky w. F56.

Windows in firmament shed light A1171.2; in heaven A661.0.6; in otherworld F165.3.5. — Extraordinary doors and w. F782ff.; ghost breaks w. E299.4; magic w. *D1145; wild hunt avoided by keeping in house with w. closed E501.17.5.3; sunlight carried into house without w. in baskets J2123; witches open w. G249.8.

Windpipe. — Murder by putting clod in person's w. K951.4.

Wine cellar entered by removing lock K317.2; -distilling wood F811.5.2; from flowers F979.9; issues from Christ's wound V211.5.1; personified Z139.3; as reward Q135; touched by heathen tabu C272.1; transformed to other object D477.0.1; used to bathe relics V221.0.1.2; needs no further water J125.1; -spilling host rebuked J1511.5. — Acquisition of w. A1428; carrying w. in basket X1756.1; at communion witches spit out w. over shoulder G285.1; country without w. F708.3; can drink only one kind of w. at a time J1511.15; consecrated w. (as magic cure) D1500.10.2, (used to discover treasure) N533.4; doctor forbids patient w., drinks himself J1433; dog turns water to w. B119.1; drinking w.-cellar empty (task) H1142.1; drinking w. tabu C272; dwarf's palm w. F451.3.4.9; everlasting w. odor D1612.13; first humans from drops of w. A1211.6; fool (lets w. run in cellar) J2176, (tries to dry up spilt w. with meal) J2176.1; father's counsel: on wishing to drink w. go to vat and drink it H588.4; fountain gives w. on feast days F716.1; fountain tasting of w. F716.1.1; four characteristics of w. A2851; host offers to send his guest a cask of w. which he has praised M206.1; host with overstock of sour w. spreads rumor of dragon at his house K484.2; identification by ring dropped in pitcher of w. H94.3; lake filled with palm w. A920.1.16; life token: w. turns to vinegar E761.6.5; magic knife stuck in tree causes w. to flow D1472.2.11; magic w. D1046; man strikes stone: w. flows D1472.1.2.1; man who only tasted w. W123.1; marvelous sensitiveness (w. shows through woman's white throat) F647.6, (w. tastes of corpse) F647.1; miser saves w. until it is strong W153.4; murder by leaving poisoned w. K929.1; odor of w. cask J34; other people's w. tastes best J1442.5; palace surrounded by rivers of w., rosewater, and honey F771.7; pig turns water into w. B184.3.2.2; priests drinking only one w. at a time J1511.15; repartee concerning w. J1310ff.; riddle: drink this w. which bird took to nest H806; river of w. F771.2.4.1; rivers of w. in otherworld *F162.2.2; rock produces w. D1472.1.2.2; sea aroma like w. F711.5; test: guessing nature of devil's w. glass H523.6; transformation: brine becomes w. D477.2; transformation by drinking w. D555.2; transformation by smelling w. D564.4; trickster sells mother's w. K499.1; trickster spits in w., given it K355.1; water becomes w. D477.1; water sold as w. in partitioned cask K476.3; well of w. D925.0.2, F162.5.1, F718.3; what is strongest? W. H631.8; where did he get w. J1321.1.

Wines. — Sickness ascribed to quarreling w. J1891.1.

Wing. — Music of bird's w. D2011.1.1.

Wings cut from flying mountains A1185; of dragon B11.2.6; of sun A726.2. — Angels' w. protect earth A1128.1; animal characteristics: w. A2377; ants ask God for w.: wind blows them away A2232.9; bird

gives shelter with w. B538.1; bird with w. of silver B101.1.1; birds beat
water with w. to honor saint B251.2.5; devil's w. G303.4.2; escape from
execution pyre by means of w. *R215; fairy comes into man's power when
he steals her w. *F302.4.2; flight on artificial w. *F1021.1; forest-spirits
with w. F441.4.4; fox's plan detected by crickets: cricket w. in his excrement K2061.10; hero enters maiden's tower by means of artificial w.
K1346; house in otherworld thatched with w. of birds F165.5; magic
birds cause sleep by shaking w. B172.9; magic object causes w. to
grow on person D1375.3; magic w. *D1022; origin of flying-fish's w.
A2136; owl's w. borrowed from rat A2241.2; person with w. F522;
raven singes feet: why its w. clap A2218.6; river contained under cock's
w. *D915.2; swan maiden finds her hidden w. and resumes her form
D361.1.1; thank God that camels have no w. J2564; thunder clouds
from w. of mountains A1142.4; trickster to give tiger w. K1013.4; winds
caused by flapping w. A1125.
Winged bull B43; chariot F861.2; dogs in wild hunt E501.4.1.7; elephant
B557.11.2; god A131.7; horse B41.1; serpent as boat: passengers within
F911.3.2; ship F841.3.1.
Wing-cornucopia B115.2.
Winking both at buyer and seller W171.1; club F835.1.
Winner. — Stakes not claimed by w. N2.0.2.
Winning, see also **Gambling;** of contest to be king P11.2; with devil's aid
G303.22.7, M217; first game to play for higher stakes K2378.1; soul
from devil in card game E756.2. — Animal w. contest for man B587;
despised boy w. race L176; magic object effects gambler's w. D1407ff.,
man granted power of w. at cards N221; punishment: w. as wife and
then killing Q411.1; suitor test: w. horse-race three times H331.5.3.
Winnings. — Bargain: to divide all w. *M241.
Winnowing peas devil's task G303.16.19.3.1; rice as royalty test H41.8.
— Animal shows w. fans as ears K1715.12; cannibal with w. tray,
pestle G11.12; origin of w. fan A1446.5.4; paramour pretends to be
returning w. basket K1517.11; witch aids w. grain G283.1.2.4.
Winter becomes summer at saint's funeral F960.2.6; magically produced
D2145.1. — Between summer and w. (i.e. between wagon and sledge)
H583.7, H1058; bringing berries (fruit, roses) in w. (task) H1023.3;
cold in w. A1135.1; continuous w. destroys race A1040ff.; cuckoo to
sing in w. H1023.3.1.1; daw waits in vain for the figs to ripen in w.
J2066.2; flowers bloom in w. F971.5; garden blooming in w. D1664,
H352, M261.1; genealogy of w. A1154; hospitality for whole w. P320.1;
for the long w. K362.1; fruit magically grows in w. *D2145.2.2; grass-
hopper builds no house for w. A2233.4; origin of w. weather A1135;
summer and w. garden D1664; storks become men in Egypt in w.
D624.1; wild hunt appears in w. E501.11.2.1.
Winters. — Year with two w. X1603.
Wiped. — Face w. dry after washing A1599.4.

Wiping hands on lame son S12.7.

Wisdom, see also **Knowledge;** from animals *J130ff.; as bride test H388; came before learning J1217.2; from children J120ff.; chosen above all else J231; from education J140ff.; from experience J10ff.; from fools J156; as God's companion A195.2; from inference J30ff.; from necessity J100ff.; from observation J50ff.; from old man J151ff.; from parable *J80ff.; personified Z128, Z139.8; or wealth more powerful? N141.2. — Acquisition and possession of w. J0—J199; Adam's seventy-two kinds of w. D1811.0.1; animals give w. *B160ff.; animals with magic w. B120—B169; book gives w. J2238; dead awaken after three days to new life and great w. E489.1; dispute of wealth, w. J461.7; found mortar taken to king reveals peasant girl's w. H561.1.2; god of w. A461; goddess of w. A461.1; magic object gives supernatural w. *D1300ff.; magic w. *D1811ff., (of extraordinary companion) D1719.4, (follows long sleep) F564.3.3, (possessed by wild man) D1719.2; man's w. puts all animals in his power A1421.1.1; moon's w. A753.3.4; origin of human w. A1481; precocious w. T615.3; quest for w. H1376.8; saint offered any gift chooses w. L212.1; seven grades of w. Z71.5.6.4; Solomon proves inferiority of woman's w. J80.1.1; stopping up mouth, ears to keep in w. J1977; streams of w. flow from magic well D1300.3.1; sun's w. A738.2.2; test of w. H501.

Wise animals B120ff.; carving of fowl H601; cleric as solver of riddles H561.8; and foolish J (entire chapter); giant as foster father of hero N812.1; eagle in earth-tree A878.3.4; man (acknowledges his ignorance) J911, (disguised as buffoon) K1818.3.1, (disguised as monk outdebates heretic) K3.4, (before entering a quarrel considers how it will end) J611, (humble in death) J912; man's advice scorned J2051; men (disguise as peasants) K1816.9.1, (of Gotham) J1700ff., (humble selves) J917, (predict rainstorm: wrong) J1714.3.1; but ugly son M93; and unwise conduct J200—J1000; woman as helper N828; words of dying father J154. — Animal gives w. example to man J133ff.; association of w. men with fools J1714; counsels proved w. by experience *J21ff.; dwarfs w. F451.3.12.3; fool passes as w. man by remaining silent N685; giants w. F531.6.17.7; king sends w. man to give rival advice K1994; land where everyone is w. F129.6; marvelously w. man F645; porter's revenge for three w. counsels J1511.6; sham w. man K1956, N611; test of cleverness: uttering three w. words H505.

Wisest. — Riddle: what is w. H659.9.

Wish for animal husband realized C26; for exalted husband realized *N201; granted before hearing it M223; for supernatural husband realized C15; for wife red as blood, white as snow, black as raven T11.6. — Conception from w. T513, (of another) T513.1; curse given to negate good w. M416; fairy ransoms self with w. F341.2; grateful fish grants mad hero his w. B375.1.1; magic last w. before death D1715.1; monster born because of hasty (inconsiderate) w. of parents

*C758.1; overheard w. realized N699.6; reward: any w. that may be asked Q115; river rises to prevent body's being carried over it against dying man's w. F932.8.1; summoning by w. D2074.2.3; transformation through w. D521; thumbling born as result of hasty w. of parents T553.

Wishes for good fortune realized N202. — Absurd w. J2070ff.; all princess's w. granted for month H313.1; deceptive bargain: three w. K175; execution evaded by using three w. J1181.1; fairies give fulfillment of w. F341; fairies make good w. for newborn child F312.1.1; fernseed makes w. come true C401.5; ghost laid when w. granted E459.3; selling soul for granting of w. M211.9; three foolish w. J2071; transformation to likeness of ruler: man so uses the last of three w. granted to him D41.1; vanquished ogre grants hero's three w. G665.

Wishing tree in otherworld F162.3.2. — Contest in w. H507.3; girl summons fairy lover by w. for him F301.1.1.1; heaven entered by trick: "w. sack" thrown in K2371.1.3; magic object from w. D852; magic results produced by w. *D1761ff.; magic w.-drum works only for owner D1651.7.2; magic w.-girdle supplies food D1472.2.1; magic w. object *D1470.1ff.; magic w.-ring loses power by touching water D877.1.

Wisp of hay transformed to bridge D451.5.7. — Magic w. D1282.2, (causes insanity) D1367.4.

Wit combat H507ff., (among sisters for dowry) H507.4; jokes over unfavorable decision J835; or learning more important? N141.1. — Hermes distributes w. L301; man buys a pennyworth of w. J163.1; one basket of w. better than twelve carloads J1662.1.

Witch *G200; abducts hero R10.4; assigns tasks H935; bone controls animals D1442.8; on broomstick G242.1; burns child's legs, magically heals them D2161.3.1; causes milk to curdle D2083.2.2; controls winds D2142.0.1; deceptively gets boy into sack K711.4; delays person's death D1855.1; in animal form G211ff.; draws rain, snow from clouds D2143.1.9; drinks boiling oil to beautify teeth G525.1; enchants bride D2062.4.1; flies with magic aids D1531.5ff.; foster mother P272.1; frightened by victim cleaving boulder K547.13; helps recover magic D885.1; imprisoned in boulder D2078.1; keeps water from boiling D2137.1; overcome or escaped G270ff.; paralyzes (mule) D2072.0.2.4, (pigs) D2072.0.2.5, (wagon) D2072.0.2.1.1; plays on jew's harp, disarmed K606.1.4; poses as beggar to steal child K764; possesses magic objects D801.1; prevents person from drinking D2072.0.5.1; produces lightning D2149.1.1; sells power to control winds D2142.0.1.1; sits atop mast D2142.0.1.2; suckles child T611.3; transforms self to hare so as to suck cows D655.2; of upper world A205; woman's son by demigod A592.1. — Allegorical game of w., devil, maiden, church Z178; beheading w. H1191.1; blinding a w. (task) H1191; bringing water from distant fountain more quickly than w. (task) H1109.1; cannibal w. G11.3; catching w. in king's garden H1191.2; child divides last loaf with w. Q42.1.1; dogs warn against w. B521.3.1; king marries w. P18.1; lending to w. tabu C784.1; man becomes w. D97; not to eat food of w.

C242; form of w. G210ff.; magic adhesion to w. *D2171.2; magic object received from w. D812.6; pipal protects against w. D1385.2.4; quest for w. stepmother H1397.1; salt bullet kills w. D1385.4.1; seeing w. tabu C311.1.6; selling to w. tabu C782.2; snow from feathers or clothes of a w. A1135.2.1; theft from w. revenged Q212.1; transformation by w. D683.2; weighing w. against Bible H234; woman promises her unborn child to appease offended w. S222.1.

Witch's aid in reaping contest F1038.2; curse M411.12; ghost chases man E261.4.1; horse-switch blossoms F971.1.2; house at border of otherworld F147.3; sabbath G243. — Breaking w. back tests strength H1562.8; curse: prince to fall in love with w. daughter M436; drawing w. blood annuls her spells D1741.2.1; earthquake at w. death F960.2.5.2, Q552.25.2; following w. fire into her power G451; mongoose leads to w. house G402.2; pasturing w. cattle, her daughters H1199.12.2; sickness of princess dependent on w. fire *D2064.2; stealing w. beautiful clothing H1151.23.

Witches G200—G299; make cows give bloody milk D2083.2.1; induce love D1901; pursued in wild hunt E501.5.1.3; steal in house D2087.7; in wild hunt E501.2.3. — Boy overhears w., gets their magic B838.9; characteristics of w. G220ff.; devil appears at meetings of w. G303.6.2.2; evil deeds of w. G260ff.; habitat of w. G230ff.; habits of w. G240ff.; magic horseshoe keeps off w. D1385.9; magic knowledge of w. D1810.0.5; maidens rescued from w. R111.1.8; men think hairy wives w. J1786.6; power of w. to see distant sights D1825.9; raja magically protected from w. D1400.1.22; recognition of w. G250ff.; secret remedy overheard in conversation of w. N452; sight of deformed w. causes man to release wife from spinning duty J51; silver bullet protects against w. D1385.4; three deformed w. invited to wedding in exchange for help *M233.

Witchcraft learning leaves man shadowless F1038.1. — Burning cut hair to prevent w. D2176.5; burning for w. Q414.0.10; churchyard mould in hat prevents w. D1385.11; charm prevents w. D1385.13; disease caused by w. A1337.0.3; door stuck by w. D1654.15; glen of w. F756.4; innocent woman accused of w. K2123; money to be regained by w. C401.3.1; origin of w. A1599.10.

Witchhazel protects against witches G272.22.

Withe at otherworld entrance F150.3.2. — Putting w. about sand Z63; recognition by carving on w. H35.4.1.

Withered. — Making w. flowers green H1023.3.2.

Withering by magic D2082.0.2; trees after tabu broken C998; of tree bad omen D1812.5.1.20. — Bird's breath w. B33.1.1, B777; flowers magically kept from w. D2167.3; hand w. after oath broken M101.4; hand w. as punishment Q559.5.2; oath w. tree M115.1.1; reason for tree's w. N452.1.1; trees w. at tragedy F979.23; witch w. arm G269.11.2.

Withershins circuit for ill luck D1791.2.

Witness always to answer "No" J1141.13. — False w. to free friend P315.2; heavens bear w. for man F961.0.5; no argument good without w. K1655.1; women disqualified as court w. A1589.1.

Witnesses bigger thieves than culprit U119.1.2. — No w. to robbery J1191.6; opposing w. have pockets filled with dung K1291.

Wizard burned, saint saved H1573.3.4; calms storm D2141.0.8.1; gives man illusion that he has been away long D2012.2; makes pupil think himself emperor W154.28. — Charm sung over flesh chewed by w. has magic power D1273.0.3; fire burns up, crackles as w. passes G229.8; magic object received from w. D812.6; storm at death of w. D2141.0.4.

Wizard's magic detection of thief D1817.0.1.1ff.; prophecy on cockfight D1814.1.1.

Wizardry. — Witches' w. cauldron G249.5.

Woe. — Idleness begets w. J21.50; quest for king's w. H1378.2.

Wolf, see also **Werwolf**; abducts person R13.1.5; acts as judge before eating the rams K579.5.1; almost locked up in the stable by the shepherd J2172.2.1; as animals' king B240.10; approaches too near to horse: kicked in face K1121; attracted to own children B751.6; bites off devil's heels G303.4.5.7; boy recovered by human parents B635.2; carries man B557.15; as commander orders all booty divided, but keeps his own U37; as dog's guest sings J581.1; boasts of having eaten horses J2351.4; brings cake from the window sill K1022.4; cut open and filled with stones as punishment Q426; defends master's child against serpent B524.1.4; does not mind dust from flock of sheep J352.1; eats devil G303.17.3.3; eats horse from rear, kicked to death K553.4; excuses killing goose by reference to saints K2055.1; executed for thefts B275.1.3; falls out of nest: cause of straight back A2211.3; flees from the wolf-head K1715.3; freezes internally from eating cold flesh J2284; as giants' dog F531.4.11.1; as God's dog A1833.3; granted patent of nobility A2546.2; hard to hold by eyebrows H659.2.1; harnessed (lie) X1216.1; in hell A671.2.6; -hounds C564.3; in human form B651.6; is the devil's craftiest enemy G303.25.1; kept at door until children have been christened K551.8; keeps well-fed leeches J215.1.3; loses interest in the sermon when he sees flock of sheep U125; makes fire as mock sunrise K1886.3; measured for clothes K551.20; not good living or dead (riddle) H841.4; objects to lion stealing sheep from him although he has himself stolen it U21.4; as ogre G352.1; offers (to act as midwife for sow) K2061.6, (to act as shepherd) *K2061.1; overeats in cellar K1022.1; persuaded to put head through jar K1022.7; persuades lamb to bring him drink: lamb to be food K815.11; poses as grandmother and kills child *K2011; poses as ram to cheat ewe K828.3; proposes abolition of dog guards for sheep K2061.1.1; punished by being married K583; punished for father's misdeeds J1863.2; punished for theft, kings honored U11.2.1; puts flour on his paw to disguise himself K1839.1; puts head in camel's mouth : killed J2131.5.5; returns sheep stolen from

saint B256.11; scorns salt meat in false expectation of other booty
J2066.4; sold as (goat) K132, (watchdog) K133.1; spares man livestock
after man aids him B381.1; steals old maid (she keeps him for husband) X755; substitutes for calf D2156.8; swears by God B251.7.1; -tail
blankets B538.2; thought to be (colt) J1752, (log of wood) J1761.5;
tied to cow's horns K1022.2; transformed to man D313.2; transformed
to object D421.1; tries (in vain to be doctor) J512.5, (to eat bowstring)
J514.2, (to drink well dry to get cheese) J1791.3.1, (to entice goat down
from high place) K2061.4, (to make friends with lion: killed) J411.5;
unjustly accuses lamb and eats him U31; waits in vain for nurse to
throw away child J2066.5; who wanted to make bread Z49.5.2; and
wolverine fight over girl B621.8; worship V1.8.5. — Alliance of dog
and w. B267.1; ass punished for stealing mouthful of grass: lion and w.
forgiven for eating sheep U11.1; blind man who feels young w.
recognizes his savage nature J33; camel lures w., crushes him K839.5;
cats unite against w. J1025.2; crane pulls bone from wolf's throat: w.
refuses payment W154.3; creation of w. A1833; curse: w. to carry off
man's genitals M442.2; death respite until w. reads horse's passport
K551.18; devil in form of w. G303.3.3.2.1; disdain of w. for dog
J953.5; dog tries to imitate w. J2413.5; dogs of w. color join wolves
J2137.2; dog refuses to help w. K231.1.3; eagle warns shepherds that
w. is eating sheep J715.1; enmity between lion and w. A2494.7.2; fairy
as w. F234.1.13; famished w. asks sheep to bring him water K2061.5;
fat w. (cumulative tale) Z33.4; fetter for Fenris w. F864.1; food of w.
A2435.3.4; fox persuades w. (to eat own brains) K1025.1, (to lie on
haycock in order to be painted) K1013.2; friendship between w. and ass
A2493.15; future hero found in w. den L111.2.4; ghost as w. E423.2.7;
giant as w. F531.1.8.1; giant w. overcome by hero B16.2.4; girl suckled
by w. has wolf's nail T611.10.1; god assumes form of w. D113.1.2; gods
battle Fenris w. A1082.2.1; hero suckled by w. A511.2.2.1; hidden w.
gives himself away by talking J2351.2; hungry w. envies fat dog until
he sees marks of his collar L451.3; why w. has straight back A2356.2.2;
helpful w. *B435.3; intruding w. (falls down chimney and kills himself)
J2133.7, K891.1; kid perched on house jeers at w. J974; lamb prefers to
be sacrificed in temple than to be eaten by w. J216.2; lion, bear, and
w. resuscitate master B515; lion kills w. who has killed mistress's sheep
B591.1; why w. lives in woods A2433.3.14; Loki's son transformed to
w. Q551.3.2.1; magic w. heart D1015.1.4; man in barrel grabs w. by
tail and is drawn out of danger X1133.3; man dreams wife attacked
by w.: so happens T255.7; man-w. B29.5; man transformed to w.
*D113.1; man turns w. inside out (lie) X1124.2; marriage to w. B601.16;
musician in w. trap B848.1; mysterious w. enters church and kills
blaspheming priest Q554.4; presumptious w. among lions J952.1;
prisoner escapes by using w. K649.10; prophecy: death by w. M341.2.6;
queen hides her child and accuses w. of eating it S332; reincarnation as

w. E612.2; saint gives calf to w. W10.2; saint's prayer causes w. to
bring back child B256.8; she-w. cares for baby in forest B535.0.11; she-
w. as child's nurse B535.0.9; sheep licking her lamb is envied by w.
J1909.5; sheep-dogs hunt w. J624.2; shepherd who cried "W!" too often
J2172.1; soul as w. E731.9; soul in w. E715.4.2; sow saves pigs from w.
coming to baptize them K1121.2; speaking w. B211.2.4; how w. got long
tail A2378.3.3; test: guessing nature of certain skin (w.-skin) H522.1.2;
test of resourcefulness: carrying w., goat, and cabbage across stream
H506.3; why w. is thief A2455.1; thieving w. sings, caught J2136.5.9;
tit for tat: lion kills w., not fox K961.1.1; transformation by striking w.-
skin glove D566.1; trouble-maker rides w. to inn K2138; wandering
soul as w. E721.5.1; wedding of w. B281.3; well-trained kid does not
open to w. J144; witch in form of w. G211.2.2; witch rides on w.
G241.1.1.

Wolf's body made smaller A2302.5; flesh renders courageous D1358.12.
— Basket tied to w. tail and filled with stones K1021.2; if the
w. tail breaks X1133.3.2; identification by w. hair H75.5; origin
of w. skin A2311.3; quest for w. milk H1361.3; ram promises to
jump into w. belly K553.3; singing w. power over humans Z33.4.2;
sword with w. image F833.7; why w. muzzle black A2335.4.5.

Wolves climb on top of one another to tree: lowest runs away and all
fall J2133.6; devour an ox without leaving a share for the rightful
owner W151.3; devour the wicked Q415.7; to eat thievish abbot
Q556.12.1; have annual (church) feast B253.2; as god's dogs
A165.2.1.1.1; guard saint's cattle B256.4.1; lick saint's shoes B251.2.3;
make false truce with sheep K2010.3; of his own country dearer than
dogs of another P711.1. — Dogs listen to hypocritical words of w.
K815.3; domesticated w. B256.4; herd of cattle transformed to w.
D412.2.1; hunting w. with rod and line X1124.4; I surely saw a
hundred w. W211.2; lies about w. X1216; ogre intimidated by alarm
of w. K42.0.1; old beggar transforms wedding party into w. T155; saint
makes covenant with w. B279.1; strong man brings w. home F615.2.5;
strong man kills w. F628.1.1.5; trickster entices w. out of stable by
music K443.5.

Wolverine. — Burnt smell of w. A2416.4; food of w. A2435.3.4; why
w. has peculiar marks on back A2356.3.3; why w. has red hair on
loins A2364.1; why w. is a thief A2455.5; wolf and w. fight over girl
B621.8.

Wolverine's — Cause of w. walk A2441.1.5.

Woman, see also **Wife;** alive by day, dead by night E155.4.1; arousing
love to be forsaken C686; with bad eyes J1169.1; becomes bird, lends
sex organ, becomes man D11.2; can be lifted only by her lover
D1654.13; carried off by water-fairy F322.0.1; changes into immortal
D1850.2; in disguise becomes pope K1961.2.1; disguised as monk
P425.3.3; disguises as man to enter enemy's camp K2357.6; as dragon-
slayer B11.11.7; exchanges horse for sack of bones J2099.1; who fell

from sky A21.1; in finery in church thinks people are standing up to see her when they rise at gospel-reading J953.8; will not follow donkey on safe path: attacked by robbers J133.4; free from trouble, worry H1195; frightens devil G303.16.19.17.1; gives jewel for salad J2093.2; gives self to riddle solver H551.2; as guardian of treasure N572; from half-drop of wine A1211.6; with horseshoe on one foot F551.1.2.1; induces men to fight over her K1086; instructs in art of arms P461.4; as leader of wild hunt E501.1.8; with lovers carried in cloak F1034.2.1; lured into forest, captured K788; masks as lawyer (judge) and frees her husband K1825.2; in the moon A751.8; plans to eat her children G72.1; satirist M402.1; seeks unknown father of her child H1381.2.1; is strongest (riddle) H631.4; subservient to husband A1571.2; in tar and feathers does not know herself J2012.3; transformed to (cat) D142.0.1, (flower) D212, (flower, recognized) H63.1, (fruit) D211ff., (island) D284, (man) D11, (pool of water) A920.1.11, D283.1, (skein of silk) D264, (tree) D215ff.; with two husbands is to be killed J1171.3; from water world B81.0.2; won and then scorned T72. — Animals from severed fingers of w. A1724.1.1; bearded w. F545.1.5; black tribe because w. put on fire A1614.8; blood as remedy for barrenness in w. D1347.2; boy behind tree tells w. about bad food he gets K1971.3; boy who had never seen w.: the Satans T371; brothers construct a w. — whose is she? Z16.1; burr-w. G311; bush by day, w. by night D621.2.1; cannibal w. devours raw buffalo H46.1; capture through wiles of w. K778; changeling addresses w. in verse and thus betrays his maturity F321.1.1.3; contract made by w. without husband void P525.2; country no w. may enter F566.1.1; creation of monkeys: old w. thrown into fire A1861.2; creation of w. from coconut A1253.2.1; death from sight of beautiful w. F1041.1.6; defeating certain old w. (task) H1149.3; devil appears when w. looks at herself in mirror after sunset G303.6.1.4; devil bargains to help man win w. M217; devil disguised as w. G303.12.6; devil in serpent form tempts first w. (Satan and Eve) A63.6; devil takes the place of w. who went to spend night with a priest G303.25.11; devil as w. G303.3.1.12; disguise as w. to enter enemy's camp K2357.8; disguise of w. in man's clothes *K1837; diving for reflection of beautiful w. J1791.6; earth gives birth to w. A1234.4; encounter with clever w. dissuades man from visit J31; every w. has her price U66.1; evil w. in glass case as last commodity K216.1; fairy as beautiful young w. F234.2.5; fairies take human midwife to attend fairy w. F372.1; fifteen characteristics of good w. Z71.6.11.1; first man catches w. in his snare A1275.10; flame indicates presence of beautiful w. F1061.1; forthputting w. imposes tabu C901.1.3.1; goddess of war in shape of w. A125.1.1; ground dries up when first w. cuts self, bleeds A856.2; guilt detected by query on possessing w. J1149.6; helping old w. tabu G745.1; impossible for w. to bear animals J1191.5.1; madness from seeing beautiful w. *F1041.8.1; magic object (draws w.

to man) D1426, (makes w. masterful) D1359.1, (received from cat-w.) D825.1, (received from old w.) D821; magician carries w. in glass coffin *D2185; man breaking oath to w. cannot be king M205.3; man creates w. from butter, sour milk, and curds A1275.5; man excels w. A1376; man made to appear to pursuers as w. carrying babe D2031.6.1; man not to look at w. C312; man-eating w. G11.6; man disguised as w. admitted to women's quarters: seduction K1321.1; man looks at copulating snakes: transformed to w. D513.1; man reincarnated as w. E605.1.2; man transformed to w. *D12; monotony of being restricted to one's favorite food (or w.) J81.0.1; mortal w. seduced by a god K1301; never have to do with w. unless wed to her J21.30; old w. F571.3, (as creator) A15.1.1, (and her pig) Z41, (builds air castle about the horse she is finally to get from sale of pail of milk) J2061.2.1, (guards gods' islands) A955.12, (guards post supporting earth: she causes earthquakes) A843, (helper) N825.3, (as prophet) M301.2, (gives chickens to devils) G303.25.6, (has control of frost) D2143.5.1, (helps on quest) H1233.1.1, (intercepts letter and takes girl's place in man's bed) K1317.2.1, (ruler of dead in lower world) E481.1.1, (supports earth on head) A842.2; only one w. on island F112.0.1.1; primeval w. cut in pieces A642.1; refusing to help w. tabu C686.1; reincarnation: w. reborn as man E605.1.1; remarkably beautiful w. F575.1; remarkably strong w. F610.0.1; race always to have illustrious w. M317; reincarnation: w. to bird, nettles, stone, woman E648.1; revenant as w. E425.1; saved soul of w. assists her husband's soul in battle against demons E756.5; seduction by man disguising as w. K1321; self-righteous w. punished L435.2; slaying w. with spear tabu C835.2.4; stupid w. swims on the roof J1972; sun a fat w. walking across sky A738.1.2; sun as w. A736.2; sun and moon born from a w. A715.1; supplies from toe of old w. D1470.2.4; tabu: eating before w. C231.3; tabu to violate w. C118; tasks performed with help of old w. H971.1; to which man does w. belong? J1153.2; there was once a w. (cumulative tale) Z49.4; transformation to seduce w. *D658; transformation to likeness of another w. D40.2; treacherous dark w. K2260.2; treacherous old w. K2293; vow to marry a certain w. M146; where devil can't reach, he sends an old w. G303.10.5; there was a wee wee w. Z39.2; wild animal will not harm chaste w. B771.0.1; wild hunter pursues a w. E501.5.1; wild w. F567.1.

Woman's garments cut off: does not know herself J2012.2.—Devil (buys w. hair) G303.25.13, (in w. train) G303.8.9; disguise of man in w. dress *K1836; dog betrays w. infidelity *B134.1; first w. mate from tree A1275.6; fish from w. severed fingers A2102; lake-serpent in w. form B91.5.2.1; Solomon proves inferiority of w. wisdom J80.1.1.

Women adorn heads, immoral below K2051.4; as best painters H659.16; disguised as ascetics escape enemy K521.9; disqualified as court witnesses A1589.1; druids P427.0.3; lead man on, then blackmail him K443.9; lure warrior aside, confederate kills him K822; poets P427.7.4;

as prime source of sin T334.1; scorned in love T71; tabu on certain island C619.4; transformed to bitches B297.2.1; transformed into flowers A2611.0.4.1; warriors F565. — Abusing w. tabu C867.1; animals punished for assaulting w. A2239.5; are there more men or w.? H708; why w. are bad A1371; birth of fifty w. prophesied M301.5.2; creation of flea: to give w. work A2032.2; death from excess of w. T99.1; don't shed blood of w. J21.2.5; dwarf w. bear children F451.3.5.5; fatal enticements of phantom w. F585.1; fox had rather meet one hen than fifty w. J488; god does not address w. A182.3.0.4; hell of w. F83; hero refuses to slay w. W11.5.12; journey to Land of W. F112; land where w. live separate from men F566.2; law requiring military service of w. P551.6; louse created to give w. work A2051.1; magic door invisible to w. D1982.1; man fishes up two blind w. from well F1065; men captive in Land of W. R7; ogre eats w. G11.6.1; origin of w. in Ireland A1611.5.4.1; portion of otherworld for w. F167.14.1; quest: what is it w. most desire H1388.1; riddle: why are there more w. than men? H774; sacred places closed to w. C51.1.10; selling three old w. (task) H1153; sterility among w. A1358; strong w. F565.2; tabu on assembly of w. C853.2; tabu confined to w. C181; tabu: w. leaving hero's land C566.3; ten w. carried in a bottle D55.2.4; three w. have among them but one (eye) F512.1.2, (tooth) F513.1.1; theft from three old w. who have but a single eye among them *K333.2; ugly ogre terrifies w. who flee, drown G476; wisdom (knowledge) from w. J155; why tigers don't kill w. who run away after quarreling with their husbands A2499.1; why witches are w. G286.1.

Women's — Besieged w. dearest possession J1545.4.1; magic protection against w. spells D1385.16.3; pope tests w. obedience: not to look into box H1557.4.

Womb. — Child in w. gives quest directions H1232.5; child speaks in mother's w. T575.1ff.; first humans from Mother Earth's w. A1234.1.1; hero enters w. of sleeping woman and is reborn T539.1; hero born by splitting mother's w. T584.7; hero in w. guides mother's direction A511.1.2.2; rebirth by crawling into w. E607.2.2; saint in w. renders woman invisible D1361.39; woman without w. F597.

Wonder that man who has been buying butcher's meat for seven years can still be alive X231; voyages F110.1. — Changeling betrays his age when his w. is excited F321.1.1.1; discovering new w. before eating C287; quest for unknown w. H1382.4.

Wonders. — Plain of w. F756.3.

Wood automatically burns D1649.4; at borders of otherworld F143; dealer prays for raja's death W153.13; enduring forever F812.7; which fire cannot consume F812.8; -gatherer K312.2; heaved on mother's head, kills her K1466; neither crooked nor straight H1378.1; turned to grain D476.1.3. — Bear builds house of w.: fox of ice J741.1; bleeding w. as Doomsday sign A1002.2.2; bundle of w. magically acts as riding

horse D1523.3; child promised to w.-spirit S213; creation of man
from w. A1252; cross of Christ made of four kinds of w.V211.4.1; devil
exorcised by burning w. G303.16.14.2.1; expensive w. burned to make
charcoal J2094; fairies give man w. that turns to gold F342.1; father
cuts w. which was burnt last year (to pay old debts) H583.2.4; fish
created from w. A2101; fool whose house is burning puts w. on the fire
J2162.2; ghosts gather w. for hell fires E755.2.4; gift w. must be split
W111.5.10; golden w. for knife H1359.1; island of rare w. F732; lake
petrifies w. F934.3; lover unloads w. on door to keep husband out
K1514.9; man in otherworld loaded down with w. F171.6.1; magic
object (found in w). D849.4, (provides w.) D1488; magic pebble splits
w. D1564.1; Mahadeo turns w. chips into insects A2002.1; man proof
against iron, stone, and w. D1841.1; magic stick of w. D956; object
transformed to w. D473; not to offend w.-spirit C43; origin of w.
carving A1465.5; piece of w. revives memory D2006.1.8; power of self-
transformation received from w.-spirit D630.1; scavenger carrying w.
bad omen D1812.5.1.29; serpent acts as rope to collect w. B579.5;
special flavor of forest w. F812.6; splitting w. suitor contest H331.12;
stacking w. from felled forest in one day H1095.2; sticks of w. become
animals D441.7; strong hero w.-spirit's son F611.1.15; sword magically
changes to w. when executioner is to decapitate innocent person H215.1;
transformation to w. C961.3; treasure buried in w.-shed N511.1.5; why
w. combustible A2782; wild hunt pursues w. spirit E501.5.3; wild man
as w. spirit F441.3; wine-distilling w. F811.5.2; wolf thought to be log
of w. J1761.5; woman becomes w. on breaking tabu C961.3; woman
charms w. stick, hides in it D1393.1.1; wound closed with w. F959.3.2.
Woods, see also **Forests.** — Animals that live in w. A2433.2.1; devil in
the w. G303.8.13; elk lives in w. A2433.3.13; king (prince) finds maiden
in w. and marries her N711.1; ogre attacks intruders in house in w.
G475.1; precept of the lion to his sons: honor the w. J22.2; wild hunt
appears in w. E501.12.1; why wolf lives in w. A2433.3.14.
Woodcutter hero L113.5. — Disguise as w. K1816.3; queen forced to
serve w. Q482.2.2.
Woodcutter's. — Disguise as cobbler to woo w. daughter K1816.10.1.
Woodcutters. — Mice win war with w. L318.
Wooden anchor would hold if it were only large, thinks the fool J2212.3;
coat F821.1.4; image V127. — City populated by w. automata D1628;
crippled cat catches mice with w. leg X1211.2; devil takes an unbaptized child and substitutes a w. log G303.9.9.4; disguise in w. covering K1821.9; dwarf rides through air on w. horse F451.6.2.2; earth
supported on w. cross A843.1; from w. spring iron bucket makes stones
from which water flows (riddle) H765; marvelous sensitiveness: fainting from noise of w. pestle and mortar F647.8; moon's w. weapons
A759.1; penance: killing oneself with w. knife Q522.2; ship built with
a w. saw J2171.1.1; Trojan w. horse K754.1; worship of w. idol V1.11.3.

Woodcock. — Color of w. A2411.2.3.1; devil in form of w. G303.3.3.3.4.

Woodcock's ugly voice A2245.1, A2421.2, A2423.1.1.

Wooddove. — Why w. has green eyes A2232.5.6.

Woodpecker in human form B652.4; punished for stinginess A2239.4; transformed to person D353.1; transformed from stingy woman A2261.4. — Why w. bores in wood A2456.1; color of w. A2411.2.4.1; creation of w. A1957; enmity of w. and weaver-bird A2494.13.8; friendship between antelope, w., and tortoise A2493.32; helpful w. B461.1; man transformed to w. D153.1; why w. has sharp beak A2343.3.2.

Woodpecker's wedding B282.3.5, B282.13. — Origin of w. crest A2321.3, A2321.11.

Woodpile. — Cat in w. prevents axe from cutting D2186.

Woodsman P458; and the gold axe Q3.1; treacherous K2259.1.

Woodworm. — Why w. bores wood A2456.2.

Wooed. — Chieftainess of too high rank to be w. P28.1; innkeeper's daughter w. by devil G303.12.1; mortal w. by fairy F302.3; wife in disguise w. by her faithless husband K1814; woman w. by trick *K1350ff.

Wooer. — Animal w. B582.1; fairies slay w. F361.6; moon as w. A753.1; respite from w. while he brings clothes all night K1227.3.

Wooing T50ff.; emissary poses as king K1952.5; not done by women A1551. — Bashful suitor w. oak T69.4; devil as woman w. man G303.12.6; devil w. woman G303.12.5.4; giant w. mortal F531.5.7.0.1; husband has friend w. his wife H492.2; king's son w. father's bride K1094; king w. through his daughter T51.2; transformation for w. *D641.1.2.

Wool on his forehead awarded sheep in lawsuit A2255.1; taken to frogs for weaving J1851.1.4. —Fairies steal w. F365.8; fish with w. coat B737; ghostly w.-packs E539.3; hedge to catch sheeps' w. J2060.2; man can hear w. grow F641.1; sheep helpful to Lord: get w. A2221.10; spinning w. still on goat's back H1024.8; task: making many shirts (clothing an army) from one hank of w. H1022.2; task: washing black w. white H1023.6; warming stove with w. J1873.3; weaving mantle from one sheep's w. H1022.4.2.

Wooly. — Mermaid has w. hair B81.9.1.

Word charm gives witch power G224.12. — Man never breaks his w. W37.0.1; transformation through magic w. D522.   ·

Words in a foreign language thought to be insults J1802; of Christian comfort cause devil and his crew to vanish G303.16.4; freeze X1623.2; as love charms D1355.18; misunderstood J1802ff.; for "stick" and "stone" confused A1333.1; from tomb E545.0.1. — Among vain w. some wisdom J263; angels from God's w. A52.0.6; death of little hen described in unusual w. Z32.2.1; devil writes down all idle w. spoken in church G303.24.1.6; disenchantment by proper w. D789.6.1; God's w. A139.6; magic power of dying man's w. *D1715; man pledged to give his

wife only good w. hits her with a prayer book J1541.1; negligent priests
buried under bags filled with w. omitted from service V5.2; poet's confounding w. J1684; power in w., herbs, and stones J1581.2; quest for
unknown magic w. H1382.1; quest to lower world for lost w. H1276;
religious w. or exercises interpreted with absurd literalness J2495;
sham parson repeats same expression over and over or says few w. of
Latin K1961.1.2; similar w. mistaken for each other J1805.1; test of
cleverness: uttering three wise w. H505; unuttered w. heard F1099.3.

Work brings happiness J21.50; of day magically overthrown at night
*D2192. — Angel shows value of w. H605; animal council assigns place
and w. to all B238; animal's daily w. A2450ff.; any w. touched automatically done D1935; boasts about brother's, father's w. capacity J2353.1;
changeling shows supernatural power to w. and thus betrays maturity
F321.1.1.4; choices: important and unimportant w. J370ff.; creation of
flea: to give women w. A2032.2; dead cannot rest until certain w. is
finished E415; deceptive labor bargain: one partner is to do all the w.
K178; devils help people at w. G303.9.3.3; dissatisfied exchange w.
U136.1; dwarfs interfere with mortal's w. F451.5.2.5; fairies leave w.
unfinished when overseen F361.3.1; god teaches people to w. A1403; intemperance in w. J553; keeping up certain w. all night (task) H1128;
king demands w. from guests P337; lazy woman resumes her w. J1011;
life without w. A1346.2.2; magic w. paralysis D2072.5; make-believe
eating, make-believe w. J1511.1; man must w. as punishment for
theft of fire A1346.1; man undertakes to do his wife's w. J2431; men
exchange w.: each cheated J2431.1; merit for charity lost by asking w.
in return V438; monk discouraged by large amount of w. to be done
persuaded to undertake but small amount each day J557.1; monk fails
to escape w. J215.4; necessity of w. J702; people taught by God to w.
C53.1; punishment: man to do woman's w. Q482.6; watching fairy at
w. tabu F348.8; wife behind tree advises husband against having his
wife w. K1971.4.1; will w. when beaten J1545.1; what kind of w.
occupies most men (riddle) H659.6; who does more w.? Husband or
wife? J1545.3.1; world's w. dependent on inequalities of fortunes
A1599.8.

Works. — Creator's w. survive him A77; devil comes and w. with man
who continues to work after night G303.22.9; devil w. backward
G303.13.2; why negro w. A1671.1.

Worked. — Ox lent by fairies must not be w. after sunset F391.1.1.

Working ghost E596.1. — Animal characteristics: punishment for w. on
holy day A2231.3; familiars w. for witch G225.0.3; miraculous w.
of the host V34; peasants punished for w. on feast day Q559.4; punishment for w. on holy day Q551.2.2; riddles about w. H588.11; stepmother w. stepdaughter to death S322.7; suitors w. for chaste wife
K1218.12.

Workmen of hell A677; rescue abandoned child R131. — Dwarfs as w.
F451.3.4ff.; gods as w. A140ff.

World at bottom of pond F725.8; calamities A1000—A1099; -columns A841; -cords A841.1; -eclipse A1046; as egg A655; -fire A1030ff.; parents A625; -soul A612.1. — Adulteress to lover, "I can see whole w." K1271.4; bringing winds from the whole w. (task) H1136; China first land in our w. A802; colors corresponding to the four w. quarters Z140.2; devil's disappearance from w. G303.17; formula for other w. "Where no man goes or crow flies" Z91; god promises never again to destroy w. by water A1113; god of the w. of the dead *A310ff.; journey of soul to w. of dead on reindeer E750.3; land of dead in lower w. *E481.1; magic knowledge from queen of other w. D1810.1; measuring the w. A1186; nun forgets to hail Mary and goes into the w. to sin V254.5; nut hits cock in head: he thinks w. is coming to an end Z43.3; prophecy of w. catastrophe M357; quest to other w. H1250ff.; renewal of w. after w. calamity A1006; rejuvenation by going to other w. and having digestive tract removed D1889.5; Satan builds another w. G303.9.1.15; sight of old home reawakens memory and brings about return from other w. *D2006.2; submarine and subterranean w. F720ff.; tear from upper w. of mortals falls on departed in lower w. E361.1.

World's — Castle at w. end F771.3.1; giants live at w. end F531.6.2.5; four gods at w. quarters support sky A665.2.1.1; quest for w. end H1371.1.

Worlds above and below A651.3. — Hierarchy of w. A651; miscellaneous w. A690ff.; nine w. tremble at rebirth F960.1.5.

World-tree *A652. — Pleiades from hunters who felled w. A773.5; spring from beneath w. A941.7.1; symbolism of roots, branches of w. H619.3.

Worldly man puts religious man out of countenance J1217.

Worm from caul born with child B714; swallowed at conception eats unborn child T579.6; transformed to other animal D418.2; transformed to person D392. — Why w. is blind A2284.3, A2332.6.4; cat's tail mistaken for w. J1759.5; conception from swallowing w. (in drink of water) T511.5.2; demon's corpse turns to w. H47; dragon from w. B11.1.3.1; earth excreted by w. A828.1; earth from w. scratched by creator's nails A828; fairy as w. F234.1.7; helpful w. B491.4; man with w. in head F511.0.7; man transformed to w. (often snake) D192; multicolored w. B731.10; mythical w. B99.2; origin of w. A2182; prophetic w. B145.3; quest for large-headed w. H1331.8; reincarnation as w. E618; seeing w. in loaf F642.3.2; transformation: demon (in human form) to w. D192.0.1; venomous w. B776.6; why thousand-legged w. avoids sun A2433.6.9.

Worm's flesh makes courageous D1358.1.2. — Horse fed with w. milk B710.2.1.

Worms. — Child born holding w. T552.2.2; lies about w. X1346; lost soul gnawed by w. E752.7; man eaten by w. as punishment Q415.3;

mankind descended from w. A1224.2; transformation to mass of w. Q551.3.2.5.

Wormwood. — Chain tale: w. rocking me to sleep Z41.7.

Worn-out broom at head of wild hunt E501.10.2; shoes as proof of long journey *H241. — Shoes miraculously w. F1015.1ff.; time measured by w. iron shoes *H1583.1; traveling till iron shoes are w. H1125.

Worry personified Z139.5. — Removing chance for w. J1396.

Worse. — Contentment with evil master for fear of w. successor J229.8; escape from one misfortune into w. N255.

Worship V0—V99. — Ancestor w. V1.3; animals praise or w. B251; devils w. host G303.24.2; intemperance in w. J564; intercourse before w. tabu C119.1.5; objects of w. V1ff.; origin of w. A1546; why Jews don't w. idols A1544.0.1.

Worshipped. — Kings w. after death P16.6.

Worshipper in trouble, goddess's throne shakes A189.5.

Worshipping. — Chain tale: brahmin w. himself Z42.3; death for w. idols Q558.12; magic results from w. D1766.10; resuscitation by w. body E63.1; sun w. God by night A722.11; witches w. demon G243.4; woman w. devil G303.9.4.10.

Worst. — Quest for w. meat H1305.1.1; what are best and w. stones (riddle) H659.3.

Worth. — Choice between w. and appearance J260ff.; what six things are not w. doing (riddle) H871.

Worthiness. — Test of w. for friendship H1558.0.1.

Worthless goods alleged to be valuable ones transformed K249.4; object substituted for valuable while owner sleeps K331.3; stones preferred to pearls J2093.3.1. — Lover pays husband w. money K1581.10; magic object exchanged for w. D871.1; robber mistakenly carries off w. goods and leaves valuable K421; sale of w. (articles) K110—K149, (services) K150ff., (animals) K130ff.; trading silver for w. cup J2096.

Worthy. — Biblical w. as giant F531.0.1; woman named "W." at communion X453.

Wound healed only by inflicter *D2161.4.10.2; healed by same spear that caused it D2161.4.10.1; masked by other wound K1872.4; received in dream F1068.2. — Birth from w. F541.2; curing w. by treating object causing it D1782.2; curse of clergy causes man to die of w. D2061.2.4.2; curse: w. not to heal M431.5; giant has w.-healing balm F531.6.5.3; identification by matching weapon, w. H101.1; insult worse than w. W185.6; lover's w. breaks while he is in bed with mistress N386; magic cure of w. D2161.2; magic object heals w. D1503ff.; miraculous cure of w. F959.3; no man with w. to be sacrificed C57.1.2; only one person able to heal w. D2161.4.10.0.1; physician describes person inflicting w. F956.4; recognition by means of ring enclosed in w. H61.3; recognition by w. H56; sham death to w. enemies K911.1; sister hidden in thigh w. F1034.3.1; surgeon can tell who inflicted w. F668.4; thorn growing in w. becomes a tree F971.3.

Wounds inflicted by certain man always fatal F693. — Beetles, barley as false remedy for w. K1016; bleeding w. don't stop hero H1507; dragon dips w. in holy well, is healed B11.12.1.2; dupe rubs salt on w. K1045.2; five w. of Christ V211.5, Z71.3.2; inflicters rather than receivers of w. chosen J481; inflaming warrior's w. K2014; king pretends to heal, really inflames ally's w. K2014.1; lovers' meeting: heroine heals hero's w. T32; magic arrow makes five w. D2092.0.1; magic girdle protects from all w. D1381.14; martyrs' w. emit milk V229.2.6; recognition by w. received in common H16.2; scratching contest: man's wife shows w. K83.1; sharing his w. J1621.

Wounded chieftain deceptively granted land K185.7.3; fairies F254.4; hero cured in peasant's house P411.3; hero restored by peasant R169.14; soldiers healed by druid P427.5.1; warrior continues fighting W33.1. — Animal cares for w. master B536; bride w. accidentally on way home T152; culture hero can be w. A526.1; curse by w. animal M411.19.1; fairy music brings sleep to w. F262.6; fairy w. by mortal F389.3; princess, w. prince abandoned in jungle T89.1.1; refusal to fight w. enemy W215.2; woman told father w., leaves, is robbed K343.1.2.

Wounding *S180ff.; animal without killing it tabu C841.0.2; self to accuse another of murder K2116.3; self from grief F1041.21.6.1. — Disenchantment by w. D712.6; foreknowledge of w. D1812.0.3; iron blessed by saint incapable of w. D1674; magic sickness from w. sick person D2064.6; symbolic w. of king Z182; trickster w. self to accuse others K2153.

Woven, see **Weaving.**

Wraiths separate from body E723ff.

Wrap. — Snake disenchanted by being allowed to w. itself three times around person's neck D759.8.

Wrapped. — Abandoned child w. in straw S336; child w. in altar coverings V135.1; coming w. in net (neither naked nor clad) H1054.1; ship w. with featherbeds and canvas F1031.

Wrapping. — Boy born in cloth w. T581.11; night from deity w. self in dark mantle A1174.4.

Wrath, see **Anger.**

Wreath. — Love through finding lady's w. T11.4.3.

Wrecked man saved on coffer of jewels becomes rich N226.

Wrecking of ship, see **Shipwreck.**

Wren as druid of the birds B242.1.2.1; helps mankind A1348.1; king of birds B242.1.2. — Fly, w., fox live with cleric B256.10; helpful w. B451.3; in burrowing contest w. goes into mouse hole K17.1.1; why w. is disliked A2522.6; why w. does not migrate A2482.3.

Wren's food A2435.4.11; wedding B282.9. — Crow's house full of w. eggs H1129.9.

Wrestler boasts he can carry mountain K1741.4. — Lie: remarkable w. X973; mighty w. F617.

Wrestling before food given strangers W213; with giant warrior H1166.1; match won by deception K12; ogre G317; as strength test H1562.9; to test son's legitimacy H218.2; with witch G275.9. — Devil and God w. at time of creation A63.3; earthquake as giant's w. F531.3.8.5.1; fairies w. with mortals F364.2; giants w. with each other F531.6.8.3.3; suitor contest: w. H331.6.

Wright. — Monk becomes w. P426.3.1.

Wrinkling. — Hills from earth w. up its feet A969.4.

Wrist. — Hand without w. F552.4.

Writer sent to heaven J225.7. — Bad w. who praises himself reprimanded J953.2.1.

Writing of Jews explained A1689.6; letter slowly because recipient can't read fast J2242.2; tablets transformed to bundle D454.11; tabu on sabbath C631.5. — Dead man w. E557; devil w. faults of man on goat skin G303.24.1.2; devil w. names of supplicants G303.6.1.2.1; genie called by w. his name on papers and burning them *D2074.2.4; ghost w. on wall E557.1; guessing magic w. H517; heavenly hand w. on wall F1036; indelible w. D1654.3.1.1; magic w. makes foster brothers enemies P273.2.4; origin of w. A1484; resuscitation by w. deity's name E75; scribe can't read own w. P425.1.

Writings. — Bird can recite sacred w. B122.3; deity authenticates sacred w. A199.6; extraordinary w. F883; magic w. *D1266.1; sacred w. V151.

Written charm renders invulnerable D1344.4. — Charm w. in blood has magic power *D1273.0.1; wife follows w. instructions J2516.3.1.

Wrong person killed N338.— Choice: apparent injustice over greater w. J225; countertask: turning jug w. side out H1923.9.1; fugitive slave takes w. road and is caught N382; one w. and five hundred good deeds J1605.

Wrongdoer. — Spring breaks forth against w. F933.6; waters drowning w. F930.2.

Wronged wife goes to wronged husband T233. — Curse by w. man M411.23; succession to fall to line that has been w. P17.7.

Wry-mouthed family X131.

Xanthippe and Socrates: "after thunder rain" T251.4.

Xylophone. — Chameleon plays x. B297.1.2.

Yak. — Magic y. tail D1029.2.1; resuscitation by y. tail E64.16.1; speaking y. B211.1.5.4.

Yaksa. — Sex exchanged with y. D592.1.

Yam cutting symbolizes daughter for marriage H611.3. — Not to heed magic y. that says not to take it up C811.2; magic y. D983.2.

Yams. — Origin of y. A1423.1, A2686.4.3; people in otherworld stand on their heads and pound y. with their heads F167.4.1; why some y. are good, some bad A2741.2, A2793.3; why y. are small and plentiful A2794.2.

Yard. — Filling y. with manure (task) H1129.1; shepherd shuts up lion in y. with livestock J2172.2.

Yards. — Giant three spans between brows and three y. between shoulders F531.2.2.

Yarn. — Husband made to believe that y. has changed to tow through his carelessness J2325; numskull ties y. around stove to keep heat from escaping J1942; pursuit of rolling ball of y. H1226.4; witch winds y. G244.1.

Yawning mouth paralyzed open D2072.0.5.2.

Yawns. — Contagious y. J1448; criminal accidentally detected: "that is the first": sleepy woman counting her y. N611.2; dupe made to believe that trickster becomes wolf when he y. three times, flees and leaves his clothes behind him K335.0.4.1.

Year added to life by eating fruit of magic tree D1338.3.3.1; and day Z72.1; seems hours in otherworld F377.2. — Bringing as many horses as there are days in y. (task) H1117; build shelter for whole y. J741; customs for the y. established A1502; disenchantment if twelve men will not leave castle for y. D759.4; door to fairyland opens once a y. F211.1.1; effects of wild hunt remedied by seeing it y. later in same place E501.19.1; formulas based on y. Z72; king for y. provides for future J711.3; kings exchange forms and kingdoms for y. D45.1; magic cauldron boils a y. D1601.10.2; magic weakness for five days each y. D1837.1.1; mermaid appears once each y. B81.12.2; one lie a y. X901; person walks unceasingly for y. F1032; prophetic dream loses force after a y. D1812.3.3.4; riddle of y. H721ff.; sinners endure hell for a y. Q560.3; strong man's labor contract: blow at end of y. F613.1; take y. to do errand: servant does J2461.4; wild hunt as omen of plentiful y. E501.20.2; windows and doors for every day in the y. F782.1.

Year's respite granted before death K551.22.1; respite for unwelcome marriage T151.

Years not counted J181; are days in Tusita world A697.2.1; seem moments while man listens to song of bird D2011.1; thought days *D2011. — Dead person visits earth every seven y. E585.1; disenchantment at end of seven y. D791.1.1; lost soul to serve as porter in hell for seven y. E755.2.3; magic pill on which one feeds self for y. D1652.1.8; moments thought y. D2012; person of remarkable sight finds tracks of swine stolen seven y. before his birth F642.2; seven y. of service imposed on suitor H317.1; talking statue, when destroyed, cannot be replaced for thirty thousand y. D1661.1.

Yearly tasks C684ff.; transformation D624. — Devil to help gambler in exchange for one task y. M214; ghost visits earth y. E585.4; wild hunt appears y. at same moment E501.11.3.2.

Yeast as an afterthought J1962. — Origin of y. A1429.2.

Yelling. — Monk y. to repel temptress T331.9.

Yellow lucky color Z148. — Blue, red, y. horses in fairyland F241.1.1.3; fairies' y. hair, clothing F233.5; why canary's eggs are y. A2391.1; why coyote has y. eyes A2332.5.1.

"Yes" C495.2.2.1. — Answering only "y." and "no" J1255.

Yesterday I was a herdsman and now I am an abbot H685.1. — Origin of y. A1178.

Yesterday's — Is today's sun same as y.? J2272.2.

Yew rod used for divination D1311.15.1. — Fairy harper in y. tree F386.1, F262.3.1.2; magic y. tree *D950.14; riddle about y. H852; sacred y. V1.7.1.3.

Yggdrasil A652. — Magic fruit from Y. D1501.4.

Yield. — God decreases plant's y. to punish man A2723.2; temporary advantage gained by pretending to y. in combat K2378.

Yielding. — Sea y. whatever people desire F931.9.2.

Ymir A642, A831.2. — Giants as sons of Y. F531.6.1.7; clouds from brain of Y. A1133.1; giants drowned in blood of Y. F531.6.12.8.1; origin of sky from skull of Y. A701.2.

Yogi advises king to use yogi blood; yogi killed J818.1; advises sacrifice of sister S260.1.2. — Contest between a y. and Musselman V351.5; thief disguised as y. K311.4.1.

Yoke. — Children in moon with y. and bucket A751.7; driving horses over ashen y. tabu C833.4; gold y. in magic tilling D1620.2.7; magic y. D1101.6, (impenetrable) D1381.10.4.

Yoked. — Old ox y. with young one J441.1; wild animals y. by saint B558.6.

Yoking stags H1154.3.6; together lion and wild boar (task) H1149.1. — Bhuiya y. cow and bullock together A1689.1; origin of custom of y. oxen A1441.2.

York. — Origin of Y. rose: from blood of War of the Roses A2656.2.

You are mine and I am yours (marriage formula) T135.1.

Young knight substitutes for old in tournament K3.2; not to precede old P633; queen murders old husband K2213.12; ravens drowned for promising father aid J267.1; wife loves young man T92.1.1. — Angel in form of y. man J225.0.3; animal neglects its y. B751.5; animal's fanciful treatment of their y. B751; animal grateful for rescue of its y. B365; army of y. men P551.1; association of y. and old J440ff.; do not go where an old man has a y. wife J21.3; man with obedient wife looks y. T254.3; old man in love with y. woman J1221; otherworld people ever y. F167.9; wisdom from y. man J175.

Younger brother asks older for health secret H596.1.1; child may not marry before elder T131.2. — Clever y. generation J1122; kingship given to y. brother P17.8; only y. son of lion keeps father's precepts and is successful J22ff.; prophecy: y. son will get throne M314.3; treacherous y. brother K2211.0.2.

Youngest brother (alone succeeds on quest) H1242, (rescues his elder brothers) R155.1, (shares wealth with older ones) W11.14, (surpasses elder as thief) K308; judge first to give decision P516; sister rescues elder R157.1. — Hero loves y. of seventy princesses T27.2; prophecy: y. brother to rule M312.2.2; victorious y. child *L0—L99; vigil for dead father: y. son alone endures frightful experiences H1462.1.

Youth, see also **Rejuvenation;** abducted by fairy F325; lamed by man whose daughter he refuses to marry Q451.2.1; made lame: had kicked his mother J225.1; meets devil in woods G303.8.13.1; promised to ogre visits his home G461; saved from death sentence R169.6; serves ogre G452; trusts self to horse over which he has no control J657.1; will answer only on throne: once there, orders king killed J1189.1. — Age and y. in love T91.4; betrayal through pretended fountain of y. K116.1; choice: suffering in y. or old age J214; conclusion: y. and age are alike J2214.2; devil (advises y. to enjoy himself and not to think of God) G303.9.7.2, (promises to help mistreated apprentice if y. will meet him by night in lonely spot) G303.22.12, (tempts y. to deny Virgin) G303.9.4.8; eagle renews y. B758; eternal y. D1883; foolish y. in love with ugly old mistress J445.1; fountain of y. D1338.1.1; god of y. A474.1; gods of y. and age A474; immortality useless without y. D1850.1; king and clever y. H561.4; land of y. D1338.7, F116.1; mature married woman in love with callow y. T91.4.1; old racehorse in mill laments vanity of y. J14; phoenix renews y. *B32.1; prophecy: either y. or mother will die M341.5; quest for the water of y. H1321.3; riddle about hastily passing y. H767.1; sun from head of sacrificed y. A718.1; token sent with y. H82.6; water of y. D1338.1.2.

Youths clever thieves K305.3; grind in mill of underworldlings F106; wear false beards K1821.4. — Devil appears among y. who jest while they say their evening prayers G303.6.2.3.

Yule. — King killed at Y. feast K913.1; vow taking at Y. festival M119.3.

Zabi's — Why z. eyes narrow: laughs so hard A2332.3.2.

Zacharias Z71.1.5.

Zadig J1661.1.1.

Zeal: temperate and intemperate J550ff.

Zebra. — Man transformed to z. D115.1; stripes of z. A2413.1; how z. got its mane A2322.3; why z. is continually eating A2478.1.

Zebra's. — Why z. ears long A2325.5; why z. mouth is large A2341.2.2.

Zenith. — Hero resides in z. A572.1.

Zeus, see also **Jove, Jupiter;** gives man modesty but it leaves when love enters T1; has embassy of dogs imprisoned for fouling his court *Q433.3; refuses wedding present from snake J411.2; smites Capaneus while he is climbing a ladder L472. — Casket with Good Luck in it given to men by Z. N113.1.1; dungbeetle keeps destroying eagle's eggs:

eagle at last goes to sky and lays eggs in lap of Z. L315.7; frogs demand live king from Z. J643.1; snake complains to Z. that people step on him J623.1.

Zise. — Feast for Z. A1541.2.1.

Zither string breaks as life token E761.5.2.

Ziz as birds' king B242.1.10. — Bird Z. B31.1.0.1.

Zodiac grows up: the Kid becomes the Goat J2212.6 — Zones of earth corresponding to Z. A881.

Zögernder Dieb J2136.5.1.

Zuñi. — Why Z. girls rub flour on their faces as they grind A1687.1.

THE END

ADDITIONS AND CORRECTIONS

(See also at end of Volume 5.)

VOLUME 1.

P. 380, 12 lines
from bottom.   *For* B131.1 *read* B131.1.1.

P. 509, line 20.   *For* D243.1 *read* C243.1.

VOLUME 3.

P. 219, 3 lines
from bottom.   *For* inexhaustible *read* inexhaustibly.

P. 409, line 13 (H363).   *For* 610B *read* 510B.

P. 501, line 5.   *For* 47 *read* 471.

VOLUME 4.

P. 90, line 36.   *For* V21 *read* U21.

P. 91, 11 lines
from bottom.   *For* pleasant *read* peasant.

P. 108, line 24 (J1364).   *For* that *read* than.

VOLUME 5.

P. 365, line 31.   *For* naivité *read* naiveté

P. 369, line 35 (T251.8).   *For* heating *read* beating

P. 377, after line 5.   *Add* T317.0.1. *Life shortened by incontinence:* 300-year old man has had intercourse every two years. India: Thompson-Balys.

Note the following Cross-References:
A123.2.1.1—N111.2.2;   A123.9—H1289.4.1;   A185.6.1.1—Q147.3, E722.2.12; A692.1—F136.2;   A751.8.6—A1142.5.1.1;   A1313.3.1—F547.1.1;   A1346.2—A1420.4;   A1423.1—A2686.4.1, A2686.4.3;   A2211.14—K952.1.2;   A2435.6.2.1—Q452;   B15.7.3—B101.1.1;   B33.1.1—B777;   B143.1.3—H1578.1.6;   B765.3—D2161.4.10.2.2;   B765.11—D1563.2.2.2;   B771—H1155;   D215—G263.2.2; D473.1—D2086.1.1;   D925.0.2—F162.5.1, F718.3;   D1442—H1155;   D1524.1.2.1 —K185.13;   D1533.1.1—D1552.4;   E629.1—E693.3;   E643.1—F1075;   F162.5.1—F718.3;   F262.3.1.2—F386.1.1;   F647.4—K2051.1;   F769.1—J21.52.1, X1503.3; F933.13.2—H251.3.9.2;   F1041.21.6—P678.1;   G254.1—Q551.2.7;   H252.1—M119.7;   H583.7—H1058;   H946.1—J1805.2.1;   J86—Z186;   J761.3—T455.3.1; J1149.2—K341.11;   J1162.3—K448;   J1805.1.1—J2489.8, K1462.2;   J1842.2—X372.4.1;   J2014—J2316.1;   K533—K1834;   K565.2—K1022.1.1,   K1973; K1023—X411.3;   K1321.1.1—K1514.16;   N317—N741.2;   T117.5—T461.3; T512.5—T533.

Note the following Inadvertant Duplications:
B301.1.2 and B301.7.1; B524.1.12 and B549.5; D452.3.1 and D476.1.11; D491.6 and F1009.4; D951 and D2178.8; F963.3 and Q147.2; H1553.5 and W185.4; J677 and U129.3; J1162.3 and K448; J1197 and U21.5; J1369.5 and J1714.5; J1603 and X372.3; V211.5 and Z271.3.2.